Lecture Notes in Computer Science 6698

Commenced Publication in 1973
Founding and Former Series Editors:
Gerhard Goos, Juris Hartmanis, and Jan van Leeuwen

Editorial Board

David Hutchison
  Lancaster University, UK
Takeo Kanade
  Carnegie Mellon University, Pittsburgh, PA, USA
Josef Kittler
  University of Surrey, Guildford, UK
Jon M. Kleinberg
  Cornell University, Ithaca, NY, USA
Alfred Kobsa
  University of California, Irvine, CA, USA
Friedemann Mattern
  ETH Zurich, Switzerland
John C. Mitchell
  Stanford University, CA, USA
Moni Naor
  Weizmann Institute of Science, Rehovot, Israel
Oscar Nierstrasz
  University of Bern, Switzerland
C. Pandu Rangan
  Indian Institute of Technology, Madras, India
Bernhard Steffen
  TU Dortmund University, Germany
Madhu Sudan
  Microsoft Research, Cambridge, MA, USA
Demetri Terzopoulos
  University of California, Los Angeles, CA, USA
Doug Tygar
  University of California, Berkeley, CA, USA
Gerhard Weikum
  Max Planck Institute for Informatics, Saarbruecken, Germany

Robert B. France Jochen M. Kuester
Behzad Bordbar Richard F. Paige (Eds.)

Modelling Foundations and Applications

7th European Conference, ECMFA 2011
Birmingham, UK, June 6-9, 2011
Proceedings

Volume Editors

Robert B. France
Colorado State University, Computer Science Department, Fort Collins, CO, USA
E-mail: france@cs.colostate.edu

Jochen M. Kuester
IBM Research Zürich, Rüschlikon, Switzerland
E-mail: jku@zurich.ibm.com

Behzad Bordbar
University of Birmingham, School of Computer Science, Birmingham, UK
E-mail: b.bordbar@cs.bham.ac.uk

Richard F. Paige
University of York, Department of Computer Science, York, UK
E-mail: paige@cs.york.ac.uk

ISSN 0302-9743 e-ISSN 1611-3349
ISBN 978-3-642-21469-1 e-ISBN 978-3-642-21470-7
DOI 10.1007/978-3-642-21470-7
Springer Heidelberg Dordrecht London New York

Library of Congress Control Number: Applied for

CR Subject Classification (1998): D.2, F.3, D.3, C.2, H.4, K.6

LNCS Sublibrary: SL 2 – Programming and Software Engineering

© Springer-Verlag Berlin Heidelberg 2011
This work is subject to copyright. All rights are reserved, whether the whole or part of the material is concerned, specifically the rights of translation, reprinting, re-use of illustrations, recitation, broadcasting, reproduction on microfilms or in any other way, and storage in data banks. Duplication of this publication or parts thereof is permitted only under the provisions of the German Copyright Law of September 9, 1965, in its current version, and permission for use must always be obtained from Springer. Violations are liable to prosecution under the German Copyright Law.
The use of general descriptive names, registered names, trademarks, etc. in this publication does not imply, even in the absence of a specific statement, that such names are exempt from the relevant protective laws and regulations and therefore free for general use.

Typesetting: Camera-ready by author, data conversion by Scientific Publishing Services, Chennai, India

Printed on acid-free paper

Springer is part of Springer Science+Business Media (www.springer.com)

Preface

The 2011 European Conference on Modelling Foundations and Applications, held at the University of Birmingham, UK, during June 6–9, 2011, focused on presenting and assessing the state of the art in the research and practice of model-driven engineering (MDE). The seventh edition of the conference (previously known as the "European Conference on Model-Driven Architecture – Foundations and Applications") covered major advances in foundational research and industrial applications of MDE.

The included papers indicate the breadth, depth and maturity of research and application of MDE, and show that the field has well-established standards, mature tool support, broad areas of application, and substantial appreciation for the challenges of transferring fundamental research results to application. ECMFA is the leading venue for publishing such research.

In 2011, the Program Committee received 61 submissions, of which 19 Foundations track papers and 5 Applications track papers were accepted. Papers on all aspects of MDE were received, including on topics such as model execution, model analysis, methodologies, model management, model transformation, architectural modelling and product lines, and domain-specific modelling. The breadth of topics, as well as the high quality of the results presented in these accepted papers, demonstrate the maturity and vibrancy of the field.

This proceedings volume also summarizes one of the conference keynote talks, given by Wilhelm Schäfer, as well as brief overviews of the tutorials and workshops held during the conference.

We are grateful to our Program Committee members for providing their expertise and quality and timely reviews. Their helpful and constructive feedback to all authors is most appreciated. We thank the ECMFA Conference Steering Committee for their advice and help. We also thank our sponsors, both keynote speakers – Wilhem Schäfer and Steve Cook – and all authors who submitted papers to ECMFA 2011.

June 2011

Robert France
Jochen Küster
Behzad Bordbar
Richard Paige

Conference Organization

ECMFA 2011 was organized by the Department of Computer Science, University of Birmingham, UK.

Program Chairs

Foundations Track	Robert France (Colorado State University, USA)
Applications Track	Jochen Küster (IBM Zurich, Switzerland)

Local Organization

Local Organization Chair	Behzad Bordbar (University of Birmingham, UK)
Workshops and Tutorials Chair	Rami Bahsoon (University of Birmingham, UK)
Publications Chair	Richard Paige (University of York, UK)
Sponsorship Chair	Nick Blundell (University of Birmingham, UK)
Finance Chair	David Oram (University of Birmingham, UK)
Tools and Consultancy Chair	Dimitris Kolovos (University of York, UK)

Program Committee

Jan Aagedal
Terry Bailey
Mariano Belaunde
Reda Bendraou
Jorn Bettin
Xavier Blanc
Behzad Bordbar
Marc Born
Phil Brooke
Jordi Cabot
Tony Clark
Benoit Combemale
Arnaud Cuccuru
Zhen Ru Dai
Miguel A. De Miguel
Birgit Demuth
Philippe Desfray
Juergen Dingel

Gregor Engels
Anne Etien
Luis Ferreira Pires
Stephan Flake
Franck Fleurey
Robert France
Mathias Fritsche
Sebastien Gerard
Marie-Pierre Gervais
Martin Gogolla
Reiko Heckel
Markus Heller
Andreas Hoffmann
Gabor Karsai
Jörg Kienzle
Andreas Korff
Jochen Kuester
Vinay Kulkarni

Ivan Kurtev
Philippe Lahire
Roberto Erick Lopez-Herrejon
Tiziana Margaria
Dragan Milicev
Parastoo Mohagheghi
Ana Moreira
Tor Neple
Ileana Ober
Richard Paige
Arend Rensink
Laurent Rioux
Tom Ritter
Julia Rubin
Bernhard Rumpe
Andrey Sadovykh
Houari Sahraoui
Andy Schürr

Bran Selic
Renuka Sindghatta
Alin Stefanescu
Gabriele Taentzer
Francois Terrier
Juha-Pekka Tolvanen
Andreas Ulrich
Antonio Vallecillo
Pieter Van Gorp
Marten J. Van Sinderen
Daniel Varro
Markus Voelter
Regis Vogel
Michael Von Der Beeck
Ksenia Wahler
Olaf Zimmermann
Steffen Zschaler

External Reviewers

Mathieu Acher
Abiar Al-Homaimeedi
Mauricio Alferez
Vincent Aranega
Camlon Asuncion
András Balogh
Olivier Barais
Jorge Barreiros
Gábor Bergmann
Luiz Olavo Bonino Da Silva Santos
Artur Boronat
Fabian Büttner
Sebastian Cech
Asma Charfi
Robert Clarisó
Mickael Clavreul
Arnaud Cuccuru
Maarten De Mol
Dolev Dotan
Hubert Dubois
Jean-Rémy Falleri
Martin Faunes
Masud Fazal-Baqaie
Silke Geisen

Christian Gerth
Amir Hossein Ghamarian
Cristina Gómez
TimGülke
Arne Haber
Lars Hamann
Ábel Hegedüs
Rim Jnidi
Stefan Jurack
Pierre Kelsen
Marouane Kessentini
Mirco Kuhlmann
Marius Lauder
Markus Look
Sebastien Mosser
Chokri Mraidha
Muhammad Naeem
Florian Noyrit
Sven Patzina
Ernesto Posse
Dirk Reiss
István Ráth
Brahmananda Sapkota
Gehan Selim

Karsten Sohr
Jeffrey Terrell
Massimo Tisi
Gergely Varro
Steven Völkel

Christian Wende
Claas Wilke
Manuel Wimmer
Mohammad Zarifi Eslami
Karolina Zurowska

Table of Contents

Keynote

Building Advanced Mechatronic Systems 1
  Wilhelm Schäfer

Model Execution

Contracts for Model Execution Verification 3
  Eric Cariou, Cyril Ballagny, Alexandre Feugas, and Franck Barbier

A FUML-Based Distributed Execution Machine for Enacting Software
Process Models 19
  *Ralf Ellner, Samir Al-Hilank, Johannes Drexler, Martin Jung,
  Detlef Kips, and Michael Philippsen*

A Generic Tool for Tracing Executions Back to a DSML's Operational
Semantics 35
  Benoît Combemale, Laure Gonnord, and Vlad Rusu

Model Analysis

Incremental Security Verification for Evolving UMLsec Models 52
  Jan Jürjens, Loïc Marchal, Martín Ochoa, and Holger Schmidt

Assessing the Kodkod Model Finder for Resolving Model
Inconsistencies 69
  Ragnhild Van Der Straeten, Jorge Pinna Puissant, and Tom Mens

Operation Based Model Representation: Experiences on Inconsistency
Detection 85
  *Jerome Le Noir, Olivier Delande, Daniel Exertier,
  Marcos Aurélio Almeida da Silva, and Xavier Blanc*

Methodology

Generating Early Design Models from Requirements Analysis Artifacts
Using Problem Frames and SysML 97
  Pietro Colombo, Ferhat Khendek, and Luigi Lavazza

Automated Transition from Use Cases to UML State Machines to
Support State-Based Testing 115
  Tao Yue, Shaukat Ali, and Lionel Briand

Transformation Rules for Translating Business Rules to OCL
Constraints 132
  Imran S. Bajwa and Mark G. Lee

Model Management (1)

Preventing Information Loss in Incremental Model Synchronization by
Reusing Elements 144
  Joel Greenyer, Sebastian Pook, and Jan Rieke

An MDE-Based Approach for Solving Configuration Problems:
An Application to the Eclipse Platform 160
  Guillaume Doux, Patrick Albert, Gabriel Barbier, Jordi Cabot,
  Marcos Didonet Del Fabro, and Scott Uk-Jin Lee

Incremental Updates for View-Based Textual Modelling 172
  Thomas Goldschmidt and Axel Uhl

Transformations

Easing Model Transformation Learning with Automatically Aligned
Examples 189
  Xavier Dolques, Aymen Dogui, Jean-Rémy Falleri,
  Marianne Huchard, Clémentine Nebut, and François Pfister

Code Generation for UML 2 Activity Diagrams: Towards a
Comprehensive Model-Driven Development Approach 205
  Dominik Gessenharter and Martin Rauscher

Tractable Model Transformation Testing 221
  Martin Gogolla and Antonio Vallecillo

Variability Analysis and ADLs

Extending SysML with AADL Concepts for Comprehensive System
Architecture Modeling 236
  Razieh Behjati, Tao Yue, Shiva Nejati, Lionel Briand, and Bran Selic

Analyzing Variability: Capturing Semantic Ripple Effects 253
  Andreas Svendsen, Øystein Haugen, and Birger Møller-Pedersen

Integrating Design and Runtime Variability Support into a System
ADL 270
  Marie Ludwig, Nicolas Farcet, Jean-Philippe Babau, and
  Joël Champeau

Domain-Specific Modelling

Domain-Specific Model Verification with QVT 282
  Maged Elaasar, Lionel Briand, and Yvan Labiche

A SysML Profile for Development and Early Validation of TLM 2.0
Models 299
  Vaibhav Jain, Anshul Kumar, and Preeti R. Panda

Taming the Confusion of Languages 312
  Rolf-Helge Pfeiffer and Andrzej Wąsowski

Model Management (2)

Table-Driven Detection and Resolution of Operation-Based Merge
Conflicts with Mirador.. 329
  Stephen C. Barrett, Patrice Chalin, and Greg Butler

Improving Naming and Grouping in UML 345
  Antonio Vallecillo

Aspect-Oriented Model Development at Different Levels of
Abstraction 361
  *Mauricio Alférez, Nuno Amálio, Selim Ciraci, Franck Fleurey,
  Jörg Kienzle, Jacques Klein, Max Kramer, Sebastien Mosser,
  Gunter Mussbacher, Ella Roubtsova, and Gefei Zhang*

Workshop Summaries

MBSDI 2011 3rd International Workshop on Model-Based Software
and Data Integration 377
  Ralf-Detlef Kutsche and Nikola Milanovic

MELO 2011 - 1st Workshop on Model-Driven Engineering, Logic and
Optimization 379
  *Jordi Cabot, Patrick Albert, Grégoire Dupé,
  Marcos Didonet del Fabro, and Scott Lee*

The Third Workshop on Behaviour Modelling - Foundations and
Applications.. 381
  Ella Roubtsova, Ashley McNeile, Ekkart Kindler, and Mehmet Aksit

Process-Centred Approaches for Model-Driven Engineering (PMDE)
–First Edition 383
  *Reda Bendraou, Redouane Lbath, Bernard Coulette, and
  Marie-Pierre Gervais*

Third International Workshop on Model-Driven Product Line
Engineering (MDPLE 2011) 385
*Goetz Botterweck, Andreas Pleuss, Julia Rubin, and
Christa Schwanninger*

Tutorial Summaries

Agile Development with Domain Specific Languages 387
*Bernhard Rumpe, Martin Schindler, Steven Völkel, and
Ingo Weisemöller*

Incremental Evaluation of Model Queries over EMF Models: A Tutorial
on EMF-IncQuery 389
Gábor Bergmann, Ákos Horváth, István Ráth, and Dániel Varró

Integrated Model Management with Epsilon 391
*Dimitrios S. Kolovos, Richard F. Paige, Louis M. Rose, and
James Williams*

Creating Domain-Specific Modelling Languages That Work:
Hands-On 393
Juha-Pekka Tolvanen

Author Index 395

Building Advanced Mechatronic Systems

Wilhelm Schäfer

Heinz Nixdorf Institute & Department of Computer Science,
University of Paderborn, Germany
wilhelm@upb.de

Mechatronics is the engineering discipline concerned with the construction of systems incorporating mechanical, electronical and information technology components. The word mechatronics as a blend of mechanics and electronics has already been invented 40 years ago by a Japanese company. Then, mechatronics just meant complementing mechanical parts with some electronical units, a typical example being a photo camera. Today, mechatronics is an area combining a large number of advanced techniques from engineering, in particular sensor and actuator technology, with computer science methods.

Typical examples of mechatronic systems are automotive applications, e.g. advanced braking systems, fly/steer-by-wire or active suspension techniques, but also DVD players or washing machines. Mechatronic systems are characterised by a combination of basic mechanical devices with a processing unit monitoring and controlling it via a number of actuators and sensors. This leads to massive improvements in product performance and flexibility. The introduction of mechatronics as a tight integration of mechanical, electronical and information-driven units allowed for turning conventionally designed mechanical components intosmart devices. The significance of mechatronics is today also reflected inuniversity education: mechatronics has become a degree on its own, and is at many places not merely taught by one area but jointly by all three. The subject managed to cross the traditional boundaries between engineering and computer science.

Today we see the first steps in the emergence of the next generation of mechatronic systems. While "intelligence" in the behaviour has so far always been achieved by gathering information (and reacting to it) from the one single machine, the usage and retrieval of information in the future will be characterised by an exchange of information between different machines. This can for instance already be seen in the automotive and rail domain: intelligent lighting systems combine information about their environment obtained from their own sensors with those collected by other cars. In the Paderborn rail system shuttles autonomously form convoys as to reduce air resistance and optimise energy consumption. This is a general trend: The smart devices of today's mechatronic systems will turn into "populations" of smart devices, exchanging information for optimising their global behaviour as well as possibly competing for limited resources. This movement imposes in particular new challenges on the computer science side in mechatronics. The mechatronic systems of the future will be characterised by the following properties:
- high degree of concurrency: Systems will consist of a large number of autonomous components, exchanging information while running in parallel. Components may form clusters to collaborate on a common goal but may also compete as to optimise their own aims.

- decentralisation: Due to the high degree of concurrency and distribution systems cannot be centrally observed and as a consequence not centrally controlled.
- Self-Coordination: As a result of the previous two points, advanced mechatronic systems will largely have to rely on principles of self-coordination.

Several disciplines in computer science are affected by this change. For achieving reliable and secure transmission of information the areas of network technology and cryptography are challenged. With respect to the issue of self-coordination it is in particular software engineering which has to make a major step towards a new design methodology. Current self-developments in software engineering are already making small steps in this direction. For the design of complex mechatronic systems of the future these have to be combined and complemented with other advanced techniques as to form an engineering method for self-coordinating systems. Such a method in particular has to involve

- modeling formalisms integrating model transformations (describing adaptation, reconfiguration etc.) themselves into the model,
- code generation techniques, operating at run-time and taking platform specific parameters into account,
- elaborate formal analysis techniques being able to cope with the high volatility of systems (and properties emerging by a continuous dynamic change).

In the talk we survey current state of the art in the development of mechatronic systems from a software engineering point of view. Based on identified weaknesses of existing approaches we present our own approach called Mechatronic UML. Mechatronic UML supports model-driven development of mechatronic systems addressing complex coordination between system components under hard real-time constraints and reconfiguration of control algorithms at runtime to adjust the system behaviour to changing system goals as well as target platform specific code generation. Modelling is based on a syntactically and semantically rigorously defined and partially refined subset of UML. It uses a slightly refined version of component diagrams, coordination patterns, and a refined version of state charts including the notion of time which are called Real time state charts. Verification of safety properties is based on a special kind of compositional model checking to make it scalable. Model checking exploits an underlying unifying semantics which is formally defined using graph transformation systems. The last part of the talk is devoted to pointing out future developments and research challenges which we believe characterise advanced mechatronic systems of the future.

Results presented in this paper and the talk evolved during many discussions with many of my PhD students and my colleagues Heike Wehrheim and Holger Giese (now with the HPI at Potsdam University) to whom I am indebted.

Biography. Dr. Wilhelm Schäfer is full Professor and chair, head of Software Engineering Group, Department of Computer Science, University of Paderborn, Chair of the International Graduate School of the University of Paderborn, Chair of the Paderborn Institute for Advanced Studies in Computer Science and Engineering (PACE), and Vice President at the University of Paderborn.

Contracts for Model Execution Verification

Eric Cariou[1], Cyril Ballagny[2], Alexandre Feugas[3], and Franck Barbier[1]

[1] University of Pau / LIUPPA, B.P. 1155, 64013 Pau Cedex, France
{Eric.Cariou,Franck.Barbier}@univ-pau.fr
[2] SOFTEAM, Objecteering Software, 8 Parc Ariane, 78284 Guyancourt Cedex, France
Cyril.Ballagny@softeam.fr
[3] INRIA Lille-Nord Europe / LIFL CNRS UMR 8022 / University of Lille 1
Cité scientifique, Bât. M3, 59655 Villeneuve d'Ascq Cedex, France
Alexandre.Feugas@inria.fr

Abstract. One of the main goals of model-driven engineering is the manipulation of models as exclusive software artifacts. Model execution is in particular a means to substitute models for code. We focus in this paper on verifying model executions. We use a contract-based approach to specify an execution semantics for a meta-model. We show that an execution semantics is a seamless extension of a rigorous meta-model specification and is composed of complementary levels, from static element definition to dynamic elements, execution specifications as well. We use model transformation contracts for controlling the dynamic consistent evolution of a model during its execution. As an illustration, we apply our approach to UML state machines using OCL as the contract expression language.

Keywords: design by contract, runtime verification, model execution, model-driven engineering, UML state machines, OCL.

1 Introduction

One of the main goals of Model-Driven Engineering (MDE) is to cope with models as final software artifacts. This can be performed by directly executing the model itself; the model is thus the "code" that is executed. Being able to execute a model is a key challenge for MDE. It also requires to ensuring that the execution has been performed correctly, by applying verification or validation techniques. In this paper, we focus on the verification of model execution.

Programming and design by contract have shown their interest in verifying the execution of software systems [2,12,13]. Contracts ensure a sufficient confidence on the software system through a lightweight verification approach at runtime. We propose to apply design by contract principles to the context of model execution. We aim at ensuring that a model execution, realized by any tool or engine, is correct with respect to the defined semantics. The first step to execute a model is thus to define its execution semantics, in a specification and verification purpose. This requires the definition of a rigorous meta-model including the specification of the state of the model during its execution. A given execution engine can then execute a model by defining its new state at each execution step. If considering that each modification of the model state is a model transformation, a model execution can be seen as a serie of endogenous model transformations. Accordingly, we can use model transformation techniques for verifying model execution, namely model transformation contracts [5].

The rest of the paper is organized as follows. Section 2 defines the requirements on meta-models for being able to execute a model and how contracts can be applied to define an execution semantics and verify a model execution. Section 3 describes the execution of UML state machines, including the required extension of the UML meta-model [16] and the associated execution engine. Section 4 defines an execution contract example, showing the feasibility of our approach. Then, before concluding, we review related works.

2 Verifying Model Execution through Contracts

In this section, we first recall the concept of contract and its application to model transformations. We next explain how a model execution can be seen as a suite of model transformations. Then we discuss the kinds of semantics we need for being able to specify the execution of a model and show that contracts – and model transformation contracts – can be used in this context.

2.1 Contracts and Model Transformation Contracts

Programming and design by contract [2,12,13] consist in specifying what a software component, a program or a model does, in order to know how to properly use it. Design by contract also allows at runtime the assessment of what has been computed with respect to the expressed contracts. A contract is composed of two kinds of constraints:

- Invariants that have to be respected by software elements;
- Specification of operations on the software elements through pre and post-conditions. A pre-condition defines the state of a system to be respected before its associated operation can be called in a safe mode. Post-conditions establish the state of a system to respect after calls. If a pre-condition is violated, post-conditions are not ensured and the system can be in an abnormal state.

In the MDE context, a meta-model is a structural diagram defining the kinds of model elements and their relations. But this structural view is rarely sufficient for expressing all relations among elements, we need to complement it with well-formedness rules. They are additional constraints expressed in a dedicated language, such as OCL (Object Constraint Language [15]). Contract invariants can be typically this kind of rules, and operations are any kind of model manipulation and modification, such as model transformations.

In [5], an approach for specifying contracts on model transformation operations using OCL has been proposed. These contracts describe expected model transformation behaviors. Formally, constraints on the state of a model before the transformation (source model) are offered. Similar constraints on the state of the model after the transformation (target model) are offered as well. Post-conditions guarantee that a target model is a valid result of a transformation with respect to a source model. Pre-conditions ensure that a source model can effectively be transformed. A couple of pre and post-conditions for specifying a transformation can also be organized via three distinct sets of constraints:

- Constraints on the source model: constraints to be respected by a model to be able to be transformed;
- Constraints on the target model: general constraints (independently of the source model) to be respected by a model for being a valid result of the transformation;
- Constraints on element evolution: constraints to be respected on the evolution of elements between the source and the target models, in order to ensure that the target model is the correct transformation result according to the source model content.

2.2 Model Execution as Model Transformations

Figure 1 shows an execution example of a UML state machine specifying the behavior of a microwave. The microwave can be in two main states depending on the state of the door: open or closed. When the door is closed, the power button allows a cycle from baking to putting the microwave off. When opening the door, if the microwave was baking, it gets in a pause mode. Otherwise, it gets in off mode. Closing the door leads to come back in the previous mode when the door was closed, either baking or being off (this is specified thanks to the history state of the state Closed). The state machine is represented in conformity with the common graphical syntax of UML state machines, except coloring leaf active states in grey. Indeed, we must know at a given time which states of the machine are currently active[1]. Then, active states fully belong to the model specification.

The figure shows several steps of the model execution. At the first step, the microwave is in baking mode with the door closed. Then, the user opens the door – the event DoorOpen is generated – and the microwave gets in the pause mode (step 2). When the user closes the door, this activates back the baking state (step 3). The last step of the example shows a particular execution step of the model: the state machine refinement. The single baking state is replaced by a composite state defining several power positions. This refinement is made during the execution of the model, at runtime. This kind of structural modification is typically what can be done for supporting adaptation at runtime [1].

As seen in the figure, each model execution step is associated with an operation: run_to_completion(Event) or refine_state(State, State). Indeed,

---

[1] The UML meta-model does not include the specification of the current active states of a state machine. We have then extended it, as described in section 3.1.

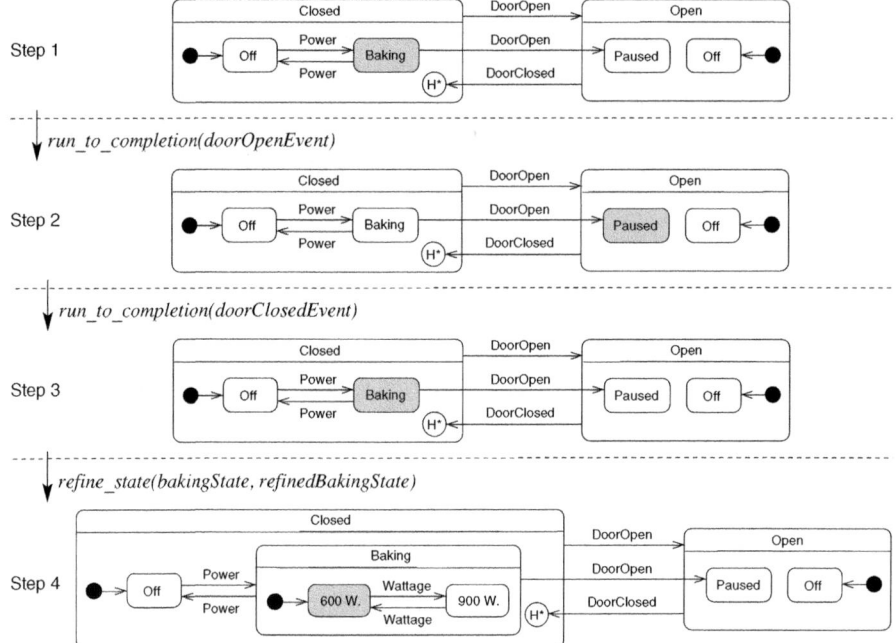

Fig. 1. Model execution example: a UML state machine of a microwave

the easiest way to specify a semantics for an execution is to link it to operations associated with meta-model elements. This allows the discretization and the reification of the execution process. Concretely, these operations are either explicitly defined on meta-elements or only implicit to be used for supporting the semantics at runtime. Here, the StateMachine UML meta-element can own these operations.

Each call of such an operation makes the model evolve by realizing an execution step. In other words, the model is transformed at each execution step. In the example, either the active states are changing (run_to_completion) or the structure of the state machine is dynamically modified (refine_state). Even if changing the active states modifies only marginally the model, it is a model transformation. As a result, an execution of a model can be considered as a suite of model transformations associated with the execution operations. These transformations are endogenous because all models conform to the same meta-model during the execution.

2.3 An Approach for Verifying Model Execution

Requirements on Meta-models for Executing Models. As already stated by previous works (such as [7,9,18]), a model execution requires that its meta-model defines several kinds of element specification, such as dynamic ones. Here, we propose our own meta-model part classification for an execution specification.

For state machines, in addition to the specification of the states, we must know at a given time which of its states are the active ones. For a model execution, its meta-model must then contain two kinds of meta-elements:

- Static part: structural definition of the model elements defining the static view of a model. For a state machine, it defines the concepts of *State, Transition, Event*, ...
- Dynamic part: structural definition of the elements specifying the execution state of a model. For a state machine, it will notably define the concept of *Active State*.

Defining the structure of the elements is not enough for specifying all the constraints on these elements and their relationships: we need to add to the meta-model structure the "well-formedness rules". They are defined through a constraint language, such as OCL for instance. Well-formedness rules are defined for the static part but also for the dynamic part of the meta-model. For instance, for the static part of a state machine, one can specify that two different transitions associated with the same event and the same guard cannot be assigned to the same source state. For the dynamic part of a state machine, one can specify that two exclusive states can not be active at the same time (like Open and Closed on Figure 1).

The meta-model structure and its well-formedness rules are not sufficient for fully specifying an execution semantics, even when including a dynamic part. For instance, in the context of state machines, if an event occurs and if associated transitions exist on current active states, the processing of this event by the execution engine implies that these transitions will be triggered. This model evolution between execution steps must also be defined as a set of constraints or rules we are calling "well-evolution rules".

These well-evolution rules can, like the well-formedness rules, be defined on the static and the dynamic parts of the meta-model. For the dynamic part, they embody constraints on the model evolution during its execution, such as the event management policy specifying which states have to be activated according to an event occurence. For the static part, this implies that the model (its "static" elements) can be modified during the execution. On a state machine, states and transitions can change during the execution (such as on Figure 1, step 4). This is what can be typically done in an adaptation context. The well-evolution rules then define the constraints of this adaptation, *i.e.*, its semantics.

Classification of Semantic Levels. Several complementary levels of semantics must be introduced in relation with the above discussion:

- Structural meta-model: definition of the static meta-elements and their relationships (the static part with the associated well-formedness rules). This structural meta-model is the common result of a meta-model definition when no model execution aspect is taken into account.

- Executable meta-model[2]: addition to the structural meta-model of elements allowing the execution of a model (the dynamic part with the associated well-formedness rules).
- Execution semantics[3]: addition to the executable meta-model of semantics of element evolution (the well-evolution rules added to the static and dynamic parts).

Figure 2 summarizes the semantics levels. We differentiate the executable meta-model from the full definition of the execution semantics. Indeed, the executable meta-model is usually unique because one single kind of representation of the model state during its execution is sufficient. However, it makes sense to define different semantics of model evolution for a same meta-model. This allows the definition of execution semantics variation points [8,10].

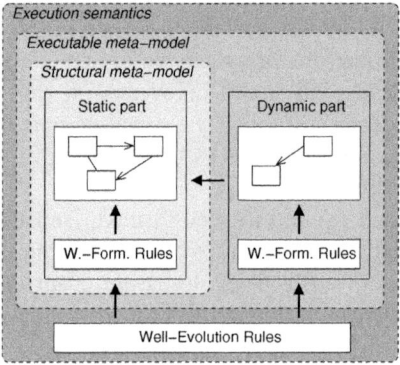

Fig. 2. Semantics levels for a meta-model

Execution Semantics as Contracts. An execution semantics can be directly expressed as a contract: a set of invariants and operation specifications through couples of pre and post-conditions. The invariants are the well-formedness rules of the executable meta-model and the specification of execution operations contains the required well-evolution rules.

An important point to notice is about defining the execution semantics of a meta-model through contracts. In our approach, this definition is done in a "seamlessly way". In other words, we use the same "technological space" to maintain in one and only one meta-model, structural aspects and the way they may be subject to a well-established evolution: the execution semantics. As an illustration, let us consider for instance the definition of a DSL (Domain Specific

---

[2] We use the term of "executable meta-model" as a shortcut for expressing that models conforming to this meta-model are executable, but the meta-model itself is not directly executable.

[3] To avoid any ambiguity: execution semantics is to be considered here as constraints to be respected during the model evolution and not as how the execution is carried out. We are not defining an operational semantics.

Language) using the EMF framework[4] and OCL. First, the Ecore meta-model and OCL constraints are used for specifying the structural part and its associated well-formedness rules. Next, making this meta-model executable leads to modifying the Ecore meta-model by adding new elements and their associated well-formedness rules by means of OCL. Finally, a concrete execution semantics for this meta-model supposes the introduction of the well-evolution rules. In this respect, we demonstrated in [5] that model transformations – here the model execution steps through associated operations – can be specified using standard OCL. So, during all these stages of execution semantics specification, one remains in the same "technological space" (Ecore and OCL) without requiring to use and know specification techniques of another technological space (Petri nets, temporal logic, graph transformations, ...) for defining some parts of the execution semantics. Moreover, these techniques are often formal and then harder to accept by the designers who define meta-models and DSLs.

Model Execution Engine Requirements. Intuitively, one can consider that managing a model execution and its contracts requires using an implementation platform offering both execution and verification capabilities (such as for the Eiffel language in a programming context [13]). This can be achieved by implementing the model execution engine with a platform, such as Kermeta[5], that contains an action language for defining executable operations associated with meta-elements and a constraint language that enables to specify invariants on meta-elements and pre/post-conditions for their operations.

Our approach allows less restricting requirements. The main issue when evaluating the contract is checking pre and post-conditions. Indeed, this task is strongly linked to the execution of the operations. As explained in [5] and section 2.1, a couple of pre and post-conditions can be written under the form of three sets of invariants. Then, an execution contract consists only of invariants. Checking invariants on a model is made independently of the way the model is handled, *i.e.*, the way by which the model is executed. We then simply require to couple the execution engine with a constraint evaluator. Besides, it is possible to check the contract at any time when the models are available, not only at the execution time. So, the contract evaluation can become an independent task of the model execution whether the execution engine is capable to store models.

As an intermediate conclusion, we rely on lesser assumptions as possible about the model execution engine or the virtual machine interpreting the model. The imposed basic requirements are the fact that the engine supports the operations characterizing the key execution steps and is able to store and manage the current state of the model before and after each execution step.

Contract Evaluation and Usage. Depending on the model execution engine capabilities, there are two main contract checking times. The first one is during the model execution: if the execution engine is coupled with a contract evaluator (typically an OCL evaluator), at each required execution step, the contract can

---
[4] Eclipse Modeling Framework: http://www.eclipse.org/emf/
[5] http://www.kermeta.org

be checked. The second one is *a posteriori*: the execution engine stores the model state after each required execution step, building in this way an execution trace. Afterwards, the contract will be checked on models from this trace.

The completeness of the contract has an influence on the contract usage for ensuring confidence on the execution engine. As defined in [12], a complete contract is a contract that detects all possible errors on models.

Depending on the moment of the contract checking and its completeness, execution contracts can be used in several ways, such as:

– In a debugging mode: for each step, a complete contract is checked and allows the designer to detect programming errors through an adequate interaction with the execution engine.
– With a complete contract and generation of execution traces, contracts can be used for model-checking: they play the role of oracles. Several traces are built with a set of different entry models. They simulate environment interactions for covering, as much as possible, most of the test cases. Contracts must then be valid for all execution traces.
– Considering a non-complete contract and evaluation at runtime, it supports the management of some execution errors and adaptations to the context during the model execution. In this case, a non-complete contract is usually preferable to avoid performance overheads. Indeed, once the execution engine tested, complete contracts are no longer required at runtime because of the prior elimination of errors.

3 Execution of UML State Machines

3.1 Extension of the UML Meta-model

To be able to execute a UML state machine, the UML meta-model – more precisely its part defining state machines ([16], Superstructure, chapter 15) – must be enhanced to become an executable meta-model.

The static part of the UML meta-model (defining that a *state machine* owns *regions* which themselves own *states* which are connected with *transitions*, ...) has been kept without modification. As for the dynamic part, it globally aims at specifying state machine instances in execution. For this, UML object diagrams are reused and extended. Figure 3 represents this dynamic part and its relationships to existing meta-elements of the UML meta-model.

An object diagram enables to specify instances. The `InstanceSpecification` meta-element represents an instance when it is associated with a `Classifier` object, namely the `Class` meta-element. In addition, a class can own a state machine in order to model its behavior. In the UML meta-model, a state machine is a kind of classifier, thus an instance specification can be linked to this state machine. Nevertheless, while there are meta-elements to specify what values of attributes are for an object, there is no meta-element to specify what the current state, a state machine object is in.

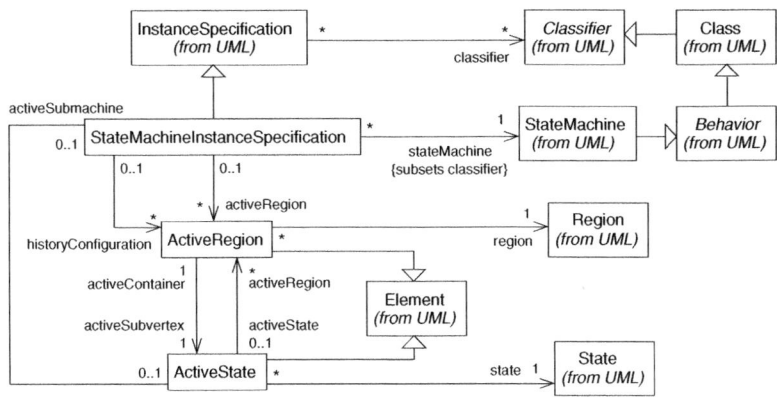

Fig. 3. UML meta-model extension for specifying state machine instances

To move forward, we specialize the InstanceSpecification meta-element to model an instance of a state machine. The association from this StateMachineInstanceSpecification meta-element to StateMachine is a subset of the pre-existing association from InstanceSpecification to Classifier. The current state of a state machine instance is characterized by an active state configuration, *i.e.*, the hierarchy of states which are active in the state machine at a particular moment. To model this configuration, we have introduced the ActiveRegion and ActiveState meta-elements. If an active state is a submachine state (*i.e.*, a state which is an alias to another state machine), a state machine instance can be referenced from this active state (association from ActiveState to StateMachineInstanceSpecification). If a region owns a history state (such as in the example of Figure 1), the last active state configuration can be store (association historyConfiguration from StateMachineInstanceSpecification to ActiveRegion). Furthermore, cardinalities of associations ensure that: 1) an active region only belongs to one state machine instance or to one active state; 2) an active region owns one and only one active state; 3) an active state is only active in one region. As an example, when the 600W leaf state is active in the microwave (cf. Figure 1, step 4), the active state configuration is the path from the state machine to this active state, including the active Closed state and the active Baking state.

Other well-formedness rules are required to complete the dynamic part definition. They ensure that: 1) the active regions and states of an instance belong to the state machine whose instance is described; 2) an active composite state (*i.e.*, a state which owns regions) owns an active state for each one of its regions; 3) an active submachine state references a state machine instance which is the submachine of this active state; 4) a history configuration is only referenced when a history state exists. These rules are concretely defined as OCL invariants. For example, here is the invariant for the well-formedness rule concerning the activation of a composite state[6]:

---

[6] The complete technical material presented in this paper is available online: http://web.univ-pau.fr/%7Eecariou/contracts/

context ActiveState **inv** activeComposite:
  state.isComposite() **implies** (activeRegion -> size() = state.region -> size()
  and activeRegion -> forAll(ar1, ar2 | state.region->exists(ar1.region) **and**
  (ar1<> ar2 **implies** ar1.region <> ar2.region)))

3.2 MOCAS: A UML State Machine Execution Engine

We have implemented an engine, MOCAS[7], for interpreting UML state machines. This engine is a Java library which relies on the Eclipse Modeling Framework implementation of UML. It supports all state machine features: transition guards, state invariants, submachine states, history states, change events, time events, signal events, call operation actions, ... The engine interprets state machine models conforming to the UML meta-model as enhanced in this paper.

MOCAS implements a "default" semantics for UML state machine execution. This supposes that some choices have been made for semantic variation points of the UML meta-model or when points have not been clearly specified in the UML documentation. However, MOCAS can be customized in order to realize different semantics. By relying on execution contracts, we are able to verify at runtime that an implementation respects the desired semantics.

Other execution engines could be used. We can for instance implement such an engine using fUML [17]. As stated in section 2.3, if these engines are able to store the executed model after each execution step or are associated with a constraint checker, our approach can be applied, independently of the way these engines are carrying out the execution and of their implementation technology.

4 Execution Contracts on UML State Machines

Checking invariants is easier compared to checking operation specifications. We then focus in this section on the definition of a contract part for an execution operation. As an example, we describe the semantics of the run_to_completion operation for the execution of UML state machines. An operation specification can be classically defined through pre and post-conditions but, as explained in section 2.3, this restricts the usability of the contract. So, we present this operation specification under the form of three sets of invariants, to widen the possibility of evaluating and using contracts. To explain how to express an operation specification in this way, we first detail some technical points.

4.1 Automatic Meta-model Modification

As stated in [5], a problem remains when evaluating OCL constraints: they are expressed for a single context and, as a result, they relate to a single model. When evaluating constraints on element evolution, we both need to reference source and target model elements. The technical solution to this problem is to concatenate all elements of these two models into a global one. This concatenation is made possible by automatically modifying their meta-model.

---

[7] http://mocasengine.sourceforge.net/

The modification consists in adding elements to an existing meta-model for which a transformation contract has to be checked (see Figure 4). First, each existing meta-element is viewed as a specialization of `ContractModelElement` (for the UML meta-model, the meta-element `Element` simply becomes a specialization of `ContractModelElement` as each meta-element of the UML meta-model inherits directly or transitively from it). Then, each element of the source or the target model will be tagged, respectively, with the "source" or "target" string value through its inherited `modelName` attribute. Secondly, we need to know the characteristics of the operation associated with the contract: this is the role of `ContractOperation` referencing elements of the global model for specifying parameters (the return value of operations as well). Lastly, the `ContractEvaluation` element is in charge of the evaluation result of the contract for embedded models. We offer the possibility of stating this result element by element, showing when necessary if an element respects (`Correct`) or not (`Error`) its part of the contract.

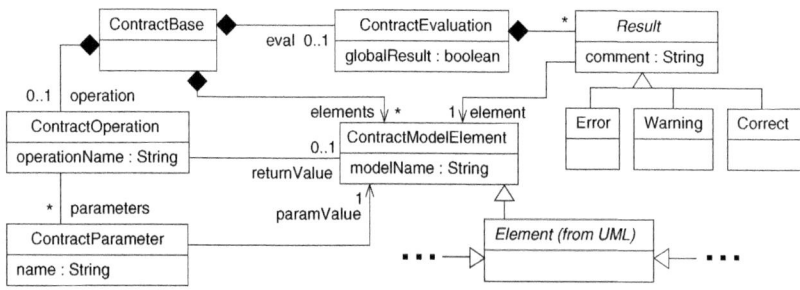

Fig. 4. Automatic meta-model modification to support contract management and its application to the UML meta-model

To sum up, when expressing the contract part for execution operations, we rely on the modified meta-model version. The modification of the meta-model is carried out automatically thanks to a dedicated tool. This tool is able to make the modification for any Ecore meta-model (including the UML implementation and then our extended version for managing state machine execution). It also realizes the concatenation of a source and a target models into a global model conforming to the modified meta-model. If instead of OCL, we use a constraint language able to handle several models simultanely, all this will not be required. Nevertheless, it will be useful to rely on it also in this case because it helps in structuring the contracts as embedding in the same global model, the source and the target models, the description of the operation and the contract evaluation result. From a practical point of view, the contract is evaluated via an ATL[8] transformation. Indeed, ATL offers a full OCL implementation and can then easily be used to check OCL constraints [3].

---

[8] ATLAS Transformation Language: http://www.eclipse.org/m2m/atl/

4.2 Specification of the run_to_completion Operation

Since there are no constraints to be respected for source and target models of the transformation corresponding to the run_to_completion operation, we only need to specify the element evolution between source and target models. The main goal is to ensure that the right transitions are triggered for active states when the associated event occurs. Figure 5 shows an extract of this specification[9]. The following description is applied to the state machine execution example of Figure 1 for the processing of the "DoorOpen" event, making the microwave state machine passing from step 1 to step 2.

The invariant to be verified on the global model (concatenating the source and the target models; each one containing one main state machine instance) is specified at line 1. First, we retrieve the event associated with the operation through contract parameters (line 2). Then (line 3), if the current state machine instance is the source one (step 1 of Figure 1), it must be valid with respect to the target one (step 2 of Figure 1) and this event, based on the transitionValidity

```
1   context StateMachineInstanceSpecification inv:
2       let evt : ContractParameter =
                    ContractParameter.allInstances() -> any( name = 'event' ) in
3       ( self = self.getSMI('source') ) implies
                    self.transitionValidity(self.getSMI('target'), evt.paramValue)

4   context StateMachineInstanceSpecification def: getSMI(name : String) :
                    StateMachineInstanceSpecification =
5   StateMachineInstanceSpecification.allInstances() -> any( smi |
                    smi.modelName = name and smi.activeState -> isEmpty())

6   context StateMachineInstanceSpecification def: transitionValidity(
            smiTarget : StateMachineInstanceSpecification, event : Event): Boolean =
7       let activeStatesForEvent : Set(ActiveState) = self.activeLeaves() -> select(s |
                    s.state.hasTransitionForEvent(event)) in
8       let activeTransitions : Set(Transition) = activeStatesForEvent -> collect(s |
                    s.state.getTransitionForEvent(event)) in
9       activeTransitions -> forAll( t | t.hasBeenPassedInTarget(smiTarget))

10  context Transition def: hasBeenPassedInTarget( smiTarget :
                    StateMachineInstanceSpecification) : Boolean =
11      let targetTransition : Transition = smiTarget.getMappedTransition(self) in
12      let states = smiTarget.getActiveStates() -> collect (state) in
13      states -> exists ( s | targetTransition.target = s) and
14      targetTransition.unactivateSourceState() implies
                    not(states -> exists ( s | targetTransition.source = s))
```

Fig. 5. OCL invariant specifying the run_to_completion operation

---

[9] For simplifying, transition guards are not taken into account.

OCL operation evaluation (specified from lines 6 to 9). Retrieving a main state machine instance in the global model is realized thanks to the getSMI OCL operation, using the modelName attribute (lines 4 and 5).

To check a transition validity, on the source side, the set of transitions that have to be triggered is computed, based on current active states and the parameter event (lines 7 and 8). In our example, two transitions can be actually triggered for the "DoorOpen" event, starting from the two active states of the state machine (the leaf state Baking and its container state Closed): the "external" one from Closed to Open leading to the Off state of Open, or the "internal" one from Baking to Paused. The choice of the transition is an execution semantic variation point. It is concretely defined in the getTransitionForEvent OCL operation. Following the UML common semantics, it returns here the most internal transition. Finally, each required transition has to be passed towards the target state machine instance (line 9), through the validation of hasBeenPassedInTarget (specified from lines 10 to 14).

A transition is passed on the target side when there is an active state associated with the target state (Paused) of this transition (line 13) and when the source state (Baking) of this transition is not anymore active[10] (line 14) except in particular cases (such as when the source and target states of the transition are the same) checked by the unactivateSourceState OCL operation. For that, we need to point to the transition on target side that is equivalent (*i.e.*, with the same associated states and event) to the one on the source side (on which the hasBeenPassedInTarget OCL operation is called, that is the current OCL context). This is achieved by the mapping function getMappedTransition. As explained in [5], mapping functions are key construction of our contracts and can be automatically generated.

Finally, one may notice that the proposed contract is not a complete contract. Indeed, not all required verifications on the model evolution are processed. We need to check that the active states that do not correspond to eligible transitions are not modified. We also need to verify that the structural part of the model – its states and its transitions – are not modified. About this issue, this simply leads to verifying that each element of the source side has an equivalent element on the target side, and vice-versa. As explained in [5], this is an unmodification contract and it can be fully and automatically generated by means of our tool. This feature greatly helps the writing of complete contracts.

5 Related Works

In the recent literature, as far as we know, there are no other design by contract (or related) approaches than ours for model execution verification at runtime, where models are considered in the context of MDE, that is UML, MOF or Ecore-like models. The closest work is [14] that proposes a global method for trusting

---

[10] To be complete, the state Closed must also be active. It is not necessary to check this here because it is already specified through the well-formedness rules ensuring the coherency of active state hierarchy (see section 3.1).

model-driven components based on contracts, notably for expressing oracles in model checking techniques. It classifies contracts as entities constituted by basic and behavioral parts that can match this paper's semantic levels. [14] points out the problem of not having a standard for expressing contracts. Our approach can be an answer to this problem since we propose a structured and implementable approach for defining well-integrated contracts in executable models.

Even if the goal of [9,11] is the definition of an operational semantics for visual models (typically UML ones), it can be adapted to be used in a verification purpose. Its interests is to define model evolution during an execution through UML collaboration diagrams. The drawback is that UML collaborations are dedicated to UML and are rarely present under an equivalent form in other technological spaces. This approach is then hard to generalize within a single technological space. Moreover, collaboration diagrams are concretely specified through graph transformations. This requires using another technological space.

Other techniques can be applied for verifying model execution. The main research field is concerned with model-checking where program verification techniques have been adapted to a modeling context. Not all of these works discuss directly model execution verification but some of them focus on model transformation verification. Indeed, as seen, model transformations are a way for expressing a part of a model execution semantics. In all these approaches, a translational semantics is defined: a model or a model transformation is specified in another technological space in order to use third-party simulation and/or verification tools. For instance, [4] verifies invariants or temporal constraints through the Maude framework and LTL properties. [7] proposes prioritized timed Petri nets while [19] stresses the expression of transformations towards colored Petri nets. [6] allows the specification of a behavioral semantics through abstract state machines (ASM). The major advantage of these approaches is the capability of using robust and efficient model-checking techniques. However, they have two main drawbacks. Firstly, the designer must master these technological spaces in addition of the technological space in which the meta-model is defined. Secondly, they require transformations of models from the meta-modeling technological space to the one of the model-checking tools, and vice-versa. This implies a supplementary work to ensure or prove the correctness of these transformations. This leads to making these approaches harder to use than integrated contracts as done in this paper, where a complete execution semantics is straightforwardly available as a logical and natural extension of a rigorous meta-model specification. Furthermore, these model checking approaches are usable at design time, but they are not at runtime. They however offer more facilities to prove the correctness of special properties, such as temporal aspects. In this respect, they can be used as a complementary approach to ours. Moreover, these model-checking or testing techniques could be used to help in validating a contract. Indeed, it can be sometimes difficult to ensure that a set of constraints covers all required specifications and that some of these constraints are not mutually contradictory.

Lastly, discussion about other model transformation contract approaches and the choice of OCL are available in the related works section of [5].

6 Conclusion

We present an approach for applying design by contract principles to model execution. In this paper, execution contracts allow the verification of model execution at runtime. They can also be used for model-checking at design time. One of the main interest of our approach is that a full execution semantics specified through a contract is realized within a single technological space, in a seamlessly way: an ordinary meta-model definition is directly enriched with execution specifications. We propose a progressive method for specifying a complete execution semantics, starting from structural part definitions to behavorial specifications. This method has the ability of defining execution semantic variants.

We have applied our approach to UML state machine execution. We have extended the UML meta-model for making state machines executable and defined the execution semantics through operation specifications in OCL. We in effect provide a support to verify the correctness of state machine execution for the MOCAS platform.

This first experimentation has shown the feasibility of our approach. The next step is to focus on usage of the contract evaluation. Notably, we plan to implement model checking techniques using our execution contracts as test oracles. The goal is to be able to execute an executable model through a framework allowing the simulation of environment interactions. Then, several traces are built with a set of different entry models and contracts must be valid for all execution traces. Another perspective is using contract for managing software adaptation at runtime. Indeed, the MOCAS platform not only executes state machines, it is dedicated to performing adaptations of software components [1]. A direct application of execution contracts is to guiding the adaptation of the executed components (*e.g.*, refining the behavior of a component or changing an operating mode of a component). Contracts can uncover a failure and lead to executing recovering policies.

References

1. Ballagny, C., Hameurlain, N., Barbier, F.: MOCAS: A State-Based Component Model for Self-Adaptation. In: Third IEEE International Conference on Self-Adaptive and Self-Organizing Systems (SASO 2009). IEEE Computer Society, Los Alamitos (2009)
2. Beugnard, A., Jézéquel, J.-M., Plouzeau, N., Watkins, D.: Making Components Contract Aware. IEEE Computer 32(7) (1999)
3. Bézivin, J., Jouault, F.: Using ATL for Checking Models. In: Intl. Workshop on Graph and Model Transformation (GraMoT 2005). ENTCS, vol. 152 (2005)
4. Boronat, A., Heckel, R., Meseguer, J.: Rewriting Logic Semantics and Verification of Model Transformations. In: Chechik, M., Wirsing, M. (eds.) FASE 2009. LNCS, vol. 5503, pp. 18–33. Springer, Heidelberg (2009)
5. Cariou, E., Belloir, N., Barbier, F., Djemam, N.: OCL Contracts for the Verification of Model Transformations. In: Proceedings of the Workshop The Pragmatics of OCL and Other Textual Specification Languages at MoDELS 2009. Electronic Communications of the EASST, vol. 24 (2009)

6. Chen, K., Sztipanovits, J., Abdelwalhed, S., Jackson, E.: Semantic anchoring with model transformations. In: Hartman, A., Kreische, D. (eds.) ECMDA-FA 2005. LNCS, vol. 3748, pp. 115–129. Springer, Heidelberg (2005)
7. Combemale, B., Crégut, X., Garoche, P.-L., Xavier, T.: Essay on Semantics Definition in MDE – An Instrumented Approach for Model Verification. Journal of Software 4(9) (2009)
8. Crane, M.L., Dingel, J.: UML vs. Classical vs. Rhapsody Statecharts: not all Models are created Equal. Software and Systems Modeling 6(4) (2007)
9. Engels, G., Hausmann, J.H., Heckel, R., Sauer, S.: Meta-Modeling: A Graphical Approach to the Operational Semantics of Behavioral Diagrams in UML. In: Evans, A., Caskurlu, B., Selic, B. (eds.) UML 2000. LNCS, vol. 1939, pp. 323–337. Springer, Heidelberg (2000)
10. France, R.B., Ghosh, S., Dinh-Trong, T., Solberg, A.: Model-Driven Development Using UML 2.0: Promises and Pitfalls. IEEE Computer 39(2) (2006)
11. Hausmann, J.H.: Dynamic Meta Modeling: A Semantics Description Technique for Visual Modeling Languages. PhD thesis, University of Paderborn (2005)
12. Le Traon, Y., Baudry, B., Jézéquel, J.-M.: Design by Contract to improve Software Vigilance. IEEE Transaction on Software Engineering 32(8) (2006)
13. Meyer, B.: Applying "Design by Contract". IEEE Computer (Special Issue on Inheritance & Classification) 25(10), 40–52 (1992)
14. Mottu, J.-M., Baudry, B., Le Traon, Y.: Reusable MDA Components: A Testing-for-Trust Approach. In: Wang, J., Whittle, J., Harel, D., Reggio, G. (eds.) MoDELS 2006. LNCS, vol. 4199, pp. 589–603. Springer, Heidelberg (2006)
15. OMG. Object Constraint Language (OCL) Specification, version 2.0 (2006), http://www.omg.org/spec/OCL/2.0/
16. OMG. Unified Modeling Language (UML) Specification, version 2.2 (2009), http://www.omg.org/spec/UML/2.2/
17. OMG. Semantics of a Foundational Subset for Executable UML Models (fUML), version 1.0 (2011), http://www.omg.org/spec/FUML/1.0/
18. Pons, C., Baum, G.: Formal Foundations of Object-Oriented Modeling Notations. In: 3rd International Conference on Formal Engineering Methods (ICFEM 2000). IEEE, Los Alamitos (2000)
19. Wimmer, M., Kappel, G., Kusel, A., Retschitzegger, W., Schoenboeck, J., Schwinger, W.: Right or Wrong? – Verification of Model Transformations using Colored Petri Nets. In: 9th OOPSLA Workshop on Domain-Specific Modeling (DSM 2009) (2009)

A FUML-Based Distributed Execution Machine for Enacting Software Process Models

Ralf Ellner[1], Samir Al-Hilank[2], Johannes Drexler[2], Martin Jung[2], Detlef Kips[1,2], and Michael Philippsen[1]

[1] University of Erlangen-Nuremberg, Computer Science Department,
Programming Systems Group, Martensstr. 3, 91058 Erlangen, Germany
{ralf.ellner,philippsen}@cs.fau.de

[2] develop group Basys GmbH, Am Weichselgarten 4, 91058 Erlangen, Germany
{alhilank,drexler,jung,kips}@develop-group.de

Abstract. OMG's SPEM standard allows for a detailed modeling of software development processes and methods, but only a rather coarse description of their behavior. This gap can be filled by extending SPEM with a fine-grained behavior modeling concept based on UML activities and state machines. In order to gain full benefit from detailed software process models including behavior, an automated enactment of these software process models is required.

In theory, the operational semantics of UML activities as defined by OMG's FUML (Semantics of a Foundational Subset for Executable UML Models) could be used to instantiate and sequentially simulate software process models on a single computer. However, FUML is insufficient to execute software process models to drive realistic projects with large and geographically spread teams. FUML lacks support for distributed execution in order to guide and support team members with their concurrent activities. FUML also does not fulfill key requirements of software processes, in particular requests for human interaction. Additionally, FUML requires explicit modeling of auxiliary user specific attributes and behavior of model elements, which is a cumbersome, repetitive and error-prone task and leads to non-reusable standard software process models.

We present the required FUML extensions to support distributed execution, human interaction, and to weave in user specific extensions of the execution machine. With these FUML extensions it becomes feasible to enact reusable standard software process models in realistic projects.

1 Introduction

Software development processes (SDPs) are widely accepted as a critical factor in the efficient development of complex and high-quality software and systems. Beginning with Osterweil's process programming [1] many process modeling languages (PMLs) have been proposed to describe SDPs in more or less abstract, (semi-)formal ways, see [2,3,4] for an overview. Some of those PMLs are standardized, for example, SEMDM [5] and SPEM [6]. In contrast to SEMDM, SPEM is based on the UML Infrastructure [7] and defines a graphical notation. Its familiar high-level notation allows practitioners to pick up SPEM easily. However, SPEM has been primarily designed to model and document the static structure of SDPs. Thus, when an SDP is modeled in detail with SPEM this results in a thorough documentation of the process. Such a well documented process is valuable or may even be required (e.g., in safety critical projects), but it does not provide much additional value for the project staff that uses the process documentation as there is no help in executing the process. Although it has been a requirement, executability is not in the scope of the current version 2.0 of SPEM, even though it would provide additional benefits (see [1,8,9]):

- Executable software process models can be simulated and thus more easily validated before using them in a project.
- A process execution machine (PEX) can guide and support the project staff.
- Since a PEX can automatically check conformance of the executed process with the modeled process, it can detect and prevent process violations.
- A PEX can track progress of the executed process. This is of great use for process audits, because proofing conformity of the actually executed process with the modeled process can be partially automated.

In [10] we presented eSPEM, a SPEM extension based on UML activities and state machines [11]. Beside the UML behavior modeling concepts (for example, decisions, exceptions, and events), eSPEM provides additional behavior modeling concepts that are specific to SDPs (e.g., task scheduling). The behavior modeling concepts in eSPEM can be used to describe the behavior of SDPs in a fine-grained, formal, but intuitive way. The formality of the SDP behavior description is required in order to execute it. Another requisite to execute an SDP is the definition of the operational semantics of the PML used to describe an SDP.

An approach to define the operational semantics of a subset of UML activities and actions is provided by the OMG standard *Semantics of a Foundational Subset for Executable UML Models* (FUML) [12]. FUML provides a mapping of UML activities and actions to Java and can instantiate and simulate UML models. However, the Java implementation is limited to a single thread in a single Java virtual machine (JVM). Consequently, FUML can be used to instantiate and locally simulate SDPs modeled in PMLs based on UML, for example eSPEM. We have verified this by implementing a simulator based on the operational semantics of the concepts we reused from UML (for example, `DecisionNode`, `ForkNode`, and `Action`), as well as the semantics of the additional behavior modeling concepts in eSPEM, like task scheduling.

While suitable for local simulation, a FUML-based implementation is insufficient to support distributed process execution needed for typical software projects that are driven by teams. In such projects, each team member has a personal workstation and is connected to a network. To be useful in such a distributed environment [13,2], a FUML-based execution machine for software processes must be able to:

- share the state of a running software process instance across several nodes in a network (R1),

- suspend and resume execution on different nodes (R2),
- interact with project staff (R3), and
- adapt to the needs of different teams in different organizations (R4).

However, FUML does not meet these requirements, because it was not designed for a distributed execution environment or to interact with humans. We discuss the problems that prevent a distributed execution in detail in Sect. 2. Section 3 presents our solutions for the insufficiencies found in FUML in order to meet all the above requirements. Sect. 4 evaluates our solutions with an exemplary SDP. In Sect. 5, we compare our execution machine to other existing approaches, before we conclude and give a brief outlook on the further steps.

2 FUML Architecture

To understand the problems that prevent a distributed execution using FUML, we start with a brief overview of FUML's architecture. FUML defines a UML model named *execution model*, that acts as a type model for models that store information about a running instance of an executed UML model. Figure 1 shows a small excerpt of FUML's execution model. The elements in the execution model (e.g., operations) are annotated with their respective Java codes. A Java-based execution machine can be generated from this annotated execution model.

In the FUML execution model, a Locus is responsible for instantiating classes from the executed UML model and for holding the instantiated Objects. FUML uses the visitor design pattern [14] to add operations (that define the operational semantics) to classes in the UML meta model. A visitor class (for example, those named *Execution, and *Activation) exists for each supported UML concept. An ActivityExecution represents a single execution of a UML::Activity(e.g.,

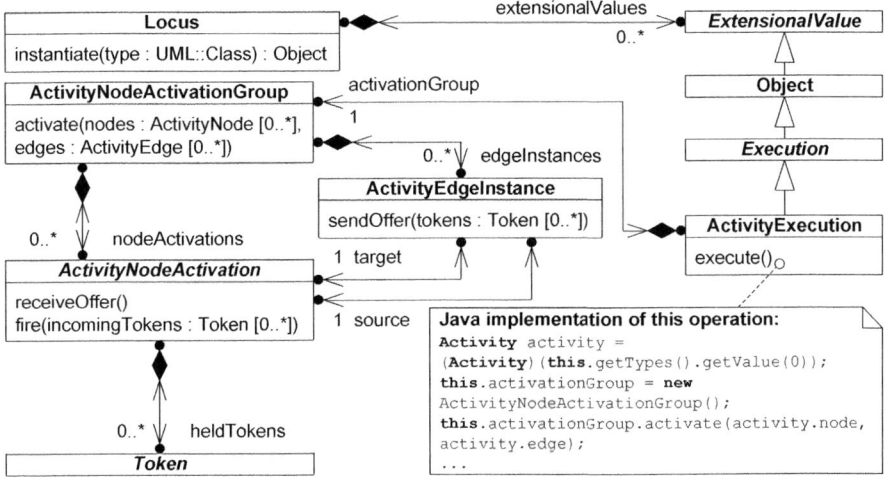

Fig. 1. Excerpt of FUML's execution model

the behavior of a UML::Class from the executed UML model). An Activity-NodeActivation represents an execution of a UML::ActivityNode. Specializations of the abstract class ActivityNodeActivation exist in FUML for the different types of ActivityNodes in UML (e.g., DecisionNode, and Action).

Since UML activity diagrams are based on Colored Petri nets [15,11], FUML makes use of the essential Petri net concepts like places, transitions, and tokens. ActivityNodeActivations are the places and can hold different types of Tokens. ActivityEdgeInstances offer these Tokens from their source to their target ActivityNodeActivation. ActivityEdgeInstances act as Petri net transitions.

Besides the problem that FUML's implementation does not provide remote access to the execution model, there are two further issues that prevent a distributed execution. First, since access to the FUML execution model instance is not protected by any locking or synchronization mechanism, the existing Java-based implementation must fail in a distributed and concurrent environment due to data corruption (P1). Second, FUML uses synchronous, sequential operation calls to propagate tokens [16]. Thus, the state of the running model instance is spread across the call stack of the machine (e.g., a JVM) that executes the FUML implementation, and the corresponding instance of FUML's execution model (P2). This contradicts traditional Petri net semantics, where the state of the Petri net is solely defined by the number of tokens in each place. Fig. 2 shows an example of a small UML activity diagram and the required interactions of the execution model objects (some omissions are made for better readability). Each of the non-UML arrows from the untyped lifelines towards nodes and edges of the activity diagram denotes the UML element that corresponds to an untyped lifeline.

A call of receiveOffer transfers tokens from one node to another. Using this design to suspend (after action A) and to resume execution later (at the workstation of another team member) requires to preserve the call stack. Another problem is that large activity diagrams or activity diagrams with cycles may lead to an overflowing stack due to the recursive receiveOffer calls.

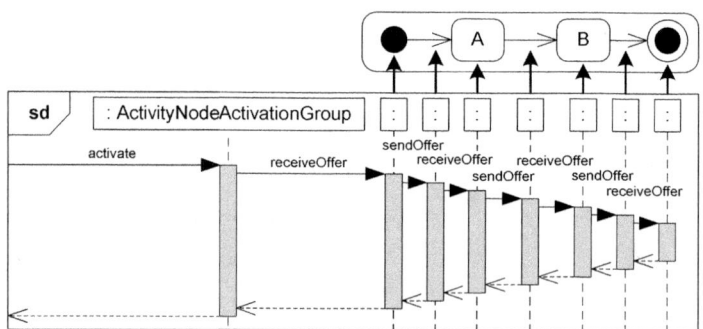

Fig. 2. Activity diagram and behavior realization in FUML

3 Distributed Execution Machine Architecture

This section presents our solutions to the two above mentioned FUML problems that prevent a distributed execution, and it discusses FUML extensions to meet all of the requirements for a PEX.

3.1 Shared Access to the Execution Model

To fulfill requirement R1 (shared execution model access), we use the Connected Data Objects (CDO) model repository [17] to manage our execution model instance. As part of the Eclipse Modeling Framework (EMF) [18], CDO provides transparent access to a shared model in a network, as well as transactions for safe model manipulations in distributed environments. With CDO we can share the state of a running software process instance in a network.

3.2 Synchronized Access to the Execution Model

Transactions are a precondition to solve the FUML problem P1 (synchronized execution model access) in the Java-based implementation. However, their use requires changes to the operational semantics of FUML, because some of the essential Petri net properties [15] need to be respected. First, it must be an atomic operation to fire a transition (to transfer a number of tokens from the source node(s) to the target node(s)). Second, different transitions may fire concurrently.

To reflect these properties, we use CDO transactions to isolate firing of single `ActivityEdge`s (transitions). This includes the `receiveOffer` call to the target `ActivityNodeActivation`, which in turn includes execution of the behavior of the target node. Thus, moving tokens from one `ActivityNodeActivation` to another is now an atomic operation on an execution model instance. This solves the FUML problem P1 (synchronized execution model access).

To solve the problem P2 (the execution state spread across the call stack and the execution model), we substitute FUML's synchronous, sequential `receiveOffer` calls (see Fig. 2) with asynchronous calls performing basic Petri net operations. This can be done, because the state of a Petri net is solely defined by the number of tokens in each place. The information stored on the call stack is redundant.

Instead of the preceding `receiveOffer` calls, our implementation triggers the firing of transitions by means of system events (different from events modeled in an SDP). Examples are user inputs, time events, and CDO events upon manipulation of the execution model instance. Depending on the type of event, the execution machine checks for transitions that can fire, and then fires them in a single transaction. Figure 3 shows how a `model changed` event is handled, if A holds one token and the edge towards B is ready to fire.

Many CDO transactions can manipulate the execution model instance concurrently, if there are different source and target nodes (places) involved. If the same source or target node is involved, it is guaranteed that at most one transaction can be committed. The other transactions are rolled back. This ensures a correct number of tokens on each place.

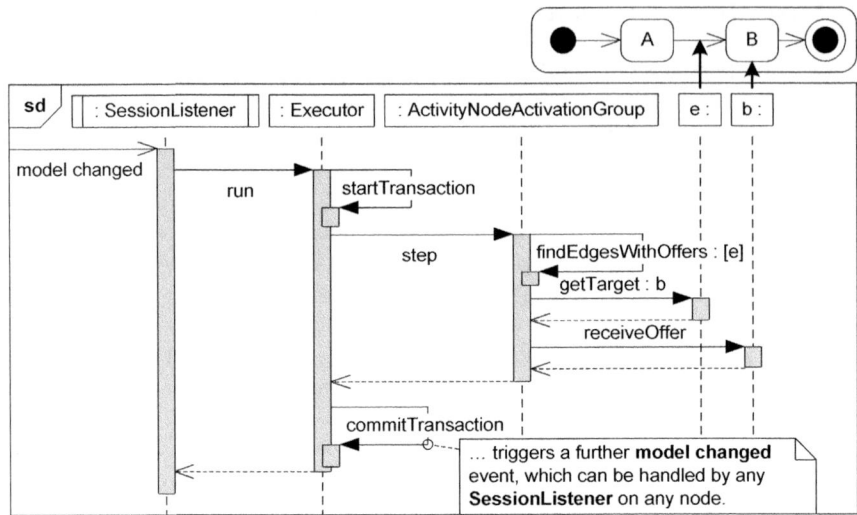

Fig. 3. Activity diagram and behavior realization in eSPEM

With these changes to FUML, we fix both problems and make the execution machine useful in distributed and concurrent environments. By using system events to trigger the firing of `ActivityEdges`, we also fulfilled requirement R2 (suspending and resuming execution on different (network) nodes), because these system events can be handled by any node in the network. After an event is handled, the node automatically suspends execution.

3.3 Human Interaction

To meet requirement R3 (human interaction), FUML has to be extended. This is due to a different focus of UML activities and actions, which are normally used to transform inputs into outputs, and must be modeled completely in order to be executable. In contrast to that, one of the essential properties of software processes is a usually incomplete formal description of their behavior. A process designer stops modeling the behavior of activities and tasks at some level of granularity. Instead, the process designer uses either natural language to describe the activities and tasks, or simply assumes that the project staff knows what to do in the course of the activities and tasks. In order to execute a software process modeled in that way, a tight interaction between the PEX and the project staff is required [1,19]. That is, the PEX is responsible to support the project staff by planning and controlling their work according to the behavior model. In opposition to the PEX, the project staff carries out the actual creative work of a software process. To support this scenario, a PEX must be able to pass control of the software process execution over to project staff and take back control when they are finished with their tasks. However, this is out of FUML's scope.

To gain support for interaction with project staff that also fits into our distributed execution concept, we added to FUML an abstract class Request and some specializations of this class (see Fig. 4).

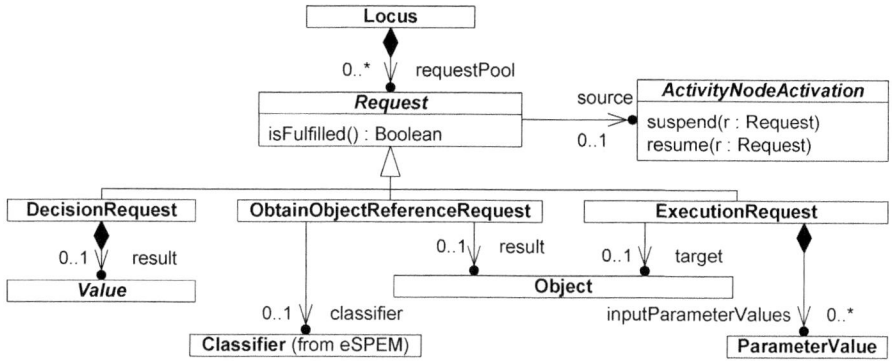

Fig. 4. Requests in our Execution Model

Execution may be suspended at any ActivityNodeActivation. Suspending adds a pending Request to the requestPool of the Locus that (transitively) contains the ActivityNodeActivation. The project staff handles these Requests by editing their properties through the graphical user interface of the PEX. Editing Requests is secured by CDO transactions and thus can take place concurrently on any of the workstations. Once a Request is fulfilled, it is removed from the Locus and execution resumes at the ActivityNodeActivation that is the source of the Request. Let us discuss the three subtypes of Requests now.

A DecisionRequest is used whenever no input value for the corresponding DecisionNode can be determined automatically. For example, a Role can be modeled [10] to choose the value for a DecisionNode as shown in Fig. 5 with one of the UML behavior modeling extensions available in eSPEM. At runtime, the PEX can offer these decisions to the ProductOwner who can choose a Value (the string Yes) as response to the DecisionRequest (see Fig. 5) through the context menu of our PEX. The PEX then selects the outgoing edge of the DecisionNode.

An ObtainObjectReferenceRequest is used whenever an Object (e.g., an instance of a Task or a WorkProduct) is required as input for an Action but

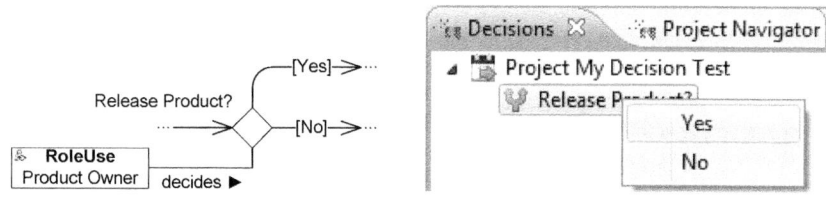

Fig. 5. Decision Modeled with eSPEM and DecisionRequest at Runtime

cannot be determined automatically. This is a quite common case when tasks are planned in advance and are dynamically selected for later execution. A project member may select an appropriate object (e.g., a pre-planned `Task`) that conforms to the `classifier`. The PEX then uses the selected object as an input to perform the `Action`.

An `ExecutionRequest` is used whenever an `ExecuteWorkAction` is invoked and the `WorkDefinition` that shall be executed has no behavior modeled. In this case control over the execution of the `target WorkDefinition` is passed to the project staff. When the staff marks the `WorkDefinition` as finished, control is passed back to the PEX.

With these extensions of FUML, we meet requirement R3: interaction with project staff. `Requests` also work in the distributed environment when handling them in CDO transactions.

3.4 Instantiation

A reasonable PEX must manage a lot of master data (for example, time spent on a task). In order to adapt to the needs of different teams and organizations (requirement R4), this data must be customizable. For example, one organization might use a PEX to track the time spent on tasks. Another organization may use a separate time-tracking software. Thus, it must be customizable whether all tasks have an attribute `timeSpent` and automatically track the time, or not. FUML's generic instantiation mechanism cannot fulfill this requirement, because it only works with attributes modeled in the instantiated model. To understand the problem, we discuss FUML's instantiation in more detail below.

Software modeling and execution using (F)UML, as well as software process modeling and execution, are engineering domains that make use of several levels of (ontological) classification [20]. For an example see Fig. 6.

The model representing the language definition (UML meta model) is an ontological type model for system models. In the same manner, a system model is an ontological type model for models that form the state of running system (instance models). To gain support for the three levels of ontological classification, FUML uses an orthogonal dimension of classification (linguistic classification) as proposed by the orthogonal classification architecture (OCA) [21]. Fig. 6 shows these orthogonal dimensions. FUML uses the prototypical concept pattern [20] to implicitly weave-in the class `Object` during linguistic instantiation. Therefore,

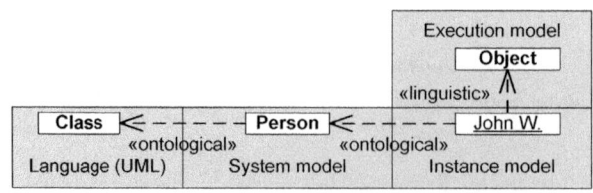

Fig. 6. Classification Levels used in UML/FUML

Object implicitly is the base class of all classes modeled in the system model. As a result, all instantiated elements in the instance model share the same base attributes and behavior of Object. This pattern can also be found in several object-oriented programming languages like Java or C#. During instantiation, FUML creates slots to hold the additional attribute values as modeled in the system model. However, there is no way to customize the base attributes and behavior of Object in FUML. The only way to do this is to explicitly model these attributes in the process model *for every class* (for example, by specializing an abstract class). This is a cumbersome, repetitive and error-prone task. The same problem occurs when FUML is used for software process execution. Missing customization support also leads to non-reusable standard process models, because they would be polluted with data specific to an organization or project.

In order to fulfill requirement R4, we add support for customization of base attributes and behavior. We create an extensible type model for the master data called *runtime model*, which is an extension of FUML's execution model. The users of the PEX can optionally extend the runtime model with a type model (*runtime model extension*). Figure 7 shows the runtime model (extension) in eSPEM's classification hierarchy.

Our runtime model provides the base attributes and behavior of the instantiable language constructs in eSPEM for example TaskDefinition and WorkProduct. These attributes are required by our PEX in order to work properly. In contrast to FUML, elements from the process model are not (ontologically) instantiated by instantiating a generic class (Object) from the execution model. Instead, when executing a process model, a type model called *process runtime model* is created on-the-fly by a configurable model-to-model (M2M) transformation. During this transformation, classes from our runtime model (or a runtime model extension) are woven-in

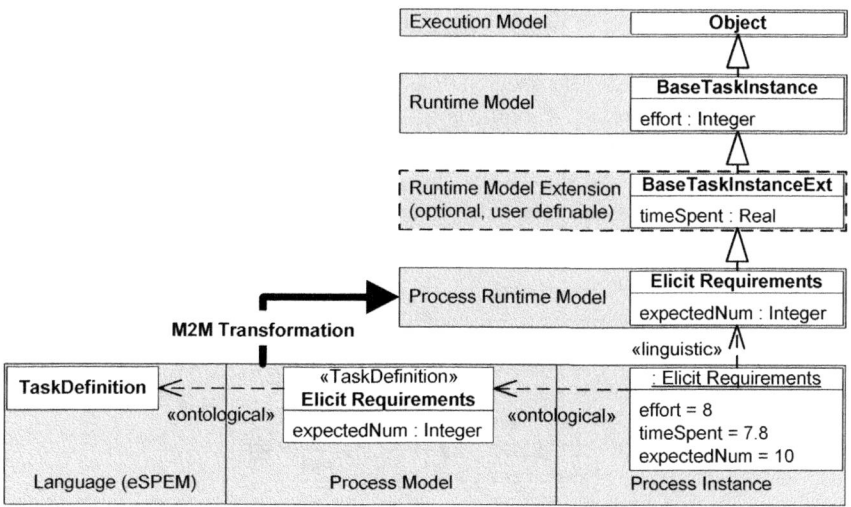

Fig. 7. Classification Levels used in eSPEM

as base classes for the classes from the process runtime model. The used base class from the runtime model (extension) is determined by the type of the corresponding process model element and the configuration of the transformation. For example, BaseTaskInstance (or BaseTaskInstanceExt) is configured as base class for all instances of TaskDefinition. Therefore, these instances share all the attributes and the behavior inherited from BaseTaskInstance (or BaseTaskInstanceExt). The behavior of the base classes can be implemented by the users of the PEX, for example, using a programming language. We use EMF models for linguistic instantiation. Thus, additional behavior of classes in a runtime model extension can be added by implementing methods in the EMF-generated Java code. For convenience, the Java code generated for a process runtime model is transparently distributed to all workstations.

With the concept presented in this section, we fulfill requirement R4: support for customization of base attributes and behavior. By weaving-in customizations contained in a runtime model extension as an aspect, there is no need to pollute SDP models with this data. Therefore, standard software process models can be easily reused by different teams and organizations.

4 Evaluation

To test our FUML-based implementation of eSPEM's operational semantics, we have implemented a test suite. Each test in this suite uses a small process model to test a specific language construct, for example, DecisionNode, ForkNode, or ExecuteActivityAction. In addition to the functional test, we also test some non-functional properties like maximum execution time.

4.1 Exemplary SDP

In addition to these tests that focus on functionality of individual language constructs, we have evaluated our PEX by executing an exemplary SDP in a controlled environment. The used SDP is based on Scrum [22] with changes to simplify automated testing. Scrum is an iterative incremental SDP. An iteration usually takes 4 weeks and is called *sprint*. At the beginning of each sprint, the features are selected that form the product increment developed in that sprint. Then, activities are planned to implement these features. Figure 8 shows the behavior of Implement Feature (with its sub-tasks) used to implement

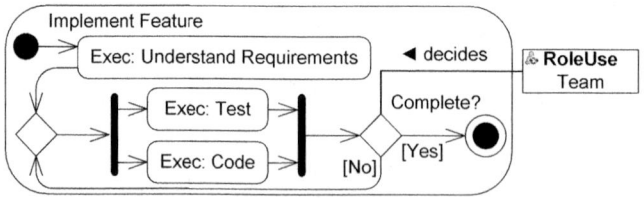

Fig. 8. Behavior of Implement Feature in the Exemplary SDP

one feature. The rest of the exemplary SDP consists of an infinite loop that instantiates and executes several Implement Feature activities.

4.2 Test Setup

Our test setup consists of 6 PCs connected by a local network. One PC acts as the server for the execution model instance and the execution machine. The other 5 PCs act as clients and simulate human interaction with the execution machine by answering Requests. Tests are performed with 1, 2, 3, 10, and 20 execution machine clients running simultaneously on each of the 5 client PCs to simulate different project sizes. We measure the execution time of each transaction on the execution model instance. The benchmark considers five different types of transactions. *Server:* The transactions that isolate the firing of transitions. These transactions are usually faster, because the execution machine is running within the same JVM as the execution model instance server (local loopback). *Planning:* These transactions isolate instantiation of Implement Feature activities on a client. *Understand* transactions isolate execution of an Understand Requirements task by a client. In the same way, *Test* and *Code* isolate execution of Test and Code tasks. The decision whether a feature is completely implemented or not, is isolated by *Finished* transactions. The average execution time for these transactions with 5, 10, 15, 50, and 100 execution machine clients concurrently working on the execution model instance, is shown in Fig. 9.

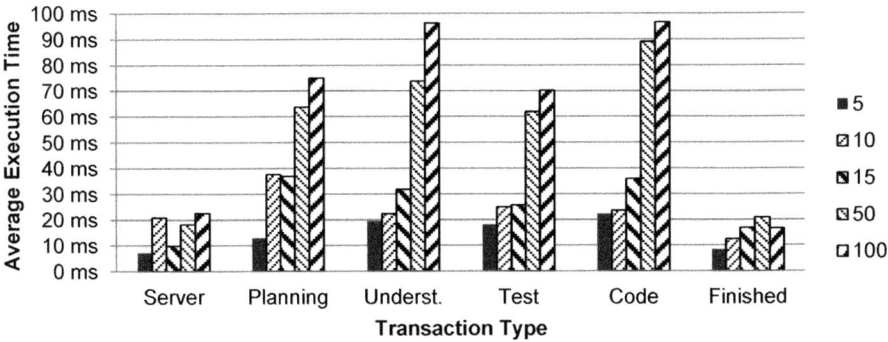

Fig. 9. Average Execution Time vs. Transaction Type for Different Numbers of Clients

Our tests show that execution time of typical transactions is below 100 ms. Hence, we consider this a sufficient response time for human interaction, even if the PEX is under high load with connections from many clients. These clients are running automated tests that handle requests within a second. In contrast, humans are considered to have a few interactions per hour with a PEX.

5 Related Work

Many authors have identified executability as highly relevant for (software) process modeling. Although first descriptions of software processes with process programming languages were executable [1] (some even supported distributed execution; see [2]), they had limited impact in industry due to their complex formalisms or low level of abstraction [13]. Therefore, below we focus on approaches that are based on standardized high-level modeling languages.

BPMN [23] or WS-BPEL [24] and its extension for People [25] were created to model and execute business processes. Although they provide a reasonable behavior modeling and execution concept, they do not provide essential concepts from SDPs, like roles, guidelines, responsibility assignments, and tools. These concepts have to be modeled by means of BPEL variables or cannot be modeled at all [19]. Thus, SDP descriptions with business process languages are incomplete and limit the support a PEX can provide when executing them.

Bendraou et al. [26] present xSPEM and focus on SDP validation with timed Petri nets. xSPEM also adds events for SPEM activities but lacks a fine-grained behavior modeling approach with decisions and task scheduling. Furthermore, no tool is provided to support direct execution of xSPEM-based models.

Seidita et al. [27] extend SPEM to support the modeling of agent oriented methodologies [28] but do not focus on executability.

UML4SPM [29] extends SPEM 1.1 with UML 2.0 behavior modeling concepts. There are two ways to make UML4SPM-based models executable. First, UML4SPM is mapped to WS-BPEL for enactment support [19]. As mentioned above, business processes lack some of the essential concepts of software processes, for example, roles, and guidelines. Moreover, the language WS-BPEL does not support human interaction during execution. Second, the operational semantics of UML4SPM is defined based on FUML. In [30], FUML's execution model concept is woven into UML4SPM using Kermeta [31]. Another implementation of UML4SPM based on FUML and Java is presented in [9]. Both implementations allow for a direct simulation and execution of UML4SPM-based process models, but they lack distributed execution support.

Di Nitto et al. [32] model SDP's with a UML 1.3-based framework. They do not use a dedicated meta model for language definition, but rather use plain UML. The proposed framework elements (e.g., `Activity`) are all instances of the UML meta class `Class`. SDPs are modeled by specializing the framework elements. This approach achieves executability by generating Java code from the diagrams (Class, Activity, and State Machine diagrams) used to describe an SDP. However, it remains vague how essential aspects of software processes (for example, precedence of activities) are translated. Another major drawback is the lack of a real modeling language definition. The sole use of UML classes may also confuse process modelers because all model elements have the same notation and semantics.

Chou [33] uses a subset of UML 1.4 activity and class diagrams to model SDPs graphically. He proposes a supplemental low-level object-oriented process programming language to execute SDPs. However, the executable code must be manually derived from the diagrams.

Besides SPEM, there is another standardized meta model driven approach for describing development methodologies: the ISO/IEC standard SEMDM [5].

However, SEMDM lacks a fine-grained behavior modeling concept and no execution support is currently provided.

Engels et al. [34] show how plain UML 2.0 can be used for process modeling. However, since essential concepts of SDP modeling are missing in UML (e.g., work products and responsibility assignments) the resulting SDPs are incomplete and imprecise so that support by a PEX must be limited.

Other approaches use UML and extensions through stereotypes for SDP modeling, for example [35] and the SPEM standard [6] itself, which also defines a UML profile. This allows to use behavior modeling concepts from UML with standard UML tools for modeling SDPs. Additionally, at least parts of the models could be executed using FUML. However, all of these approaches suffer from the fact that stereotypes change the semantics of the UML elements they are applied to but have no influence on the language structure as defined by the UML meta model. This results in two drawbacks: First, the SDP modeling language structure has to be re-implemented, for example, as constraints for the stereotypes. Second, the operational semantics of the stereotypes has to be defined and integrated with FUML in order to provide reasonable execution support. As outlined above, FUML also has a different focus and does not provide essential concepts like human interaction.

Benyahia et al. [16] extend FUML to reflect additional requirements on the execution semantics for real-time systems (e.g., scheduling, and concurrency). The authors highlight similar problems with FUML's Java mapping using synchronous, sequential method calls for token and event propagation. They introduce the class `Scheduler` in the execution model that is responsible to dispatch actions and therefore break the strictly sequential execution in FUML. However, they do not support distributed execution.

Regarding instantiation, several other approaches exist that enable multi-level modeling. Atkinson and Kühne discuss some of them in [21]. We briefly discuss the two most prominent of them below.

The powertype pattern [36] (used by SEMDM [5,37]) uses a special relationship between two classes (powertype and partitioned type). The powertype instantiates objects that form the process model. In conjunction with a specialization of the partitioned type, these objects form a so called *clabject*. The name is derived from class and object, because a clabject has both a class facet and an object facet. Objects at process instance level are instantiated from the class facet. The powertype pattern still uses one level of instantiation (shallow instantiation), but with generalization relationships crossing the ontological instantiation layers. This violates a strict separation of classification levels as requested by strict meta modeling [20] and may lead to confusion [38]. FUML and our approach use an instantiation concept well aligned with orthogonal classification architecture that also conforms to the rules of strict meta modeling.

Atkinson and Kühne [21,39] present another approach to multi-level modeling called *deep instantiation*, which allows to annotate elements of type models (for example, classes and attributes) with a non-negative number called *potency*. With each instantiation step, potency is decreased by 1. An element with potency above 0 can be further instantiated. With potency 0, it behaves like a normal object or attribute instance. Although this is a generic approach for multi-level classification, its application to established standards like UML and SPEM is problematic [40,41].

6 Conclusion and Future Work

In this paper, we have identified why pure FUML cannot be used to execute software process models to drive realistic projects with large and distributed teams. The presented FUML extension supports distributed execution with synchronized access to a shared execution model instance. In addition, it supports suspending and resuming execution on different nodes, as well as requests to interact with project staff. Our extension of FUML's instantiation concept allows organizations and projects to easily weave-in their specific attributes and behavior in order to tailor the execution machine to their needs. As a result, the extended FUML can be used to enact reusable standard software process models in realistic projects.

Our work is also useful for other PMLs based on UML behavior modeling concepts and for a concurrent execution of UML models in general. With small modifications of the M2M transformation, our instantiation concept could also be used to weave-in specific behavior for UML elements with stereotypes and therefore implement the semantics of the stereotypes.

In the future, we will focus on implementing the operational semantics of state machines, which are currently missing in both FUML and our FUML-extension. We also plan to enhance our PEX to integrate existing tools and their data formats. Another topic of our future work is process evolution: Process evolution is considered crucial if a model is executed over a long time (duration of the development project) and the process model or the runtime extension model has to be changed, for example, due to an error in the process model. Process evolution should allow for an (semi-)automatic adaptation of the process instance model to the changed process model or runtime extension model.

References

1. Osterweil, L.J.: Software processes are software too. In: Proc. 9th Intl. Conf. on Softw. Eng., Monterey, CA, pp. 2–13 (April 1987)
2. Zamli, K., Lee, P.: Taxonomy of Process Modeling Languages. In: Proc. ACS/IEEE Intl. Conf. on Computer Sys. and Appl., Beirut, Lebanon, 435–437 (June 2001)
3. Acuña, S.T., Ferré, X.: Software Process Modelling. In: Proc. World Multiconf. on Systemics, Cybernetics and Informatics, Orlando, FL, pp. 237–242 (July 2001)
4. Bendraou, R., Jezequel, J.M., Gervais, M.P., Blanc, X.: A Comparison of Six UML-Based Languages for Software Process Modeling. IEEE Trans. Softw. Eng. 36, 662–675 (2010)
5. ISO/IEC: ISO/IEC 24744:2007 – Software Engineering – Metamodel for Development Methodologies (February 2007)

6. Object Management Group: Software & Systems Process Engineering Meta-Model Specification v2.0 (April 2008)
7. Object Management Group: UML: Infrastructure v2.2 (February 2009)
8. Almeida da Silva, M.A., Bendraou, R., Blanc, X., Gervais, M.-P.: Early Deviation Detection in Modeling Activities of MDE Processes. In: Petriu, D.C., Rouquette, N., Haugen, Ø. (eds.) MODELS 2010. LNCS, vol. 6395, pp. 303–317. Springer, Heidelberg (2010)
9. Bendraou, R., Jezéquél, J.M., Fleurey, F.: Achieving process modeling and execution through the combination of aspect and model-driven engineering approaches. J. of Softw. Maintenance and Evolution: Research & Practice (2010) (preprint) n/a
10. Ellner, R., Al-Hilank, S., Drexler, J., Jung, M., Kips, D., Philippsen, M.: eSPEM – A SPEM Extension for Enactable Behavior Modeling. In: Kühne, T., Selic, B., Gervais, M.-P., Terrier, F. (eds.) ECMFA 2010. LNCS, vol. 6138, pp. 116–131. Springer, Heidelberg (2010)
11. Object Management Group: UML: Superstructure v2.2 (February 2009)
12. Object Management Group: Semantics of a Foundational Subset for Executable UML Models v1.0 Beta 3 (March 2010)
13. Gruhn, V.: Process Centered Software Engineering Environments – A Brief History and Future Challenges. Annals of Softw. Eng. 14(1-4), 363–382 (2002)
14. Gamma, E., Helm, R., Johnson, R., Vlissides, J.: Design Patterns: Elements of Reusable Object-Oriented Software. Addison-Wesley, Reading (1994)
15. Jensen, K.: Coloured Petri nets. Springer, Heidelberg (1995)
16. Benyahia, A., Cuccuru, A., Taha, S., Terrier, F., Boulanger, F., Gérard, S.: Extending the Standard Execution Model of UML for Real-Time Systems. In: Hinchey, M., Kleinjohann, B., Kleinjohann, L., Lindsay, P.A., Rammig, F.J., Timmis, J., Wolf, M. (eds.) DIPES 2010. IFIP Advances in Information and Communication Technology, vol. 329, pp. 43–54. Springer, Heidelberg (2010)
17. Eclipse Foundation: Connected Data Objects (CDO) Model Repository, http://www.eclipse.org/cdo/
18. Eclipse Foundation: Eclipse Modeling Framework (EMF), http://www.eclipse.org/modeling/emf/
19. Bendraou, R., Sadovykh, A., Gervais, M.P., Blanc, X.: Software Process Modeling and Execution: The UML4SPM to WS-BPEL Approach. In: Proc. 33rd EUROMICRO Conf. on Softw. Eng. and Adv. Appl., Lübeck, Germany, pp. 314–321 (August 2007)
20. Atkinson, C., Kühne, T.: Processes and products in a multi-level metamodeling architecture. Intl. J. Softw. Eng. and Knowledge Eng. 11(6), 761–783 (2001)
21. Atkinson, C., Kühne, T.: The essence of multilevel metamodeling. In: Gogolla, M., Kobryn, C. (eds.) UML 2001. LNCS, vol. 2185, pp. 19–33. Springer, Heidelberg (2001)
22. Schwaber, K.: Agile Project Management with Scrum. Microsoft Press, Redmond (2004)
23. Object Management Group: Business Process Modeling Notation v1.2 (January 2009)
24. OASIS: Web Services Business Process Execution Language v2.0 (April 2007)
25. Active Endpoints Inc., Adobe Systems Inc., BEA Systems Inc., IBM Corp., Oracle Inc., and SAP AG: WS-BPEL Extension for People (BPEL4People), v1.0 (June 2007)
26. Bendraou, R., Combemale, B., Crégut, X., Gervais, M.P.: Definition of an Executable SPEM 2.0. In: Proc. 14th Asia-Pacific Softw. Eng. Conf., Nagoya, Japan, pp. 390–397 (December 2007)

27. Seidita, V., Cossentino, M., Gaglio, S.: Using and Extending the SPEM Specifications to Represent Agent Oriented Methodologies. In: Proc. 9th Intl. Workshop Agent-Oriented Softw. Eng., Estoril, Portugal, pp. 46–59 (May 2008)
28. Henderson-Sellers, B., Giorgini, P.: Agent-Oriented Methodologies. Idea Group, USA (2005)
29. Bendraou, R., Gervais, M.P., Blanc, X.: UML4SPM: A UML2.0-Based Metamodel for Software Process Modelling. In: Briand, L.C., Williams, C. (eds.) MoDELS 2005. LNCS, vol. 3713, pp. 17–38. Springer, Heidelberg (2005)
30. Bendraou, R., Jezéquél, J.M., Fleurey, F.: Combining Aspect and Model-Driven Engineering Approaches for Software Process Modeling and Execution. In: Wang, Q., Garousi, V., Madachy, R., Pfahl, D. (eds.) ICSP 2009. LNCS, vol. 5543, pp. 148–160. Springer, Heidelberg (2009)
31. Muller, P.A., Fleurey, F., Jezéquél, J.M.: Weaving Executability into Object-Oriented Meta-languages. In: Briand, L.C., Williams, C. (eds.) MoDELS 2005. LNCS, vol. 3713, pp. 264–278. Springer, Heidelberg (2005)
32. Di Nitto, E., Lavazza, L., Schiavoni, M., Tracanella, E., Trombetta, M.: Deriving executable process descriptions from UML. In: Proc. 24th Intl. Conf. on Softw. Eng., Orlando, FL, pp. 155–165 (May 2002)
33. Chou, S.C.: A Process Modeling Language Consisting of High Level UML-based Diagrams and Low Level Process Language. J. of Object Technology 1(4), 137–163 (2002)
34. Engels, G., Förster, A., Heckel, R., Thöne, S.: Process Modeling using UML. In: Dumas, M., van der Aalst, W., ter Hofstede, A. (eds.) Process-Aware Information Sys., pp. 85–117. John Wiley & Sons, Chichester (2005)
35. Jäger, D., Schleicher, A., Westfechtel, B.: Using UML for Software Process Modeling. In: Proc. 7th European Softw. Eng. Conf., Toulouse, France, pp. 91–108 (September 1999)
36. Odell, J.J.: Power types. J. of Object-Oriented Programming 7(2), 8–12 (1994)
37. Henderson-Sellers, B., Gonzalez-Perez, C.: The Rationale of Powertype-based Metamodelling to Underpin Software Development Methodologies. In: Proc. 2nd Asia-Pacific Conf. on Conceptual Model., Newcastle, Australia, pp. 7–16 (January 2005)
38. Kühne, T.: Contrasting classification with generalisation. In: Proc. 6th Asia-Pacific Conf. on Conceptual Model., Wellington, New Zealand, pp. 71–78 (January 2009)
39. Atkinson, C., Kühne, T.: Rearchitecting the UML infrastructure. ACM Trans. Model. Comput. Simul. 12(4), 290–321 (2002)
40. Gutheil, M., Kennel, B., Atkinson, C.: A systematic approach to connectors in a multi-level modeling environment. In: Czarnecki, K., Ober, I., Bruel, J.-M., Uhl, A., Völter, M. (eds.) MODELS 2008. LNCS, vol. 5301, pp. 843–857. Springer, Heidelberg (2008)
41. Atkinson, C., Gutheil, M., Kennel, B.: A flexible infrastructure for multilevel language engineering. IEEE Trans. Softw. Eng. 35, 742–755 (2009)

A Generic Tool for Tracing Executions Back to a DSML's Operational Semantics

Benoît Combemale[1,*], Laure Gonnord[2], and Vlad Rusu[2]

[1] University of Rennes 1, IRISA, Campus de Beaulieu, Rennes, France
INRIA Rennes - Bretagne Atlantique (Triskell Project)
[2] LIFL - UMR CNRS/USTL 8022, INRIA Lille - Nord Europe
(DaRT Project) 40 avenue Halley, 59650 Villeneuve d'Ascq, France
First.Last@inria.fr

Abstract. The increasing complexity of software development requires rigorously defined *domain specific modeling languages* (DSML). Model-driven engineering (MDE) allows users to define a DSML's syntax in terms of *metamodels*. The behaviour of a language can also be described, either operationally, or via transformations to other languages (e.g., by code generation). If the first approach requires to redefine analysis tools for each DSML (simulator, model-checker...), the second approach allows to reuse existing tools in the targeted language. However, the second approach (also called *translational semantics*) imply that the results (e.g., a program crash log, or a counterexample returned by a model checker) may not be straightforward to interpret by the users of a DSML. We propose in this paper a generic tool for formally tracing such analysis/execution results back to the original DSML's syntax and operational semantics, and we illustrate it on xSPEM, a timed process modeling language.

1 Introduction

The design of a Domain-Specific Modeling Language (DSML) involves the definition of a metamodel, which identifies the domain-specific concepts and the relations between them. The metamodel formally defines the language's abstract syntax. Several works - [6,11,16], among others - have focused on how to help users define operational semantics for their languages in order to enable model execution and formal analyses such as model checking. Such analyses are especially important when the domain addressed by a language is safety critical.

However, grounding a formal analysis on a DSML's syntax and operational semantics would require building a specific verification tool for each DSML; for example, a model checker that "reads" the syntax of the DSML and "understands" the DSML's operational semantics. This is not realistic in practice.

Also, any realistic language will eventually have to be executed, and this usually involves code generation to some other language. Hence, model execution, resp. formal analyses, are performed via transformations of a *source* DSML to

---

[*] This work has been partially supported by the ITEA2 OPEES project.

some *target* language (the language chosen for code generation, resp. the input language of a model checker). The consequence is that execution and analysis results are typically not understandable by the source DSML practitioners. Hence, there should be a translation of the execution/analysis results back to the source.

In this paper we address the problem of formally tracing back results that are finite executions of a target language (that could have been obtained, e.g., as counterexamples to safety properties in a model checker, or as program crash logs) to executions of a source DSML, thereby allowing the DSML users to understand the results and to take action based on them. We propose a generic algorithm and its implementation in a DSML-independent tool to achieve this.

Our approach is illustrated in Figure 1. A *forward translation* typically implemented as a model transformation translates a DSML to a target language. Consider then an execution of that language, represented at the bottom of Figure 1. The *back-tracing algorithm* maps that execution to one that *matches* it in the source DSML, according to its syntax and operational semantics. We formally define this algorithm in the paper, and implement it in an MDE framework, using an aspect-oriented paradigm to make it reusable and generic for a broad class of DSML: those whose operational semantics are definable as finitely-branching transition systems (i.e., allowing for finite nondeterminism), and for executions of the target language presented as finite, totally ordered sequences of states.

The algorithm is parameterized by a relation R (depicted in Figure 1 using dashed lines) between states of the DSML and states of the target language; and by a natural number n that encodes an upper bound on the allowed "difference in granularity" between executions of the DSML and of the target language.

Our algorithm does not require the precondition that R is a bisimulation or a simulation relation between transition systems; indeed, detects situations where R is not so. However, in the case that R was proved to be such a relation (typically, in a theorem prover, as in, e.g., [5]) , our algorithm nicely complements the proof, by obtaining the parameters R and n that it needs, and by explicitly finding *which* DSML executions match a given target-language execution. Specifically,

- our algorithm requires the parameters R and n as inputs, and one can reasonably assume that these parameters characterise the bisimulation relation against which the model transformations was verified; hence, our algorithm benefits from that verification by obtaining two of its crucial inputs;
- our algorithm provides information that model transformation verification does not: DSML executions that correspond to given target-language ones.

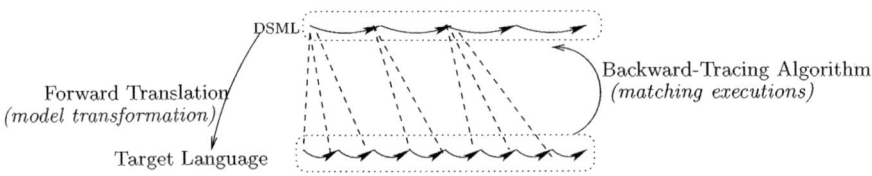

Fig. 1. Back-tracing executions

Also, by combining model transformation verification with our back-tracing algorithm, we completely relieve DSML users of having to know *anything* about the target language. This is important for such formal methods to be accepted in practice. A typical use of the combined approach by a DSML user would be:

- the user chooses a model conforming to the DSML, and a safety property;
- the model transformation automatically maps the model and property to the target language, here assumed to be the language of a model checker;
- the model checker runs automatically, producing the following output:
  - either *ok*, meaning that the property holds on the domain-specific model;
  - or a counterexample (in terms of the target language), that our tool automatically maps to an execution in terms of the source DSML.

This is an interesting (in our opinion) combination of theorem proving (for model transformation) and model checking (for model verification), set in the MDE and aspect-oriented paradigms to provide a DSML-independent implementation.

The rest of the paper is organized as follows. In Section 2 we illustrate our approach on an example (borrowed from [5]) of a process modeling language called xSPEM, transformed into Prioritized Time Petri Nets for verification by model checking. In Section 3 we present the generic implementation of our tool based on the advanced MDE capabilities and aspect-oriented features provided by the KERMETA environment [11], and we show the results of the implementation on the example discussed in Section 2. In Section 4 we detail the back-tracing algorithm implemented by the tool, and formally state its correctness. In Section 5 we present related work, and we conclude and suggest future work in Section 6.

2 Running Example

In this section we present a running example and briefly illustrate our approach on it. The example is a DSML called xSPEM [1], an executable version of the SPEM standard [14]. A transformation from xSPEM to Prioritized Time Petri Nets (PrTPN) was defined in [5] in order to benefit from the TINA verification toolsuite [2]. They have also proved (using the COQ proof assistant) that this model transformation induces a *weak bisimulation* between any xSPEM model's behavior and the behavior of the corresponding PrTPN. This implies in particular that for every PrTPN P and every execution of P returned by TINA - for instance, as a counterexample to a safety property - there *exists* a *matching* execution in the xSPEM model that transforms to P. However, their approach does not exhibit *which* xSPEM execution matches a given PrTPN execution.

This is the problem we address in this paper, with a generic approach that we instantiate on the particular case of the xSPEM-to-PrTPN transformation.

In the rest of this section we briefly describe the xSPEM language (Section 2.1): its abstract syntax, defined by the metamodel shown in Figure 2, and its operational semantics. After recalling a brief description of PrTPN (Section 2.2), we illustrate the model transformation on a model (Section 2.3). Finally, we show the expected result of our algorithm on this example (Section 2.4).

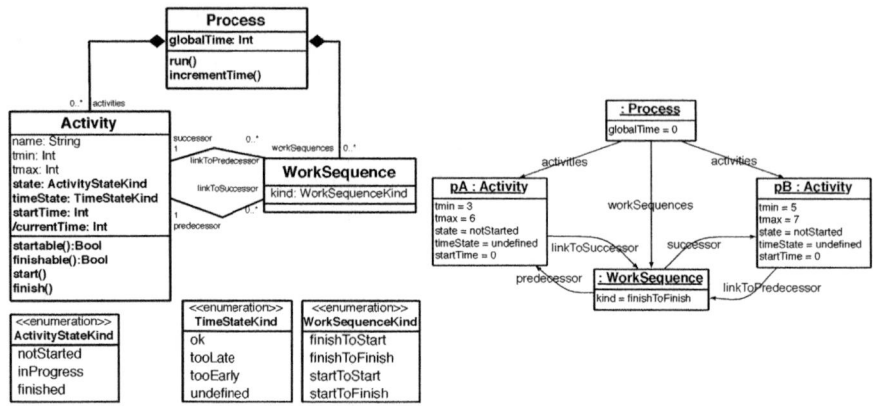

Fig. 2. xSPEM (simplified) metamodel and a model example

2.1 The xSPEM Language and Its Operational Semantics

In the metamodel shown in Figure 2 (left), an *Activity* represents a general unit of work assignable to specific performers. Activities are ordered thanks to the *WorkSequence* concept, whose attribute *kind* indicates when an activity can be started or finished. The values of *kind* are defined by the *WorkSequenceKind* enumeration. Values have the form *stateToAction* where *state* indicates the state of the work sequence's source activity that allows to perform the *action* on the work sequence's target activity. For example, in the right-hand side of Figure 2, the two activities *pA* and *pB* are linked by a *WorkSequence* of kind *finishToFinish*, which expresses that *pB* will be allowed to complete its execution only when *pA* is finished. The *tmin* and *tmax* attributes of the *Activity* class denote the minimum and, respectively, the maximum duration of activities.

Operational Semantics. The following attributes and methods (written in bold font in Figure 2) are used for defining the system's state and operational semantics[1]. An activity can be *notStarted*, *inProgress*, or *finished* (*state* attribute). When it is finished an activity can be *tooEarly*, *ok*, or *tooLate* (*timeState* attribute), depending on whether it has completed its execution in the intervals $[0, tmin[$, $[tmin, tmax[$, or $[tmax, \infty[$ respectively (all intervals are left-closed, right-open). The *timeState* value is *undefined* while an activity is not *finished*.

Time is measured by a global clock, encoded by the *globalTime* attribute of the *Process* class, which is incremented by the *incrementTime()* method of the class. The remaining attributes and methods are used to implement the state and time changes for each activity; *startTime* denotes the starting moment of a given activity, and the derived attribute *currentTime* records (for implementation reasons) the difference between *globalTime* and *startTime* (i.e., the current execution time of a given activity). Finally, the *startable()* (resp. *finishable()*)

---

[1] Defining state and operational semantics using attributes and methods is consistent with the Kermeta framework [11] in which we implement our tool.

methods check whether an activity can be started (resp. finished), and the *start()* and *finish()* methods change the activity's state accordingly.

Definition 1. *The state of an* xSPEM *model defining the set of activities A is the Cartesian product* $\{globalTime\} \times \Pi_{a \in A}(a.state, a.timeState, a.currentTime)$.

The initial state is $\{0\} \times \Pi_{a \in A}\{(notStarted,\ undefined,\ 0)\}$. The method *run* of the *Process* class implements this initialisation (Figure 2). The transition relation consists of the following transitions, implemented by the following methods:
- for each activity $a \in A$, the transitions shown in Figure 3. The first one starts the activity (implemented by the method *start* of the *Activity* class). An activity can be started when its associated constraints (written in the OCL language in Figure 3) are satisfied. These constraints are implemented in the *startable()* method of the metamodel. The three remaining transitions deal with finishing activities, depending on whether the activity ends too early, in time, or too late.
- the method *incrementTime* of *Process* increments the *globalTime*. It can be called at any moment. The values of $a.currentTime$ are derived accordingly.

$\forall ws \in a.linkToPredecessor,$
$\quad (ws.linkType = startToStart\ \&\&\ ws.predecessor.state \in \{inProgress, finished\})$
$\|\ (ws.linkType = finishToStart\ \&\&\ ws.predecessor.state = finished)$
$\quad (notStarted, undefined, a.currentTime) \xrightarrow{start} (inProgress, tooEarly, 0)$

$\forall ws \in a.linkToPredecessor,$
$\quad (ws.linkType = startToFinish\ \&\&\ ws.predecessor.state \in \{inProgress, finished\})$
$\|\ (ws.linkType = finishToFinish\ \&\&\ ws.predecessor.state = finished)$
$\quad$ if $a.currentTime < a.tmin$ then
$\quad (inProgress, tooEarly, a.currentTime) \xrightarrow{finish} (finished, tooEarly, a.currentTime)$
$\quad$ if $a.currentTime \in [a.tmin, a.tmax[$ then
$\quad (inProgress, ok, a.currentTime) \xrightarrow{finish} (finished, ok, a.currentTime)$
$\quad$ if $a.currentTime \geq a.tmax$ then
$\quad (inProgress, tooLate, a.currentTime) \xrightarrow{finish} (finished, tooLate, a.currentTime)$

Fig. 3. Event-based Transition Relation for Activities

2.2 Prioritized Time Petri Nets

We translate xSPEM to *Prioritized Time Petri Nets* (PrTPN) for model checking.

A Petri Net (PN) example is shown in the left-hand side of Figure 4. Let us quickly and informally recall their vocabulary and semantics. A PN is composed of *places* and *transitions*, connected by oriented *Arcs*. A *marking* is a mapping from places to natural numbers, expressing the number of tokens in each place (represented by bullet in a place). A transition is *enabled* in a marking when all its predecessor (a.k.a. input) places contain at least the number of tokens specified by the arc connecting the place to the transition (1 by default when not represented). If this is the case then the transition can be *fired*, thereby removing the number of tokens specified by the input arc from each of its input places, and adding the number of tokens specified by the output arc to each of its successor (a.k.a. output) places. In the extended Petri net formalism that we

Fig. 4. A Petri Net and a Prioritized Time Petri Net

are using there is an exception to this transition-firing rule: if an input place is connected by a *read-arc* (denoted by a black circle) to a transition, then the number of tokens in this input place remains unchanged when the transition is fired. An *execution* of a Petri net is then a sequence of markings and transitions $m_0, t_1, m_1, \ldots, t_n, m_n$ (for $n \geq 0$) starting from a given initial marking m_0, such that each marking m_i is obtained by firing the transition t_i from the marking m_{i-1} (for $i = 0, \ldots, n$) according to the transition-firing rule.

Time Petri Nets (TPN) [9] are an extension of Petri Nets, dedicated to the specification of real-time systems. TPN are PN in which each transition t_i is associated to a *firing interval* that has non-negative rational end-points. Executions are now sequences of the form $(m_0, \tau_0), t_1, (m_1, \tau_1) \ldots, t_n, (m_n, \tau_n)$ (for $n \geq 0$), starting from a given initial marking m_0 at time $\tau_0 = 0$, and such that each marking m_i is obtained by firing the transition t_i at time τ_i from the marking m_{i-1} (for $i = 1, \ldots, n$) according to the transition-firing rule.

Finally, Prioritized Time Petri Nets (PrTPN) [3] allows for *priorities* between transitions. When two transitions can both be fired at the same time, the one that is actually fired is the one that has higher priority (the priorities are denoted by dotted arrows in the right-hand side of Figure 4 - the source of the arrow denotes the higher priority).

2.3 A Transformation from xSPEM to PrTPN

In [5] we have defined a model transformation from xSPEM to PrTPN. We illustrate this transformation by presenting its output when given as input the xSPEM model shown in the right-hand side of Figure 2. The result is shown in Figure 5. Each *Activity* is translated into seven places, connected by four transitions:

– Three places characterize the value of *state* attribute (*NotStarted*, *InProgress*, *Finished*). One additional place called *Started* is added to record the fact that the activity has been started, and may be either *inProgress* or *finished*.
– The three remaining places characterize the value of the *time* attribute: *tooEarly* when the activity ends before *tmin*, *tooLate* when the activity ends after *tmax*, and *ok* when the activity ends in due time.

We rely on *priorities* among transitions to encode temporal constraints. As an example, the *deadline* transition has a priority over the *finish* one (cf. Figure 5). This encodes the fact that the termination interval [*tmin*, *tmax*[is right-open.

Finally, a *WorkSequence* instance becomes a *read-arc* from one place of the source activity, to a transition of the target activity according to the *kind* attribute of the *WorkSequence*. In our example, *kind* equals *finishToFinish*,

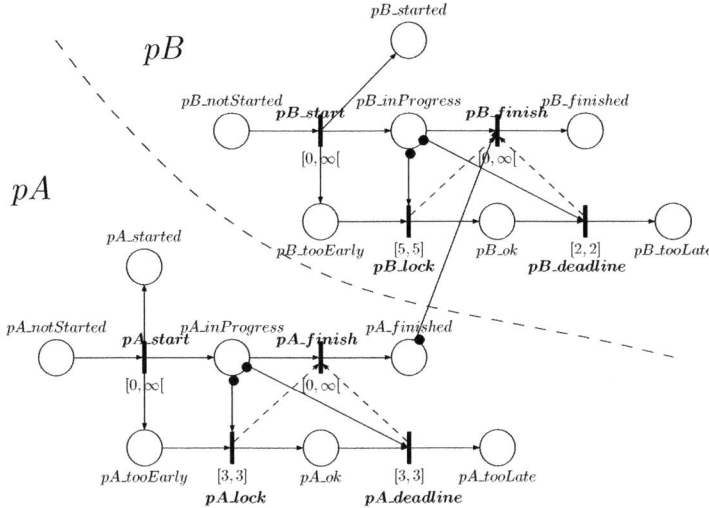

Fig. 5. PrTPN obtained from the XSPEM model in Figure 2 (right). The initial marking has one token in each of the *pA_notStarted* and *pB_notStarted* places.

meaning that *pA* has to complete its execution before *pB* finishes; hence the read-arc in Figure 5 from the *pA_finished* place to the *pB_finish* transition.

2.4 An Illustration of Our Back-Tracing Algorithm

The PrTPN obtained from the transformation of a given XSPEM model can be analyzed by the TINA model checker. For example, to exhibit an execution where both activities end on time, we challenge TINA to prove that such an execution does not exist. This is expressed by the following temporal-logic formula:

$\Box \neg (pA\_finished \wedge pA\_ok \wedge pB\_finished \wedge pB\_ok)$

The tool returns *false*, and chooses one PrTPN execution that contradicts the temporal-logic property - that is, an execution where both activities end on time. For sake of simplicity, the markings m_i of the execution are not shown:

(m_0,0),pA_start,(m_1,0),pA_lock,(m_2,3),pA_finish,(m_3,3),
pB_start,(m_4,3),pB_lock,(m_5,8),pB_finish,(m_6,8).

That is, pA_start fires at time 0, then pA_lock, pA_finish, pB_start fire in sequence at time 3, and finally pB_lock, pB_finish fire in sequence at time 8.

Our back-tracing algorithm (cf. Section 4.2) takes this input together with a relation R between XSPEM and PrTPN states, and a natural-number bound n that captures the difference in granularity between XSPEM and PrTPN executions. Two states are in the relation R if for each activity, the value of its *state* attribute is encoded by a token in the corresponding place of the PrTPN, and when an activity is *finished*, the value of its *timeState* attribute is encoded by a token in the corresponding place of the PrTPN (cf. Section 2.3). For instance, $A.state = notStarted$ is encoded by a token in the *pA_nonStarted* place;

and similarly for the *inProgress* and *finished* state values; and $A.timeState = ok$ is encoded by a token in the pA_ok place; and similarly for the *tooEarly* and *tooLate* time state values. Regarding the bound n, it is here set to 5 - because in XSPEM executions *globalTime* advances by at most one time unit, but in the given PrTPN execution, the maximum difference between two consecutive timestamps is $5 = 8 - 3$. Then, our algorithm returns the following XSPEM execution:

globalTime	XSPEM states : $(state_i, timeState_i, currentTime_i)$	
	$i = p_A$	$i = p_B$
0	$(notStarted, undefined, 0)$	$(notStarted, undefined, 0)$
0	$(inProgress, tooEarly, 0)$	$(notStarted, undefined, 0)$
3	$(inProgress, ok, 3)$	$(notStarted, undefined, 0)$
3	$(finished, ok, 3)$	$(notStarted, undefined, 0)$
3	$(finished, ok, 3)$	$(inProgress, tooEarly, 0)$
8	$(finished, ok, 3)$	$(inProgress, ok, 5)$
8	$(finished, ok, 3)$	$(finished, ok, 8)$

Note that indeed both processes finish in due time: pA starts at 0 and finishes at 3 (its $tmin = 3$); and pB starts at 3 and finishes at 8 (its $tmin = 5 = 8 - 3$).

3 A Generic Tool for Tracing Executions in Kermeta

Our implementation takes as input an execution of the target language and returns as output a corresponding execution of the source DSML. In our running example, the input execution trace comes from the TINA toolsuite and the tool returns an XSPEM model execution, as shown in the previous section.

3.1 Generic Implementation Using Executable Metamodeling

Kermeta is a language for specifying metamodels, models, and model transformations that are compliant to the Meta Object Facility (MOF) standard [12]. The abstract syntax of a DSML is specified by means of metamodels possibly enriched with constraints written in an OCL-like language [13]. Kermeta also proposes an imperative language for describing the operational semantics of DSML [11].

We implement in Kermeta the back-tracing algorithm given in detail in Section 4. Here, we focus more specifically on the genericity of the implementation. Accordingly, our implementation relies on a generic tree-based structure (cf. Figure 6, left). The algorithm is generically defined in the *treeLoading* method of the *SimulationTree* class. To use this method, the *SourceExecution* and its sequence of *SourceState* have to be specialized by an execution coming from an execution platform (*e.g.*, a verification tool), and the *TargetState* have to be specialized by the corresponding concept in the DSML[2].

The *treeLoading* method builds a simulation tree by calling the method *findStates* for each tree node. This method *findStates* computes the set of target states

---

[2] We assume in this work a naive definition of the domain-specific model state by specializing *TargetState* by *Process*. This work could be extended to well-distinguish the dynamic information in order to store only this one.

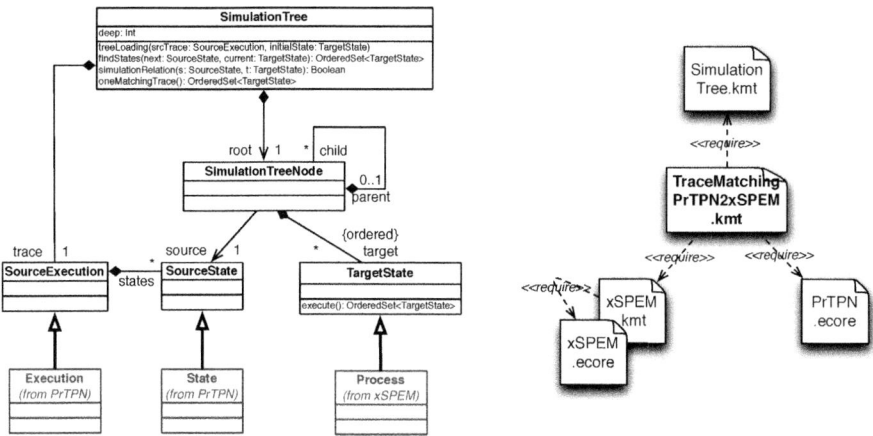

Fig. 6. The generic *SimulationTree* class (left) and how to use it (right)

that are in relation with the next source state. The generic computation is based on calling the abstract method *execute* on the current *TargetState*. For a given DSML (XSPEM in our case), the method *execute* needs to be implemented to define one execution step according to the DSML operational semantics. This method depends on a given relation R (in our example, the one discussed in Section 2.4) defined in the method *simulationRelation* between *sourceState* and *targetState*. It also depends on a given maximal depth of search defined by the attribute *deep*. Once the simulation tree is built, a DSML execution that matches any execution provided by the verification tool can be generated by the method *oneMatchingTrace*.

3.2 Tool Specialization for a Given Example Using Aspect-Oriented (Meta)Modeling

Among others, one key feature of Kermeta is its ability to extend an existing metamodel with constraints, new structural elements (meta-classes, classes, properties, and operations), and functionalities defined with other languages using the *require* keyword. This keyword permits the composition of corresponding code within the underlying metamodel as if it was a native element of it. This feature offers flexibility to developers by enabling them to easily manipulate and reuse existing metamodels. The static introduction operator *aspect* allows for defining these various aspects in separate units and integrating them automatically into the metamodel. The composition is performed statically and the composed metamodel is type-checked to ensure the safe integration of all units.

We use both model weaving and static introduction to specialize our generic implementation of the back-tracing algorithm to the particular context of computing XSPEM executions from a PrTPN execution. As described in Figure 6 (right) and in Listing 1.1, the *TraceMatchingPrTPN2xSPEM.kmt* program weaves the XSPEM metamodel (*xSPEM.ecore*) and its operational semantics (*xSPEM.kmt*), together with a metamodel for PrTPN (*PrTPN.ecore*) and our generic implementation for the back-tracing algorithm (*SimulationTree.kmt*) – cf. lines 4 to 7 in Listing 1.1.

In addition to weaving the different artifacts, *TraceMatchingPrTPN2xSPEM.kmt* also defines the links between them. Thus we define the inheritance relations (cf. Figure 6, left) between *Execution* (from *PrTPN.ecore*) and *SourceExecution*, between *State* (from *PrTPN.ecore*) and *SourceState*, and between *Process* (from *xSPEM.ecore*) and *TargetState* – cf. lines 9 to 11 in Listing 1.1. We also define the relation *R* by specializing the method *simulationRelation*) (cf. lines 13 to 18 in Listing 1.1) and the value of the attribute *deep* (cf. line 35 in Listing 1.1). Finally, we illustrate the content of the method *main* of *TraceMatchingPrTPN2xSPEM.kmt* in Listing 1.1, that loads a given PrTPN execution trace, a given process initial state, and computes a corresponding process execution trace.

Listing 1.1. *TraceMatchingPrTPN2xSPEM.kmt*

```
1   package prtpn2xspem;
2
3   require kermeta
4   require "./traceMatching.kmt"
5   require "./prtpn.ecore"
6   require "./xSPEM.ecore"
7   require "./xSPEM.kmt"
8
9   aspect class prtpn::Execution inherits traceMatching::SourceExecution { }
10  aspect class prtpn::State inherits traceMatching::SourceState { }
11  aspect class xspem::Process inherits traceMatching::TargetState { }
12
13  aspect class traceMatching::SimulationTree {
14      operation simulationRelation(next: SourceState, current: TargetState)
              : Boolean is do
15          // specification of the simulation relation between xSPEM and
              PrTPN
16          // ...
17      end
18  }
19
20  class TraceMatching
21  {
22      // Tracing a Petri net execution trace to an xSPEM process execution
23      operation main(inputTrace: String, initialState: String, deep:
              Integer) : Void is do
24          var rep : EMFRepository init EMFRepository.new
25          // loading of the Petri net trace  (using EMF API)
26          var resPN : Resource init rep.createResource(inputTrace, "./prtpn
              .ecore")
27          var pnTrace : prtpn::Execution
28          tracePN ?= resPN.load.one
29          // loading of the xSPEM process initial state (using EMF API)
30          var resProcess : Resource init rep.createResource(initialState, "
              ./xSPEM.ecore")
31          var processInitState : xspem::Process
32          processInitState ?= resProcess.load.one
33          // trace matching
34          var prtpn2xspem : traceMatching::SimulationTree init
              traceMatching::SimulationTree.new
35          prtpn2xspem.deep := 5
36          prtpn2xspem.treeloading(pnTrace, processInitState)
37          // one possible result
38          prtpn2xspem.oneMatchingTrace()
39      end
40  }
41  endpackage
```

Thus, *TraceMatchingPrTPN2xSPEM.kmt* may be used for a given execution of PrTPN conforming to *PrTPN.ecore*, in our case, the TINA execution obtained in Section 2.4). As TINA only provides textual output, we had to parse and pretty-print it in the right format (XMI - *XML Metadata Interchange*). This was done in OCaml[3]. After running the method *SimulationTree*, we obtain the following input (and corresponding model) using the method *oneMatchingTrace*:

```
Console
simulationTree.kmt_mtverification____Main_main [Kermeta Application] platform:/resource/fr.inria.mt.ver
One matching trace:
(0, {(pB, notStarted), (pA, notStarted)})  -->  (0, {(pA, inProgress), (pB, notS
tarted)})  -->  (3, {(pB, notStarted), (pA, inProgress)})  -->  (3, {(pA, finish
ed@3=>ok), (pB, notStarted)})  -->  (3, {(pB, inProgress), (pA, finished@3=>ok)}
)  -->  (8, {(pA, finished@3=>ok), (pB, inProgress)})  -->  (8, {(pA, finished@3
=>ok), (pB, finished@5=>ok)})
```

4 Formalizing the Problem

In this section we formally define our back-tracing algorithm and prove its correctness. We start by recapping the definition of *transition systems* and give a notion of *matching* an execution of a transition system with a given (abstract) sequence of states, modulo a given relation between states.

4.1 Transition Systems and Execution Matching

Definition 2 (transition system). *A transition system is a tuple* $\mathcal{A} = (A, a_{init}, \rightarrow_{\mathcal{A}})$ *where A is a possibly infinite set of states, a_{init} is the initial state, and* $\rightarrow_{\mathcal{A}} \subseteq A \times A$ *is the transition relation.*

Notations. $\mathbb{N}$ is the set of natural numbers. We write $a \rightarrow_{\mathcal{A}} a'$ for $(a, a') \in \rightarrow_{\mathcal{A}}$. An execution is a sequence of states $\rho = a_0, \ldots a_n \in A$, for some $n \in \mathbb{N}$, such that $a_i \rightarrow_{\mathcal{A}} a_{i+1}$ for $i = 0, \ldots, n-1$; $length(\rho) = n$ is the *length* of the execution ρ. Executions of length 0 are states. We denote by $exec(a)$ the subset of executions that start in the state a, i.e., the set of executions ρ of $\mathcal{A}$ such that $\rho(0) = a$. We restrict ourselves to *finitely branching* transition systems, meaning that for all states a there are at most finitely many states a' such that $a \rightarrow_{\mathcal{A}} a'$.

Definition 3 (*R-matching*). *Given a transition system* $\mathcal{B} = (B, b_{init}, \rightarrow_{\mathcal{B}})$, *a set A with $A \cap B = \emptyset$, an element $a_{init} \in A$, a relation $R \subseteq A \times B$, and two sequences $\rho \in a_{init}A^*$, $\pi \in exec(b)$, we say that ρ is R-matched by π if there exists a (possibly, non strictly) increasing function $\alpha : [0, \ldots, length(\rho)] \rightarrow \mathbb{N}$ with $\alpha(0) = 0$, such that for all $i \in [0, \ldots, length(\rho)]$, $(a_i, b_{\alpha(i)}) \in R$.*

Example 1. In Figure 7 we represent two sequences ρ and π. A relation R is denoted using dashed lines. The function $\alpha : [0, \ldots, 5] \rightarrow \mathbb{N}$ defined by $\alpha(i) = 0$ for $i \in [0, 3]$, $\alpha(4) = 1$, and $\alpha(5) = 5$ ensures that ρ is R-matched by π.

---
[3] http://caml.inria.fr/ocaml/

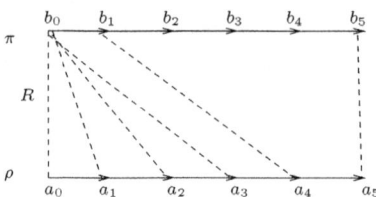

Fig. 7. R-matching of sequences. The relation R is represented by dashed lines. Note that R-matching does not require all π-states to be in relation to ρ-states.

In our framework, $\mathcal{B} = (B, b_{init}, \to_{\mathcal{B}})$ is the transition system denoting a DSML $\mathcal{L}$ (in our running example, XSPEM) and its operational semantics, with b_{init} being the initial state of a particular model $m \in \mathcal{L}$ (in our example, the model depicted in the right-hand side of Figure 2). The model m is transformed by some model transformation ϕ (in our example, the model transformation defined in [5]) to a target language (say, $\mathcal{L}'$; in our example, PrTPN, the input language of the TINA model checker). About $\mathcal{L}'$, we only assume that it has a notion of *state* and that its state-space is a given set A. Then, $\rho \in a_{init} A^*$ is the execution of the tool that we are trying to match, where a_{init} is the initial state of the model $\phi(m) \in \mathcal{L}'$ (here, the PrTPN illustrated in Figure 5 with the initial marking specified in the figure). The relation R can be thought of as a matching criterion between states of a DSML and those of the target language; it has to be specified by users of our back-tracing algorithm.

Remark 1. We do not assume that the operational semantics of $\mathcal{L}'$ is known. This is important, because is saves us the effort of giving operational semantics to the target language, which can be quite hard if the language is complex.

4.2 The Back-Tracing Problem

Our back-tracing problem can now be formally stated as follows: given
- a transition system $\mathcal{B} = (B, b_{init}, \to_{\mathcal{B}})$
- a set A, an element $a_{init} \in A$, and a sequence $\rho \in a_{init} A^*$
- a relation $R \subseteq A \times B$,

does there exist an execution $\pi \in exec(b_{init})$ such that ρ is R-matched by π; and if this is the case, then, construct such an execution π.

Unfortunately, this problem is not decidable/solvable. This is because an execution π that R-matches a sequence ρ can be arbitrarily long; the function α in Definition 3 is responsible for this. One way to make the problem decidable is to impose that, in Definition 3, the function α satisfies a "bounded monotonicity property" : $\forall i \in [0, length(\rho) - 1] \, \alpha(i+1) - \alpha(i) \leq n$ for some given $n \in \mathbb{N}$. In this way, the candidate executions π that may match ρ become finitely many.

Definition 4 ((n, R)-matching). *With the notations of Definition 3, and given a natural number $n \in \mathbb{N}$ we say that the sequence ρ is (n, R)-matched by the execution π if the function α satisfies $\forall i \in [0, length(\rho) - 1] \, \alpha(i+1) - \alpha(i) \leq n$.*

In Example 1 (Figure 7), ρ is $(5, R)$-matched (but not $(4, R)$-matched) by π.

4.3 Back-Tracing Algorithm

For a set $S \subseteq A$ of states of a transition system $\mathcal{A}$, we denote by $\rightarrow_{\mathcal{A}}^{n} (S)$ ($n \in \mathbb{N}$) the set of states $\{a' \in A | \exists a \in S. \exists \rho \in exec(a). length(\rho) \leq n \wedge \rho(length(\rho)) = a'\}$; it is the set of successors of states in S by executions of length at most n. Also, for a relation $R \subseteq A \times B$ and $a \in A$ we denote by $R(a)$ the set $\{b \in B | (a,b) \in R\}$. We denote the empty sequence by ε, whose length is undefined; and, for a nonempty sequence ρ, we let $last(\rho) \triangleq \rho(length(\rho))$ denote its last element.

Algorithm 1. Return an execution $\pi \in exec(b_{init})$ of $\mathcal{B}$ that (n, R)-matches the longest prefix of a sequence $\rho \in a_{init} A^*$ that can be (n, R)-matched.

Require: $\mathcal{B} = (B, b_{init}, \rightarrow_{\mathcal{B}}); A; a_{init} \in A; \rho \in a_{init} A^*; n \in \mathbb{N}; R \subseteq A \times B$
    Local Variable: $\alpha : [0..length(\rho)] \rightarrow \mathbb{N}; \pi \in B^*; S, S' \subseteq B; \ell \in \mathbb{N}$
1: **if** $(a_{init}, b_{init}) \notin R$ **then return** ε
2: **else**
3:     $\alpha(0) \leftarrow 0, k \leftarrow 0, \pi \leftarrow b_{init}, S \leftarrow \{b_{init}\}$
4:     **while** $k < length(\rho)$ and $S \neq \emptyset$ **do**
5:         $k \leftarrow k + 1$
6:         $S' \leftarrow R(\rho(k)) \cap \rightarrow_{\mathcal{B}}^{n} (last(\pi))$
7:         **if** $S' \neq \emptyset$ **then**
8:             Choose $\hat{\pi} \in exec(last(\pi))$
                such that $\ell = length(\hat{\pi}) \leq n$ and $\hat{\pi}(\ell) \in S'$ ▷ ℓ can be 0
9:             $\alpha(k) \leftarrow \alpha(k-1) + \ell$
10:            $\pi_{\alpha(k-1)+1..\alpha(k)} \leftarrow \hat{\pi}_{1..l}$ ▷ effect of this assignment is null if $\ell = 0$
11:         **end if**
12:         $S \leftarrow S'$
13:     **end while**;
14:     **return** π
15: **end if**

Theorem 1 (Algorithm for matching executions). *Consider a transition system $\mathcal{B} = (B, b_{init}, \rightarrow_{\mathcal{B}})$, a set A with $A \cap B = \emptyset$, an element $a_{init} \in A$, a relation $R \subseteq A \times B$, and a natural number $n \in \mathbb{N}$. Consider also a sequence $\rho \in a_{init} A^*$. Then, Algorithm 1 returns an execution $\pi \in exec(b_{init})$ of $\mathcal{B}$ that (n, R) matches the longest prefix of ρ that can be (n, R)-matched.*

A proof can be found in the extended version of this paper [18]. In particular, if there exists an execution in $exec(b_{init})$ that (n, R)-matches the whole sequence ρ then our algorithm returns one; otherwise, the algorithm says there is none. Regarding the algorithm's complexity, it is worst-case exponential in the bound n, with the base of the exponent being the maximum branching of the transition system denoting the operational semantics of the source DSML. For deterministic DSML, the exponential disappears. In practice, n may be known if a proof of (bi)simulation between source and target semantics was performed; this is why our algorithm works best when combined with a theorem prover (as discussed in the introduction). If n is unknown, one can start with $n = 1$ and gradually increase n until a matching execution is found or until resources are exhausted.

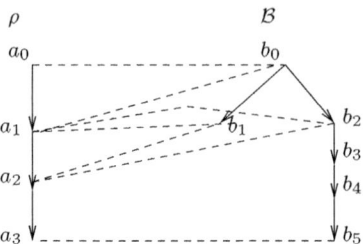

Fig. 8. Attempting to match execution ρ

Example 2. We illustrate several runs of our algorithm on the execution ρ depicted in the left-hand side of Figure 8, with the transition system $\mathcal{B}$ depicted in the right-hand side of the figure, and the relation R depicted using dashed lines. In the algorithm, let $n = 3$. The set S is initialized to $S = \{b_0\}$. For the first step of the algorithm - i.e., when $k = 1$ in the while loop - we choose $b = b_0$ and the execution $\hat{\pi} = b_0$; we obtain $\alpha(1) = 0$, $\pi(0) = b_0$ and $S' = R(a_1) \cap \{b_0, b_1, b_2, b_3, b_4\} = \{b_0, b_1, b_2\}$. At the second step, we choose $b = b_0$ and, say, $\hat{\pi} = b_0, b_2$; we obtain $\alpha(2) = 1$, $\pi(1) = b_2$ and $S' = R(a_2) \cap \{b_2, b_3, b_4, b_5\} = \{b_2\}$. At the third step, we can only choose $b = b_2$ and $\hat{\pi} = b_2, b_3, b_4, b_5$; we obtain $\alpha(3) = 4$, $\pi_{2..4} = \hat{\pi}$, and $S' = \{b_5\}$, and now we are done: the matching execution π for ρ is $\pi = b_0, b_2 \ldots b_5$. Note that our non-deterministic algorithm is allowed to make the "most inspired choices" as above. A deterministic algorithm may make "less inspired choices" and backtrack from them; for example, had we chosen $\hat{\pi} = b_0, b_1$ at the second step, we would have ended up failing locally because of the impossibility of matching the last step $a_2 a_3$ of ρ; backtracking to $\hat{\pi} = b_0, b_2$ solves this problem. Finally, note that with $n < 3$, the algorithm fails globally - it cannot match the last step of ρ.

Remark 2. The implementation of our algorithm amounts to implementing nondeterministic choice via state-space exploration. A natural question that arises is then: why not use state-space exploration to perform the model checking itself, instead of using an external model checker and trying to match its result (as we propose to do)? One reason is that it is typically more efficient to use the external model checker to come up with an execution, and to match that execution with our algorithm, than performing model checking using our (typically, less efficient) state-space exploration. Another reason is that the execution we are trying to match may be produced by something else than a model checker, e.g., a program crash log can also serve as an input to our algorithm.

5 Related work

The problem of tracing executions from a given target back to a domain-specific language has been addressed in several papers of the MDE community. Most of the proposed methods are either dedicated to only one pair metamodel/verification tool ([7], [10]) or they compute an "explanation" of the execution in a more abstract way.

In [8], the authors propose a general method based on a *traceability* mechanism of model transformations. It relies on a relation between elements of the source and the target metamodel, implemented by means of annotations in the transformation's source codes.essentially By contrast, our approach does not require instrumenting the model transformation code, and is formally grounded on operational semantics, a feature that allows us to prove its correctness.

In the formal methods area, Translation Validation ([15]) has also the purpose of validating a compiler by performing a verification *after each run of the compiler* to ensure that the output code produced by the compilation is a correct translation of the source program. The method is fully automatic for the developer, who has no additional information to provide in order to prove the translation: all the semantics of the two languages and the relation between states are embedded inside the "validator" (thus it cannot be generic). Contrary to our work, Translation Validation only focuses on proving correctness, and does not provide any useful information if the verification fails. Also, the Counterexample-Guided Abstraction Refinement (CEGAR) verification method ([4]) also consists in matching model-checking counterexamples to program executions. The difference between CEGAR and our approach is that CEGAR makes a specific assumption - that the target representation is an abstract interpretation of the source representation; whereas we do not make this assumption.

Finally, in the paper [17] we describe, among others, an approach for back-tracing executions, which differs from the one presented here in several aspects: the theoretical framework of [17] is based on observational transition systems and the relation between states is restricted to observational equality, whereas here we allow for more general relations between states; and in in [17], the relation is restricted such that the parameter n is always one, which means that one step in the source may match several steps in the target, but not the other way around. The are also practical differences: Maude is less likely to be familiar and acceptable to software engineers; and Maude allows for a direct implementation of the nondeterministic back-tracing algorithm, whereas in Kermeta a deterministic version of the algorithm had to be designed first.

6 Conclusion and Future Work

DSML are often translated to other languages for efficient execution and/or analysis. We address the problem of formally tracing executions of a given target language tool back into an execution of a DSML. Our solution is a generic tool implementing an algorithm that requires that the DSML's semantics be defined formally, and that a relation R be defined between states of the DSML and of the target language. The algorithm also takes as input a natural-number bound n, which estimates a "difference of granularity" between semantics of the DSML and of the target language. Then, given a finite execution ρ of the target language (e.g., a counterexample to a safety property, or program crash log), our algorithm returns an (n, R) *matching* execution π in terms of the DSML's operational semantics - if there is one - or it reports that no such execution exists, otherwise.

We implement our algorithm in Kermeta, a framework for defining operational semantics of DSML (among other features). Using Kermeta's abilities for aspect-oriented metamodeling, our implementation is generic: the user has to provide the appropriate metamodels, as well as the estimated bound n and relation R between the states of DSML and verification tool; the rest is automatic.

We illustrate our tool on an example where the DSML is xSPEM, a timed process modeling language, and the target language is Prioritized Time Petri Nets (PrTPN), the input language of the TINA model checker.

Regarding future work, the main direction is to exploit the combination of theorem proving (for model transformation) and model checking (for model verification) as described in the introduction. Another orthogonal research direction is to optimise our currently naive implementation in Kermeta in order to avoid copying whole models when only parts of them (their "state") change.

References

1. Bendraou, R., Combemale, B., Crégut, X., Gervais, M.-P.: Definition of an eXecutable SPEM2.0. In: 14th APSEC. IEEE, Los Alamitos (2007)
2. Berthomieu, B., Ribet, P.-O., Vernadat, F.: The tool TINA – construction of abstract state spaces for Petri nets and time Petri nets. Int. Journal of Production Research 42(14), 2741–2756 (2004)
3. Berthomieu, B., Peres, F., Vernadat, F.: Model checking bounded prioritized time petri nets. In: Namjoshi, K.S., Yoneda, T., Higashino, T., Okamura, Y. (eds.) ATVA 2007. LNCS, vol. 4762, pp. 523–532. Springer, Heidelberg (2007)
4. Clarke, E., Grumberg, O., Jha, S., Lu, Y., Veith, H.: Counterexample-guided abstraction refinement. In: Emerson, E.A., Sistla, A.P. (eds.) CAV 2000. LNCS, vol. 1855, pp. 154–169. Springer, Heidelberg (2000)
5. Combemale, B., Crégut, X., Garoche, P.-L., Thirioux, X.: Essay on Semantics Definition in MDE. An Instrumented Approach for Model Verification. Journal of Software 4(9), 943–958 (2009)
6. Csertán, G., Huszerl, G., Majzik, I., Pap, Z., Pataricza, A., Varró, D.: VIATRA - visual automated transformations for formal verification and validation of UML models. In: 17th ASE, pp. 267–270. IEEE, Los Alamitos (2002)
7. Guerra, E., de Lara, J., Malizia, A., Daz, P.: Supporting user-oriented analysis for multi view domain specific visual languages. Information & Software Technology 51(4), 769–784 (2009)
8. Hegedüs, A., Bergmann, G., Ráth, I., Varró, D.: Back-annotation of simulation traces with change-driven model transformations. In: SEFM 2010 (September 2010)
9. Merlin, P.M.: A Study of the Recoverability of Computing Systems. Irvine: Univ. California, PhD Thesis (1974)
10. Moe, J., Carr, D.A.: Understanding distributed systems via execution trace data. In: Proceedings of the 9th International Workshop on Program Comprehension IWPC 2001. IEEE Computer Society, Los Alamitos (2001)
11. Muller, P.-A., Fleurey, F., Jézéquel, J.-M.: Weaving Executability into Object-Oriented Meta-languages. In: Briand, L.C., Williams, C. (eds.) MoDELS 2005. LNCS, vol. 3713, pp. 264–278. Springer, Heidelberg (2005)
12. Object Management Group. Meta Object Facility 2.0 (2006)
13. Object Management Group. Object Constraint Language 2.0 (2006)

14. Object Management Group. Software Process Engineering Metamodel 2.0 (2007)
15. Pnueli, A., Shtrichman, O., Siegel, M.D.: Translation validation: From SIGNAL to C. In: Olderog, E.-R., Steffen, B. (eds.) Correct System Design. LNCS, vol. 1710, pp. 231–255. Springer, Heidelberg (1999)
16. Rivera, J.E., Vicente-Chicote, C., Vallecillo, A.: Extending visual modeling languages with timed behavior specifications. In: CIbSE, pp. 87–100 (2009)
17. Rusu, V.: Embedding domain-specific modelling languages into Maude specifications, http://researchers.lille.inria.fr/~rusu/SoSym
18. Rusu, V., Gonnord, L., Combemale, B.: Formally Tracing Executions From an Analysis Tool Back to a Domain Specific Modeling Language's Operational Semantics. Technical Report RR-7423, INRIA (October 2010)

Incremental Security Verification for Evolving UMLsec models[*]

Jan Jürjens[1,2], Loïc Marchal[3], Martín Ochoa[1], and Holger Schmidt[1]

[1] Software Engineering, Department of Computer Science,
TU Dortmund, Germany
[2] Fraunhofer ISST, Germany
[3] Hermès Engineering, Belgium
{jan.jurjens,martin.ochoa,holger.schmidt}@cs.tu-dortmund.de
loic.marchal@hermes-ecs.com

Abstract. There exists a substantial amount of work on methods, techniques and tools for developing security-critical systems. However, these approaches focus on ensuring that the security properties are enforced during the initial system development and they usually have a significant cost associated with their use (in time and resources). In order to enforce that the systems remain secure despite their later evolution, it would be infeasible to re-apply the whole secure software development methodology from scratch. This work presents results towards addressing this challenge in the context of the UML security extension UMLsec. We investigate the security analysis of UMLsec models by means of a change-specific notation allowing multiple evolution paths and sound algorithms supporting the incremental verification process of evolving models. The approach is validated by a tool implementation of these verification techniques that extends the existing UMLsec tool support.

1 Introduction

The task of *evolving secure software systems* such that the desired security requirements are preserved through a system's lifetime is of great importance in practice. We propose a *model-based approach to support the evolution of secure software systems*. Our approach allows the verification of *potential future evolutions* using an automatic analysis tool. An explicit model evolution implies the transformation of the model and defines a difference Δ between the original model and the transformed one. The proposed approach supports the definition of multiple evolution paths, and provides tool support to verify evolved models based on the delta of changes. This idea is visualized in Fig. 1: The starting point of our approach is a Software System Model which was already verified against certain security properties. Then, this model can evolve within a range of possible

---

[*] This research was partially supported by the EU project Security Engineering for Lifelong Evolvable Systems (Secure Change, ICT-FET-231101).

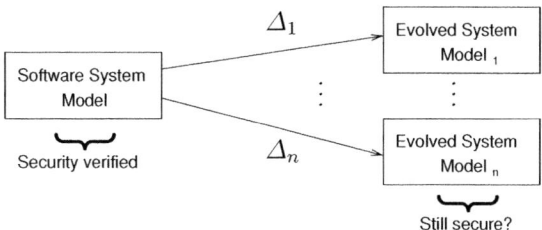

Fig. 1. Model verification problem for n possible evolution paths

evolutions (the evolution space). We consider the different possible evolutions as *evolution paths* each of which defines a *delta* Δ_i. The result is a number of evolved Evolved System Model$_i$. The main research question is "Which of the evolution paths leads to a target model that still fulfills the security properties of the source model?".

Theoretically, one could simply re-run the security analysis done to establish the security of the original model on the evolved model to decide whether these properties are preserved after evolution. This would, however, result in general in a high resource consumption for models of realistic size, in particular since the goal in general is to investigate the complete potential evolution space (rather than just one particular evolution) in order to determine which of the possible evolutions preserve security. Also, verification efficiency is very critical if a continuous verification is desired (i.e. it should be determined in real-time and in parallel to the modelling activity whether the modelled change preserves security).

We use models specified using the Unified Modeling Language (UML) [1] and the security extension UMLsec [6]. The UMLsec profile offers new UML language elements (i.e., *stereotypes*, *tags*, and *constraints*) to specify typical security requirements such as secrecy, integrity, and authenticity, and other security-relevant information. Based on UMLsec models and the semantics defined for the different UMLsec language elements, possible security vulnerabilities can be identified at an early stage of software development. One can thus verify that the desired security requirements, if fulfilled, enforce a given security policy. This verification is supported by a tool suite [2] [8].

In this paper we present a general approach for the incremental security verification of UML models against security requirements inserted as UMLsec stereotypes. We discuss the possible atomic (i.e. single model element) evolutions annotated with certain security requirements according to UMLsec. Moreover, we present *sufficient conditions* for a set of model evolutions, which, if satisfied, ensure that the desired security properties of the original model are preserved under evolution. We demonstrate our general approach by applying it to a representative UMLsec stereotype, « secure dependency ». As one result of our work, we demonstrate that the security checks defined for UMLsec allow significant efficiency gains by considering this incremental verification technique.

---

[1] The Unified Modeling Language http://www.uml.org/
[2] Available online via http://www-jj.cs.tu-dortmund.de/jj/umlsectool

To explicitly specify possible evolution paths, we have developed a further extension of the UMLsec profile (called UMLseCh) that allows a precise definition of which model elements are to be *added*, *deleted*, and *substituted* in a model. Constraints in first-order predicate logic allow to coordinate and define more than one evolution path (and thus obtaining the deltas for the analysis).

Note that UMLseCh is not intended as a general-purpose evolution modeling language: it is specifically intended to model the evolution in a security-oriented context in order to investigate the research questions wrt. security preservation by evolution (in particular, it is an extension of UMLsec and requires the UMLsec profile as prerequisite profile). Thus, UMLseCh does not aim to be an alternative for any existing general-purpose evolution specification or model transformation approaches (such as [4,1,2,14,9]). It will be interesting future work to demonstrate how the results presented in this paper can be used in the context of those approaches.

This paper is organized as follows: The change-specific extension UMLseCh is defined in Sect. 2. Sect. 3 explains our general approach for evolution-specific security verification. Using class diagrams as an example application, this approach is instantiated in Sect. 4. In Sect.5, we give an overview of the UMLsec verification tool and how this tool has been extended to support our reasoning for evolving systems based on UMLseCh. We conclude with an overview of the related work (Sect. 6) and a brief discussion of the results presented (Sect. 7).

2 UMLseCh: Supporting Evolution of UMLsec Models

In this section we present a further extension of the UML security profile UMLsec to deal with potential model evolutions, called UMLseCh (that is, an extension to UML which itself includes the UMLsec profile). Figure 2 shows the list of UMLseCh stereotypes, together with their tags and constraints, while Fig. 3 describes the tags.

The UMLseCh tagged values associated to the tags {add} and {substitute} are strings, their role is to describe possible future model evolutions. UMLseCh describes **possible future changes**, thus conceptually, the substitutive or additive model elements are not actually part of the current system design model, but only an attribute value inside a change stereotype[3]. At the concrete level, i.e. in a tool, this value is either the model element itself if it can be represented with a sequence of characters (for example an attribute or an operation within a class), or a namespace containing the model element.

Note that the UMLseCh notation is complete in the sense that any kind of evolution between two UMLsec models can be captured by adding a suitable number of UMLseCh annotations to the initial UMLsec model. This can be seen by considering that for any two UML models M and N there exists a sequence of deletions, additions, and substitutions through which the model M can be transformed to the model N. In fact, this is true even when only

---

[3] The type change represents a type of stereotype that includes «change», «substitute», «add» or «delete».

Stereotype	Base Class	Tags	Constraints	Description
change	all	ref, change	FOL formula	execute sub-changes in parallel
substitute	all	ref, substitute,	FOL formula	substitute a model element
add	all	ref, add,	FOL formula	add a model element
delete	all	ref, delete	FOL formula	delete a model element
substitute-all	all	ref, substitute,	FOL formula	substitute a group of elements
add-all	all	ref, add,	FOL formula	add a group of elements
delete-all	all	ref, delete	FOL formula	delete a group of elements

Fig. 2. UMLseCh stereotypes

Tag	Stereotype	Type	Multip.	Description
ref	change, substitute, add, delete, substitute-all, add-all, delete-all	list of strings	1	List of labels identifying a change
substitute	substitute, substitute-all	list of pairs of model elements	1	List of substitutions
add	add, add-all	list of pairs of model elements	1	List of additions
delete	delete, delete-all	list of pairs of model elements	1	List of deletions
change	change	list of references	1	List of simultaneous changes

Fig. 3. UMLseCh tags

considering deletions and additions: the trivial solution would be to sequentially remove all model elements from M by subsequent atomic deletions, and then to add all model elements needed in N by subsequent additions. Of course, this is only a thereotical argument supporting the theoretical expressiveness of the UMLseCh notation, and this approach would neither be useful from a modelling perspective, nor would it result in a meaningful incremental verification strategy. This is the reason that the substitution of model elements has also been added to the UMLseCh notation, and the incremental verification strategy explained later in this paper will crucially rely on this.

2.1 Description of the Notation

In the following we give an informal description of the notation and its semantics.

substitute. The stereotype «substitute» attached to a model element denotes the possibility for that model element to evolve over time and defines what the possible changes are. It has two associated tags, namely ref and substitute. These tags are of the form { ref = CHANGE-REFERENCE } and

$$\{ \text{substitute} = (\text{ELEMENT}_1,\ \text{NEW}_1),\ \ldots\ ,\ (\text{ELEMENT}_n,\ \text{NEW}_n) \}$$

with $n \in \mathbb{N}$. The tag ref takes a list of sequences of characters as value, each element of this list being simply used as a reference of one of the changes modeled by the stereotype «substitute». In other words, the values contained in this tag can be seen as labels identifying the changes. The values of this tag can also be considered as predicates which take a truth value that can be used to evaluate conditions on other changes (as we will explain in the following). The tag substitute has a list of pairs of model element as value, which represent the substitutions that will happen if the related change occurs. The pairs are of the form (e, e'), where e is the element to substitute and e' is the substitutive model element [4]. For the notation of this list, two possibilities exist: The elements of the pair are written textually using the abstract syntax of a fragment of UML defined in [6] or alternatively the name of a namespace containing an element is used instead. The *namespace notation* allows UMLseCh stereotypes to graphically model more complex changes (cf. Sect. 2.2).

If the model element to substitute is the one to which the stereotype «substitute» is attached, the element e of the pair (e, e') is not necessary. In this case the list consists only of the second elements e' in the tagged value, instead of the pairs (this notational variation is just syntactic sugar). If a change is specified, it is important that it leaves the resulting model in a syntactically consistent state. In this paper however we focus only on the preservation of security.

Example. We illustrate the UMLseCh notation with the following example. Assume that we want to specify the change of a link stereotyped «Internet» so that it will instead be stereotyped «encrypted». For this, the following three annotations are attached to the link concerned by the change (cf. Figure 4):

«substitute», { ref = encrypt-link }, { substitute = («encrypted», «Internet») }

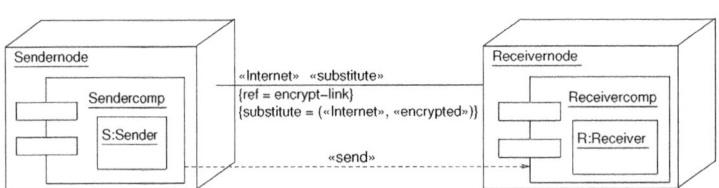

Fig. 4. Example of stereotype substitute

---

[4] More than one occurrence of the same e in the list is allowed. However, two occurrences of the same pair (e, e') cannot exist in the list, since it would model the same change twice.

The stereotype «substitute» also has a list of optional constraints formulated in first order logic. This list of constraints is written between square brackets and is of the form [(ref$_1$, CONDITION$_1$), ..., (ref$_n$, CONDITION$_n$)], $n \in \mathbb{N}$, where, $\forall i : 1 \leq i \leq n$, ref$_i$ is a value of the list of a tag ref and CONDITION$_n$ can be any type of first order logic expression, such as $A \wedge B$, $A \vee B$, $A \wedge (B \vee \neg C)$, $(A \wedge B) \Rightarrow C$, $\forall x \in N.P(x)$, etc. Its intended use is to define under which conditions the change is allowed to happen (i.e. if the condition is evaluated to true, the change is allowed, otherwise the change is not allowed). As mentioned earlier, an element of the list used as the value of the tag ref of a stereotype «substitute» can be used as an atomic predicate for the constraint of another stereotype «substitute». The truth value of that predicate is true if the change represented by the stereotype «substitute» to which the tag ref is associated occurred, false otherwise.

To illustrate the use of the constraint, the previous example can be refined. Assume that to allow the change with reference encrypt-link, another change, simply referenced as change for the example, has to occur. The constraint [change] can then be attached to the link concerned by the change. To express for example that two changes, referenced respectively by change$_1$ and change$_2$, have to occur first in order to allow the change referenced encrypt-link to happen, the constraint [change$_1 \wedge$ change$_2$] is added to the stereotype «substitute» modeling the change.

add and delete. Both «add» and «delete» can be seen as syntactic sugar for «substitute». The stereotype «add» attached to a parent model element describes a list of possible sub-model elements to be added as children to the parent model element. It thus substitutes a collection of sub-model elements with a new, extended collection.

The stereotype «delete» attached to a (sub)-model element marks this element for deletion. Deleting a model element could be expressed as the substitution of the model element by the empty model element $\emptyset$. Both stereotypes «add» and «delete» may also have associated constraints in first order logic.

substitute-all. The stereotype «substitute-all» is an extension of the stereotype «substitute». It denotes the possibility for **a set of model elements of same type and sharing common characteristics** to evolve over time. In this case, «substitute-all» will always be attached to the super-element to which the sub-elements concerned by the substitution belong. As the stereotype «substitute», it has the two associated tags ref and substitute, of the form { ref = CHANGE-REFERENCE } and

{ substitute = (ELEMENT$_1$, NEW$_1$), ..., (ELEMENT$_n$, NEW$_n$) }.

The tags ref has the same meaning as in the case of the stereotype «substitute». For the tag substitute the element e of a pair representing a substitution does not represent one model element but **a set of model elements** to substitute if a change occurs. This set can be, for example, a set of classes, a set of methods of a class, a set of links, a set of states, etc. All the elements of the set share common characteristics. For instance, the elements to substitute are the methods having the integer argument *"count"*, the links being stereotyped «Internet» or the classes having the stereotype «critical» with the associated tag secrecy. Again, in order to identify the model element precisely, we can use, if necessary, either the UML namespaces notation or, if this notation is insufficient, the abstract syntax of UMLseCh.

Example. To replace all the links stereotyped «Internet» of a subsystem so that they are now stereotyped «encrypted», the following three annotations can be attached to the subsystem: «substitute-all», { ref = encrypt-all-links }, and { substitute = («Internet», «encrypted») }. This is shown in Figure 5.

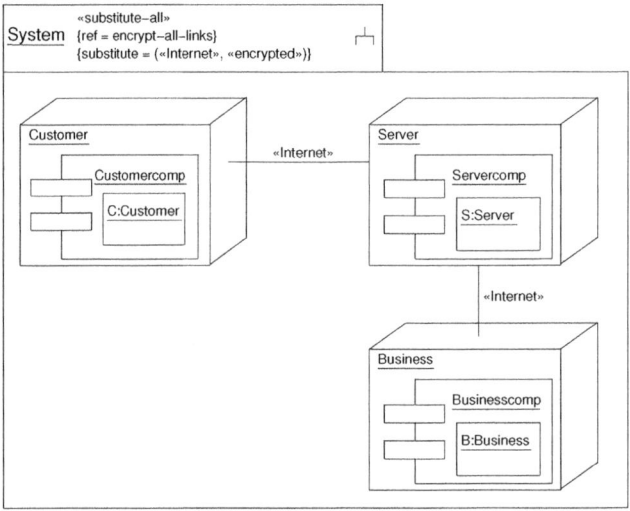

Fig. 5. Example of stereotype substitute-all

A pair (e, e') of the list of values of a tag substitute here allows us a parameterization of the values e and e' in order to keep information of the different model elements of the subsystem concerned by the substitution. To allow this, variables can be used in the value of both the elements of a pair. The following example illustrates the use of the parameterization in the stereotype «substitute-all». To substitute all the tags secrecy of stereotypes «critical» by tags integrity, but in a way that it keeps the values given to the tags secrecy (e.g. { secrecy = d }), the following three annotations can be attached to the subsystem containing the class diagram: «substitute-all», { ref = secrecy-to-integrity }, and { substitute = ({ secrecy = X }, { integrity = X }) }.

The stereotype «substitute-all» also has a list of constraints formulated in first order logic, which represents the same information as for the stereotype «substitute».

change. The stereotype «change» is a particular stereotype that represents a *composite change*. It has two associated tags, namely ref and change. These tags are of the form { ref = CHANGE-REFERENCES } and { change = CHANGE-REFERENCES$_1$, ..., CHANGE-REFERENCES$_n$ }, with $n \in \mathbb{N}$. The tag ref has the same meaning as in the case of a stereotype «substitute». The tag change takes a list of lists of strings as value. Each element of a list is a value of a tag ref from another stereotype of type change.[5] Each list thus represents the list of *sub-changes* of a *composite change* modeled by the stereotype «change». Applying a change modeled by «change» hence consists in applying all of the concerned *sub-changes* **in parallel**.

Any change being a *sub-change* of a change modeled by «change» **must** have the value of the tag ref of that change in its condition. Therefore, any change modeled by a *sub-change* can only happen if the change modeled by the *super-stereotype* takes place. However, if this change happens, the *sub-changes* will be applied and the *sub-changes* will thus be removed from the model. This ensures that *sub-changes* cannot be applied by themselves, independently from their *super-stereotype* «change» modeling the *composite change*.

2.2 Complex Substitutive Elements

As mentioned above, using a complex model element as substitutive element requires a syntactic notation as well as an adapted semantics. An element is complex if it is not represented by a sequence of characters (i.e. it is represented by a graphical icon, such as a class, an activity or a transition). Such complex model elements cannot be represented in a tagged value since tag definitions have a string-based notation. To allow such complex model elements to be used as substitutive elements, they will be placed in a UML namespace. The name of this namespace being a sequence of characters, it can thus be used in a pair of a tag substitute where it will then represent a reference to the complex model element. Of course, this is just a notational mechanism that allows the UMLseCh stereotypes to graphically model more complex changes. From a semantic point of view, when an element in a pair representing a substitution is the name of a namespace, the model element concerned by the change will be substituted by the content of the namespace, and not the namespace itself. This type of change will request a special semantics, depending on the type of element. For details about this complex substitutions we refer to [15].

3 Verification Strategy

As stated in the previous section, evolving a model means that we either *add*, *delete*, or / and *substitute* elements of this model. To distinguish between big-step and small-step evolutions, we will call "atomic" the modifications involving only one model element (or sub-element, e.g. adding a method to an existing class or deleting a dependency). In general there exist evolutions from diagram A to diagram B such that there is no sequence of atomic modifications for which

---

[5] By type change, we mean the type that includes «substitute», «add», «delete» and «change».

security is preserved when applying them one after another, but such that both A and B are secure. Therefore the goal of our verification is to allow some modifications to happen *simultaneously*.

Since the evolution is defined by additions, deletion and substitutions of model elements, we introduce the sets **Add**, **Del**, and **Subs**, where **Add** and **Del** contain objects representing model elements together with methods id, type, path, parent returning respectively an identifier for the model element, its type, its path within the diagram, and its parent model element. These objects also contain all the relevant information of the model element according to its type (for example, if it represents a class, we can query for its associated stereotypes, methods, and attributes). For example, the class "Customer" in Fig. 6 can be seen as an object with the subsystem "Book a flight" as its parent. It has associated a list of methods (empty in this case), a list of attributes ("Name" of type String, which is in turn an model element object), a list of stereotypes («critical») and a list of dependencies («call» dependency with "Airport Server") attached to it. By recursively comparing all the attributes of two objects, we can establish whether they are equal.

The set **Subs** contains pairs of objects as above, where the type, path (and therefore parent) methods of both objects must coincide. We assume that there are no conflicts between the three sets, more specifically, the following condition guarantees that one does not delete and add the same model element:

$$\nexists\, o, o' (o \in \mathbf{Add} \wedge o' \in \mathbf{Del} \wedge o = o')$$

Additionally, the following condition prevents adding/deleting a model element present in a substitution (as target or as substitutive element):

$$\nexists\, o, o' (o \in \mathbf{Add} \vee o \in \mathbf{Del}) \wedge ((o, o') \in \mathbf{Subs} \vee (o', o) \in \mathbf{Subs})$$

As explained above, in general, an "atomic" modification (that is the action represented by a single model element in any of the sets above) could by itself harm the security of the model. So, one has to take into account other modifications in order to establish the security status of the resulting model. We proceed algorithmically as follows: we iterate over the modification sets starting with an object $o \in \mathbf{Del}$, and if the relevant simultaneous changes that preserve security are found in the delta, then we perform the operation on the original model

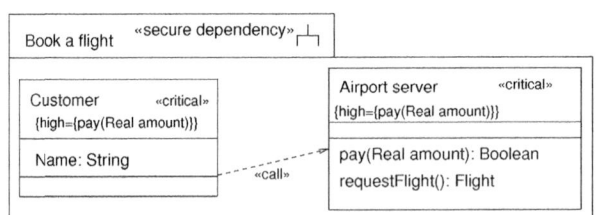

Fig. 6. Class Diagram Annotated with «secure dependency»

(delete o and necessary simultaneous changes) and remove the processed objects until **Del** is empty. We then continue similarly with **Add** and finally with **Subs**. If at any point we establish the security is not preserved by the evolution we conclude the analysis. Given a diagram M and a set Δ of atomic modifications we denote $M[\Delta]$ the diagram resulting after the modifications have taken place. So in general let P be a diagram property. We express the fact that M enforces P by $P(M)$. *Soundness* of the security preserving rules R for a property P on diagram M can be formalized as follows:

$$P(M) \wedge R(M, \Delta) \Rightarrow P(M[\Delta]).$$

To prove that the algorithm described above is sound with respect to a given property P, we show that every set of simultaneous changes accepted by the algorithm preserves P. Then, transitively, if all steps were sound until the delta is empty, we reach the desired $P(M[\Delta])$.

One can obtain these deltas by interpreting the UMLseCh annotations presented in the previous section. Alternatively, one could compute the difference between an original diagram M and the modified M'. This is nevertheless not central to this analysis, which focuses on the verification of evolving systems rather than on model transformation itself.

To define the set of rules R, one can reason inductively by cases given a security requirement on UML models, by considering incremental atomic changes and distinguishing them according to *a)* their *evolution* type (addition, deletion, substitution) and *b)* their *UML diagram* type. In the following section we will spell-out a set of possible sufficient rules for the sound and secure evolution of class diagrams annotated with the «secure dependency» stereotype.

4 Application to <<secure dependency>>

In this section we demonstrate the verification strategy explained in the previous section by applying it to the case of the UMLsec stereotype «secure dependency» applied to class diagrams. The associated constraint requires for every communication dependency (i.e. a dependency annotated «send» or «call») between two classes in a class diagram the following condition holds: if a method or attribute is annotated with a security requirement in one of both classes (for example { secrecy = {method()} }), then the other class has the same tag for this method/attribute as well (see Fig. 6 for an example). It follows that the computational cost associated with verifying this property depends on the number of *dependencies*. We analyze the possible changes involving classes, dependencies and security requirements as specified by tags and their consequences to the security properties of the class diagram.

Formally, we can express this property as follows:

$$P(M): \forall C, C' \in M.\mathsf{Classes}\ (\exists d \in M.\mathsf{dependencies}(C, C') \Rightarrow C.\mathsf{critical} = C'.\mathsf{critical})$$

where $M.\mathsf{Classes}$ is the set of classes of diagram M, $M.\mathsf{dependencies}(C, C')$ returns the set of dependencies between classes C and C' and $C.\mathsf{critical}$ returns the set of pairs (m, s) where m is a method or an object shared in the dependency and $s \in \{\text{high}, \text{secrecy}, \text{integrity}\}$ as specified in the «critical» stereotype for that class.

We now analyse the set Δ of modifications by distinguishing cases on the evolution type (deletion, addition, substitution) and the UML type.

Deletion

Class. We assume that if a class $\bar{C}$ is deleted then also the dependencies coming in and out of the class are deleted, say by deletions $D = \{o_1, ..., o_n\}$, and therefore, after the execution of o and D in the model M (expressed $M[o, D]$) property P holds since:

$$P(M[o, D]):$$

$$\forall C, C' \in M.\text{Classes} \setminus \bar{C} \ (\exists d \in M[o, D].\text{dependencies}(C, C') \Rightarrow C.\text{critical} = C'.\text{critical})$$

and this predicate holds given $P(M)$, because the new set of dependencies of $M[o, D]$ does not contain any pair of the type $(x, \bar{C})$, $(\bar{C}, x)$.

Tag in Critical. If a security requirement (m, s) associated to in class $\bar{C}$ is deleted then it must also be removed from other methods having dependencies with C (and so on recursively for all classes $C_{\bar{C}}$ associated through dependencies to $\bar{C}$) in order to preserve the secure dependencies requirement. We assume $P(M)$ holds, and since clearly $M.\text{Classes} = (M.\text{Classes} \setminus C_{\bar{C}}) \cup C_{\bar{C}}$ it follows $P(M[o, D])$ because the only modified objects in the diagram are the classes in $C_{\bar{C}}$ and for that set we deleted symmetrically (m, s), thus respecting P.

Dependency. The deletion of a dependency does not alter the property P since by assumption we had a statement quantifying over all dependencies (C, C'), that trivially also holds for a subset.

Addition

Class. The addition of a class, without any dependency, clearly preserves the security of P since this property depends only on the classes with dependencies associated to them.

Tag in Critical. To preserve the security of the system, every time a method is tagged within the «critical» stereotype in a class C, the same tag referring to the same method should be added to every class with dependencies to and from C (and recursively to all dependent classes). The execution of these simultaneous additions preserves P since the symmetry of the critical tags is respected through all dependency-connected classes.

Dependency. Whenever a dependency is added between classes C and C', for every security tagged method in C (C') the same method must be tagged (with the same security requirement) in C' (C) to preserve P. So if in the original model this is not the case, we check for simultaneous additions that preserve this symmetry for C and C' and transitively on all their dependent classes.

Substitution

Class. If class C is substituted with class C' and class C' has the same security tagged methods as C then the security of the diagram is preserved.

Tag in Critical. If we substitute { requirement = method() } by { requirement' = method()' } in class C, then the same substitution must be made in every class linked to C by a dependency.

Dependency. If a «call» («send») dependency is substituted by «send» («call») then P is clearly preserved.

Example. The example in Fig. 7 shows the Client side of a communication channel between two parties. At first (disregarding the evolution stereotypes) the communication is unsecured. In the packages Symmetric and Asymmetric, we have classes providing cryptographic mechanisms to the Client class. Here the stereotype «add» marked with the reference tag {ref} with value add_encryption specifies two possible evolution paths: merging the classes contained in the current package (Channel) with either Symmetric or Asymmetric. There exists also a stereotype «add» associated with the Client class adding either a pre-shared private key k or a public key K_S of the server. To coordinate the intended evolution paths for these two stereotypes, we can use the following first-order logic constraint (associated with add_encryption):

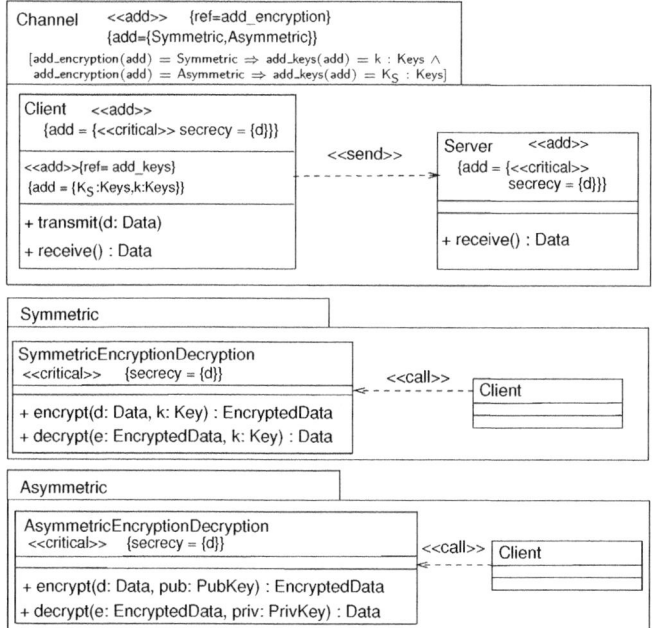

Fig. 7. An evolving class diagram with two possible evolution paths

$$[\mathsf{add\_encryption(add)} = \mathsf{Symmetric} \Rightarrow \mathsf{add\_keys(add)} = \mathsf{k} : \mathsf{Keys} \land$$
$$\mathsf{add\_encryption(add)} = \mathsf{Asymmetric} \Rightarrow \mathsf{add\_keys(add)} = \mathsf{K_S} : \mathsf{Keys}]$$

The two deltas, representing two possible evolution paths induced by this notation, can be then given as input to the decision procedure described for checking «secure dependency». Both evolution paths respect sufficient conditions for this security requirement to be satisfied.

5 Tool Support

The UMLsec extension [6] together with its formal semantics offers the possibility to verify models against security requirements. Currently, there exists tool support to verify a wide range of diagrams and requirements. Such requirements can be specified in the UML model using the UMLsec extension (created with the ArgoUML editor) or within the source-code (Java or C) as annotations. As explained in this paper, the UMLsec extension has been further extended to include evolution stereotypes that precisely define which model elements are to be added, deleted, or substituted in a model (see also the UMLseCh profile in [15]). To support the UMLseCh notation, the UMLsec Tool Suite has been extended to process UML models including annotations for possible future evolutions.[6]

Given the sufficient conditions presented in the previous sections, if the transformation does not violate them then the resulting model preserves security. Nevertheless, security preserving evolutions may fail to pass the tests discussed, and be however valid: With respect to the security preservation analysis procedures, there is a trade-off between their efficiency and their completeness. Essentially, if one would require a security preservation analysis which is complete in the sense that every specified evolution which preserves security is actually shown to preserve security, the computational difficulty of this analysis could be comparable to a simple re-verification of the evolved model using the UMLsec tools. Therefore if a specified evolution could not be established to preserve security, there is still the option to re-verify the evolved model.

It is of interest that the duration of the check for «secure dependency» implemented in the UMLsec tool behaves in a more than linear way depending on the number of dependencies. In Fig. 8 we present a comparison between the running time of the verification[7] on a class diagram where only 10% of the model elements were modified. One should note that the inefficiency of a simple re-verification would prevent analyzing evolution spaces of significant size, or to support online verification (i.e. verifying security evolution in parallel to the modelling activity), which provides the motivation to profit from the gains provided by the delta-verification presented in this paper. Similar gains can be achieved for

---

[6] Available online at http://www-jj.cs.tu-dortmund.de/jj/umlsectool/manuals_new/UMLseCh_Static_Check_SecureDependency/index.htm

[7] On a 2.26 GhZ dual core processor

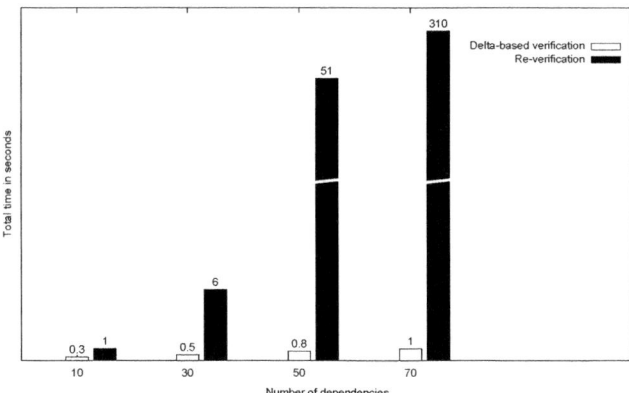

Fig. 8. Running time comparison of the verification

other UMLsec checks such as «rbac», «secure links» and other domain-specific security properties for smart-cards, for which sound decision procedures under evolution have been worked out (see [15]).

6 Related Work

There are different approaches to deal with evolution that are related to our work. Within *Software Evolution Approaches*, [10] derives several *laws of software evolution* such as "Continuing Change" and "Declining Quality". [12] argue that it is necessary to treat and support evolution throughout all development phases. They extend the UML metamodel by *evolution contracts* to automatically detect conflicts that may arise when evolving the same UML model in parallel. [16] proposes an approach for transforming non-secure applications into secure applications through requirements and software architecture models using UML. However, the further evolution of the secure applications is not considered, nor verification of the UML models. [5] discussed consistency of models for incremental changes of models. This work is not security-specific and it considers one evolution path only.

Also related is the large body of work on software verification based on *Assume-Guarantee reasoning*. A difference is that our approach can reason incrementally without the need for the user to explicitly formulate assume-guarantee conditions.

In the context of *Requirements Engineering for Secure Evolution* there exists some recent work on requirements engineering for secure systems evolution such as [17]. However, this does not target the security verification of evolving design models. A research topic related to software evolution is *software product lines*, where different versions of a software are considered. For example, Mellado et al. [11] consider product lines and security requirements engineering. However, their approach does not target the verification of UML models for security properties.

Evolving Architectures is a similar context with a different level of abstraction. [3] discusses different evolution styles for high-level architectural views of the system. It also discusses the possibility of having more than one evolution path and describes tool support for choosing the "correct" paths with respect to properties described in temporal logic (similar to our constraints in FOL). However, this approach is not security specific. On a similar fashion, but more focused on critical properties, [13] also discusses the evolution of Architectures.

The UMLseCh notation is informally introduced in [7], however no details about verification are given. Both the notation and the verification aspects are treated in more detail in the (unpublished) technical report [15] of the SecureChange Project. Note that UMLseCh does not aim to be an alternative for any existing general-purpose evolution specification or model transformation approaches (such as [4,1,2,14,9]) or model transformation languages such as QVT [8] or ATL [9]. It will be interesting future work to demonstrate how the results presented in this paper can be used in the context of those approaches.

To summarize, to the extent of our knowledge there is so far no published work that considers evolution in the context of a model-based development approach for security-critical software involving more than one evolution path and automated model verification.

7 Conclusion

This paper concerns the preservation of security properties of models in different evolution scenarios. We considered selected classes of model evolutions such as addition, deletion, and substitution of model elements based on UMLsec diagrams. Assuming that the starting UMLsec diagrams are secure, which one can verify using the UMLsec tool framework, our goal is to re-use these existing verification results to minimize the effort for the security verification of the evolved UMLsec diagrams. This is critical since simple re-verification would in general result in a high resource consumption for models of realistic size, specially if a continuous verification is desired (i.e. it should be determined in real-time and in parallel to the modelling activity whether the modelled change preserves security).

We achieved this goal by providing a general approach for the specification and analysis of a number of sufficient conditions for the preservation of different security properties of the starting models in the evolved models. We demonstrated this approach at the hand of the UMLsec stereotype «secure dependency». This work has been used as a basis to extend the existing UMLsec tool framework by the ability to support secure model evolution. This extended tool supports the development of evolving systems by pointing out possible security-violating modifications of secure models. We also show that the implementation of the techniques described in this paper leads to a significant efficiency gain compared to the simple re-verification of the entire model.

---

[8] Query/View/Transformation Specification http://www.omg.org/spec/QVT/
[9] The ATLAS Transformation Language http://www.eclipse.org/atl/

Our work can be extended in different directions. For example, we plan to increase the completeness of the approach by analyzing additional interesting model evolution classes. Also, it would be interesting to generalize our approach to handle other kinds of properties beyond security properties.

References

1. Andries, M., Engels, G., Habel, A., Hoffmann, B., Kreowski, H.-J., Kuske, S., Plump, D., Schürr, A., Taentzer, G.: Graph transformation for specification and programming. Science of Computer Programming 34(1), 1–54 (1999)
2. Bézivin, J., Büttner, F., Gogolla, M., Jouault, F., Kurtev, I., Lindow, A.: Model transformations? Transformation models! In: Wang, J., Whittle, J., Harel, D., Reggio, G. (eds.) MoDELS 2006. LNCS, vol. 4199, pp. 440–453. Springer, Heidelberg (2006)
3. Garlan, D., Barnes, J., Schmerl, B., Celiku, O.: Evolution styles: Foundations and tool support for software architecture evolution. In: WICSA/ECSA 2009, pp. 131 –140 (September 2009)
4. Heckel, R.: Compositional verification of reactive systems specified by graph transformation. In: Astesiano, E. (ed.) ETAPS 1998 and FASE 1998. LNCS, vol. 1382, pp. 138–153. Springer, Heidelberg (1998)
5. Johann, S., Egyed, A.: Instant and incremental transformation of models. In: Proceedings of the International Conference on Automated Software Engineering (ASE), pp. 362–365. IEEE Computer Society, Washington, DC, USA (2004)
6. Jürjens, J.: Principles for Secure Systems Design. PhD thesis, Oxford University Computing Laboratory (2002)
7. Jürjens, J., Ochoa, M., Schmidt, H., Marchal, L., Houmb, S., Islam, S.: Modelling secure systems evolution: Abstract and concrete change specifications (invited lecture). In: Bernardo, I. (ed.) 11th School on Formal Methods (SFM 2011), Bertinoro, Italy, June 13-18. LNCS. Springer, Heidelberg (2011)
8. Jürjens, J., Shabalin, P.: Tools for secure systems development with UML. Intern. Journal on Software Tools for Technology Transfer 9(5-6), 527–544 (2007); Invited submission to the special issue for FASE 2004/05
9. Kolovos, D.S., Paige, R.F., Polack, F., Rose, L.M.: Update transformations in the small with the epsilon wizard language. Journal of Object Technology 6(9), 53–69 (2007)
10. Lehman, M.M., Ramil, J.F., Wernick, P.D., Perry, D.E., Turski, W.M.: Metrics and Laws of Software Evolution – The Nineties View. In: METRICS 1997, pp. 20–32. IEEE Computer Society, Washington, DC, USA (1997)
11. Mellado, D., Rodriguez, J., Fernandez-Medina, E., Piattini, M.: Automated Support for Security Requirements Engineering in Software Product Line Domain Engineering. In: AReS 2009, pp. 224–231. IEEE Computer Society, Los Alamitos, CA, USA (2009)
12. Mens, T., D'Hondt, T.: Automating support for software evolution in UML. Automated Software Engineering Journal 7(1), 39–59 (2000)
13. Mens, T., Magee, J., Rumpe, B.: Evolving Software Architecture Descriptions of Critical Systems. Computer 43(5), 42–48 (2010)
14. Rensink, A., Schmidt, Á., Varró, D.: Model checking graph transformations: A comparison of two approaches. In: Ehrig, H., Engels, G., Parisi-Presicce, F., Rozenberg, G. (eds.) ICGT 2004. LNCS, vol. 3256, pp. 226–241. Springer, Heidelberg (2004)

15. Secure Change Project. Deliverable 4.2, http://www-jj.cs.tu-dortmund.de/jj/deliverable_4_2.pdf
16. Shin, M.E., Gomaa, H.: Software requirements and architecture modeling for evolving non-secure applications into secure applications. Science of Computer Programming 66(1), 60–70 (2007)
17. Tun, T.T., Yu, Y., Haley, C.B., Nuseibeh, B.: Model-based argument analysis for evolving security requirements. In: SSIRI 2010, pp. 88–97. IEEE Computer Society, Los Alamitos (2010)

Assessing the Kodkod Model Finder for Resolving Model Inconsistencies*

Ragnhild Van Der Straeten[1,2], Jorge Pinna Puissant[2], and Tom Mens[2]

[1] Vrije Universiteit Brussel & Université Libre de Bruxelles, Belgium
rvdstrae@vub.ac.be
[2] Université de Mons, Belgium
{jorge.pinnapuissant,tom.mens}@umons.ac.be

Abstract. In model-driven software engineering (MDE), software is built through the incremental development, composition and transformation of a variety of models. We are inevitably confronted with design models that contain a wide variety of inconsistencies. Interactive and automated support for detecting and resolving these inconsistencies is indispensable. We evaluate an approach to automate the generation of concrete models in which structural inconsistencies are resolved. We implemented this approach in the model finder Kodkod and assessed its suitability for model inconsistency resolution based on an objective set of criteria.

Keywords: model-driven engineering, model finder, inconsistency resolution.

1 Introduction

Model-driven engineering (MDE) is an approach to software engineering where the primary assets are models, describing particular aspects of the system, and being expressed in one or more modelling languages. An important challenge in MDE is the ability to tolerate the presence of certain model inconsistencies, while being able to resolve others. This is for example necessary in the early stages of software design, where design models will be incomplete and contain a lot of inconsistencies that can only be resolved in later phases of the development process. It is the task of the software designer to decide when to detect inconsistencies and when to resolve them.

This article focuses on resolution of model inconsistencies using formal methods. The research question we address is which formal techniques can be used for inconsistency resolution without requiring a lot of effort or customisation. Examples of such formal methods are fragments of first order logic, logic programming, SAT solving, graph transformation, automated planning and constraint

---

* This work has been partially supported by (i) Interuniversity Attraction Poles Programme - Belgian State – Belgian Science Policy; (ii) Action de Recherche Concertée AUWB-08/12-UMH 19 funded by the Ministère de la Communauté française - Direction générale de l'Enseignement non obligatoire et de la Recherche scientifique.

satisfaction. In the past, we attacked inconsistency resolution using graph transformation [13] and Description Logics, a fragment of first-order logic [23]. Both approaches exhibited the same problem: resolution rules were specified manually, which is an error-prone process.

To tackle this problem, we aim to generate consistent models without the need of writing or generating resolution rules. Based on an inconsistent model and a set of inconsistencies that need to be resolved, the approach should be able to generate well-formed models in a reasonable time. The underlying idea is that model inconsistencies can be resolved by finding models that satisfy the consistencies. Currently, we are investigating the automated generation of resolution plans [17] and the use of model finders. The latter is the focus of this article. After having explained when and how inconsistencies can be resolved (Section 3), we introduce *Kodkod* [21] a SAT-based constraint solver for first-order logic with relations, transitive closure, and partial models (Section 4). We assess this model finder in the context of inconsistency resolution (Section 5). This experiment reveals the complexity of the inconsistency resolution problem in general and the scalability problem of the model finder in this context (Section 6 and Section 7).

2 Related Work

First, we discuss existing approaches to inconsistency resolution using formal methods. Finkelstein et al. [15] generate inconsistency resolution actions automatically from inconsistency detection rules. These resolution actions are described as first-order logic formulae. The execution of these formulae only allows to resolve one inconsistency at a time and the resulting models do not necessarily conform to their metamodels. Kleiner [10] proposes an approach that aims at modifying a model that partially conforms to a constrained metamodel in order to make it fully conform. A constrained metamodel is a classical metamodel associated with a set of constraints. The approach uses two types of solvers: a SAT solver and a CSP solver to automatically modify the model. In the current article we focus on SAT solvers. Kleiner uses *Alloy* [9], an expressive relational language that can be used with different SAT solvers. His experiments result in a small SAT predicate (753 variables and 1271 clauses).

Other approaches to inconsistency resolution that do not use formal techniques exist in the literature. Xiong et al. [25] define a language to specify inconsistency rules and the possibilities to resolve the inconsistencies. This requires inconsistency rules to be annotated with resolution information. The approach is completely automatic, i.e., without requiring user interaction, which makes it only usable for a small subset of inconsistencies. Instead of explicitly defining or generating resolution rules, a set of models satisfying a set of consistency rules can be generated and presented to the user. Almeida da Silva et al. [1] define such an approach for resolving inconsistencies in UML models. They generate so-called resolution plans for inconsistent models. Egyed et al. [7] define a similar approach that, given an inconsistency and using choice generation functions, generates possible resolution choices, i.e., possible consistent models. All these approaches exhibit similar problems as the ones that use formal methods: the choice generation functions depend on the modelling language; they only consider the impact of one consistency rule at a time; and they need to be implemented manually.

3 Background

We use the UML to express design models because it is the de-facto general-purpose modelling language [16]. Figure 1 presents a UML class diagram and sequence diagram, respectively, which are part of the design model of an automatic teller machine (ATM). The interaction shows how a *Session* object is created when a card is inserted in the ATM and how the card and PIN code is read. The model contains an occurrence of the *NavigationIncompatibility* inconsistency [7, 16, 24]. This inconsistency arises because the message *performSession()* is sent by an *ATM* object to a *Session* object over a link typed by the association that exists between the *ATM* and *Session* class. This association is only navigable from *Session* to *ATM* and not in the other direction.

The set of inconsistencies considered in our study is based on what we found in the state-of-the-art literature [4, 7, 18, 24, 25]. These inconsistencies specify constraints expressed in terms of UML metamodel elements. For example, the previously mentioned *NavigationIncompatibility* inconsistency boils down to the following logic formula over the UML metamodel:

```
Message.receiveEvent.theLine.theObject.ownedType not in
Message.sentConnector.typedAssoc.navigableOwnedEnd.ownedType
```

The part of the model accessed during evaluation of this formula is depicted in the lower part of Figure 2 showing the abstract syntax of part of the sequence diagram of Figure 1. The upper part of Figure 2 shows part of the UML metamodel defining metaclasses, meta-associations and meta-attributes.

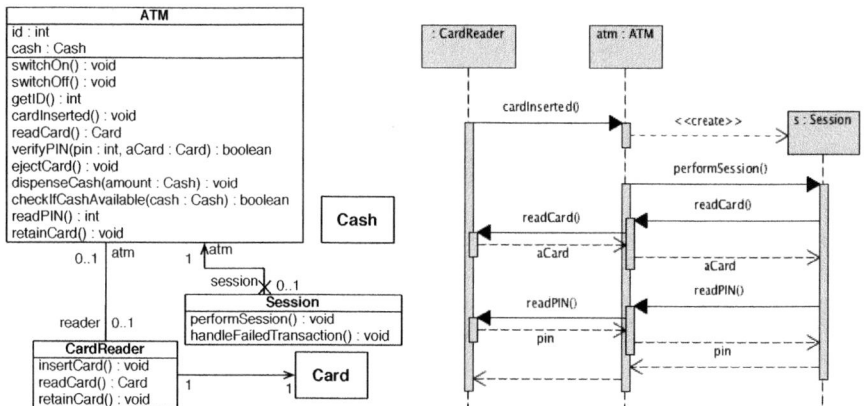

Fig. 1. UML model containing a class diagram (left) and sequence diagram (right). The model contains a *NavigationIncompatibility* inconsistency.

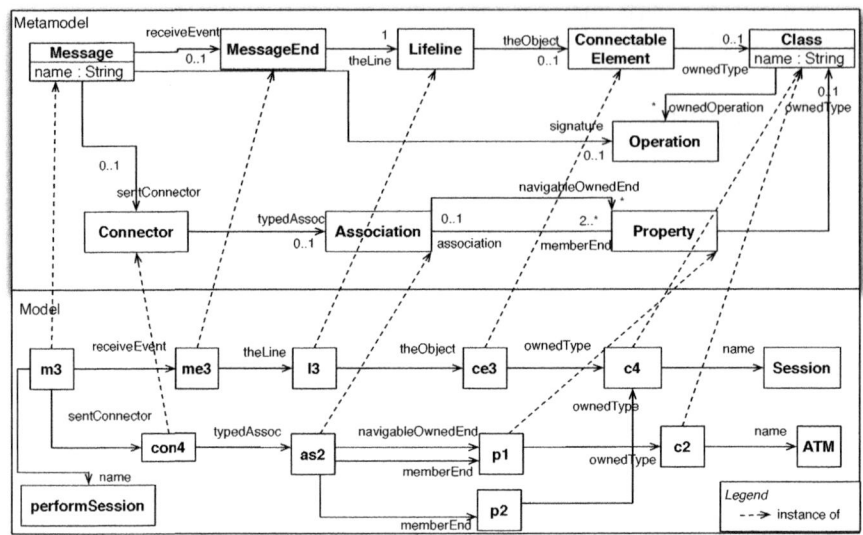

Fig. 2. Abstract syntax for model involved in a *NavigationIncompatibility* inconsistency

To be able to resolve an inconsistency occurrence, we need to know *where* and *how* to resolve it. In the remainder of the paper, we use the word *inconsistency* to denote a particular inconsistency occurrence and *inconsistency rule* to denote the definition of an inconsistency. Model elements where potentially an inconsistency can be resolved, are called *locations* in the literature [7]. A difference is made between the location *type* in the metamodel and the exact location in the model [7]. The location *types* for the *NavigationIncompatibility* inconsistency rule for example, can be read from the aforementioned logic formula. It is much harder to find all the locations for a certain inconsistency. Egyed et al. [7] used model profiling to determine the locations. In [24], we demonstrated an approach to inconsistency detection where inconsistency rules are expressed as logic queries. These queries return the model elements connected through metamodel relations involved in the inconsistency. Consequently, the *locations*, i.e., the model elements connected through metamodel relations involved in the inconsistency, are known.

If the *NavigationIncompatibility* rule would be executed as a query over our inconsistent UML design model using that approach, it would return the elements connected through metamodel relations shown in Figure 2 (except for the memberEnd relation, because this relation does not appear in the inconsistency rule). These elements are all possible locations. An inconsistency resolution needs to change at least one of these elements. For example, a possible location is navigableOwnedEnd(as2,p1) (navigableOwnedEnd is the location type of the tuple (as2,p1)) and a possible resolution is to include in the set of navigable owned ends of the as2 association the property p2 typed by the class c4. These values of a location resolving an inconsistency are called *choices* [7]. Current approaches specify these choices manually or generate them by manually written choice generation functions.

4 Inconsistency Resolution Using Kodkod

This section presents how UML model inconsistency resolution can be automated using the *Kodkod* model solver, without the need of manually writing any inconsistency resolution rule or resolution generation functions. *Kodkod* is a constraint solver. The logic accepted by *Kodkod* is a core subset of the *Alloy* modelling language supporting first order quantifiers, connectives, arbitrary-arity relations and transitive closure. *Kodkod*, in contrast to *Alloy*, makes no distinction between unary and non-unary relational variables, and all relations are untyped. In addition, the purely syntactic conventions of the *Alloy* language, i.e., predicates, functions and facts, are not part of the *Kodkod* logic [20]. *Kodkod* searches for model instances by completing a user-specified partial solution as opposed to *Alloy*. It has been shown that *Kodkod* outperforms *Alloy* dramatically [21] due to a new symmetry detection scheme, a new sparse-matrix translation to boolean encoding and a new sharing detection mechanism.

4.1 Specification of Models

First, we explain how a UML model can be specified as a *Kodkod* problem. Next, we show how to adapt this translation for inconsistency resolution. The left-hand side of Figure 3 shows the *Kodkod* formulation of the UML model of Figure 2.

A *Kodkod* problem consists of a universe declaration, i.e., a set of atoms, a set of relation declarations and a formula. The universe of a *Kodkod* problem representing a UML model contains an atom for each model element. A relation in a *Kodkod*

{m3, me3, l3, ce3, con4, as2, p1, c2, c4, Session, ATM}
Message :$_1$ [{⟨m3⟩}, {⟨m3⟩}]
MessageEnd :$_1$ [{⟨me3⟩}, {⟨me3⟩}]
Lifeline :$_1$ [{⟨l3⟩}, {⟨l3⟩}]
ConnectableElement :$_1$ [{⟨ce3⟩}, {⟨ce3⟩}]
Connector :$_1$ [{⟨con4⟩}, {⟨con4⟩}]
Association :$_1$ [{⟨as2⟩}, {⟨as2⟩}]
Property :$_1$ [{⟨p1⟩}, {⟨p1⟩}]
Class :$_1$ [{⟨c2⟩,⟨c4⟩}, {⟨c2⟩,⟨c4⟩}]
receiveEvent :$_2$ [{⟨m3, me3⟩}, {⟨m3, me3⟩}]
theLine :$_2$ [{⟨me3,l3⟩}, {⟨me3, l3⟩}]
theObject :$_2$ [{⟨l3,ce3⟩}, {⟨l3, ce3⟩}]
ownedType :$_2$ [{⟨ce3,c4⟩⟨p1, c2⟩⟨p2, c4⟩}, {⟨ce3, c4⟩⟨p1, c2⟩⟨p2, c4⟩}]
sentConnector :$_2$ [{⟨m3, con4⟩}, {⟨m3, con4⟩}]
typedAssoc :$_2$ [{⟨con4, as2⟩}, {⟨con4, as2⟩}]
navigableOwnedEnd :$_2$ [{⟨as2, p1⟩}, {⟨as2, p1⟩}]
memberEnd :$_2$ [{⟨as2, p1⟩⟨as2, p2⟩}, {⟨as2, p1⟩⟨as2, p2⟩}]
name :$_2$ [{⟨c2, ATM⟩, ⟨c4, Session⟩}, {⟨c2, ATM⟩, ⟨c4, Session⟩}]
(all m : Message | lone m.receiveEvent) and
(all me: MessageEnd | one me.theLine) and
(all a : Association | ♯(a.memberEnd) ≥ 2)

{m3, me3, l3, ce3, con4, as2, p1, c2, c4, Session, ATM}
Message :$_1$ [{⟨m3⟩}, {⟨m3⟩}]
MessageEnd :$_1$ [{⟨me3⟩}, {⟨me3⟩}]
Lifeline :$_1$ [{⟨l3⟩}, {⟨l3⟩}]
ConnectableElement :$_1$ [{⟨ce3⟩}, {⟨ce3⟩}]
Connector :$_1$ [{⟨con4⟩}, {⟨con4⟩}]
Association :$_1$ [{⟨as2⟩}, {⟨as2⟩}]
Property :$_1$ [{⟨p1⟩}, {⟨p1⟩}]
Class :$_1$ [{⟨c2⟩,⟨c4⟩}, {⟨c2⟩,⟨c4⟩}]
receiveEvent :$_2$ [{⟨m3, me3⟩}, {⟨m3, me3⟩}]
theLine :$_2$ [{⟨me3, l3⟩}, {⟨me3, l3⟩}]
theObject :$_2$ [{⟨l3, ce3⟩}, {⟨l3, ce3⟩}]
ownedType :$_2$ [{⟨ce3, c4⟩⟨p1, c2⟩⟨p2, c4⟩}, {⟨ce3, c4⟩⟨p1, c2⟩⟨p2, c4⟩}]
sentConnector :$_2$ [{⟨m3, con4⟩}, {⟨m3, con4⟩}]
typedAssoc :$_2$ [{⟨con4, as2⟩}, {⟨con4, as2⟩}]
navigableOwnedEnd :$_2$ [{}, {as2} → {p1, p2}]
memberEnd :$_2$ [{⟨as2, p1⟩⟨as2, p2⟩}, {⟨as2, p1⟩⟨as2, p2⟩}]
name :$_2$ [{⟨c2, ATM⟩, ⟨c4, Session⟩}, {⟨c2, ATM⟩, ⟨c4, Session⟩}]
(all m : Message | lone m.receiveEvent) and
(all me: MessageEnd | one me.theLine) and
(all a : Association | ♯(a.memberEnd) ≥ 2) and
all m: Message | m.receiveEvent.theLine.theObject.
ownedType in m.sentConnector.typedAssoc.
navigableOwnedEnd.ownedType)

Fig. 3. On the left: inconsistent UML model expressed as a *Kodkod* problem. On the right: a *Kodkod* problem used for resolving an *NavigationIncompatibility*.

problem is declared through a relational variable name, its arity and bounds on its value. *Kodkod* requires the relational variables to be bound prior to analysis. Every relational variable must be bound from above by a relational constant, a fixed set of tuples drawn from the universe of atoms. Each relation must also be bound from below by a relational constant, i.e., a lower bound containing the tuples that the variable's value must include in an instance of the formula. The union of all relations' lower bounds forms a problem's partial instance [21]. Each UML metaclass is expressed as a unary relation. Its value is the set of model elements that represent its instances. For example, the variable Class in the *Kodkod* problem in Figure 3 represents the metaclass *Class* and serves as a handle to the unary constant $\{\langle c2 \rangle, \langle c4 \rangle\}$ that represents the set of all classes in the model. The UML meta-association ends and attributes are translated into the corresponding k-arity relational variables. The values of these relational variables are tuples containing the UML model elements involved in the corresponding UML meta-associations or meta-attributes. For example, the binary variable navigableOwnedEnd in Figure 3 represents the meta-association end *navigableOwnedEnd* and encodes the ends of an association that are navigable.

The cardinality constraints specified on the UML meta-associations are encoded in the formula of the *Kodkod* problem. For example, cardinalities such as 1, 0..1 and 1..∗ map onto the *Kodkod* keywords **one**, **lone** and **some** respectively. The formula specified in the left-hand side of Figure 3 (last three lines) expresses that each *Message* optionally has a *receiveEvent*, each *MessageEnd* has exactly one *theLine*, and each *Association* has at least two *memberEnds*. The ♯ operator is the *Kodkod* set cardinality operator, the **in** keyword represents the set inclusion operator. An instance of a formula is a binding of the declared relational variables to relational constants, that makes the formula true. *Kodkod*'s analysis will search for such an instance within the provided upper and lower bounds. Remark that there is no conceptual difference between the above translation and existing translations of UML diagrams and OCL constraints to *Alloy* (e.g., [2]). We have built an Eclipse plugin to generate the corresponding *Kodkod* problem automatically given a (set of) UML model(s). Our plugin uses the UML2 Eclipse plug-in API[1].

4.2 Inconsistency Resolution

In order to generate consistent models w.r.t. a consistency rule, we need to specify the consistency rule as part of the *Kodkod* problem's formula. In our approach, the notion of inconsistency rule and consistency rule can be used interchangeably. Because a consistency rule is the negation of an inconsistency rule, only the logic connectives and quantifiers differ but not the metamodel elements. For example, the following formula represents the negation of *NavigationIncompatibility*.

```
(all m: Message | m.receiveEvent.theLine.theObject.ownedType
in m.sentConnector.typedAssoc.navigableOwnedEnd.ownedType)
```

---

[1] http://www.eclipse.org/modeling/mdt/?project=uml2

Currently, the translation of such a consistency rule to a *Kodkod* formula is done manually. However, an automatic translation can be envisioned similar to the automatic translation of OCL constraints to *Alloy* as defined in [2].

Each relational variable in a *Kodkod* problem representing a UML model element has the same lower and upper bound (cf. Section 4.1). This means that the model is static and the size is fixed. For resolving inconsistencies, we want *Kodkod* to generate consistent models by adding model elements or adding elements to a meta-association/attribute or changing the value of a meta-association/attribute.

Considering the translation specified above, for *Kodkod* to be able to find models for the given consistency rule, the lower bound of certain relations needs to be changed. As explained in Section 3, each element involved in an inconsistency is a possible location for resolving the inconsistency. After having identified the possible locations, one or several of these can be chosen and will be excluded from the corresponding relations' lower bounds. For example, given the location navigableOwnedEnd(as2,p1), the tuple ⟨as2,p1⟩ will be excluded from the navigableOwnedEnd's lower bound in the corresponding *Kodkod* problem. This results in an empty set as shown in the right-hand side of Figure 3. The upper bound of the relational variable representing the location type needs to be changed too. It becomes the Cartesian product of its domain and its range. In the example, the upper bound of the navigableOwnedEnd relation is the Cartesian product of all atoms that represent associations and all atoms that represent properties. The right-hand side of Figure 3 shows the *Kodkod* problem with modified navigableOwnedEnd relation (the *Kodkod* → operator represents the set product operation) and the negation of the *NavigationIncompatibility* rule included in the formula. *Kodkod*'s analysis will search for an instance of this consistency within the provided upper and lower bounds.

Considering the Cartesian product as the upper bound of a relation can result in models not contributing to the consistency of the model. This is the case when the cardinality of the UML meta-association ends of the considered meta-association is of the form $n..m$ with $m > 1$. Consider the superClass meta-association ([16], pg. 50) giving the superclasses of a class. Both ends of this meta-association have an unlimited cardinality (*). Suppose the aim is to add subclasses to a certain class and suppose we set the upper bound of such a relation to the Cartesian product of the set of classes. *Kodkod* will return not only models that add subclasses to the class under study but also models which additionally add subclasses to other classes of the model. The latter models do not contribute to our goal. Consequently, in the case of an association with ends of cardinality $n..m$ with $m > 1$, the upper bound of the corresponding relation equals the lower bound of the relation union the Cartesian product of the model element (i.e., a singleton) and the range of the relation.

Remark that multiple inconsistency locations can be considered by the approach by excluding the corresponding tuples from the lower bound of the corresponding relational variables. Currently, modifying the lower and upper bound is done manually, we envision to automate this step.

5 Case Study

5.1 Cases

Due to lack of access to sufficiently large and realistic UML models, we evaluate our approach on UML models obtained by reverse engineering five software systems (Table 1). We opt for open source software systems in order to have reproducible results. These systems cover finance, chat, modelling and web development applications. Reverse engineering was done through Together 2006 Release 2 for Eclipse resulting in class diagrams and sequence diagrams. Although our approach is applicable to all kinds of UML diagrams, the models considered only contain class and sequence diagrams. The model sizes range from 2064 to 8572 elements.

Table 1. Reverse engineered open source models

	software system	version	model size
m_1	Chipchat	1.0 beta 2	2064
m_2	Cleansheets	1.4b	7387
m_3	SweetRules	2.0	6342
m_4	Thinwire	1.2	8572
m_5	UMLet	9beta	4890

We consider 12 model inconsistency rules, borrowed from [4, 13, 16, 24] and described in [22]. They cover the main constraints that can be expressed in *Kodkod*: cardinality constraints, quantified constraints, comparison constraints, negated constraints and compound constraints using the logic connectives.

Each reverse engineered model m_i was consistent with respect to the 12 considered inconsistency rules, except for *Rule9*: *NavigationIncompatibility*. Inconsistencies of this type were caused by the absence of associations in the reversed engineered models. This resulted in 191 inconsistencies in m_1, 14 in m_2, 103 in m_3, 12 in m_4 and 36 in m_5.

To carry out our experiment, we first removed all these inconsistencies (by adding the necessary associations), and next we manually added one inconsistency of each different type to each of the five models. A model inconsistency typically affects only part of a model. As a result, we only took into consideration relational variables that were involved in the inconsistencies we wanted to resolve when translating the models into a *Kodkod* problem. We used the translation explained in Section 4, but we translated only metamodel elements (i.e., meta-classes, meta-associations, meta-attributes) occurring in the consistency rules, and only model elements that are instances of these metaclasses and related through the considered meta-relations. For example, if a user wants to resolve a *NavigationIncompatibility* inconsistency (*Rule9*), only the elements that are instances of the metamodel elements shown in the upper part of Figure 2 are considered. The formula of the corresponding *Kodkod* problem contains the considered consistency rule and the cardinality constraints involving the considered metamodel elements. This reduces the resulting number of *Kodkod* elements.

Figure 4 shows, for each model, the percentage of model elements involved in the *Kodkod* problem. For each inconsistency rule there is a cluster of five bars, each bar corresponding to one of the 5 models. Only considering the elements that are instances of the metaclasses that are in the rule definition results in sizes between 5% and 60% of the original model size. The only exception is *Rule4: OwnedElement* that uses almost the entire model[2] because it considers the metaclass *Element* and each model element is an instance of this metaclass.

Figure 5 shows the number of model elements and references (i.e., instantiations of meta-associations and meta-attributes) involved in each generated *Kodkod* problem per rule and per model as a percentage of the model size (i.e., the number of model elements). This chart shows the importance of the references between model elements: they more or less double the size of the elements involved in the translation.

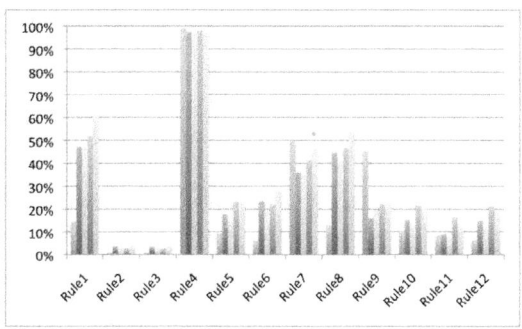

Fig. 4. Percentage of model elements that need to be considered per inconsistency rule, for each of the five considered models

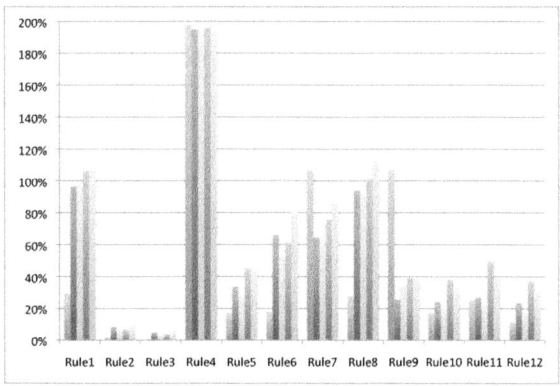

Fig. 5. Percentage of model elements and references per rule and per model

---

[2] *Rule4* searches for model elements that directly or indirectly own themselves.

The considered (in)consistency rules contain 44 location types in total, of which 28 distinct location types. This is not exhaustive because the considered inconsistencies only reason over a part of the UML metamodel. Resolving an inconsistency at a certain location gives rise to a set of consistent models, called *choices*. Table 2 shows the average number of choices per inconsistency rule and per model. This table needs more explanation. First of all, remark that the number of choices is independent of the chosen resolution technique or approach. The number of choices is infinite for *Rule*11: *MultiplicityIncompatibility* dealing with the upper and lower cardinality of properties. *Kodkod* lets us deal with this infinity through its scope bounds that limit the number of choices returned. The number of choices for *Rule*2: *CyclicInheritance* and *Rule*3: *NoConcreteSubclass* for m_1 are not relevant (NR) because the rules deal with inheritance and the model does not contain any inheritance hierarchies. For the remaining models the number of choices for *Rule*2 and *Rule*3 have a complexity of $\mathcal{O}(2^n)$ with n the number of classes not involved in the inheritance hierarchy under study. As an example, inconsistency *Rule*3: *NoConcreteSubclass* searches for abstract leaf classes (implying that the class has no concrete implementation). A possible resolution is to make a concrete existing class subclass of the abstract class. The number of choices is the number of concrete classes available in the model and all possible combinations of classes available in the model. So the total number of choices equals 2^n with n the number of concrete classes in the model. The number of choices for *Rule*4: *OwnedElement* are about half the size of the models. The number of choices for *Rule*1: *DanglingParameterType* and *Rule*12: *DanglingPropertyType* depend on the number of types or properties in the model. The number of choices for *Rule*5 till *Rule*10 is not that large because elements of sequence diagrams are involved, and these elements constitute a minority of the elements in the model.

Table 2. Average number of choices per (in)consistency rule and model

	Rule1	Rule2	Rule3	Rule4	Rule5	Rule6	Rule7	Rule8	Rule9	Rule10	Rule11	Rule12
m_1	47	NR	NR	1021	10	1	3	18	10	3	∞	20
m_2	572	$\mathcal{O}(2^n)$	$\mathcal{O}(2^n)$	3600	119	2	35	19	8	14	∞	237
m_3	487	$\mathcal{O}(2^n)$	$\mathcal{O}(2^n)$	3092	92	7	10	17	9	15	∞	183
m_4	695	$\mathcal{O}(2^n)$	$\mathcal{O}(2^n)$	4201	113	10	57	18	10	20	∞	226
m_5	442	$\mathcal{O}(2^n)$	$\mathcal{O}(2^n)$	2369	86	3	8	20	9	16	∞	172

5.2 Timing Results

We used the Kodkodi [11] front-end for *Kodkod* and we used the MiniSat solver [6] available in *Kodkod* because of its faster performance compared to the other available SAT solvers (according to the SAT competitions in 2009 and 2010[3]). Each experiment consisted of the introduction of one inconsistency of a certain

---

[3] http://www.satcompetition.org/

type in the consistent model and selecting a location. We executed the resolutions on a MacBook Pro with a 2.33 GHz Intel Core 2 Duo Processor and 4GB of memory. For each model and consistency rule, we resolved one inconsistency by considering the different possible locations. The aggregations of these experiments resulted in 220 (44 location types × 5 models) timing results.

Figure 6 shows the timing results we obtained. Each dot in the plot represents the time for generating choices for a certain location type for each rule (the numbers on the x-axis correspond to the rule numbers, time is expressed in ms) and per model. All results that took more than 6 minutes of execution time or that resulted in an out of memory are excluded from Figure 6. Only in case of *Rule*4, several experiments ran out of memory. 25% of the experiments resulted in a time greater than 6 minutes. In 17% of the remaining cases it took more than one minute to execute a resolution. In general, we conclude that the approach does not provide instantaneous resolution on medium scale models.

Another question we raised is whether the size of a model has an influence on the performance of the model finder. Figure 7 shows the timing results again per rule and per model but the values of the x-axis indicate the size of the considered models. To verify whether there is a correlation between the size of the models and the performance results we used three statistical methods. Pearson's correlation coefficient, indicating the degree of linear correlation between the two considered variables, resulted in a value of 0.063. Being very close to 0, there is no linear correlation between the two variables. We used Spearman's rank correlation coefficient to assess how well the relationship between the two variables can be described using a monotonic function. A perfect Spearman correlation of +1 or -1 occurs when each of the variables is a perfect monotone function of the other. We obtained a value of 0.489. Finally, we used Kendall's rank correlation to measure the strength of dependence between two variables.

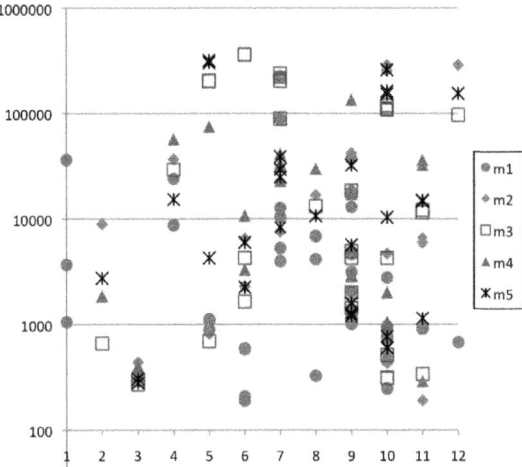

Fig. 6. Timing results in ms (y-axis) for each rule (x-axis) per location type and model

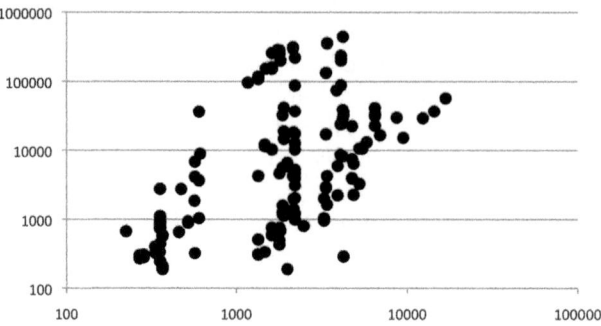

Fig. 7. Timing results in ms (y-axis) in function of model size (x-axis), using log-log scale

A value of +1 or -1 indicates a perfect correlation while 0 indicates no correlation at all. The value obtained for Kendall's rank correlation based on our data is 0.349. Summarising, we did not observe any convincing correlation between the size of the model and the timing results.

6 Threats to Validity

External Validity. To determine whether our results are generalisable to other models (in particular, models that have not been reverse engineered from the code, and models of a larger size) or other types of models, more experiments are needed. The same is true for the inconsistency rules. We considered only a limited set of rules, but tried to include a variety of different expressions and constraints. We can easily extend our list of inconsistency rules with new ones, as long as they can be expressed in *Kodkod*. It remains an open question to which extent the obtained results depend on the model finder (*Kodkod*) and the SAT solver (*MiniSat*) used.

Internal Validity. Because we obtained our models by *reverse engineering source code*, associations were absent in the resulting models and we had to change these models before they became usable for our experiments. We added the necessary associations including association ends manually to the models such that all models were consistent before starting the experiments. An alternative would be to generate large models using a model generator such as the one proposed in [14]. However, this generator generates class diagrams only.

Our approach is restricted in the sense that it does not generate choices that remove model elements. This is intrinsic to *Kodkod* because it starts with a partial model and it will not remove elements from the lower bound of the problem. On the other hand, the fact that we only consider partial models not removing elements from the model has the advantage that we do not end up with dangling references in the complete model.

7 Discussion and Future Work

The combination of a model finder with a SAT solver has several advantages. The strengths of using *Kodkod* for our purposes are (1) its relational logic extended with a mechanism for specifying partial models, (2) its new translation to SAT that uses sparse-matrices resulting in a significantly faster to produce and easier to solve boolean encoding and new algorithms for identifying symmetries and for finding minimal unsatisfiable cores [19].

The use of a SAT-based constraint solver enables us to discuss *correctness* and *completeness* of the approach. A generated resolution model is *correct* if it no longer contains the particular inconsistency selected for resolution. The correctness of the generated models is guaranteed by the SAT solver. Because *Kodkod* translates relational logic to Boolean logic and invokes an off-the-shelf SAT solver, it is the correctness of the SAT solver that will guarantee the correctness of *Kodkod*. State-of-the-art SAT solvers implement formally proven correct algorithms [12]. The set of generated models after resolution should be *complete*, i.e., no other consistent model can be found. *Kodkod* is complete within the considered lower and upper bounds of the relations defined in a *Kodkod* problem: *Kodkod* will generate all the consistent models with values of the considered relations within the relations' lower and upper bound. Of course, there can be other consistent models consisting of model elements not within the specified lower and upper bound of a relation. However, our approach is conceived such that the original model and the generated models only differ at one or several locations of certain location types. Consequently, other consistent models either involve other locations or will only add model elements of the considered location types to the generated models not contributing to the consistency of the model. When no models are generated by *Kodkod*, either more locations need to be specified (resulting in a smaller lower bound of the considered location type(s)) in order to resolve the inconsistency, or no consistent models w.r.t. the given consistency rule can be found. This would mean that the model is over-constrained.

A major limitation of the proposed approach is its poor performance and lack of scalability. For 80% of the timing results the generation of the CNF (conjunctive normal form) took more than 90% of the total time. As future work, several optimisations can be envisioned to make model finders more performant and hence more suitable for inconsistency resolution. A first optimisation would be to build the CNF incrementally. Another possible optimisation is to refine the given constraints and trying to resolve the refinements.

Our experiment focused on a single location type and resolved one inconsistency at a time. We could optimise the given translation (cf. Section 4) further by considering as an upper bound for the relation to be modified not the Cartesian product of its domain and range but the given lower bound plus the Cartesian product of the model element under study and its range. However, this optimisation is not possible when considering multiple locations or multiple inconsistencies. These inconsistencies can be instances of the same rule or of different rules. In future work we aim to extend our approach to multiple inconsistencies and multiple location types.

Next to considering multiple inconsistencies, we will extend the set of rules. This should give us more statistically relevant information about the correlation between inconsistencies and models on the one hand and the corresponding translation and solving time on the other hand. We want to come up with a classification of inconsistency rules together with a benchmark of suitable models on which to compare different approaches implementing these rules.

Another way to tackle the scalability would be to limit the number of generated choices. As our brute-force approach revealed, in some cases large sets of models are returned to the user, for example, in case of *Rule*3 where all possible inheritance hierarchies based on the available classes are returned for one inconsistency. Most of these inheritance hierarchies do not make sense in the application domain. Consequently, any inconsistency resolution technique generating models needs to be able to filter the generated set of models or to define heuristics to restrict the generation. In the first case the set of models is generated and afterwards a filter is applied, in the latter case the input of the model finder is restricted such that a smaller set of models is generated. For example, enabling end-users to declaratively express relations between the original model and the desired resulting model(s) would result in only meaningful models being returned to the end users.

Our approach is strongly related to CSP because *Kodkod* is used to generate a set of models satisfying a set of consistency rules. In [5] the tool UMLtoCSP is presented. Given a UML class diagram annotated with OCL constraints, UMLtoCSP automatically checks several correctness properties. The tool uses Constraint Logic Programming and the constraint solver ECL^iPS^e [3]. We believe that this constraint solver could be used for resolving model inconsistencies too. Another issue of further research is the use of search-based approaches advocated by Harman [8]. Such approaches include a wide variety of different techniques such as metaheuristics, local search algorithms, automated learning, genetic algorithms. These techniques could be applied to the problem of model inconsistency resolution, as it satisfies at least three important properties that motivate the need for search-based software engineering: the presence of a large search space, the need for algorithms with a low computational complexity, and the absence of known optimal solutions.

8 Conclusion

Resolution of model inconsistencies is an important and truly challenging activity in MDE, necessitating interactive and automated support. This article explored the use of the *Kodkod* model finder for automatically generating consistent models starting from an inconsistent model and a set of inconsistencies. The approach was validated on a set of medium-size models, and the proposed technique does not appear to be viable for interactive model development.

Because we cannot generalise conclusions from our validation, our initial assessment results call for the initiation of a research path in this area. For example, it is necessary to extend the experiment with more inconsistency rules, more models and to consider multiple inconsistencies at a time. This will allow a correlation analysis between performance and multiple inconsistencies and to classify inconsistency rules.

References

1. Almeida da Silva, M., Mougenot, A., Blanc, X., Bendraou, R.: Towards automated inconsistency handling in design models. In: Pernici, B. (ed.) CAiSE 2010. LNCS, vol. 6051, pp. 348–362. Springer, Heidelberg (2010)
2. Anastasakis, K., Bordbar, B., Georg, G., Ray, I.: On Challenges of Model Transformation from UML to Alloy. Software and Systems Modeling, Special Issue on MoDELS 2007 9(1), 69–86 (2008)
3. Apt, K., Wallace, M.: Constraint Logic Programming using ECL^iPS^e. Cambridge University Press, Cambridge (2006)
4. Blanc, X., Mounier, I., Mougenot, A., Mens, T.: Detecting model inconsistency through operation-based model construction. In: Int'l Conf. Software Engineering, pp. 511–520. ACM, New York (2008)
5. Cabot, J., Clarisó, R., Riera, D.: UMLtoCSP: a tool for the formal verification of UML/OCL models using constraint programming. In: ASE, pp. 547–548. ACM, New York (2007)
6. Eén, N., Sörensson, N.: An extensible SAT-solver. In: Giunchiglia, E., Tacchella, A. (eds.) SAT 2003. LNCS, vol. 2919, pp. 502–518. Springer, Heidelberg (2004)
7. Egyed, A., Letier, E., Finkelstein, A.: Generating and evaluating choices for fixing inconsistencies in UML design models. In: ASE, pp. 99–108. IEEE, Los Alamitos (2008)
8. Harman, M.: Search based software engineering. In: Alexandrov, V.N., van Albada, G.D., Sloot, P.M.A., Dongarra, J. (eds.) ICCS 2006. LNCS, vol. 3994, pp. 740–747. Springer, Heidelberg (2006)
9. Jackson, D. (ed.): Software Abstractions. Logic, Language and Analysis. MIT Press, Cambridge (2006)
10. Kleiner, M., Didonet Del Fabro, M., Albert, P.: Model search: Formalizing and automating constraint solving in MDE platforms. In: Kühne, T., Selic, B., Gervais, M.-P., Terrier, F. (eds.) ECMFA 2010. LNCS, vol. 6138, pp. 173–188. Springer, Heidelberg (2010)
11. Kodkodi: version 1.2.11 (March 2010), www4.in.tum.de/~blanchet/#kodkodi
12. Marić, F.: Formalization and implementation of modern SAT solvers. J. Autom. Reason. 43(1), 81–119 (2009)
13. Mens, T., Van Der Straeten, R., D'Hondt, M.: Detecting and resolving model inconsistencies using transformation dependency analysis. In: Wang, J., Whittle, J., Harel, D., Reggio, G. (eds.) MoDELS 2006. LNCS, vol. 4199, pp. 200–214. Springer, Heidelberg (2006)
14. Mougenot, A., Darrasse, A., Blanc, X., Soria, M.: Uniform random generation of huge metamodel instances. In: Paige, R.F., Hartman, A., Rensink, A. (eds.) ECMDA-FA 2009. LNCS, vol. 5562, pp. 130–145. Springer, Heidelberg (2009)
15. Nentwich, C., Emmerich, W., Finkelstein, A.: Consistency management with repair actions. In: ICSE, pp. 455–464. IEEE Computer Society, Los Alamitos (May 2003)
16. Object Management Group: Unified Modeling Language 2.1.2 Superstructure Specification. formal/2007-11-02 (November 2007), www.omg.org

17. Pinna Puissant, J., Mens, T., Van Der Straeten, R.: Resolving model inconsistencies with automated planning. In: 3rd Workshop on Living with Inconsistencies in Software Development, CEUR Workshop Proceeding (September 2010)
18. Sabetzadeh, M., Nejati, S., Liaskos, S., Easterbrook, S.M., Chechik, M.: Consistency checking of conceptual models via model merging. In: ER, pp. 221–230. IEEE, Los Alamitos (2007)
19. Torlak, E.: A Constraint Solver for Software Engineering: Finding Models and Cores of Large Relational Specifications. Ph.D. thesis, MIT (February 2009)
20. Torlak, E., Dennis, G.: Kodkod for alloy users. In: First ACM Alloy Workshop (2006)
21. Torlak, E., Jackson, D.: Kodkod: A relational model finder. In: Grumberg, O., Huth, M. (eds.) TACAS 2007. LNCS, vol. 4424, pp. 632–647. Springer, Heidelberg (2007)
22. Van Der Straeten, R.: Description of UML model inconsistencies. Tech. rep., Vrije Universiteit Brussel, Belgium (2011),
http://soft.vub.ac.be/soft/members/ragnhildvanderstraeten/bibliography
23. Van Der Straeten, R., D'Hondt, M.: Model refactorings through rule-based inconsistency resolution. In: ACM Symposium on Applied Computing (SAC 2006), pp. 1210–1217. ACM, New York (2006)
24. Van Der Straeten, R., Mens, T., Simmonds, J., Jonckers, V.: Using description logic to maintain consistency between UML models. In: Stevens, P., Whittle, J., Booch, G. (eds.) UML 2003. LNCS, vol. 2863, pp. 326–340. Springer, Heidelberg (2003)
25. Xiong, Y., Hu, Z., Zhao, H., Song, H., Takeichi, M., Mei, H.: Supporting automatic model inconsistency fixing. In: ESEC/FSE, pp. 315–324. ACM, New York (2009)

Operation Based Model Representation: Experiences on Inconsistency Detection

Jerome Le Noir[1], Olivier Delande[1], Daniel Exertier[2],
Marcos Aurélio Almeida da Silva[3], and Xavier Blanc[4]

[1] Thales Research and Technology, France
[2] Thales Corporate Services, France
[3] LIP6, UPMC Paris Universitas, France
[4] LABRI, Université de Bordeaux 1, France

Abstract. Keeping the consistency between design models is paramount in complex contexts. It turns out that the underlying Model Representation Strategy has an impact on the inconsistency detection activity. The Operation Based strategy represents models as the sequence of atomic editing actions that lead to its current state. Claims have been made about gains in time and space complexity and in versatility by using this kind of representation when compared to the traditional object based one. However, this hypothesis has never been tested in an industrial context before. In this paper, we detail our experience evaluating an Operation Based consistency engine (Praxis) when compared with a legacy system based on EMF. We evaluated a set of industrial models under inconsistency rules written in both Java (for EMF) and PraxisRules (the DSL – Domain Specific Language – for describing inconsistency rules in Praxis). Our results partially confirm the gains claimed by the Operation Based engines.

1 Introduction

Current large scale software projects involve hundreds of developers working in a distributed environment over several models that need to conform to several meta-models (e.g. SysML, UML, Petri nets, business process) [1]. In such context keeping the consistency between models and with their respective meta-models is mandatory[2].

Models are usually represented as sets of *objects* along with their *attributes* and mutual *associations* [3,4]. A model is considered to be inconsistent if and only if it contains undesirable patterns, which are specified by the so called *inconsistency rules* [5]. Even if these rules may be represented in many different ways, such as the well-formedness rules of [6], the structural rules of [7], the detection rules of [4], the syntactic rules of [8], and the inconsistency detection rules of [9], approaches that deal with detection of inconsistencies irremediably consist in browsing the model in order to detect undesirable patterns.

The underlying strategy used to represent the model is then very likely to have significant effects on the performance of inconsistency detection algorithms. Under the Operation Based model representation strategy[9,10], instead of keeping track of the current configuration of the objects, their attributes and associations, one records the sequence of atomic editing actions that were performed in order to obtain the current configuration.

Operation Based checkers claim to be as efficient as Object Based ones, and very adequate for Incremental inconsistency detection mode[11]. This mode, consists in, instead of checking every inconsistency rule over the complete model every time the model has been modified, limiting the search to a subset of this problem. The search for inconsistencies is performed on the subset of the model that was modified since the last check and using the subset of the inconsistency rules that are concerned by this modification. The efficiency gains claimed by these checkers would come from the fact that identifying the scope of an incremental check reduces to looking at the sequences of actions appended to the current model by the uses (these sequences are called *increments*)[12].

Unfortunately, none of these claims has ever been tested in an industrial context before, specially on non-UML models. In this paper we report our experiences on the impact of the underlying strategy for model representation to the overall performance of the inconsistency checker. These experiences have been synthesized in a case study in which we compare an operation based consistency checker (Praxis [9]) with the one provided by the Eclipse Modeling Framework (EMF)[1]. Our tests included industrial models ranging from 1.000 to 50.000 model elements. We have carried out the approach on the engineering meta-model defined by Thales composed of about 400 meta-classes. This meta-model contains 114 inconsistency rules implemented in Java, from which 30 mandatory ones were selected, re-implemented and checked in models coming from operational contexts. Our results partially confirm the gains claimed by Operation Based consistency engines: the overall performance gains were identified in the incremental mode but no significant gains were identified in the batch mode.

This paper is organized as follows: Section 2 details the operation model representation strategy used in Praxis and compares it to the object based one used in EMF. Section 3 presents the design and results of our case study. Section 4 concludes.

2 Praxis: An Operation Based Model Representation Strategy

The objective of this section is introducing Praxis, an operation based model representation strategy and PraxisRules, the rule based DSL – Domain Specific Language – for representing consistency rules in Praxis. Our objective is not presenting them in details, but to present their basics in comparison to traditional object based model representation and consistency rules as provided by EMF, for example.

---

[1] The Eclipse Modeling Framework, http://eclipse.org/emf

2.1 Praxis

Praxis[9] is a meta-model independent consistency checking strategy whose internal model representation is based on the operation based model representation. In Praxis, a model is represented as the sequence of atomic editing actions that lead to its current state. This approach uses 6 kinds of atomic actions which were inspired on the MOF reflective API [3].

The $create(me, mc, t)$ and $delete(me, t)$ actions respectively create and delete a model element me, that is an instance of the meta-class mc at the time-stamp t. The time-stamp which indicates the moment when it was executed by the user. The actions $addProperty(me, p, value, t)$ and $remProperty(me, p, value, t)$ add or remove the value $value$ to or from the property p of the model element me at time-stamp t. Similarly, the actions $addReference(me, r, target, t)$ and $remReference(me, r, target, t)$ add or remove the model element $target$ as a reference r from the model element me.

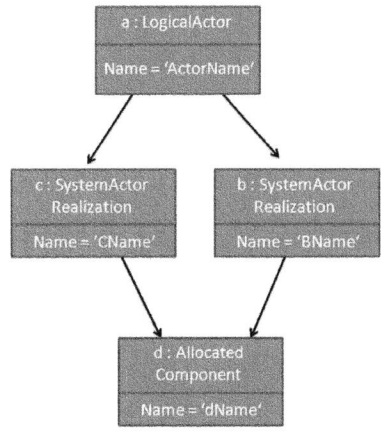

create(a,logicalActor,1)
addProperty(a,name, 'ActorName',2)
create(b,systemActorRealization,3)
addProperty(b,name, 'BName',4))
create(c,systemActorRealization,5)
addProperty(c,name,'CName',6)
addReference(a,systemActorRealization,b,7)
addReference(a,systemActorRealization,c,8)
create(d,allocatedComponent,10)
addProperty(d,name, 'dName', 11)
addReference(b, allocatedComponent, d, 12)
addReference(c, allocatedComponent, d, 13)

Fig. 1. Sample model   **Fig. 2.** Model construction operationsequence

Figures 1 and 2 represent the same model in the form of respectively a set of objects along with attributes and associations and a sequence of editing actions. Both represent the *LogicalActor* a, the *SystemActorRealizations* b and c and the *AllocatedComponent* d. They also represent the *name* attribute of each object. The actions in timestamps 1 and 2 create the a object and set its name. The actions $3-6$ create the b and c objects and set their *name* attributes. The actions in timestamps 7 and 8 create the associations between a, b and c. Finally, the actions in timestamps $10-13$ create the c object and associate it as the *allocatedComponent* of b and c.

2.2 PraxisRules: The Consistency Rules DSL for Praxis

PraxisRules is a rule-based logical DSL used to define consistency rules over Praxis sequences. This language is able to represent constraints over the order of the actions in a sequence or over the configuration of objects implied by it.

The Java code snippet below represents a consistency rule over the model in Figure 1. This rule makes sure that every *ActorRealization* of a *LogicalActor* is an instance of *Actor*. This is done by navigating through a logical actor (represented by the *logicalActor* variable whose declaration is not shown), obtaining the list of its realizations (line 4) and iterating through it (lines 5 − 8) and checking if every realization has an associated allocated component that is an instance of *Actor* (lines 9 − 13).

```
1  /* Ensures that the Actor Realization of a Logical Actor always
2   *    realizes an Actor (at the system analysis level).
3   */
4     EList<SystemActorRealization> actorRealisations =
              logicalActor.getSystemActorRealizations();
5     Iterator<SystemActorRealization> iterator =
              actorRealisations.iterator();
6
7     while (iterator.hasNext()) {
8             SystemActorRealization next = iterator.next();
9             Component allocatedComponent =
                  next.getAllocatedComponent();
10
11            if (null == allocatedComponent ||
                  !(allocatedComponent instanceof Actor)) {
12                return createFailureStatus(ctx_p,
                      new Object[] { logicalActor.getName() });
13            }
14    }
15 }
```

The following PraxisRule code snippet illustrates the definition of the same rule under an operation based model representation strategy. This code defines a rule called check_LogicalActor_ActorRealization which detects logical actors realized by a system realization that is allocated to an object that is not an actor or that is not realized by any system actor realization.

First of all, notice that this rule defines a logical expression based on logical connectives (and{} for conjunction, or{} for disjunction and not{} for negation). Capitalized terms represent variables and terms starting with the # sign represent meta-classes or associations. Another important fact is that Praxis actions are used as predicates in this logical expression.

```
1 ["Ensures that the Actor Realization of a Logical Actor always
      realizes an Actor (at the system analysis level)"]
2 public check_LogicalActor_ActorRealization(A, R)
3    <=>
4    and {
5        create(A, #LogicalActor),
6        addReference(A, #systemActorRealizations, R),
7        or {
8            not {addReference(R, #allocatedComponent, _)},
```

```
9            and {
10               addReference(R, #allocatedComponent, A),
11               create(A, #Actor)
12           }
13      }
14 }.
```

The most important difference between this rule and the previous one is that this one is not based on navigating through the objects in the current configuration, but in looking for actions in the sequence that represents the current model.

The main advantage of this kind of rule is that it is possible to identify which rules need to be rechecked (and which parameters need to be rechecked) by a simple inspection of the rules. For example, every time an action *addReference* for the association *systemActorRealization* is performed this rule needs to be rechecked, because if a new system actor realization is being added to a logical actor, it is necessary to verify if it does not violate this rule.

3 Case Study

The advantages of the operation based model representation presented in the last section have been empirically validated on randomly generated UML models in [12]. However they have never been investigated in real industrial models. That is then the main motivation for the present study.

This section is organized as follows: Section 3.1 details the industrial context in which this study has been realized; Section 3.2 lists its main objectives and planning. Finally, Section 3.3 describes the environment in which it was effectively performed and Section 3.4 discusses its results.

3.1 Industrial Context

In order to build an architecture of a software intensive system, many stakeholders contribute to the description of the system architecture. Following a model-based engineering approach, the different stakeholders will use modelling tools to describe the architecture and analysis tools to evaluate some properties of the architecture.

Thales has defined a model-based architecture engineering approach for software intensive systems, the ARCADIA method [13]. It defines a model organization of five abstraction levels (viewpoints) for mainstream engineering and a set of others viewpoints for speciality engineering, depending typically on non-functional constraints applied on the system to be engineered. The views conforming to these viewpoints are used by different stakeholders during the system definition process. Therefore, techniques and tools to manage the consistency of an information bulk made of several views on a system are necessary. The ARCADIA method adopts a viewpoint-based architectural description such as described in the conceptual foundations of ISO/IEC 42010, Systems and Software Engineering - Architecture Description [2].

This ongoing standard attempts to specify the manner in which architecture descriptions of systems are expressed. This standard provides key concepts and their relationships to document an architecture. Its key concepts (ArchitectureFramework, ArchitectureDescription, Viewpoint, View and Correspondence rule) are defined thanks to the conceptual model illustrated by the Figure 3. This conceptual model defines the semantics of the different concepts we overview here. An architecture description aggregates several Architecture Views. A view addresses one or more system concerns that are relevant to some of the system's stakeholders. A view aggregates one or more Architecture Models. Each view is defined following the conventions of an Architecture Viewpoint. The viewpoint defines the Model Kinds used for that view to represent the architecture addresses stakeholders' concerns.

As stated in this standard, in architecture descriptions, one consequence of employing multiple views is the need to express and maintain the consistency between these views. The standard introduces the Correspondence Rule concept that states a constraint that must be enforced on a correspondence to express relation between architecture description elements (Views, Architectural Model, etc.). Correspondences can be used to express consistency, traceability, composition, refinement and model transformation, or dependencies of any type spanning more than a single model kind.

Considering this industrial context, it can be considered that there are 3 major types of model coherency to be managed:

– The first one aims at ensuring that a model conforms to its metamodel, i.e. that it addresses the well-formedness of the model. Since the modeling

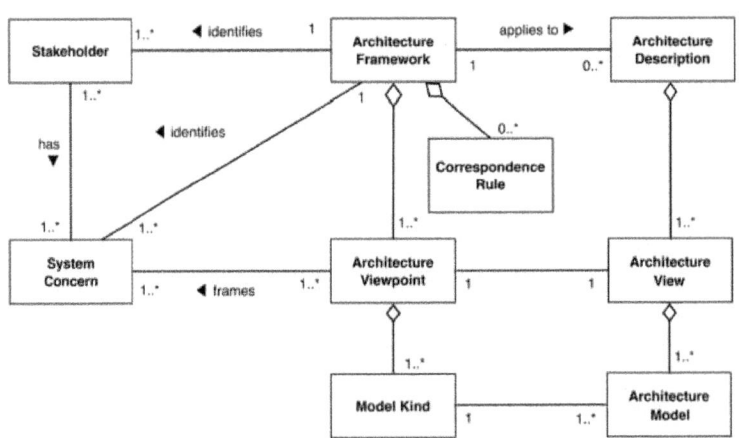

Fig. 3. ISO-IEC 42010 Architecture Framework overview

environment is DSL based (i.e. not profile based using a general purpose language), the well-formedness can be de facto ensured.
- The second one aims at ensuring that a model conforms to a coherent set of engineering rules; i.e. that the engineer conforms to a defined engineering method; in order to capitalize and reuse standard and domain specific engineering best practices.
- The third one aims at ensuring information consistency between distributed engineering environments, i.e. when there is not a unique centralized data reference. The main purpose here is to ensure coherency of all engineering activities across engineering domains, typically mainstream architecting and speciality engineering activities.

3.2 Objectives and Planning

Our experimentation focused on the second type of model coherency which consists in determining if a given configuration of set of views (models) are coherent with a set of consistency rules or not. This study consisted in detecting the inconsistencies between views conforms to the engineering meta-model defined by Thales and composed of a set of 20 meta-models and about 400 meta-classes involved in the five viewpoints defined in ARCADIA. The purpose of this study was assessing the benefits of Praxis Rules over Praxis strategy when compared to the traditional Java over EMF one. In terms of benefits, we study the efficiency to compute the set of inconsistencies in a given model and the usability of the approach.

In order to evaluate the effectiveness of the operation-based approach, we have validated the approach against our case study and the experiment environment with one Prolog expert and two Java developers from Thales. A set of 30 existing consistency rules initially implemented in Java over EMF have translated in Praxis Rules thanks to the praxis rule editor. We validated the consistency engine with models coming from operational contexts. We used three different models (ranging from 1.000 to 50.000 model elements) to determine the performance of the consistency engine tool for different model sizes.

3.3 Environment

Our experiment environment consisted of the Praxis consistency engine and a System engineering tool dedicated to this industrial context. This latter tool has been built on the top on the Eclipse Obeo Designer tool[2] and exposes a dedicated engineering language providing user-friendly ergonomics.

It allows engineers to define the architecture description of a software system by providing the five following views:

- The "Operational Analysis" model level, where the customer needs are defined and/or clarified in terms of tasks to accomplish by the System/Software, in its environment, for its users.

---
[2] http://obeo.fr/pages/obeo-designer

- The "System Analysis" model level, that provides a "black box" view of the System where the System limits are defined and/or clarified in terms of actors and external interfaces, the System capabilities and functional and non-functional needs and expectations; allowing to identify the more constraining/impacting requirements.
- The "Logical Architecture" model level, which provides a "white box" view of the System. It defines a technical and material independent decomposition of the System into components, and where the non-functional constraints are refined and allocated.
- The "Physical Architecture" model level, which is defined by the structuring architecture of the System. It takes into account non-functional constraints, reuses legacy assets and applies product policies.
- The "EPBS (End Product Breakdown Structure)" model level is an organizational view identifying the configuration items for development contracts and further Integration, Verification and Validation.

The Praxis Consistency engine has been integrated on top of this tool. It has been written in Java and is coupled with SWI-Prolog. From any given model, a equivalent sequence of editing operations is generated and passed to SWI Prolog. The Prolog engine then executes a set of queries representing consistency rules (also described in Prolog) and returns the list of detected inconsistencies to the user.

In the point of view of users, the Praxis Consistency engine provides two main components or features: the ConsistencyRule editor and the Consistency View. The first one allows the description of consistency rules using the PraxisRules DSL. These rules are then compiled into Prolog and are used by the Consistency engine. The Consistency View shows the number of inconsistencies found in the model and the model information that are not conform to the engineering rules.

A screen shot of the integrated tool is displayed in Figure 4. It shows an architecture description model that is being edited by an engineer (on the top) and the set of detected inconsistencies (the list on the bottom right). The only modification on this tool needed to this experiment was the inclusion of a timer that precisely indicated the time needed to perform each consistency verification.

3.4 Results and Evaluation

This section details the results of our experiments and the evaluation of the usability and applicability of Praxis in the industrial context under study. This section is divided into three parts, in the first one we analyze the comparison of the performance results obtained by Praxis and EMF. In the second part we analyze the adaptation of the rules written in the first part to the incremental checking model provided by Praxis. Finally, the third part describes our overall evaluation about the difficulty of rewriting part of our existing Java consistency rules in PraxisRules.

Detecting model inconsistency. Table 1 describes the different metrics of the models used in our experiment. The model A is a toy model provided with

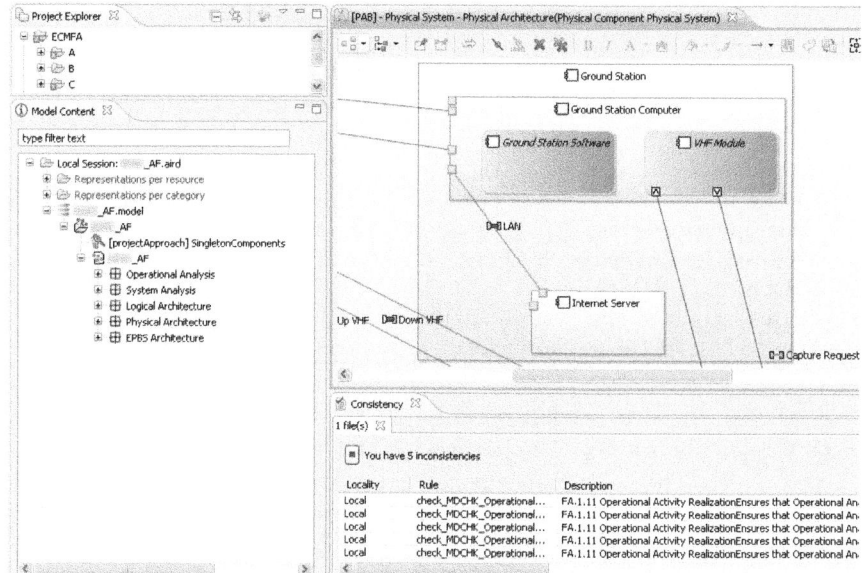

Fig. 4. Experiment Environment

the environment and the two others (B and C) are realistic models. The first three lines describe respectively the number of model elements in each model; the size of the model as represented as an EMF model and as a Praxis sequence of actions. Notice that the Praxis representation is in average four times more verbose than the EMF one. That happens because much more information is stored in Praxis, namely the order and the time-stamp of execution of each action.

The fourth, fifth, sixth and seventh lines display respectively the time needed to generate the actions file from the EMF model; the time needed to load it along with the translated consistency rules into the SWI Prolog engine and the amount of memory in MB necessary for the Eclipse process and the Prolog process to open each representation of it. These memory related numbers have been obtained by subtracting the amount of memory used by the process before and after loading the model. The amount of memory used before loading the EMF file averaged in 261 MB and before loading the Praxis sequences of actions averaged in 6MB.

Finally, the two last lines compare the time taken by each consistency engine to verify each model. Notice that, the "Java Overall check time" is always lesser than the "Praxis Overall check time".Nevertheless, we consider that the "Praxis Overall check time " is acceptable for the set of rules in this context.

As an overall evaluation, the main limitation of the Praxis consistency engine lies in the fact that it works with another model representation, a file containing the sequence of editing actions represented as Prolog facts. This file has to be generated and loaded into the Prolog engine every time the model has been

Table 1. Experimentation metrics

	Model A	Model B	Model C
Number of model elements	986	48 616	52 703
EMF model file size (KB)	326	11 282	13 724
Praxis action file size (KB)	1 398	37 589	66 562
Time to generate actions file (ms)	265	7 625	9 610
Loading time (ms)	1 516	11 968	12 031
eclipse.exe (MB)	41	63	62
plcon.exe (MB)	0,6	85,4	89,6
Praxis Overall check time(ms)	63	1 172	1 640
Java Overall check time (ms)	13	292	332

modified. For the two realistic models (B and C), the time to generate the praxis actions file is about 7 to 10 seconds and the time taken to load this file is about 12 sec. The performance penalty thus induced means that it would be impractical to use Praxis in an industrial usage by generating the action file from scratch and to load the actions files for each check.

Incremental detection of model inconsistencies. Since testing the incremental mode in EMF would require the adaptation of the existing Java rules to this mode we decided to evaluate only the usability of the Praxis consistency engine, without comparing it to EMF.

After having opened the model in incremental mode, the user needs to wait for a batch mode check that computes the initial set of inconsistencies in the model. From this point on, when any modification is made to the model the incremental check is executed, taking into consideration only the subset of the models and of the inconsistency rules that is concerned by the modification that was performed. We evaluated both the time necessary to perform the initial batch verification and the time needed to verify the increments. The performance obtained by the former was equivalent to the performance of the batch checker already displayed in Table 1. The performance for the later averaged in 100ms.

As an overall evaluation, we concluded that the time needed to perform the initial batch verification to be reasonable and comparable to the time already needed to load the model on Eclipse. With respect to the incremental checking time, we considered it to be quite transparent and independent of the number of rules that need to be re-checked. We consider that the main drawbacks of the praxis approach can be mitigated with the incremental mode.

Inconsistency rules. Thanks to the consistency rule editor, 30 rules have been written by two Java developers without knowledge of Prolog in the beginning of the study and one Logic Programming expert. Java and PraxisRules are languages built on very different paradigms. Java is imperative in nature, and querying or checking a model typically consists in iteratively navigating and inspecting the model elements with the explicit use of loops and collections. PraxisRules, being built on top of Prolog, inherits its declarative nature, which means that the typical querying or checking code consists of a pattern to be identified in the sequence of actions.

In the present study, 60% of the inconsistency rules were dedicated to verify some realization relationship between the five views (i.e. verifying if an element in a view correctly realizes other elements in other views). This kind of rule is easy to write with the PraxisRule syntax. Nevertheless, the rules that have been written by the Prolog expert were more efficient in terms of performance than the ones written by the Java programmers. 4 rules could not be written without the Prolog expert because they required to use of language constructs that were not available in the basic PraxisRules *library*. These constructs needed to be implemented in Prolog and added to that library by the Prolog expert. In spite of the language not being typed, the Consistency Rule editor helped to overcome this limitation by adding warnings to the references in the PraxisRule code that were not found of the imported metamodels.

As an overall evaluation, we considered that knowledge of Prolog is a very important prerequisite to write PraxisRules consistency rules. Furthermore, for more advanced cases it could become difficult to translate rules from Java to Praxis, especially for complex engineering rules which were considered to be hard to implement. This difference is counterbalanced by the fact that no rules needed to be rewritten in order to use Praxis on the incremental mode. Our evaluation is that for some classes of rules (like the ones detecting simple patterns between different views) it is worth to write the them in PraxisRules.

4 Conclusion

This paper described our experiences on the impact of the Operation based underlying model representation strategy to the efficiency of the inconsistency detection task. We use the Eclipse Modeling Framework (EMF) as the reference for our study, which consisted in testing Praxis, an operation based consistency management, by reimplementing a set of 30 consistency rules from the engineering meta-model defined by Thales and comparing the time necessary to compute its consistency with the time needed by EMF. This case study was executed in an industrial context, with non-UML models.

Our results show that, in terms of computation time, the operation based approach is not better than the object based on. The difficulty of adapting these rules to being used in the incremental verification was also compared. Our results show that the work necessary to write the consistency rules is reduced by the use of the operation based approach, since they usually do not need to be rewritten to work on incremental mode.

As future works, we intend to compare the Praxis incremental model with the EMF one. We also intend to repeat this evaluation in non-EMF contexts.

Acknowledgments. This work was partly funded by ANR project MOVIDA under the convention N° 2008 SEGI 011.

References

1. Selic, B.: The pragmatics of model-driven development. IEEE Software 20(5), 19–25 (2003)
2. International Organization for Standardization: ISO/IEC FCD 42010: Systems and software engineering - Architecture Description (June 2010)
3. OMG: Meta Object Facility (MOF) 2.0 Core Specification (January 2006)
4. Mens, T., Van Der Straeten, R., D'Hondt, M.: Detecting and resolving model inconsistencies using transformation dependency analysis. In: Wang, J., Whittle, J., Harel, D., Reggio, G. (eds.) MoDELS 2006. LNCS, vol. 4199, pp. 200–214. Springer, Heidelberg (2006)
5. Balzer, R.: Tolerating inconsistency. In: Proc. Int' Conf. Software engineering (ICSE 1991), vol. 1, pp. 158–165 (1991)
6. Spanoudakis, G., Zisman, A.: Inconsistency management in software engineering: Survey and open research issues. In: Handbook of Software Engineering and Knowledge Engineering, pp. 329–380. World Scientific, Singapore
7. Van Der Straeten, R., Mens, T., Simmonds, J., Jonckers, V.: Using description logic to maintain consistency between UML models. In: Stevens, P., Whittle, J., Booch, G. (eds.) UML 2003. LNCS, vol. 2863, pp. 326–340. Springer, Heidelberg (2003)
8. Elaasar, M., Brian, L.: An overview of UML consistency management. Technical Report SCE-04-18 (August 2004)
9. Blanc, X., Mougenot, A., Mounier, I., Mens, T.: Detecting model inconsistency through operation-based model construction. In: Robby (ed.) Proc. Int'l Conf. Software Engineering (ICSE 2008), vol. 1, pp. 511–520. ACM, New York (2008)
10. Finkelstein, A., Kramer, J., Nuseibeh, B., Finkelstein, L., Goedicke, M.: Viewpoints: A Framework for Integrating Multiple Perspectives in System Development. International Journal of Software Engineering and Knowledge Engineering 2(1), 31–57 (1992)
11. Egyed, A.: Fixing inconsistencies in UML design models. In: Proc. Int'l Conf. Software Engineering (ICSE 2007), pp. 292–301. IEEE Computer Society, Los Alamitos (2007)
12. Blanc, X., Mougenot, A., Mounier, I., Mens, T.: Incremental detection of model inconsistencies based on model operations. In: van Eck, P., Gordijn, J., Wieringa, R. (eds.) CAiSE 2009. LNCS, vol. 5565, pp. 32–46. Springer, Heidelberg (2009)
13. Voirin, J.L.: Model-driven architecture building for constrained systems. In: CSDM 2010 (2010)

Generating Early Design Models from Requirements Analysis Artifacts Using Problem Frames and SysML

Pietro Colombo[1], Ferhat Khendek[2], and Luigi Lavazza[1]

[1] Dipartimento di Informatica e Comunicazione, Università degli Studi dell'Insubria
Via Mazzini 5, 21100 Varese, Italy
{pietro.colombo,luigi.lavazza}@uninsubria.it
[2] Department of Electrical and Computer Engineering, Concordia University
1455, de Maisonneuve W., Montreal, Canada H3G 1M8
khendek@encs.concordia.ca

Abstract. The relationship between requirement specifications and design models has been widely investigated with the aim of bridging (semi) automatically the gap between the two artifacts. The work reported in this paper contributes to this research stream with an approach for generating early design models from requirement artifacts and analysis criteria. The approach is based on Problem Frames, decomposition and re-composition analysis patterns and is supported by SysML.

Keywords: Problem Frames, Decomposition Criteria, Architectural Patterns, Blackboard, SysML.

1 Introduction

Problem Frames (PFs) [9] are a requirement analysis approach that helps developers in understanding, mastering and describing problems. PFs have the potential of improving the early phases of software development processes. However they have some limitations that may hinder their application in real scale projects. In fact, the approach provides a set of methodological suggestions that have to be integrated with the languages and methods used in industrial software development. In [14,15,6] the integration of PFs with UML [19] was explored: the experience showed that UML –although quite rich in diagrams– is not always expressive enough to represent well problem frames concepts. The combination of PFs with SysML [18] was found to be more effective [3,4].

In [5] an analysis approach based on PFs and supported by SysML has been applied to a realistic size case study. The experience allowed us to identify decomposition and re-composition guidelines that can be generalized and drive the analysis of problems and mitigate their complexity. Based on that experience, this paper proposes an approach to develop an early design model from the requirement artifacts and the decomposition decisions made during the analysis.

Stakeholders look at the requirements analysis from different points of view. This brought to the specialization of the concept of requirements [13] according to the level of abstraction. For instance, a high level manager is concerned with *business goals*, while the software analyst is concerned with the responsibilities of the software system in satisfying *user needs*. Our analysis approach is based on *user requirements*. It requires reasoning on the problem domain to define the specifications of a *machine* that satisfies the requirements through the interaction with the problem *environment* [13]. In our approach the requirements analysis and design activities are strictly connected. In fact, the design consists of modeling the machine's internals and refining the specifications.

The original problem is decomposed into simpler sub-problems by means of the problem projection [9] and using given decomposition criteria. The identified sub-problems, which may have overlapping parts, are individually analyzed and a machine specification that satisfies their requirements is defined. The specification of the original problem is defined by composing and coordinating the identified machines, each of which helps solving a particular aspect of the entire problem. The design model is defined through the enhancement of the machine specifications. The model is structured according to the blackboard architecture. This choice allows executing the analysis and the design in parallel and incrementally. The machines are designed as "knowledge sources" that collaborate exchanging information by means of a central repository, "the blackboard".

SysML is used as modeling language for both the analysis and the design phases. The benefits are manifolds. SysML supports well the modeling of requirements and design artifacts in an intuitive and expressive manner. Moreover, the usage of one notation eases the cooperation of analysts and designers; it also enables traceability and a better integration of the modeled artifacts.

The rest of the paper is organized into four sections. Section 2 introduces the example used throughout the paper and the analysis approach. In Section 3, we propose our approach for generating early design models from requirement models. Section 4 discusses related works. In Section 5, we conclude the paper.

Because of space limits, we do not report here the machine specifications (in many cases they are similar to the requirements). Moreover, only the most representative diagrams illustrating the requirements and design models are shown.

2 The Analysis Process

This section summarizes the problem analysis approach based on PFs, SysML and decomposition and re-composition criteria [5]. The original problem is decomposed into sub-problems in a recursive manner. The goal is to tackle each sub-problem separately. Once sub-problems have been identified, analyzed and a machine specification is defined, their descriptions are recomposed.

The example of a controller for a road intersection will be used throughout the paper. An intersection controller manages the traffic lights at a four way intersection. The intersection is composed of two approaches, named NS and EW, equipped with traffic lights and detectors to sense the approaching of emergency vehicles. The intersection controller operates the traffic lights according to criteria defined by the "Fixed cycle" and "Preempted" operation modes.

The aggregation of the states of the traffic lights represents a state of the intersection and is called a phase. The system goes through several phases. In the Fixed cycle mode, the controller issues commands at predefined time intervals to move from the current phase to the next. Whenever an emergency vehicle is detected the controller enables the Preempted operation mode, sets to green the traffic lights for (one of) the emergency vehicles and switches to red the other ones. The Fixed cycle operation mode resumes after the emergency vehicle has crossed the intersection. The intersection controller also checks the state of the traffic lights for compliance with the last commands issued. If a malfunction is detected it sets all the traffic lights into flashing yellow states.

2.1 Structural Analysis

The structural characteristics of a problem are modeled using Problem diagrams [9], SysML Block Definition Diagram and Internal Block diagram [18]. These diagrams describe problem domains, shared phenomena and the allocation of requirements. The behavior of each problem domain is specified using SysML behavioral diagrams.

The road intersection system is composed of three domains: 1) the Intersection Controller, which is the machine in Jacksons terminology, and the target of the specification activity, 2) the Emergency Vehicle Detector, which notifies the controller whenever an emergency vehicle is approaching and when it has crossed the intersection and is moving away, and 3) the Traffic Lights, which besides setting their lamps according to the commands from the controller, also monitor the states of the lamps, informing the controller of the current state and of possible malfunctions. Fig. 1 shows the Problem diagram that describes the context of the problem.

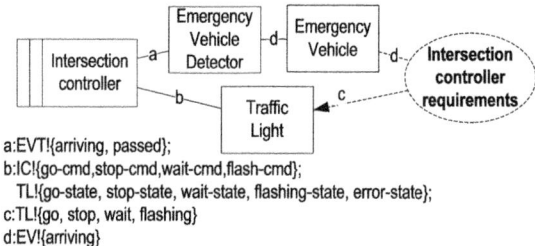

a:EVT!{arriving, passed};
b:IC!{go-cmd,stop-cmd,wait-cmd,flash-cmd};
  TL!{go-state, stop-state, wait-state, flashing-state, error-state};
c:TL!{go, stop, wait, flashing}
d:EV!{arriving}

Fig. 1. The problem diagram describing the domain of the problem

2.2 Problem Decomposition

The decomposition of a problem is guided by the nature of its internal activities and leads to the identification of parallel and sequential sub-problems characterized by a set of requirements, a machine and a projection of domains and phenomena of the original problem. The decomposition stops when the identified sub-problems meet the characteristics of basic PFs.

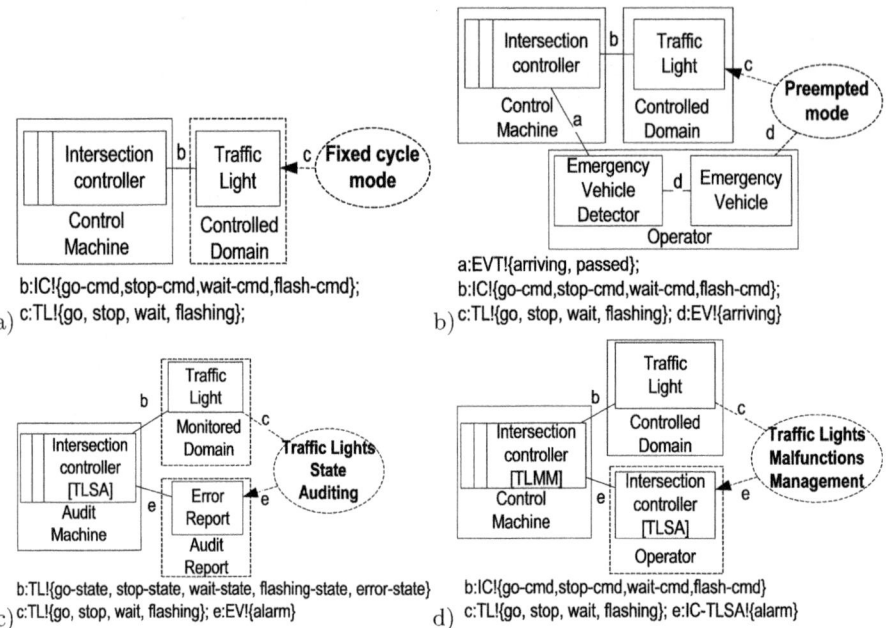

Fig. 2. Problem diagrams of the sub-problems: a) Fixed cycle mode, b) Preempted mode, c) Traffic Lights States Auditing, d) Traffic Lights Malfunctions Management

At any point in time the controller manages the phases of the intersection and concurrently checks the state of the traffic lights and reacts when a malfunction is detected. In the management phase the controller operates the traffic lights alternating the Fixed cycle mode and the Preempted mode. Each operation mode is a sequential sub-problem described by a basic frame. The Fixed cycle sub-problem is described (in Fig. 2a) by the Required behavior frame [9], while the Preempted mode sub-problem is described (in Fig. 2b) by the Commanded behavior Frame [9]. The monitoring of the traffic light states (Traffic Light State Auditing - TLSA) is an Information display problem (Fig. 2c) [9], while the management of malfunctions (Traffic Light Malfunctions Management - TLMM) is a Commanded behavior problem (Fig. 2d).

The decomposition process is illustrated using a decomposition tree. The root represents the original problem while the other nodes represent its sub-problems. The leaves represent basic problems that do not require further decomposition. The decomposition of the intersection controller problem is illustrated in Fig. 3.

2.3 Sub-problem Analysis

The analysis is performed for each sub-problem separately –i.e., as if the problem were independent from the others–by specifying its requirements and the machine that satisfies such requirements when connected to the problem domains.

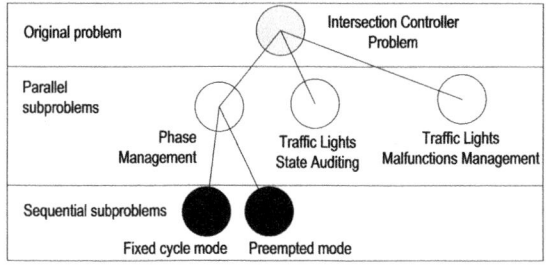

Fig. 3. The decomposition tree for the intersection controller problem

Fixed cycle mode
In this operation mode the controller repeatedly executes a predefined control pattern that consists of the sequence of the intersection phases. The requirements of the problem specify the duration of each phase and are defined with the State Machine diagram (*stm*) in Fig. 4.

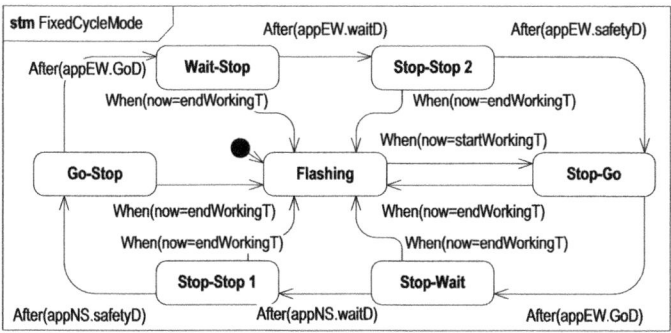

Fig. 4. The requirements of the Fixed cycle mode problem

Preempted mode
In this operation mode, when an emergency vehicle approaches, the controller has to set the Go signal for the concerned approach and the Stop for the other one as soon as possible.

The requirements are described using two parallel *stm* as shown in Fig. 5. The first *stm* keeps track of the emergency condition while the second one orchestrates the phases.

Traffic lights states auditing
The controller has to check if the current state of the traffic lights complies with the last issued command. The requirements are specified using the activity *CheckTL* shown in Fig. 6, which takes as input, as a continuous flow, the states of the traffic lights and checks if they are coherent with the last issued command. In case of misbehaviors the event *Alarm* is generated.

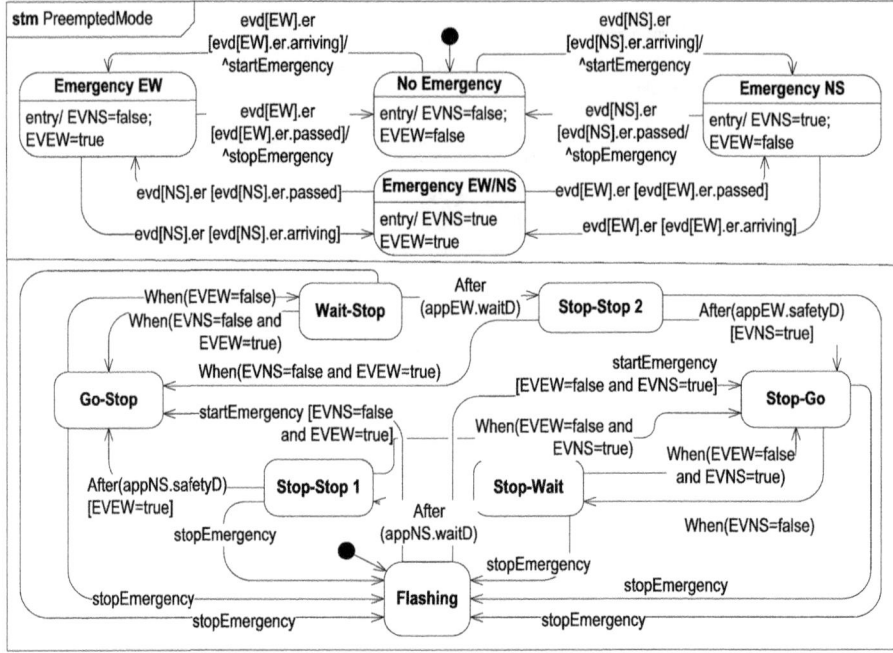

Fig. 5. The requirements of the Preempted mode problem

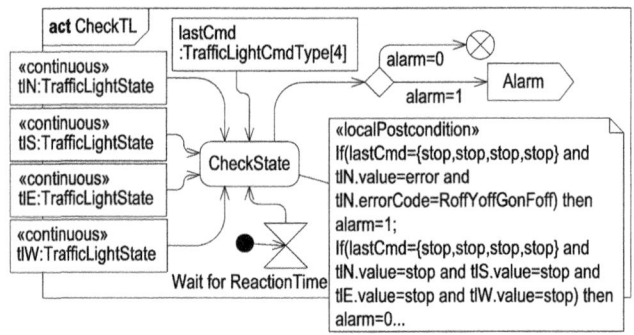

Fig. 6. The requirements of the Traffic lights state auditing problem

Traffic lights malfunctions management

The controller has to switch to phase Flashing whenever a malfunction is detected. Malfunctions are notified via event *Alarm* generated by the machine of the auditing sub-problem. The requirements are defined using a *stm* with the same states as the Fixed cycle problem, and transitions triggered by the event *Alarm*, which causes the transition to the Flashing phase from any other phase.

2.4 Sub Problem Composition

At this stage the sub-problems are composed together. The recomposed problem, obtained using a Composition Frame [12], coordinates the activities of the machines of the sub-problems and manages possible interferences.

The composition requirements specify how interferences have to be handled. The recomposed problem is characterized by the union of the problem domains and machines of the sub-problems and by a new machine. The sub-problems machines are coordinated by the new machine according to the composition requirements. The composition process is driven by the decomposition tree using a bottom up approach.

The composition starts with the sub-problems that manage the phases of the intersection, namely the Fixed cycle mode and the Preempted mode subproblems (step 1). Once they are recomposed by means of a Sequential Coordinator (SC) (step 2), we move into the composition of the parallel sub-problems: TLSA, TLMM and SC (step 3). We end up with the recomposed problem that coordinates the execution of the parallel sub-problems (step 4).

Composing sequential sub-problems

The composition of the sequential sub-problems is described by the Sequential Coordinator (SC) problem diagram in Fig. 7. The machines of the sub-problems are labeled with the initial letter of the problems name [FC] for Fixed cycle mode, [PM] for Preempted mode and [SC] for Sequential Coordinator.

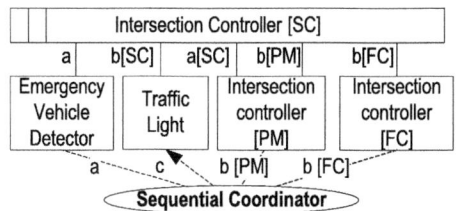

Fig. 7. Sequential Coordinator problem diagram

The composition requirements specify that the change of operating mode should not cause losing memory of the current phase. The requirements also constrain the changes in operation modes. For instance, whenever an emergency vehicle approaches the intersection, the controller has to switch to Preempted mode and, as soon as the emergency is over, the controller has to re-enable the Fixed cycle mode.

The requirements are described by two parallel *stm*. The first *stm*, shown in Fig. 8, keeps track of the operating mode and of the emergency conditions.

The second *stm* not shown because of space limits describes the phase transitions according to the commands issued by the coordinated machines and the current operation mode.

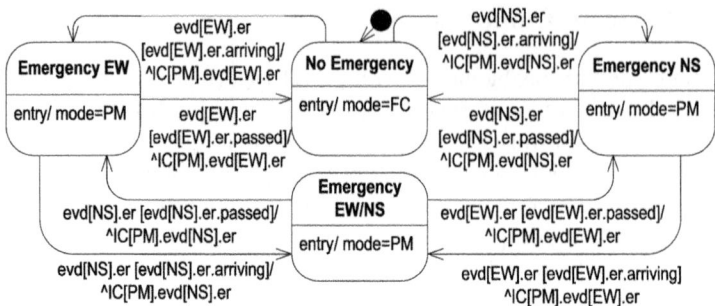

Fig. 8. Mode change requirements

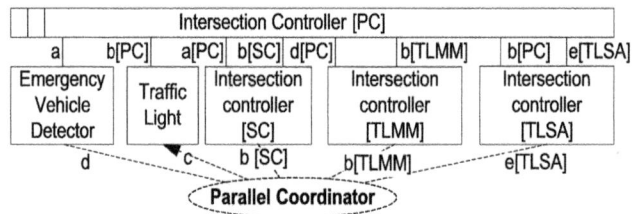

Fig. 9. Parallel Coordinator Problem diagram

Composing parallel sub-problems

The composition of parallel sub-problems is defined by the Parallel Coordinator (PC) problem diagram in Fig. 9. The problem is characterized by the machines of the TLSA, TLMM, and SC problems, by the problem domains Traffic Light and Emergency Vehicle Detector and by a new machine Parallel Coordinator.

An interference may occur whenever the controller reacts to a malfunction by setting the phase Flashing, and at the same time the approaching of an emergency vehicle causes the controller to switch to the Preempted mode and to force the transition to the phase that favors the passage of the emergency vehicle: the two target phases are different!

The composition requirements address this conflict by specifying that once entered the Flashing phase upon a failure, it should not be abandoned until the malfunction is fixed. The requirements of the problem are described with a *stm* not shown here because of space limits.

3 The Design Process

The decomposition and composition decisions performed during the analysis and the resulting artifacts can be exploited to generate an early design model. The recomposed problem is characterized by the problem domains and the machines of the identified sub-problems.

The behaviors of the machines contribute to the definition of the general behavior of the controller. The composite machines orchestrate the execution of the recomposed ones by sending and receiving information. This situation where several agents contribute to the solution of a problem by sharing information can be seen as a representation of the blackboard approach [10]. This architectural pattern takes its name from the central data structure, namely the blackboard, which is accessed and modified by components called knowledge sources.

The blackboard keeps track of the current state of the whole system, which in turn triggers the execution of knowledge sources that access and possibly modify the central data structure. This structure is the only interaction and information exchange medium for these components.

The adoption of this architectural style for defining an early design model based on our analysis and its artifacts is therefore a straightforward choice. The machines of the analyzed (sub-) problems represent the independent components playing the role of knowledge sources, while the blackboard is the component containing the shared phenomena observed and controlled by the machines of the (sub-) problems.

The design process starts towards the end of the decomposition process of the analysis phase (in Section 2.3), when all the basic sub-problems are identified.

The machine of each basic sub-problem is modeled as a knowledge source specifying both its structural characteristics and contextualizing the behavioral specification provided during analysis (the contextualization concept will be further elaborated later on). The design starts with the definition of the knowledge sources corresponding to the machines of the sub-problems FC, PM, TLSA and TLMM. Concurrently, the blackboard component is defined in an incremental manner through the modeling of the shared phenomena controlled or observed by the machines of each sub-problem. The design process is synchronized with the composition activity of the analysis phase and follows a similar bottom up approach.

The final step of the design consists of generating a component that integrates and connects the blackboard data structure and all the generated knowledge sources. Such a component represents the machine of the original problem. The behavior of this machine accomplishes the dynamics of the blackboard problem solving approach. The internal parts of this component are interconnected according to the rules of the blackboard architectural style.

3.1 Blackboard Generation

The blackboard is the central data structure for exchanging information. The blackboard has to keep track of phenomena controlled and observed by the machines of the sub-problems as well as of their internal states.

The design process consists of 1) identifying the data types that suitably represent internal states and shared phenomena, and 2) using such data types for the design of the blackboard structure. First, suitable attributes of the blackboard are defined, to represent the machines internal states. Next, a type representing the shared phenomena controlled or observed by machines is identified.

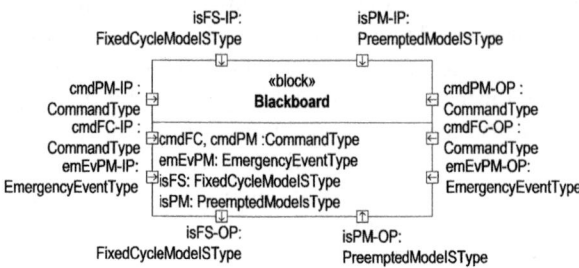

Fig. 10. The blackboard component after the analysis of the sequential problems

An attribute having such type is added to the blackboard. For instance, let us consider the *Blackboard* component represented in Fig. 10. The data type *CommandType* models the commands to change the state of the traffic lights; *cmdFC* and *cmdPM* represent the last commands that are issued by the knowledge sources representing the machines of the Fixed Cycle and the Preempted Mode sub-problems, respectively.

Internal states and Shared Phenomena type identification
The machine specification of each sub-problem is described using state machines. States can be either simple or composite, i.e. they may contain sub-machines. For instance, a single *stm* is associated with the Fixed cycle mode problem, while two parallel *stms* describe the Preempted mode problem. Stms characterized by simple states are defined by means of enumerative types whose literals correspond to states. For instance the *stm* of the Fixed cycle mode involves literals *Stop-Go*, *Stop-Wait*, *Stop-Stop 1*, *Go-Stop*, *Wait-Stop*, *Stop-Stop 2* and *Flashing*. Specifications characterized by parallel *stms* or *stms* with composite states are defined using data types that keep track of the current state of each *stm* using enumerative variables. For instance, the machine of the Preempted mode problem consists of a *stm* that keeps track of the emergency conditions (*NoEmergency*, *Emergency NS*, *Emergency EW*, and *Emergency EW/NS*) and a *stm* that as in the Fixed cycle keeps track of the current phase. Therefore, two enumerative variables are necessary.

The shared phenomena too are represented using data types. Phenomena representing states are specified using types that range over the list of the states. Phenomena representing values are defined using types that characterize their domains. Finally, phenomena representing events are defined by data structures composed of fields that characterize the data carried by the event.

Modeling internal states and shared phenomena
The data types representing internal states and shared phenomena are used to define the internals of the blackboard, namely the types of the attributes that represent the information exchanged by knowledge sources.

For a given machine, an attribute is defined for each internal state type. The attribute is named using the identifiers of the machine and the internal state type. For instance, the attribute *isPM* of type *PreemtedModeISType*, shown in Fig. 10, models the internal state of the Preempted mode machine. An attribute is defined also for each identified phenomenon. The attribute is named using the identifiers of the phenomenon and the machine, and typed accordingly.

The blackboard component is modeled in SysML using a Block characterized by different properties (the term "property" is used in SysML to indicate an attribute). For each property one input and one output Atomic Port are also defined. Such ports represent interaction points through which the knowledge sources get access to the internals of the blackboard. For instance, Fig. 10 illustrates the blackboard component generated after the analysis of the sequential basic problem. Such component stores the internal states of the Fixed cycle mode machine and of the Preempted mode machine, as well as phenomena observed and controlled by such machines. A set of I/O ports allows for accessing the content of each property.

3.2 Knowledge Source Generation

The knowledge sources to be modeled correspond to the machines of the different (sub-)problems identified during decomposition and re-composition. Once the original problem is fully decomposed, knowledge sources are generated starting from the specification of the machines of the analyzed (sub-)problems (both basic and recomposed).

Knowledge sources are modeled as components. Their generation concerns structural and behavioral aspects.

Structural aspects
The structural definition depends on the interface of the machine, i.e. on the phenomena that are shared by the machine and the problem domains to which it is connected.

The machine is modeled as a component equipped with one port for each of its shared phenomena and internal states. The machine can either control the phenomena or it may simply observe them. This determines whether the port is defined as an input or an output port.

The type associated with the port is the same one used to classify the phenomenon. The component definition is supported in SysML by a Block equipped with one SysML Atomic Port for each shared phenomenon and internal state. For instance, the knowledge source corresponding to the machine of the Preempted mode sub-problem (shown in Fig. 11) is modeled as a component characterized by: *cmdPM-OP*, an output port through which the commands to set the state of the traffic lights are propagated; *isPM-IP*, an input port to provide access to the internal states of the machine (i.e., the phase and the emergency condition); *emEvPM-IP*, an input port that routes the events generated by the emergency vehicle detector; and finally, *mode*, an input port that specifies the mode.

The generation of the static aspects of the knowledge sources may also exploit the usage of architectural patterns for PFs. Architectural patterns are general solution structures that match the problem structures represented by basic PFs.

Fig. 11. The component representing the machine of the Preempted mode problem

In [2] an architectural pattern is proposed for each frame proposed in the catalogue of basic frames defined by Jackson [9]. Architectural patterns can be directly applied whenever the target machine is defined in a problem that fits the characteristics of a basic frame.

Behavioral aspects
The definition of the behavioral aspects is based on the specification of actions that adapt the machine specifications of the different sub-problems to be executed in the context of the blackboard architecture. The generation technique reflects the sequential and parallel nature of the problems.

Modeling the machine of sequential problems. The behavior of a knowledge source representing sequential machines is modeled using two distinct parallel actions. The first action continuously monitors the state of the blackboard and tests the conditions for exercising the behavior of the machine. Since only one sequential machine can be active at any time, these conditions express the execution turn. The second action adapts the machine specification to the context of the blackboard architecture, making the behavior step-based and interruptible. The generation of the model involves the definition of actions named *WatchDog*, *CheckTurn* and *MachineBehaviorStep*.

WatchDog continuously checks the state of the shared phenomena whose values trigger the execution of the machine (see Fig. 12a). *WatchDog* takes as input the value carried by the input parameter *Turn* that identifies the execution turn of the sequential machines: in our application, the turn identifies the current operation mode.

Each sequential sub-machine is characterized by an internal property *Id* that uniquely identifies the machine. For instance, *Id* is set to *FC* for the Fixed cycle machine and *PM* for the Preempted mode. In case *Turn* is equal to *Id* the actions *MachineBehaviorStep* and *CheckTurn* are invoked.

The definition of *WatchDog* does not depend on the specification of the original machine. *MachineBehaviorStep* models the behavior defined in the machine

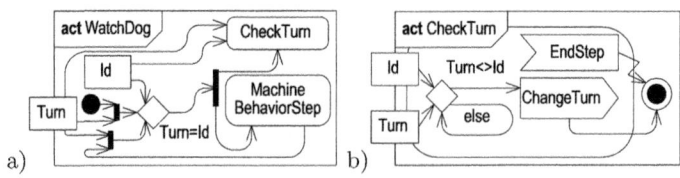

Fig. 12. The act diagrams that define the actions: a) WatchDog and b) CheckTurn

specification, while *CheckTurn* supervises such behavior, interrupting it in case the value of *Turn* changes during the execution (see Fig. 12b). *MachineBehaviorStep* is responsible for executing a single step of the behavior of the involved machine. For instance, in the Fixed cycle mode problem, the action is responsible for changing the current phase when timing conditions are met.

MachineBehaviorStep specifies input and output parameters corresponding to the internal states and shared phenomena of the current machine. These parameters, are assigned to the input and output port of the component, and will be assigned to the internal states and shared phenomena defined in the blackboard at architecture definition time (see Section 3.3). For instance, for the Preempted mode machine, the parameters are allocated to the I/O ports shown in Fig. 11 that route phases, emergency states, commands, and emergency events.

MachineBehaviorStep is generated from the *stm* used to specify the behavior of sequential machines. A different flow is defined for each of the states in the original *stm*. The flow to be executed depends on the current value of the internal state at invocation time.

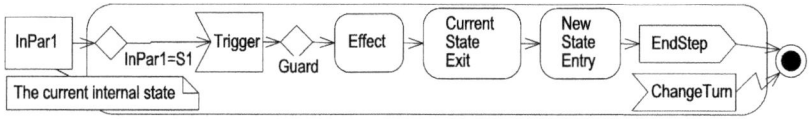

Fig. 13. Characterization of the control flow

Fig. 13 shows the characterization of a generic control flow. Each flow is organized into three sections. The first section specifies the trigger and the conditions that enable the firing of the transition (*Trigger* and *Guard* elements in Fig. 13). The second section models behaviors associated with the firing of a transition (action *Effect* in Fig. 13). More specifically, Action *Effect* specifies the firing effect of the transition, *CurrentStateExit* specifies the behavior executed while exiting from the current state, and action *NewStateEntry* specifies the behavior performed while entering the new state. Finally, before terminating the execution the event *EndStep* is generated to interrupt the execution of the action *CheckTurn*. The behavior is defined within an interruptible region, since *MachineBehaviorStep* can be interrupted as a consequence of the event *ChangeTurn*. Fig. 14 shows a portion of the *MachineBehaviorStep* definition for the Preempted mode machine, namely the flow generated for the state *NoEmergency*.

Modeling the machine of parallel problems. The definition follows the same process used for the modeling of sequential machines, i.e., it is based on the definition of the action *MachineBehaviorStep*. However, differently from the sequential machine case, the execution is not regulated by execution turns. Since *MachineBehaviorStep* realizes a single step of the behavior defined by the machine specification, the action is continuously re-invoked as soon as it completes its task. The invocation is managed by a second action named *ExecutionManager*. *ExecutionManager* is executed in parallel by all the parallel knowledge sources.

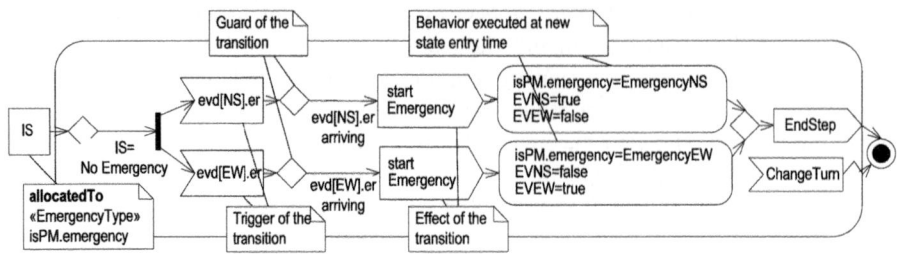

Fig. 14. A portion of MachineBehaviorStep defined for the Preempted mode machine

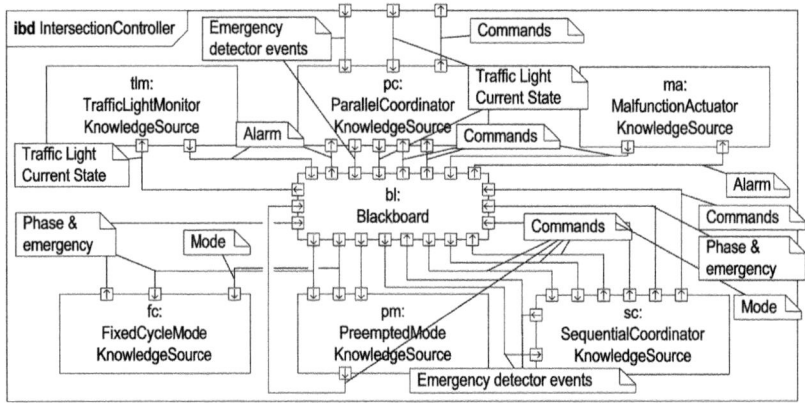

Fig. 15. A view of the internal architecture of Intersection Controller

3.3 Composing the Architecture of the System

This phase of the design process aims at instantiating and connecting the blackboard and knowledge sources.

The blackboard data structure, the knowledge sources representing the machines of parallel and sequential sub-problems and the ones that coordinate their execution are modeled as internal parts of a component. This component is simply a container that includes all the different artifacts that contribute to the definition of the solution.

The component is characterized by the same interface of the machine of the original problem, hence it will have one input port for each phenomenon controlled by the problem domains and one output port for each observed phenomenon. Therefore, the Intersection Controller component is characterized by one input port through which it receives the signals generated by the emergency detector, one through which it gets the current state of the traffic lights, and one output port used to route the commands to the traffic lights.

A connection is defined between input (output) ports of the container and those input (output) ports of the knowledge source at the root of the decomposition tree. As a consequence, Parallel Coordinator directly receives the events generated by the emergency detector and the state of the traffic lights through the input ports of the Intersection Controller container components and issues commands to the traffic lights through its output ports.

All the communications between the different knowledge sources are mediated by the blackboard. The generation of the connections among the communication ports of knowledge sources and the blackboard is a stepwise activity based on the breadth first visit of the decomposition tree. Each step considers a different knowledge source.

The input (output) ports of the knowledge source generated for its observed (controlled) phenomena are connected to the output (input) ports of the blackboard. The input ports of the knowledge sources generated for the internal states are connected to output ports of the blackboard.

If the knowledge source models a machine that has not been recomposed, its output ports exposing the internal states are connected to the co-respective input ports of the blackboard. In other words, the coordinator machines specify the current internal state shared with the coordinated machine, while the coordinated machines which are not allowed to modify the state simply access this property. For instance, Sequential Coordinator observes the movements of emergency vehicles via the blackboard, and forwards the movement information in the area of the blackboard that provides input to the sequential machine Preempted mode.

Sequential Coordinator publishes on the blackboard also the controlled phenomenon representing the current operation mode and internal state (phase and emergency condition) to be shared with the coordinated machine. Fig. 15 shows a partial view of the internal architecture of the controller.

4 Related Work

Several researchers investigated the relationship between requirements and architectures. For instance, the approach in [16] refines a set of requirements containing rationale into skeletons of architectures, namely, into preliminary architectural models that need to be completed and refined. The Twin Peaks model [17] investigates how the requirements engineering and architecture design can be combined to achieve incremental development. These proposals help understanding the relationship between requirements and design, but they do not support the transition from the former to the latter.

Researchers have also proposed formal methodologies to generate design models incrementally and (semi-) automatically. Authors in [7] propose a technique based on Behavior trees. The approach supports the automatic transition from the problem to the solution domain but it does not consider structural properties that represent a fundamental aspect of the design.

The approach reported in [11] generates automatically the behavior of SDL processes from high level Message Sequence Charts (MSC) and the target system architecture. This approach does not deal with the analysis phase and assumes the requirement specification is given; therefore no knowledge about the problem is reused. Moreover, these techniques focus mainly on behavioral aspects and can be hardly adapted to general purpose systems for which the structural aspects of design are crucial characteristics to be considered.

The method proposed in [1] transforms the requirements specification into an intermediate artifact called architectural prescription, which specifies the most important and critical aspects of the architecture. An additional step is required to generate the architecture from this intermediate artifact.

Some other proposals aim at extending the PFs analysis approach to support the definition of machine architectures. [20] proposes the integration of architectural styles to guide the analysis of the problem by means of Architectural Frame, a crosscutting element characterized by the properties of the problem and the architecture. In [8] an extension is proposed to consider architectural aspects as part of the problem domain, enhancing machine domain with architectural elements. These proposals look into the transition from a different and complementary perspective to integrate at the analysis level existing architectures.

5 Conclusions

The transition from requirements specification to an early design is an open research issue. This paper proposes an approach for generating an early design model structured according to the blackboard architectural pattern. It starts from artifacts identified during the analysis phase and exploits the decomposition and composition criteria and decisions made during that phase.

The proposed approach targets the definition of a structure composed of 1) knowledge sources corresponding to the machine domains in the original problem and sub-problems and 2) the blackboard component, a data-structure used by the knowledge sources for communication purposes.

The approach aims at easing the design effort by reusing some knowledge and decisions from the analysis phase. It is incremental: a knowledge source is generated as soon as the machine specification of a (sub)problem is defined, at the same time each (sub)problem contributes to the definition of a part of the blackboard data structure. The approach allows analysts and designers to work partially in parallel, thus potentially shortening the development time and reducing the cost. The approach is model-based and uses SysML as the modeling language. SysML was preferred to UML for its support of PFs [3][4]. The SysML artifacts of the design model are elaborated from the models defined in the requirements analysis phase. This favors traceability. Finally, the approach can be automated. To this aim we are refining the approach into a model-based transformation process.

Although the benefits of the proposed solution are manifolds, the selected architectural style is of limited applicability when resource efficiency is critical. In fact, due to the distributed nature of the blackboard architecture, solutions defined implementing the generated design model may suffer from low performances and high use of resources such as memory consumption and bandwith.

In order to address these shortcomings, we are analyzing additional architectural styles and (de)composition criteria. Our final goal is the definition of a framework supporting the automatic generation of design solutions using multiple (de)composition guidelines and architectures.

As future work, we will test the scalability and generality of the framework targeting other case studies.

Acknowledgement

The work described in this paper has been done during a post doctoral term of Pietro Colombo at Concordia University, Montreal (Canada). The work has been partially supported by the Natural Sciences and Engineering Research Council (NSERC) of Canada and by the project "Metodi e tecniche per la modellazione, lo sviluppo e la valutazione di sistemi software" funded by Università degli Studi dell'Insubria.

References

1. Brandozzi, M., Perry, D.E.: Transforming goal oriented requirements specifications into architectural prescriptions. In: STRAW (2001)
2. Choppy, C., Hatebur, D., Heisel, M.: Architectural patterns for problem frames. IEE Proceedings - Software 152(4), 198–208 (2005)
3. Colombo, P., del Bianco, V., Lavazza, L., Coen-Porisini, A.: A methodological framework for SysML: a Problem Frames-based approach. In: APSEC 2007 (2007)
4. Colombo, P., del Bianco, V., Lavazza, L., Coen-Porisini, A.: Towards the integration of SysML and Problem Frames. In: IWAAPF 2008 (2008)
5. Colombo, P., Khendek, F., Lavazza, L.: Requirements analysis and modeling with Problem Frames and SysML: A case study. In: Kühne, T., Selic, B., Gervais, M.-P., Terrier, F. (eds.) ECMFA 2010. LNCS, vol. 6138, pp. 74–89. Springer, Heidelberg (2010)
6. Del Bianco, V., Lavazza, L.: Enhancing Problem Frames with Scenarios and Histories in UML-based software development. Expert Systems 25(1) (2008)
7. Dromey, R.G.: Formalizing the transition from requirements to design. In: He, J., Liu, Z. (eds.) Mathematical Frameworks for Component Software Models for Analysis and Synthesis, pp. 173–205. World Scientific, Singapore
8. Hall, J.G., Jackson, M., Laney, R.C., Nuseibeh, B., Rapanotti, L.: Relating software requirements and architectures using Problem Frames. In: RE 2002 (2002)
9. Jackson, M.: Problem Frames: Analyzing and Structuring Software Development Problems. ACM Press Books, New York (2001)
10. Jagannathan, V., Dodhiawala, R., Baum, L.S.: Blackboard Architectures and Applications. Academic Press, London (1989)
11. Khendek, F., Zhang, X.J.: From MSC to SDL: Overview and an application to the autonomous shuttle transport system. In: Leue, S., Systä, T.J. (eds.) Scenarios: Models, Transformations and Tools. LNCS, vol. 3466, pp. 228–254. Springer, Heidelberg (2005)
12. Laney, R., Barroca, R., Jackson, M., Nuseibeh, B.: Composing Requirements Using Problem Frames. In: RE 2004 (2004)
13. Lavazza, L.: User needs vs. user requirements: a Problem Frame-based View. In: IWAAPO 2010 (2010)

14. Lavazza, L., Del Bianco, V.: A UML-based Approach for Representing Problem Frames. In: IWAAPF 2004 (2004)
15. Lavazza, L., Del Bianco, V.: Combining Problem Frames and UML in the Description of Software Requirements. In: Baresi, L., Heckel, R. (eds.) FASE 2006. LNCS, vol. 3922, pp. 199–213. Springer, Heidelberg (2006)
16. Medvidovic, N., Grnbacher, P., Egyed, A., Boehm, B.W.: Bridging models across the software lifecycle. Journal of Systems and Software 68(3), 199–215 (2003)
17. Nuseibeh, B.: Weaving together requirements and architectures. IEEE Computer 34(3) (2001)
18. OMG SysML, V. 1.2, http://www.omg.org/spec/SysML/1.2/
19. OMG UML, V. 2.3, http://www.omg.org/spec/UML/2.3/
20. Rapanotti, L., Hall, J.G., Jackson, M., Nuseibeh, B.: Architecture-driven problem decomposition. In: RE 2004 (2004)

Automated Transition from Use Cases to UML State Machines to Support State-Based Testing

Tao Yue[1], Shaukat Ali[1,2], and Lionel Briand[1,2]

[1] Simula Research Laboratory
P.O. Box 134, 1325, Lysaker, Norway
[2]Department of Informatics, University of Oslo, Oslo, Norway
{tao,shaukat,briand}@simula.no

Abstract. Use cases are commonly used to structure and document requirements while UML state machine diagrams often describe the behavior of a system and serve as a basis to automate test case generation in many model-based testing (MBT) tools. Therefore, automated support for the transition from use cases to state machines would provide significant, practical help for testing system requirements. Additionally, traceability could be established through automated transformations, which could then be used for instance to link requirements to design decisions and test cases, and assess the impact of requirements changes. In this paper, we propose an approach to automatically generate state machine diagrams from use cases while establishing traceability links. Our approach is implemented in a tool, which we used to perform three case studies, including an industrial case study. The results show that high quality state machine diagrams can be generated, which can be manually refined at reasonable cost to support MBT. Automatically generated state machines showed to largely conform to the actual system behavior as evaluated by a domain expert.

Keywords: Use Case Modeling; UML; State Machine; Model-Based Testing (MBT); State-based Testing; Transformation; Natural Language Processing.

1 Introduction

In the last decade, model-based testing (MBT) has attracted much attention in both industry and academia. This can be seen from a large number of MBT tools which have been produced in recent years [1]. In addition, several MBT test strategies have been shown to be highly effective [2]. MBT however relies on complete and precise models for executable test case generation. Developing such models has always been a challenge, especially for large-scale industrial systems, and entails a thorough domain understanding and solid modeling expertise. Oftentimes, developing such models is difficult for Software Quality Assurance teams as they are often not sufficiently acquainted with modeling. On the other hand, these teams are comparatively much more familiar with writing textual use cases and the application domain. This paper is part of an automated methodology (aToucan [3, 4]) to assist the development of high-level (system-level) models from use case models (UCMods). The focus here is on generating UML state machines, which are subsequently refined such that executable test cases can be generated using existing MBT tools.

The original motivation of this work was to support test automation for a video conferencing system (VCS) at Cisco Norway [5]. Since video conferencing systems at Cisco exhibits state-driven behavior, it is natural to provide support for state-based testing and therefore the behavior of the system is captured using mostly UML state machines. Besides, state machines is the most commonly used notation for model-based test case generation and particularly so in control and communication systems. However, the construction of such state machines is manual, expensive, and error-prone. In this paper, we provide support for automated transformation from UCMods to system-level UML state machines. We targeted system-level state machines since our focus was on system testing to address the needs of our industry partner; however lower level state machines can also be generated provided that more detailed use cases are provided as the input for the transformation.

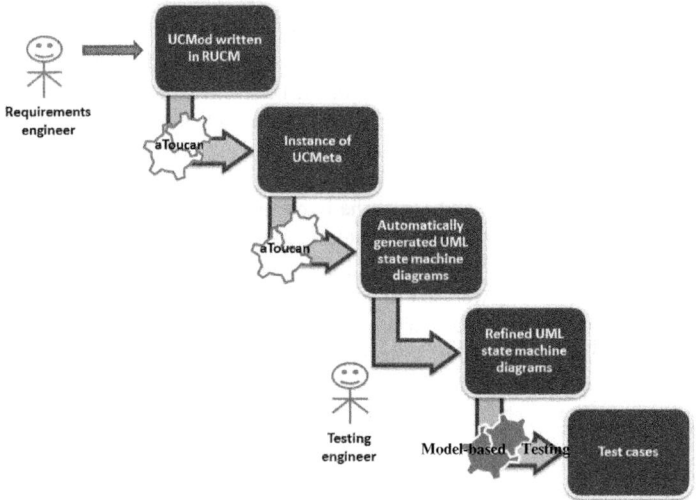

Fig. 1. Roadmap from requirements to test cases

Automated transformation from use cases to UML state machines would also enable automated traceability from requirements to state machine diagrams. Traceability is important during software development since it allows engineers to understand the connections between various artifacts of a software system. Traceability is also mandated by numerous standards (e.g., IEEE Std. 830-1998 [6]) to support, for example, change impact analysis or safety verification [7].

The basis of our approach is a use case modeling approach, named RUCM [8], which relies on a use case template and a set of restriction rules for textual Use Case Specifications (UCSs) to reduce the imprecision and incompleteness inherent to UCSs. We have conducted a controlled experiment with human subjects [8] to evaluate RUCM and results indicate that RUCM, though it enforces a template and restriction rules, has enough expressive power, is easy to use, and helps improve the understandability of use cases.

The current work is part of the aToucan approach and tool [3], which aims to transform a UCMod produced with RUCM into a UML analysis model (e.g., class and sequence diagrams). aToucan involves three steps. As shown in Figure 1, first, requirements engineers manually define use cases complying with RUCM [8]. Second, aToucan reads these textual UCSs to identify Part-Of-Speech (POS) and grammatical relation dependencies of sentences, and then records that information into an instance of UCMeta (our intermediate metamodel) (Section 3.3). The third step is to transform the instance of UCMeta into a UML state machine. During these transformations, aToucan establishes traceability links between the UCMod and the generated UML state machine diagrams. These state machines are then refined by test engineers such that executable test cases can be generated [1, 9, 10]. In this work, we focus on the transformation from an instance of UCMeta to a UML state machine diagram.

Two initial case studies were first performed to evaluate the state machine diagrams generated by aToucan. Results show that syntactically correct and largely complete state machine diagrams were generated. In addition, we also automatically generated a system-level UML state machine in one industrial case study at Cisco Norway. The generated state machine was evaluated by a domain expert, who assessed it to mostly conform to the existing, manually developed UML state machine. The latter case study also showed that refining the generated state machine to get it ready for test generation took less than one hour.

The rest of the paper is organized as follows. The related work is presented in Section 2. In Section 3, we briefly discuss RUCM, UCMeta and the running example being used to exemplify the transformation. The transformation approach is discussed in Section 4, followed by tool support (Section 5). The evaluation of our approach and promising future work are discussed in Section 6. Section 7 concludes the paper.

2 Related Work

We conducted a systematic literature review [11] on transformations of textual requirements into analysis models, represented as class, sequence, state machine, and activity diagrams. A carefully designed paper selection procedure in scientific journals and conferences from 1996 to 2008 and Software Engineering textbooks identified 20 primary studies (16 approaches). The method proposed here is based on the results of this review, with a focus on automatically deriving state machine diagrams from UCMods.

A series of methods is proposed in [12] (one of the primary studies of our systematic review [11]) to precisely capture requirements and then manually transform requirements into a conceptual model composed of object models (e.g., class diagrams), dynamic models (i.e., state machines and sequence diagrams), and functional diagrams. The approach does not purport to provide a solution for transforming requirements into analysis models. Instead, it proposes a set of techniques for users to precisely specify requirements and conceptual models, and also proposes a process to guide the users in deriving the conceptual models from the requirements. No transformation method is reported in the paper.

Somé [13], another primary study of our systematic review, proposes an approach to generate finite state machines from use cases in restricted Natural Language (NL).

The approach requires the existence of a domain model. The domain model serves two purposes: a lexicon for the NL analysis of use cases, and the structural basis of the state transition graphs being generated. The domain model acts as the lexicon for NL analysis of the use cases, because the model elements of the domain model are used to document the use cases. For example, actors of the use cases refer to the classes of the domain model. Interactions between the system and the actors are defined as one type of use case operations (also including branching statements, use case inclusion statements) which correspond to class operations in the domain model. One can see that a great deal of user effort is needed to obtain a domain model containing classes, associations, and operations, which are all indispensable for generating state machines. An algorithm is described in the paper to explain how to automatically transform the use cases plus the domain model into state machines. A working example is used to explain the approach. No case study is presented to evaluate the approach.

In summary, none of the existing approaches is able to fully and automatically generate state machine diagrams from a UCMod while establishing traceability links, which is what we are proposing in the paper.

3 Background

In this section, we briefly review the use case modeling approach RUCM (Section 3.2) and the intermediate model (UCMeta) (Section 3.3) of our transformations (Section 4). The detailed description of RUCM and UCMeta are provided in [8] and [3], respectively. A running example will be presented in Section 3.1 to exemplify RUCM, UCMeta and the transformations.

3.1 Running Example

The running example is a simplified subsystem (called Saturn) of a communication system (video conferencing system) developed by Tandberg [5] (now part of Cisco Norway), which is a leading global provider of telepresence, high-definition video conferencing and mobile video products and services. This subsystem is the industrial case study used to evaluate this work (Section 6).

The core functionality of a typical video conferencing system in Tandberg is sending and receiving multimedia streams. The use case diagram capturing the main functionalities of the simplified subsystem Saturn is given in Figure 2. Saturn deals with establishing video conferencing calls, disconnecting calls, and starting/stopping presentation. It can also receive requests for establishing calls, disconnecting calls, and starting/stopping presentation from other video conferencing systems (Endpoints) participating in a videoconference. The endpoints communicating with Saturn are modeled as secondary actors in the use case diagram in Figure 2.

3.2 RUCM

RUCM encompasses a use case template and 26 well-defined restriction rules [8]. Rules are classified into two groups: restrictions on the use of Natural Language (NL), and rules enforcing the use of specific keywords for specifying control structures. The goal of

RUCM is to reduce ambiguity and facilitate automated analysis. Two controlled experiment evaluated RUCM in terms of its ease of application and the quality of the analysis models derived by trained individuals [8, 14]. Results showed that RUCM is overall easy to apply and that it results in significant improvements over the use of a standard use case template (without restrictions to the use of NL), in terms of the quality of derived class and sequence diagrams. Below we discuss the features of RUCM that are particularly helpful to generate state machine diagrams. An example of UCS documented with RUCM of use case *Disconnect* (Figure 2) is presented in Table 1. The complete list of UCSs of the use cases in Figure 2 is provided in Appendix A for reference.

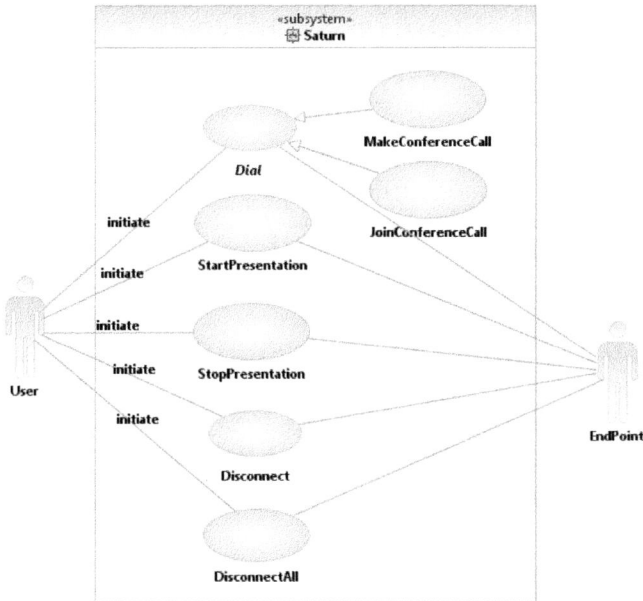

Fig. 2. Use case diagram of Saturn

A UCS has one basic flow and can have one or more alternative flows (first column in Table 1). An alternative flow always depends on a condition occurring in a specific step in a flow of reference, referred to as *reference flow*, which is either the basic flow or an alternative flow itself. We classify alternative flows into three types: A *specific alternative flow* refers to a specific step in the reference flow; A *bounded alternative flow* refers to more than one step in the reference flow–consecutive steps or not; A *global alternative flow* (called *general alternative flow* in [15]) refers to any step in the reference flow. For example, as shown in Table 1, use case *Disconnect* has one basic flow and two specific alternative flows, which branch from Step 1 and Step 5 of the basic flow, respectively. For specific and bounded alternative flows, a RFS (Reference Flow Step) section specifies one or more (reference flow) step numbers (e.g., *RFS Basic flow 2*). Whether and where the flow merges back to the reference flow or terminates the use case must be specified as the last step of the alternative flow. Branching condition, merging and termination are specified by following restriction rules that impose the use of specific keywords (see below). Each alternative flow and the basic flow must have a postcondition.

RUCM defines a set of keywords to specify conditional logic sentences (IF-THEN-ELSE-ELSEIF-ENDIF), concurrency sentences (MEANWHILE), condition checking sentences (VALIDATES THAT), and iteration sentences (DO-UNTIL). An alternative flow ends either with ABORT or RESUME STEP, which means that the last step of the alternative flow should clearly specify whether the flow returns back to the reference flow and where (using keywords RESUME STEP followed by a returning step number) or terminates (using keyword ABORT).

Table 1. Use case Disconnect

Use Case Name	Disconnect		
Brief Description	User disconnects an Endpoint participating in a conference call.		
Precondition	The system is in a conference call.		
Primary Actor	User	Secondary Actors	EndPoint
Dependency	INCLUDE USE CASE StopPresentation	Generalization	None
Basic flow steps	1) User sends a message to the system to disconnect an Endpoint. 2) The system VALIDATES THAT Endpoint to be disconnected is in the conference call. 3) The system sends a disconnection notification to Endpoint. 4) Endpoint sends an acknowledgement message back to the system. 5) The system VALIDATES THAT The conference call has only one EndPoint. 6) The system disconnects Endpoint. **Postcondition**: The system is idle.		
Specific Alt. Flow (RFS Basic flow 2)	1) The system sends a failure message to User. 2) ABORT. **Postcondition**: The system is in a conference call.		
Specific Alt. Flow (RFS Basic flow 5)	1) The system disconnects Endpoint. 2) ABORT **Postcondition:** The system is in a conference call.		

3.3 UCMeta

UCMeta is the intermediate model in aToucan [3], used to bridge the gap between a textual UCMod and a UML analysis model (class, sequence, activity, and state machine diagrams). As a result, we have two transformations: from the textual UCMod to the intermediate model, and from the intermediate model to the analysis model (Figure 1). Metamodel UCMeta complies with the restrictions and use case template of RUCM. UCMeta is currently composed of 108 metaclasses and is expected to evolve over time. The detailed description of UCMeta is given in [3].

UCMeta is hierarchical and contains five packages: UML::UseCases, UCSTemplate, SentencePatterns, SentenceSemantics, and SentenceStructure. UML::UseCases is a package of UML 2 superstructure [16], which defines the key concepts used for modeling use cases such as actors and use cases. Package UCSTemplate models the concepts of the use case template of RUCM: those concepts model the structure that one can observe in Table 1. SentencePatterns is a package describing different types of sentence patterns, which uniquely specify the grammatical structure of simple sentences, e.g., SVDO (subject-verb-direct object) (Table 1, Basic flow, step 6). SentenceSemantics is a package modeling the classification of sentences from the aspect of their semantic functions in a UCMod. Each sentence in a UCS can either be a `ConditionSentence` or an `ActionSentence`. Package `SentenceStructure` takes care of NL concepts in sentences such as subject or Noun Phrase (NP). Package `UCSTemplate` is mostly related to the generation of state machine diagrams and therefore it is the only package discussed below due to space limitation.

Package `UCSTemplate` not only models the concepts of the use case template but also specifies three kinds of sentences: `SimpleSentence`s, `ComplexSentence`s, and `SpecialSentence`s. In linguistics, a `SimpleSentence` has one independent clause and no dependent clauses [17]: one `Subject` and one `Predicate`. UCMeta has four types of `ComplexSentence`s: `ConditionCheckSentence`, `ConditionalSentence`, `IterativeSentence`, and `ParallelSentence`, which correspond to four keywords that are specified in RUCM (Section 3.1) to model conditions (IF-THEN-ELSE-ELSEIF-THEN-ENDIF), iterations (DO-UNTIL), concurrency (MEANWHILE), and validations (VALIDATES THAT) in UCS sentences. UCMeta also has four types of special sentences to specify how flows in a use case or between use cases relate to one another. They correspond to the keywords RESUME STEP, ABORT, INCLUDE USE CASE, EXTENDED BY USE CASE, and RFS (Reference Flow Step).

4 Approach

Recall that our objective is to automatically transform a textual UCMod expressed using RUCM into UML state machine diagrams, while establishing traceability links. Notice that the transformation from the textual UCMod to the instance of UCMeta is not discussed in this paper, but provided in [3] for reference. In this section, we however only focus on the transformation from instances of UCMeta to UML state machine diagrams. We present detailed transformation rules in Section 4.1. The steps required transforming automatically-generated state machine diagrams into the state machines that can be used for automated test case generation in Section 4.2.

4.1 Transformation Rules

The transformation from an instance of UCMeta to a state machine diagram involves 12 rules, which are summarized in Table 2. Subscripts on rule numbers (Column 1, Table 2) indicate the type of the rule: "c" and "a" denote composite and atomic rules, respectively; a composite rule is decomposed, whereas an atomic rule is not.

Rule 1 generates an instance of UML `StateMachine` for a UCMod, which can then be visualized as a state machine diagram. Rules 2-4 generate the initial state (an instance of `Pseudostate`), the start state (an instance of `State`), and the transition (an instance of `Transition`) from the initial state to the start state, respectively. The reason of requiring the start state is that for a state machine, it is typically required to transit from the start state to more than one state through more than one transition. However, an initial state of UML can have at most one outgoing transition [16].

Composite rule 5 invokes atomic rules 5.1-5.4 to process each use case of the UCMod. Notice that we generate a single state machine for the whole UCMod. The generated state machine is a system-level state machine where we model the states of the system as a whole and the system-level calls (e.g., APIs) as transitions. In contrast, in class-level state machines, states are modeled based on class instance variables and transitions have triggers with, for instance, call events as method calls. System-level state machines are at a higher level of abstraction than class-level state machines and are more suitable for system-level testing - the main motivation of this paper. To automatically generate system-level state machines, we utilize the information mostly contained in the precondition and postconditions of all the use cases of a UCMod to generate states. We generate an instance of State for each sentence of the precondition and the postconditions, but making sure that no duplicate states are generated. Since the precondition of a use case indicates what must happen before the use case can start and the postconditions of the use case specify what must be satisfied after the use case completes, we define rule 5.3 to generate transitions between the states derived from the precondition and the states derived from the postcondition of the basic flow.

Figure 3 presents an excerpt of Kermeta [18] code implementing rule 5.3 to generate an instance of Transition (pre2post_transition : uml::Transition). The first section of the excerpt is to show how we determine the guard condition of a transition (*S1*). As shown in Figure 3, if the steps of the basic flow of a use case contains ConditionalSentences (step.asType(ConditionalSentence)) and/or ConditionCheckSentences (step.isInstanceOf(ConditionCheckSentence)), then the guard condition of the generated transition should be the conjunction of the conditions of these sentences. For example, as shown in the state machine diagram generated for the subsystem of Saturn in Appendix B, the transition from state The system is in a conference call (the precondition of use case *Disconnect*, as shown in Table 1) to state The system is idle (the postcondition of the basic flow of *Disconnect*) with trigger Disconnect and effect The system disconnect Endpoint, has the guard condition: Endpoint to be disconnected is in the conference call. AND The conference call has only one Endpoint. The guard condition is the conjunction of the two condition checking sentences (i.e., VALIDATES THAT sentences) of steps 2 and 5 of the basic flow (Table 1). Thanks to RUCM and UCMeta, the generation of precise guard conditions becomes feasible and easier. This is because RUCM defines a set of keywords (e.g., VALIDATES THAT) and UCMeta formalizes them as metaclasses (e.g., ConditionCheckSentence). Recall that the transformation from a UCMod expressed with RUCM to an instance of UCMeta is automated and presented in [3].

The second section of the excerpt (*S2*) in Figure 3 shows how the guard condition is instantiated as an instance of uml::Constraint. The third section of the excerpt (*S3*) generates the trigger of the transition. Its name is assigned as the name of the use case, which is reasonable because the use case triggers the transition from its precondition to the postcondition of its basic flow. The fourth section of the excerpt (*S4*) generates the effect of the transition. The effect is determined by the last step of the basic flow. One may argue that the steps in the basic flow (except the condition sentences) all together should be considered as the effect. However, according to our experience in developing the tool, we noticed that in most cases, the last step is sufficient to indicate the effect of the transition. In the future, when more case studies are performed, this transformation is expected to be refined. The last fragment (*S5*) of the excerpt invokes an operation to generate the transition.

Table 2. Summary of transformation rules

Rule #	Description
1_a	Generate an instance of *StateMachine* for the use case model.
2_a	Generate the initial state (instance of Pseudostate with PseudostateKind = initial) for the state machine.
3_a	Generate an instance of State, named as 'start', representing the start state of the state machine.
4_a	Generate an instance of Transition. Its trigger is named as 'construct'. This transition connects the initial state to the start state.
5_c	Invoke rules 5.1-5.4 to process each use case of the use case model.
5.1_a	Generate an instance of State for each sentence of the precondition of the use case, as long as such a state has not been generated, which is possible because two use cases might have the same preconditions.
5.2_a	Generate an instance of State for each sentence of the postcondition of the basic flow of the use case, as long as such a state has not been generated.
5.3_a	Connect the states corresponding to the precondition to the states representing the postcondition of the basic flow of the use case with the transition whose trigger is the name of use case. See Figure 3 for the corresponding Kermeta code.
5.4_c	Process the postcondition of each alternative flow of the use case.
$5.4.1_a$	Generate an instance of State for each sentence of the postcondition of each alternative flow.
$5.4.2_a$	Connect the states corresponding to the precondition of the basic flow to the states corresponding to the postconditions of the alternative flows with the transition whose trigger is the name of use case. See Figure 4 for how guard conditions are determined.
6_a	Connect the precondition of the including use case to its postcondition through a transition. Its trigger is the including use case. Its effect is the included use case, and the guard is the conjunction of all the conditions of the condition sentences of the previous steps of the step containing the INCLUDE USE CASE sentence.

Rule 5.4 processes the postconditions of each alternative flow of the use case. Notice that RUCM enforces that each flow of events (both basic flow and alternative flows) of a UCS contains its own postcondition (Section 3.2). This characteristic of RUCM makes the transformation (rule 5.4) systematic. For a traditional use case template without enforcing this RUCM characteristic, the UCSs expressed with it would have a single postcondition for a use case. Therefore unavoidably the postcondition will combine all the conditions of the basic flow and the alternative flows, hence resulting in a single state corresponding for the postcondition of the use case. Such a state is imprecise because it encapsulates all the interesting states that a system can transit to while executing a particular use case. It is desirable (both for testing and in general) to have separate states and separate transitions with different conditions to handle alternative flows. This is exactly what our transformation does with the help of RUCM.

The reason of handling the postconditions of the alternative flows separately from the transformation rules of handling the basic flow is that guard conditions are processed in a different way. Rule 5.4 further invokes rules 5.4.1 and 5.4.2 to generate states for the postcondition of each alternative flow and connect these states to the already generated states corresponding to the precondition of the basic flow through transitions, respectively. An excerpt of Kermeta code of this rule is provided in Figure 4, which is mainly

```
precondition_states.each{precondition_state|
  postcondition_states.each{postcondition_state|
    var pre2post_transition : uml::Transition
    var guard_string : uml::String init uml::String.new
    //S1: Determine the guard condition
    basicflow.steps.each{step|
      if step.isInstanceOf(ConditionalSentence) and
          guard_string := guard_string + " AND " + step.
                    asType(ConditionalSentence).IFcondition.description
      end
      if step.isInstanceOf(ConditionCheckSentence) then
          guard_string := guard_string + " AND " + step.
       asType(ConditionCheckSentence).condition.description
      end
    }
    //S2: Generate the guard condition of the transition
    var guard_expression : uml::OpaqueExpression init uml::OpaqueExpression.new
    guard_expression.body.add(guard_string)
    var guard : uml::Constraint init uml::Constraint.new
    guard.specification := guard_expression
    //S3: Generate the trigger of the transition
    var trigger : uml::Trigger init uml::Trigger.new
    trigger.name := uc.name
    //S4: Generate the effect of the transition
    var effect : uml::OpaqueBehavior init uml::OpaqueBehavior.new
    var lastStep : String init String.new
    lastStep := basicflow.steps.at(basicflow.steps.size()-1).
          asType(Sentence).description
    effect.body.add(lastStep)
    effect.name := lastStep
    //S5: Generate the transition
    pre2post_transition := createTransition(statemachine, region,
       precondition_state, postcondition_state, uml::TransitionKind.external,
              guard, trigger, effect)
  }
}
```

Fig. 3. Excerpt of Kermeta code for implementing rule 5.3

```
var guard_string1 : uml::String init uml::String.new
altflow.postCondition.postCondtionSentences.each{sen|
  var alt_postcondition_state : uml::State
  alt_postcondition_state := createState(statemachine, region, sen.description)
    precondition_states.each{source|
      altflow.bfs.each{bfs|
        if bfs.isInstanceOf(ConditionalSentence) then
            guard_string1 := "NOT " 
                 bfs.asType(ConditionalSentence).IFcondition.description
        end
        if bfs.isInstanceOf(ConditionCheckSentence) then
            guard_string1 := "NOT " +
                 bfs.asType(ConditionCheckSentence).condition.description
        end
        ...
    }
  }
```

Fig. 4. Excerpt of Kermeta code for implementing rule 5.4.2

used to explain how the guard conditions of the transitions are determined. As one can see for the code, the guard condition of a transition from a state generated for the precondition of the use case and a state generated for the postcondition of an alternative flow is determined by negating the condition sentence (either a ConditionalSentence or a ConditionCheckSentence) of the basic flow that the alternative flow branches from (indicated using keyword RFS in the UCS of the use case) (Section 3.2). For example, as shown in the state machine diagram in Appendix B, the transition of state The system is in a conference call (representing the precondition of use case *Disconnect*, as shown in Table 1) to itself (representing the postcondition of the first specific alternative flow of *Disconnect*) with trigger Disconnect and effect The system sends a failure message to User, has the guard condition: NOT Endpoint to be disconnected is in the conference call.

Rule 6 processes each include relationship of the UCMod. For each include relationship, transitions are generated to link the precondition of the including use case to its postcondition, with the trigger named as the name of the including use case, the effect named as the name of the included use case, and the guard being as the conjunction of all the conditions of the condition sentences of the previous steps of the step INCLUDE USE CASE. As shown in Figure 5, use case *ReturnVideo* includes use case *ReadBarCode* at the basic flow step 2. Transitions are created to connect the precondition of use case *ReturnVideo* to its postconditions. For example, a transition is generated to connect the precondition of *ReturnVideo* ('Employee is authenticated') to its basic flow postcondition (sentence 'A video copy has been returned.' and sentence 'The video copy is available for rent.'), with trigger '*ReadBarCode*', effect '*ReturnVideo*'. Since there is no condition sentence before the basic flow step 2, no guard condition should be generated. Due to space limitation, we cannot provide the complete UCS in the paper.

In terms of Extend relationships between use cases, we don't need specific rules to handle them. As shown in Figure 5, use case *VideoOverdue* extends use case *ReturnVideo* in the alternative flow 1, when 'The system VALIDATES THAT the video

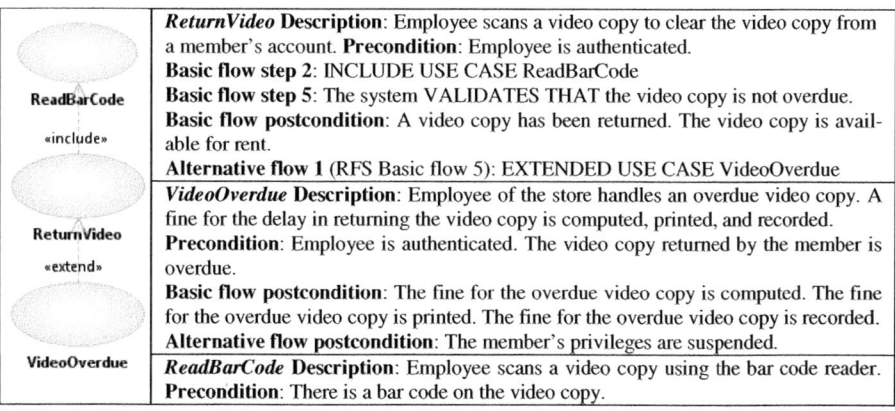

Fig. 5. Example of the Include and Extend relationships among use cases

copy is not overdue' (Basic flow step 5) is not true. When we follow rules 5.3 and 5.4.2, transitions are generated to connect the precondition of *VideoOverdue* and its postconditions of both the basic and alternative flows. Notice that the precondition of *VideoOverdue* is the combination of the precondition of *ReturnVideo* and the negative condition of the basic flow step 5. Therefore, there is no need to create transitions from the precondition of *ReturnVideo* to the postconditions of *VideoOverdue* and therefore we don't see a need to have a rule to particularly handle Extend relationships.

4.2 Transition to State Machine Diagrams for Automated Test Generation

After the system-level state machine diagram is generated for a UCMod, we need to follow the following steps to refine the state machine diagram so that it can be used as an input to automatically generate test cases.

1. We need to add missing transitions and states, remove extra states and transitions, or modify incorrect ones in the generated state machine, if required.
2. Second, we need to add state invariants using the Object Constraint Language (OCL) [19] for each state of the generated state machine based on the actual state variables of a system. For example, *NumberOfActiveCall* is a state variable of Saturn that determines how many systems are currently in a video conference. This information is mandatory in state-based testing for automated oracle generation. However this information cannot be captured in the UCMod and is therefore missing in the state machine diagram generated by aToucan.
3. The third step is to map all the triggers in the state machine diagram to the actual API calls of the SUT so that the API of the system can be invoked while executing test cases generated from the state machine.
4. Last, it is also required to replace textual guard conditions of the generated state machine with corresponding OCL constraints, based on the state variables and/or input parameters of the triggers associated with the guards.

An effort estimate for these steps is provided on an industrial case study in Section 6.

5 Tool Support

Our approach has been implemented as part of aToucan [3]. aToucan aims to automatically transform requirements given as a UCMod in RUCM into a UML analysis model including a class diagram, a set of sequence and activity diagrams, and a state machine diagram. It relies on a number of existing open source technologies. aToucan is built as an Eclipse plug-in, using the Eclipse development platform. UCMeta is implemented as an Ecore model, using Eclipse EMF [20], which generates code as Eclipse plug-ins. The Stanford Parser [21] is used as a NL parser in aToucan. It is written in Java and generates a syntactic parse tree for a sentence and the sentence's grammatical dependencies (e.g., *subject, direct object*). The generation of the UML analysis model relies on Kermeta [18]. It is a metamodeling language, also built on top of the Eclipse platform and EMF. The target UML analysis model is instantiated using the Eclipse UML2 project, which is an EMF-Based implementation of the UML 2 standard.

The architecture of aToucan is easy to extend and can accommodate certain types of changes. Transformation rules for generating different types of diagrams are structured into different packages to facilitate their modifications and extensions. Thanks to the generation of an Eclipse UML2 analysis model, generated UML models can be imported and visualized by many open source and commercial tools. Similarly, though UCSs are currently provided as text files, a specific package to import UCSs will allow integration with open source and commercial requirement management tools. More details on the design of aToucan can be found in [3].

We adapted the traceability model proposed in the traceability component (fr.irisa.triskell.traceability.model) of Kermeta [18] to establish traceability links. Details of the traceability model is discussed in [3].

6 Evaluation, Discussion, and Future Work

Our goal here is to assess 1) whether the tool does generate system-level state machine diagrams based on UCMods, 2) whether our transformation rules are semantically complete, 3) whether our transformation rules lead to state machine diagrams that are syntactically correct, and 4) whether the automatically generated state machine diagrams can be refined by engineers to support MBT with reasonable effort. Regarding point 3, syntactic correctness means that a generated state machine diagram conforms to the UML 2.2 state machine diagram notation. Regarding point 2, semantic correctness means that a generated state machine diagram correctly represents its UCMod; all the constructs that are related to the transformation in the UCMod are correctly transformed by following the transformation rules and no redundant model elements are generated.

Regarding the first three evaluation points, two software system descriptions (ATM and Elevator, called Banking System and Elevator System in [22]) were used to evaluate them. UCSs of these systems were re-written by applying RUCM so that they could be used as input of the transformations. These UCSs have also been used to generate class and sequence diagrams [3], and activity diagrams [4]. As the state machines provided in the textbook do not fully correspond to the UCMods also provided in the same textbook, we cannot compare the state machine diagrams automatically generated by our tool with the ones provided in the textbook. However, we carefully examined our state machines, and we could verify that the generated state machines were syntactically correct and mostly but not entirely semantically complete. More importantly, this allowed us to identify the following limitations:

- The quality of UCSs has direct impact on the quality of the generated state machine diagrams. For example, correct preconditions and postconditions of UCSs are required in order to generate meaningful state machine diagrams. In our future work, we plan to propose guidelines on how to write UCSs using RUCM for the purpose of generating state machine diagrams, so that higher quality of UCSs will be defined and lead to higher quality state machines.
- In order to reduce redundant states and transitions, using advanced lexical analysis techniques such as WordNet [23] (an electronic lexical database) are needed to identify similar words and sentences, so as to eliminate redundancy

among model elements in generated state machine diagrams. This is also one of our future research directions.
- Use case diagrams cannot model possible sequences of use case executions. However such information is sometimes needed in order to generate more complete and precise system-level state machine diagrams. For example, it is always an issue to identify the set of states where a state machine should transition from the start state (Section 4.1, rule 3). As shown in the state machine diagram in Appendix B, the automatically generated state machine diagram does not have any transition going from the start state to the other states of the state machine. The reason is that in order to create such transitions, we need to identify the possible sequences of executing use cases. Using our case study as example, we need to answer questions such as: is use case *MakeConferenceCall* executed before use case *StartPresentation*? A use case diagram cannot capture such information; therefore, using for example activity diagrams to capture such sequential constraints is needed. From a testing perspective, such information is required to generate feasible test cases from state machine diagrams. For example, a test case generated from a state machine diagram should correspond to an infeasible path, e.g., executing use case *StartPresentation* before use case *MakeConferenceCall*.

We also conducted an industrial case study to automatically generate a state machine diagram from the UCMod of a video conferencing systems (Saturn) developed at Cisco Norway. The UCMod contains seven use cases as shown in Figure 2 and the generated state machines contains five states and ten transitions. The automatically generated state machine was manually refined by one domain expert and one modeling expert working together by following the steps described in Section 4.2. More specifically, one transition from the Start state to state The system is idle, with trigger PowerOn, was manually added to the automatically generated state machine diagram (Appendix B). One transition from state The system is idle to state The presentation is started, with trigger Start presentation, was also added. This transition means that Saturn can start a presentation without being in any conference call. Notice that these two transitions were not automatically generated, because the required information was not described in the UCMod. In total, it took around 40 minutes for them to complete the refinement process. In addition, they did not meet any difficulty in applying RUCM and they took less than three hours to complete the UCMod of Saturn. aToucan took less than 200 seconds to generate the state machine diagram for Saturn. In the future, we plan to conduct controlled experiments to compare the quality of aToucan-generated state machines with the ones manually derived by engineers.

7 Conclusion

Over the last decade, model-based testing (MBT) has been shown to be effective as a test automation strategy. However, the success of MBT relies on developing complete and precise input models. Developing such models from scratch can be a challenging task, especially when testers are not acquainted with modeling. To assist the initial modeling required for MBT, we propose an approach to transform use case specifications into UML state machines, the most common notation used for MBT.

A more precise and rigorous use case modeling approach (RUCM) was proposed in [8] and was used in this paper to automatically generate UML state machines diagrams from textual use case specifications. This work is part of the aToucan approach [3], which aims to transform a use case model produced with RUCM into an initial UML analysis model that so far included class and sequence diagrams [3], and activity diagrams [4]. We first evaluated our state machine transformations on two case studies from Gomaa's textbook [22]. We manually assessed the quality of generated state machines and found them largely consistent with the source use cases. In addition, we evaluated our approach on an industrial application, where we modeled use case specifications of a video conferencing system developed by Cisco Norway. These use case specifications were automatically transformed into initial state machine diagrams using our tool, which were then refined by a domain expert and a modeling expert to support test case generation. Our industry partner benefited not only from the executable test cases, but also from the system specification expressed as UML state machine diagrams and precise requirements expressed with RUCM, all this for an overall cost of less than four hours, including documenting the use case model and refining the generated state machine diagram.

In the future, we are planning to provide detailed guidelines to help write use case specifications using RUCM. We are also planning to extend RUCM to allow the specification of use case execution sequences, which can further help in improving completeness of generated state machine diagrams. Empirical studies will be conducted to evaluate the quality of automatically generated state machine diagrams compared to the ones manually generated by engineers.

Acknowledgments

We are grateful to Cisco Norway for their support and help on performing the industrial case study.

References

1. Shafique, M., Labiche, Y.: A Systematic Review of Model Based Testing Tool Support. Carleton University, Technical Report SCE-10-04
2. Neto, A.C.D., Subramanyan, R., Vieira, M., Travassos, G.H.: A survey on model-based testing approaches: a systematic review. In: The 1st ACM International Workshop on Empirical Assessment of Software Engineering Languages and Technologies. ACM, Atlanta (2007)
3. Yue, T., Briand, L.C., Labiche, Y.: Automatically Deriving a UML Analysis Model from a Use Case Model. Simula Research Laboratory, Technical Report 2010-15 (2010)
4. Yue, T., Briand, L.C., Labiche, Y.: An Automated Approach to Transform Use Cases into Activity Diagrams. In: Kühne, T., Selic, B., Gervais, M.-P., Terrier, F. (eds.) ECMFA 2010. LNCS, vol. 6138, pp. 337–353. Springer, Heidelberg (2010)
5. Cisco Norway (Tandberg), http://www.tandberg.no/
6. IEEE Std. 830-1998, IEEE Standard for Software Requirement Specification (1998)
7. Olsen, G.K., Oldevik, J.: Scenarios of traceability in model to text transformations. In: Akehurst, D.H., Vogel, R., Paige, R.F. (eds.) ECMDA-FA. LNCS, vol. 4530, pp. 144–156. Springer, Heidelberg (2007)

8. Yue, T., Briand, L.C., Labiche, Y.: A use case modeling approach to facilitate the transition towards analysis models: Concepts and empirical evaluation. In: Schürr, A., Selic, B. (eds.) MODELS 2009. LNCS, vol. 5795, pp. 484–498. Springer, Heidelberg (2009)
9. Ali, S., Hemmati, H., Holt, N.E., Arisholm, E., Briand, L.: Model Transformations as a Strategy to Automate Model-Based Testing - A Tool and Industrial Case Studies, Simula Research Laboratory, Technical Report (2010-01) (2010)
10. Smartesting, http://www.smartesting.com
11. Yue, T., Briand, L.C., Labiche, Y.: A systematic review of transformation approaches between user requirements and analysis models. Accepted for publication in Requirements Engineering (Online first) (2011)
12. Insfrán, E., Pastor, O., Wieringa, R.: Requirements Engineering-Based Conceptual Modelling. Requirements Engineering 7, 61–72 (2002)
13. Some, S.S.: An approach for the synthesis of state transition graphs from use cases, vol. 1, pp. 456–462. CSREA Press, Las Vegas (2003)
14. Yue, T., Briand, L., Labiche, Y.: Facilitating the Transition from Use Case Models to Analysis Models: Approach and Experiments, Simula Research Laboratory, Technical Report (2010-12) (2010)
15. Bittner, K., Spence, I.: Use Case Modeling. Addison-Wesley, Boston (2002)
16. OMG: UML 2.2 Superstructure Specification (formal/2009-02-04)
17. Brown, E.K., Miller, J.E.: Syntax: a linguistic introduction to sentence structure. Routledge, London (1992)
18. Kermeta: Kermeta metaprogramming environment
19. OMG: OCL 2.0 Specification
20. Eclipse Foundation: Eclipse Modeling Framework
21. The Stanford Natural Language Processing Group: The Stanford Parser version 1.6
22. Gomaa, H.: Designing Concurrent, Distributed, and Real-Time Applications with UML. Addison-Wesley, Reading (2000)
23. Princeton University, WordNet: A lexical database for English, http://wordnet.princeton.edu/

Appendix A. Use Case Specifications of Saturn

The following use case specifications only contain the fields with important information to understand our approach due to space limitation.

Table 3. Use case Dial

Brief Description	User dials the system.
Precondition	The system is powered on.
Basic flow steps	1) User dials the system. **Postcondition**: The system is in a conference call.

Table 4. Use case MakeConferenceCall

Brief Description	The system is idle.
Precondition	User dials the system to make a conference call.
Basic flow steps	1) User dials the system. 2) The system makes a conference call to Endpoint. **Postcondition**: The system is in a conference call.

Table 5. Use case JoinConferenceCall

Brief Description	User dials the system to join a conference call.
Precondition	The system is in a conference call.
Basic flow steps	1) User dials the system. 2) The system VALIDATES THAT the maximum number of Endpoint to the conference call is not reached. 3) The system adds Endpoint to the conference call. **Postcondition**: The system is in a conference call.
Specific Alt. Flow (RFS Basic flow 2)	1) The system sends a message to User. 2) ABORT. **Postcondition**: The system is in a conference call.

Table 6. Use case StartPresentation

Brief Description	User wants to start the presentation.
Precondition	The system is in a conference call.
Basic flow steps	1) User requests the system to start a presentation. 2) The system sends the presentation to Endpoint. **Postcondition**: The presentation is started.

Table 7. Use case StopPresentation

Brief Description	User wants to stop the presentation.
Precondition	The presentation is started.
Basic flow steps	1) User requests the system to stop a presentation. 2) The system stops the presentation to Endpoint. **Postcondition**: The system is in a conference call.

Table 8. Use case DisconnectAll

Brief Description	User disconnects all Endpoint participating in a conference call.
Precondition	The system is in a conference call.
Basic flow steps	1) The system disconnects all connected EndPoints. 2) ABORT **Postcondition**: The system is idle.

Appendix B. Generated State Machine Diagram for Saturn

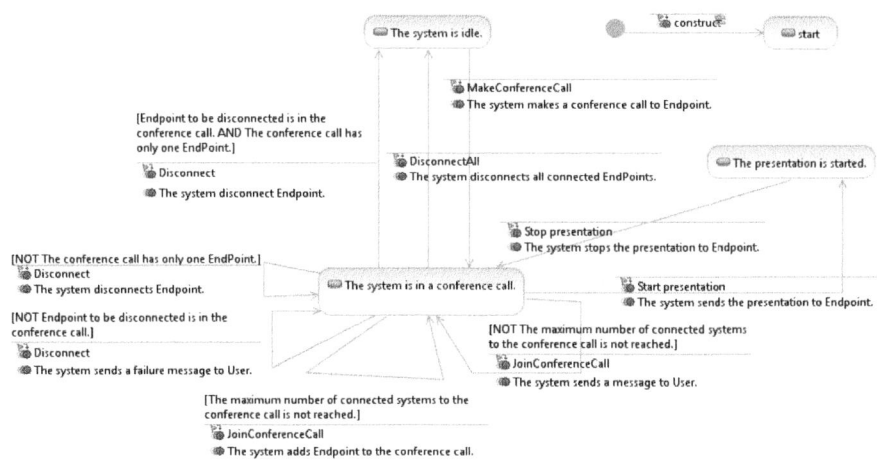

Transformation Rules for Translating Business Rules to OCL Constraints

Imran S. Bajwa and Mark G. Lee

School of Computer Science, University of Birmingham, B15 2T, Birmingham, UK
{i.s.bajwa,m.g.lee}@cs.bham.ac.uk

Abstract. In design of component based applications, the designers have to produce visual such as Unified Modeling Language (UML) models, and describe the software component interfaces. Business rules and constraints are the key components in the skeletons of software components. Semantic of Business Vocabulary and Rules (SBVR) language is typically used to express constraints in natural language and then a software engineer manually maps SBVR business rules to other formal languages such as UML, Object Constraint Language (OCL) expressions. However, OCL is the only medium used to write constraints for UML models but manual translation of SBVR rules to OCL constraints is difficult, complex and time consuming. Moreover, the lack of tool support for automated creation of OCL constraints from SBVR makes this scenario more complex. As, both SBVR and OCL are based on First-Order Logic (FOL), model transformation technology can be used to automate the transformation of SBVR to OCL. In this research paper, we present a transformation rules based approach to automate the process of SBVR to OCL transformation. The presented approach implemented in SBVR2OCL prototype tool as a proof of concept. The presented method softens the process of creating OCL constraints and also assists the designers by simplifying software designing process.

Keywords: Model Transformation, Transformation Rules, OCL constraints, SBVR business rules, SBVR business design.

1 Introduction

Software modeling is a major phase of software development and the growing complexity of large software systems can be handled using the modeling approach. Unified Modeling Language (UML) is an essential tool for developing high-quality, possibly error-free, and highly accurate models of complex and mammoth-sized software systems. However, a UML model remains semantically incomplete without constraints. Constraints further restrict the behavior of objects in a UML model. Object Constraint Language (OCL) is a formal specification language [1] used to define constraints for a UML model. But adaptability of OCL has been a major issue since it has emerged into an Object Management Group (OMG) standard [2]. Less adaptability of OCL is due to unfamiliar syntax of OCL [11] and lack of built-in support in OCL specification for standardized semantic verification [3]. Existing OCL tools just perform type checking and parsing of OCL expressions [12], [13].

Currently, there is no tool that facilitates easy creation of OCL constraints from business rules.

SBVR (Semantic of Business Vocabulary in Rules) [7] is an OMG specification used for expressing business/software requirements for business/software models in the form of business rules. A Business rule is key element of SBVR based business/software models. SBVR has replaced the natural languages to capture business/software requirements due to inherent support of formal semantics in SBVR. The business/software constraints can also be represented using SBVR (rules) as SBVR promises semantically consistent representation to the software/business constraint specifications. In SBVR, semantic consistency is achieved due to SBVR's inherent support of formal approaches: typed predicate logic; arithmetic; set and bag comprehension, and with some additional basic results from modal logic [7]. As the logic is essentially classical logic, so mapping to other logic-based specifications such as OCL should be simple as OCL is also based on typed logic, First-Order-Logic (FOL) [3].

This work is extension of the automated generation of natural language specification to OCL constraint via SBVR [19], [22]. The automated transformation of SBVR rules to OCL constraints simplifies the process of manually generating OCL constraints from SBVR representation as manual generation is not only difficult and complex but also causes erroneous OCL expressions [3], [11]. The proposed methodology for the transformation of SBVR rules to OCL constraints is based on set of transformation rules. Transformation rules based SBVR to OCL mapping is shown in Figure 1.

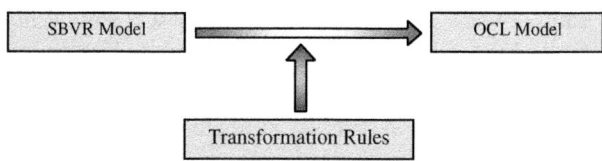

Fig. 1. Transformation rules to map source model (SBVR) to target model (OCL)

Following section gives the brief description of SBVR and OCL elements.

1.1 SBVR Constraints

SBVR [7] is typically used by business people to capture business requirements specifications and constraints. In business models, constraints are represented using business rules. The business rules in SBVR are assembled on facts, and facts build on concepts as expressed by terms. Terms express business concepts; facts make assertions about these concepts; rules constrain and support these facts. For example in a business rule "customer *uses* a credit card", used concepts are 'customer' and 'credit card' and this rule is based on a fact-type 'customer *uses* card' while '*uses*' is a verb concept. In this example, given concepts are noun concepts. Concepts can also be individual concept e.g. 'VISA card'.

In SBVR, a business rule can be of two types: structural rule and behavioral rule [7]. A *structural rule* is used to express state or structure of a noun concept for example a structural rule "customer has a bank account" expresses the state of a noun concept 'customer' who has a 'bank account'. A *behavioral rule* principally describes the operations or actions performed by a noun concept. For example in a behavioral rule "customer *deposits* money" it is given that a noun concept 'customer' performs an action of depositing 'money'.

Two notations are proposed for SBVR rules in SBVR 1.0 [7]: Structured English and RuleSpeak. In this paper, we have used Structured English as a formal notation for SBVR rules [10]. The SBVR structured English notation proposes to underline the noun concepts, italicize the *verb concepts*, double underline the individual concepts, and bold the SBVR **keywords**. The above SBVR rules with logical formulations are written using defined notation of Structured English.

1.2 OCL Constraints

The Object Constraint Language (OCL) is another important standard from OMG used to annotate UML models with logical constraints to avoid semantic ambiguities. OCL is a declarative language that is mainly used to define constraints on a UML class models, and define queries for it.

OCL Syntax: To define the basic structure of n OCL expression, OCL syntax is defined in OCL 2.0 [3]. The syntax of a typical OCL expression is mainly composed of the following three components.

Context: A context [3] in an OCL expression specifies the scope of the expression. The OCL context limits a world of an expression in which it is valid using a keyword 'context'. A keyword 'self' is used to refer a particular class or operation of a class specified in a context.

Property: An OCL property [3] represents an attributes or operation of a class. '.' operator is used to specify these properties e.g. customer.account or customer.deposit()

Keyword: The OCL keywords [3] e.g. if, then, else, and, or, not, implies are typically used to specify the conditional expressions.

OCL Constraints: An OCL constraint defines a Boolean expression that can result in True or False. If a constraint is always true, the system remains in a valid state. An OCL constraint can have following 3 types:

Invariants: The invariants [3] are conditions those need to be True always. Keyword 'inv' is used in invariants.

```
context customer
inv: self.age >= 18
```

Precondition: A precondition [3] is a constraint that should be True before the execution of a method starts. Keyword 'pre' is used in preconditions.

```
context customer :: isAdult(dDOB: Integer): Boolean
pre: dDOB >= 1990
```

Postcondition: A postcondition [3] is a constraint that should be True after the execution of a method has finished. Keyword 'post' is used in postconditions.

```
context customer :: isAdult(dDOB: Integer): Boolean
post: result >= 18
```

The rest of the paper is structured as follows. Section 2 describes the methodology for the translation of UML class diagrams into SBVR rules and transformation rules used to translate the SBVR abstract syntax into the OCL abstract syntax. All the transformation rules are illustrated by examples. Section 3 describes a prototype translation tool OCL-Builder, whereas section 4 describes experiments, results and analysis. Section 5 presents the related work to our research and the paper is closed with the conclusion section.

2 SBVR to OCL Transformation

SBVR to OCL transformation is performed in two phases. In first phase, the SBVR constraints specification is mapped to the target UML model and in second phase the SBVR information is mapped to OCL constraints using a set of transformation rules. Detailed description of both phases is given here:

2.1 Mapping SBVR Rules to UML Model

In this phase, the SBVR rules are mapped to UML models for semantic verification before the SBVR rules are mapped to OCL constraints. Semantic verification is essential to validate that the target OCL constraints will be semantically verified with the target UML model. To illustrate the process of mapping SBVR rules to the UML model we have taken an example shown in Figure 2.

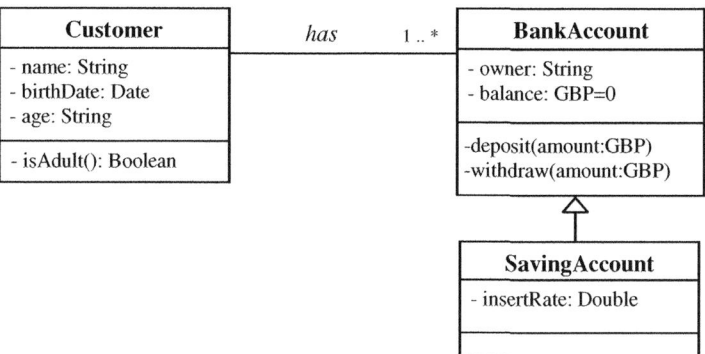

Fig. 2. A UML class model

The mapping process starts with the syntax analysis of SBVR rules to extract various elements of the SBVR rule i.e. noun concepts, verb concepts, fact types, etc.

Following section describes the process of mapping classes and their respective associations with a common SBVR rule.

Mapping Classes: The general noun concepts in SBVR rules represent the UML classes. Verb concepts specify methods of a class. Adjectives are tagged as attributes. An example of a SBVR rule is given below:

It is obligatory that each <u>customer</u> *can have* **at least one** <u>bank account</u> **only if** <u>customer</u> *is* **18** <u>years old</u>.

In the above shown SBVR rule, both noun concepts '<u>customer</u>' and '<u>bank account</u>' are matched to all classes in the UML class model shown in the figure 2 and the noun concepts are replaced with the names of the classes, if matched.

Mapping Class Associations: Associations in a UML class model express relationship of two entities in a particular scenario. A UML class model may consists of different types of associations e.g. packages, associations, generalizations, and instances. Typically, these associations are involved in defining the context of an OCL constraint, so it is pertinent to map these associations in the target SBVR specification of business rules.

Mapping Packages: A package in a UML class model organizes the model's classifiers into namespaces [20]. In SBVR, there is no specific representation of a package. Hence user has to manually specify the package name for a set of classes. The package names are also defined in the OCL constraints, so the package information is also mapped to the SBVR rules.

Mapping Associations: Associations in a UML model specify relationships between two classes [20]. Simple associations can be unidirectional, bidirectional, and reflexive [18]. Unidirectional associations in UML are mapped with unary (based on one noun concept) fact types in SBVR and the bidirectional associations in UML are mapped with binary (based on two noun concepts) fact types in SBVR. Direction of the association is determined by the position (subject or object) of the noun concepts and object types in SBVR.

Mapping Generalizations: Generalization or inheritance is an association between two classes that defines the property of one class inheriting the functionalities of the other [20]. In SBVR the relationship of general noun concept (super class in UML) and individual noun concept (sub class in UML) is used to identify the inheritance feature. If a class A inherits the class B then the class B will also be the part of OCL context of class A.

Mapping Instances: The instances of the classes can also appear in a UML class model. The individual concepts in SBVR are mapped to the instances (objects). The defined instances also become part of the OCL contexts and OCL constraints. So, the instances are also mapped in SBVR rules.

In SBVR to UML mapping, the classes that do not map to the given UML class model are ignored.

2.2 Mapping SBVR Rules into OCL Constraints

We present an automated approach for the translation of the SBVR specification into the OCL constraints. Our approach not only softens the process of creating the OCL syntax but also verifies the formal semantics of the OCL expressions with respect to the target UML class model. As OCL is a side-effect free language, hence it is important that each OCL expression should be semantically verified to the target UML model. A prototype tool "SBVR2OCL" is also presented that performs the target transformation. Figure 3 shows a *SiTra* library [21] based Model Transformation Framework for SBVR to OCL Transformation using (SBVR to OCL) mapping rules.

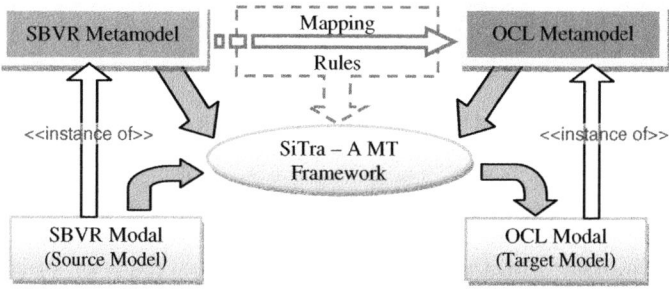

Fig. 3. A SiTra based Model Transformation Framework for SBVR to OCL Transformation

Mapping of SBVR rules to OCL code is carried out by creating different fragments of OCL expression and then concatenating these fragments to compile a complete OCL expression. Typically, OCL expression can be of two types: OCL invariant and OCL query operation. In this paper, we will present only the creation of OCL invariants and the creation of OCL query operation is part of the future work.

The SBVR rules' specification created in section 2 is further analyzed to extract the business information as follows:

It is obligatory that each <actor> <action> **at least** one <thematic-object> only if <actor> <action> <thematic-object>

The analyzed SBVR rule is further transformed to the logical representation after omitting the SBVR keywords as following

$p \Rightarrow q$ if $p \rightarrow function1()$ AND $q \rightarrow q.function2()$

This logical representation can be further generalized as follows:

$p \Rightarrow q$ if condition1 = *TRUE* AND condition2=*TRUE*

This generalized representation is finally transformed to the OCL constraint by using the defined transformation rules. A typical transformation rule comprises of the variables, predicates, queries, etc [9]. A typical transformation rule consists of two parts: a left-hand side (LHS) and a right-hand side (RHS). The LHS is used to access the source model element, whereas the RHS expands it to an element in the target model. The transformation rules for each part of the OCL constraints are based on the abstract syntax of SBVR and OCL that are given in the following section.

Generating OCL Context: The context of an OCL expression defines the scope of the given invariant or pre/post condition. To specify the context of an OCL invariant, the major actor in the SBVR rule is extracted to specify the context. To specify the context of an OCL pre/post condition, the action performed by the actor in a SBVR rule is considered as the context. Rule 1.1 shows the OCL context for invariant expressions and Rule 1.2 shows the context of for the pre/post condition of an operation:

> Rule 1.1
> T[*context*-inv(object type)] = *context-name*
> Rule 1.2
> T[*context*-cond(object type, verb concept)] = *context-name* :: *operation-name*

Precondition and postcondition can co-exist in a single an OCL expression than the both precondition and postcondition share the same context.

Generating OCL Constraints: Transformation rules for mapping of the SBVR specification to OCL constraints are defined in this section. There are two basic types of an OCL constraints; invariant of a class, and pre/post condition of an operation. Constraint on a class is a restriction or limitation on a particular attribute, operation or association of that class with any other class in a model. An expression for these constraints consists of two elements: context of the constraint and body of the constraint.

> R0u
> le 2.1
> T[*invariant*(*context-inv, inv-body*)] =   context *context-inv*
>   inv: *inv-body*
> Rule 2.2
> T[*pre-cond* (*context-cond, pre-cond-body*)] = context *context-cond*
>   pre: *pre-cond-body*
> Rule 2.3
> T[*post-cond* (*context-cond, post-cond-body*)] =   context *context-cond*
>   post: *post-cond-body*

Generating OCL Invariants: The OCL invariant specifies a condition on a class's attribute or association. Typically, an invariant is a predicate that should be TRUE in all possible worlds in UML class model's domain. The OCL context is specified in the invariants by using `self` keyword in place of the local variables.

> Rule 3.1
> T[*inv-body* (*ocl-exp*)] = inv: *ocl-exp*

An invariant can be expressed in a single attribute or set of attributes from a class. In OCL, collection operations are used to perform basic operations on the set of attributes.

Rule 3.2
T[*ocl*-exp()] = self.(*Expression | collection-exp | if-exp*)
Rule 3.3
T[*collection-exp(Expression)*] = *Expression* → *collection-op* |
$\qquad\qquad\qquad\qquad\qquad\qquad$ *Expression* → *collection-op* → *collection-exp* | ""
Rule 3.4

T[*if-exp(Condition, Expression*)] = If *Condition* then *Expression-1*
$\qquad\qquad\qquad\qquad\qquad\qquad\quad$ else *Expression-2*   endif

Generating OCL Pre/Post Conditions: Similar to the OCL invariant, the OCL preconditions and the OCL postcondition are used specify conditions on operations of a class. Typically, a precondition is a predicate that should be TRUE before an operation starts its execution, while a postcondition is a predicate that should be TRUE after an operation completes its execution.

Rule 4.1
T[*pre-cond-body(ocl-exp*)] = pre: *ocl-exp*
Rule 4.2
T[*post-cond-body(ocl-exp, value*)] = post: *ocl-exp* | post: result = *value*
Rule 4.3
T[*value*(thematic-object)] = *Integer-value | Double-value | String-value | Boolean-value*

A pre/post condition can be expressed in a single attribute or set of attributes from a class. Rule 3.2 and 3.3 are reused here to accompany Rule 4.1 and 4.2. In rule 4.3 the attribute value is verified that the provided value is of accurate type e.g. integer, double, or String, etc.

Generating OCL Expressions: The OCL expressions express basic operations that can be performed on available attributes of a class. An OCL expression in the OCL invariant can be used to represent arithmetic, and logical operations. OCL arithmetic expressions are based on arithmetic operators e.g. '+', '-', '/', etc, while, logical expressions use relational operators e.g. '<', '>', '=', '<>', etc and logical operators e.g. 'AND', 'implies', etc.

Rule 5.1
T[*Expression(Expression*)] = *Expression infix-oper Expression | prefix-oper Expression*
Rule 5.2
T[*infix-oper(Quantification*)] = + | - | * | / | = | > | < | >= | <= | <> | OR | AND | implies
Rule 5.3
T[*prefix*-oper(*Quantification*)] = - | NOT
Rule 5.4
T[*Quantification*(Keyword)] = at least *n* | at most *n* | exactly *n*

Generating OCL Operations: The OCL collections represent a set of attributes of a class. A number of operations can be performed on the OCL collections e.g. sum, size, count, isEmpty, etc.

Rule 6.1

T[*collection-op(Expression*)] = forAll(*Expression*) | exists(*Expression*) | select(*Expression*) | allInstances(*Expression*) | include(*Expression*) |....

3 Tool Support

SBVR2OCL tool was implemented to translate SBVR to OCL constraints. Translation rules and the abstract syntax of OCL and SBVR were implemented in java as an Eclipse plugin using EMF (Eclipse Modeling Framework). A rule based parser (that we used in [16]) was employed to syntactically analyze SBVR rules and map them with given UML class Model in EMF UML 2.0 format. SBVR2OCL tool then finally translates the SBVR specification to OCL constraints by using translation rules. Figure 4 and 5 shows screen-shots of the tool.

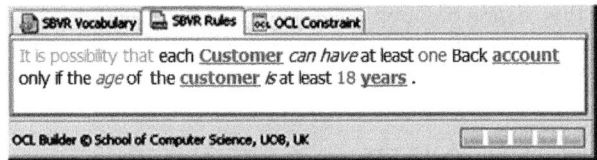

Fig. 4. SBVR2OCL – Input SBVR Rule

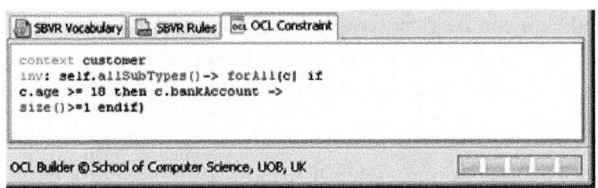

Fig. 5. SBVR2OCL – Output OCL Constraint

Limitation of SBVR2OCL tool is that it generates one OCL constraint for one SBVR specification at a time.

4 Experiments and Results

To find the bugs in the working of the tool experiments were performed to carry out the dynamic verification of the software tool. To test the accuracy of the OCL constraints generated by the designed system three classes were defined: invariants, preconditions and post-conditions. Various complexity levels of input i.e. simple, compound and complex SBVR rules were also defined to verify the consistency of tool's output. Both, the simple and complex constraints contain only one fact type. Moreover, the simple constraints do not involve association and generalizations but complex business constraints involve associations and generalizations. Compound constraints are complex constraints with multiple fact types. Examples of defined complexity levels are following:

Simple: **It is necessary that each** customer *has* **at most** one BankAccount.

Complex: **It is obligatory that each** customer *can have* **at least one** BankAccount **only if** age of customer *is* **18** years.

Compound: **It is permitted that** if **each** customer *has* **at least** one bankAccount and account balance *is* **at least** GBP 500 *can apply* for **at least** one credit card.

In the above examples, 'necessary', 'obligatory', and 'permitted' are SBVR keywords used to represent modality formulation [7]. To test tools accuracy 10 examples of each complexity-level were used. Constraint types for each 10 examples were generated. Each generated OCL constraint from each category was type-checked. For type checking OCLarity [16] tool was used that is an OCL type checking tool. For the sake of type checking in OCLarity, the used class model and the generated OCL constraint were given as input. A matrix representing OCL constraints accuracy test (%) for invariants, preconditions, and post conditions has been constructed. Overall accuracy for all types of OCL constraints is determined by adding total accuracy of all categories and calculating its average that is 88.33%.

Table 1. Testing results of OCL constraints

Complexity level/ Constraint Type	Invariant	Precondition	Postcondition	Total
Simple	94.1%	91.5%	89.3%	91.63%
Complex	91.2%	90.2%	87.8%	89.73%
Compound	86.6%	84.7%	79.8%	83.7%

OverAll Accuracy = 88.33%

The graph above is showing the accuracy ratio of various diagram types in terms of invariants, pre-condition, and post-condition parameters. The correctness of the software tool was verified though static verification by performing the analysis.

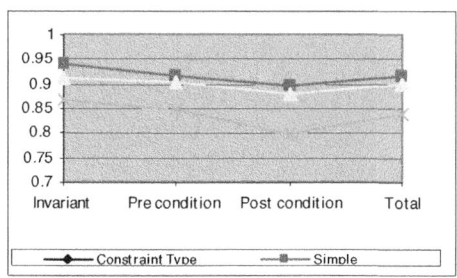

Fig. 6. SBVR2OCL tool Results

5 Related Work

Transformation of SBVR Business design to the formal representations i.e. UML, OCL, Java, etc is a relatively new area. In last decade, many automated solutions for transformation of natural language based informal specification to formal specification have been presented [15, 17]. Introduction of frameworks and tools for automated transformation NL to UML model have made things very easy and time saving for the software designers.

Amit presented his work to transform SBVR business design to UML models [5]. He has used model driven engineering approach to transform SBVR specification into different UML diagrams e.g. activity diagram, sequence diagram, class diagram. His research work is a millstone in reducing gap between SBVR and UML based software modeling. Linehan's work [14] for the transformation of SBVR rules into formal languages e.g. Java is one of the only case. In this work, Java code is generated from the SBVR rules through OCL representation. SBeaVeR is an [18] another open-source tool that translates the SBVR rules into Prolog rules. This also provides facility of expressing SBVR rule in "Structured English". This tool lacks the support for transformation to standard middleware artifacts.

6 Conclusion

This paper presents a transformation rules based approach to create OCL constraints from UML based SBVR rules' specification. SBVR to OCL transformation is based on transformation rules. The transformation rules are derived from the abstract syntax of SBVR and OCL. Presented approach is fully automated as user provides only the input business rules and target UML model. The presented work helps in achieving the objective of providing a simple means of analysis and verification of the given UML model. The proposed approach also ensures the creation of consistent OCL expressions. This automated transformation not only softens the process of creating OCL but also improves the usability of OCL by providing automatic mechanism of semantic verification with a UML model. The presented tool, SBVR2OCL performs transformation of SBVR rules to OCL after semantic verification with a given UML model. The use of automated transformations ensures seamless creation of OCL statements and deemed to be non-intrusive. Our tool is used to evaluate usability of the presented approach.

References

[1] OMG: Object Constraint Language (OCL), OMG Standard, v. 2.0 (2006)
[2] Warmer, J., Kleppe, A.: The Object Constraint Language – Getting Your Models Ready for MDA, 2nd edn. Addison Wesley, Reading (2003)
[3] Cabot J., et al.: UML/OCL to SBVR Specification: A challenging Transformation. Journal of Information systems (2009) doi:10.1016/j.is.2008.12.002
[4] Linehan, M.: SBVR Use Cases. In: Bassiliades, N., Governatori, G., Paschke, A. (eds.) RuleML 2008. LNCS, vol. 5321, pp. 182–196. Springer, Heidelberg (2008)

[5] Raj, A., Prabharkar, T., Hendryx, S.: Transformation of SBVR Business Design to UML Models. In: ACM Conference on India software engineering, pp. 29–38 (2008)
[6] Cabot, J., Teniente, E.: Transformation Techniques for OCL constraints. J. of Science of Computer Programming 68(03), 152–168 (2007)
[7] OMG: Semantics of Business vocabulary and Rules (SBVR), OMG Standard, v. 1.0 (2008)
[8] Pau, R., Cabot, J.: Paraphrasing OCL Expressions with SBVR. In: Kapetanios, E., Sugumaran, V., Spiliopoulou, M. (eds.) NLDB 2008. LNCS, vol. 5039, pp. 311–316. Springer, Heidelberg (2008)
[9] Marcano, R.: Transformation Rules of OCL Constraints in to B Formal Expression. In: Fifth International Conference on UML – the langauge and its Applications, Workshop on Critical Systems Development with UML, Dresden, Germany (September 2003)
[10] Enterprise Architect, http://www.sparxsystems.com/products/ea/
[11] Wahler M.: Using Patterns to Develop Consistent Design Constraints, PhD Thesis, ETH Zurich, Switzerland (2008)
[12] Demuth B, Wilke C.: Model and Object Verification by Using Dresden OCL. In R.G. Workshop on Innovation Information Technologies: Theory and Practice, pp. 81–89 (2009)
[13] IBM OCL Parser (September 2009), http://www-01.ibm.com/software/awdtools/library/standards/ocl-download.html
[14] Linehan, M.H.: Ontologies and Rules in Business Models, edocw. In: Eleventh International IEEE EDOC Conference Workshop, pp. 149–156 (2007)
[15] Bajwa, I., Samad, A., Mumtaz, S.: Object Oriented Software modeling Using NLP based Knowledge Extraction. European Journal of Scientific Research 35(01), 22–33 (2009)
[16] EmPowerTec, OCLarity, http://www.empowertec.de/index.htm
[17] Bryant, B., et al.: From Natural Language Requirements to Executable Models of Software Components. In: Workshop on S. E. for Embedded Systems, pp. 51–58 (2008)
[18] De Tomassi, M., Pierpaolo, C.: Sbeaver Business Modeler Editor, http://www.sbeaver.sourceforge.net
[19] Bajwa I., Behzad B., Lee M.: OCL Constraints Generation from Natural Lanauge Specification. In: EDOC 2010 – 14th IEEE EDOC Conference, Vitoria, Brazil, pp. 204–213 (2010)
[20] OMG: Unified Modeling Langauge (UML), OMG Standard, v. 2.1 (2007)
[21] Akehurst, D.H., Boardbar, B., et al.: SiTra: Simple Transformations in Java. In: Wang, J., Whittle, J., Harel, D., Reggio, G. (eds.) MoDELS 2006. LNCS, vol. 4199, pp. 351–364. Springer, Heidelberg (2006)
[22] Bajwa, I., Lee M., Behzad B.: SBVR Business Rules Generation from Natural Lanauge Specification. In: AAAI 2011 Spring Symposium – AI for Business Agility, San Francisco, USA, pp. 2–8 (2011)

Preventing Information Loss in Incremental Model Synchronization by Reusing Elements*

Joel Greenyer[1,**], Sebastian Pook[2], and Jan Rieke[1,**]

[1] Software Engineering Group, Department of Computer Science
University of Paderborn, 33098 Paderborn, Germany
{jgreen,jrieke}@uni-paderborn.de
[2] Heinz Nixdorf Institute
University of Paderborn, 33098 Paderborn, Germany
Sebastian.Pook@hni.uni-paderborn.de

Abstract. The development of complex mechatronic systems requires the close collaboration of multiple engineering disciplines. Hence, multidisciplinary system engineering approaches have been developed. However, the refinement of discipline-specific aspects of the system, for example the implementation of software controllers, still requires discipline-specific models and tools. During the development, changes in these discipline-specific models may affect other disciplines' models. Thus, inconsistencies are likely to occur, leading to increased development time and costs if they remain undetected. Bidirectional model synchronization techniques aim at automatically resolving such inconsistencies. Existing synchronization algorithms today, however, fail in this application scenario, because synchronization steps often unnecessarily destroy and re-create elements, which damages parts of the models that are not subject to the synchronization. In order to solve these issues, we present a novel synchronization technique based on Triple Graph Grammars with improvements regarding the reuse of model elements.

Keywords: Incremental Model Synchronization, Mechatronic System Design, Triple Graph Grammars (TGG), Information Retainment in the Target.

1 Introduction

The development of mechatronic systems, from modern household aids to transportation systems, requires the close collaboration of multiple disciplines, such as mechanical engineering, electrical engineering, control engineering, and software engineering. Usually, in a first development phase, called *conceptual design*, all disciplines collaborate in creating a discipline-spanning *system model*. In the

---

* This work was developed in the course of the Collaborative Research Center 614 – Self-optimizing Concepts and Structures in Mechanical Engineering – University of Paderborn, funded by the Deutsche Forschungsgemeinschaft.
** supported by the International Graduate School Dynamic Intelligent Systems.

following *refinement* phase, engineers from each discipline develop discipline-specific models in parallel, using different modeling languages and tools. As changes during the refinement are likely to affect other disciplines, avoiding inconsistencies during the refinement is crucial. Synchronizing changes among the models is often done manually today, being prone to errors and inconsistencies.

To automatically synchronize the different models used during the development, a concept is needed to bidirectionally propagate changes between the different models: if, for instance, the discipline-spanning system model is changed, these changes must be propagated from this (*source*) model to the discipline-specific (*target*) models. Bidirectional model transformation techniques are a promising approach for such synchronization scenarios. However, existing synchronization algorithms [4,5,18,8] are not sufficient for such a scenario: When changes to a source model are propagated, often too many elements of the target models are unnecessarily deleted and recreated. This severely damages parts of the target model which referenced the deleted elements. Such synchronization issues arise in many model-based development scenarios: different models are created for different purposes, and overlap in the information they contain, e.g., models for specification and models for testing. We present an improved synchronization algorithm based on Triple Graph Grammars (TGGs) [14], a rule-based formalism for declaratively specifying relations between models. This algorithm prevents unnecessary deletions by providing flexible repair operations.

The paper is structured as follows. Sec. 2 describes the development of mechatronic systems and introduces the example. In Sec. 3, we give a short introduction to TGGs and model synchronization approaches. The main contribution, our improved synchronization algorithm, is described in detail in Sec. 4. Finally, we summarize related work in Sec. 5 and conclude the paper in Sec. 6.

2 Development of Mechatronic Systems

Design guidelines for mechatronic systems, like VDI 2206 [17], or development methods elaborated in the Collaborative Research Center (CRC) 614 "Self-Optimizing Concepts and Structures in Mechanical Engineering" in Paderborn, propose that experts from all disciplines collaborate in a first development phase, called the *conceptual design*. Together, they work out the *principle solution*, a system model that captures all interdisciplinary concerns. A core part of this interdisciplinary system model is the *active structure*, which shows how the system is composed of different system elements, how they are hierarchically structured, and how they affect each other by flows (e.g., information or energy flows).

The principle solution then serves as a basis for the discipline-specific *refinement* phase. However, the principle solution rarely captures all interdisciplinary concerns and, therefore, cross-disciplinary changes may become necessary during the discipline-specific refinement phase. These changes then have to be propagated among the discipline-specific models. This is realized by first updating the interdisciplinary system model with the information relevant to other disciplines and then propagating these changes to the other affected discipline-specific models. Gausemeier et al. [3] described such a process from a methodological viewpoint, showing the applicability of model transformation techniques in general.

Let us consider an example in the following. One project which serves as a case study for the CRC 614 is the *RailCab*.[1] Its vision is that, in the future, the schedule-based railway traffic will be replaced by small, autonomous RailCabs, which transport passengers and goods on demand, being more energy efficient by dynamically forming convoys. Fig. 1 shows the active structure of a RailCab. This diagram kind is part of an interdisciplinary specification language that was developed to model the principle solution of mechatronic systems [2]. In the following, we call this specification language the *Mechatronic Modeling Language* (MML). We consider the refinement of this model in the discipline of software engineering using *Mechatronic UML*. Mechatronic UML is a modeling language for the development of distributed, safety-critical real-time systems, especially to model the software architecture and the behavior of the system and its components [1]. It allows us to specify *hybrid components*, which include both discrete and continuous behavior, and dynamic *reconfigurations* of components.

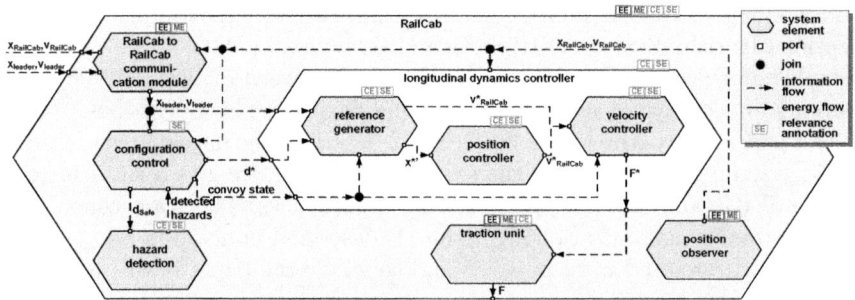

Fig. 1. Parts of the active structure of the RailCab system

Let us take a closer look at the active structure. The longitudinal dynamics controller is responsible for controlling the traction unit. The control strategy for the velocity is reconfigured based on the current convoy state: Usually, a setpoint value for the speed, $v^*_{RailCab}$, is used, calculated by the reference generator. During convoy mode, the controllers are reconfigured so that the position controller becomes active and the velocity is controlled based on the distance to the leading RailCab. The basic reconfiguration behavior is described in the principle solution, but the details are implemented later during the discipline-specific refinement. For details, we refer to Gausemeier et al. [3]. The small *relevance annotations* at the top of each system element mark which system element is relevant to which discipline (e.g., "SE" denotes Software Engineering). Thus, these annotations define discipline-specific views on the active structure.

Inconsistencies may easily arise during the development. Consider the following process as an example.

---

[1] Neue Bahntechnik Paderborn/RailCab: http://www-nbp.uni-paderborn.de/

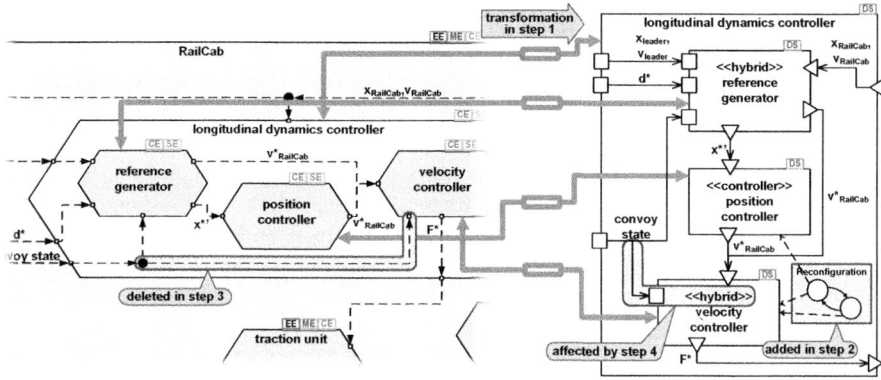

Fig. 2. Transition from the active structure to a Mechatronic UML component diagram

1. The discipline-specific models are generated from the principle solution by different *initial* model transformations. Fig. 2 shows how different elements of the active structure correspond to Mechatronic UML model elements.
2. The disciplines' engineers start refining their models. E.g., the software engineer defines behavior for components; especially he elaborates on the reconfiguration behavior for the longitudinal dynamics controller. This discipline-specific information is typically not reflected back to the principle solution.
3. A flaw is identified within the original principle solution: the velocity controller inside the longitudinal dynamics controller receives information about the current convoy state, but this is unwanted and possibly misleading for the engineers implementing it. So the principle solution is changed, and this information flow and its ports are removed.
4. After the only discrete port of the velocity controller has been removed, the corresponding component in Mechatronic UML must not be a hybrid component anymore, but a simple controller component. (Controller components, in contrast to hybrid components, are not further refined by the software engineers, but entirely implemented by control engineering. Thus, it is just a placeholder for controller code.) Therefore, the model synchronization updates the software model and changes the hybrid component to a controller.

The main challenge in step 4 is that the model synchronization has to replace some parts of the Mechatronic UML model, *but in a way that the discipline-specific information introduced in step 2 is not destroyed or becomes invalid.* Here, the reconfiguration chart developed in step 2 references the hybrid component velocity controller. Deleting this hybrid component and recreating it as a controller component would *damage this reconfiguration chart*, because the chart would still reference the deleted hybrid component.

3 Triple Graph Grammars

Bidirectional model transformation techniques are a promising approach for automatically synchronizing the different models during the development. Model synchronization is an intensively researched topic today, and several techniques and approaches exist. Here, we use a concept called *Triple Graph Grammars* (TGGs) [14]. TGGs are a rule-based formalism that allows us to specify how corresponding graphs or models can be produced "in parallel" by linking together two graph grammar rules from two different graph grammars. More specifically, a TGG rule is formed by inserting a third graph grammar rule to produce the so-called *correspondence* graph that links the nodes of the other two graphs. TGGs can be interpreted for different transformation and synchronization scenarios. Before we describe these scenarios, let us consider the structure of TGG rules.

3.1 Triple Graph Grammar Rules

Fig. 3a illustrates a TGG rule, SystemElementToHybridComponent, which is taken from a TGG that defines the mapping between MML and Mechatronic UML.

TGG rules are non-deleting graph grammar rules that have a left-hand side (lhs) and a right-hand side (rhs) graph pattern. The nodes appearing on the lhs and the rhs are called *context nodes*, displayed by white boxes. The nodes appearing on the rhs only are called *produced nodes*, displayed by green boxes, labeled by "++". Accordingly, there are *context edges*, displayed by black arrows, and *produced edges*, displayed by green arrows and "++" labels.

In TGGs, graphs are *typed* and *attributed*. When working with models and meta-models in terms of MOF [11], this means that the host or *instance* model contains objects and links that are instances of classes and references of a given meta-model. Accordingly, the nodes and edges in the rules are typed over the classes and references in a meta-model. Nodes are labeled in the form "*Name:Type*". For instance, the nodes in the left column of rule SystemElement-ToHybridComponent are typed by the classes Package and SystemElement from the MML meta-model. The edge is typed over the reference packagedElement.

The columns of a TGG rule describe model patterns of different meta-models and are called *domains*. The left-column production states that when there is a

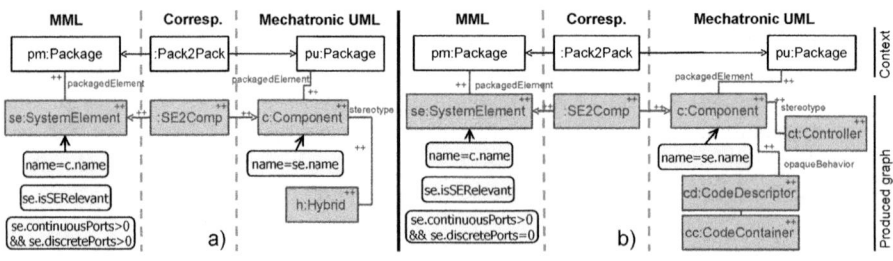

Fig. 3. a) SystemElementToHybridComponent, b) SystemElementToController

package in MML, we can add a system element and a link between them. The right column of the rule represents the graph grammar production for creating components in packages in Mechatronic UML. In the middle, there is the production of the correspondence structure between the models.

Our TGG rules further introduce the concept of *attribute constraints* and *application conditions* (depicted by yellow, rounded rectangles in Fig. 3). Attribute constraints are attached to nodes and have expressions of the form $\langle prop \rangle = \langle expr \rangle$, where $\langle prop \rangle$ is a property of the node's type class, and $\langle expr \rangle$ is an OCL expression that must conform to the type of $\langle prop \rangle$. Node names can be used as variables in the OCL expression. Attribute constraints constrain the attribute value of an object, e.g., rule SystemElementToHybridComponent has two constraints that express that the name of the component has to be equal to the name of the opposite component. A rule application is not valid if the attributes do not equal the specified values. Application conditions are OCL expressions over model properties that evaluate to a Boolean value. A rule application is not valid if an application condition evaluates to false. E.g., the constraints on the left of the rule SystemElementToHybridComponent restrict the applicability to cases where there are both continuous and discrete ports at the system element and where the component is relevant to software engineering.

For the transformation from MML to Mechatronic UML, we defined a set of TGG rules. Rule SystemElementToHybridComponent defines how system elements with both discrete and continuous information flows correspond to hybrid components. Rule SystemElementToController (Fig. 3b) relates system elements without discrete but with continuous flows to controller components.

3.2 Application Scenarios

We can interpret TGGs for different *application scenarios*. One application scenario, called *forward transformation*, is to create one "target" graph corresponding to a given "source" graph. In this case, a TGG rule is interpreted as follows: First, the context pattern and the produced source domain pattern of the rule are matched, adhering to the following conditions: First, the context pattern of the rule must only be matched to *bound* model elements. Bound nodes and edges are those that were previously matched by another rule application. Second, the source produced pattern may only be matched to yet *unbound* parts in the source model. If a matching respecting these conditions is found, the produced target and correspondence patterns are created and bindings are created for the newly matched and created elements.[2] The *backward* direction works accordingly, reversing the notion of source and target. We refer to Greenyer and Kindler [6] for further details on TGGs and the binding semantics.

Our TGG engine interprets attribute constraints (of the form $\langle prop \rangle = \langle expr \rangle$) as assignments in the target domain. If a TGG rule shall support both transformations directions, assignments must be specified for both directions.

---
[2] In the following, we use the term *binding* when referring to a single node-to-object or edge-to-link match, and *matching* for a set of those bindings (i.e., when a whole pattern is matched to several elements).

3.3 Incremental Model Synchronization

In a situation where a triple of corresponding models is given and a change occurs in one domain model, this change can be propagated by *incrementally updating* only the affected parts of the model. Algorithms for this problem have been described before [5,4,18,8]. In the following, we explain the shortcomings of existing incremental synchronization approaches.

Giese and Wagner suggest the following approach [5]. When a change occurs in the source model, the rule application(s) which are violated by the change (i.e., there is no longer a valid match of the rule) are revoked. Second, all rule applications that depend on the revoked rule(s) are also revoked. During that process, the target model elements created by the revoked rule applications are destroyed, and the source model elements become unbound. Finally, the transformation is re-run for the unbound source model elements.

Giese and Hildebrandt present another algorithm [4]. When a change occurs in the source model, it tries to repair the rule applications that are violated by the change. For instance, if the change is a move of an element on the source side, a rule application can be repaired by changing the link from the corresponding (target-side) element to its old (target-side) parent such that it is now linked to the new corresponding parent on the target side. These repairs are performed by pre-generated repair operations that are derived from the rules. Only if such a repair operation is not possible, the rule application is revoked. Then the algorithm tries to apply another rule to these unbound source model elements. However, these repair operations are only able to modify links; whenever it is not possible to repair a rule application by changing a link, the rule must be revoked and the target model elements are destroyed. In the following, we present an example where this approach leads to the unwanted loss of information in the target model. Our improved algorithm resolves this problem.

4 Improved Synchronization

As the deletion of elements should be prevented if possible, it is reasonable not to immediately destroy elements when a rule application is revoked. Thus, these elements are just *marked for deletion* by our improved synchronization algorithm. The novelty of our algorithm is that it can reuse these removed objects and links during later rule application by explicitly *searching for matches in the set of elements that are marked for deletion*. Only if such a (deletion-marked) element cannot be reused (i.e., bound again) by a new rule application, it will be ultimately destroyed. The problem is that there may be several ways of how the elements marked for deletion can be reused. A particular challenge is then to determine the "best" way to reuse these elements.

The remainder of the section is structured as follows. First, we present an example, and overview the improved synchronization algorithm. Then we give an extended example with different ways of reusing elements and we discuss heuristics to determine which reusable pattern may be best. Finally, we discuss the details of the *partially reusable pattern search* and conclude with a runtime evaluation.

4.1 Improved Synchronization Example

We assume that our models are in a consistent state, e.g., after an initial transformation as shown in Fig. 2. In particular, all elements are bound by a TGG rule application. Then, as described in Sec. 2, the information flow convoy state to the system element velocity controller is deleted, and with it its corresponding port (crossed-out in Fig. 4a). The rule applications that previously translated the information flow and the information flow port are now structurally invalid[3]. Therefore, these rule applications are revoked, which means removing all its bindings and marking the (correspondence and target) produced objects and links as deleted (denoted by dashed lines in Fig. 4a). Additionally, the application of SystemElementToHybridComponent that mapped the velocity controller system element to a hybrid component becomes invalid because the constraint `continuousPorts>0&&discretePorts>0` is violated (as there is no discrete port any more). So, this rule application has to be revoked by marking its produced part as deleted, too.

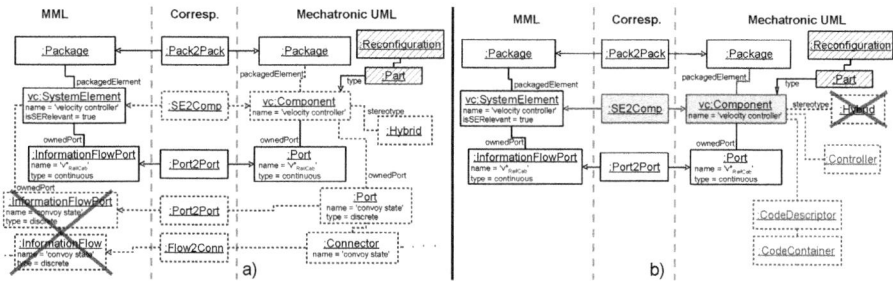

Fig. 4. Abstract syntax after rule revocation, a) after deleting a flow and the revocation of rules, b) after applying the new rule (with reusing elements by repair operations)

We now try to apply new rules immediately, instead of first revoking depended rule applications. In this case, SystemElementToController (see Fig. 3b) can be applied: Its context is matched onto the package objects in MML and UML and the correspondence :Pack2Pack. As we are incrementally updating in forward direction, the produced source (MML) pattern (se:SystemElement) is matched onto the velocity controller system element (as this element is now unbound due to the revocation of SystemElementToHybridComponent). Also the constraints are valid, as they require no discrete port. A normal rule application would simply create the correspondence and target patterns. Instead, our improved synchronization first searches for a pattern matching in the set of elements marked for deletion. Two elements in this set can be reused: Starting the search from the velocity controller system element, our algorithm finds and reuses the (deleted) :SE2Comp correspondence and the velocity controller component.

No other previously deleted element can be reused by this rule. Unfortunately the matching is not complete yet, as there are no existing objects to match the

---
[3] We refrain from showing these TGG rules, as they simply translate one information flow (resp. one information port) to one connector (resp. one port).

Controller, CodeDescriptor, and CodeContainer nodes of rule SystemElementToController. The algorithm uses this *partial pattern matching* anyway. Now we can apply the rule as follows. First, removing the "deleted" flag from everything that has been reused and binding these elements again. Second, because the match of the TGG rule is not yet complete, additional links and objects are created as required for this rule. Unfitting links of single-valued references are moved. This process is called *repair operation*.

Fig. 4b shows the situation after the rule application. The algorithm reused the :SE2Comp correspondence and the velocity controller component (shaded in Fig. 4b). It created new instances of Controller, CodeDescriptor, and CodeContainer, and set the appropriate links (dashed in Fig. 4b), as no reusable element could be found for them. The Hybrid stereotype object could not be reused. Thus, it is ultimately deleted (crossed-out in Fig. 4b).

By reusing the velocity controller component, which was previously marked for deletion, a dangling edge from the model-specific reconfiguration specification (hatched in Fig. 4a and 4b) is prevented. Additionally, any further model-specific information that is attached to the component is also preserved. Furthermore, a deletion and recreation of the component would have rendered the context for the PortToPort rule invalid. Thus, the old synchronization algorithm would have to revoke this and possibly further rule application.

4.2 Improved Synchronization Algorithm

In summary, our improved synchronization algorithm works as follows:
1. Iterate over all TGG rule applications in the order they were applied, and if the application has become invalid due to changes in the source model
   a. Remove the bindings of the produced graph, and mark the correspondence and target produced elements previously bound to this graph as deleted.
   b. If the same or other rules are applicable in the forward direction, i.e., the context and the source produced graph match,
      i. search for a pattern of elements marked for deletion that "best" matches part of the rule's correspondence/target graph structure.
      ii. apply the rule by reusing this pattern, creating the remaining target/correspondence pattern, and enforcing attribute value constraints

   Continue checking the next rule application or terminate if all applications have been checked.
2. Finally, effectively destroy elements that are still marked for deletion.

The concept to "mark for deletion" allows us to remember the elements that might be reusable. It is the basis for intelligently reusing model elements during the synchronization, which is the main improvement over previous approaches.

In the example above there was only one possible partially reusable pattern, but often there are several partial matchings that reuse more or less elements. In fact, some partial matchings may reuse elements in an unintended way. Therefore, we first calculate all possible partial matchings, and then choose the most reasonable. In the following, we present an extended example in which two reuse possibilities occur. Next, we discuss the implementation details of the partially reusable pattern search, which computes the different reuse options (step 1b-i).

4.3 Selection of Elements to be Reused

The heuristic for the "best" partial matching is generally to take the partial matching that reuses most elements. However, also considering existing correspondence information can be vital, as we show in the following example. Let us assume that we start with a consistent state, as in the previous example. First, as before, the discrete port and its information flow are deleted from the MML velocity controller. Second, for some reason the position controller's relevance flag for the software engineering discipline is removed. Therefore the application of rule SystemElementToHybridComponent for the velocity controller and the application of rule SystemElementToController for the position controller is revoked. The result is shown in Fig. 5, with user deletions crossed-out and deletion-marked elements depicted by dashed lines.

As explained before, rule SystemElementToController is now applicable at the MML velocity controller. In addition to the partial pattern match described before (see Fig. 4b), there is a second promising partial match now (marked with $\sqrt{}$s in Fig. 5). It is found by the partial pattern matching search starting from the context :Package object of Mechatronic UML. This partial match reuses the deleted position controller component, its controller, code descriptor and code container. However, the existing correspondence node does not fit (marked with a ⊛): It points to the MML position controller, but it must be connected to the MML velocity controller (because the node se:SystemElement is already matched to the velocity controller). Additionally, the attribute constraint must be repaired, changing the component's name to "velocity controller" (also marked with ⊛).

Although this alternative partial matching reuses more elements than the partial matching used in Fig. 4b, it is in fact an example where the reuse is unintended, because it creates a correspondence between the "wrong" elements. At first glance, this may not seem to be a problem, because the change propagation will adapt all links and attribute values in the target model to satisfy the constraints posed by the TGG. However, there may be elements in the target model that are not subject to the transformation which reference these reused elements. A "wrong" reuse means that these elements now reference completely altered objects that have changed in meaning. Therefore, it is reasonable to favor such partial matchings where a correspondence node is reused without changing

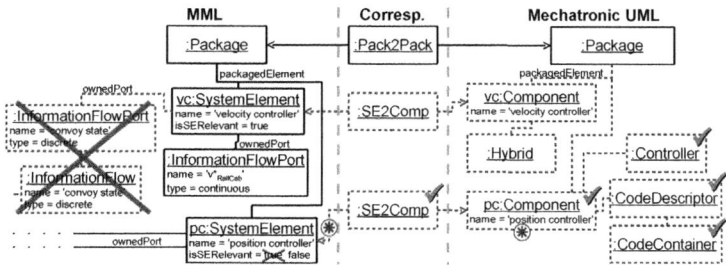

Fig. 5. "Wrong" partial pattern match

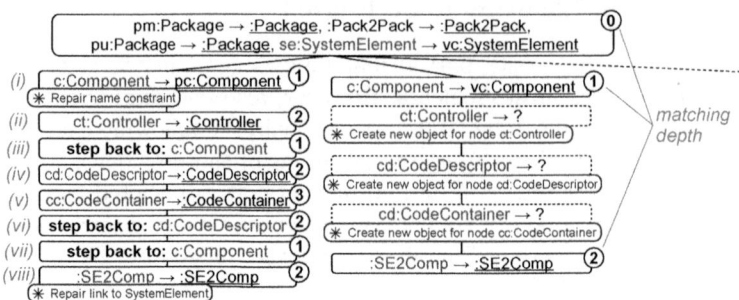

Fig. 6. Matching tree resulting from searching the produced pattern of SystemElement-ToController in the set of deleted elements from Fig. 5

its correspondence links. In this way, only previously corresponding elements are reused, typically resulting in the intended reuse of elements.

Note that in terms of the TGG semantics, it is not relevant in which way existing elements are reused (or whether reused at all). Because of this fact, also our synchronization algorithm does not change the TGG semantics, because (a) when a rule is applied, reused objects and links will be modified so that they fit the rules, and (b) at the end of a synchronization run, unused objects marked for deletion will be actually destroyed, so they won't interfere with other rule applications. Therefore, after a successful transformation, every rule holds, and no remainders of revoked rules exist. Thus, arguing informally, fundamental TGG transformation properties like termination, correctness, completeness are unaffected by our new algorithm. However, a formal proof that the algorithm does not violate these properties has yet to be elaborated.

4.4 Partial Reusable Pattern Matching Algorithm

In the following, we describe the data structure we use for the partially reusable pattern search and discuss how the algorithm searches for partial matchings.

All possible partial matchings are computed by creating a tree structure. The root of this tree is a vertex which represents the matching of the context and the source produced domain pattern (computed in step 1b). Each edge of the tree represents a step of the pattern matching which binds a new node. Each other vertex is labeled with a single node binding (a node-object tuple). Additionally, it is labeled with its pattern matching *depth*, which is the depth in the recursion of a depth-first pattern matching algorithm. Each vertex of the tree therefore represents a (partial) matching of the rule, recursively defined by the node binding of the vertex and those of its parent.

The resulting tree reflects the pattern matching search: When traversing the rule, the algorithm adds a new child vertex for each successful pattern matching step (i.e., whenever it finds a new candidate object for a node). Thus, a vertex has more than one child when there are different possibilities to match a node.

Fig. 6 shows a part of the matching tree that is the result of a partial pattern matching search of rule SystemElementToController (Fig. 3b) in the set of deleted elements from Fig. 5. As described, the root of this tree contains the matching of the context and the source produced domain pattern. The different bindings of this matching are shown in the form "*Node:NodeType* → *Object:ObjectType*", where *Node* represent a node from the TGG rule and *Object* is the matched object. The algorithm starts a search from every binding in the root. Let us assume it first tries to match the TGG rule node pu:Package and finds the not yet bound outgoing edge packagedElement to c:Component (Fig. 3b). The algorithm now has two options on how to match this node: Both the objects position controller and the velocity controller components match. So a new vertex is created for both (the left one is marked with (i) in Fig. 6), each with $depth = 1$ (denoted as the circled number in the upper right corner of the vertices in Fig. 6).

The left subtree contains the "wrong" partial matching possibility (see Fig. 5): The algorithm continues with matching the ct:Controller node to the controller object and adding a vertex with $depth = 2$ for it (ii). Then, as there is no unbound node connected to the ct:Controller node, the search must be continued at the previous node, decreasing the *depth* (iii). Here, the previous node is simply the node of the parent vertex, c:Component. Next, the cd:CodeDescriptor (iv) and the cc:CodeContainer (v) is matched. Again, as no unbound node connected to cc:CodeContainer exists, the algorithm steps back in the pattern matching, i.e., returns to the previous node, cd:CodeDescriptor (vi). There is also no unbound node connected to cd:CodeDescriptor. At this point, the previous node is not the node of the parent vertex. Therefore, the previous node is identified using the *depth* counter: we walk up the tree and select the first vertex v with $v.\text{depth} < currentVertex.\text{depth}$, which is c:Component (vii).

The :SE2Comp correspondence node matches (viii), but its link to the position controller system element does not, because there is already a binding for the node se:SystemElement that binds a different object. So this must be repaired if this partial matching should be applied, denoted with the ⊛. Furthermore, the attribute constraint that ensures the equality of the system element's and the component's name must be enforced by changing the name of the pc:Component (again marked with a ⊛ at the first vertex (i) of the left subtree).

The right subtree represents the other partial matching from the previous example, where the ct:Controller, cd:CodeDescriptor, and ct:CodeContainer nodes could not be matched. Note that there are no real vertices for these unmatchable nodes in the tree. They are depicted dashed in Fig. 6 only to illustrate the repair operations needed to be performed to create a valid rule matching.

In fact, there is a third subtree (not shown in the figure). The search starts at every node of the root's matching (remember it contains bindings for all context and produced source graph nodes). Thus, starting from the se:SystemElement node, the algorithm would create this third subtree which contains the same matching as the second subtree, just in opposite direction.

Every vertex of the matching tree represents a possible repair operation. The number of reused elements is equal to the depth of a vertex in the tree (not the value of the *depth* counter), not counting the "step back to" vertices. Thus, using the root would not reuse deleted elements, but create the whole produced pattern. Once the tree is computed, it has to be decided which of the several partial matchings (i.e., which vertex of the tree) should be used. We have discussed above that a reasonable heuristic is to select the partial matching which does not damage reusable correspondences and which reuses most elements, i.e., will require the least repair operations. In this way, it is likely that only previously related elements are reused, which is probably the intention of the user.

Further details including the algorithm's pseudocode can be found in [7].

4.5 Runtime Evaluation

With our improved synchronization, we intend to address the issue of information loss during update operations, and focus less on performance improvements. Some operations of our solution turn out to be relatively time-consuming. Especially, building a complete search tree is exponential in the number of nodes and candidate objects (objects marked for deletion), but all techniques that calculate different matchings resp. repair alternatives will suffer from the general complexity of this problem. To estimate the performance impact, we implemented both our algorithm and the one by Giese and Wagner [5] in our TGG INTERPRETER[4]. Due to lack of space, we only give a short summary of the runtime evaluation here. Detailed results can be found in [7].

In summary, our algorithm works best when there are only few altered elements, because then the number of candidate objects is small. There could even be performance improvements when a large amount of revocations of dependent rules is prevented. Overall, the prevention of information loss comes with a performance decrease in most cases. However, in typical editing cases, the maximum performance drop was only 30 % in comparison with the old algorithm.

In our examples, we observed that good partial matchings were often found early in the partially reusable pattern search. Thus, additional heuristics could be used to determine the quality of a partial matching already during the search. When a good-quality matching is found, we could even decide to terminate the search, possibly long before the complete matching tree is build up. Then we may miss the intended way of reusing the elements, but we believe that there are many examples where adequate heuristics could determine the "best" matching early, improving the overall performance significantly. However, elaborating these heuristics is planned for future work.

5 Related Work

Model synchronization has become an important research topic during the last years. Several concepts of incremental updates, which are mandatory for preserving model-specific information, have been proposed. However, as discussed in this paper, simply updating incrementally can still be insufficient. To the best of our knowledge, there are only few solutions that address these further issues.

---

[4] http://www.cs.uni-paderborn.de/index.php?id=12842&L=1

As described in Sec. 4, the approach of Giese and Hildebrandt [4] is similar, but their main focus is performance and not optimizing the reuse of elements. Their approach is only able to cover cases similar to an element move (which means essentially repairing edges). It does not allow for more complex scenarios: either a rule application can be repaired by changing links or attributes value, or the rule is revoked and all elements are unrecoverably deleted.

Körtgen [10] developed a synchronization tool for simultaneous evolution of both models. She defines several kinds of damage types that may occur and gives abstract repair rules for these cases. At runtime, these general repair rules are used to derive concrete repair operations for a specific case. The synchronization itself, however, is a highly user-guided process, even if changes are propagated in just one direction. Our aim is to avoid unnecessary user interaction where that is possible. For ambiguous cases, however, we would also like to incorporate means for user interaction.

Xiong et al. [18] present a synchronization technique that also allows for the simultaneous evolution of both models in parallel. Basically, they run a backward transformation into a new source model, and then use model merging techniques to create the updated final source model. The same is done in forward direction. Other approaches (e.g., Jimenez [9]) also rely on model merging. In general, using model merging techniques in combination with (possibly non-incremental) transformations is another possibility to solve the issues discussed in this paper: a simple transformation propagates changes from the source model to a working copy of the target model. Then the model merger is responsible for merging the changes in the target model. However, this puts additional requirements on the model merger: first, it must identify "identical" elements without using unique IDs, because these IDs change when elements are recreated in a transformation. Second, discipline-specific information is lost in the working copy of the target model during a simple transformation, but still contained in the original target model. The model merger must be aware of this discipline-specific information in order not to overwrite it unintentionally. As model merging techniques evolve, it will be interesting to compare such techniques with our solution.

Another approach to the problem is using information on the editing operations that took place on a model. Ráth et al. [13] propose a solution which does not define the transformation between models any more, but maps between model manipulation operations. The problem with this approach is that a model transformation must be described in terms of corresponding editing operations, which may be a tedious and error-prone task.

Varró et al. [15] describe a graph pattern matching algorithm similar to ours. They also use a tree structure to store partial matchings. When (in-place) graph transformation rules are applied, the matching tree is updated to reflect the changed graph, allowing the pattern matching itself to be incremental.

QVT-Relations [12] has a "check-before-enforce" transformation semantics which says that a pattern in the target model must be reused when there is an exact match with the target rule pattern. Nothing is reused if only parts of the target pattern can be matched. With this semantics, also QVT would delete and re-create the Mechatronic UML component in the above example. Even if we would change the semantics of QVT-Relations to allow for a better reuse of elements, algorithms for this semantics would yet have to be developed. Such an algorithm could use an approach similar to the one presented in this paper.

As mentioned before, performance was not in focus when developing the new synchronization. Therefore, it is likely that the heuristics and the search can still be improved. There exist several approaches for improving the performance of pattern matching. Varró et al. [16] use model-sensitive search plans that are selected during runtime. Especially when there are many elements marked for deletion that can possibly be reused, a dynamically selected search plan could also help increasing the performance in our case.

6 Conclusion and Future Work

We presented an improved incremental update mechanism that aims at minimizing the amount of unnecessarily deleted elements in the target model. In this way, much of the discipline-specific information that is not covered by the transformation can be preserved. The method is applicable not only for comparatively simple cases, like move operations, but also for more complex cases which involve alternative rule applications. One advantage of the technique is that it does not require the repair operations to be specified manually, but is a general solution and independent of the meta-models and the TGG rules.

The technique cannot prevent every possible inconsistency or loss of information. Therefore, are several improvements that plan to investigate in the future. One extension is to involve the use if it is not clear how existing element have to be reused. Furthermore, the heuristic presented in Sec. 4 can be improved. For instance, we have described that the best partial match is the one that reuses most correspondence nodes. But as different TGG rules may have different correspondence node types, it is reasonable to reuse correspondence information even if the types do not match (and thus the correspondence object as such cannot be reused). Last, the technique presented here only considers one single rule application when building the partial matching search tree. The algorithm could be extended to find a best partial match over several rule applications and in this way further increase the amount of elements that are reused. This basically requires backtracking over rule applications.

The presented technique works only for changes in a single model. We are currently working on extending our TGG approach to support scenarios where two concurrently modified models must be synchronized.

References

1. Burmester, S., Giese, H., Tichy, M.: Model-Driven Development of Reconfigurable Mechatronic Systems with Mechatronic UML. In: Aßmann, U., Rensink, A., Aksit, M. (eds.) MDAFA 2003. LNCS, vol. 3599, pp. 47–61. Springer, Heidelberg (2005)

2. Gausemeier, J., Frank, U., Donoth, J., Kahl, S.: Specification technique for the description of self-optimizing mechatronic systems. Research in Engineering Design 20(4), 201–223 (2009)
3. Gausemeier, J., Schäfer, W., Greenyer, J., Kahl, S., Pook, S., Rieke, J.: Management of Cross-Domain Model Consistency During the Development of Advanced Mechatronic Systems. In: Proc. of the 17th Int. Conference on Engineering Design (ICED 2009) (2009)
4. Giese, H., Hildebrandt, S.: Efficient Model Synchronization of Large-Scale Models. Tech. Rep. 28, Hasso Plattner Institute at the University of Potsdam (2009)
5. Giese, H., Wagner, R.: From model transformation to incremental bidirectional model synchronization. Software and Systems Modeling 8(1) (2009)
6. Greenyer, J., Kindler, E.: Comparing relational model transformation technologies: implementing Query/View/Transformation with Triple Graph Grammars. Software and Systems Modeling (SoSyM) 9(1) (2010)
7. Greenyer, J., Rieke, J.: Improved algorithm for preventing information loss in incremental model synchronization. Tech. Rep. tr-ri-11-324, Software Engineering Group, Department of Computer Science, University of Paderborn (2011)
8. Hearnden, D., Lawley, M., Raymond, K.: Incremental Model Transformation for the Evolution of Model-Driven Systems. In: Wang, J., Whittle, J., Harel, D., Reggio, G. (eds.) MoDELS 2006. LNCS, vol. 4199, pp. 321–335. Springer, Heidelberg (2006)
9. Jimenez, A.M.: Change Propagation in the MDA: A Model Merging Approach. Master's thesis, University of Queensland (2005)
10. Körtgen, A.T.: Modellierung und Realisierung von Konsistenzsicherungswerkzeugen für simultane Dokumentenentwicklung. Ph.D. thesis, RWTH Aachen University (2009)
11. Object Management Group (OMG): Meta Object Facility (MOF) Core 2.0 Specification (2006), http://www.omg.org/spec/MOF/2.0/
12. Object Management Group (OMG): MOF Query/View/Transformation (QVT) 1.0 Specification (2008), http://www.omg.org/spec/QVT/1.0/
13. Ráth, I., Varró, G., Varró, D.: Change-driven model transformations. In: Schürr, A., Selic, B. (eds.) MODELS 2009. LNCS, vol. 5795, pp. 342–356. Springer, Heidelberg (2009)
14. Schürr, A.: Specification of Graph Translators with Triple Graph Grammars. In: Mayr, E.W., Schmidt, G., Tinhofer, G. (eds.) WG 1994. LNCS, vol. 903. Springer, Heidelberg (1995)
15. Varró, G., Varró, D., Schürr, A.: Incremental Graph Pattern Matching: Data Structures and Initial Experiments. Graph and Model Transformation (2006)
16. Varró, G., Friedl, K., Varró, D.: Adaptive graph pattern matching for model transformations using model-sensitive search plans. Electronic Notes in Theoretical Computer Science 152 (2006)
17. Verein Deutscher Ingenieure: Design Methodology for Mechatronic Systems (2004)
18. Xiong, Y., Song, H., Hu, Z., Takeichi, M.: Supporting Parallel Updates with Bidirectional Model Transformations. In: Paige, R.F. (ed.) ICMT 2009. LNCS, vol. 5563, pp. 213–228. Springer, Heidelberg (2009)

An MDE-Based Approach for Solving Configuration Problems: An Application to the Eclipse Platform

Guillaume Doux[1], Patrick Albert[2], Gabriel Barbier[3], Jordi Cabot[1],
Marcos Didonet Del Fabro[4], and Scott Uk-Jin Lee[5]

[1] AtlanMod, INRIA & EMN, Nantes
[2] IBM France, Paris
[3] Mia-software, Nantes
[4] Universidade Federal do Paraná
[5] CEA, LIST, Gif-sur-Yvette

{Guillaume.Doux,Jordi.Cabot}@inria.fr, AlbertPa@fr.ibm.com,
gbarbier@mia-software.com, marcos.ddf@inf.ufpr.br,
Scott.Lee@cea.fr

Abstract. – Most of us have experienced configuration issues when installing new software applications. Finding the right configuration is often a challenging task since we need to deal with many dependencies between plug-ins, components, libraries, packages, etc; sometimes even regarding specific versions of the involved artefacts. Right now, most configuration engines are adhoc tools designed for specific configuration scenarios. This makes their reuse in different contexts very difficult. In this paper we report on our experience in following a MDE-based approach to solve configuration problems. In our approach, the configuration problem is represented as a model that abstracts all irrelevant technological details and facilitates the use of generic (constraint) solvers to find optimal solutions. This approach has been applied by an industrial partner to the management of plug-ins in the Eclipse framework, a big issue for all the technology providers that distribute Eclipse-based tools.

Keywords: Configuration, MDE, Eclipse, Plug-in, Cartography.

1 Introduction

Complex software systems are built by assembling components (components in a broad sense, i.e. COTS, libraries, plug-ins,...) coming from different repositories. This simplifies the development of the system but inevitably introduces an additional complexity dimension due to the need of managing these components. Each component can evolve independently and new releases can introduce/break dependencies with other components.

In particular, this is becoming a huge problem in the Eclipse community where new tools are built on top of several other plug-ins already available in the platform, many times requiring a specific version of the plug-ins. Therefore, releasing a new Eclipse tool implies a precise build definition for the tool that must be continuously evolved.

Therefore, technology providers commercializing Eclipse tools are looking for solutions that help them to automate and optimize the build definitions for their tools so that end-users do not need to suffer all these configuration problems. Right now, this very costly and time-consuming task requires a dedicated engineer in the provider company. This engineer needs to manually provide all the information regarding the tool dependencies, the plug-ins that can satisfy those dependencies and also the repositories where the plug-ins are available. Moreover, once everything is defined, the generated build definition needs to be empirically tested. Clearly, for non-trivial projects, this process does not scale.

In this paper, we propose to overcome this situation by means of using Model Driven Engineering and Constraint Programming techniques to automate the generation of build definitions. This work has been done in collaboration with two industrial partners: Mia-Software[1], a well-known technology provider in the Eclipse community that leads several Eclipse projects and IBM that has contributed its expertise in commercial constraint programming tools.

This paper is structured as follows. Section 2 discusses the motivations of our solution in an industrial environment. Section 3 presents the overall approach used to manage our Eclipse plug-ins configuration problem. Section 4 is focused on the management of the configuration as a Constraint Satisfaction Problem (CSP) whereas Section 5 describes the decision tree approach for finding configurations, and Section 6 illustrates the tool used to visualize the configurations. Section 7 presents the implementation, a comparison between the resolution approach described and the lessons learnt. Section 8 focuses on the related works and Section 9 concludes this study.

2 Motivation: Industrial Challenge

This work has been motivated by the need of Mia-Software to configure and control build definitions for its tools and to be able to update such definitions during the tool lifecycle.

A second (and more complex) requirement is to be able to tailor build definitions to different scenarios, such as targeting the minimal subset of elements to run the application in a headless mode (using scripts on a server), or selecting only non-GPL component to allow integration in proprietary applications.

The results of this work are being integrated in the MoDisco[2] and EMF Facet[3] Eclipse projects and in the custom developments the company builds internally for its clients.

As an example, the MoDisco Eclipse project alone contains 94 plug-ins (without the 30 test plug-ins) and depends directly or indirectly on around 920 additional plug-ins. For the time being, the MoDisco project has a dedicated plug-in to configure the build definition. This plug-in contains more than ten types of files to do so (ant files, xml files, properties files, cspec files, cquery files, mspec files, rmap files, xsl files, sh files and txt files). To be able to maintain all of these artifacts and to reproduce in a

---

[1] Mia-Software: http://www.mia-software.com/
[2] The MoDisco project: http://www.eclipse.org/MoDisco/
[3] The EMF Facet project: http://www.eclipse.org/modeling/emft/facet/

server environment the behavior of a development environment, a dedicated engineer is now assigned to the task. To initially configure the build definition one full month of the engineer was required. Unfortunately, due to the continuous evolution of the Eclipse platform this is not just a one-time effort. Every time there are new relevant plug-in versions or a new release of the Eclipse platform available, two or three additional days are spent in adapting the configuration (e.g. to update the locations of update sites for dependencies). Furthermore, the correctness of the process cannot be detected until the application is rebuilt again.

Therefore, MoDisco is clearly a tool that could benefit from the results of our work. It is worth to note that this kind of complex dependencies scenario is not the exception but the norm and thus, any tool that improves the current state of the art could have a real impact on current industrial practices of Mia-Software and similar technology providers.

3 Overall Approach

This section gives an overview of our Model Driven approach for solving Eclipse plug-ins configuration problems. Adopting an MDE approach has several advantages. First, it provides a homogeneous representation for all the technologies involved in the solution. Secondly, it allows designers to deal with the problem at a higher-abstraction level where some irrelevant details are omitted. And finally, the own Eclipse platform is moving more and more towards the adoption of model-based solutions (as the b3 Eclipse models used to define build generations) so an MDE approach perfectly fits in this scenario.

Our approach follows a three step process (see Fig. 1).

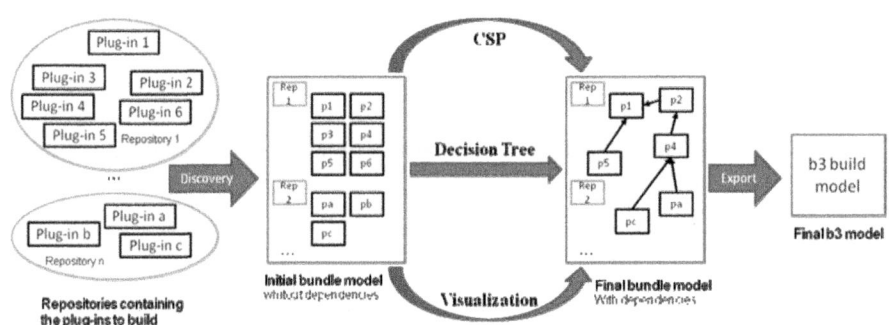

Fig. 1. Overview of the Eclipse plug-ins build generation process

In the first step, a discovery phase allows the designer to express the requirements for the tool/component/plug-in she wants to build and the possible locations (i.e. repositories) where to find plug-ins that satisfy those requirements. The information concerning these plug-ins such as the dependencies they need, the name, the version or every other useful information is stored in a plug-in model conforming to the metamodel presented in Figure 2. This metamodel allows the representation of the different elements needed for the plug-ins configuration representation. The main entity of this metamodel is the *Plugin* class whereas the main relationship between plug-ins is represented by the *PluginDependency* class. This class allows linking the plug-ins according to their dependencies. A second set of entities and relations is expressed with the *JavaPackage* and the *JavaPackageDependencies* classes. A *JavaPackageDependency* element allows the representation of the relation between a *Plugin* element and the imported *JavaPackage* elements. At this stage, we just have the "raw data", i.e. we have the candidate plug-ins but not yet the selected configuration.

This is done in the second step: a possible combination of the candidate plug-ins (i.e. respecting all their dependencies) is created either manually (visualization option), interactively (decision tree option) or automatically (constraint programming option). When several configurations are possible, the final selection can be driven by additional search criteria like newest versions of the plug-ins (default option), license or cost. We propose these three different ways to obtain a configuration since each one offers a different trade-off as explained later on. As a result of this step we get a refined plug-in model with information from the selected configuration for the build generation.

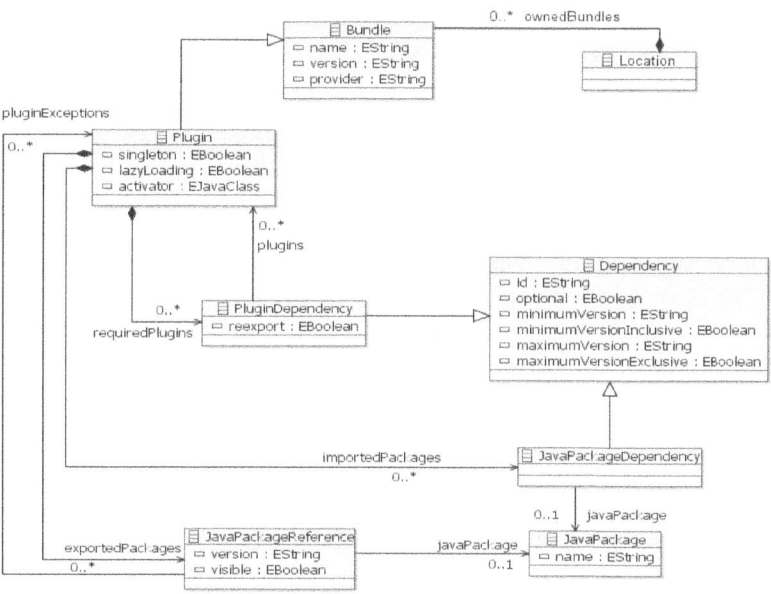

Fig. 2. Metamodel to represent the plug-ins

The last step is the generation of the final configuration file from the refined plug-in model. In our case the configuration will be expressed as a b3 model but it could easily be expressed as a Maven[4] file or Ant[5] script. The b3 Eclipse project focuses on

---

[4] The Maven project, http://maven.apache.org/
[5] The ANT project, http://ant.apache.org/

the development of a new generation of Eclipse technology to help building and assembling software. It proposes an approach using model driven engineering to represent the different artifacts that are relevant for building applications. More specifically, b3 proposes a metamodel to represent all of artifacts needed for the build, and execution support for these build models. Therefore in our approach the generation of the final configuration file is realized using model to model (or model to text in the case of Maven and ANT) transformations.

4 Configuration as a CSP

Constraint Programming [8] is a declarative problem solving paradigm where the programming process is limited to the definition of the set of requirements (constraints). A constraint solver is in charge of finding a solution that satisfies the requirements. Problems addressed by Constraint Programming are called constraint satisfaction problems (CSPs). A CSP is represented by the tuple CSP = <V,D,C> where V denotes the finite set of variables of the CSP, D the set of domains, one for each variable, and C the set of constraints over the variables. A solution to a CSP is an assignment of values to variables that satisfies all constraints, with each value within the domain of the corresponding variable.

We can represent the problem of configuration of Eclipse plug-ins as a CSP. This solution is a practical instantiation of the approach called *Model Search* [4].

The problem can be stated as follows: given a set of partially-connected Eclipse-plug-ins and a set of constraints that must be satisfied, find one (or the optimal, according to a given property) valid and executable build distribution. The constraints may be of different nature. For instance, defining version dependencies between the plug-ins, or specifying one desired vendor.

The constraints are written using OCL++. OCL++ is an adaptation of OCL (Object Constraint Language) [6]. OCL++ simplifies OCL for writing CSP problems. For instance, it enables writing multi-class invariants, which is a common construct in CSP problems. It also enables writing optimization functions.

More specifically, the re-expression of a configuration Eclipse problem in terms of a CSP is implemented as a chain of transformation operations over the initial plug-in model. Since Existing CSP solvers cannot directly read EMF models and OCL++ constraints as input, we need to translate the input artifacts into the CP language supported by the constraint solver of the ILOG OPL-CPLEX development bundle [7] engine, which is OPL (Optimization Programming Language). The OPL engine enables adding optimization functions, i.e., to find the best solution given an optimization criterion. The main steps of the process are:

1. Transformation of the Eclipse plug-in metamodel and the constraints into the OPL language.
2. Transformation of the input model into the OPL data format. The separation of the input model and metamodels into two transformations enables having independence between the problem specification (metamodels + constraints) and the input models with the initial data to start the CP process.
3. Execution of the CSP engine. This operation is called *model search*. During this phase the input model is extended with the solutions found by the engine.

However, the result produced by the CP engine is expressed as sets of integers, String and floats (the OPL output format).
4. Transformation of the output into a model conforming to the Eclipse plug-ins metamodel.

To facilitate the execution of these different steps a predefined script in charge of chaining the transformations is provided.

This approach combines the benefits of CSP with the advantages of expressing the problem at the model level (e.g. writing the constraints in OCL++). Moreover, the transformation chain makes the CP solver transparent to the user who provides and receives models as input/output of the process. Clearly, it would be even better that the transformation from the models to the CSP included an additional intermediate step where the CSP is expressed as instance of a solver-independent CSP metamodel. This would facilitate the utilization of different CSP solvers.

5 Decision Tree

Decision Trees is a strategy used in the field of Software Product Line (SPL) to illustrate all possible product configurations in terms of decisions on variations. It enables interactive configurations where user selects an appropriate decision for each variation to configure a particular product. The main benefits of utilizing decision tree in configuration are the clear presentation of all possible configurations and the ability to customize the configuration by allowing each decision made on variation to be based on different criteria. As only valid configurations are proposed in the decision tree, the build engineer work becomes simpler and safer using this approach. On the other hand, the strategy main limitation, compared to the CSP one, appears when there are a large number of choice criteria involving an important number of choices for the engineer. In that case, it can become difficult to manage efficiently a big configuration.

In order to take advantage of these benefits, we adapt the concept of decision tree and Sequoia, a UML based SPL tool embedded in Papyrus, to our configuration challenge. The main difference with the CSP implementation is in the generation of several build configurations instead of only one. This characteristic involves some user interactions for the final configuration choice. The process of Eclipse plug-ins configuration with Sequoia consists of different steps as described below:

1. **Construction of the initial bundle model in UML** – The initial bundle model obtained from the discovery phase must be transformed into a UML model since Sequoia is a UML specific tool. As in the Eclipse plug-ins problem, several versions of the same plug-in can exist, and thus, a way to identify plug-ins conforming to the same unique plug-in definition is needed. The plug-in definition can be seen as a "formal" plug-in having several "instance" plug-ins, corresponding to the different available version of this plug-in. In the transformation, formal plug-ins are defined as classes to type all the instance plug-ins of the model. Then, plug-in locations are defined as packages to group all plug-ins in the same location. Plug-in classes include useful metadata such as version, price and license. Each possible instantiation of the plug-in (i.e. different versions or vendors for the plug-in) instantiate these

classes with the appropriate information to be considered during the configuration. Dependencies for a plug-in are represented as a dependency relationship from the depender plug-in to the dependee plug-in class.
2. **Extraction of dependency constraints** – Once the initial bundle model is constructed in UML, the dependency constraints are extracted following the specific profile defined in Sequoia. In addition, the extraction process can also accommodate the dependencies with constraints on criteria by allocating all the instances of the class that meet the constraints. For example, a dependency from the plug-in instance 'a' to a plug-in class 'B' with the constraint limiting the version of 'B' to be less than 3.0 will be converted into the set of dependencies from 'a' to 'b' with version 1.0 and 'b' with version 2.0.
3. **Computation of dependency constraints** – Once all dependencies are expressed as constraints, Sequoia uses the formal verification tool Alloy Analyzer [8] to produce all feasible configurations. The result of the calculation represents all possible configuration of the plug-ins computed based on their dependencies and represented in a textual format.
4. **Decision tree creation** – After the computation, the extracted dependency constraints are analyzed against the textual result of the calculation to construct a decision tree with decision nodes representing dependency constraints and its resolution edges representing all the configuration decisions that satisfy that dependency. In addition, values of various plug-in criteria are calculated and indicated for each resolution edge. Users can use these values to make more informed choices when interacting with the tree.
5. **Transformation of decision tree into final bundle model** – Finally, an Eclipse plug-in configuration interactively generated from the decision tree is transformed into a final bundle model.

6 Visualization

The visualization mechanism allows quickly checking if the obtained configuration fits the user needs and, if several possible configurations have been produced, the user can choose the one he prefers from the visualizations. For simple configuration problems, the visualization of the plug-ins suffices to manually define the optimal configuration. Nevertheless, this kind of approach cannot be used to manage configurations involving an important number of elements, as the generated graph becomes too complex to be understandable. As an example, a visualization of an initial bundle model is shown Figure 3.

This visualization component relies on the cartography plug-in Portolan[6]. Integration with Portolan is easy since Portolan uses a model driven approach for the cartography analysis and visualization.

To visualize plug-in data we just need to link the plug-in metamodel with the generic cartography metamodel provided with Portolan and, optionally, configure the view definitions that filter the input data and specify how this data will be visualized. The relationship between the plug-in and the cartography metamodels is done by

---

[6] Portolan website: http://code.google.com/a/eclipselabs.org/p/portolan/

defining the plug-in metaclasses as subclasses of the two main cartography metaclasses (entity and relationship). Once this is done, transforming data conforming to the plug-in metamodel to data conforming to the cartography metamodel is trivial (it is mainly a simple copy transformation).

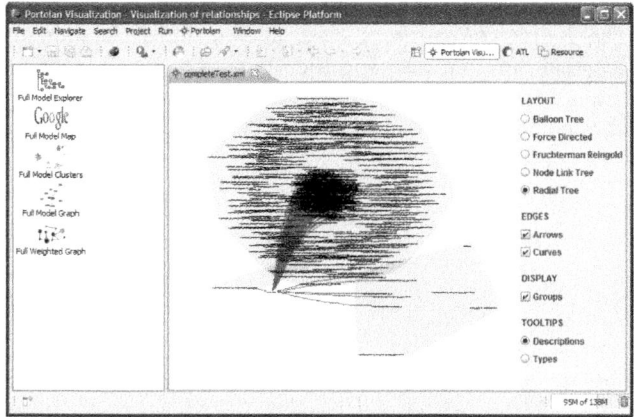

Fig. 3. Screenshot of the visualization tool

7 Implementation and Preliminary Results

The MDE-based approach presented here for solving Eclipse configuration problems has been implemented as an Eclipse set of plug-ins that provide the discovery of available plug-ins, the computation of possible dependencies, their visualization and the final build generation services. These functionalities are briefly presented in this section.

The discovery functionality is implemented as an Eclipse file creation wizard. This wizard proposes the creation of a model which is conforming to our metamodel dedicated to the Eclipse bundles representation (presented in Figure 2). To this aim, it allows selecting several plug-ins present in the workspace and then choosing the update sites that have to be considered when discovering candidate plug-ins for the bundle model.

The connection with the configuration engines (both the CSP and the decision tree versions) has been implemented as described in their respective sections. Also, as indicated, the visualization service is implemented using a model driven cartography tool called Portolan. A specific extension of Portolan has been designed for this study to be able to visualize configuration models.

The build generation functionality takes the feedback from the previous configuration plug-ins and generates a b3 model representing the selected configuration. This is mainly done by executing an ATL transformation between the internal model conforming to the plug-in metamodel (presented in Figure 2) and the final b3 model conforming to the b3 metamodel. This b3 model will be processed by the b3 engine to drive the build generation (by retrieving the needed plug-ins and launching the different steps of the application build). An excerpt of the b3 metamodel (Figure 4) presents the main elements used for the build generation. The *BeeModel* class represents the build model root; this class contains references to the *BuildUnit* and *Repository* elements used. In the model, a *BuildUnit* represents something to build with b3, in our case it will be a bundle (in the general case, it can also be a library or any other kind of component). The *repositories* reference of *BuildUnit* allows knowing which repositories can be used for the build unit's resolution. The *BuildUnitRepository* class allows the declaration of a build unit repository location in b3. A specific type of it is represented by the *BeeModelRepository* class; this repository declaration refers to the *BeeModel* to use for building the components contained in the repository.

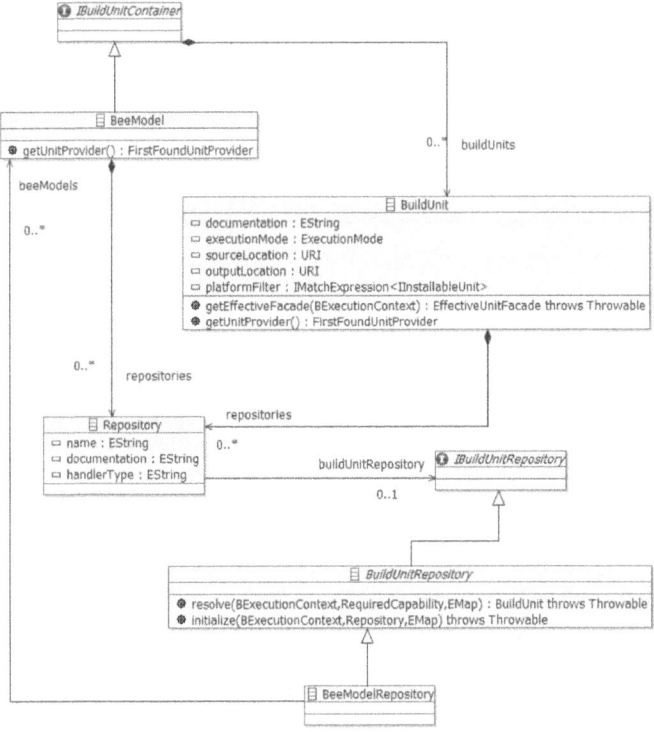

Fig. 4. Representative Excerpt of the b3 Metamodel

Of course, other alternative implementations (e.g. Maven, ANT) of this service could easily be provided using the own Eclipse extension mechanisms.

After the initial set of experiments we have been able to validate that all three strategies (CSP, decision tress and purely visualization) can be used to solve the configuration problem. Each one has its own trade-offs and is best suited to address a specific kind of configuration problem. This is exactly the reason why we decided to keep the three of them in the framework without clearly favoring any of them.

The CSP-based approach is the best option when looking for a completely automatic solution. It is also recommended when looking for a single solution according to a specific criteria and when dealing with very complex problems (on which human interaction is not feasible).

Decision trees is an intermediate solution. It does most part of the job automatically (calculating all possible solutions) but still gives some flexibility to the designer to influence the final choice.

Visualization per se is only useful for simple solutions as an aid for the designer but it is a good complement to the other two as a visualization tool for the computer-generated solutions.

Besides this, the realization of this project has also shown the benefits of MDE when used as a tool for the unification of heterogeneous domain, such as the Eclipse plug-ins and the constraint programming domains. By expressing both domains (i.e. technical spaces) as models, we obtain a homogeneous representation that facilitates the transformation/communication between them.

Nevertheless, these first experiments have also pointed out some challenges that need to be addressed in the future. Reasoning tools usually suffer from scalability problems and our scenario is not an exception. Sometimes user interaction is required just because the search space is too big to get an answer from the solver in a reasonable time and the designer must help to reduce it by providing additional constraints to limit the search.

Also, our approach suffers from the lack of standards in the constraint programming domain. Even if part of the transformation chain is generic, the last steps are solver-dependent and need to be reimplemented if the development team decides to use a different solver in the future.

We are now working in both aspects. For instance, regarding the second one we are adopting the idea of a CSP solver-independent metamodel that abstracts until the last step the specificities of the solver to use. The translation of the configuration information present in a solver independent model into solver specific models becomes easy to specify using model transformations and should permit to choose the most appropriated solver for the configuration resolution.

8 Related Work

An alternative solution for plug-in management in Eclipse is called p2 [2]. This solution proposes to use the metadata of the plug-ins to create a set of constraints that are solved with the SAT solver SAT4j[7]. In this approach there is no explicit modeling of the problem so designers cannot define additional constraints about the desired characteristics of the solution (e.g. to get an optimal configuration). Moreover, since the translation is adhoc cannot be reused. Besides this, this approach only focuses on one of the alternative strategies we have explored.

Another interesting proposal is [1]. It proposes to use a model driven approach to represent the configuration and available packages for FOSS distributions. These models are then used to predict the effect of changes on the installed package base

---

[7] Sat4j website: http://www.sat4j.org/

(e.g. upgrades) on the system configuration. As our own work, this approach brings the advantages of working at a higher abstraction level when compared with approaches that rely on a direct manipulation of the available metadata. Nevertheless, our approach is able to deal with a more general problem since we are able to create the entire configuration and not only simulate/predict what would happen if something changes.

The topic of translating models into other formalisms for an automatic analysis has been explored in several previous approaches (e.g. [10-13]) but they mostly focus on specific kinds of UML diagrams. Some of these techniques could be adapted to our configuration models and integrated in our framework to provide additional analysis capabilities.

9 Conclusions

This paper reports a collaboration between industrial and research partners to solve configuration problems faced by technology providers using a combination of model-driven engineering and constraint programming techniques.

We have focused on the specific configuration problems for tools developed on top of the Eclipse platform that need to manage and solve a lot of plug-in dependencies. This use case has been provided by Mia-software, a software editor specialized in the application Model Driven approaches for the software lifecycle industrialization with plenty of experience in the development of Eclipse projects.

As further work, we plan to generalize our framework to deal with configuration problems in other domains. The core of the approach can be easily reused but specific metamodels (e.g. Linux packages metamodel for Linux distributions configuration) need to be developed for each specific application domain.

Acknowledgement. This work has been partially funded by ANR IdM++ project.

References

1. Cicchetti, A., Di Ruscio, D., Pelliccione, P., Pierantonio, A., Zacchiroli, S.: Towards a model driven approach to upgrade complex software systems. In: Maciaszek, L.A., González-Pérez, C., Jablonski, S. (eds.) ENASE 2008/2009. Communications in Computer and Information Science, vol. 69, pp. 262–276. Springer, Heidelberg (2010)
2. Le Berre, D., Rapicault, P.: Dependency management for the eclipse ecosystem. In: Proceedings of IWOCE 2009, International workshop on Open Component Ecosystems (2009)
3. Gruber, O., Hargrave, B.J., McAffer, J., Rappicault, P., Watson, T.: The eclipse 3.0 platform: Adopting osgi technology. IBM Systems Journal 44(2) (2005)
4. Kleiner, M., Del Fabro, M.D., Albert, P.: Model Search: Formalizing and Automating Constraint Solving in MDE Platforms. In: Kühne, T., Selic, B., Gervais, M.-P., Terrier, F. (eds.) ECMFA 2010. LNCS, vol. 6138, pp. 173–188. Springer, Heidelberg (2010)
5. EMF. Eclipse Modeling Project. Reference site, http://www.eclipse.org/emf
6. OCL 2.0 specification (2008), http://www.omg.org/spec/OCL/2.0/

7. ILOG OPL-CPLEX development bundle (January 2010), http://www-01.ibm.com/software/integration/optimization/cplex-dev-bundles/
8. Jackson, D.: Alloy: a lightweight object modelling notation. ACM Transactions on Software Engineering and Methodology 11(2), 256–290 (2002)
9. Apt, K.R.: Principle of Constraint Programming. Cambridge University Press, Cambridge (2003)
10. Brucker, A.D., Wolff, B.: The HOL-OCL book. Technical Report 525, ETH Zurich (2006)
11. Cabot, J., Clarisó, R., Riera, D.: UMLtoCSP: a tool for the formal verification of UML/OCL models using constraint programming. In: ASE 2007, pp. 547–548 (2007)
12. Van Der Straeten, R., Mens, T., Simmonds, J., Jonckers, V.: Using description logic to maintain consistency between UML models. In: Stevens, P., Whittle, J., Booch, G. (eds.) UML 2003. LNCS, vol. 2863, pp. 326–340. Springer, Heidelberg (2003)
13. Anastasakis, K., Bordbar, B., Georg, G., Ray, I.: Uml2alloy: A challenging model transformation. In: ACM/IEEE 10th International Conference on Model Driven Engineering Languages and Systems, pp. 436–450 (2007)

Incremental Updates for View-Based Textual Modelling

Thomas Goldschmidt[1] and Axel Uhl[2]

[1] ABB Corporate Research, Ladenburg, Germany
thomas.goldschmidt@de.abb.com
[2] SAP AG, Walldorf, Germany
axel.uhl@sap.com

Abstract. Model-Driven Engineering (MDE) aims at improving the development of software systems. Within this context textual concrete syntaxes for models are beneficial for many reasons. They foster usability and productivity because of their fast editing style, their usage of error markers, autocompletion and quick fixes. Several frameworks and tools from different communities for creating concrete textual syntaxes for models emerged during recent years. On the other side, view-based modelling enables for different views on a central model which helps modellers to focus on specific aspects. However, combining textual and view-based modelling has not been tackled by research to a satisfying extent. Open issues include the handling and synchronisation of partial and federated textual views with the underlying model. In this paper we present an approach for concrete textual syntaxes that makes use of incremental parsing and transformation techniques. Thus, we circumvent problems that occur when dealing with concrete textual syntaxes in view-based modelling.

1 Introduction

Today Model-Driven Engineering (MDE) gains a considerable momentum in software industries. MDE provides means to create, view and manipulate models at different levels of abstraction as well as different development roles. An important part of a modelling language apart from the metamodel itself is its concrete syntax. Today's languages mostly have either a graphical or a textual concrete syntax. As a manifestation of syntaxes, specialised views on a common underlying model may foster the understanding and productivity [1] of model engineers. Recent work [2] even promoted view-based aspects of modelling as core paradigm. For graphical concrete syntaxes view-based modelling, which enables modellers to focus on specific aspects, is a state-of-the-art technique. However, textual modelling does not yet profit from this paradigm.

A challenge that needs to be solved in order to develop a textual, view-based modelling approach is the synchronisation of the textual representation with an underlying model. Within partial views on a model, not all of the model's information is represented in a single view. Only the combination of all views allows to give a complete picture of the model. Thus, traditional textual modelling tools (see [3]) fail to support view-based modelling as they will discard and re-create all model elements upon re-parsing of the textual representation. As this representation may be incomplete, i.e., being a partial view, a complete reconstruction of such model elements is not possible.

Approaches for incremental parsing and the creation of development environments including language specific editors have been developed in the compiler construction community many years ago [4,5,6,7]. However, such incremental parsing techniques focus on optimizing the performance of syntactic and semantic analysis and do not consider the identity of elements that are constructed. This is also the way current textual modelling techniques [8,9] employ these techniques. An adoption to the specific problems of view-based, textual modelling is still lacking. Other approaches [10], follow a syntax directed editing[1] approach, allowing only editing commands which are atomic w.r.t. the underlying model. Thus keeping the model and its representation in synch at all times. However, this restricts the freedom of editing to only write text that is syntactically correct.

The approach presented in this paper is based on a view-based, textual modelling approach called FURCAS[2][11] that combines textual syntaxes with view-based modelling. In [12] we presented an approach that allows for the representation of models as textual views. Now, within this paper we base on our existing work and present an approach that implements the synchronisation from textual views to the underlying model.

The contribution of this paper is the following. By using incremental parsing techniques and analysis of the changes that occurred since the last parsing we retain model elements from the previous version of the model. This novel technique is not constrained by the atomicity of editing commands, as syntax directed approaches are. Thus, allowing for more freedom for modellers when working with textual views. With the presented approach we enable for multiple, partial views on an underlying model within textual modelling.

The remainder of this paper is structured as follows. Section 2 deals with related work. Some background information on FURCAS is presented in Section 3. Section 4 introduces our running example. We describe the developed incremental update technique in Section 5. A discussion on the validation of the approach is presented in Section 6. Section 7 concludes and presents future work.

2 Related Work

Several approaches for defining concrete textual syntaxes for metamodels emerged from the model-driven community [13,9,14] (see [3] for a complete list). An assumption made by these approaches is that it is possible to re-create model elements from the textual representation without losing information. As for view-based modelling, this assumption does not hold, neither of them supports this paradigm.

The idea of having a tighter integration of concrete and abstract syntax was already thoroughly researched in the compiler construction community several years ago. For example, the IPSEN approach [5] introduced a tightly integrated software development environment, including incremental update and storage of the abstract syntax elements as leading entities. Also the generation of the environment including editors featuring

---

[1] In syntax directed editing, the user is guided through the creation process using some kind of completion menu. That means the only way to change the text is by invoking predefined commands on the text. No free editing is possible.
[2] **F**ramework for **UUID-R**etaining Concrete to **A**bstract **S**yntax Mappings)

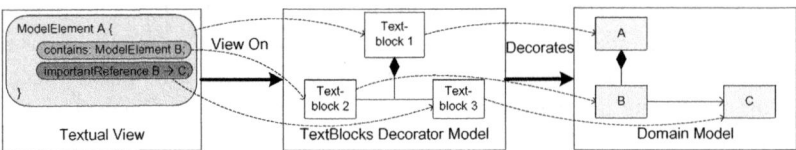

Fig. 1. Overview on the FURCAS decorator approach

syntax directed autocompletion and error checking could already be generated out of an attributed grammar. Another approach that is based on this idea is the Cornell Language Synthesizer (CLS) [6]. The incremental update processes of this approach were mainly focused on reducing the effective compilation time of programs. Furthermore, the way of editing within the CLS approach was completely restricted to syntax directed editing.

A more recent approach that works using the syntax-directed editing is the Meta Programming System (MPS) [10] that allows to define languages that consist of syntactical elements that look like dynamically-arranged table cells. This means that the elements of the language are predefined boxes which can be filled with a value. MPS follows the MVC updating approach that allows for direct editing of the underlying model. This allows the editor to easily provide features such as syntax highlighting or code completion. However, it is not possible to write code freely and save intermediate inconsistent states. Furthermore, it is not possible to define partial or overlapping views that go beyond the sheer hiding of the underlying UUIDs.

Previous work on FURCAS deals with a more specific problem definition of the textual, view-based modelling problem [15], i.e., the retainment of UUIDs of model elements in textual modelling. The UUID of a model element can be seen as a special property that is hidden in the concrete representation of a model element. Thus, we can consider all concrete syntaxes not showing the UUID as being partial. This work also introduces ideas to classify the editing events in order to identify the users intention when doing textual modelling. Furthermore, the textual view approach used by FURCAS was defined in [12]. A tool-oriented view on FURCAS was presented in [11]. We presented an initial idea on how to realise an incremental update process for textual views in [16]. However, a detailed presentation of the approach is still missing.

3 Background on FURCAS

FURCAS employs a decorator approach for view-based textual modelling. This means that an additional model called *TextBlocks(TB)-Model* annotates the underlying model and tells the FURCAS editor how the model should be presented as text. This is comparable to the approach that is used in the Graphical Modelling Framework (GMF) that decorates models with information on how to render them as diagrams. Figure 1 depicts an overview on the decorator concept. It shows that the textual representation is only a transient view based on the information stored in the domain model and the annotating TextBlocks model.

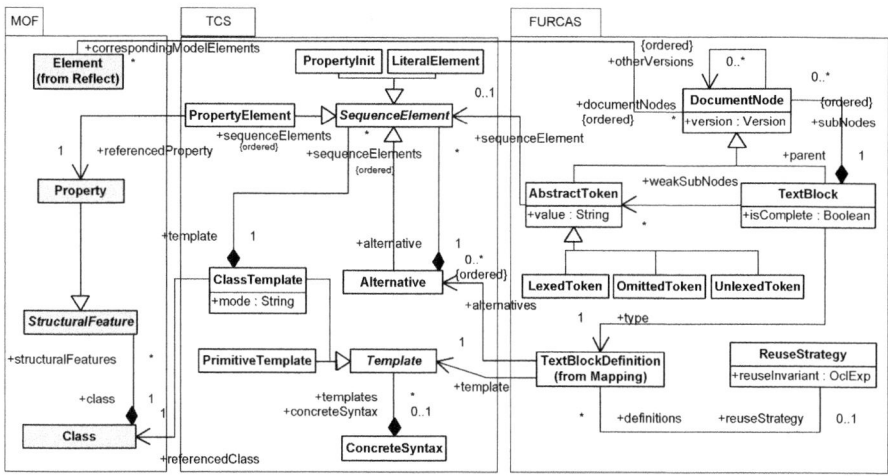

Fig. 2. Simplified version of the TCS and TextBlocks metamodels

TCS: FURCAS is based on the Textual Concrete Syntax (TCS) approach published by Jouault et al [13]. TCS is used to define the mappings between the domain metamodel and its textual syntax. A simplified version of the TCS metamodel is shown in the TCS package in figure 2. TCS is a template language that has a grammar-like structure in which it defines rules (`ClassTemplate`) for the metamodel classes that should get a textual syntax. Within these templates it is possible to define `Alternatives`, literals (`LiteralRef`) as well as `PropertyElements` which serve as expansions to the corresponding templates of the property's type.

There are many more additional features that are not explained in this short overview, we refer to [13] for a detailed description of the concepts of TCS. FURCAS extends the mapping concepts of TCS by adding constructs that define how partial and overlapping views as well as the construction of TextBlocks should be handled.

From such a syntax definition, we generate a parser grammar and from that a parser implementation (we use ANTLR [17] as parser generator). This includes a lexer part as well as a LL(1) parser with syntactic predicates.

TextBlocks: The FURCAS package in figure 2 presents the TextBlocks metamodel. It defines `TextBlocks` which represent the major building blocks of the decorator model as well as several subtypes of `AbstractToken` which are used to store format information and represent textual values. Both elements define references to `Elements` of an underlying model and through this reference decide whether it appears in the textual representation. So-called TextBlockDefinition elements from the connection between a TextBlock-Model and the concrete syntax definition. Therefore, each TextBlock has a `type` which transitively refers to a `Template` of the syntax definiton. For tokens, this connection is resembled by the `sequenceElement` property which refers to the corresponding `Property` or `LiteralRef` elements of the syntax. A more detailed explanation of the TextBlocks metamodel can be found in [12].

4 Running Example

The syntax definition given in Figure 3 will serve as running example to explain the update approach. It defines a view type for the representation a part of the example metamodel also given in Figure 3. The view type is partial, some elements from the metamodel (marked in grey) are not included in the textual syntax,

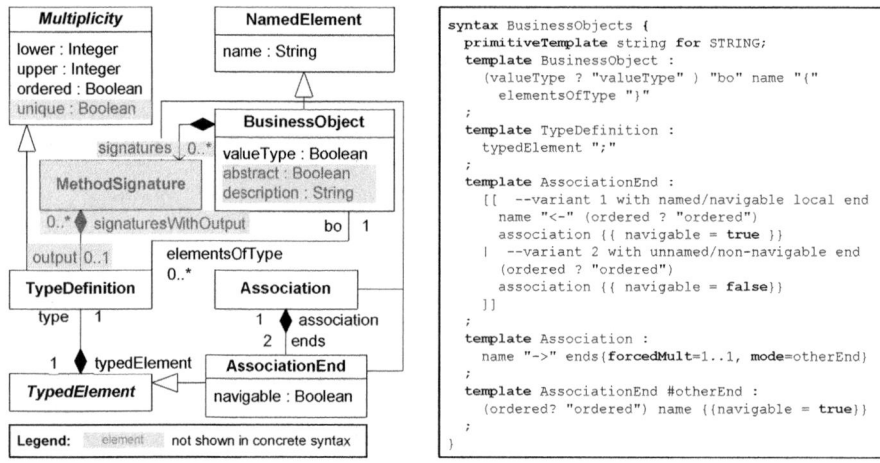

Fig. 3. Example businessobjects metamodel and textual view definition

The given syntax allows to specify Associations between *BusinessObjects*. These Associations may be navigable in both directions depending on whether a name is specified for the local end (variant 1) or not (variant 2). The metamodel also allows that a BusinessObject has signatures and other attributes that the syntax does not show. This is to demonstrate the requirement for retaining partially viewed model elements upon updates from the textual syntax, as not all information is contained in the textual view.

An example instance (*CustomerModel*) of the business objects metamodel is given in Figure 4. This example shows the textual representation, the corresponding Text-Block-Model (*CustomerView*) as well as the relation of the TextBlock-Model to the underlying domain model. There are two scenarios how this setting could have been produced. First, the *CustomerModel* was pre-existing and a modeller opened it in the FURCAS editor, which led to the creation of the *CustomerView* which serves as basis for the FURCAS editor that shows the textual representation. In the second scenario, the modeller started from an empty FURCAS editor and created the textual represenation leading to an initial *CustomerModel*. Then the (or a different) modeller edited the model in a different view adding all information that is not editable through the *CustomerView*.

As the TypeDefinition does not have a syntax contribution of its own, the element is included in the corresponding model elements of the respective AssociationEnd. The elements and attributes marked in grey are not shown in the textual representation. Therefore, simply re-creating all elements from the text would lead to loosing those

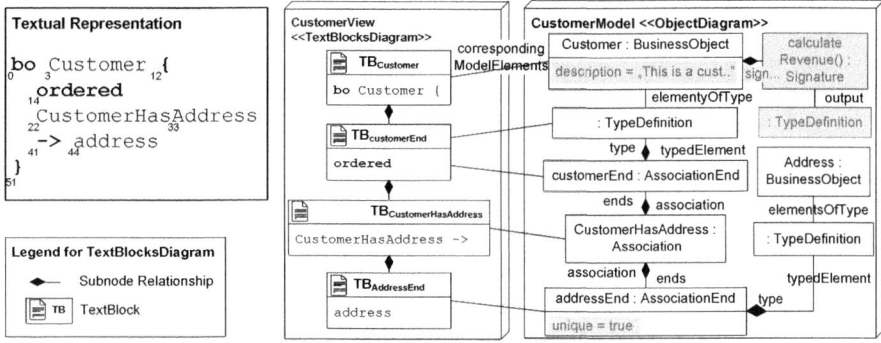

Fig. 4. TextBlock-Model for the running example

elements and values. For example, just from re-parsing the text it is not known whether the *addressEnd* element was *unique* or not.

5 Synchronisation from Textual View to Model

Given an existing TextBlock-Model for an underlying model a modeller can make modifications to the textual representation which are then directly reflected in the TextBlock-Model. To be able to react to all possible editing events and perform the incremental update to the model accordingly we first present a classification of such changes based on their scope. According to these categories we define the incremental update approach in subsequent sections. The validation presented in Section 6, then elaborates on the completeness of our approach based on these categories.

5.1 Classification of Changes to the Textual Representation of a Model

The incremental update approach is based on the possible modifications that a TextBlock-Model may be subject to. We distinguishes between three different scopes of changes to a TextBlock-Model *tokens*, *blocks* and *regions*.

A token is the smallest entity which can be affected by a change. For example, given a token with the value "Customer", a change on token level may affect the value to be changed to "valueType Customer". Still, depending on the rules for the lexical analysis such a change may also lead to the creation of a new token, resulting in the tokens "valueType" and "Customer".

Changes on *block* level are modifications of more than one token at a time but still belonging to a single root TextBlock. A TextBlock may include subblocks as well as tokens. However, a change on block level must always include *all* subblocks and (transitive) tokens of a given block. For example the deletion of the text "ordered CustomerHasAddress -> address" which conforms to one complete block of our running example would be considered a change on block level. Thus, changes on block level are creation/deletion/move move events of TextBlocks.

Changes that occur on *region* level can span over more than one block but do not include the whole block. For example, the cutting of the last three of four tokens of one block including the first token and the first subblock of the subsequent block would be a modification on region level. Changes that occur on region level but are not at the same time only on block level or only on token level are changes to an *inconsistent region*.

5.2 Incremental Update Approach

The FURCAS incremental update process depicted in Figure 5 is, after reacting to a modification event through the editor (0), divided into the following phases: (I) *self-versioning of TextBlocks* , (II) *incremental lexing*, (III) *incremental parsing*, (IV) *TextBlock merging* and (V) *model update*. The following sections will explain these phases step by step in detail. We will explain each step using the running example.

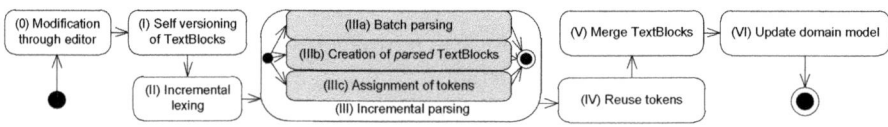

Fig. 5. Overview on the phases of the incremental textual view to domain model update process

(0) Modification Through Editor. The FURCAS text editor projects its underlying TextBlock-Model to a textual view. By typing or deleting characters, the modeller produces events that are passed to the appropriated places in the TextBlock-Model. These events can be denoted as $Event(o, l, t)$. In this form the offset o denotes the index starting from the first character of the text where the change occurred, the length l denotes how many characters, starting from the character at o are overwritten and the text t gives the set of characters to be replaced. Depending on the range of characters that are overwritten, FURCAS determines the scope of the change according to the classification presented in Section 5.1. For the elements in the determined scope, the self-versioning phase is triggered.

(I) Self Versioning of the TextBlock-Model. To be able to analyse the changes to the TextBlock-Model in later phases, we use a change history based on an in-place versioning of the TextBlock-Model. The FURCAS meta-model (Figure 2) incorporates capabilities of so-called self-versioning documents [4]. Self-versioning documents are characterised by the ability to navigate back and forth in the change history of a document by means of the document itself. To achieve this in FURCAS, we use the `DocumentNodeHasVersions` association for linking different versions of a Text-Block or a token to each other. Each `DocumentNode` furthermore includes an attribute `version` that determines the version of the node. Other versions of a node can be retrieved by traversing the `DocumentNodeHasVersions` association transitively until the desired version of a node is reached.

The different phases work on four different versions of nodes in a TextBlock-Model:

Reference is the version of the node in its last consistent state. This means that the TextBlock-Model forms a consistent view on the underlying model. Thus, each

TextBlock has at least one link to a corresponding model element and all tokens within the TextBlock are valid w.r.t. the lexer of the current syntax. Furthermore, the type of the TextBlock, i.e., the corresponding TextBlockDefinition, is correctly set. The same applies for tokens referring to the SequenceElements of the syntax.

Edited is the version after one or more editing events were received. Thus, this version already contains the textual change information in a raw format, as it is just text that is either placed in the value of the tokens at the targeted offset of the event.

Lexed is the version that the incremental lexer produces during the incremental lexing process. In this version, tokens already get their lexical type assigned and thus are valid tokens. However, the SequenceElements have not yet been assigned. TextBlocks are just copies of the *edited* version responsible for organising the tokens into a tree structure.

Parsed is the version that the incremental parser produces during the incremental parsing process. In this version, each TextBlock has its TextBlockDefinition and chosen alternative assigned.

The self-versioning phase will create a new version for each token and/or TextBlock within the scope of a given change event. Even if the scope of a change is limited to a single token, the token's parent TextBlock will also get a new version. Still, the new TextBlock will then only have this single token as child. The versioning of these parent TextBlocks is required for the comparison of the merge phase.

The self-versioning phase reacts to the different event types as follows. For *token level* changes we simply update the targeted token accordingly. Note, that for deletion of text, i.e., using events of the form $Event(o, l > 0, "")$, the targeted tokens will receive an empty value and are in this way marked for deletion. Analogously, this applies for changes on *block level*, meaning that all (transitive sub-)tokens of the targeted block will get empty values. Finally, for changes on *region level*, self-versioning is performed up to a common ancestor of the modified nodes. This may also be the root element of the document. All tokens and TextBlocks directly affected by a change event are modified as on *block* and *token* level, respectively.

Figure 6 shows the running example after the following two editing events: $Event(0, 0, "valueType\_")$ and $Event(12, 7, "customer\_<-\_ordered")$. The tokens at the positions to where the editing events point are self-versioned into their *edited* version. The self-versioning mechanism also creates *edited* versions for the TextBlocks that contain the modified tokens. These TextBlocks then contain the *edited* tokens.

(II) Incremental Lexing. The incremental lexing process is based on an algorithm presented by Wagner in [4]. Basically, this approach works as follows: In Wagner's approach the self versioned documents support the incremental lexing process. The information of the newer versions are compared to the reference versions. The outcome of this comparison is then used to decide where new tokens have to be produced. Wagner proofs that the lexing process is always optimal with respect to complexity. In FURCAS, we reuse Wagner's approach and extend it for the purpose of synchronising textual views with their underlying model. The extension mainly consists in the adoption of the approach to the TextBlock metamodel as well as the maintenance of the links between TextBlocks, tokens and their corresponding model elements.

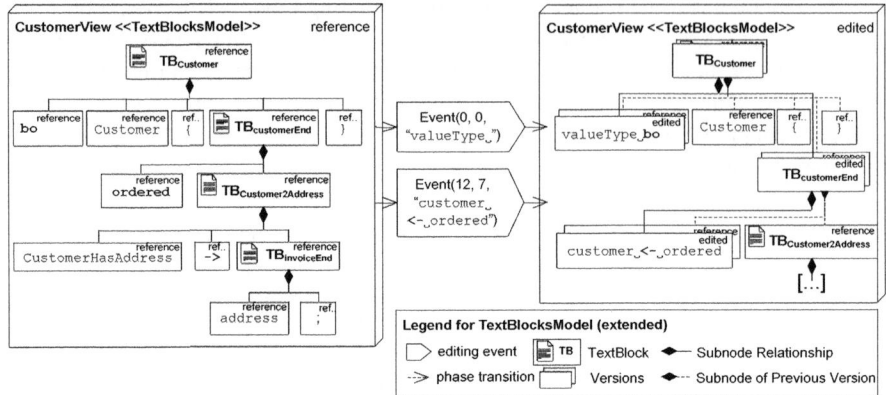

Fig. 6. TextBlock-Model for the running example after the self versioning phase I

The incremental lexing process creates new tokens for the modified tokens based on the lexical rules of the syntax. The incrementality of Wagner's lexing approach ensures that we only create new tokens where required.

For change events on *token level*, the new tokens will have the token of the *edited* version as originating version. Thus, all new tokens created from a token in *edited* version will reference that token in their otherVersions property. For *block* and *region level* changes, the versioning links will resemble a fully meshed network between the newly created *lexed* and the overwritten *edited* version. This ensures that in phase (IV), all possibly reusable tokens can be reached from each of the *lexed* tokens. Note, that by referencing the *edited* version, the versioning also transitively reaches the corresponding *reference* version.

In the running example (depicted in Figure 7) a token "ordered"$_{reference}$ is modified to "customer <- ordered"$_{edited}$ by the insertion of the new text "customer <-". The incremental lexer then creates three tokens "customer"$_{lexed}$, "<-"$_{lexed}$ and "ordered"$_{lexed}$ from that token. All three *lexed* tokens will then refer to "ordered"$_{reference}$ as their *reference* and "customer <- ordered"$_{edited}$ as their *edited* version.

(III) Incremental Parsing. The incremental parsing process is, opposed to conventional incremental parsing algorithms like [18], not based on pruning and grafting subtrees of the abstract syntax tree. Instead, in phase (IIIa) a conventional LL parser (see Section 3) is used to parse the tokens coming from phase (II). During phase (IIIa) two parallel phases (IIIb) and (IIIc) receive information about matched parse rules and consumed tokens through callbacks from the parser. Based on the matched parse rules of that parser FURCAS instantiates a new version, i.e., the *parsed* version, of the TextBlock-Model. Most importantly, during this sub-phase, FURCAS assigns the TextBlock-Definitions and chosen alternatives to the created TextBlocks. Sub-phase (IIIc) assigns tokens consumed by the parser in phase (IIIa) to the TextBlocks created in phase (IIIb). Furthermore, phase (IIIc) assigns the SequenceElements to which the tokens conform.

(IIIa) The Batch Parsing Process. The batch parsing process uses the the tokens as they result from the *lexed* version of the TextBlock-Model. Thus, the parser only runs on

those parts of the TextBlock-Model which were affected by changes in previous phases. However, this may require to call parse rules of common parents of the changed regions. Calling the parser only on sub-trees of the TextBlock-Model is not a requirement of our approach, we use this technique only to improve performance of the incremental update process. Later phases would also work if the parser runs for the complete TextBlock-Model. Therefore, this phase is also independent from the actual change scope and works on *token*, *block* and *region* level alike.

(IIIb) Creation of the Parsed *Version of a TextBlock-Model.* During the parsing process the parser instantiates TextBlock in their *parsed* version. Basis for the creation of this blocks is the selection of parse rules the parser decides to take. Each generated parse rule contains a parse action that identifies the template from which the rule was generated. This action attaches the corresponding TextBlockDefinition for that template to the newly instantiated TextBlock. The same applies to the alternatives that the parse rule chose during its execution.

(IIIc) Assignment of Tokens to Parsed *TextBlocks.* This phase assigns the consumed, *lexed* version tokens to the new *parsed* version of the TextBlocks. For this assignment we use the separate `weakSubNodes` property (see metamodel in Figure 2). Therefore, these tokens still keep their original TextBlock (*lexed* version) as composite parent. The combination of this assignment and the original assignment of tokens to their parent TextBlocks then serves as basis for the merging phase (V).

(IV) Reuse Tokens. To be able to decide which modified parts of a TextBlock-Model still represent the same decorated model element we need to analyse the semantics of the performed modifications. This analysis starts on token level by identifying which tokens from the *reference* version can be reused for the *lexed* version. A precondition for the correct assignment of *lexed* tokens to their *reference* version correspondents is that each token has its corresponding sequence element assigned. The sequence element represents the location of an element within the syntax and therefore the meaning of a token. As shown in the metamodel in Figure 2 a token has two properties that may be subject to change, `sequenceElement` and `value`. Thus, there are different cases

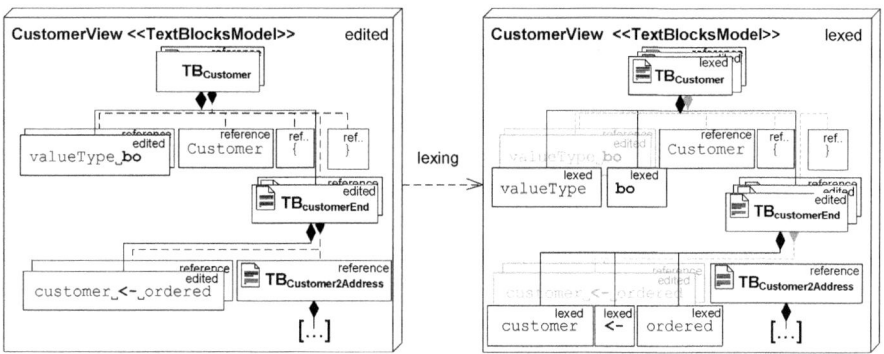

Fig. 7. TextBlock-Model for the running example after the incremental lexing phase II

that may qualify a token for reuse, each based on the values of these properties. Ordered by priority, these cases, which we call *reuse qualifiers*, are:

1. The `sequenceElement` of both tokens is the same. Tokens may refer to the *same sequence element*, thus having the same semantics, which qualifies for reuse.
2. Even if a token has a different sequence element, this sequence element may be a corresponding sequence element in a different alternative that represents the same property/literal (see running example in Figure 8). This also qualifies for reuse.
3. In the first two cases `value` may or may not have changed. However, if `sequenceElement` is different and not comparable through alternatives the token may still have the same `value` which also qualifies for reuse.

If there are multiple candidate tokens that match these criteria FURCAS takes the priority of the qualifiers into account. The token which matches the qualifier with the highest priority wins. If there are multiple tokens matching the same property, the overall amount of matching qualifiers weighted by their priorities determines which token to reuse. The following formula determines this reuse factor for a given token tok over the set of reuse qualifiers Q where $priority(q)$ gives the priority of a qualifier and $matches_q(tok)$ determins whether tok matches the qualifier q:

$$reuseFactor(tok) = \sum_{q \in Q} \begin{cases} 10^{priority(q)} & \text{if } matches_q(tok) \\ 0 & \text{else} \end{cases}$$

For example, a token matching the priority 1 as well as 3 would have a reuse factor of $10^{-1} + 0 + 10^{-3} = 0.101$.

In the running example, Figure 8 depicts the reusability of the *edited/reference* tokens. For the first change event two candidates for token reusability exist. Both tokens, `valueType` as well as bo, stem from the same *reference* version which originally was bo. For the latter token several criteria for token reuse are fulfilled: The sequence element for $bo^{reference}$ is the same as bo^{lexed} because during the incremental parsing phase assigned the sequence element for the literal bo to the *lexed* version of bo^{lexed}. Additionally the value of the token is the same as before. Therefore, the reuse factor of bo^{lexed} w.r.t. $bo^{reference}$ is 0.101. Whereas the reuse factor for the `valueType` token is 0. Therefore, FURCAS will retain the versioning link for the bo^{lexed} token while removing it from the `valueType` token. For the second change event there are three candidates for token reuse `customer`, `< -` and `ordered`. Obviously the last token is the one with the highest reuse factor as it matches qualifiers 2 and 3 which results in a factor of 0.011 which is higher than those of the other tokens, which is 0. Therefore, FURCAS will retain the versioning link of `ordered` whereas removing it from the other two.

Note that, due to the fully meshed version connections of tokens for change events on *block* and *region* level, all *edited* tokens in the scope of a change events are candidates for reuse on these levels.

(V) TextBlock Merging. This phase merges the *reference* TextBlock-Model with its *parsed* version. A TextBlock β^{lexed} is considered *mergeable* for with a TextBlock β^{parsed} if both represent the same element in the underlying model and only differ

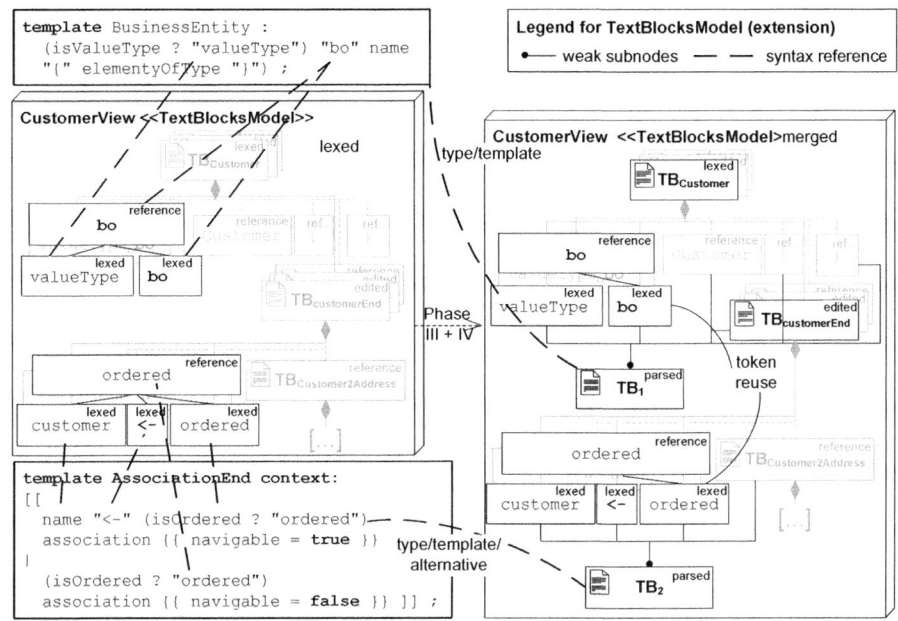

Fig. 8. Application of phases III and IV to the running example

in changes that would still retain the identity of the element. Based on a computed *mergeability factor* FURCAS will decide if and which TextBlock to merge.

Comparable to the reuse factor of tokens, the *mergeability* factor for TextBlocks is based on the possibly modified properties of the TextBlock metaclass. For a TextBlock this is its type (transitively referring to the template used to instantiate it), the Alternative within its template, the mode of the template and finally the tokens assigned to that TextBlock. The following list represents also the priority in which FURCAS checks the candidate TextBlocks for mergeability.

1. The type and therefore the template of β^{lexed} and β^{parsed} are the same, which means that b and b^{parsed} were produced according to the same template within the mapping definition.
2. The chosen alternatives within the same template. A TextBlock may be constructed using a different alternative than its previous version while still being mergeable. However, if there is more than one reuse candidate which only differ in the chosen alternative of the same template, FURCAS will choose the one where the chosen alternatives still match best. A best match of alternatives is determined starting from the top level alternatives going down the sub alternatives. In the following example template Alts : [[top$_{1,a}$ | top$_{1,b}$]] [[top$_{2,a}$ | top$_{2,b}$]] ;, there are two top level alternative sequences top$_1$ and top$_2$. Note that in this case it is possible that for a TextBlock with alternatives top$_{1,a}$, top$_{2,a}$ there is TextBlock β_1^{parsed} that matches top$_{1,a}$, top$_{2,b}$ and one TextBlock β_2^{parsed}

that matches $top_{1,b}$, $top_{2,a}$. In this case the mergeability depends on the next lower prioritised mergeability features.
3. It might by the case that through changes in the call hierarchy of the templates a template with a different `mode` for the same class was triggered. However, the element can still be considered the same and be mergeable with each other.
4. The number of tokens reachable through the `weakAssignment` association that were *reused* within the TextBlock also impacts the mergeability. The more, tokens β^{parsed} reuses from β^{lexed} the higher is the mergeability factor for this combination. If up to this point in the decision hierarchy two β^{parsed} are still considered equal the one with the higher number of reusable tokens is preferred.

The index in the list of mergeability properties also represents their priority when it comes to the determination of the *mergeability factor* mf of TextBlocks. The computation works the same way as the *reusability factor* for tokens. The β^{lexed} with the highest $mf > 0$ will be considered *mergeable* for a given β^{parsed}. If there is no block with $mf > 0$, FURCAS considers all old blocks for deletion.

The *mergeability factor* mf is computed as follows:

$$mergeabilityFactor(\beta^{lexed}, \beta^{parsed}) = \sum_{q \in mergeabilityQualifiers} \begin{cases} \#(reusedTokens(\beta^{lexed}, \beta^{parsed})) * 10^{priority(q)} & \text{if } matches_q(\beta^{parsed}) \wedge q = 4 \\ 10^{priority(q)} & \text{if } matches_q(\beta^{parsed}) \\ 0 & \text{else} \end{cases}$$

For each pair of TextBlocks from the *lexed* and *parsed* versions within the same scope, FURCAS performs the above mergability computation. The scope is defined depending on the type of the change. For *token level*, all transitively connected TextBlocks through the versioning links of its tokens are considered in one scope. For *block level* the complete block from the *lexed* version including its transitive children determins this scope. Finally, on *region level*, all TextBlocks transitively contained under the determined common ancestor are considered for the reuse scope.

In the running example, the changes applied to the TextBlock-Model through the different previous phases lead to the merging of two pairs of TextBlocks as illustrated in Figure 8. In phase (III) FURCAS creates TextBlock TB_1 and TB_2 according to the batch parser production rules and assigns the consumed tokens as `weakSubnodes` to the newly created TextBlocks. After phase (IV) determined the reusable tokens, phase (V) FURCAS computes the mergeability factor for all candidate TextBlocks. Thus, TB_1 will have a mergeability factor of $10^{-1} + 10^{-2} + 0 + (5*10^{-4}) + 0 = 0.1104$. As there is no other merge candidate for this TextBlock, TB_1 will be merged with $TB_{Customer}$. The same applies for TB_2 which has a mergeability factor of $10^{-1} + 0 + 0 + (2*10^{-4}) + 0 = 0.1002$ and the only candidate for merging is $TB_{customerEnd}$.

(VI) Model Update. After the mergeable TextBlocks have been prepared in the TextBlock merging phase, it is now possible to update the domain model according to the mergeable and new TextBlocks. This is done by a model to model transformation which uses as input both the reference TextBlock-model as well as the parsed version of the TextBlock-model. The transformation will delete model elements for not-mergeable *reference* TextBlocks, update properties for merged TextBlocks and create new model elements for new, unmerged *parsed* TextBlocks.

The model update phase performs property update based on the changed or newly created token values and subblock relationships. As each token as well as each TextBlock refers to the corresponding sequence element in the syntax definition, which may be a PropertyElement referring to a property from the metamodel, the property to update, can easily be determined. The same applies for the model elements on which to update the properties. These are the elements referenced by the TextBlocks' correspondingElements.

In the running example, this will result in setting the valueType property of Customer to true and setting the name of the local AssociationEnd to "customer" and its navigable property to true. Due to the mergeability decision in the previous phase elements such as the addressEnd are retained even though their textual representation was completely overwritten. Thus, also their information, in this case the unique = true attribute is retained. This shows the how view-based modelling is supported by FURCAS' incremental update approach.

6 Validation

The following main threats offend the validity of our approach: (I) We assumed that all modifications handled by the incremental update process start from the threefold classification of change scopes into *token, block* and *region* level. If a mapping from textual change events to this kind of basic change scopes is not possible, our approach may not be applicable. (II) Employing parsing techniques into the incremental update approach while allowing arbitrary changes to the textual representation that the parser should analyse may lead to errors in lexing, and parsing if the textual structure is not syntactically correct. (III) The approach may prove unusable in practice as the update approach takes to much time and modellers are blocked in their development efforts. (IV) The restrictions on the language to be mappable to a LL(1) parser with syntactic predicates may prevent language engineers from developing complex languages.

To address these threats, we discuss them in the following paragraphs.

Mapping Change Events to Change Scopes. As defined in Section 5.2 in phase (0), changes made in a textual editor can be described as: $Event(o, l, t)$, using the offset o, the length l and the inserted text t. Using this structure, we can map every possible editing event to our previously defined change scopes of a TextBlock-Model. Using the following classification we classify a given event e in form $Event(o, l, t)$ into one of the scopes $Event_{token}, Event_{block}, Event_{region}$ by applying function s:

$$s(e) = \begin{cases} Event_{token} & \text{if } l = 0 \\ Event_{token} & \text{if } l > 0 \text{ and there is a token } \tau \text{ so that } \mathit{offset}(\tau) = o \text{ and } \\ & \mathit{length}(\tau) <= l \\ Event_{block} & \text{if } l > 0 \text{ and there is a TextBlock } \beta \text{ so that } \mathit{offset}(\beta) = o \\ & \text{and } \mathit{length}(\beta) = l \\ Event_{region} & \text{else} \end{cases}$$

Note that for a TextBlock having exactly one token cases 2 and 3 both match. To resolve this FURCAS will chose case 3.

Some examples for editing events and their classification into these categories are the following, including changes applied to the running example from Figure 4:

- Insertions of a sequence of characters of arbitrary length at specific position are changes on *token* level, for example $Event(12, 0, \text{"ordered "})$.
- Deletions of a sequence of characters at a specific position are changes on *token* level, for example $Event(14, 7, \text{""})$.
- Replacements of a sequence of characters within the boundary of a token are changes token level, for example $Event(3, 7, \text{"Client"})$.
- Deletions of larger sequences of may also be on block level, for example $Event(14, 37, \text{""})$ which deletes the block for the "CustomerHasAddress" association from the textual representation.
- More disruptive changes, being replacements may span over multiple, but incomplete blocks and are therefore *region*-level changes. For example, $Event(33, 18, \text{"Phone -> phone"})$ will overwrite parts of the $TB_{CustomerHasAddress}$ block as well as the whole $TB_{AddressEnd}$ block.

Handling of Errors and Inconsistencies in the Lexing and Parsing Phases. If during the batch parsing phase a parse error occurs, for example because no matching template was found for a given modified stream of tokens, a TextBlock will be marked as isComplete = false (see metamodel in Figure 2). As soon as the textual representation of the inconsistent region is again in a parseable state a merge based on both versions can be performed. This merge is based directly on the underlying model, as there may be multiple representations overlapping on the model. And as these representations may be partial a text based merge is not possible. The actual model merging process is beyond the scope of this paper. However, there are multiple publications that deal with that problem.

Parsing Performance for Complex Languages. In the case studies explained in the subsequent paragraph we implemented complex, industrial languages with FURCAS. When developing sample applications with those languages we measured the time required for the incremental update process. The values ranged from 100ms up to 5 seconds. The latter parsing time made us investigate where the performance decrease actually comes from. We identified the instantiation of new versions of larger parts of the TextBlock-Model as one of the main cost factors w.r.t. parsing performance. To address this issue we are currently investigating the use of light-weighted plain objects instead of full blown model elements for the intermediate states of the TextBlock-Model.

Application to Practice. We applied our framework within multiple industrial case study which we conducted at SAP AG in the area of business information systems. Within this case study three different metamodels with eight different textual views for a rather large metamodels were created. In total metamodel 1 has 34, metamodel 2 has 136 and metamodel 3 has 87 classes that are relevant for the mapping definitions. The mapping definitions were partially overlapping to each other and in some parts only showed a partial view on a common domain model. Based on this created language a proof of concept application was built using the FURCAS editors. Within the third case study we also let untrained (w.r.t. FURCAS) language engineers develop the language mappings. In total we could implement each of the case studies using the FURCAS approach. However, some language constructs required complex workarounds to fulfil the requirements. To ease the development with FURCAS is a task for future work.

7 Conclusions and Future Work

In this paper we presented an approach that enables for textual modelling in combination with a view-based paradigm. We provided an incremental update process that allows to retain model elements that take part in partial views upon changes to the textual view representation. To evaluate our approach we implemented a prototype facilitating all features that were presented here which is available from the FURCAS website [19]. Additionally the prototype was evaluated within several case studies conducted in cooperation with the SAP AG.

Currently the transformations between the TextBlocks model and the domain model are hand written. However, given the complexity of these transformations, their incremental character as well as their operation on models we are currently experimenting with several approaches (QVT-Relational as well as Triple-Graph-Grammars) that may be suitable for expressing and executing these transformations. The idea is to automatically generate a transformation from a mapping definition.

References

1. Finkelstein, A., Kramer, J., Nuseibeh, B., Finkelstein, L., Goedicke, M.: Viewpoints: A framework for integrating multiple perspectives in system development. International Journal of Software Engineering and Knowledge Engineering 2 (1992)
2. Atkinson, C., Stoll, D., Bostan, P.: Supporting view-based development through orthographic software modeling. In: ENASE, pp. 71–86. INSTICC Press (2009)
3. Goldschmidt, T., Becker, S., Uhl, A.: Classification of Concrete Textual Syntax Mapping Approaches. In: Schieferdecker, I., Hartman, A. (eds.) ECMDA-FA 2008. LNCS, vol. 5095, pp. 169–184. Springer, Heidelberg (2008)
4. Wagner, T.A.: Practical Algorithms for Incremental Software Development Environments. PhD thesis, University of California at Berkeley (1998)
5. Nagl, M. (ed.): Building tightly integrated software development environments: the IPSEN approach. Springer-Verlag New York, Inc., New York (1996)
6. Teitelbaum, T., Reps, T.: The cornell program synthesizer: a syntax-directed programming environment. Commun. ACM 24(9), 563–573 (1981)
7. Bahlke, R., Snelting, G.: The PSG - Programming System Generator. SIGPLAN Not. 20(7), 28–33 (1985)
8. Kats, L., Visser, E.: The Spoofax language workbench. Rules for declarative specification of languages and IDEs. In: Proceedings of OOPSLA, pp. 444–463 (2010)
9. Foundation, E.: Eclipse XText Website (2010), http://www.eclipse.org/Xtext/ (last retrieved 2010-07-06)
10. Dimitriev, S.: Language oriented programming: The next programming paradigm. Onboard Magazine 2 (2005)

11. Goldschmidt, T., Becker, S., Uhl, A.: FURCAS: Framework for UUID-Retaining Concrete to Abstract Syntax Mappings. In: Proceedings of the 5th European Conference on Model Driven Architecture - Foundations and Applications (ECMDA 2009) - Tools and Consultancy Track, pp. 100–106. CTIT (2009)
12. Goldschmidt, T., Becker, S., Uhl, A.: Textual views in model driven engineering. In: Proceedings of the 35th EUROMICRO Conference on Software Engineering and Advanced Applications (SEAA). IEEE, Los Alamitos (2009)
13. Jouault, F., Bézivin, J., Kurtev, I.: TCS: a DSL for the specification of textual concrete syntaxes in model engineering. In: GPCE 2006, pp. 249–254 (2006)
14. Heidenreich, F., Johannes, J., Karol, S., Seifert, M., Wende, C.: Derivation and refinement of textual syntax for models. In: Paige, R.F., Hartman, A., Rensink, A. (eds.) ECMDA-FA 2009. LNCS, vol. 5562, pp. 114–129. Springer, Heidelberg (2009)
15. Goldschmidt, T.: Towards an incremental update approach for concrete textual syntaxes for UUID-based model repositories. In: Gašević, D., Lämmel, R., Van Wyk, E. (eds.) SLE 2008. LNCS, vol. 5452, pp. 168–177. Springer, Heidelberg (2009)
16. Goldschmidt, T., Becker, S., Uhl, A.: Incremental Updates for Textual Modeling of Large Scale Models. In: Proceedings of the 15th IEEE International Conference on Engineering of Complex Computer Systems (ICECCS 2010), pp. 247–248. IEEE, Los Alamitos (2010)
17. Parr, T.: The Definitive ANTLR Reference. The Pragmatic Bookshelf (2007)
18. Cook, P., Welsh, J.: Incremental parsing in language-based editors: user needs and how to meet them. Software: Practice and Experience 31, 1461–1486 (2001)
19. Goldschmidt, T., Uhl, A.: The FURCAS website (2011), http://www.furcas.org (last retrieved 2011-01-20)

Easing Model Transformation Learning with Automatically Aligned Examples*

Xavier Dolques[1], Aymen Dogui[2], Jean-Rémy Falleri[3],
Marianne Huchard[4], Clémentine Nebut[4], and François Pfister[5]

[1] INRIA, Centre Inria Rennes - Bretagne Atlantique,
Campus universitaire de Beaulieu, 35042 Rennes, France
xavier.dolques@inria.fr
[2] Supélec Paris, France
aymen.dogui@supelec.fr
[3] Université de Bordeaux, France
falleri@labri.fr
[4] LIRMM, Université de Montpellier 2 et CNRS,
Montpellier, France
first.last@lirmm.fr
[5] LGI2P, Ecole des Mines d'Alès, Nîmes, France
francois.pfister@mines-ales.fr

Abstract. Model Based Transformation Example (MTBE) is a recent track of research aiming at learning a transformation from examples. In most MTBE processes, a transformation example is given in the form of a source model, a transformed model and links between source elements and the corresponding transformed elements. Building the links is done manually, which is a tedious task, while in many cases, they can be deduced from the examination of the source and transformed models, by using relevant attributes, like names or identifiers. We exploit this characteristic by proposing a semi-automatic matching operation, suitable for discovering matches between the source model and the transformed model. Our technique is inspired by and extends the Anchor-Prompt approach, and is based on the automatic discovery of pairs of anchors (pairs of elements for which there is a strong assumption of matching) to support the whole matching discovery. An implementation of the approach is provided for validation on a case study.

1 Introduction

Model transformations are the operational, often automated, part of Model Driven Engineering (MDE), and several transformation languages have been proposed to introduce useful concepts to develop transformations. The QVT standard [1] has been proposed by the OMG to unify the field.

Writing a transformation requires two important skills: firstly a strong knowledge in transformation languages and metamodeling and secondly a good

---

* This research was partially supported by the european project OPEES.

comprehension of the semantics of the source and target domains. While transformation developers have the first skill, the second one is usually owned by the domain experts. This fact makes the development of a model transformation difficult and time-consuming, because the transformation developers have to interact, on abstract concepts of a specific domain, with the domain experts, so as to obtain a correct transformation.

Two kinds of approaches have recently been introduced to assist the development of model transformations. The first kind of approach operates at the metamodel level [2,3] and exploits an alignment between the source and target metamodels. It assumes (thus is efficient when) the source and target metamodels are very similar in their structure and terminology. The second approach, Model Transformation By Example (MTBE), uses metamodels and models. It aims at inferring either the transformation [4,5,6], or the result of a transformation [7], by using a set of transformation examples. In this paper we focus on this second kind of approaches.

Applying MTBE requires to have transformation examples: a source model, a transformed model and the links between source and transformed elements. While having a source and a target model is quite easy (a domain expert can create them), retrieving the links between the elements of these models is tedious and time-consuming, because no mainstream metamodeling environment is capable of creating them when models are manually edited. Therefore, these links are usually manually looked for and added. We believe that the major part of these links can be automatically retrieved. Indeed, when the transformed model is created, the names of the transformed elements are usually equal or very similar to the ones of the source elements, maybe using different naming conventions. Also, the underlying metamodels are different but often neighbors of an element in the source model (understood as the instantiation of the metamodel) are transformed into neighbors of the transformed element.

In this paper, after the context description (Section 2), we propose an approach (Section 3), that combines string similarity and schema matching techniques to automatically retrieve the links going from the elements of a source model to their corresponding elements in the transformed model. This approach helps the transformation developers to gather transformation examples, allowing them to benefit from the MTBE approaches. We describe our tool and case study in Section 4. Related work is discussed in Section 5, and we conclude in Section 6.

2 Problem Statement

The MTBE process aims at inferring a rule-based transformation from transformation examples. A classical version of the process is presented in the l.h.s of Figure 1. The input of the process is a transformation example, defined by a source model, a transformed (target) model and matching links between the two models. It results into transformation rules, deduced from the example, that can transform any model conforming to the source metamodel to a model conforming to the target metamodel. Several proposals for the MTBE engine can be used, *e.g.* [4,5,6].

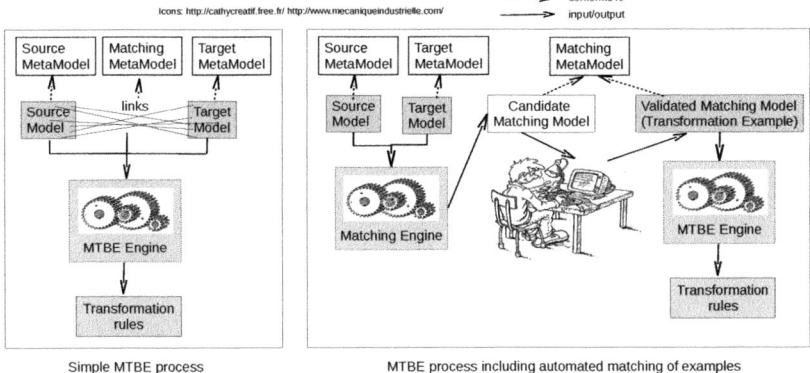

Fig. 1. The MTBE process: a simple view (l.h.s) and including assistance for matching (r.h.s)

We illustrate this section and the rest of the paper with a classical example of transformation from UML class model to entity-relationship model. The input is thus an example of a UML model, and the corresponding transformed entity-relationship model. Figures 2 and 3 give the used metamodels (in ecore format) for UML class diagrams and entity-relationship models.

The chosen example models literary texts (novels or poetry), written by (and with a foreword from) authors. Each text has one or several styles. The examples are given with concrete syntax in Figures 4 and 5, and an excerpt is given with abstract syntax in Figures 6 and 7 (in the form of an instance of the metamodels). Though less readable, the abstract syntax is the one actually handled by the tools. The presented excerpts show the authors writing texts but hide the poetry, the style, and the fact that authors write a foreword for texts.

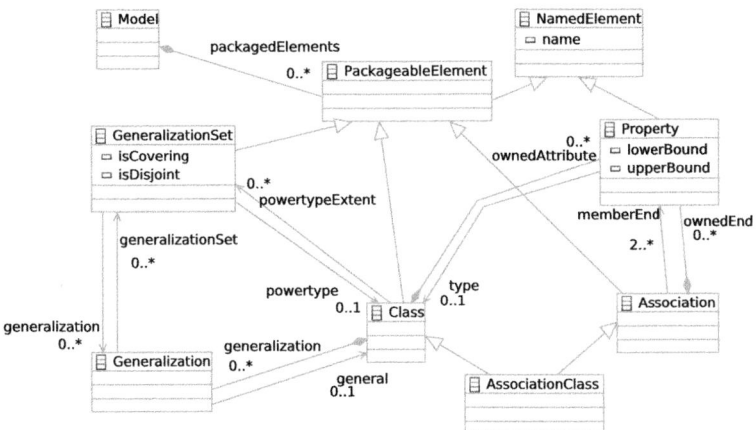

Fig. 2. A metamodel for UML class diagrams (drastic simplification of the UML metamodel)

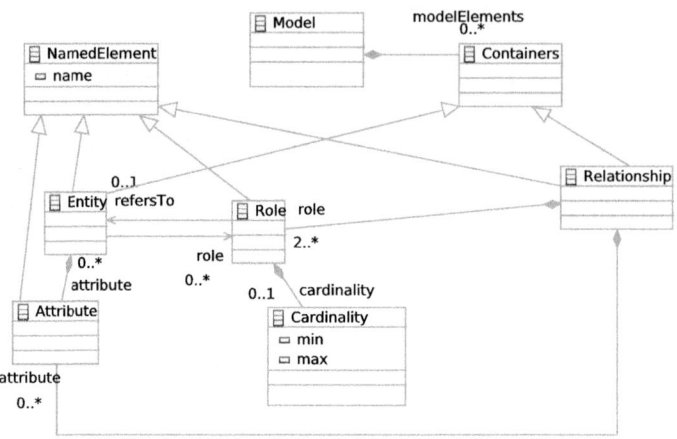

Fig. 3. A metamodel for Entity-Relationship models

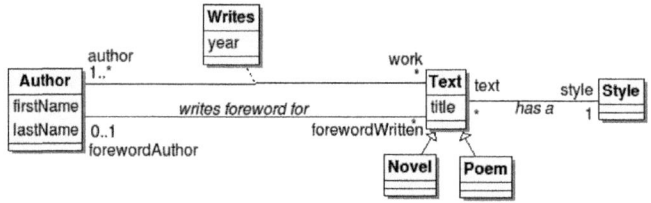

Fig. 4. An example UML model for the UML2ER transformation

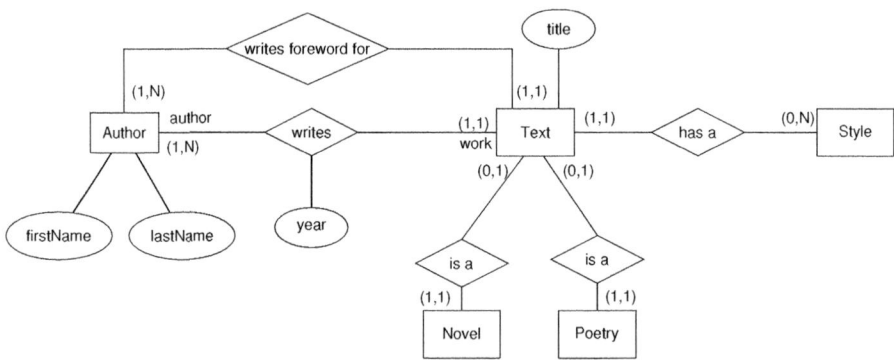

Fig. 5. An example of Entity-relation model for the UML2ER transformation

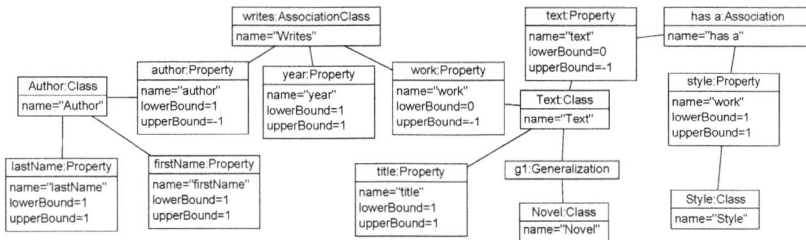

Fig. 6. Excerpt of the UML example with abstract syntax

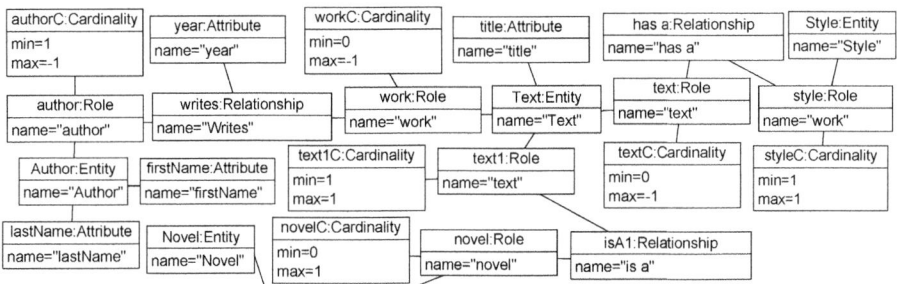

Fig. 7. Excerpt of the ER example with abstract syntax

The examples are quite easy to build, moreover they will be useful for testing or documentation purposes. However, to feed the MTBE process, the transformation links have to be given. For example, one has to specify that the Author class from Figure 4 has to be transformed into the Author entity from Figure 5, and that the inheritance link from Novel to Text has to be transformed into an is_a relationship (and in fact using the abstract syntax shown in Figures 6 and 7: the generalization element has to be transformed into the is_a relationship and the two linked roles). This is a tedious task, and only dedicated to the MTBE process. Our purpose is to use string similarity and alignment methods to generate part of those links. The resulting architecture for the MTBE process is presented in the r.h.s of Figure 1. The links from the source model to the transformed model are partly generated by a matching engine. The generated links are checked by an expert. The *matching engine* takes source models and target (transformed) models, and provides a candidate matching model (matching links). This candidate matching model is proposed to an expert who validates and fixes the matching model, producing the validated matching model which composes (together with the source and target model) the transformation example. Our aim is to assist the domain expert as far as possible, providing him with an initial matching solution where nearly obvious matches are included. For example, with the example of the literary texts, we discover all the "obvious" matchings (the class Text maps to the entity Text, the firstName property maps to the firstName attribute, ...) and also more sophisticated mappings such that: the generalization from Novel to Text maps to an is_a relationship and the two roles text and novel. Even if the complete mappings are not discovered (as explained in the case study, we have for the UML2ER example a precision of 1.0 and a recall of 0.7), the generation of a partial mapping is a valuable help in a MTBE process.

To sum up, we study a matching problem that considers two models that on one hand come from two different metamodels (maybe very divergent), with relations differently named and organized; and on the other hand contain a large set of common underlying entities and a large set of similarly named entities, due to the common underlying natural semantics.

3 The Model Matching Approach

The literature offers several approaches to build a matching between two structures [8,9]. Due to the specificities of our problem, we propose a tool inspired by the Anchor-Prompt approach [10]. The original approach is a two-step process designed to match ontologies. The first step is the discovery of matches with a high confidence rate (anchors), while the second one propagates those anchors so as to discover other matchings. Our approach follows the same two steps and improves the second, they are described below.

3.1 Anchor Discovery

This first step consists in finding pairs of anchors, i.e. initial matchings. The original Anchor-Prompt approach does not specify a process to discover pairs of anchors. In our case, the target model is the result of the transformation of the source model, and the entities and their values, are very close. Although the source and target metamodels are different, it is common that model entities have an identifying attribute (such as the name) and that this attribute value does not change much during the transformation. In values, we can have slight variations due to naming conventions: prefixes or suffixes can often be added, but it is mostly improbable that both a prefix and a suffix is added so we assume that they are not very different. A high confidence rate is needed for this subset since the next step strongly depends on the quality of those pairs of elements. Those matchings cannot be detected using types, as the two models may be instances of different metamodels, thus we need to rely on some attribute values of those elements, e.g. the attribute name of the UML metaclass NamedElement, that we assume to remain nearly unchanged after transformation.

Let Att_{src} and Att_{tgt} be the sets of all the attributes of all the elements respectively in the source and target models. Let $P = Att_{src} \times Att_{tgt}$. We want to extract $M \subset P$, a set of attribute pairs validating a matching test. From this set M we generate a set of pairs of anchors A by replacing each attribute value in the pairs of M by the entity containing this value. A general algorithm for the anchor discovery is given in Figure 8.

```
proc Anchor-Discovery (In : AttSrc set of Attribute values,
                            AttTgt set of Attribute values,
                       Out: A set of Entity pairs)
M := AttSrc x AttTgt;
P := empty set;
A := empty set;
for pair in M do
   if match(pair.source, pair.target)
      then P.add(pair);
for pair in P do
   A.add( (pair.source.entity, pair.target.entity) );
```

Fig. 8. General process of anchor discovery

We tested several matching operations and we present here the most relevant:

- **equality:** the most obvious matching operation is the equality. If two elements share exactly the same value, then they are likely to be matched. But this test is worthless if we do not check the occurrence frequency of the values matched. Indeed it appears in our tests that some values are not relevant, such as stereotypes or cardinalities in class diagrams. Thus, another condition for two attributes to be matched is that their value appears once and only once in the source and target models. This matching operation appears to be reliable as it brings a precision of 1 in most of our tests.
- **substring:** the drawback of the previous operation is that it may pass through simple renaming transformations, that may add or delete a prefix or a suffix. To tackle this issue after the equality test we check, if the values are character strings, if one value is a substring of the other. As with the previous operation, we must be cautious on the obtained results, and check if the substring exists as an attribute value in the model that contains the longest string value of the couple. This method is once again reliable in most of the cases, and in our tests it always gave a precision of 1.

We also experimented with other matching operations that use the longest common substring or the Levenshtein distance, but our context implies that values in the target model remain really close to values from the source model, even capital or lowercase letters are important. To find highly reliable matchings we cannot afford to use distance methods that may lower the precision of the matchings.

At the end of this step, for our example, A includes, among others, the pairs of anchors (`Text:Class, Text:Entity`) or (`has a:Association, has a:Relationship`).

3.2 Anchor Propagation

Considering the anchors as a nearly correct match, we propagate this information on paths outgoing from an anchor and leading to another close anchor to discover other potential matches. Indeed, we assume that on a path between two anchors, even if the metamodels are different, when an entity e is close to another entity f in the source model, it is likely that the entity which results from the transformation of e is close to the entity which results from the transformation of f. Due to the differences between the metamodels, the path between the two entities is likely to be differently labeled. The process cannot be correct in all the cases, because during the transformation some elements can be removed or added, but it is likely to produce many correct matches.

Source and target models may be seen as two labeled graphs G_{src} and G_{tgt}, in which a node represents an instance of a class from the metamodel, and an edge represents an association between class instances (cf. graphs in Figures 6 and 7). We enumerate from the two graphs all the paths connecting two anchors and whose length is less than a constant α.

We align the nodes from a path between two anchors a_1 and a_2 of G_{src} with the nodes from a path between the anchors a'_1 and a'_2 if $(a_1, a'_1) \in A$ and $(a_2, a'_2) \in A$. For example we will align a path between Text:Class and has a:Association with a path between Text:Entity and has a:Relationship. One difference from the original Anchor-Prompt approach is in the alignment of paths with different lengths, for which Anchor-Prompt only aligns pairs of paths of identical length. This way the original approach leads to match elements that are on the same position on the path. More generally, in our approach, when aligning two paths, we consider each pair of nodes as shown in Figure 9, but not with the same weight: we are giving the maximum weight to pairs of nodes that are in the same position relatively to each node's path length.

Let X and Y be two lists of nodes, respectively from G_{src} and G_{tgt} and representing two paths to be aligned. X and Y are starting by two anchors that are matched together. Let $x \in X$ and $y \in Y$. $index(x)$ and $index(y)$ are the position of the nodes in the list starting from 1. The weight of the pair (x, y) is defined by:

$$W(x,y) = 1 - \left| \frac{index(x)}{length(X)+1} - \frac{index(y)}{length(Y)+1} \right|$$

For instance, $W(x1, y1) = 1 - \left|\frac{1}{6} - \frac{1}{4}\right| = 0.92$ and $W(x1, y2) = 1 - \left|\frac{1}{6} - \frac{2}{4}\right| = 0.67$, showing that $x1$ is more likely to match with $y1$ rather than with $y2$.

We align each pair of paths whose extremities are anchors, incrementing the similarity coefficient of a pair of elements each time the elements appear in two paths to be aligned. The increment is computed depending on the weight of the pair.

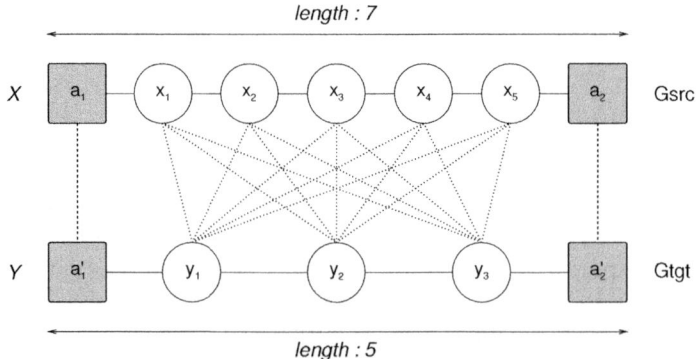

Fig. 9. Aligning two paths

At the end of the process we have a set of node pairs with similarity coefficients. The similarity coefficients have no meaning if compared globally. If a node appears only in one path between two anchors, then all the pairs containing this node will have a similarity coefficient that may be lower than ones with nodes appearing in many paths between two anchors, making difficult to decide which pairs are important. However, comparing the similarity coefficients of all the pairs containing one node is more meaningful. Indeed, the pair with the highest similarity coefficient is more likely to be a matching, so all the similarity coefficients of this node should be compared relative to it.

Figure 10 shows in the case of the object of name "text" and type *Property* in our example how it is deduced that its matching element in the target model is the object of name "text" of type *Role* attached to the *RelationShip* named "hasa". We see that for all the matching links containing the *Property* "text", the highest similarity coefficient is obtained with the *Role* "text", and none of the other matching links pass over a threshold that, after some experiments, we fixed at 80% of the highest value for an object. The same principle can be used symmetrically for the *Role* "text" that validates the choice of this matching.

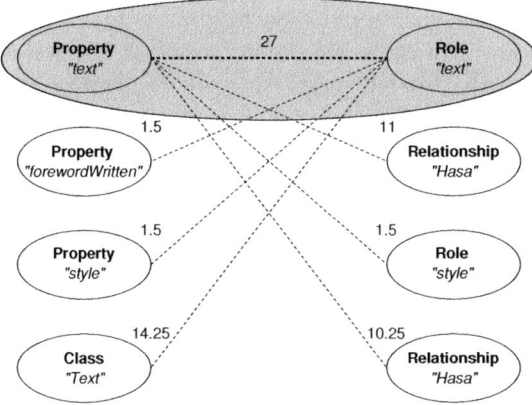

Fig. 10. Filtering of the similarity coefficient

4 Case Study

This section presents the experimental results obtained with our approach. We present the implementation used to run the experimentation, then the experimental protocol and data, and the obtained results with their interpretation.

4.1 Tool Implementation

A tool called MANDARINE[1] has been developed based on the approach described above, with the objective of improving MTBE processes. It has been

---

[1] Model AligNement Disseminating AttRibute INstances Equivalences

designed to be efficiently integrated with the approach described in [11] by using a part of its metamodel but it can also be used as a standalone tool for an integration with another approach. It is based on the Eclipse Modeling Framework, as it is a modeling facility widely adopted by the MDE community, and has been implemented in JAVA.

The tool takes as input the source and target example models of the transformation and returns the computed matchings between the models as a model conforming to *Matching Model*, the metamodel described in Figure 12. This metamodel is also used to describe the input of the MTBE process from [11]. Technically, the only requirement for the input models is that they must be recognized by EMF as instances of an Ecore Model.

An informal representation of the architecture of the tool is provided in Figure 11. The process of matching is split in two distinct steps: the first one implements the anchor discovery process from section 3.1 with the ability to choose the matching operation between attributes. This step returns a Matching Model as a result. The second part implements our adaptation of Anchor-Prompt from section 3.2, where the maximum length of the considered paths and the threshold for filtering the similarity coefficients may be passed as input with a Matching Model. Although the two processes are designed to be launched one after another, they are independently implemented to allow flexibility of use and further evolution.

The *Matching Evaluation* tool is the infrastructure to evaluate the discovered matchings against an expert matchings, it will be discussed in Section 4.

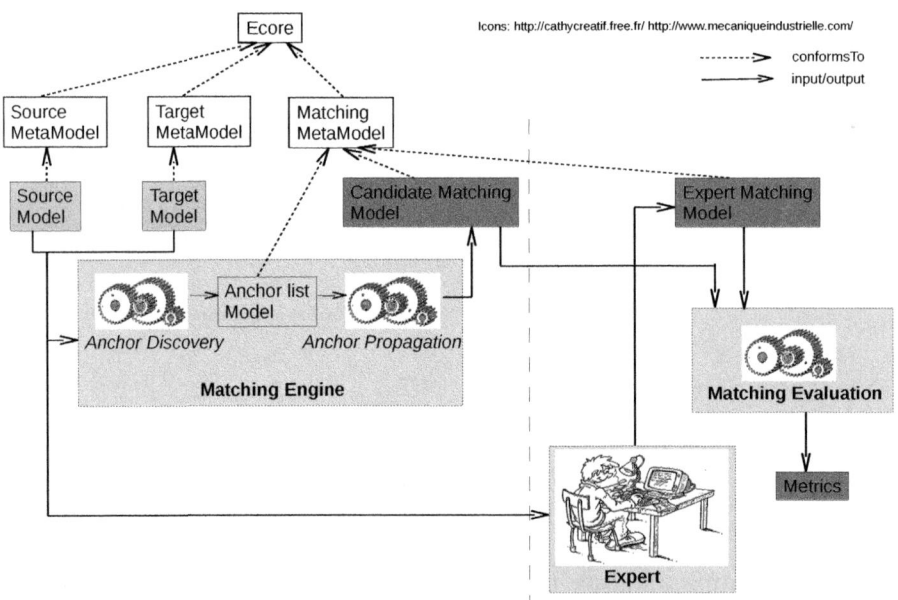

Fig. 11. An architecture for the anchor-based matching tool

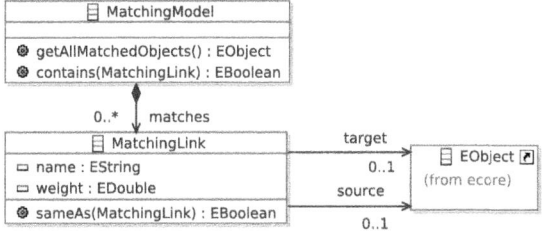

Fig. 12. Metamodel describing the matching used in our tool

4.2 Testing Protocol and Metrics

As an extension of the tool previously described, we designed a testing platform presented on the right hand side of Figure 11. This platform takes as input two matching models, one created by an expert that gives a reference result and that we will refer to as A_{expert}, and another one automatically computed that will be called A_{auto} and of which we want to measure the quality. Those two models are then automatically compared according to several metrics. Model matching being similar with schema matching or ontology matching, we propose here to use metrics from those last two domains. We will especially refer to the metrics described in [12]: precision, recall and overall. In the following we will use $A_{positives} = A_{auto} \cap A_{expert}$ as the set of matching links that are present in both expert and automatically obtained matchings (see Figure 13).

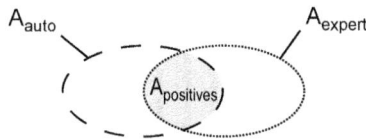

Fig. 13. Schematic illustration of matching comparison

Precision. The precision calculates the ratio of correct matchings in A_{auto} over the size of A_{auto}. Therefore this metric depends on the quantity of bad matchings introduced by the approach. It is a rational number going from 0 (if all the obtained matchings are wrong) to 1 (if there are no wrong matchings at all *i.e.* $A_{auto} \subseteq A_{expert}$). It is calculated by the formula: $precision = \frac{|A_{positives}|}{|A_{auto}|}$

Recall. The recall calculates the ratio of correct matchings in A_{auto} over the number of correct matchings, *i.e.* the size of A_{expert}. Therefore this metric depends on the quantity of matchings from A_{expert} missed by the approach. It is a rational number going from 0 (if there are no matchings from A_{expert} in A_{auto}) to 1 (if all the matchings from A_{expert} have been discovered, *i.e* if $A_{expert} \subseteq A_{auto}$). It is calculated with the following formula: $recall = \frac{|A_{positives}|}{|A_{expert}|}$

Overall. The overall combines precision and recall to quantify the needed effort to go from A_{auto} to A_{expert}, relatively to the size of the expert model. It is a rational number bounded between $-\infty$ and 1. Overall is 1 if $precision = recall$, and 0 if the number of wrong matchings in A_{auto} added to the number of missing matchings is equal to the size of A_{expert}. If this number is greater than the size of A_{expert} then overall is a negative number. It is calculated with the following formula: $overall = 1 - \frac{(|A_{auto}|-|A_{positives}|)+(|A_{expert}|-|A_{positives}|)}{|A_{expert}|}$

4.3 Data

We propose here to validate our approach by applying it on 22 model transformations[2]. The data used for this case study comes from several sources: home made transformations, UML refactorings [13] and transformations from the ATL zoo of transformations [14]. In the latter case, the models used as examples are given with the transformation.

4.4 Results

The evaluation program has been applied twice for each transformation, first to evaluate the anchor discovery result and then the whole process result. Precision and recall have been measured in each case, and the overall has been calculated from them. Figures 14, 15, and 16 present the obtained results. For the anchor discovery step, we only show the results obtained with the substring similarity metrics, since it is the one giving the best results. We can see in Fig. 14 that

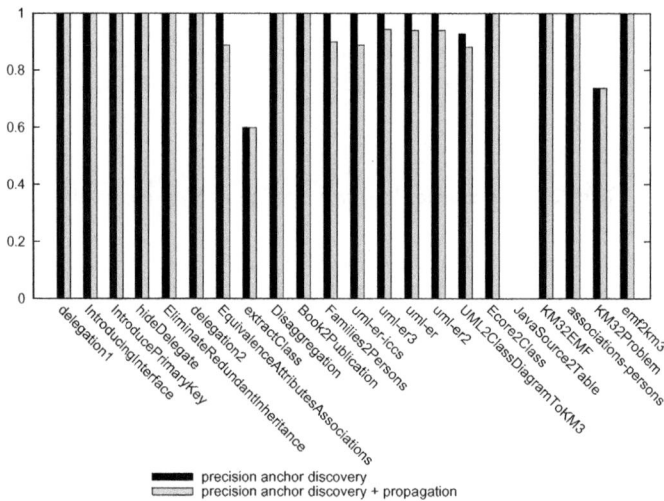

Fig. 14. Precision measured on the case study

---

[2] The detail of all the transformations is given at: http://www.lirmm.fr/%7Enebut/Publications/ArticleSupplements/ECMFA2011/examples-casestudy.html

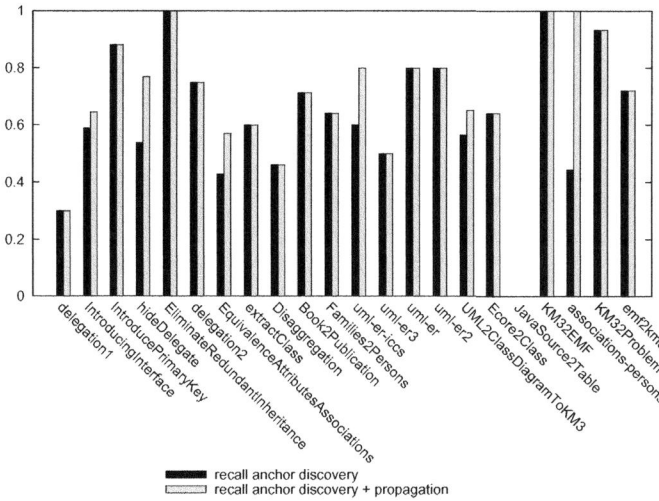

Fig. 15. Recall measured on the case study

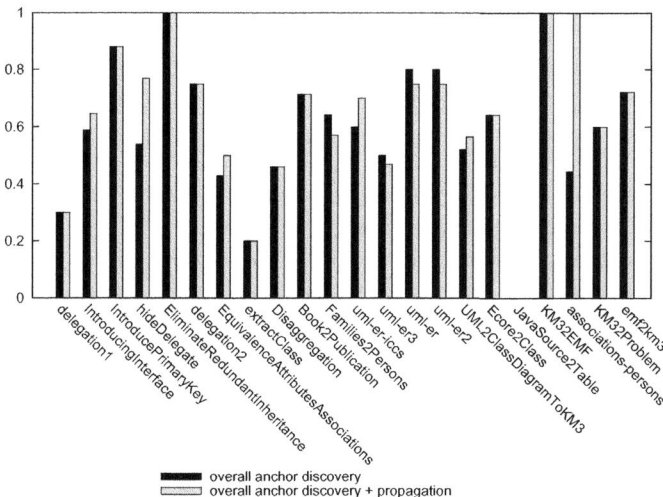

Fig. 16. Overall measured on the case study

the precision obtained is good, with a value of 1 in many cases, especially for the anchor discovery process. It enforces our hypothesis that the anchor discovery result can be considered as reliable. On the other hand, the recall values are not as good, but it was expected as our approach intends to assist the matching creation and not to completely automate it. It sometimes occurs that for a same transformation, the propagation of the anchors degrades the precision, while not increasing the recall. That shows that this step could be enhanced; ways to enhance this step are given in conclusion. We can also see that one of the transformation gives no results at all. This transformation, named *JavaSource2 Table* is an extraction of statistics from a Java program and therefore does not keep the structure of the source model at all during the transformation.

The overall values are all positives, so if we consider adding or removing a match as an atomic operation with the same cost, then in each case our approach is decreasing the cost of matching two models completely by hand, in many cases by half or more. However, with the good results obtained for the precision, the correction operations of the matching model are mainly adding operations.

5 Related Work

Automating the discovery of mappings between database and XML schemas, ontologies, or (meta)models has been thoroughly investigated. We encourage the reader to refer to [8] or [9] for an in-depth description of the existing work. Most of the main approaches such as [15,16,17,18,19] make the assumption that the relations between the two models being compared are identical. The basic idea exploited by these approaches is to compute first a similarity between the elements using their names, and to compute then a similarity using the structure. To compute this second kind of similarity, they assume that the relations between the elements have the same kind in the two compared models. In the MDE terminology, it could be translated as: *the models being compared have the same meta-model*. In our case the models being compared conform to two different meta-models. Therefore, a straightforward use of one of these techniques may not exploit all the potential of those approaches. In [20], they use (among other similarity calculations) the similarity flooding ([15]) and they construct adequate propagation models that capture the semantics of the relationships. These propagation models are nevertheless specific to the studied meta-models (and their meta-meta-model(s)) and are designed by an expert.

Moreover, our alignment problem has two characteristics to exploit: since the source and target models are supposed to be written by the same person, the identifiers and names should be nearly identical. Second, since the target model results from a transformation from the source model (this is a main difference with approaches that study the meta-model matching), the structures of the two models are supposed not to be radically different one from the other. That is why we adapted another kind of approach [10]. Indeed, due to the first characteristic of the problem, the anchors should be easy to detect, and due to the second characteristic, the mapping algorithm exploiting the anchors should be efficient.

Concerning the context of application of our matching approach (model transformation by example), several proposals [21,5,6,7] aim at inferring the rules of a transformation or its result using a set of examples. In all these approaches, an example consists at least of a source model, a transformed model, and the links between the elements of these two models. None of those approaches include an assistance to build those last links, and all of them would benefit from the approach proposed in this paper.

In [22], a By-Demonstration approach is proposed to generate model transformations. It consists in building step by step examples of transformations, following strong naming constraints. Thus examples are incrementally built, and both the increments and the naming constraints allow links to be deduced and rules to be inferred.

6 Conclusion

Model transformation by example (MTBE) is a promising approach to ease the development of model transformations. Several proposals have been developed to make MTBE feasible. Those approaches take as input examples of a transformation composed of source models, target (transformed) models, and the transformation links from source model elements to target model elements. While designing the source and target models is a simple and valuable task (the models can later reused for documentation or testing purpose), making explicit the transformation links is a tedious and error-prone task. In this paper, we detailed an approach and a tool using text analysis and alignment techniques to partly generate those links. Such a mapping engine provides valuable help to the expert in charge of designing an example for an MTBE process. In order to validate the proposed approach, we performed experiments on a set of model transformations, and compared, based on metrics such as precision and recall, the matchings generated by our matching tool to reference (manually built) matchings. The results obtained are promising: we obtain very good precision results and fairly good recall results. The experiments also show that the propagation step could be more efficient (loss of precision, for sometimes no gain in recall), while the step of discovery of the anchors is sufficiently efficient (precision of 1, and sufficient recall). Future work will consist in enhancing the propagation step, first integrating in it the similarity metrics between the values of elements computed in the first step, and secondly taking into account attributes that are not of String type, like cardinalities.

References

1. OMG: MOF QVT Final Adopted Specification. Object Modeling Group (2005)
2. Lopes, D., Hammoudi, S., Bézivin, J., Jouault, F.: Generating transformation definition from mapping specification: Application to web service platform. In: Pastor, Ó., Falcão e Cunha, J. (eds.) CAiSE 2005. LNCS, vol. 3520, pp. 309–325. Springer, Heidelberg (2005)
3. Falleri, J.R., Huchard, M., Lafourcade, M., Nebut, C.: Metamodel matching for automatic model transformation generation. In: Busch, C., Ober, I., Bruel, J.-M., Uhl, A., Völter, M. (eds.) MODELS 2008. LNCS, vol. 5301, pp. 326–340. Springer, Heidelberg (2008)
4. Wimmer, M., Strommer, M., Kargl, H., Kramler, G.: Towards model transformation generation by-example. In: HICSS 2007: Proc. of the 40th Annual Hawaii International Conf. on System Sciences, p. 285b. IEEE Computer Society, Los Alamitos (2007)

5. Balogh, Z., Varró, D.: Model transformation by example using inductive logic programming. Software and Systems Modeling (2008) (appeared online)
6. Dolques, X., Huchard, M., Nebut, C.: From transformation traces to transformation rules: Assisting model driven engineering approach with formal concept analysis. In: Proceedings of ICCS 2009 Supplementary, pp. 15–29 (2009)
7. Kessentini, M., Sahraoui, H., Boukadoum, M.: Model Transformation as an Optimization Problem. In: Busch, C., Ober, I., Bruel, J.-M., Uhl, A., Völter, M. (eds.) MODELS 2008. LNCS, vol. 5301, pp. 159–173. Springer, Heidelberg (2008)
8. Rahm, E., Bernstein, P.A.: A survey of approaches to automatic schema matching. VLDB J. 10(4), 334–350 (2001)
9. Shvaiko, P., Euzenat, J.: A survey of schema-based matching approaches. In: Spaccapietra, S. (ed.) Journal on Data Semantics IV. LNCS, vol. 3730, pp. 146–171. Springer, Heidelberg (2005)
10. Noy, N.F., Musen, M.A.: Anchor-prompt: Using non-local context for semantic matching. In: Proc. of the Workshop on Ontologies and Information Sharing at IJCAI 2001, Seattle, USA, pp. 63–70 (2001)
11. Dolques, X., Huchard, M., Nebut, C., Reitz, P.: Learning transformation rules from transformation examples: An approach based on relational concept analysis. In: 14th IEEE International Enterprise Distributed Object Computing Conference Workshops of EDOC 2010, pp. 27–32. IEEE Computer Society Press, Los Alamitos (2010)
12. Do, H.H., Melnik, S., Rahm, E.: Comparison of schema matching evaluations. In: Chaudhri, A.B., Jeckle, M., Rahm, E., Unland, R. (eds.) NODe-WS 2002. LNCS, vol. 2593, pp. 221–237. Springer, Heidelberg (2003)
13. Fowler, M., Beck, K., Brant, J., Opdyke, W., Roberts, D.: Refactoring: Improving the Design of Existing Code. Addison-Wesley, Reading (2000)
14. ATL transformation zoo, http://www.eclipse.org/m2m/atl/atlTransformations/
15. Melnik, S., Garcia-Molina, H., Rahm, E.: Similarity flooding: A versatile graph matching algorithm and its application to schema matching. In: ICDE, pp. 117–128. IEEE Computer Society, Los Alamitos (2002)
16. Do, H.H., Rahm, E.: Coma - a system for flexible combination of schema matching approaches. In: VLDB, pp. 610–621. Morgan Kaufmann, San Francisco (2002)
17. Madhavan, J., Bernstein, P.A., Rahm, E.: Generic schema matching with cupid. In: VLDB, pp. 49–58. Morgan Kaufmann, San Francisco (2001)
18. Ehrig, M., Staab, S.: QOM – quick ontology mapping. In: McIlraith, S.A., Plexousakis, D., van Harmelen, F. (eds.) ISWC 2004. LNCS, vol. 3298, pp. 683–697. Springer, Heidelberg (2004)
19. Euzenat, J., Loup, D., Touzani, M., Valtchev, P.: Ontology Alignment with OLA. In: Proc. of the 3rd EON Workshop, 3rd Int. Semantic Web Conf, pp. 333–337 (2004)
20. Fabro, M.D.D., Valduriez, P.: Towards the efficient development of model transformations using model weaving and matching transformations. Software and System Modeling 8(3), 305–324 (2009)
21. Wimmer, M., Strommer, M., Kargl, H., Kramler, G.: Towards model transformation generation by-example. In: HICSS, p. 285. IEEE Computer Society, Los Alamitos (2007)
22. Langer, P., Wimmer, M., Kappel, G.: Model-to-model transformations by demonstration. In: Tratt, L., Gogolla, M. (eds.) ICMT 2010. LNCS, vol. 6142, pp. 153–167. Springer, Heidelberg (2010)

Code Generation for UML 2 Activity Diagrams
Towards a Comprehensive Model-Driven Development Approach

Dominik Gessenharter and Martin Rauscher

Institute of Software Engineering and Compiler Construction,
Ulm University, Ulm Germany
{Dominik.Gessenharter,Martin.Rauscher}@uni-ulm.de

Abstract. Modeling static structure and modeling behavior are often regarded as two distinct topics, however, in UML[1] they are not. They are even tightly coupled as can be seen e.g. by looking at attributes: That an attribute holds values at runtime is defined within the *Classes* language unit whereas the act of setting or getting a concrete value of an attribute is defined in the *Actions* language unit.

Tool support for modeling static structure is far more advanced than for modeling behavior. In particular, further model processing for activities like transformations or code generation is in a rudimentary stage.

In this paper, we present an approach for code generation for activities preceded by model transformations. Besides advancing model-driven development to properly include behavior, our contribution also enhances structural modeling by providing generation of code for accessing structural features based on the UML semantics of *Actions*.

Keywords: UML, Actions, Activities, Code Generation.

1 Introduction

"Modeling is the designing of software applications before coding. Modeling is an essential part of large software projects, and helpful to medium and even small projects as well. (. . .) Models help us by letting us work at a higher level of abstraction. A model may do this by hiding or masking details, bringing out the big picture, or by focusing on different aspects of the prototype." [16]

This characterization of modeling is verbalized in the introduction to the probably most widely-used modeling language – OMG's (Object Management Group) UML, which currently is the de facto standard for modeling software systems. "Built upon fundamental OO concepts including class and operation, it is a natural fit for object-oriented languages and environments." [16] Object oriented programming bases on objects which inherently couple data (values of attributes) and methods for data manipulation.

---

[1] Unified Modeling Language [18], http://www.uml.org

UML supports structural modeling [18, §7] as well as behavioral modeling by defining *Actions* [18, §11] and *Behaviors*. Actions are basic concepts provided by UML whereas behaviors are user-defined. Since *Activity* [18, §12] is the only behavior directly containing actions [2], it is essential for behavioral modeling.

The relation of classes, actions and activities can be seen in Fig. 1 showing the semantic areas of UML as three distinct composite layers. Each layer depends on lower layers, but not on upper ones. The bottom layer is structural. Actions are the behavioral base for the higher-level behavioral formalisms of UML contained in the top layer. Clearly mapping actions to the structural foundation makes it easy to define the semantics of behavioral formalisms based on actions [4].

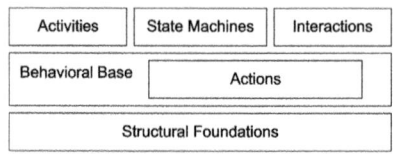

Fig. 1. A schematic of the UML semantic areas and their dependencies

Since modeling a system's structure and behavior gives rise to automatic generation of the full runnable code [11], UML is well suited for Model-Driven Development (MDD). In Sect. 2, we discuss modeling using UML at a glance. As for a comprehensive approach to MDD, tools are required supporting further processing of models [3] including both, structure and behavior, we present our code generation for static structures, *Actions*, and *Activities* in Sect. 3. To keep the code generation process straight forward, a preceding model transformation is used as in Sect. 4. We provide some results of an evaluation of our approach in Sect. 5, followed by a discussion of our contribution and related work.

2 Modeling with UML

2.1 Structural Modeling

The predominant elements of structural models are *Classes* and *Relationships* between classes, most often *Generalizations* and *Associations*. *Property* is used to define the structure of classes and associations. According to its upper bound, a property represents a single value or a collection of values when instantiated.

Another important feature available for classes only is *Operation*. It is a *BehavioralFeature* which may have a behavior associated [18, §13.2.22]. Calling an operation at runtime results in executing its specified behavior, e.g. an activity, a state machine or an *OpaqueBehavior*, i.e. a code fragment of any language.

2.2 Activities

UML defines the semantics of a number of specialized actions which serve as fundamental units of behavior specification. According to the UML metamodel [18]

and Bock[2], actions are directly contained only in activities. The sequence of action executions is defined by control flows or object flows which additionally provide input to actions from outputs of other actions (see Fig. 2(a)).

Our approach focuses on three concepts which make activities a very expressive formalism: *ObjectFlow*, concurrency, and *InterruptibleActivityRegions*. Dedicated object flows are convenient as they clearly show the locations of data creation and consumption and make activities well suited for modeling behaviors where object flows are extensively used. Concurrency may be a result of either explicit or implicit modeling. Fig. 2(b) shows the use of a *ForkNode* and a *JoinNode* for explicitly modeling concurrency and synchronization as well as an implicit fork (outgoing flows of a) and an implicit join (incoming flows of d). *InterruptibleActivityRegions* support aborting executions of actions which are grouped inside the region. Since aborting an execution might prevent locked resources from being released, aborting actions is risky.

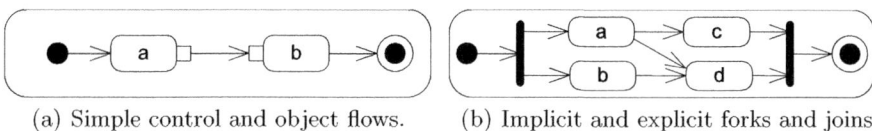

(a) Simple control and object flows.   (b) Implicit and explicit forks and joins

Fig. 2. Two examples of basic activities

2.3 Actions

Actions are the fundamental units of executable functionality. UML's specification contains 37 concrete actions for various purposes. Specializations of *StructuralFeatureAction* support insertion and removal of single attribute values, removal of all values of an attribute and the retrieval of attribute values. Specializations of *LinkAction* provide similar functionality for links of associations. *CallOperationAction* causes a behavior which implements the operation to execute, *CallBehaviorAction* directly invokes another behavior.

Besides graphical modeling, UML encourages the use of a surface action language which encompasses both primitive actions and the control mechanisms provided by behaviors. Furthermore it may introduce higher-level constructs like e.g. a creation operation with initialization as a single unit as a shorthand for the create action to create an object and further actions to initialize attribute values and create objects for mandatory associations [18, §11, p.217].

Foundational UML (fUML)[19], a subset of UML, and the Action Language for Foundational UML (Alf)[17] both have been specified by the OMG. Although only very few new constructs have been introduced, using Alf may have advantages compared to traditional graphical modelling.

Fig. 3(a) shows an activity for setting the value of an attribute of the context object, Fig. 3(b) shows the same activity in Alf. Here, the graphical notation is more complex than a textual, code-like representation. The quicksort example of

(a) Graphical UML notation.

(b) Implementation in Alf

```
1 activity SetName(in _name: String)
2 {
3   this.name = _name;
4 }
```

Fig. 3. Graphical vs. textual representation of an activity writing an attribute value

the Alf specification [17, pp. 366, 368] contrasts an Alf implementation of 10 lines with a graphical representation consuming a whole page of this paper's format. Another advantage of Alf is that it can be seen which feature is updated. In the graphical notation of UML, this detail is not presented.

But even though the level of abstraction differs between graphical representation and Alf, two problems are still unsolved: 1) behavioral modeling in UML is based on very fine grained actions which are not suitable to reach a higher level of abstraction or bringing out a big picture and 2) the poor tool support of activities is not addressed by introducing another representation of activities.

2.4 Interplay of Structures, Actions and Behaviors

Behavioral models depend on structural models if actions access structural features. They may also serve as an implementation of operations contained in structural models. This is illustrated in Fig. 4: The metamodel is given on the left, a concrete instance on the right. Gray shaded beams connect meta classes with their instances in the model. The bold framed actions *read* and *write* are instances of specializations of the bold framed *StructuralFeatureAction*.

Dashed lines pointing from *StructuralFeatureActions* to associated *Structural Features* and from *Operations* to associated *Activities* represent instances of the bold printed meta associations between the corresponding meta classes.

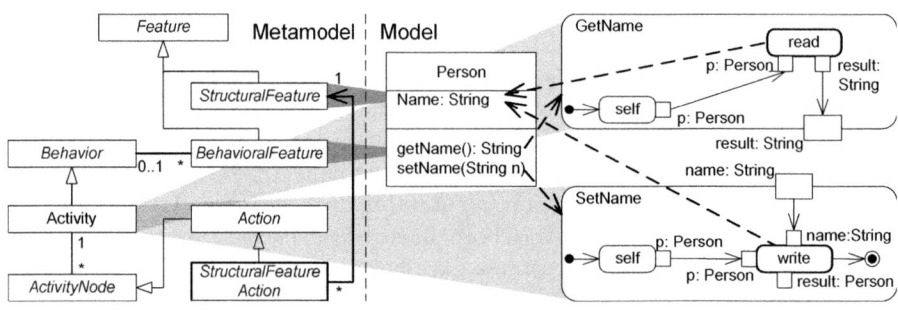

Fig. 4. Dependencies and relationships between metamodel and model elements

3 Code Generation for UML Models

3.1 Implementing Structural Models

Our code generator handles classes with attributes, associations and association classes based on the code patterns presented in our previous works [8]. For attributes, methods for writing and reading values are generated. If an attribute's upper bound is 1, set and get methods are generated, for upper bounds greater than 1, add, get and remove methods are generated. A get method returns a single value or a set of values according to the attribute's upper bound.

Associations are represented as dedicated classes managing a list of tuples representing the links between instances. Association classes are implemented by adding its features to the tuple representing the links.

Methods for creating or destroying links are contained in the implementation class of an association but are only visible to classes participating the association. Within these classes, get as well as set or add and remove methods are generated according to the association end's multiplicity, their visibility is determined by the end's visibility as shown in Fig. 5. The methods generated for association ends delegate calls to the association implementation class which creates or destroys tuples or arranges a result set of instances for get method calls.

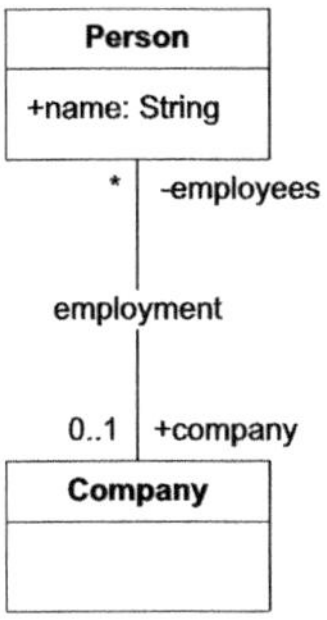

```
1  public class employee{
2      private String name;
3      public void setName(String n){...}
4      public String getName(){...}
5      public void setCompany(Company c){...}
6      public Company getCompany(){...}
7  }
8  public class Company{
9      private void addEmployees(Employee e){...}
10     private void removeEmployees(Employee e){...}
11     private Employee[] getEmployees(){...}
12 }
```

(a) Class Diagram   (b) Implementation of classes Employee and Company

Fig. 5. An example of a structural model and its implementation. Note that for the association *employment* no implementation is contained in Fig. 5(b).

3.2 Code Generation for Actions

Generating code for accessing attributes or associations is close to an implementation of actions. To fit to the specification, set, get, add, and remove methods must be mapped to *StructuralFeatureActions* and *LinkActions* and thus be called when an *Action* associated with the corresponding attribute is executed.

Actions are implemented as part of the static structure by inserting code into those classes which are affected by an action, e.g. a *StructuralFeatureAction* is implemented in the class owning the associated feature.

In Sect. 2.3, we refer to the idea of using a surface action language. We avoid the development of such a language as well as supporting an existing one by using *OpaqueActions* for coupling models and code: for each *OpaqueAction*, an equally named method within the activity's context is called, i. e. code written by the user when implementing the method. Within this code, methods to which action executions are mapped can directly be called, i. e. actions can be used in models as well as in code. Generated code is located in generated classes whereas user written code is located in a subclass thereof. Thus, both kinds of code are separated from each other while generated code is still accessible to the user.

3.3 Basic Token Flow Concept

The semantics of the abstract metaclass *Action* from *FundamentalActivities* defines four steps of executing an action [18], of which the first is to create an action execution. The creation of an execution requires all object flow and control flow prerequisites to be satisfied, i. e. tokens must be available at all incoming edges. The second step is the consumption of the tokens which are removed from the original sources. The third step is executing the action until it terminates. After termination, the last step is to offer tokens to all outgoing edges.

A sequence of actions a and b with a single flow from a to b as shown in Fig. 6(a) is implemented as a sequence of statements (Fig. 6(b)).

Object flows may be implemented by explicitly using a variable or by nesting calls, as shown for c and d in Fig. 6(b) and Fig. 6(c).

If multiple object flows exist between two actions, this still can be implemented as a sequence of statements. Depending on the implementation language, processing of the parameters requires appropriate techniques. Considering Java which only supports a single return value and no out parameters, a class is required to hold the return values as shown in Fig. 6(b). The class XY has two attributes representing the values of x and y, action e must create an instance of that class and write its output to the attributes. Fig. 6(c) shows an alternative implementation suitable for languages providing *out* parameters.

A basic flow, i. e. a flow from one action to another without any control nodes in between, sequences actions so that two sequential statements calling the according methods is a suitable implementation. Such sequences can be implemented in a single thread and as threads may be executed concurrently, a flow of multiple tokens can be implemented. For a proper implementation of the token flow semantics, it is necessary to properly implement guards as well as control nodes, as explained in the following.

3.4 Guards

If the guard of an edge does not hold, it prevents tokens from traversing that edge. Applied to Fig. 6, if a guard is annotated to the edge from a to b (or c to d or e to f respectively) the call of b() (d() or f()) is deferred as long as the guard is not satisfied. A proper implementation requires to pause the execution of code, if a guard prevents a token from flowing. This is important in particular

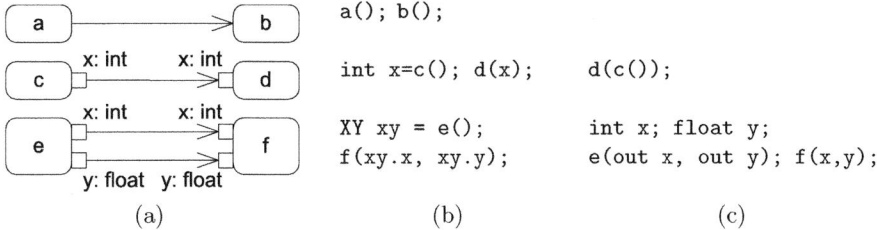

Fig. 6. Three examples of sequences of actions and implementations

if concurrency occurs in an activity: The evaluation of a guard may depend on other concurrently executed sequences of actions. An implementation using if is insufficient as this does not cause the control flow of an application to pause.

Regarding Fig. 6, inserting while (!<guard>){;} after a();, c();, and e(); pauses the activity execution. A more sophisticated approach is to let a thread wait until the guard holds. As a waiting thread cannot evaluate the guard, all waiting threads must be notified if a guard might evaluate to true. Therefore, all actions writing values to attributes or variables contain code to notify waiting threads which immediately re-evaluate guards. Depending on the result of this evaluation, threads continue executing or waiting for another notification.

Besides deferring the execution of an action in a sequence of actions, guards have a far more complex impact on the execution of actions if used in combination with control nodes. This is discussed in detail later.

3.5 Token Flow at Control Nodes

UML defines four kinds of control nodes: *DecisionNode*, *MergeNode*, *ForkNode*, and *JoinNode*. Before going into detail, we roughly give the implication of control nodes. A *DecisionNode* is used to choose between multiple alternatives from which only one may be taken. A *ForkNode* splits an incoming flow into multiple concurrent outgoing flows. Multiple flows are combined to one single flow by a *MergeNode*. A token arriving at one incoming edge results in a token flow on the outgoing edge. When combining multiple flows with a *JoinNode*, a token must be available at each incoming edge to emit a single token at the outgoing edge.

Tokens cannot rest at control nodes. A control token always flows from one action to another action, a data token may flow to a central buffer. An exception to this rule is the *ForkNode*, where tokens may be buffered. We discuss this in detail when looking closer at fork nodes later.

Note that two or more incoming edges of an action represent an implicit join, i.e. tokens must be offered to all incoming edges. This implicit join may be made explicit either by modeling so or by a model transformation. Therefore, we consider activities to be free of implicit joins. Analogously, two or more outgoing edges represent an implicit fork. For the same reason as for implicit joins, we consider all forks to be explicitly modeled.

3.6 Code Generation Based on Token Flow Semantics

Generating code for sequences of actions is easy. When considering control nodes, the situation gets more complex, depending on how complex flows are composed: 1) at most one control node is used in a flow from one action to another; 2) flows may contain any quantity of control nodes, but the flow from the source to the target is acyclic; 3) any quantity of control nodes and cycles may occur.

The code generation as presented in this paper is designed for activities where flows contain at most one control node. However, it can be adapted to handle more complex flows, but remarkable effort is required. We provide additional information to this issue where necessary.

Our prototype is implemented in Java, but the general idea can be applied to any other object oriented language supporting threads. Sequences of actions are translated to sequences of method calls, each method being the implementation of the corresponding action (see above). Between sequences, control nodes occur so that at the end of each sequence, depending on the semantics of that control node, subsequent sequence(s) to execute must be determined and started.

As sequences might be executed concurrently, they must be implemented as dedicated threads. Separating the code for sequences in individual classes causes a large number of classes being created. We prefer to include all code in one class and to determine at runtime, which lines of code to execute. For this purpose, an id is introduced which is used to identify the sequence to run, as indicated by the grey boxes in Fig. 7. Setting the id to -1 causes the thread to terminate.

```
1  class ActThread extends Thread {
2    private int id = 1;
3    public ActThread(int id) {
4      this.id = id;}
5    public void run() {
6      while(id >= 0) {
7        switch(id) {
8          case 1: a();
9                  new ActThread(2).start();
10                 id = 3;
11                 break;
12         case 2: b1();
13                 b2();
14                 id=4;
15                 break;
16         case 3: c1();
17                 c2();
18                 id=4;
19                 break;
20         case 4: d();
21                 id = -1;    } } } }
```

Fig. 7. An activity and the generated code for its implementation

Changing the id to another value causes the thread to execute another sequence of actions. If two sequences are to be started concurrently, a new thread is created with the appropriate id and the id of the current thread is changed according to the other sequence (cf Fig. 7, ll. 9–10). If a thread needs input data due to an object flow, id and data must be provided as parameters when creating it.

3.7 Token Flow at Control Nodes in Detail

Implementing a merge node is achieved by changing the value of id, as can be seen in Fig. 7, line 14 and line 18.

A token arriving at a decision node may traverse any of the outgoing edges, but only one of them. If guards are annotated to outgoing edges – what typically is the case as these guards define the decision to take – the token may traverse any edge the guard of which evaluates to true. If one of the outgoing edges is labeled with an else guard as is in Fig. 8(a), at least one edge may always be traversed. A suitable implementation is:

```
a();    if (x>0) id = ...;    else    id = ...;
```

Fig. 8(b) shows a situation in which none of the outgoing edges may be traversed if x=0. The decision shown in Fig. 8(c) is non-deterministic if x=0. To consider this while code generation requires an analysis of the guards which is difficult as guards may be any boolean expression evaluated within the context of the activity. We prefer to test guards of all edges for holding until a guard is found that is satisfied. If none of the guards holds, the thread waits until receiving a notification which is sent when attribute or variable values are changed.

```
while (true){
  if (<guard1>) { id = ...; break; }
  if (<guard2>) { id = ...; break; }
  ...
  wait(); }
```

A very complex semantics is that of the fork node. A token offered to its incoming edge is offered to the targets of its outgoing edges, if the corresponding guards hold. If at least one token is accepted by a target, a copy of this token is buffered at each outgoing edge which guard holds, but the target of which cannot accept the token. An example for this is given later on the basis of Fig. 9. If at most one control node appears between two actions, the implementation of the fork

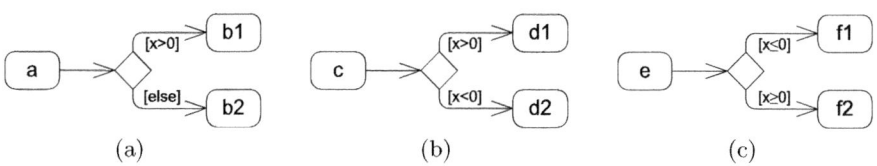

Fig. 8. Three examples of the use of a *DecisionNode*

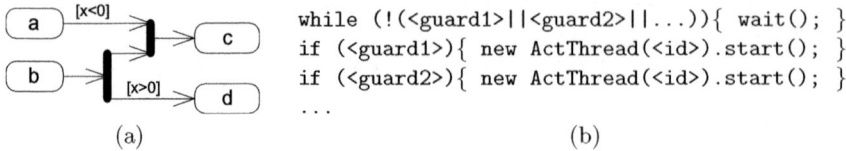

Fig. 9. Use of fork and join nodes invalidating a simple fork node implementation

node is similar to that of the decision node as can be seen in Fig. 9(b). Items in angle brackets must be replaced by actual values.

If a flow from one action to another contains more than one control node, not only the guards of an edge determine whether a target action accepts a token. Subsequent *JoinNodes* may prevent a token from flowing, too. An example is given in Fig. 9(a).

A) If a token is offered only to the outgoing edge of a and x<0 holds, c cannot accept that token as an additional token from b is required.

B) If a token is available at b but not at a, d is executed if x>0 and a token is buffered at the edge from the fork node to the join node; if x<0, the offered token at b cannot flow.

C) If tokens are available from a and b and x<0 holds, c is executed and no token is buffered at the fork node as the guard of the edge to d fails.

D) If, under conditions of C), x>0 holds, d is executed and a token is buffered at the fork node. As soon as x<0 holds, c is executed.

Note that the implementation of Fig. 9(b) is sufficient for a single fork node, but not if a fork node is used together with other control nodes in the same flow.

A proper implementation considering token buffering must represent control nodes as objects able to propagate tokens to subsequent control nodes and to indicate consumption of tokens to precedent nodes.

The *JoinNode* is the most complex node with regard to implementation. Although it is known which sequences must be executed before the join node is reached, it is not known, which threads will be the first ones reaching the join node. Our implementation of a join node is a class with lists of objects. Each list represents an incoming edge. Whenever one of the sequences ending at the join nodes terminates, a token is added to the appropriate list. After that, the join implementation checks all lists and if each list contains at least one token and all guards are satisfied, the next sequence is started and tokens are removed from the lists.

3.8 Implementing InterruptibleActivityRegions

When entering an *InterruptibleActivityRegion*, i.e. before executing the first action inside it, the current thread adds itself to a list of active threads inside the region (Fig. 10(b), l. 2). When leaving the region, the thread removes itself from the list as aborting the region no longer affects this thread (Fig. 10(b), l. 4). For convenience, the list is managed by an object representing the group (ir1).

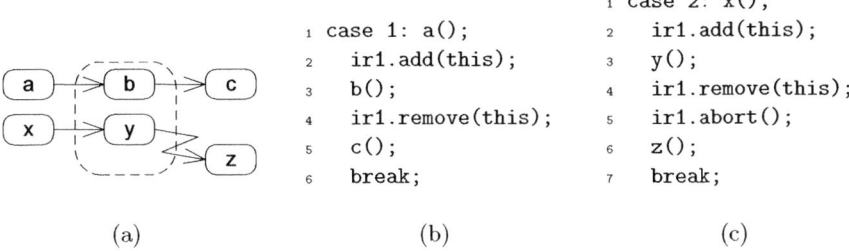

Fig. 10. Code for supporting *InterruptibleActivityRegions*

The implementation of a sequence which leaves the region via an edge interrupting the region contains lines for adding and removing the thread in the list as well (Fig. 10(c), ll. 2 and 4). For actually causing all actions inside the region to be aborted, ir1.abort(); is called (Fig. 10(c), l. 6). The implementation of that method might either kill all threads, sent a message requesting the threads to terminate, or set a flag which is checked before new actions are executed. One of the two latter options probably is preferable as killing threads – although closer to the specification – is quite risky.

A proper implementation of interruptible regions requires, when interrupted, to clear those lists of join nodes which represent edges having their source located inside the region and fork nodes within the region to discard buffered tokens.

4 Preparing Models by Model Transformations

A model transformation can keep our code generation straight forward by applying three steps: 1) make implicit forks and joins explicit; 2) move sequences such as shown in Fig. 6(a) to separate behaviors and replace them by *CallBehaviorActions*; 3) if possible, replace multiple control nodes by a single one.

An activity and the result of the transformation is shown in Fig. 11. Note that the two object flows between a1 and a2 are not handled as an implicit fork and subsequent join since both flows can be implemented as in Fig. 6.

The transformation A^t of activity A only contains *CallBehaviorActions* which implement simple sequences of actions. If A contained a *CallBehaviorAction* (say action a2), it was moved to activity X. Consequently, each *CallBehaviorAction* of A^t is mapped to a sequence of actions, each *CallBehaviorAction* occurring in a sequence represents a call of another behavior. All control nodes sequencing the sequences of actions remain in A^t. Thus, finding sequences is part of the transformation whereas sequencing of sequences is part of the code generation. Both conversions are solved purely programmatic by prototypically implementations.

Since all actions still persist – even though at a different location – mapping actions of A^t to actions of A can easily be done if necessary e.g. for the development of a debugger. In our approach, debugging is done by using our interpreter, but adding debug information to the generated code in principle is possible.

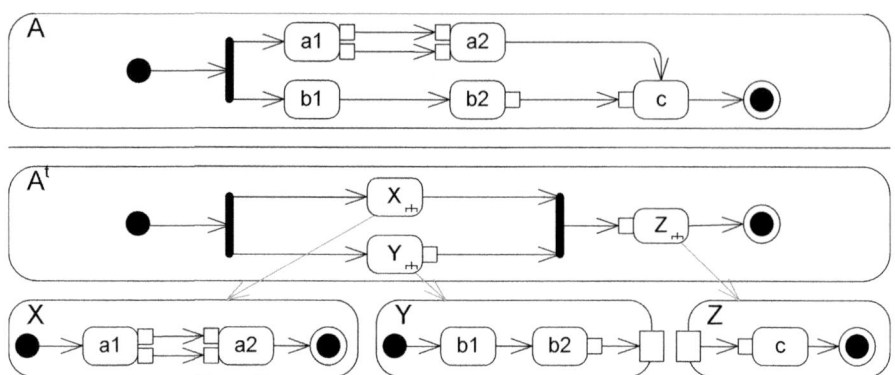

Fig. 11. Activity A and its transformation A^t with Activities X, Y, and Z

5 Evaluation

We consider the question of semantic correctness of model transformations and code generation as well as a comparison of generated code and model interpreters.

This does not include a formal verification of the semantic correctness, but our work is based on the formalization of the semantics of UML2 activities by Sarstedt [20] which we compared to the fUML specification. Since fUML is a subset of UML introducing additional constraints, its semantic is less complex. E. g. for fork nodes, the influence of guards on token buffering is dropped as fUML allows guards only at edges outgoing from a decision node.

The token flow formalization [20] serving as a foundation for our work is not UML compliant with regard to token buffering at fork nodes. This issue is considered in this work and tests show that for all elements presented here, the effects of generated code are equal to those of interpreters resulting from our own previous work as well as to that of a reference implementation of fUML[2].

An evaluation of our model transformation is done on a metalevel by the following consideration: moving sequences of actions to activities which are associated to a *CallBehaviorAction* is equivalent to the mapping of fUML where sequences of actions are moved into a structured node [19, §A.3.1].

Compared to Alf, UML activities are more expressive. E. g. in Alf, parallel flows are always arranged in a block structure, i. e. Fig. 2(b) cannot be expressed in Alf as in its syntax block statements may have a *parallel* annotation to force concurrent execution and synchronization of these blocks. In UML, *JoinNodes* wait for tokens on each incoming edge for synchronization. These tokens not necessarily have to be a copy of the same source token built at a *ForkNode*.

For evaluation of our prototype, we modeled an information system for public transportation of an imaginary city and generated code from that model. The structural model consists of 17 classes, 14 associations and 3 association classes,

---

[2] http://portal.modeldriven.org/content/fuml-reference-implementation-download

the behavioral model consists of a single activity of 14 Actions, 8 control flows and 15 object flows. Applying our code generation approach, the output is 1700 lines of code for the structural model including the implementation of actions and another 700 lines of code for the implementation of the activity.

The implementation of the static structure and of the behavior makes up more than 75% of the entire project code excluding the GUI. If excluding behavior, generated code amounts to only about 15%. For more details about the sample project as well as its implementation, we refer to our previous work [9].

Another aspect worth evaluating are runtime characteristics and size of the generated code. Numbers of these characteristics are only interesting if compared to those of other approaches. We compare our code generation approach with different kinds of activity interpreters: 1) an interpreter computing each token flow step by propagating tokens along edges; 2) an enhanced interpreter using lookup tables for flow computation – both results of our previous work – and 3) the fUML reference implementation.

The code generated by our prototype executes faster than interpreters as expected since interpreting causes additional overhead whereas generated code may be optimized by the compiler. The numerous console outputs of the fUML reference implementation were considered by adding console output to our code generator. Increasing complexity of models has fewer impact on the execution time of generated code. However, our own interpreters allocate less memory than the generated code if activities are complex; in case of small activities, memory allocation of generated code may be better as that of interpreters[3]. For a more detailed comparison of generated code and interpreters, we refer to our previous work [10].

6 Discussion and Related Work

In UML, only actions provide access to structural features. Some tools, e.g. Fujaba [25] provide access to attributes or even to associations by additional lines of code [7], which is a proprietary add-on not based on the UML specification. Such extra code can be seen as an implementation of actions if being mapped to the actions they represent, thus becoming applicable for behavioral modeling. Since *Activities* are the only behavior containing *Actions*, code implementing actions must be called when executing corresponding actions in an activity.

Our eclipse based prototype uses *UML2* of the *Modeling Development Tools (MDT)* [5] and can be coupled with a compatible editor such as *Eclipse UML2 Tools* or Papyrus [26] in order to provide a user friendly modeling interface with our model processing facilities. A survey giving a detailed analysis of current tools [6] reveals, that support of activities w.r.t. modeling is well supported in very few tools, e.g. Papyrus [26]. Further processing of activities, in particular their execution by interpreters or code generation is only rudimentary supported, if at all. If generating code for actions and compiling activities to code as presented, for some essential modeling elements the execution semantics of activities can be fully preserved when building applications from UML models.

---

[3] fUML reference implementation is excluded from this comparison

Activities are often associated with business processes. Our approach is probably not feasible for implementing business workflows. There are workflow engines available to which such processes might be deployed. But activities can also be used to describe short workflows were failover features with process state preservation etc. is not needed. E. g. the workflow of purchasing a ticket required to use a public transportation system: using a workflow engine for the process of selecting a departure and a destination station, a departure or arrival time and selecting a connection fitting the given constraints is oversized. For such purposes, we consider generating code a good idea.

Some advantages of generating code are that we can profit from compiler technique benefits like code optimizations which would have to be re-implemented in an interpreter if runtime characteristics of compiled code are desired. Not building an interpreter but transforming activities to code and thus making the Java virtual machine to the model interpreter is our goal.

Our approach supports implementations for accessing structural features and maps it to corresponding actions, thus achieving the coupling of structures and behaviors. By additionally accurately considering the subtleties of the UML token flow semantics, our approach supports behavioral modeling according to the specification. However, as composing complex flows by combining multiple control nodes between actions makes code generation very difficult – if not impossible – our approach is limited to a single control node between two actions. This limitation may be dropped when implementing control nodes as dedicated classes with methods for token propagation and token consumption.

Although other approaches dealing with code generation for activities exist, these approaches most often focus on some special application in which code generation for activities is only a minor part. UML based Web Engineering (UWE) [12,13] is concerned with this issue, but even claiming being based on standards, UWE only uses the notation but as can be seen in examples, the semantics of implicit joins is not considered [13, pp. 171,176][14]. Blu Age [23] which is based on executable UML suffers the same restriction.

Another approach for comprehensive MDD is implemented in UJECTOR. Since the provided examples only consist of simple sequences of actions [22, pp. 30,34], we can not assess the value of code generation for activities of this tool.

Sulistyo and Prinz propose *recursive modeling* to obtain complete code [21], but the introduced code patterns neither support concurrency nor a delay of token flow due to not holding guards.

Bhattacharjee and Shyamasundar present an approach for *validated code generation for activity diagrams* [1]. Mapping activities to Esterel, a language supporting concurrency, this approach overcomes limitations of the so far mentioned works. However, even here some problems are not addressed, e. g. the fact that it can not be statically decided which threads will be joined when reaching a join node. A delay of a token flow due to not satisfied guard conditions as well as the token buffering semantics of fork nodes are not considered.

Executable UML [15] gives detailed advice how to build executable UML models, but without addressing details of compiling models to code. BridgePoint[24] is a tool based on executable UML, but modeling UML2 activities is not supported. Instead, Object Action Language (OAL) is used, which is less expressive than Alf as concurrency is not supported on the same level. Deferring an activity execution due to non satisfied guards is not possible in OAL, too. Thus, central concepts which we address in this paper are not applicable there.

Summing up we can find the token flow semantics of activities being not sufficiently implemented in current approaches or tools using more restrictive formalisms such as subsets of the UML specification of activities or action languages. As explained, a decision node cannot be implemented only by using an `if-then-else` statement. If the guard of each outgoing edge is not satisfied, the decision is delayed until one guard holds. Suchlike effects of the token flow semantics are very different to what programmers are used to and possibly therefore often not considered – but dealing with them is the essence of this contribution.

7 Conclusion and Future Work

Since code for behavior amounts for over 50% of the complete code of our sample project, better tool support for behaviors is a promising perspective. Furthermore, according to the specifiaction, activities couple behavior and structure. Thus, for comprehensive MDD, supporting activities is indispensible. Runtime characteristics of generated code show that including activities in an MDD approach by code generation offers some advantages which interpreters do not.

Our approach is currently limited with regard to a complex composition of flows by using control nodes. Pushing this boundary by analyzing complex flows which can – if matching special patterns – be implemented without explicit token propagation is our next step. Depending on the limitations remaining after that, a decision of whether implementing flows explicitly or not will be taken. A major objection is, that generating code for token propagation may become close to generating an interpreter which computes each step at runtime.

Apart from that, supporting additional modeling concepts like e.g. *Streaming* of object flows are further steps to take. Even architectural aspects like deployment raising the complexity of communication between instances might be considered, thus integrating behavior, structure and other aspects of UML.

References

1. Bhattacharjee, A., Shyamasundar, R.: Validated Code Generation for Activity Diagrams. In: Chakraborty, G. (ed.) ICDCIT 2005. LNCS, vol. 3816, pp. 508–521. Springer, Heidelberg (2005)
2. Bock, C.: UML 2 Activity and Action Models Part 2: Actions. Journal of Object Technology 2(5), 41–56 (2003)
3. Broy, M.: Challenges in Automotive Software Engineering. Proceedings of the ICSE 2006, pp. 33–42 (2006)
4. Crane, M.L.: Slicing UML's Three-layer Architecture: A Semantic Foundation for Behavioural Specification. PhD thesis, Queen's University, Kingston, Ontario, Canada (January 2009)

5. Eclipse Foundation, Inc. Eclipse Model Development Tools (MDT) (2011), http://www.eclipse.org
6. Eichelberger, H., Eldogan, Y., Schmid, K.: A Comprehensive Analysis of UML Tools, their Capabilities and their Compliance. Software Systems Engineering, Institut für Informatik, Universität Hildesheim (2009)
7. Fujaba Associations Specification (2005), http://www.se.eecs.uni-kassel.de/~fujabawiki/index.php/Fujaba/ Associations/~Specification
8. Gessenharter, D.: Implementing UML Associations in Java: A Slim Code Pattern for a Complex Modeling Concept. In: RAOOL 2009: Proceedings of the Workshop on Relationships and Associations in Object-Oriented Languages, pp. 17–24. ACM, New York (2009)
9. Gessenharter, D.: Extending The UML Semantics for a Better Support of Model Driven Software Development. In: Software Engineering Research and Practice, pp. 45–51 (2010)
10. Gessenharter, D.: UML Activities at Runtime - Experiences of Using Interpreters and Running Generated Code. In: Trujillo, J., Dobbie, G., Kangassalo, H., Hartmann, S., Kirchberg, M., Rossi, M., Reinhartz-Berger, I., Zimányi, E., Frasincar, F. (eds.) ER 2010. LNCS, vol. 6413, pp. 275–284. Springer, Heidelberg (2010)
11. Harel, D.: From Play-In Scenarios to Code: An Achievable Dream. Computer 34, 53–60 (2001)
12. Koch, N., Kraus, A.: The Expressive Power of UML-based Web Engineering (2002)
13. Koch, N., Zhang, G., Baumeister, H.: UML-Based Web Engineering: An Approach Based on Standards. In: Web Engineering: Modelling and Implementing Web Applications, pp. 157–191 (2008)
14. LMU: Ludwig-Maximilians-Universität München, Institute for Informatics Programming and Software Engineering. UWE Examples (December 2009), http://uwe.pst.ifi.lmu.de/exampleAddressBookWithContentUpdates.html
15. Mellor, S.J., Balcer, M.: Executable UML: A Foundation for Model-Driven Architectures. Addison-Wesley Longman Publishing Co., Inc., Boston (2002); Foreword By-Jacoboson, Ivar
16. Object Management Group. Introduction to OMG's Unified Modeling Language (UML) (July 2005), http://www.omg.org/gettingstarted/what_is_uml.htm
17. Object Management Group. Action Language for Foundational UML (Alf), Concrete Syntax for a UML Action Language, FTF Beta 1, OMG Document Number: ptc/2010-10-05 (2010)
18. Object Management Group. Unified Modeling Language (OMG UML), Superstructure Version 2.3 (2010), OMG Document Number: formal/2010-05-05
19. Object Management Group. Semantics of a Foundational Subset for Executable UML Models (fUML), v1.0 (2011), OMG Document Number: formal/2011-02-01
20. Sarstedt, S.: Semantic Foundation and Tool Support for Model-Driven Development with UML 2 Activity Diagrams. PhD thesis, Ulm University (2006)
21. Sulistyo, S., Prinz, A.: Recursive Modeling for Completed Code Generation. In: Proceedings of the 1st Workshop on Behaviour Modelling in Model-Driven Architecture, BM-MDA 2009, pp. 6:1–6:7. ACM, New York (2009)
22. Usman, M., Nadeem, A.: Automatic Generation of Java Code from UML Diagrams using UJECTOR. International Journal of Software Engineering and Its Applications 3(2), 21–37 (2009)
23. Blu Age Corp., Blu Age (2011), http://wiki.bluage.com/, §3.5.1
24. Mentor Graphics Corp., BridgePoint UML Suite (2010), http://www.mentor.com
25. Fujaba Development Group, Fujaba Tool Suite 4.3.2 (2007), http://www.fujaba.de/
26. Papyrus, Open Source Tool (2011), http://www.papyrusuml.org

*Tract*able Model Transformation Testing

Martin Gogolla[1] and Antonio Vallecillo[2]

[1] Database Systems Group, University of Bremen, Germany
[2] GISUM/Atenea Research Group, Universidad de Málaga, Spain
gogolla@informatik.uni-bremen.de, av@lcc.uma.es

Abstract. Model transformation (MT) testing is gaining interest as the size and complexity of MTs grows. In general it is very difficult and expensive (time and computational complexity-wise) to validate in full the correctness of a MT. This paper presents a MT testing approach based on the concept of Tract, which is a generalization of the concept of Model Transformation Contract. A Tract defines a set of constraints on the source and target metamodels, a set of source-target constraints, and a tract test suite, i.e., a collection of source models satisfying the source constraints. We automatically generate input test suite models, which are then transformed into output models by the transformation under test, and the results checked with the USE tool (UML-based Specification Environment) against the constraints defined for the transformation. We show the different kinds of tests that can be conducted over a MT using this automated process, and the kinds of problems it can help uncovering.

1 Introduction

Model transformations are key elements of Model-driven Engineering (MDE). They allow querying, synthesizing and transforming models into other models or into code, and can also be composed in chains for building new and more powerful model transformations.

As the size and complexity of model transformations grow, there is an increasing need to count on mechanisms and tools for testing their correctness. This is specially important in case of transformations with hundreds or thousands of rules, for which manual debugging is no longer possible—but for which we still need to check whether the produced models conform to the target metamodel, or whether some essential properties are preserved by the transformation.

Testing model transformations is not an easy task and present numerous challenges [1,2,3,4]. In the literature there are two main approaches to model transformation testing (see also Section 5). In the first place we have the works that aim at fully *validating* the behaviour of the transformation and its associated properties (confluence of the rules, termination, etc.) using formal methods and their associated toolkits (see, e.g., [5,6,7,8,9,10,11]). The potential limitations with these proposals lies in their inherent computational complexity, which makes them inappropriate for fully testing large and complex model transformations. An alternative approach (proposed in, e.g., [12,13,14,15,16]) consists of trying to *certify* that a transformation works for a selected set of test input models, without trying to validate it for the full input space. Although such a certification approach cannot fully prove correctness, it can be very useful for identifying bugs in a very cost-effective manner, and can deal with industrial-size transformations without having to abstract away any of the structural or behavioural properties of the transformations.

In this paper we will follow this latter approach, making use of some of the concepts, languages and tools that have proved to be very useful in the case of model validation [17]. In particular, we generalize *model transformation contracts* [2,18] for the specification of the properties that need to be checked for a transformation, and then apply the ASSL language [19] to generate input test models, which are then automatically transformed into output models and checked against the set of contracts defined for the transformation, using the USE tool [20].

This paper is organized as follows. After this introduction, Section 2 describes the context of our work and introduces the running example that will be used throughout the paper to illustrate our approach. Section 3 presents our proposal and describes the prototype we have developed as a proof-of-concept. Then, Section 4 discusses the kinds of tests that can be conducted and how to perform them. Finally, Section 5 compares our work with other related proposals and Section 6 draws the final conclusions and outlines some lines for future work.

2 Context

2.1 Models and Metamodels

In MDE, models are defined in the language of their metamodels. In this paper we consider that metamodels are defined by a set of classes, binary associations between them, and a set of integrity constraints.

In Figure 1 we show our running example as handled by the tool USE [20]. The aim of the example is to transform a Person source metamodel shown in the upper part of the class diagram into a Family target metamodel displayed in the middle part. The source permits representing people and their relations (marriage, parents, children) while the target focuses on families and their members.

Some integrity constraints are expressed as multiplicity constraints in the metamodels, such as the ones that state that a family always has to have one mother and one father, or that a person (either female or male) can be married to at most one person.

There are other constraints that require specialized notations because they imply more complex expressions. In this paper we will use OCL [21] as the language for stating constraints. In order to keep matters simple, we have decided to include only one source metamodel constraint (SMM) and one target metamodel constraint (TMM). On the Person side (source), we require that, if two parents are present, they must have different gender (SMM_parentsFM). On the Family side (target), we require an analogous condition (TMM_mumFemale_dadMale). Many further constraints (like acyclicity of parenthood or exclusion of marriage between parents and children or between siblings) could be stated for the two models.

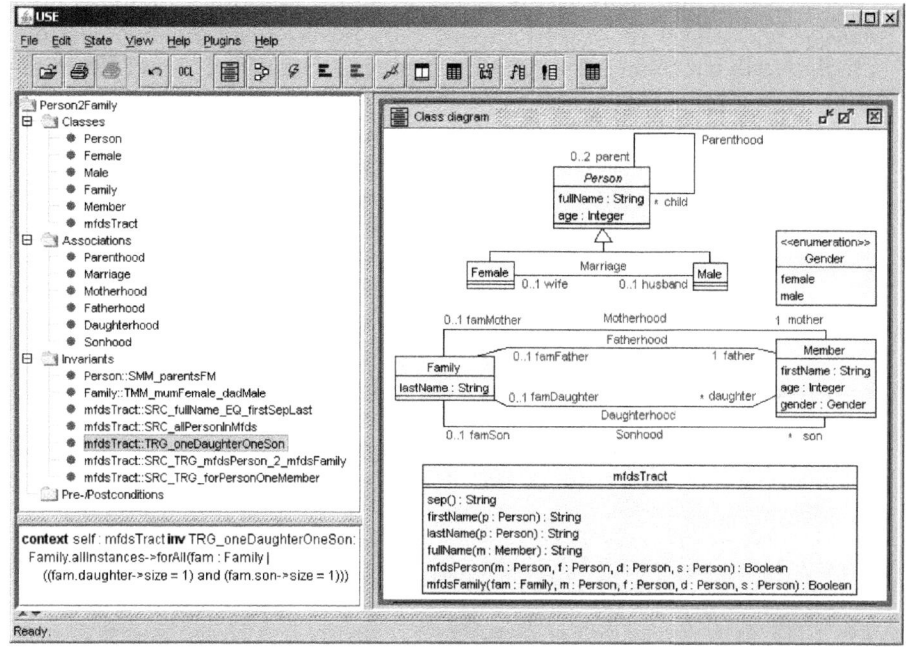

Fig. 1. USE Screenshot

```
context Person inv SMM_parentsFM:
  parent->size()=2 implies
    parent->select(oclIsTypeOf(Female))->size()=1 and
    parent->select(oclIsTypeOf(Male))->size()=1
context Family inv TMM_mumFemale_dadMale:
  mother.gender = #female and father.gender = #male
```

2.2 Model Transformations

In a nutshell, a model transformation is an algorithmic specification (either declarative or operational) of the relationship between models, and more specifically the mapping from one model to another. A model transformation involves at least two models (the source and the target), which may conform to the same or to different metamodels. The transformation specification is often given by a set of model transformation rules, which describe how a model in the source language can be transformed into a model in the target language.

One of the challenges of model transformation testing is the heterogeneity of model transformation languages and techniques [4]. This problem is aggravated by the possibility of having to test model transformations which are defined as a composition of several model transformations chained together. In our proposal we use a black-box testing approach, by which a model transformation is just a program that we invoke. The main advantages of this approach are that we can deal with any transformation language and that we will be able to test the model transformation *as-is*, i.e., without having to transform it into any other language, represent it using any formalism, or abstract away any of its features.

To illustrate our proposal we will use a running example of a model transformation that, given a Family model, creates a Person model. The goal is to show how this transformation can be tested. For this place we asked some students to write such a transformation, and the resulting code is shown below. It is written in ATL [22], a hybrid model transformation language containing a mixture of declarative and imperative constructs which is widely used in industry and academia.

```
module Persons2Families ;
create OUT : Families from IN : Persons ;

rule Father2Family{
 from f : Persons!Male (not f.child -> isEmpty())
 to fam : Families!Family (
     lastName <-f.name.substring(f.name.lastIndexOf(' ')+2,
                                 f.name.size()) ),
    mb : Families!Member (
     firstName <- f.name.substring(1,f.name.lastIndexOf(' ')),
     age <- f.age, gender <- #male, famFather <- fam )
}
rule Mother2Family{
 from m : Persons!Female (not m.child -> isEmpty())
 to mb : Families!Member (
     firstName <- m.name.substring(1,m.name.lastIndexOf(' ')),
     age <- m.age, gender <- #female, famMother <- m.husband )
}
rule Son2Family{
 from s : Persons!Male (s.child -> isEmpty())
 to mb : Families!Member (
     firstName <- s.name.substring(1,s.name.lastIndexOf(' ')),
     age <- s.age, gender <- #male,
     famSon <-s.parent->select(e|e.oclIsTypeOf(Persons!Male)) )
}
rule Daughter2Family{
 from d : Persons!Female (d.child -> isEmpty())
 to mb : Families!Member (
     firstName <-d.name.substring(1,d.name.lastIndexOf(' ')),
     age <- d.age, gender <- #female,
     famDaughter <- d.parent->select(e|e.oclIsTypeOf(Persons!Male)) )
}
```

This transformation is defined in terms of four basic rules, each one responsible for building the corresponding target model elements depending on the four kinds of role a source person can play in a family: father, mother, son or daughter. The attributes and references of every target element are calculated using the information of the source elements. Target elements that represent families are created with the last name of the father (in rule Father2Family).

3 Tracts for Model Transformations

3.1 Model Transformation Contracts

In Figure 2 we have displayed the central ingredients of our approach for transformation testing: a source and target metamodel, the transformation T under test, and a transformation contract, for short *tract*, which consists of a tract test suite and a set of tract constraints. The test suite and its transformation result

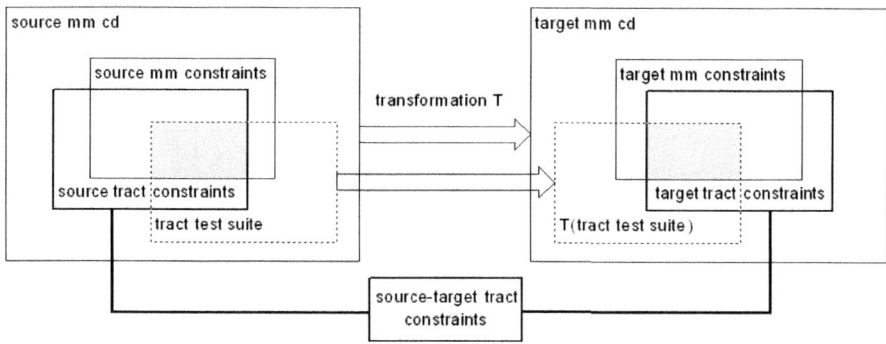

Fig. 2. Building Blocks of a Tract

are shown with dashed lines and the different tract constraints with thick lines. Five different kinds of constraints are present: the source and target class diagrams are restricted by source and target metamodels constraints, and the tract imposes source, target, and source-target tract constraints. Such constraints are expressed by means of OCL invariants. The context of these invariants is a class representing a transformation tract, a so-called tract class. An example of a tract class called mfdsTract is shown in Figure 1.

Assume a source model M being an element of the test suite and satisfying the metamodel source and the tract source constraints is given. Then, the tract essentially requires that the result $T(M)$ of applying transformation T satisfies the target metamodel and the target tract constraints and the pair $(M,T(M))$ satisfies the source-target tract constraints. The source-target tract constraints are crucial insofar that they can establish a correspondence between a source element and a target element in a declarative way by means of a formula. Note that this declarative correspondence between source and target has to be made explicit in other transformation approaches like the triple graph grammar (TGG) proposal [23] or the Epsilon framework [24]. In technical terms, a source tract constraint is basically an OCL expression with free variables over source elements, a target tract constraint has free variables over target elements, and a source-target tract constraint possesses free variables over source and target elements. Figure 3 gives an overview on the used concepts and their connection.

In Figure 2, the rectangles indicate possible overlap (resp. disjointness) of source and target models. Basically, the tract — consisting of the test suite and the three kinds of constraints — checks for the correctness of the transformation in the sense that correct source models from the test suite are transformed to correct target models, i.e., our approach checks that in Figure 2 the grey source section is transformed into the grey target section. In general, there will be more than one tract for a single transformation because particular source models are constructed in the test suite which then induce particular tract constraints.

Let us go back to our example in Figure 1. The lower part of the class diagram pictures the tract metamodel represented by the class mfdsTract where mfds is

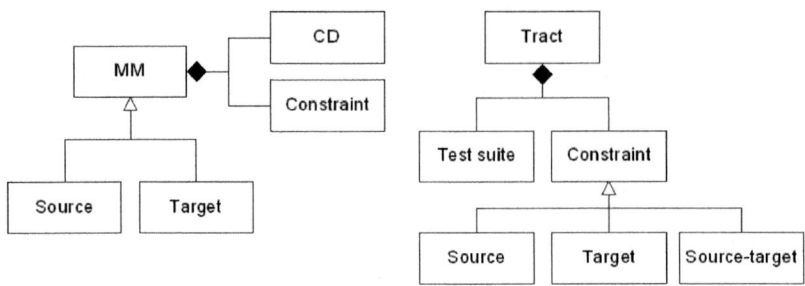

Fig. 3. Concepts in a Tract

a shortcut for mother-father-daughter-son expressing that our tract and our testing (for demonstration purposes) concentrates on conventional families with exactly one person in the respective role. The operations in class mfdsTract are helper operations for formulating the tract constraints which are shown as invariants on the left in the project browser. The five different kinds of constraints are reflected by different prefixes for invariant names: SMM for source metamodel constraints, TMM for target metamodel constraints, SRC for source tract constraints, TRG for target tract constraints, and SRC_TRG for source-target tract constraints.

Note that concepts like father or mother are not explicitly present in the Person metamodel (through attributes or association ends). Besides, please be warned: both metamodels and their transformation seem simple, but intricate complications live under the surface. Roughly speaking, the transformation must (a) split one source attribute into two target attributes in different target classes; (b) merge two source associations into one target class and four target associations; (c) map a source generalization hierarchy into a target attribute. The following listing details the five OCL invariants that constitute the mfdsTract.

```
inv SRC_fullName_EQ_firstSepLast:
  Person.allInstances->forAll(p|
    p.fullName=firstName(p).concat(sep()).concat(lastName(p)))
inv SRC_allPersonInMfds:
  let allFs=Female.allInstances in let allMs=Male.allInstances in
  Person.allInstances->forAll(p|
    Bag{allFs->exists(d  | allMs->exists(f,s| mfdsPerson(p,f,d,s))),
        allFs->exists(m,d| allMs->exists(s  | mfdsPerson(m,p,d,s))),
        allFs->exists(m  | allMs->exists(f,s| mfdsPerson(m,f,p,s))),
        allFs->exists(m,d| allMs->exists(f  | mfdsPerson(m,f,d,p)))} =
    Bag{true,false,false,false})
inv TRG_oneDaughterOneSon:
  Family.allInstances->forAll(fam |
    fam.daughter->size()=1 and fam.son->size()=1)
inv SRC_TRG_mfdsPerson_2_mfdsFamily:
  Female.allInstances->forAll(m,d| Male.allInstances->forAll(f,s|
    mfdsPerson(m,f,d,s) implies
    Family.allInstances->exists(fam|mfdsFamily(fam,m,f,d,s))))
inv SRC_TRG_forPersonOneMember:
  Female.allInstances->forAll(p| Member.allInstances->one(m|
    p.fullName=fullName(m) and p.age=m.age and m.gender = #female and
    (p.child->notEmpty() implies (let fam=m.famMother in
      p.child->size()=fam.daughter->union(fam.son)->size())) and
    (p.parent->notEmpty() implies m.famDaughter.isDefined()) and
    (p.husband.isDefined() implies m.famMother.isDefined()) )) and
```

```
Male.allInstances->forAll(p| Member.allInstances->one(m|
  p.fullName=fullName(m) and p.age=m.age and m.gender = #male and
  (p.child->notEmpty() implies (let fam=m.famFather in
    p.child->size()=fam.daughter->union(fam.son)->size())) and
  (p.parent->notEmpty() implies m.famSon.isDefined()) and
  (p.wife.isDefined() implies m.famFather.isDefined()) ))
```

There are two source, one target, and two source-target tract constraints. The source constraint `SRC_fullName_EQ_firstSepLast` guarantees that one can decompose the `fullName` into a `firstName`, a separator, and a `lastName`. The source constraint `SRC_allPersonInMfds` requires that every Person appears exactly once in a `mfdsPerson` pattern. `mfdsPerson` patterns are described by the boolean operation `mfdsPerson` which characterizes an isolated mother-father-daughter-son pattern having no further links to other persons.

The constraint `SRC_allPersonInMfds` is universally quantified on Person objects. Each Person must appear either as a mother or as a father or as a daughter or as a son. This exclusive-or requirement is formulated as a comparison between bags of Boolean values. From the four possible cases, exactly one case must be true. Technically this is realized by requiring that the bag of truth values, which arises from the evaluation of the respective sub-formluas, contains exactly once the Boolean value `true` and three times the Boolean value `false`.

```
mfdsTract :: mfdsPerson(m:Person,f:Person,d:Person,s:Person):Boolean=
  Set{m,f,d,s}->excluding(null)->size()=4 and
  m.oclIsTypeOf(Female) and f.oclIsTypeOf(Male) and
  m.oclAsType(Female).husband=f and
  d.oclIsTypeOf(Female) and s.oclIsTypeOf(Male) and
  m.child=Set{d,s} and f.child=Set{d,s} and
  d.parent=Set{m,f} and s.parent=Set{m,f}
mfdsTract ::
  mfdsFamily(fam:Family,m:Person,f:Person,d:Person,s:Person):Boolean=
  fam.lastName=lastName(m) and fam.lastName=lastName(f) and
  fam.lastName=lastName(d) and fam.lastName=lastName(s) and
  fam.mother.firstName=firstName(m) and
  fam.father.firstName=firstName(f) and
  fam.daughter.firstName=Bag{firstName(d)} and
  fam.son.firstName=Bag{firstName(s)}
```

Both source constraints reduce the range of source models to be tested. The target tract constraint `TRG_oneDaughterOneSon` basically focusses the target on models in which the multiplicity * on the daughter and son roles are changed to the multiplicity 1. The first central source-target constraint `SRC_TRG_mfds-Person_2_mfdsFamily` demands that a `mfdsPerson` pattern must be found in transformed form as a mfds `Family` pattern in the resulting target model. The second central source-target constraint `SRC_TRG_forPersonOneMember` requires that a Person must be transformed into exactly one Member having comparable attribute values and roles as the originating Person. Both source-target tract constraints are central insofar that they establish a correspondence between a Person (from the source) and a Family Member (from the target) in a declarative way by means of a formula.

3.2 Generating Test Input Models

The generation of source models for testing purposes is done by means of the language ASSL (A Snapshot Sequence Language) [19]. ASSL was developed to generate object diagrams for a given class diagram in a flexible way. Positive and negative test cases can be built, i.e., object diagrams satisfying all constraints or violating at least one constraint. ASSL is basically an imperative programming language with features for randomly choosing attribute values or association ends. Furthermore ASSL supports backtracking for finding object diagrams with particular properties.

For the example, we concentrate on the generation of (possibly) isolated mfds patterns representing families with exactly one mother, father, daughter, and son in the respective role. The procedure genMfdsPerson shown below is parameterized by the number of mfds patterns to be generated. It creates four Person objects for the respective roles, assigns attribute values to the objects, links the generated objects in order to build a family, and finally links two generated mfds patterns by either two parenthood links or one parenthood link or no parenthood link at all. The decision is taken in a random way. For example, for a call to genMfdsPerson(2) a generated model could look like one of the three possibilities shown in Figure 4. Marriage links are always displayed horizontally, whereas parenthood links are shown vertically or diagonally.

```
procedure genMfdsPerson(numMFDS:Integer)     -- number of mfds patterns
  var lastNames:Sequence(String), m:Person ... -- further variables
begin
---------------------------------------------- variable initialization
lastNames:=[Sequence{'Kennedy' ... 'Obama'}];        -- more
firstFemales:=[Sequence{'Jacqueline' ... 'Michelle'}]; -- constants
firstMales:=[Sequence{'John' ... 'Barrack'}];        -- instead
ages:=[Sequence{30,36,42,48,54,60,66,72,78}];        -- of ...
mums:=[Sequence{}]; dads:=[Sequence{}];

-------------------------------------------------- creation of objects
for i:Integer in [Sequence{1..numMFDS}] begin
  m:=Create(Female); f:=Create(Male);              -- mother father
  d:=Create(Female); s:=Create(Male);              -- daughter son
  mums:=[mums->append(m)]; dads:=[dads->append(f)];

-- - - - - - - - - - - - - - - - - - - - assignment of attributes
lastN:=Any([lastNames]); firstN:=Any([firstFemales]);
[m].fullName:=[firstN.concat('_').concat(lastN)];[m].age:=Any([ages]);
firstN:=Any([firstMales]);
[f].fullName:=[firstN.concat('_').concat(lastN)];[f].age:=Any([ages]);
...                    -- analogous handling of daughter d and son s

-- - - - - - - - - - - - - - - - - - - - - creation of mfds links
Insert(Marriage,[m],[f]);
Insert(Parenthood,[m],[d]); Insert(Parenthood,[f],[d]);
Insert(Parenthood,[m],[s]); Insert(Parenthood,[f],[s]);
---------- random generation of additional links between mfds patterns
------------------------------ such links lead to negative test cases
flagA:=Any([Sequence{0,1,2,3}]); -- 0 none, 1 mother, 2 father, 3 both
  if [i>1 and flagA>0] then begin
    if [flagA=1 or flagA=3] then begin
      flagB:=Any([Sequence{0,1}]);   -- 1 give daughter, 0 give son
      if [flagB=1] then begin
        Insert(Parenthood,[mums->at(i-1)],[mums->at(i)]); end
      else begin
```

```
        Insert(Parenthood,[mums->at(i-1)],[dads->at(i)]); end;
      end;  ...
end;
end;
```

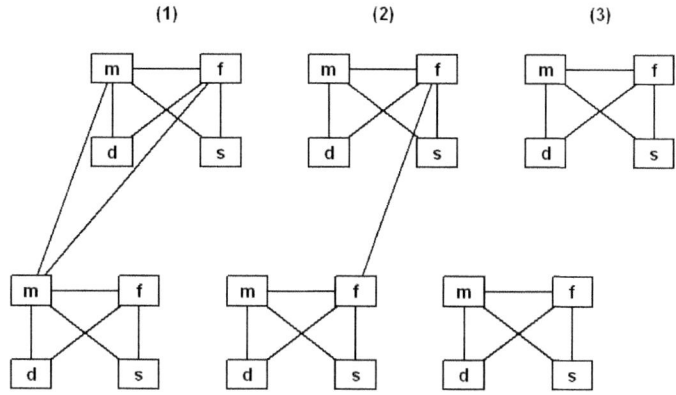

Fig. 4. Three Possibilities for Linking Two mfds Patterns

3.3 Proof of Concept

The approach we have presented in this paper allows modellers to check the behaviour of a transformation by specifying a set of tracts that should be fulfilled. For each of these tracts we generate the tract test suite mentioned in the previous section, i.e. the sample input models for the tract, and then we check that the corresponding output models (i.e., the ones produced by the transformation) fulfil the tract invariants.

As a proof-of-concept of our proposal we have built a prototype that allows testing a transformation in an automated way, chaining three tools. In the first place, the tract classes and their associated invariants are specified using USE. The ASSL program that generates the tract test suite is also specified within the USE environment, and then executed within it. The second tool is a script that takes the input models generated by the ASSL procedure (which are in the textual format that both ASSL and USE understand, .cmd), converts them into the Ecore format so that they can be manipulated by ATL, invokes the ATL transformation under test, and converts the resulting target model into the USE .cmd format again (using an ATL query). Finally, the correctness of these output models is checked against the OCL invariants specified in the transformation tract using USE.

4 Analysis

Counting on mechanisms for specifying tract invariants on the source and target metamodels, and on the relationship that should be established between them, has proved to be beneficial when combined with the testing process defined above.

Transformation Code Errors: In the first place, we can look for errors due to either bugs in the transformation code that lead to misbehaviours, or to hidden assumptions made by the developers due to some vagueness in the (verbal) specification of the transformation. These errors are normally detected by observing how valid input models (i.e., belonging to the grey area in the left hand side of Figure 1) are transformed into target models that break either the target metamodel constraints or the source-target constraints. This is the normal kind of errors pursued by most MT testing approaches.

Transformation Tract Errors: The second kind of errors can be due to the tract specifications themselves. Writing the OCL invariants that comprise a given tract can be as complex as writing the transformation code itself (sometimes even more). This is similar to what happens with the specification of the contract for a program: there are cases in which the detailed description of the expected behaviour of a program can be as complex as the program itself. However, counting on a high-level specification of what the transformation should do at the tract level (independently of how it actually implements it) becomes beneficial because both descriptions provide two complementary views (specifications) of the behaviour of the transformation. In addition, during the checking process the tract specifications and the code help testing each other. In this sense, we believe in an incremental and iterative approach to model transformation testing, where tracts are progressively specified and the transformation checked against them. The errors found during the testing process are carefully analyzed and either the tract or the transformation refined accordingly.

Issues due to Source-Target Semantic Mismatch: This process also helps revealing a third kind of issues, probably the most difficult problems to cope with. They are due neither to the transformation code nor the tract invariant specifications, but to the semantic gap between the source and target metamodels. We already mentioned that the metamodels used to illustrate our proposal look simple but hide some subtle complications. For example, one of the tracts we tried to specify was for input source models that represented three-generation families, i.e., mfds patterns linked together by parenthood relations (see Figure 5 representing a generated negative test case failing to fulfill SRC_allPersonInMfds; without the links ('Elizabeth Reagan', 'Ronald Reagan'), ('Alta Reagan', 'John Carter'), and ('Ronald Reagan', 'John Carter') we would obtain a valid mfds source model). This revealed the fact that valid source models do not admit in general persons with grandchildren. More precisely, after careful examination of the problem we discovered that such patterns are valid inputs for the transformation only if the last name of all persons in the family is the same. This is because the transformed model will consist of three families, where one of the members should end up, for example, playing the role of a daughter in one family and the role

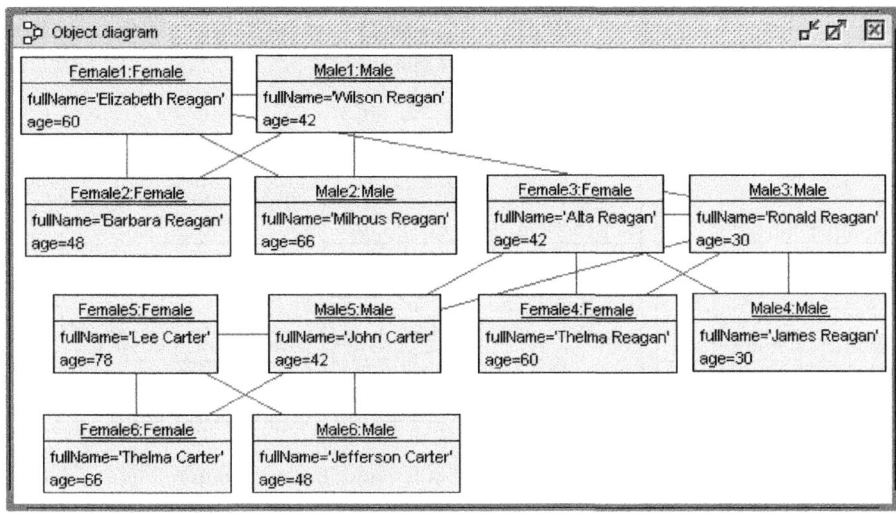

Fig. 5. Generated Negative Test Case with Linked mfds Patterns

of mother in the other. Since all members of a family should share the same last name, and due to the fact that a person should belong to two families, the last names of the two families should coincide.

Examples of these problems can also happen because of more restrictive constraints in the target metamodel. For instance a family in the target metamodel should have both a father and a mother, and they should share the same last name. This significantly restricts the set of source models that can be transformed by *any* transformation because it does not allow unmarried couples to be transformed, nor families with a single father or mother. Married couples whose members have maintained their last names cannot be transformed, either. Another problem happens with persons with only a single name (i.e., neither a first nor last name, but a name only), because they cannot be transformed. These are good examples of semantic mismatches between the two metamodels that we try to relate through the transformation. How to deal with (and solve) this latter kind of problems is out of the scope of this paper, here we are concerned only with the detection of such problems. A visual representation of some semantic differences between the example metamodels is shown in Figure 6.

Being able to select particular patterns of source models (the ones defined for a tract test suite) offers a fine-grained mechanism for specifying the behaviour of the transformation, and allows the MT tester to concentrate on specific behaviours. In this way we are able to partition the full input space of the transformation into smaller, more focused behavioural units, and to define specific tests for them. By selecting particular patterns we can traverse the full input space, checking specific spots. This is how we discovered that the size of the grey area in Figure 1 was much smaller than we initially thought, as mentioned above.

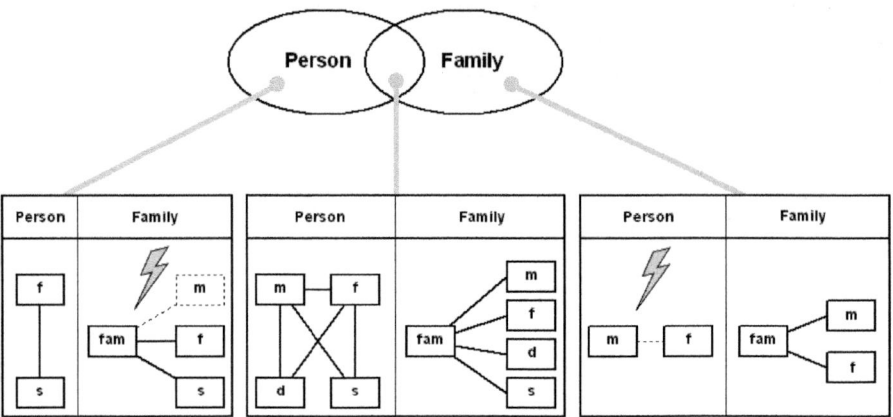

Fig. 6. Semantic Differences between Source and Target Example Metamodels

This approach also opens up the possibility of testing the transformation with invalid inputs, to check its behaviour. For example, we defined a tract where people could have two male parents, being able to check whether the transformation produced output models that violated the target metamodel constraints or not, or just hanged. In this way we can easily define both positive and negative tests for the transformation.

5 Related Work

There are several kinds of contributions that can be related to our work. In the first place we have the works that define contracts for model transformations, using different notations. One of the earlier works [18] introduces the concept of "transformation contract" in a similar way to ours—although without incorporating test suites. However, the authors propose to specify contracts by means of OCL operations, which causes many technical problems for writing contracts—as the own authors discuss in their paper. Besides, they do not discuss any practical way of using their contract specifications for model testing. The work in [2] also proposes OCL for defining transformation contracts. Their ideas are also close to [18] and to ours, but in their paper they just provide a general view of what they think that could be done with model transformation contracts, but without delving into the details about how to achieve it.

The proposal presented in [9] is also of interest. The authors show how to derive some invariant-based verification properties that should be preserved by the transformation (which are similar to our tracts) by analysing the internal rules that compose a transformation. Although they follow a white-box approach to model transformation testing, it could probably be combined with ours if their approach could help us identify some more tracts for a transformation written in any of the languages they deal with (TGG and QVT).

Other group of works (see, e.g., [5,6,7,8,10,11]) also use a white-box approach to model-transformation testing, aiming at fully validating the behaviour of the transformation (including other properties such as confluence of the rules, termination, etc.) using formal methods and their associated toolkits—which include, e.g., Alloy, Maude, or graph rewriting techniques. Although more powerful than our approach from a theoretical perspective, their computational complexity generally makes them inappropriate for testing large model transformations. In addition, the drawback of a white-box approach is that it is tightly coupled to the transformation language and thus it would need to be adapted or completely redefined for another transformation language [4].

Alternative approaches validate the transformation under test with only a selected set of test input models, as we do in our approach, but focusing more on how to generate input models [7,12,13,14,15,16] and how to reason about some of the properties of the generated set (e.g, coverage). They can be related to what we achieve with the ASSL language, although in this paper we have also shown how these input suites can be integrated into a complete testing process such as the one presented here. Complementing our current ASSL procedures with some of the ideas and algorithms proposed in these works is something we would like to explore as part of our future work.

6 Conclusions

In this paper we have introduced the concept of *Tract*, a generalization of model transformation contracts, and showed how it can be used for model transformation black-box testing. A tract defines a set of constraints on the source and target metamodels, a set of source-target constraints, and a tract test suite, i.e., a collection of source models satisfying the source constraints. To test a transformation T we automatically generate the input test suite models using the ASSL language, and then transform them into their corresponding target models. These models are checked with the USE tool against the constraints defined for the transformation. The checking process can be automated, allowing the model transformation tester to process a large number of models in a mechanical way.

Although this approach to testing does not guarantee full correctness, it provides very interesting benefits. In particular, it can be useful for identifying bugs in a cost-effective manner. Moreover, it allows dealing with industrial-size transformations without having to transform them into any other formalism or to abstract away any of its features. Furthermore, tracts provide a modular approach to testing, allowing to partition the full input space of the transformation into smaller, more focused behavioural units, and to define specific tests for them. These are important advantages over other approaches that aim at proving full correctness but at a higher-cost: their computational complexity normally make them *untractable*.

There are several lines of work that we plan to address next. In particular, we would like to study how to improve our proposal by incorporating some of the existing works on the effective generation of input test cases. We expect this to help us enhance the definition of our tract test suites. Larger case studies will be carried out in order to stress the applicability of our approach and to obtain more extensive feedback. In this sense, we would like to conduct some empirical studies on the effects of the use of tracts in the lifecycle of model transformations. Concerning the tracts, we also plan to investigate some of their properties, such as their composability, subsumption, refinement or coverage. Finally, we plan to improve the current tool support for tracts, incorporating the creation and maintenance of libraries of tracts, and the concurrent execution of the tests using sets of distributed machines.

Acknowledgements. The authors would like to thank the anonymous for their useful comments and suggestions, and to Lars Hamann, Mirco Kuhlmann, Fernando López and Javier Troya for their help and support during the preparation of the paper. This work is supported by Research Projects TIN2008-03107 and P07-TIC-03184.

References

1. Lin, Y., Zhang, J., Gray, J.: Model comparison: A key challenge for transformation testing and version control in model driven software development. In: OOPSLA/GPCE: Best Practices for Model-Driven Software Development, Control in Model Driven Software Development, pp. 219–236. Springer, Heidelberg (2004)
2. Baudry, B., Dinh-Trong, T., Mottu, J.M., Simmonds, D., France, R., Ghosh, S., Fleurey, F., Traon, Y.L.: Model transformation testing challenges. In: Proc. of the ECMDA workshop on Integration of Model Driven Development and Model Driven Testing, Barcelona, Spain (2006), http://www.cs.colostate.edu/~france/publications/TransTesting.pdf
3. Stevens, P.: A landscape of bidirectional model transformations. In: Lämmel, R., Visser, J., Saraiva, J. (eds.) GTTSE II. LNCS, vol. 5235, pp. 408–424. Springer, Heidelberg (2008)
4. Baudry, B., Ghosh, S., Fleurey, F., France, R., Traon, Y.L., Mottu, J.M.: Barriers to systematic model transformation testing. Communications of the ACM 53(6), 139–143 (2010)
5. Baresi, L., Ehrig, K., Heckel, R.: Verification of model transformations: A case study with BPEL. In: Montanari, U., Sannella, D., Bruni, R. (eds.) TGC 2006. LNCS, vol. 4661, pp. 183–199. Springer, Heidelberg (2007)
6. Ehrig, H., Ehrig, K., Lara, J.D., Taentzer, G., Varró, D., Varró-Gyapay, S.: Termination criteria for model transformation. In: Cerioli, M. (ed.) FASE 2005. LNCS, vol. 3442, pp. 49–63. Springer, Heidelberg (2005)
7. Ehrig, K., Küster, J.M., Taentzer, G.: Generating instance models from meta models. Software and Systems Modeling 8, 479–500 (2009)
8. Küster, J.M.: Definition and validation of model transformations. Software and Systems Modeling 5(3), 233–259 (2006)
9. Cabot, J., Clarisó, R., Guerra, E., de Lara, J.: Verification and validation of declarative model-to-model transformations through invariants. Journal of Systems and Software 83(2), 283–302 (2010)

10. Anastasakis, K., Bordbar, B., Küster, J.M.: Analysis of model transformations via Alloy. In: Proc. of MODEVVA (2007), http://www.cs.bham.ac.uk/~bxb/Papres/Modevva07.pdf
11. Troya, J., Vallecillo, A.: Towards a rewriting logic semantics for ATL. In: Tratt, L., Gogolla, M. (eds.) ICMT 2010. LNCS, vol. 6142, pp. 230–244. Springer, Heidelberg (2010)
12. Brottier, E., Fleurey, F., Steel, J., Baudry, B., Traon, Y.L.: Metamodel-based test generation for model transformations: an algorithm and a tool. In: Proc. of the 17th International Symposium on Software Reliability Engineering (ISSRE 2006), pp. 85–94 (2006)
13. Solberg, A., Reddy, R., Simmonds, D., France, R., Ghosh, S.: Developing distributed services using an aspect-oriented model driven framework. International Journal of Cooperative Information Systems 15(4), 535–564 (2006)
14. Mottu, J.M., Baudry, B., Traon, Y.L.: Reusable MDA components: A testing-for-trust approach. In: Wang, J., Whittle, J., Harel, D., Reggio, G. (eds.) MoDELS 2006. LNCS, vol. 4199, pp. 589–603. Springer, Heidelberg (2006)
15. Fleurey, F., Baudry, B., Muller, P.A., Traon, Y.L.: Qualifying input test data for model transformations. Software and Systems Modeling 8(2), 185–203 (2009)
16. Küster, J.M., Abd-El-Razik, M.: Validation of model transformations – first experiences using a white box approach. In: Auletta, V. (ed.) MoDELS 2006. LNCS, vol. 4364, pp. 193–204. Springer, Heidelberg (2007)
17. Gogolla, M., Hamann, L., Kuhlmann, M.: Proving and visualizing OCL invariant independence by automatically generated test cases. In: Fraser, G., Gargantini, A. (eds.) TAP 2010. LNCS, vol. 6143, pp. 38–54. Springer, Heidelberg (2010)
18. Cariou, E., Marvie, R., Seinturier, L., Duchien, L.: OCL for the specification of model transformation contracts. In: Proc. of the OCL and Model Driven Engineering Workshop (2004), http://web.univ-pau.fr/~ecariou/papers/workshop-ocl-mde-uml2004-paper.pdf
19. Gogolla, M., Bohling, J., Richters, M.: Validating UML and OCL Models in USE by Automatic Snapshot Generation. Software and Systems Modeling 4(4), 386–398 (2005)
20. Gogolla, M., Büttner, F., Richters, M.: USE: A UML-based specification environment for validating UML and OCL. Science of Computer Programming 69, 27–34 (2007)
21. Object Management Group: Object Constraint Language (OCL) Specification. Version 2.2. (2010), OMG Document formal/2010-02-01
22. Jouault, F., Allilaire, F., Bézivin, J., Kurtev, I.: ATL: A model transformation tool. Science of Computer Programming 72(1-2), 31–39 (2008)
23. Schürr, A.: Specification of graph translators with triple graph grammars. In: Mayr, E.W., Schmidt, G., Tinhofer, G. (eds.) WG 1994. LNCS, vol. 903, pp. 151–163. Springer, Heidelberg (1995)
24. Kolovos, D.S., Rose, L.M., Paige, R.F.: The Epsilon Book (2010), http://www.eclipse.org/gmt/epsilon/doc/book/

Extending SysML with AADL Concepts for Comprehensive System Architecture Modeling

Razieh Behjati[1,2], Tao Yue[1], Shiva Nejati[1],
Lionel Briand[1,2], and Bran Selic[1,3]

[1] Simula Research Laboratory, Lysaker, Norway
[2] University of Oslo, Oslo, Norway
[3] Malina Software Corp., Ottawa, Canada
{raziehb,tao,shiva,briand,bselic}@simula.no

Abstract. Recent years have seen a proliferation of languages for describing embedded systems. Some of these languages have emerged from domain-specific frameworks, and some are adaptions or extensions of more general-purpose languages. In this paper, we focus on two widely-used standard languages: the Architecture Analysis and Design Language (AADL) and the Systems Modeling Language (SysML). AADL was born as an avionics-focused domain-specific language and later on has been revised to represent and support a more general category of embedded real-time systems. SysML is an extension of the Unified Modeling Language (UML) intended to support system engineering and modeling. We propose the ExSAM profile that extends SysML by adding AADL concepts to it with the goal of exploiting the key advantages of both languages in a seamless way. More precisely, by using ExSAM and any SysML modeling environment, we will be able to both model system engineering concepts and use AADL analysis tools where needed. We describe the ExSAM profile through several examples and compare it with existing alternatives. We have implemented ExSAM using IBM Rational Rhapsody and evaluated its completeness and usefulness through two case studies.

Keywords: Integrated Control Systems (ICSs), Systems modeling languages, Architecture modeling languages, Embedded control systems, AADL, SysML.

1 Introduction

Many control applications are systems-of-systems, integrating various mechanical, electronic, and software systems. The design of these systems, classified as Integrated Control Systems (ICSs), depends more and more on effective solutions that can address heterogeneity and interplay of physical and software elements. In particular, design languages used for specifying ICSs should incorporate, in a consistent manner, essential concepts from multiple disciplines, such as mechanical, electronic, and software engineering.

Model-Driven Engineering (MDE) approaches to system development have been adopted in diverse domains, in particular, ICSs. This is because the use of models has shown to be promising in addressing the above issues, as well as, in handling the increasing complexity of ICSs, reducing their cost of construction, and supporting efficient maintenance and evolution [17,15].

A number of modeling languages have been proposed to help engineers from different disciplines to communicate and compare their perspectives, to reason about properties of heterogeneous ICSs, and to develop optimized system-level solutions by assessing multidisciplinary design trade-offs. Of particular interest in our work are *standardized* languages, which are generally preferred by industry because they can reduce training costs, and reduce the risk of vendor lock in. In recent years, a number of modelling languages targeting ICSs have been standardized, but, to the best of our knowledge, none of them provide the full range required to deal effectively with the kinds of ICSs that we have encountered. Some of them, such as Systems Modeling Language (SysML) [7], focus on the "big picture" requirements and architectural views, whereas others, such as Architecture Analysis and Design Language (AADL) [14] address the more detailed platform-oriented and physical aspects of such systems.

Consequently, we investigated the possibility of combining these two languages, SysML and AADL, since they are both widely used in industry with adequate tool support. However, since it is generally preferable for system engineers to work with a single internally consistent formalism within one modeling environment, we chose to merge the two into a single unified language as a SysML profile. Concrete objectives include the ability to use AADL analysis tools while performing system engineering modeling in any SysML modeling environment.

Figure 1 illustrates the relationship between the capabilities of the two languages, showing that they are mutually complementary. SysML, an extension of Unified Modeling Language (UML), version 2, is a standardized language for systems engineering. In addition to retaining much of UML, it also pro-

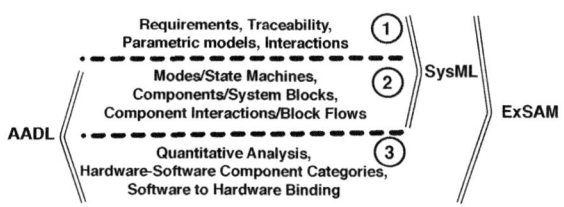

Fig. 1. The relationship between SysML, AADL, and the combined profile ExSAM

vides specialized support for requirements engineering, traceability, and precise modeling of diverse physical phenomena. AADL, on the other hand, is oriented towards the modeling of real-time embedded systems and includes a comprehensive catalogue of hardware and software elements common in such systems and their characteristics, allowing relatively precise and dependable analyses of different system properties such as performance, timing, or power consumption.

Although both SysML and AADL have extension mechanisms, in unifying the two languages, we chose to extend SysML. This is because its extension mechanism (profiles) comes from UML, which is much more widespread and better supported by tools, and which is also more powerful compared to that of AADL (annexes). We propose a SysML profile, Extended SysML for Architecture Analysis Modeling (ExSAM), that combines all the modeling capabilities of AADL and SysML (Figure 1). Specifically, ExSAM extends SysML to cover all AADL concepts, by expressing these concepts using SysML constructs.

Since SysML and AADL both target modeling embedded software systems, there are conceptual overlaps between them. Figure 1, level 2, represents an overview of the overlapping constructs between these two languages. These constructs seemingly specify the same concepts, however they tend to have different meanings, usages, or design rationales. In general, AADL has a well defined semantics compared to SysML, which inherits the main bulk of its semantics from UML with several semantic variation points. Hence, in the ExSAM profile, we opt for the AADL semantics whenever the corresponding SysML elements are not precisely defined or have a semantics different from that of AADL. We do so by defining appropriate Object Constraint Language (OCL) [6] constraints. For example, realization relation is used both in AADL and SysML. In AADL, realization allows the reuse of attributes of physical components, whereas in SysML, the physical attributes cannot be manipulated through realization relations because such attributes appear at the instance-level while realization is defined at the block-level (UML class-level). Hence, to model AADL realization, SysML realization must be extended and constrained (Section 3.1). In ExSAM, we have made several such alignments to fully embed AADL constructs into SysML.

To evaluate the completeness and usefulness of ExSAM for ICSs, we have applied it to two case studies: One is a benchmark case study and the other is a large-scale, industrial case study. The first case study showed that ExSAM was adequate to capture all the used AADL concepts. The second case study showed that ExSAM was sufficient to satisfy the modeling needs of our industrial partner, while AADL and SysML alone were not.

The reminder of the paper is organized as follows. We provide a brief introduction to SysML and AADL in Section 2. In Section 3, we present ExSAM and illustrate its use. We describe the tool support and an evaluation of ExSAM through two case studies in Section 4. We compare ExSAM with other alternatives in Section 5. Finally, we conclude the paper in Section 6.

2 Background

In this section, we provide a brief introduction to SysML (Section 2.1) and to AADL (Section 2.2).

2.1 SysML

SysML is a modeling language with a graphical syntax developed and standardized by the Object Management Group (OMG). It was designed to, among other things, capture the interactions of software with physical entities, and is widely used for systems engineering [16]. Compared to UML 2, SysML adds support for systems engineering (e.g. through requirements engineering, and quantitative analysis of physical aspects of the system), while removing many of UML's object-oriented constructs. In ExSAM, we have particularly benefited from the following SysML-specific constructs:

SysML blocks. Blocks are modular units of system descriptions in SysML and are generalizations of the UML class concept. The notion of block in SysML enables better expression of Systems engineering semantics compared to UML, and particularly, reduces the UML bias towards software. Blocks and their relationships are visualized in SyML **block definition diagrams** (bdds). The definition of a block in SysML can be further detailed by specifying its **parts**; **ports**, specifying its interaction points; and **connectors**, specifying the connections among its parts and ports. This information is visualized using SysML **internal block diagrams** (ibds).

SysML flows ports and SysML item flows. The SysML flow port concept extends the UML port concept and is intended to describe an interaction point for a block through which the block interacts with its environment [18]. The rationale for having flow ports is that some interactions of a block may not involve message passing or service calls, but rather phenomena such as continuous or discrete energy flows. In particular, a block can have interaction points over which it supplies or is supplied with electric power, fuel, air, or any other kind of streaming input or output. SysML **FlowPort**s are typed by **FlowSpecification**s, which specify the types of flows that can pass through them. The SysML **ItemFlow** concept extends the UML **InformationFlow** concept, which has the ability to be explicitly associated with **Connectors** via the **realizingConnector** dependency [8]. This capability allows us to describe the detailed implementation of an item flow through connectors and flows realizing it.

2.2 AADL

AADL, is a modeling language originally designed for and used in avionics. It was standardized by the Society of Automotive Engineers (SAE) and has been used to describe software execution platforms (e.g., processors, memory, buses, devices) as well as the physical environments of embedded software systems (e.g., electronic and mechanical parts interacting with ICSs). In addition, AADL supports the early prediction and analysis of critical system qualities – such as performance, schedulability, and reliability [14].

In this section, we provide an overview of AADL using a domain model representing the main AADL concepts and their relationships. We have developed this domain model based on the AADL reference manual [14]. A fragment of this domain model capturing the main AADL concepts is shown in Figure 2. A complete domain model is available in [10]. Below, we discuss the concepts shown in Figure 2 and illustrate them using the AADL example in Figure 3.

AADL provides abstractions for describing a system in terms of its components, their interfaces, and the connectors between the interfaces. AADL provides two mechanism for declaring components: using the *component type* construct,

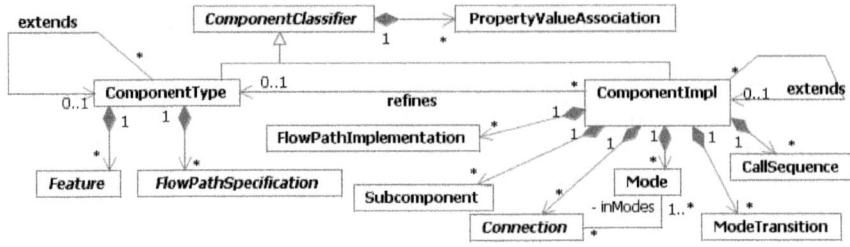

Fig. 2. The core AADL concepts

which specifies a component by describing only its interface, or using the *component implementation* construct, which specifies a component by describing its internal structure. ComponentType and ComponentImpl in Figure 2, respectively, represent these concepts. In Figure 3, lines 1-10 specify a component type named redundant_pattern, and lines 11-32 specify a component implementation named redundant_pattern.primary_backup. In AADL, components are declared as a type or implementation within a particular *component category* [14]. These core concepts are elaborated further below.

```
1   system redundant_pattern
2   features
3      indata: in data port;
4      outdata: out data port;
5      reinitialize: in event port;
6   flows
7      primary_flow: flow path indata -> outdata;
8   properties
9      Period => 20ms;
10  end redundant_pattern;

11  system implementation redundant_pattern.primary_backup
12  subcomponents
13     primary_system: system principal_functions;
14     backup_system: system principal_functions;
15     observer: process observer_pattern;
16  connections
17     in_nom:data port indata -> primary_system.indata in modes nominal;
18     in_fail: data port indata -> backup_system.indata in modes backup, reinit;
19     out_nom:data port primary_system.outdata -> outdata in modes nominal;
20     out_bk: data port backup_system.outdata -> outdata in modes backup, reinit;
21     indata_p: data port primary_system.outdata -≫ observer.indata_P;
22     indata_b: data port backup_system.outdata -≫ observer.indata_B;
23  flows
24     primary_flow: flow path indata -> in_nom -> primary_system.flow1 -> out_nom -> outdata;
25  modes
26     primary: initial mode;
27     backup: mode;
28     reinit: mode;
29     primary -[observer.primary_fail]-> backup;
30     backup -[reinitialize]-> reinit;
31     reinit -[observer.primary_ok] -> primary;
32  end redundant_pattern.primary_backup;
```

Fig. 3. An example AADL model

Component categories. AADL provides ten component categories to define the runtime nature of software, hardware, and composite components. Software component categories are *data, subprogram, thread, thread group* and *process*. Hardware component categories are *memory, processor, bus* and *device*. A special component category named *system* indicates either a system consisting of several software components only, or a system consisting of both hardware and software components. In Figure 3, the component type `redundant_pattern` (Line 1) and the component implementation `redundant_pattern.primary_backup` (Line 11) both belong to the component category `system`.

Component types. A component type specifies the externally visible characteristics of a component in terms of features, flow specifications, and property value associations (Figure 2).

- **Features.** Different types of features are used to specify the interfaces of a component. Ports and port groups (collections of ports or other port groups) are hardware features that represent the directional exchange of data, events, or both. Subprograms, server subprograms, and their parameters are used to specify the software features of a component. In Figure 3, lines 3-5 specify the `features` of the component type `redundant_pattern`.
- **Flow specifications.** In a component type, flows are directional and designate a source or a sink, which are features of a component, or a flow path, which represents a flow through a component from one feature to another. Line 7 in Figure 3 declares a flow path connecting `indata` to `outdata`, which are declared as features of the component type.
- **Property value associations.** Property value associations are used to assign a value or a list of values to properties. Note that these properties are defined as part of the component categories. Line 9 in Figure 3 shows a property value association.

Component implementations. As shown in Figure 2, component implementations refine component types by specifying subcomponents, interactions (connections and call sequences), flow path implementations, property value associations and modes. In Figure 3, `redundant_pattern.primary_backup` implements the component type `redundant_pattern`.

- **Subcomponents and interactions.** Subcomponents in a component implementation can be other component types or component implementations. Connections and call sequences are used to describe the interactions among subcomponents. In Figure 3, subcomponents of the component implementation `redundant_pattern.primary_backup` are listed in lines 13-15. Connections among these subcomponents are declared in lines 17-22.
- **Flow path implementations.** A flow path implementation describes a sequence of paths through and connections among subcomponents within a component implementation. This path is a realization of the corresponding flow path declared in the component type declaration [14]. In Figure 3, the flow path implementation declared in line 24 refines the flow path specification declared in line 7.

Modes. An AADL component implementation declaration may contain the declaration of modes and mode transitions. Modes represent alternative operational states of a system or component [14]. Transition from one mode to another is triggered by events. In Figure 3, lines 26-28 declare three modes of redundant_pattern.primary_backup. In addition, lines 29-31 show the mode transitions among these three modes.

In AADL, a mode is an explicit configuration of its contained elements, e.g., subcomponents and connections. The in modes clause in the declaration of a component implementation is used to specify the active elements in each mode. The declarations of the connections in lines 17-20, in Figure 3, also contain the specification of the modes these connections are active in.

3 Profile Description

In this section we describe how we extend SysML using a profile, ExSAM, with the purpose of combining architecture design and analysis concepts of AADL with the system modeling concepts of SysML. This profile is resulted from our practice of mapping AADL to SysML and based on our observations of SysML limitations in addressing important AADL concepts discussed in Section 2.2. In this section, we briefly describe the most important features of ExSAM. A complete description of the profile, and illustration of its usage is provided in [10]. Here, we first describe the mapping for AADL components in Section 3.1. In Section 3.2 we describe the mapping for AADL component extension and generalizations. Section 3.3 is dedicated to the mapping of AADL modes. In Section 3.4 we present the mapping for AADL bindings. Finally, in Section 3.5 we explain how we can use ExSAM to benefit from AADL analysis capabilities for SysML models.

3.1 Mapping Component Types and Component Implementations

Recall from Section 2.2 that in AADL, component types and component implementations describe a component, respectively, through its externally visible interface and its internal structure. In ExSAM, we use SysML blocks to model both AADL component types and AADL component implementations. To distinguish between component types and component implementations, we use two newly defined stereotypes, «ComponentType» and «ComponentImpl», both extending SysML block as shown in Figure 4[1]. SysML blocks extend UML classes, and are chosen to model components because they can describe both structural and behavioral features of a system or component. In addition, using blocks for modeling components allows us to easily use other SysML constructs (e.g. parts and ports) to model AADL constructs (e.g. subcomponents and ports) associated with a component in a consistent and straightforward manner.

---

[1] In Figures 4 and 7, the stereotypes in gray are introduced by us, and the rest are from SysML. Also, in these two figures, a solid line ending in a filled triangle shows UML extension and a solid line ending in a hollow triangle shows UML generalization.

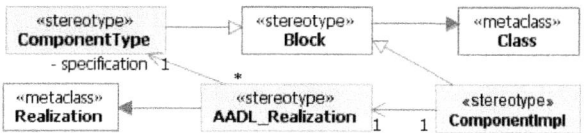

Fig. 4. Metamodel for mapping AADL concepts: component type and component implementation

As mentioned in Section 2.2, AADL provides ten different component categories. In ExSAM, we dedicate to each AADL component category a stereotype with a set of attributes representing the properties of the corresponding component category. AADL property value associations are then automatically mapped to the values assigned to the attributes of stereotypes applied to blocks. In the rest of this section, we refer to this set of stereotypes as *category identifier stereotypes*. In ExSAM, all category identifier stereotypes generalize «ComponentType» and «ComponentImpl». We apply two stereotypes to each block: one stereotype specifies whether it is a component type («ComponentType») or a component implementation («ComponentImpl»), and the other specifies its component category.

As shown in Figure 2, a component implementation in AADL can realize and refine a component type specification by adding implementation details to it, namely, by specifying its **subcomponents**, **connections**, **modes**, **properties**, and **flow paths**. A realization relationship in AADL transfers all property value associations from the component type to the component implementation, and makes all features and flow specifications of the component type accessible from the component implementation. In ExSAM, we capture this refinement using a UML/SysML realization relationship between a block stereotyped by «ComponentImpl» and a block stereotyped by «ComponentType». However, the semantics of UML/SysML realization is different from that of AADL realization. For example, it does not support the transfer of property value associations from the block stereotyped by «ComponentType» to the block stereotyped by «ComponentImpl». In addition, for the realization to be meaningful in this context, the involved blocks should be stereotyped by the same category identifier stereotype. In ExSAM, we have specialized and constrained UML/SysML realization using «AADL_Realization» (Figure 4) to capture these detailed semantics. Each realization relationship in an ExSAM model, should, therefore, be stereotyped by «AADL_Realization» to represent an AADL realization.

Figure 5 shows an excerpt of the ExSAM model created for the AADL model in Figure 3. In this model, a block named redundant_pattern, stereotyped by «ComponentType» and «System», represents the AADL component type redundant_pattern. The value of the attribute period, defined in «System», is set to 20ms in this block. The other block, redundant_patternPrimary_backup, realizes redundant_pattern, and is stereotyped by «ComponentImpl» and «System». Note that the realization relation between the two blocks is also stereotyped by «AADL_Realization», which, as shown in Figure 5, ensures that in redundant_patternPrimary_backup the value of period is 20ms.

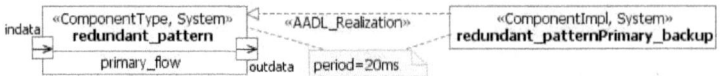

Fig. 5. A fragment of the ExSAM model for the AADL model in Fig. 3. Having «AADL_Realization» applied to the realization relation ensures that in redundant_patternPrimary_backup the value of period is set to 20ms, which is the same value as in redundant_pattern.

As mentioned in Section 2.2 and shown in Figure 2, a component type declaration in AADL defines the interface of a component in terms of features and flow specifications. In ExSAM, we use attributes and operations of a SysML block to model AADL software features (e.g. subprograms and parameters), and ports (i.e. SysML **FlowPorts** and UML **StandardPorts**) to model AADL hardware features (e.g. ports). Specifically, for modeling an AADL port group in ExSAM, we use a port typed by a SysML **FlowSpecification**.

In AADL, flow specifications are used to specify flow sources, flow sinks, and flow paths that connect flow sources to flow sinks. Since, flow sources and flow sinks are hardware features of a component, according to the mapping specified earlier in this section, they are mapped to ports in ExSAM. To model a flow path connecting a flow source to a flow sink, we use a SysML **ItemFlow** connecting the two ports representing the flow source and the flow sink. For example, in the ExSAM model created for the AADL model in Figure 3, there is an **ItemFlow** named primary_flow in the block named redundant_pattern connecting the ports representing indata and outdata (Figure 5). Note that in SysML, **ItemFlow** is a stereotype that can be applied to both associations and connectors. In this particular example, it is applied to a connector specifying that there is a data transferring between two ports of a block.

Recall from Section 2.2 that in AADL, a component implementation specifies the internal structure of a component through its subcomponents and the connections among them. Subcomponents of an AADL component implementation are naturally mapped to parts of a SysML block in ExSAM. The connections among AADL subcomponents are then captured through SysML ports (owned by the parts or by the encompassing block) and connectors connecting them. SysML ibds are used to visualize this information.

As mentioned in Section 2.2, an AADL component implementation can declare flow path implementations (e.g. line 24 in Figure 3) to refine and implement the flow path specifications (e.g. line 7 in Figure 3) declared in the component type that it implements. A flow path implementation involves connections that specify a flow path starting from a flow source, passing through a number of subcomponents and their specified flows and finally reaching the flow sink. In ExSAM, an AADL flow path implementation is mapped to a set of connectors that are associated to the **ItemFlow** representing the AADL flow path specification, which is implemented by the flow path implementation. In addition, for each flow path implementation we create an ibd in the ExSAM model to visualize these connectors and the way they connect parts and ports, as shown in

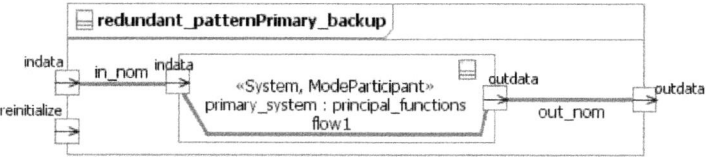

Fig. 6. An ibd in the ExSAM model created for the AADL model in Fig. 3. This ibd shows the internal structure of redundant_patternPrimary_backup in the nominal mode.

Figure 6. The highlighted connectors in Figure 6, in_nom, out_nom, and flow1, are used to realize the primary_flow ItemFlow depicted in Figure 5.

We use ItemFlows to model flow path specifications because SysML ItemFlow extends UML InformationFlow, which according to UML metamodel [8], can be realized using a set of connectors named realizingConnectors. In our mapping, the realizingConnectors of SysML ItemFlows are used to model AADL flow path implementations.

A component implementation in AADL can also declare call sequences. In ExSAM, we use SysML activities or interactions to model call sequences.

3.2 Extension and Generalization

As shown in Figure 2, in AADL, a component type can extend another component type. A component type inherits all the features, flow specifications and property value associations from its base component. Similarly, a component implementation can extend another component implementation. A component implementation inherits subcomponents, flow path implementations, call sequences, modes and property value associations from its base component implementation.

In an ExSAM model, we can use UML/SysML generalization to model the extension relationships between AADL components. However, the semantics of UML/SysML Generalization is different from that of AADL extension. For example, using UML/SysML Generalization we cannot capture the inheritance of property value associations. To address this semantic difference, in ExSAM, we define a new stereotype named «AADL_Generalization» that specializes UML/SysML Generalization and implements the semantics of AADL extension using an OCL constraint. Such an OCL constraint specifies that: 1) a block can extend another if they both have the same category identifier stereotype, 2) if the blocks are component types, the sub block must inherit from its supper block all the attributes, ports, item flows, and values assigned to the attributes of the category identifier stereotype applied to its super block, 3) if the blocks are component implementations, the sub block must inherit from its super block all parts, item flows and their realizing connectors, interactions, modes, and values assigned to the attributes of the category identifier stereotype applied to its super block.

3.3 Modes

As mentioned in Section 2.2, a component implementation can operate in several modes. Each mode represents one configuration of the component. The component can transit from one mode to another in response to the occurrence of an event. In ExSAM, we use states to model modes and state machine transitions to capture mode transitions. Such a state machine is associated with the block - stereotyped by «ComponentImpl» - representing the component implementation with modal behavior. The association between «ComponentImpl» and StateMachine in Figure 7 shows this.

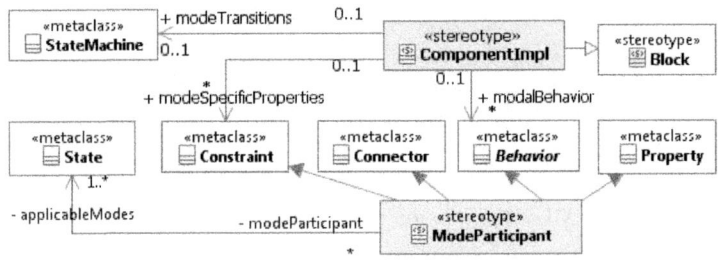

Fig. 7. Metamodel for mapping AADL concepts: modes

In addition, in AADL, the in modes clause is used to specify the active subcomponents and connections in each mode. Notice that a state machine can only model modes and the transitions among them, but have no way to link modes (states in state machine) to their own structure, behavior, and/or constraints. Therefore, to model the AADL in modes concept in ExSAM, we have introduced a stereotype named «ModeParticipant». As shown in Figure 7, the «ModeParticipant» stereotype has a relation to the UML State metaclass. This relation shows the set of modes that an element stereotyped by «ModeParticipant» can be active in. Notice that a «ModeParticipant» can be active in one or more modes.

There are three different types of modes in AADL: (1) mode-specific structure of subcomponents and connections, which describes alternative configurations of active components and connections; (2) modal configurations of call sequences, which describe alternative behavioral interactions of subcomponents; and (3) mode-specific properties, which define alternative characteristics and behaviors of the components. To support these modeling capabilities in ExSAM, we use the «ModeParticipant» stereotype, which, as shown in Figure 7, extends the UML metaclasses Property, Connector, Behavior, and Constraint. Being able to model properties, including parts and ports, as well as connectors as mode participants allows us to precisely model the mode specific structure in each state. Similarly stereotyping behaviors, including interactions and activities as mode participants allows us to precisely specify AADL behaviors, e.g. call sequences, and associate them to the appropriate state.

Figure 6 shows an excerpt of the ExSAM model depicting an ibd for the internal structure of the component redundant_pattern.primary_backup (Figure 3) in the nominal mode. In this ibd the part named primary_system represents the subcomponent primary_system in the AADL model. Note that the other subcomponents are not shown in this ibd, since the purpose of this ibd is to visualize only the elements that are involved in the mode nominal. The part primary_system is stereotyped by «System» to show its component category. Figure 8 shows another ibd, which is used to visualize the active part and connectors (e.g. backup_system, in_fail, out_bk) in the backup mode. Table 1, lists model elements of Figures 6 and 8 that are stereotyped by «ModeParticipant». For each element in the table, the modes in which that element is active are indicated using ✓. Note that this information is not shown in Figures 6 and 8 to minimize cluttering the figures.

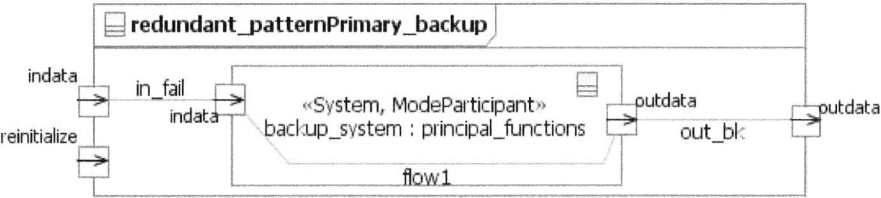

Fig. 8. An ibd visualizing the part and connectors that are active in the backup mode

Table 1. Mode participants and their active modes

	indata	in_fail	backup_system	out_bk	outdata	in_nom	primary_system	out_nom
nominal	✓				✓	✓	✓	✓
backup	✓	✓	✓	✓	✓		✓	
reinit	✓	✓	✓	✓	✓		✓	

Note that in the development of ExSAM, we were restricted by the design choices of SysML, including the fact that only a subset of UML constructs are imported into SysML. The most interesting UML concepts that are, in our opinion, missing in SysML are Collaboration and CollaborationUse, which can be used to capture AADL modes in UML. The solution we proposed in this section, however, uses the «ModeParticipant» stereotype and applies it to several metaclasses, mentioned above, to precisely convey the semantics of AADL modes in ExSAM models.

3.4 Mapping for Bindings

An important aspect of AADL is the ability to model the deployment of software components to hardware components. In AADL it is done through value associations to specific properties of certain, deployable component categories.

For example, in AADL to model that process FlightDirector is deployed to the processor named Xeon_solo, in the component FlightDirector we set the value of the property bound_processor to Xeon_solo.

In order to model this information in ExSAM, we use SysML allocation relationships. For example, in the example mentioned above, we add a dependency stereotyped by SysML «allocate» to the model, connecting the block representing FlightDirector to the block representing Xeon_solo. Note that this mapping is an exception to the general rule on mapping property value associations (Section 3.1), which is done through values assigned to the attributes of stereotypes. This is because allocation is an important piece of information in ICSs, and it is crucial to explicitly capture and visualize it using dependencies stereotyped by «allocate».

3.5 Support for AADL Analysis

As mentioned in Section 2.2, AADL supports quantitative analysis of non-functional properties as well as early prediction of critical systems qualities. In order to take advantage of the analysis capabilities of AADL, we can use ExSAM to extract the fragment of a SysML or an ExSAM model that conforms to AADL. One can then transform this fragment to AADL using the mappings specified in ExSAM, and apply AADL analysis tools to the result of transformation. Note that the only modeling elements of SysML that are translatable to AADL are those in level 2 of Figure 1 because these are the only concepts that have corresponding elements in AADL.

4 Application and Evaluation of the Profile

The ExSAM profile presented in Section 3 is implemented and its applicability and usefulness are evaluated through two case studies. The first case study, presented in Section 4.1, is taken from the Carnegie Mellon Software Engineering Institute (SEI) report [13] on applying AADL to analyze an avionics system design. The purpose of this case study is to evaluate the ability of ExSAM in capturing all the AADL concepts. The next case study, presented in Section 4.2, is a real industrial case study, in which we applied ExSAM to model one of the Subsea Production Systems of FMC Technologies [3]. The goal of this case study is to evaluate the ability of ExSAM in addressing the modeling requirements of large, distributed, integrated control systems (ICSs).

We have implemented ExSAM as a set of stereotypes and constraints using IBM Rational Rhapsody Architect for Systems Engineers, version 7.5.1 [4], which supports SysML.

4.1 The Avionics Case Study

In the first case study, we used ExSAM to model an avionics system. The AADL model for this system is presented in [13] and is accessible from [1]. An avionics system typically consists of a collection of hardware and software components that controls the flight, navigation, and radio communication [13].

The SysML features used in this case study are bdds and ibds to show the blocks, their relationships, and their internal structures. In addition, the model consists of a total of six SysML **FlowSpecifications** for modeling AADL port groups and 49 blocks for capturing the components. The blocks are all stereotyped by either «ComponentType» or «ComponentImpl». In addition, each block is stereotyped by one of the category identifier stereotypes specified in Section 3.1. There are 10 realization relationships that are stereotyped by the newly proposed «AADL_Realization», and four generalization relationships that are stereotyped by «AADL_Generalization». The ExSAM model and diagrams created for this case study are provided in our technical report [10].

From the above description, we can conclude that the developed ExSAM model captured all the features and details in the AADL model for the avionics system. As expected, many aspects of the AADL model required that we use ExSAM features since SysML turned out to be insufficient.

4.2 The FMC Case Study

As a typical integrated control system, one of the subsea control systems of FMC Technologies (henceforth referred to simply as FMC) is selected as the industrial case study in this work. FMC is a leading global provider of technology solutions for the energy industry. One of the key technologies of FMC subsea systems is the Subsea Production System (SPS), which is used for managing and improving oil production fields. The main component of the system is the Subsea Control Module (SCM), which contains electronics and instrumentation for safe and efficient operation of subsea valves, chokes, etc. FMC subsea systems are large-scale, integrated and distributed systems of systems connected through high speed electric and fiber-optic network communication links. In this case study, we focused on FMC SPS, which according to the characteristics listed above, is a typical, complex ICS, which is representative in terms of modeling requirements. Based on the characteristics of SPS and results of the detailed domain analysis we conducted, the main requirements for modeling the architecture of such complex ICSs are:

– Req-1) For a particular installation, we need to model how the SPS is configured into a deployable product by capturing how its software and hardware components are connected and what roles they play,
– Req-2) For a particular installation, we must specify the software deployment across distributed hardware computing resources, which in our case consists of many instances of the SCM,
– Req-3) We need to model the behavior of the SPS in several possible modes of operation. For example, the SPS can be operated by different topside control modules, requiring operation in different control modes. It can also operate in the maintenance mode or the normal operation mode. In each mode, we need to identify which hardware and software components are actively operating, and identify constraints and behavior related to this mode.
– Req-4) We need to specify requirements and link them to the SPS architecture and design. This is very important to support safety inspection and certification in the maritime and energy sectors.

- Req-5) The hardware characteristics on which the software will be deployed need to be specified to facilitate the actual configuration of the SPS and to enable performance and resource consumption analysis.

In addition, there are practical considerations that should be accounted for. FMC wishes to use well-supported commercial tools with graphical notations for modeling SPS.

We applied ExSAM to model the architecture of the FMC SPS. In the model, we have a total of 13 bdds, 15 ibds, two state machine diagrams for describing modes and mode transitions, three sequence diagrams and two activity diagrams for describing behaviors. We used, 104 blocks stereotyped by category identifier stereotypes of ExSAM to model different components of the system. In this model, 43 realization relationships are stereotyped by «AADL_Realization», and 18 generalization relationships are stereotyped by «AADL_Generalization». Deployment of software to processors, and processors to underlying hardware for one part of the system is modeled using seven SysML allocation links, and is visualized in an ibd.

The description of the ExSAM model for the FMC case study suggests that SysML provides the basis for achieving the above requirements with its block concept, various diagram types (e.g., ibd, bdd, state machine diagram), and allocation modeling capabilities. SysML blocks, bdds and ibds can together be used to describe an FMC product through its physical and logical elements, their relationships, and internal structures, addressing Req-1. As pointed in Req-2, an important modeling requirement for the FMC case study is to capture software deployment to distributed hardware computing resources. In the ExSAM model, this is done through SysML allocations, which are equivalent to AADL bindings. Req-4 can be fulfilled using SysML requirements modeling capability, including the specification of requirements, their relationships (e.g., decomposition), and the traceability links between requirements or between them and other model elements.

In addition to the above, the FMC case study illustrated that SysML alone does not have the necessary mechanisms to satisfy Req-3 and Req-5, while ExSAM does. Using the «ModeParticipant» stereotype and its association to UML **State** metaclass (Figure 7), ExSAM can explicitly identify the components that are currently active in a mode and also link each mode to its own behavior, structure, and/or constraints (Section 3.3). Regarding Req-5, using newly introduced stereotypes and their attributes in ExSAM (e.g., «Memory», «Device») allows us to capture the hardware characteristics of the SPS such that system configuration can be facilitated and performance and resource consumption analysis can then be supported.

As mentioned earlier in this section, one practical consideration at FMC is the need for well-supported commercial modeling tools. To the best of our knowledge, however, AADL lacks professional tool support and a well-defined, complete graphical notation. AADL tool support is restricted to only one commercial tool and a few open-source ones. In contrast, SysML is supported by an increasing number of commercial (e.g. [2,4,5]) and open source tools justifying our choice for using SysML as the basis for ExSAM. In addition, AADL has no mechanisms to model requirements and traceability. However, AADL has some important features such as modes, and detailed component categories that are missing from SysML, thus justifying their reuse in ExSAM.

In sum, ExSAM brings missing features from AADL into SysML so that we can benefit from both AADL and SysML strengths. We applied ExSAM to model the architecture of the FMC SPS, which is a typical and complex ICS, and is representative in terms of architecture modeling requirements in ICSs domain. According to the two domain experts who reviewed the resulting architecture models, ExSAM is able to fulfill the five requirements mentioned above.

5 Related Work

MARTE is a UML profile for modeling real-time and embedded systems [9]. The two approaches presented in [9] and [12], that have used MARTE to create AADL-like models, suggest that MARTE is an interesting alternative to ExSAM. MARTE can indeed be extended with AADL-like constructs, as we did with SysML. However, in this work we chose to focus on SysML because of its wide acceptance in a wide spectrum of industrial sectors, as well as its support for systems engineering through features such as traceable requirements and parametric diagrams.

Combining SySML and MARTE is another alternative to bring together SysML's systems engineering constructs and MARTE's ability in specifying non-functional aspects, thus enabling quantitative analysis. The combination of SySML and MARTE is currently investigated and discussed in [11] in the context of four usage scenarios. A comparison of ExSAM with such alternatives would be interesting but is out of the scope of this paper.

6 Conclusion and Future Work

The increasing complexity of integrated control systems demands more effective design languages that can address, in a consistent manner, the heterogeneity resulting from the multidisciplinary nature of such systems.

In this paper, we describe how we combined two highly complementary standard modeling languages, SysML and AADL, to provide a common modeling language (in the form of the ExSAM profile) for specifying embedded systems at different abstraction levels, and from different stakeholder perspectives.

In Section 3, we specified ExSAM, which extends SysML with AADL-like concepts. The applicability and usefulness of ExSAM were investigated through two case studies. One benchmark case study showed that ExSAM can fully cover all AADL aspects and one large-scale industrial case study, performed in collaboration with an industrial partner developing integrated control systems, showed that ExSAM could successfully address all their modeling requirements, whereas neither SysML nor AADL could do so in isolation.

Future work will include the development of tool support for translating ExSAM models into AADL models by abstracting away the ExSAM constructs that fall in level 1 of Figure 1 (i.e., requirements, traceability, parametric models, interactions). The resulting AADL models can therefore be analyzed using AADL analysis tools.

Acknowledgments

This work was supported by a grant from Det Norske Veritas (DNV) and Simula Research Laboratory, Norway, in the context of the ModelME! project. We are grateful to FMC Technologies Inc. for their support and help on performing the industrial case study.

References

1. Aadl model for the avionics case study, http://aadl.sei.cmu.edu/aadl/downloads/Models/IntegratedModel10292007.zip
2. Enterprise Architect Tool, http://www.sparxsystems.com/
3. FMC Technologies, Inc., http://www.fmctechnologies.com/
4. IBM Rational Rhapsody Architect for Systems Engineers, http://www-01.ibm.com/software/rational/products/rhapsody/sysarchitect/
5. MagicDraw SysML Plugin, http://www.magicdraw.com/sysml
6. OMG Object Constraint Language, http://www.omg.org/spec/OCL/2.2/
7. OMG Systems Modeling Language, http://www.omgsysml.org/
8. UML 2.0 Superstructure Specification (August 2005)
9. A UML profile for MARTE: Modeling and analysis of real-time embedded systems (May 2009)
10. Behjati, R., Yue, T., Nejati, S., Briand, L., Selic, B.: An AADL-based SysML profile for architecture level systems engineering: Approach, metamodels, and experiments. Technical Report 2011-03, Simula Research Laboratory (2011), http://vefur.simula.no/~raziehb/ExSAM-11.pdf
11. Espinoza, H., Cancila, D., Selic, B., Gérard, S.: Challenges in combining sysML and MARTE for model-based design of embedded systems. In: Paige, R.F., Hartman, A., Rensink, A. (eds.) ECMDA-FA 2009. LNCS, vol. 5562, pp. 98–113. Springer, Heidelberg (2009)
12. Faugere, M., Bourbeau, T., de Simone, R., Gérard, S.: MARTE: Also an UML profile for modeling AADL applications. In: IEEE International Conference on Engineering of Complex Computer Systems, pp. 359–364 (2007)
13. Feiler, P.H., Gluch, D., Hudak, J.J., Lewis, B.A.: Embedded system architecture analysis using SAE AADL. Technical report, CMU/SEI (2004)
14. Feiler, P.H., Gluch, D.P., Hudak, J.J.: The Architecture Analysis & Design Language (AADL): An Introduction. Technical report, CMU/SEI (2006)
15. Nunes, N.J., Selic, B., da Silva, A.R., Álvarez, J.A.T. (eds.): UML Satellite Activities 2004. LNCS, vol. 3297. Springer, Heidelberg (2005)
16. Schafer, W., Wehrheim, H.: The challenges of building advanced mechatronic systems. In: FOSE 2007, pp. 72–84 (2007)
17. Weigert, T., Weil, F.: Practical experience in using model-driven engineering to develop trustworthy computing systems. In: IEEE International Conference on Sensor Networks, Ubiquitous, and Trustworthy Computing, pp. 208–217 (2006)
18. Weilkiens, T.: Systems Engineering with SysML/UML: Modeling, Analysis, Design. Morgan Kaufmann Publishers Inc., San Francisco (2008)

Analyzing Variability:
Capturing Semantic Ripple Effects

Andreas Svendsen[1,2], Øystein Haugen[1], and Birger Møller-Pedersen[2]

[1] SINTEF, Pb. 124 Blindern, 0314 Oslo, Norway
[2] Department of Informatics, University of Oslo, Pb. 1080 Blindern, 0316 Oslo, Norway
{andreas.svendsen,oystein.haugen}@sintef.no,
birger@ifi.uio.no

Abstract. This paper shows how to incrementally analyze how variability described in the Common Variability Language (CVL) affects the semantics of a model in a domain-specific language (DSL). CVL is a generic language for modeling variability. Using Alloy for definition of semantics we perform analysis to capture the elements in the model, which are semantically affected by applying the variabilities specified by the CVL model. An extension to the CVL editor is provided to automate the analysis. To illustrate the approach, we combine CVL with the Train Control Language (TCL) to capture how the semantics of TCL models are affected when applying CVL to them. We show how the analysis can be applied e.g., for testing.

Keywords: Language composition, model analysis, semantic modifications, Alloy, Common Variability Language, Train Control Language.

1 Introduction

Software product line engineering aims to define the commonalities and variabilities between software systems. A software product line can often be realized by using model transformations to transform a product line model into product models. The model transformation typically defines a transformation of a model by the means of a set of rules based on a description of variability. In general, structural modifications are explicitly expressed by the transformation, while the operational semantics of the model are implicitly modified. When a model is transformed, other applications, depending on the semantics of the model, may need to be modified accordingly. E.g., if thorough testing of a model (through test cases) has been performed, and the model is transformed, how will the semantic ripple effects of the transformed model affect the test cases and their results?

The Common Variability Language (CVL) [6] is a generic language for modeling variability in base models (a model defined by a domain-specific language (DSL)). A CVL model has one-way references to the base model, describing how the base model elements can vary. The base model is thus oblivious of the added variability by the CVL model. Executing a CVL model (with resolution of the variabilities) yields a model transformation from the base model to another model (the product model) in the same DSL, where the structure of some of the base model elements is modified.

In this paper we discuss how we can capture the semantic ripple effects when using CVL for modeling the variability in a model in a DSL and executing the CVL model with resolutions of the variabilities. We use the Alloy Analyzer to formally combine CVL with the base language, to perform the analysis. As an example base DSL we use the Train Control Language (TCL) [18] [5], which enables the modeling of train stations. We look at a concrete example where we transform a two-track station into a three-track station, to see how the operational semantics of the two-track station is affected by the transformation. The approach is evaluated by integrating the analysis with the CVL editor, and by performing the analysis on the example.

The contribution of this paper is as follows: We give a formalization of CVL and a formalization of the base language TCL, including the operational semantics. In addition we discuss how these already existing languages can be combined in Alloy, such that analysis of how CVL models affect the operational semantics of TCL models can be performed. We also discuss how this can be used to examine whether test cases related to the base model ought to be modified and re-run after a CVL transformation.

The outline of the paper is as follows: Section 2 describes the background for this work, including an introduction to CVL and TCL, and the challenges leading to the need for formal analysis. Section 3 introduces the formal language Alloy and Section 4 presents how CVL and TCL are combined formally in Alloy. Section 5 illustrates analysis that can be performed by Alloy to capture the semantic ripple effects of CVL models. Finally, Section 6 gives some related work before Section 7 concludes and gives some indications of future work.

2 Background

2.1 Common Variability Language

CVL is a language for modeling variability in models in any DSL where separate variability models define variability on a base model, and resolution models define how this variability should be resolved to form specific product models [10]. CVL includes concepts for abstraction, to be able to model e.g. feature diagrams, and concepts for concrete specification of how base model elements, in form of concrete repository objects, should be substituted with other model elements to form product models with the required features. CVL has three kinds of substitutions: Fragment substitution, reference substitution and value substitution. A fragment substitution replaces a placement fragment, which is a set of base model elements, with a replacement fragment, which is another set of base model elements. A reference substitution replaces a reference with another reference (redirect a reference). A value substitution replaces an attribute value in the model with another value. CVL has been developed as an Eclipse plug-in based on Eclipse Modeling Framework (EMF) [4] and Graphical Modeling Framework (GMF) [9], and allows definitions of variability of models in DSLs defined in Ecore. MOFScript [15] is used to perform the model transformation from a base model to product models.

For the purpose of the analysis presented later, we will in this paper use a simplified version of CVL, with minimal support for abstraction, and only fragment substitution with its placement and replacement fragment. However, reference and value substitutions can be obtained by a fragment substitution, though in a less convenient way. Thus, we will not lose generality relative to the full CVL.

The metamodel for the simplified CVL is illustrated in Fig. 1. A *CVLModel* contains a *variability specification*, which is specialized into *composite variability, fragment substitution, placement fragment* and *replacement fragment*. Composite variability allows a hierarchy of variability specifications, while fragment substitution binds (through *ToBinding* and *FromBinding*) a placement fragment and a replacement fragment, thereby replacing the placement fragment with the replacement fragment.

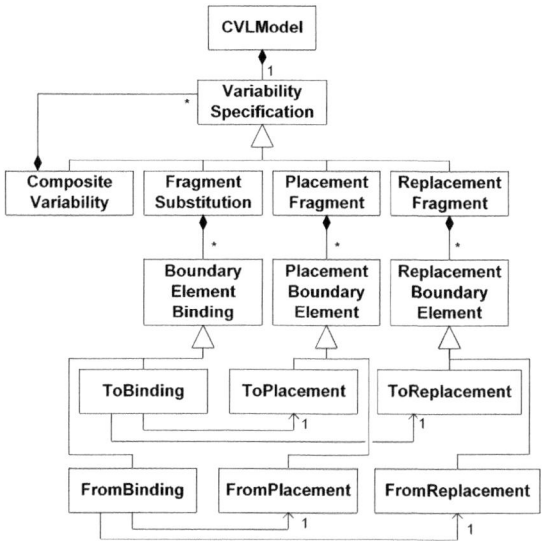

Fig. 1. Simplified CVL metamodel

A placement fragment defines a set of base model elements (objects in the model repository) to be replaced, by recording all references into and out of this fragment of elements. References going to the fragment are recorded by *ToPlacement*, which stores the element outside and the elements inside the fragment (see Fig. 2 and Fig. 3). References going out of the fragment are recorded by *FromPlacement*, storing the elements outside the fragment. Similarly, references into and out from a replacement fragment are recorded by *ToReplacement* and *FromReplacement*. Notice that a placement stores the context for where a replacement can be added, while a replacement stores the elements to be added to the placement context. Fig. 2 illustrates the references from CVL into the base model (*ModelElement*) and Fig. 3 illustrates how a fragment substitution binds a placement fragment with a replacement fragment to form a new product model.

As illustrated in Fig. 3, executing a CVL model involves substituting placements with replacements, by modifying the recorded references. E.g., the reference from A to C is bound to, and thus substituted with, the reference to H. Notice that CVL explicitly models where the variability is, and no algorithm for e.g. pattern matching is used. This will ease the possibility for performing the analysis presented later. For specification of the full CVL language and tool support, we refer to [6] for further information. A case study of CVL is given in [19].

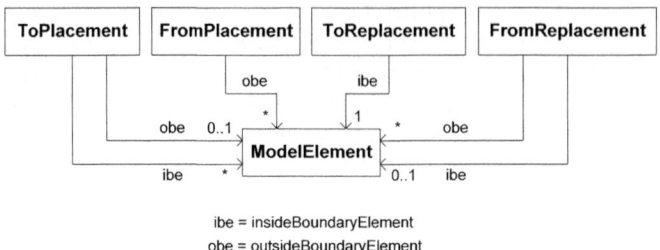

Fig. 2. CVL references to base model

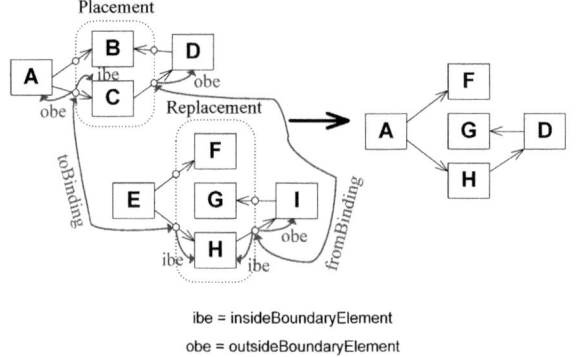

Fig. 3. A fragment substitution replaces a placement fragment with a replacement fragment

2.2 Train Control Language

As our base language we will use TCL, which is a DSL for modeling train stations. TCL has been developed in cooperation with ABB, Norway, to automate the development of interlocking source code, used to control signaling systems on train stations. TCL is defined by a metamodel (see Fig. 4), and is developed as an Eclipse plug-in using EMF and GMF. The TCL generator, transforming a station model into source code, is written in MOFScript.

The top concept of the metamodel is *station*, containing all the other concepts. A *train route* is a route that a train is given before it can move into or out of the station. The train route is divided into *track circuits*, which consists of a certain amount of *tracks* where a train can be located. A track can either be *a line segment* or a *switch*, which are connected by *endpoints*. Each train route starts and ends at an endpoint, which is connected to a *signal*. This signal will only give a clear signal (green light) if the requested route is safe. The concrete syntax of TCL is illustrated in Fig. 5.

Intuitively, a train will stop at a signal giving red light. The train will then request a route. Given that no conflicting train routes are already allocated, and no track circuits in the route are occupied, the train can be given the route and get a clear signal. As the train moves through the route, each visited track circuit will be occupied and freed afterwards. For further information about TCL, we refer to [18] and [5].

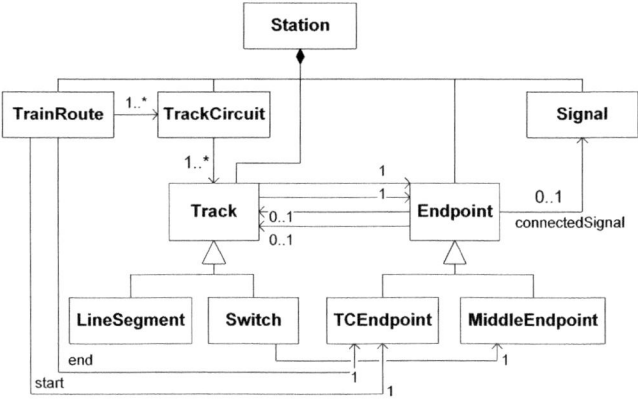

Fig. 4. TCL metamodel excerpt

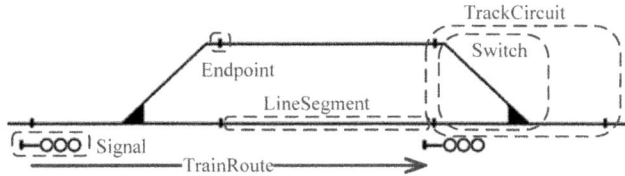

Fig. 5. TCL concrete syntax

2.3 Need for Analysis of CVL Models

Since the train domain is safety-critical, testing is a big part of the development of new train stations. A huge amount of resources is used to ensure that a station is well tested against some predefined criteria. Examples of such test cases can be to place trains on certain tracks, and let another train try to allocate a route using these tracks. If the amount of time and resources used to test these stations can be reduced, the cost and time-to-market can be drastically reduced.

Instead of modeling each station manually, CVL offers the possibility to specify the modifications from an existing station more formally, in such a way that the new station model can be transformed from an existing base station model. However, applications depending on the existing model (e.g., test cases) will often need to be redesigned (and retested) to apply to the new station model. By analyzing the semantic ripple effects of the CVL model, we can foresee how these applications should be modified as well. [16] presents some initial thoughts in this area, and based on this work, we present an approach for analyzing CVL models to find semantic ripple effects of these models.

To perform analysis of CVL models, we need a formal representation of CVL and of the base language to which CVL is applied. Due to its fully automatic analyzer and uniform notation, we use Alloy to specify these languages and to automate the analysis. This approach builds directly upon the work by Kelsen and Ma [14] presenting how to formalize modeling languages using Alloy.

3 Alloy

Alloy is a light-weight declarative constraint-solving language offering automatic and incremental analysis through relational calculus and first-order logic [13]. Unlike traditional theorem proving techniques, Alloy gives fully automatic analysis ranging over a finite space of cases. Thus, Alloy guarantees that the analysis is complete and correct up to a given scope (which bounds the number of elements of each type). However, the small scope hypothesis ensures that if there is a solution to a request, this solution will be in a scope of small size [2].

A system can be defined in Alloy using *signatures*, where a signature defines a type. A type hierarchy can be realized by letting a signature extend another signature. Signatures can contain *fields*, which refer to other signatures. Global constraints for the system may be added as *facts*. Parameterized constraints can be defined as *predicates*, which will evaluate to true only if all the contained constraints are evaluated to true. Predicates can thus be used as operations, where it constrains some behavior. Alloy also allows assertions, where an assertion is a claim that some constraints must hold.

There are two kinds of analysis performed by the Alloy Analyzer: either search for a solution that satisfies a predicate, or search for a counter-example to an assertion. The Alloy Analyzer performs these analyses automatically by populating the signatures with elements up to the given scope, to find either a solution or a counter-example. If an analysis does not give any solution or counter-example, there may not be any solution or counter-example within the scope, or the constraints (facts/predicates) may over-constrain the model. The Alloy model can therefore be built stepwise based on the feedback from the Alloy Analyzer.

4 Combining CVL and TCL in Alloy

TCL and CVL are two DSLs that are already operational in Eclipse, where we have combined models of CVL with models of TCL to describe product lines of TCL models [19]. In this paper we use an example with a two-track station as our TCL base model. We add a CVL model on top of this base model to substitute the second track with another two-track, yielding a three-track station. Fig. 6 illustrates the CVL model on the right side, which defines a fragment substitution on the TCL model on the left side. By selecting the placement fragment, the TCL editor highlights the model elements to be substituted (red color) and the model elements that are involved in this substitution (orange color). Notice that the two rows of rectangles represent the train routes and the track circuits. The naming of train routes and track circuits follows the convention from the train domain, where names are based on the related signal. The result of executing the CVL model is a three-track station (see Fig. 7).

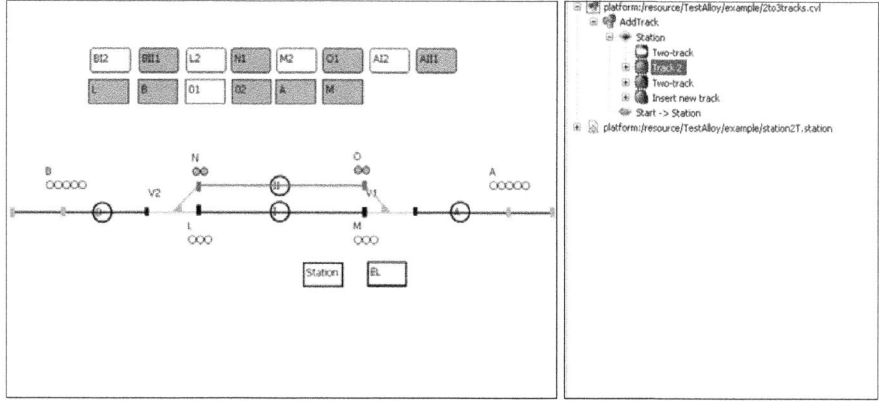

Fig. 6. CVL (right) on TCL (left) in Eclipse

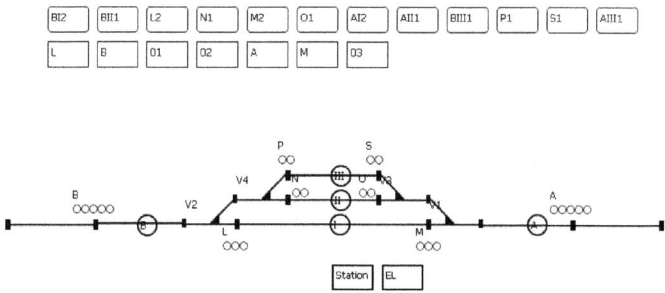

Fig. 7. A three-track station is the result of executing the CVL model

4.1 Formalizing TCL

The formalization of TCL involves three Alloy models; static model, dynamic model and instance model (see Fig. 8). The TCL static model gives the static semantics for the TCL language. This model represents the concepts of TCL (e.g., train routes, track circuits, etc.) as signatures, the references between the model elements as fields and additional constraints as facts. As an example, in the TCL metamodel (Fig. 4) a train route is contained by *Station* and has references to track circuit, *start* endpoint and *end* endpoint, with cardinality 1..*, 1 and 1 respectively. Fig. 9 illustrates how this train route is defined in the Alloy model: as a signature, with *trackCircuits*, *start*, *end* and *direction* as fields with the appropriate cardinalities. In addition, two constraints are defined on this signature. The first constraint states that the train route has to be referred from one Station element. The second constraint ensures that no model can be instantiated with a train route starting and ending at the same endpoint.

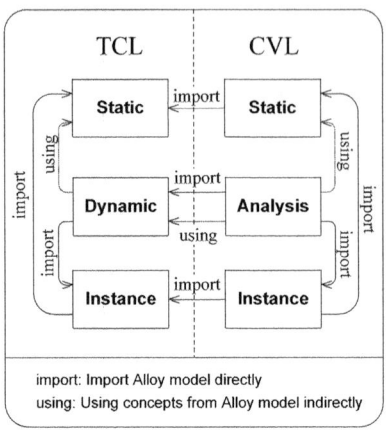

Fig. 8. Alloy specification divided into six models

```
abstract sig TrainRoute extends Element {
  trackCircuits: some TrackCircuit,
  start: one TrackCircuitEndpoint,
  end: one TrackCircuitEndpoint,
  direction: one Direction
}{one st:Station | this in st.trainRoutes}

//trainroutes have to refer different endpoints
fact {no t:TrainRoute, e:t.start, e2:t.end | e in e2}
```

Fig. 9. Definition of a train route with additional constraints

When Alloy searches for solutions or counter-examples, it will try to populate the signatures with elements satisfying all constraints. Thus, with the static semantics of TCL the Alloy Analyzer instantiates an arbitrary TCL model. However, the purpose of our analysis is to perform analysis on a given model in the base language. Therefore, we force Alloy to instantiate the model instance that has been created in the TCL editor. Our approach for instantiating such a model is to extend the static model with a TCL instance model, extending each concept with its instances. Fig. 10 illustrates the train route instance "BI2", which extends train route and constrains the fields to refer other instances. Constraining all the concepts in such a manner, gives the Alloy Analyzer only one valid instance. Thus, the instance model imports the static model in order to extend its elements (see Fig. 8). In this paper, this particular instance model is a model of a two-track station (illustrated in Fig. 6).

The dynamic TCL model contains the dynamic (operational) semantics of TCL. We have simplified the TCL dynamic semantics for the purpose of applying analysis. We will omit some elements and only concentrate on the core elements for train movement. Intuitively, our dynamic semantics for TCL is as follows: A train has to allocate a train route before it is allowed to enter or exit the station. The train route will only be given to the train if no other conflicting train routes are already allocated. If the train gets the route, it can move and occupy one track after another. When it

```
one sig tr_BI2 extends TrainRoute{} {#trackCircuits = 2}
fact {all tr:tr_BI2, st:Station2T | tr in st.trainRoutes}
fact {all tr:tr_BI2, e:ep_TCE1 | e in tr.start}
fact {all tr:tr_BI2, e:ep_TCE4 | e in tr.end}
fact {all tr:tr_BI2, tc:tc_B | tc in tr.trackCircuits}
fact {all tr:tr_BI2, tc:tc_01 | tc in tr.trackCircuits}
fact {all tr:tr_BI2, dir:Right | dir in tr.direction}
```

Fig. 10. Definition of a train route instance

reaches its destination, the train route is freed. If the train is entering the station, it will try to allocate the subsequent route to exit the station. Several trains can move at the same time, as long as train routes are not mutually conflicting.

The dynamic model, representing the TCL operational semantics, constrains how the elements defined by the TCL static model can behave by defining a state machine. Since the static model elements are defined as abstract types, and the instance model defines subtypes of them, the dynamic semantics can constrain the static model elements while the Alloy Analyzer will use the instance elements in the solution. Therefore, we import the instance model, but specify how the static elements can behave. We also import the Alloy library *util/ordering[State]* to get a set of ordered states. The State signature contains fields referring to sets of trains, train routes, tracks for storing the current location of the trains and their status. For instance, there are four sets of trains; *initial trains* that have not yet arrived at the station, *idle trains* that have arrived but are waiting for a train route, *moving trains* that have a train route and are currently moving, and *final trains* that have left the station.

To be able to simulate the movement of trains, the Alloy model contains three predicates that act as operations; *newTrain*, *allocateRoute* and *moveTrain*. The predicate newTrain describes the movement of a train from the initial train set to the idle train set and the location of the train on either side of the station. The predicate allocateRoute defines the allocation of a route to an idle train if this satisfies all constraints for route allocation, and the movement of the train from the idle train set to the moving train set. The predicate moveTrain describes the movement of a train one track for each transition, and movement of the train either to the idle train set or the final train set when it reaches its destination.

Fig. 11 illustrates how we obtain the Alloy models. The static TCL model is produced by traversing the metamodel of TCL and generating the proper signatures, fields and constraints. The dynamic TCL model is manually produced. The TCL instance model (in Alloy) is fully transformed from a TCL model. This ensures that other Alloy instances of TCL can be generated automatically from a TCL model created in the TCL editor. We refer to [17] for more information about how to perform analysis on station models.

4.2 Formalizing CVL and Relation to Base Language

We follow the same principles when formalizing CVL, dividing it into a static model, an instance model and an analysis model. The CVL static model contains signatures for the elements in the CVL metamodel, associations as fields with proper cardinalities and additional constraints. The CVL static model also imports the TCL static model to define the reference to TCL model elements. In CVL the references to the base model are realized through boundary elements (see Fig. 2), which are referring to ModelElements (EObjects in the Eclipse implementation). We follow this strategy for the Alloy model by introducing a signature as a supertype to the TCL elements. This is illustrated in Fig. 9, where a train route extends *Element*. Fig. 12 illustrates how the references to the base model in the boundary element ToPlacement (see Fig. 2) are realized in Alloy.

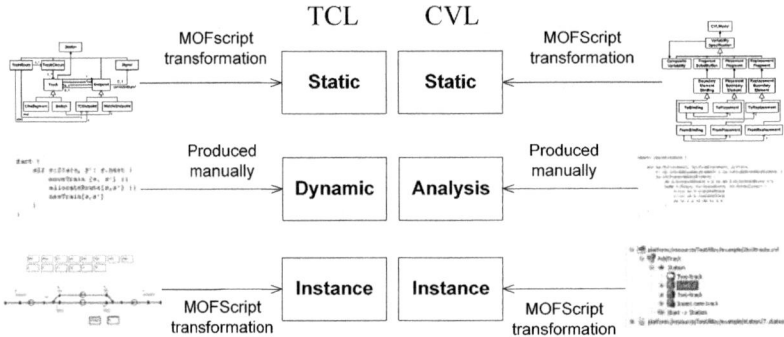

Fig. 11. Development of the Alloy models

```
abstract sig ToPlacement extends PlacementBoundaryElement {
    insideBoundaryElement: set Element,
    outsideBoundaryElement: lone Element
}
```

Fig. 12. CVL boundary element refers the base model through Element

The CVL instance model constrains the CVL model such that the Alloy Analyzer only finds one instance of it. Similar to the TCL instance model, the CVL instance model imports the CVL static model and extends the static elements. In addition it imports the TCL instance model, to constrain the connection to the TCL model (see Fig. 8). In this paper, the CVL instance model contains a fragment substitution which replaces a track with another two-track fragment, yielding a three-track station.

As illustrated in Fig. 11, the CVL static model is obtained by traversing the CVL metamodel and generating the Alloy signatures, fields and constraints. Notice that the same transformation is used here as for TCL, since it is written generally for Ecore models. The CVL analysis model is produced manually, and will be further discussed in Section 5. The CVL instance model is fully transformed from a CVL model. As for TCL, this ensures that other instances of CVL models can be generated automatically from CVL models created in the CVL editor.

4.3 Optimizing the Instance Models

When performing analysis by using Alloy, we notice that when the base model grows, and thus the scope of number of Element (root of base model, see Fig. 9), the time needed to perform the analysis increases rapidly. Typical TCL models range from about 50 to more than 100 model elements. The approach followed in this paper specifies a general language, and specializes this language into an instance model by constraining how the instance model elements are connected. This will force the Alloy Analyzer to populate all possible instances, and discard the ones that violate the constraints.

Instead of using constraints to specify our instance, we optimize the instance models by defining fixed functions defining relations between the instance model elements. The optimization considerably improves the analysis time to about 1/10 of original time (SAT solving time can be variable), such that the approach scales better.

5 Analyzing Semantic Ripple Effects

We have created a formal model for the TCL and CVL languages, for models in these languages and for the behavior of the TCL models. We can now write analyses of these models to be executed by the Alloy Analyzer. Our motivation for this work is to analyze the semantic ripple effects of a CVL transformation. The CVL model specifies explicitly which base model elements should be substituted for other elements, meaning that the modifications of the static semantics of the model are obvious. However, whether the transformed TCL model will have semantic ripple effects still needs to be investigated, and this is the target for our analysis.

The operational semantics of a TCL model is defined by the set of all traces defining legal train movement through the model. Following the STAIRS approach [11] these traces can be formalized and possibly refined. Positive traces then define the intended train movement, while negative traces define unintended train movement. Fig. 13 illustrates a trace defining train movement of one train from the left through the main track, by describing the movement of the train T1 on the tracks. Note that the trace also explicitly defines the position of the switches in the route, which is either in normal (for main track) or divert (for second track) position. For explanation of the composition of line segments and switches, see Fig. 14.

<{T1,LS1}, {T1,LS3}, {V2,normal}, {T1,V2}, {T1,LS5},
{V1,normal}, {T1,V1}, {T1,LS4}, {T1,LS2}>

Fig. 13. Positive trace defining train movement from left through the main track

In the CVL analysis model we have written assertions to check whether the CVL transformation will affect the traces of the TCL model. Fig. 15 illustrates a simple assertion claiming that no base model element inside or referring to the placement fragment is included in any trace of the TCL operational semantics. The boundary elements record which elements are inside the fragment (red elements in Fig. 6) and which elements are involved (orange elements in Fig. 6).

To evaluate and automate this analysis we have extended the CVL editor with menu options to perform the analysis (see Fig. 16). The menu allows the user to export the Alloy models, perform analysis to get a list of affected elements and do custom analysis by providing a file containing the custom analysis. Choosing to perform analysis (to get the affected elements) involves executing the Alloy Analyzer with the assertion in Fig. 15, which will yield a counter-example with the first affected element. This analysis is then reiterated, excluding the discovered element, until there are no more affected elements.

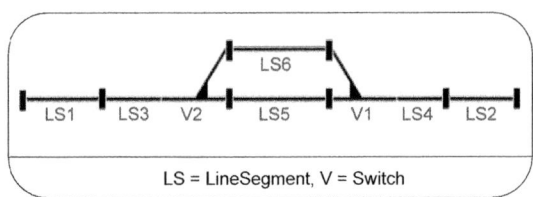

Fig. 14. Composition of LineSegments and Switches

```
assert checkElements {
    all tp:ToPlacement, s:State,
        e: tp.insidePlacementBoundaryElement +
           tp.outsidePlacementBoundaryElement {
                no (s.occupiedTrack) & e
                no (s.allocatedRoute) & e
        }
}
```

Fig. 15. Check if the TCL dynamic semantics is affected by the modified elements

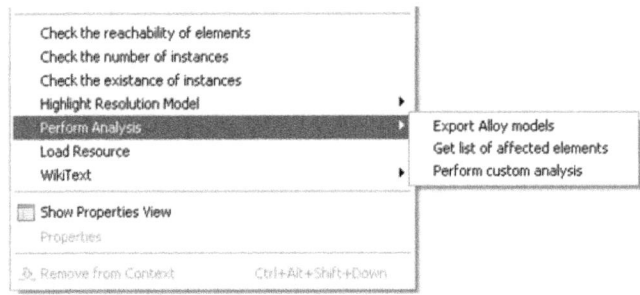

Fig. 16. Performing analysis in the CVL editor

Applying the assertion in Fig. 15 on the example, the Alloy Analyzer gives us counter-examples indicating that the following elements are affected: Train routes BII1, N1, O1, AII1 and tracks (line segments and switches) LS6, V2, V1 (see Fig. 17). The analysis also gives the affected attribute names given by the boundary elements and which elements they refer to. E.g. switch V1 is affected on the attribute *divert*, which is referring to track circuit endpoint TCE5. Notice that these train routes are the routes entering and leaving the second track of the station. The line segment LS6 is placed on the second track, while switches V2 and V1 are located on each side of it. From this we observe that train movement to and from the main track is not affected by the transformation, unlike train movement to and from the second track.

The affected line segment LS6 is placed on the second track, and analysis of the replacement fragment is necessary to determine whether the transformation will affect the traces including this line segment. E.g., the line segment can be replaced by two line segments, changing the trace through the second track. Furthermore, we observe that switches V2 and V1 are affected with the divert property, stating that if the traces do not include this attribute, they cannot change. Therefore, even though these switches are indicated to be affected, there is no possibility that the traces using the normal position will be affected. In other words, the analysis shows that all traces through the main track of the station are not affected by the change, while it requires further analysis of the replacement fragment to determine the effect on the traces through the second track. Similarly, it requires further analysis of the replacement fragment to verify the additional traces through the third track.

```
Analysis performed in 6 seconds.
The following elements are affected:

LS6 (inside PF)
BII1 : end : TCE5
N1 : start : TCE3
O1 : start : TCE5
AII1 : end : TCE3
V2 : divert : TCE3
V1 : divert : TCE5

Traces not including any of the listed properties of these
elements are still valid after the CVL transformation.
```

Fig. 17. The result of the analysis

As discussed in Section 2.3, the train domain is a safety-critical domain. Therefore testing the behavior of the station is a big and time-consuming part of the development. When a station is well tested, manually implementing a similar station will require all the tests to be modified and executed again. However, if the new station can be expressed in CVL with the well-tested station as a base model, we can perform analysis on how the operational semantics of the base model has been affected. Then we can determine whether the test cases also have been affected. A test case in TCL involves testing a particular train movement using either positive traces (a successful train movement) or negative traces (a disastrous train movement). An example of such a test case, given by a positive trace, is illustrated in Fig. 13, showing a successful train movement from left through the main track. Fig. 18 illustrates a negative trace where train T1 moves from left into the main track followed by movement of train T2 from right into the main track.

<{T1,LS1}, {T1,LS3}, {V2,normal}, {T1,V2}, {T1,LS5},
{T2,LS2}, {T2,LS4}, {V1,normal}, {T2,V1}, {T2,LS5}>

Fig. 18. Negative trace defining two trains moving into the main track

For the two-track station there are test cases which test whether train routes entering the station to the main track can be allocated if there are trains located on this track, and similar for the second track of the station. Based on the analysis performed we know that the test cases involving train movement through the main track are not affected, and a re-test of these on the transformed station can be avoided. The train routes to the second track have, however, been affected by the transformation, and we cannot safely determine whether a re-test can be avoided. E.g., the analysis has confirmed that the test case (negative trace) in Fig. 18 involving the main track will yield the same result for the three-track station as for the two-track station, causing a re-test to be redundant. Since there are large numbers of such test cases, testing all possible combinations, the analysis performed can reduce the effort needed to perform testing.

Another issue is the completeness of the test cases for the transformed model. In our example the transformed model contains three tracks. However, the test cases testing the base model are designed for only two tracks, leaving all train movement to and from the third track, and the behavior of the added model elements, untested. Careful analysis of the replacement fragment and the current test cases can give information of how to add new test cases testing the added functionality. Such analysis may reveal whether a CVL substitution yields a refinement of the traces representing the test cases. In this case, it may be possible to determine that even more traces will remain unaffected and whether new traces can be established based on the already existing ones. Further information is given in Section 7 as future work.

Notice that transformations on base models with relatively small changes (modeled in CVL models) are quite common. In this kind of situation, such incremental analysis of the CVL models has a potential of reducing the total amount of analysis necessary.

6 Related Work

Kelsen and Ma [14] present a comparison between traditional techniques and an Alloy approach for formalizing modeling languages. Their findings state that the Alloy approach enables automatic analysis and a uniform notation. They claim that this approach is more accessible and has the potential of making formal analysis of modeling languages more widely adopted. Our approach is based on the work by Kelsen and Ma, and we use an Alloy formalization of CVL and TCL to perform the presented analysis.

Several approaches use Alloy to perform analysis on product line models and model transformations. Baresi and Spoletini [3] propose an approach for using Alloy to analyze graph transformation systems. They check reachability of paths, whether sequences of rules are valid, etc. Anastasakis et al. [1] describe an approach for using Alloy to analyze a model transformation and the well-formedness of the target model. Gheyi et al. [8] specify a theory for feature models in Alloy. The Alloy Analyzer is used to check well-formedness and refactoring rules. Our approach analyzes how the semantics of the base model is affected by a transformation instead of analyzing the well-formedness of the transformation itself.

Uzuncaova et al. [20] [21] present an approach using incremental test generation to test product line models represented by feature models. Each feature of a program is defined as an Alloy formula, which is used to generate incremental tests. Instead of incrementally building tests, we use the description of variability on a model to decide the semantic ripple effect, and thus which test cases which need to be reconsidered.

Fraser et al. [7] present and evaluates methods to identify obsolete test cases using model-checkers. In this approach, only test cases that are related to the model changes are selected for the updated test case suite, avoiding a retest of the unaffected test cases. This is similar to the approach discussed in this paper; using the Alloy Analyzer (model finder) to obtain the updates in operational semantics, to observe whether test cases are affected. However, unlike their approach, we analyze the CVL model (representing the differences), without comparing the base model with the transformed model. This may be more efficient and result in more accurate results.

In [12] Jackson presents a case study where Alloy is used to model railway safety. The main purpose of this case study was to show that Alloy can analyze a structural aspect. The formalization of this railway system is quite similar to the formalization of the operational semantics of TCL. However, TCL includes more elements and is more complex, e.g., bidirectional train movement on a track, because it is modeling an actual train system.

7 Conclusion and Future Work

This paper presented an approach for discovering modification in operational semantics in CVL transformations. We gave a formalization (both static and dynamic) of the Train Control Language using the light-weight formal language Alloy. We then formalized the Common Variability Language and connected it to TCL. Analysis for discovering semantic ripple effects when applying CVL was conducted. A discussion about the purpose of this analysis, for use with test case evolution, was also given, in which we discovered that re-testing of some test cases can be avoided. Thus, we observed that by using CVL to follow an incremental approach of developing station models and performing analysis, the cost of testing the stations can be reduced.

As current and future work we will extend the analysis of the CVL models in order to obtain more precise information about the semantic ripple effects. This includes further analysis of the replacement fragments, which is needed for this approach to further support evolution of test cases. Such analysis can reveal whether more of the traces are unaffected, and if they represent a refinement of the existing traces. Additional traces can then be determined to be unaffected, causing a re-test of test cases based on these traces to be redundant.

In addition extending the CVL formalization to include other CVL concepts will be investigated. CVL concepts for abstraction will then allow specification of SPLs.

A case study comparing this incremental approach with redesigning station models from scratch is also important future work.

Acknowledgements. The work presented here has been developed within the MoSiS project ITEA 2 – ip06035 and the Verde project ITEA 2 – ip8020 parts of the Eureka framework.

References

1. Anastasakis, K., Bordbar, B., Küster, J.M.: Analysis of Model Transformations Via Alloy. In: Baudry, B., Faivre, A., Ghosh, S., Pretschner, A. (eds.) 4th International Workshop on Model Driven Engineering, Verification and Validation, in conjunction with MoDELS 2007, Nashville, TN, USA. Springer, Heidelberg (2008)
2. Andoni, A., Daniliuc, D., Khurshid, S., Marinov, D.: Evaluating the Small Scope Hypothesis. MIT CSAIL MIT-LCS-TR-921 (2003)
3. Baresi, L., Spoletini, P.: On the Use of Alloy to Analyze Graph Transformation Systems. In: Corradini, A., Ehrig, H., Montanari, U., Ribeiro, L., Rozenberg, G. (eds.) ICGT 2006. LNCS, vol. 4178, pp. 306–320. Springer, Heidelberg (2006)
4. EMF, Eclipse Modeling Framework (Emf), http://www.eclipse.org/modeling/emf/
5. Endresen, J., Carlson, E., Moen, T., Alme, K.-J., Haugen, Ø., Olsen, G.K., Svendsen, A.: Train Control Language - Teaching Computers Interlocking. In: Computers in Railways XI (COMPRAIL 2008), Toledo, Spain (2008)
6. Fleurey, F., Haugen, Ø., Møller-Pedersen, B., Olsen, G.K., Svendsen, A., Zhang, X.: A Generic Language and Tool for Variability Modeling, SINTEF, Oslo, Norway, Technical Report SINTEF A13505 (2009)
7. Fraser, G., Aichernig, B.K., Wotawa, F.: Handling Model Changes: Regression Testing and Test-Suite Update with Model-Checkers. Electronic Notes in Theoretical Computer Science 190, 33–46 (2007)
8. Gheyi, R., Massoni, T., Borba, P.: A Theory for Feature Models in Alloy. In: First Alloy Workshop, Portland, United States, pp. 71–80 (2006)
9. GMF, Eclipse Graphical Modeling Framework (Gmf), http://www.eclipse.org/modeling/gmf/
10. Haugen, O., Møller-Pedersen, B., Oldevik, J., Olsen, G.K., and Svendsen, A.: Adding Standardized Variability to Domain Specific Languages. In: SPLC 2008, Limerick, Ireland (2008)
11. Haugen, Ø., Husa, K., Runde, R., Stølen, K.: Stairs Towards Formal Design with Sequence Diagrams. Software and Systems Modeling 4, 355–357 (2005)
12. Jackson, D.: Micromodels of Software. In: Broy, M., Pizka, M. (eds.) Models, Algebras and Logic of Engineering Software, pp. 351–384. IOS Press, Amsterdam (2003)
13. Jackson, D.: Software Abstractions: Logic, Language, and Analysis. The MIT Press, Cambridge (2006)
14. Kelsen, P., Ma, Q.: A Lightweight Approach for Defining the Formal Semantics of a Modeling Language. In: Busch, C., Ober, I., Bruel, J.-M., Uhl, A., Völter, M. (eds.) MODELS 2008. LNCS, vol. 5301, pp. 690–704. Springer, Heidelberg (2008)
15. Oldevik, J.: Mofscript Eclipse Plug-In: Metamodel-Based Code Generation. In: Eclipse Technology Workshop (EtX) at ECOOP 2006, Nantes (2006)
16. Svendsen, A.: Application Reconfiguration Based on Variability Transformations, School of Computing, Queen's University, Kingston, Canada, Technical Report 2009-566 (2009)

17. Svendsen, A., Møller-Pedersen, B., Haugen, Ø., Endresen, J., Carlson, E.: Formalizing Train Control Language: Automating Analysis of Train Stations. In: Comprail 2010, Beijing, China (2010)
18. Svendsen, A., Olsen, G.K., Endresen, J., Moen, T., Carlson, E., Alme, K.-J., Haugen, O.: The Future of Train Signaling. In: Busch, C., Ober, I., Bruel, J.-M., Uhl, A., Völter, M. (eds.) MODELS 2008. LNCS, vol. 5301, pp. 128–142. Springer, Heidelberg (2008)
19. Svendsen, A., Zhang, X., Lind-Tviberg, R., Fleurey, F., Haugen, Ø., Møller-Pedersen, B., Olsen, G.K.: Developing a Software Product Line for Train Control: A Case Study of Cvl. In: Bosch, J., Lee, J. (eds.) SPLC 2010. LNCS, vol. 6287, pp. 106–120. Springer, Heidelberg (2010)
20. Uzuncaova, E., Garcia, D., Khurshid, S., Batory, D.: Testing Software Product Lines Using Incremental Test Generation. In: Proceedings of the 2008 19th International Symposium on Software Reliability Engineering, pp. 249–258. IEEE Computer Society, Los Alamitos (2008)
21. Uzuncaova, E., Khurshid, S., Batory, D.: Incremental Test Generation for Software Product Lines. IEEE Trans. Softw. Eng. 36, 309–322 (2010)

Integrating Design and Runtime Variability Support into a System ADL

Marie Ludwig[1], Nicolas Farcet[1],
Jean-Philippe Babau[2], and Joël Champeau[3]

[1] Thales Communications, 148 boulevard de Valmy
92704 Colombes Cedex, France
{marie.ludwig,nicolasfarcet}@fr.thalesgroup.com
[2] LISyC, UBO, UEB, 20 avenue Le Gorgeu
29200 Brest, France
jean-philippe.babau@univ-brest.fr
[3] LISyC, ENSTA Bretagne, 2 rue François Verny
29200 Brest, France
joel.champeau@ensta-bretagne.fr

Abstract. As the complexity of modern large systems or System of Systems increases, it becomes challenging to capture their whole dimension and to identify their key aspects. Architecture models provide a legible description of the system, and help describing its properties in a representation shared and understood by most stakeholders. In our case, we intend to evaluate system architectures through model execution. Since evolutionary design and configuration are key challenges of such systems, variability needs a way to be expressed in architecture models. Variability can be solved either at design time (derive a system from the family), or at runtime (reconfigure the system). This paper presents our experience in integrating variability aspects in a system architecture description Domain-Specific Language.

Keywords: Systems of Systems, architecture modelling, variability.

1 Introduction

Architecting and engineering large systems or Systems of Systems [1] face multiple complexity issues. During the early stages of enterprise[1] architecting, there is a need for a gradual understanding of its structure and confidence in its ability to fulfill its missions and satisfy its objectives. Model-Based Systems Engineering (MBSE) approaches [2], which are currently mainly used in IT enterprises, emphasize the use of an architecture model to provide a legible description of the studied system, shared and understood by most of the stakeholders.

In [3], we presented an approach to use architecture modelling as a support for system architects as well as business experts for the design and evaluation of enterprise

---

[1] In the remaining of the paper, we will use 'enterprise' as a generic term comprising large systems and systems of systems.

architecture in the early stages of architecting. This approach is based on rapid prototyping and short and incremental design / simulation loops using an executable architecture model. In our case, by *executable* model we mean an architecture model that can be simulated as a whole (i.e. by taking into account all its aspects) without model transformation. In particular, we execute operational processes in correlation with enterprise operational entities, services, roles, and command and control organizations.

According to Maier's criteria for identifying Systems of Systems [1], *evolutionary design* is an inherent challenge to such systems: for example they have to adapt to unpredictable environments and evolving missions, enable dynamic collaborations, master critical services chains, and mitigate vulnerabilities. Running an architecture model in a convincing way thus requires the ability to express the possible reconfigurations and variations of the enterprise.

Based on ongoing works on Variability and Product Line engineering [5][6][8][9], this paper presents the integration in an enterprise architecture metamodel of concepts and activities dedicated to variability description and reconfiguration at runtime. In particular, we will focus on using variability as a support for the reconfiguration of sub-systems. Section 2 introduces the background of the project. Section 3 presents the variability challenges in this context, while Section 4 addresses the approach and implementation we adopted. Section 5 exposes an overview of related works and Section 6 concludes with future works and perspectives.

2 Background

To support rapid prototyping and iterative analysis of architecture models, we have designed a modelling framework and tools. The corresponding approach is based on the execution of semi-formal models and is part of a process named IDEA, bridging wider Concept Development & Experimentation (CD&E) and system engineering through architecting [3].

Because the proposed tools are intended to be used by stakeholders that may be operational experts with limited abilities in modelling, we had to go for a Domain-Specific Language (DSL) instead of using a general purpose language such as the UML. The DSL underlying metamodel is based on a core set of architectural concepts chosen for their simplicity and expressiveness for the participants of CD&E sessions. This metamodel will be referred to as the *IDEA Metamodel* in the rest of this paper. The specific models conforming to this metamodel will be referred to as *IDEA Models*.

From a technological point of view, our tool suite has been developed using the Microsoft .NET framework. The metamodel has been designed with the DSL Tools add-in for Visual Studio 2010, and the model execution engine is based on a set of .NET technologies – principally Windows Workflow Foundation (WF) and Windows Communications Foundation (WCF).

2.1 IDEA Metamodel Overview

The core concepts of the IDEA metamodel are close or similar to the ones described in the Architecture Frameworks such as the NATO Architecture Framework (NAF) [13]. They are meant to describe *what* the enterprise is supposed to do (*e.g.* capabilities), *how* it can achieve its goals (*e.g.* collaborations) and *who* performs the tasks (*e.g.* humans or systems). A synthetic view of the core concepts and their relationships is presented in Fig.1.

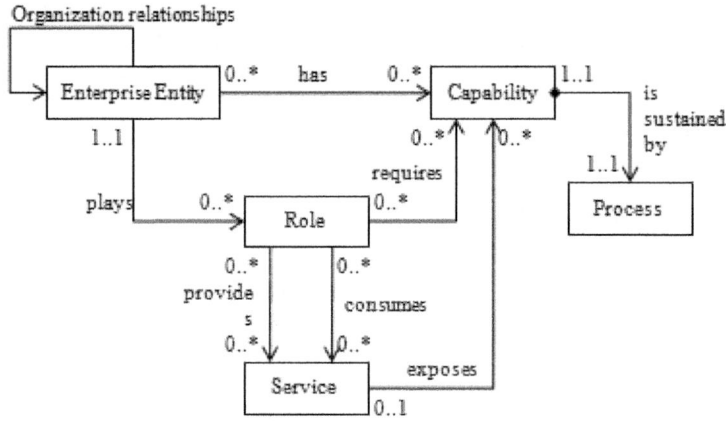

Fig. 1. IDEA Enterprise Architecture metamodel core concepts and relationships

Enterprise Entities Organization. Enterprise Entities represent the actors who achieve the tasks the enterprise is intended to realize. In particular, the systems composing a system of system are seen as Enterprise Entities. Enterprise Entities can be physical (such as vehicles) or logical (such as groups like patrols). The structure of the Enterprise Entities organization is based on several kinds of decomposition relationships, whose properties, behaviors and operational meanings are different depending on the kind of entity being decomposed. For the sake of simplicity, in this paper all these kinds of relationships will be equally referred to using the generic term Enterprise Entity *decomposition relationship*.

In order to introduce flexibility and modularity in the architecture model, all functional and collaborative aspects (operational processes, service interactions…) are assigned to *Roles*. Indeed, Roles supports the selection of role players while retaining the same collaboration scheme.

Model execution. While the general structure of the IDEA Metamodel is based on the Prototype Language paradigm [19], the elements used for the execution are based on a type / instance dichotomy. Most IDEA Metamodel concepts can be used to create either type or instance model elements. For example, the same Enterprise Entity concept is used to model a type of Entity – *e.g.* a police patrol car – and an instance derived from this type – *e.g.* a specific unmarked police car.

Processes are defined to describe and simulate the operational behaviors of the Entities. During model execution, each Enterprise Entity instance performs one or more Process(es) instance(s) in the context of a Role instance.

Due to collaborations defined between Roles, the Processes of different Entities may interact with each other (e.g. synchronize or exchange information or products). A Process may also contain Activities dedicated to the modification of an instance element in the model, for example changing an interaction between two entity instances. The modifications such an Activity can perform are constrained by the consistency rules inherent to the metamodel and to the specification of the corresponding type element.

3 Variability Challenges in IDEA Models

A priori, all elements of an enterprise architecture model are potential subjects to variation. However, in our case the models are not intended to be exhaustive architecture descriptions, but to be used for rapid prototyping by stakeholders who may not be familiar with modelling. Therefore, for model simplicity and legibility reasons, we decided to allow defining variability only for a subset of elements. In this paper, we will focus on variability related to the operational Enterprise Entities organization.

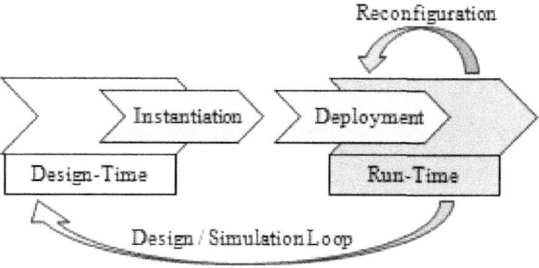

Fig. 2. IDEA Model lifecycle stages

3.1 Variability during the Model Lifecycle

As illustrated on Fig.2, the lifecycle of an IDEA architecture model is based on four stages:

- *Design-Time* – The user identifies the system Capabilities, Processes and Services, defines the type of Entities and their organization, and creates the map of the collaborating Roles.
- *Instantiation* – The user instantiates the Entities and Roles that will be deployed for the simulation.
- *Deployment* – The Entities are located on a simulated operation theatre. If relevant, they might consequently be attributed geographical properties.
- *Run-Time* – The Processes are simulated. Their execution takes into account all relevant operational context information available in the model (e.g. the condition of the entities).
- *Reconfiguration* may occur if a Process being executed modifies the model.
- After a simulation, the model can be refined or completed through a new cycle.

Design and Runtime Configuration. While the description of the variability will usually be done at Design-Time, the resolution may need to be solved at different stages of the model lifecycle.

Solving variability at Design-Time during the Instantiation produces configurations likely to be un-modifiable for the remaining of the entity lifecycle, and thus usually concerns lower granularity-leveled elements such as vehicles. In the remaining of the paper, we will use the term *Design Configuration* to mention a configuration resulting from variability resolution at Design-Time.

Solving variability at runtime is a way of performing Reconfiguration. As resulting configurations can still change again during the simulation, the Entity needs to keep track of all possible configurations compliant to its type. In the remaining of the paper, we will use the term *Runtime Configuration* to mention a configuration resulting from variability resolution at runtime.

3.2 Use Case Presentation

The examples used in this paper will be based on a simplified use case close to one of our current industrial projects in the domain of public safety.

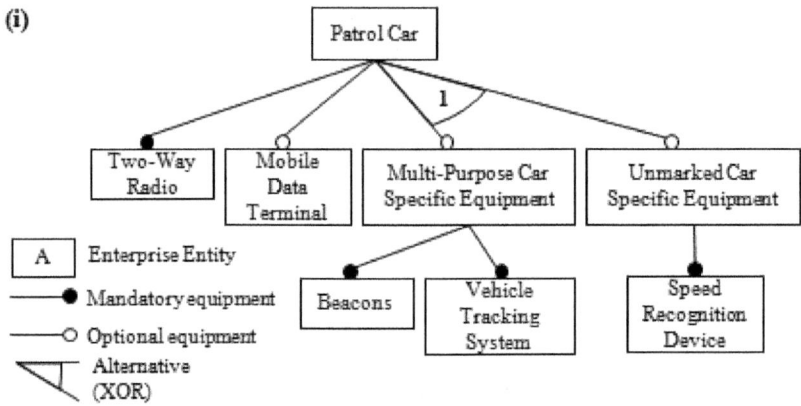

Fig. 3. Design Configuration: the example of Patrol Car equipments

(i) Design Configuration Example. A set of Enterprise Entities belong to the same product family. The model has to describe their common and variable characteristics in terms of sub-system decomposition.

In the domain of public safety, we consider several types of police cars that may embed different kinds of equipments depending on the type of mission they have been designed for. All these equipments are physically attached to the car and are un-removable and un-exchangeable in the duration of an operation: the equipment set of an instantiated police car from this family represents a Design Configuration.

In this model, *Patrol Cars* are equipped with a *Two-Way Radio*, and possibly a *Mobile Data Terminal*. They also embed either both *Beacons* and a *Vehicle Tracking System*, or a *Speed Recognition Device*. This example will be referred to as Example (i) in the following of the paper. It is illustrated in Fig.3 using the FODA Feature

Diagram notation [10] and the notation for cardinalities in Feature Diagrams proposed by Riebisch et al. in [7].

(ii) Runtime Configuration Example. In case of a given operational event, an opportunist collaborative group of Enterprise Entities has to be constituted from already deployed Entities to face the situation. Defining the way the enterprise is intended to respond to such a situation – *i.e.* what is the structure of the opportunist organization in terms of interactions and which processes it will perform – is one of the usual goals of enterprise architecture prototyping.

In the domain of public safety, we consider the example of a *Surveillance Patrol* who detects a suspicious package near a station and calls for reinforcement. Depending on the location of the threat, the supervision of the mission is either done by the *Station Security HQ* or by the *Police HQ*. A collaborative group composed of the *Patrol*, the *HQ* in charge of the supervision and a *Demining Squad* is created to handle the threat. This scenario will be referred to as Example (ii) in the following of the paper. Fig.4 illustrates the composition of the group and the Roles played by its members, using the same base notation as Fig.3.

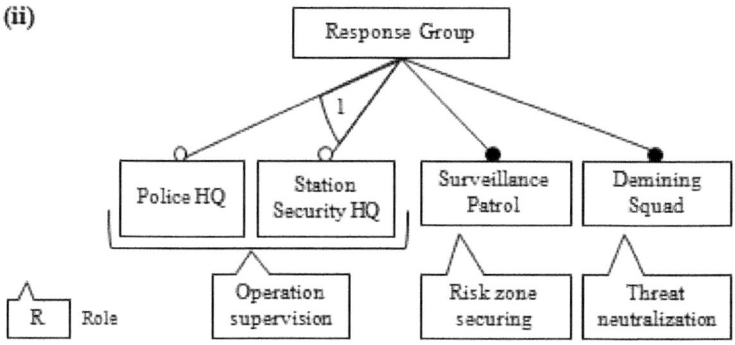

Fig. 4. Runtime Configuration: the example of a suspicious package alert response group

4 Approach and Implementation

Recent approaches to variability support for DSL frequently prone to separate the variability-related metamodel from the domain metamodel [6][8][9]. In our case, variability is intended to be used to model different operational configurations for some particular aspects of the enterprise (*e.g.* the Enterprise Entity organization), and thus we considered its expression as part of the domain itself.

In the case of *Mandatory* and *Optional* equipment specifications, cardinalities alone are sufficient – mandatory equipments being affected a (1..1) cardinality and optional equipments a (0..1). In Example (ii) there is a need for a *variation point* concept that supports the information that the Entity chosen between the *Police HQ* and the *Station Security HQ* will play the *Operation Supervision* Role.

Solving the variability expressed by such a variation point means substituting the chosen variant to the variation point, which involves the redirection of all relevant links it had to other model elements (especially links to played Roles). Therefore the variation point shall be able to contain all relevant structural information to enable a seamless substitution.

This approach to variation modelling is close to the substitution considered as the simplest form of operation in the variability language proposed by Fleurey et al. [9]. While in their case the variability language is generic and designed to work with any other language defined by a metamodel, in our case simplicity concerns lead us to integrate the substitution mechanism directly in the IDEA Metamodel.

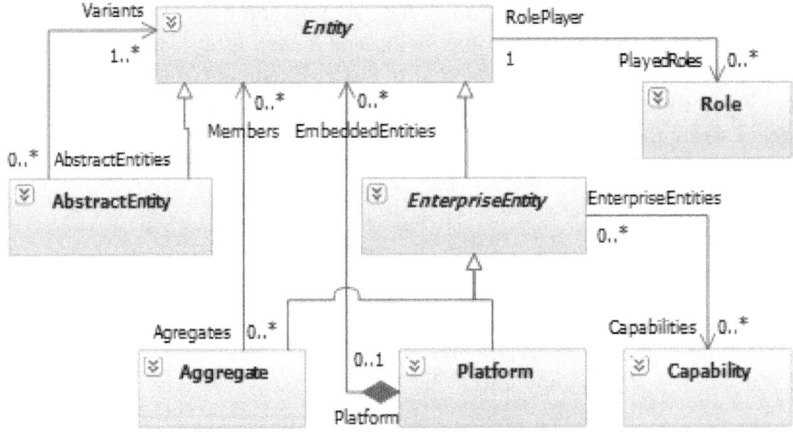

Fig. 5. Abstract Entity in the IDEA Metamodel

4.1 The Abstract Entity concept

We introduced a dedicated concept named *Abstract Entity* that represents a location in the enterprise organization where an Enterprise Entity may be substituted for another. For a given *Abstract Entity*, the substitution options are restrained to an identified set of Enterprise Entities referred to as its *Variants*.

When introducing variability in a model, it cannot always be inferred whether it will have to be resolved at Design-Time or at Runtime. For example, modelling different types of car useable for a same kind of police patrol could be either solved at Design-Time by directly instantiating a patrol with a multi-purpose car, or being left unsolved until, at Runtime, a process decides which type of car is more suitable in the patrol for the current mission. The same concept Abstract Entity shall be able to support both Design and Runtime Configurations.

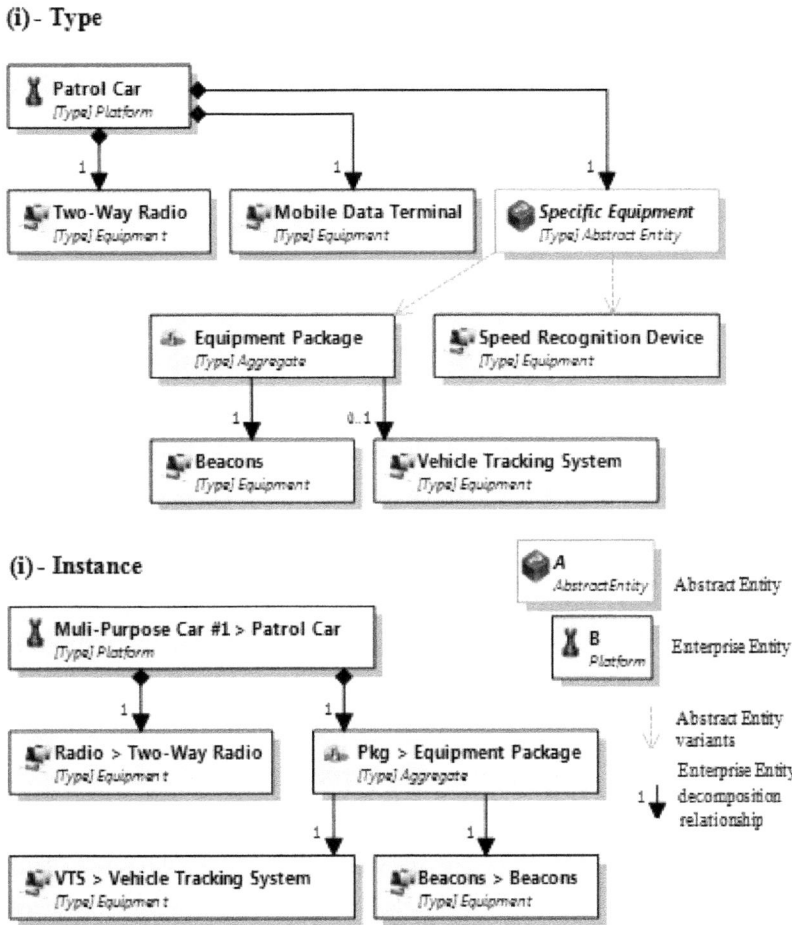

Fig. 6. Example (i) – Using IDEA Abstract Entities

4.2 Design Configurations

The car equipment alternative in Example (i) can be modeled using an Abstract Entity, with the two *Specific Equipment* sets as its variants. The indication that the alternative is intended to be solved at Design-Time can be added as an attribute on the Abstract Entity.

An instance from the type Patrol Car modeled as presented on Fig.6 does not contain an Abstract Entity anymore: the Patrol Car directly embeds either a Speed Recognition Device or the Equipment Package. The specific instance illustrated on the figure has also been created without the optional Mobile Data Terminal equipment.

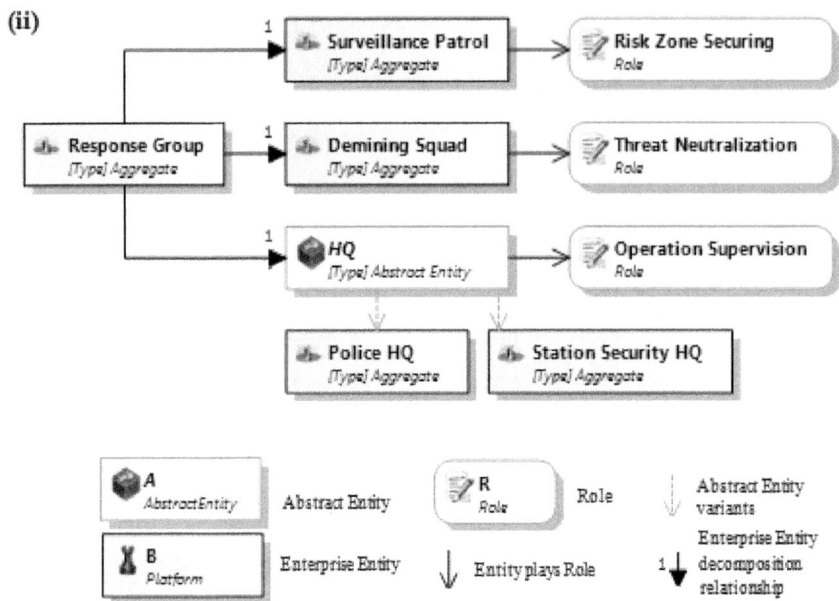

Fig. 7. Example (ii) – Using IDEA Abstract Entities

4.3 Runtime Configurations

Operational behaviors are captured in IDEA models by processes, *i.e.* series of activities performed to achieve a given task. At runtime, Entities execute Processes in the context of collaborating operational Roles.

IDEA process toolbox includes activities providing functionalities to undertake actions on the structure of the enterprise, also called System of System Management Activities (SoSM Activities). The conditions to be realized to trigger the reconfiguration performed by SoSM Activities are identified and evaluated using the usual process decision activities. The main SoSM Activities related to the Enterprise Entities are *Entity Instantiation*, *Role Restaffing* and *Abstract Entity Configuration*.

- The execution of an *Entity Instantiation Activity* creates a new Enterprise Entity instance of a given type defined in the model. The instantiation is propagated along some of the Enterprise Entities decomposition relationships, for example the embedding relationship of an *Equipment* on a *Vehicle*. If one of these relationships targets an Abstract Entity, the Abstract Entity is instantiated but not configured. This default behavior can be customized.
- The execution of a *Role Restaffing Activity* changes the Enterprise Entity instance role player for a given Role instance.
- The execution of an *Abstract Entity Configuration Activity* sets or changes the Variant that stands for a given Abstract Entity instance.

In the case of the two latter, the new Entity is chosen either manually by the simulation operator or by an algorithm that takes into account the simulation context.

Modelling the type of Response Group as introduced in Example (ii) can be done using an Abstract Entity as illustrated in Fig.7.

At runtime, the reconfiguration process is triggered by an operational event simulating the discovery of the suspicious package. The reconfiguration itself first implies instantiating a Response Group, where the Operation Supervision Role is initially played by an HQ Abstract Entity instance. After evaluating the location of the threat to choose the actual HQ Entity in charge, this Abstract Entity instance is deleted and replaced by an instance of the actual HQ Entity – for example, a Police HQ instance. The role-playing link between the Abstract Entity and the Operation Supervision Role is redirected to the Police HQ instance. Fig.8 schematizes the sequence of SoSM Activities used for this reconfiguration process.

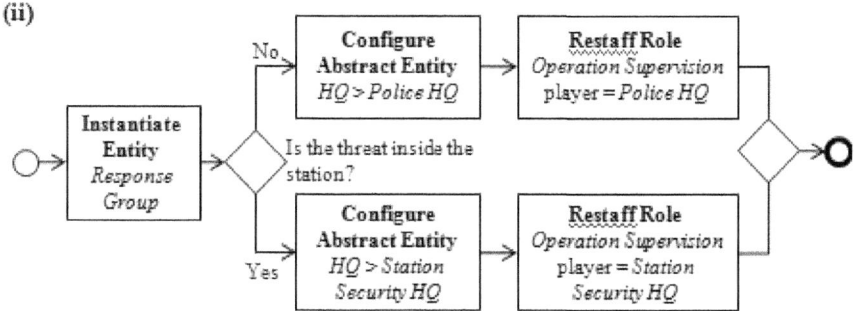

Fig. 8. Example (ii) – Reconfiguration process overview

5 Related Works

Variability in Systems Engineering. Variation has been primarily studied in the context of Software Product Line engineering. As highlighted in [4], handling variability is not limited to Product Lines, but is an essential concern when dealing with most systems and systems of systems, at all stages of their lifecycle. Model-Based Systems Engineering (MBSE) approaches have a need for modelling mechanisms to cope with variability in software as well as physical systems.

OMG language System Modelling Language (SysML) [12] is a general-purpose systems engineering modelling language widely used for MBSE applications. Krueger et al. handled variability in SysML models using the variation point notion provided by the IBM Rational Rhapsody/Gears Bridge [14], and successfully applied it in the industrial domain of wind turbines [15].

The multiple viewpoints paradigm, widely used in MBSE, permits a separated representation of the different concerns of a system. The MOVIDA (MOdelling VIews and Decision support for Architects) project tackles the problem of dealing with variability in multi-views engineering [16]. Their approach proposes the use feature models to model families of views, each view being a model of the system relevant to a given concern and designed with a DSL. The project also includes the specification and realization of a tool-suite that supports modelling variability of views and product derivation.

Runtime Variability. Runtime variability have been identified as a major ongoing challenge for modern Software Product Lines in the future Common Variability Language (CVL) OMG specification [11]. The objective of the CVL is to enable the specification of the variability in software product line models, variability being described as a model separate from the base model on which it applies. In particular, the language should support variability resolution resulting in alterations at runtime of an executing product.

The challenge of runtime adaptation is also being addressed in many software engineering domains, in various contexts and granularity levels. Software systems that have to dynamically adapt their behavior to their context execution are referred to as Dynamic Adaptive Systems (DAS). In [17], Acher et al. investigate the use of feature models as a support for DAS adaptive configuration. The proposed approach is based on modelling both the DAS and its context, and capture adaption through the interrelations of the two models. In [18], Navas et al. leverage the specific issues raised by evolution at execution time for resource-constrained embedded system, and propose a component-based approach to manage it.

6 Conclusion

This paper presents an approach and implementation to integrate variability aspects into a metamodel dedicated for executable enterprise architecture models. Modelling variability in the enterprise organization is used to produce Enterprise Entities configurations at design-time as well as reconfigure them at runtime. The introduction of an Abstract Entity point of variation combined with the use of cardinalities has proven successful in expressing our needs. Future work includes achieving a better support for the specification of variation constraints. The approach and tools based on this metamodel are also going to be used in additional industrial business cases.

References

1. Maier, M.W.: Architecting Principles for System of Systems. INCOSE Systems Engineering Journal 1(4), 267–284 (1998)
2. International Council on Systems Engineering (INCOSE): Systems Engineering Vision 2020. Technical Report INCOSE-TP-2004-004-02 (2007)
3. Ludwig, M., Farcet, N.: Evaluating Enterprise Architectures through Executable Models. In: 15th ICCRTS – International Command and Control Research and Technology Symposium (2010)
4. Hilliard, R.: On Representing Variation. In: ECSA 2010 – Proceedings of the Fourth European Conference on Software Architecture Companion Volume (2010)
5. Morin, B., Barais, O., Jézéquel, J.-M., Fleurey, F., Solberg, A.: Models at Runtime to Support Dynamic Adapatation. Computer, 46–53 (October 2009)
6. Morin, B., Perrouin, G., Lahire, P., Barais, O., Vanwormhoudt, G., Jézéquel, J.-M.: Weaving Variability into Domain Metamodels. In: Schürr, A., Selic, B. (eds.) MODELS 2009. LNCS, vol. 5795, pp. 690–705. Springer, Heidelberg (2009)

7. Riebisch, M., Böllert, K., Streitferdt, D., Philippow, I.: Extending Feature Diagrams With UML Multiplicities. In: IDPT 2002 – 6th World Conference on Integrated Design & Process Technology (2002)
8. Haugen, Ø., Møller-Pedersen, B., Oldevil, J., Olsen, G.K., Svendsen, A.: Adding Standardized Variability to Domain Specific Languages. In: 12th International Software Product Line Conference (2008)
9. Fleurey, F., Haugen, Ø., Møller-Pedersen, B., Olsen, G.K., Svendsen, A., Zhang, X.: A Generic Language and Tool for Variability Modeling. SINTEF Report A13505 (2009)
10. Kang, K, Cohen, S., Hess, J., Novak, W, Peterson, S.: Feature-Oriented Domain Analysis (FODA) Feasibility Study, report CMU/SEI-90-TR-21, Software Engineering Institute (1990)
11. OMG Common Variability Language (CVL), http://www.omgwiki.org/variability/doku.php
12. OMG System Modeling Language (SysML), http://www.omgsysml.org
13. NATO Architecture Framework (NAF), http://www.nhqc3s.nato.int/
14. Krueger, C.W., Bakal, M.: Systems and Software Product Line Engineering with SysML, UML and the IBM Rational Rhapsody / BigLever Gears Bridge. IBM White Paper (2009)
15. Trujillo, S., Garate, J.M., Lopez-Herrejon, R.E., Mendialdua, X., Rosado, A., Egyed, A., Krueger, C.W., de Sosa, J.: Coping with Variability in Model-Based Systems Engineering: An Experience in Green Energy. In: Kühne, T., Selic, B., Gervais, M.-P., Terrier, F. (eds.) ECMFA 2010. LNCS, vol. 6138, pp. 293–304. Springer, Heidelberg (2010)
16. Gouyette, M., Barais, O., Le Noir, J., Jézéquel, J.-M.: Managing Variability in Multi-Views Engineering. Journées Lignes de Produits (2010)
17. Acher, M., Collet, P., Fleurey, F., Lahire, P., Moisan, S., Rigault, J.-P.: Modeling Context and Dynamic Adaptations with Feature Models. In: MODELS 2009 – 12th International Conference on Model Driven Engineering Languages and Systems, Models@run.time Workshop (2009)
18. Navas, J.F., Babau, J.-P., Pulou, J.: A Component-Based Run-Time Evolution Infrastructure for Resource-Constrained Embedded Systems. In: GPCE 2010 (2010)
19. Ungar, D., Chambers, C., Chang, B-W., Hölze, U.: Organizing Programs Without Classes. Lisp and Symbolic Computation 4(3) (1991)

Domain-Specific Model Verification with QVT

Maged Elaasar[1,3], Lionel Briand[2], and Yvan Labiche[3]

[1] IBM Canada Ltd, Rational Software, Ottawa Lab
770 Palladium Dr., Kanata, ON. K2V 1C8, Canada
melaasar@ca.ibm.com
[2] Simula Research Laboratory & U. of Oslo,
Martin Linges v 17, Fornebu, P.O.Box 134, 1325 Lysaker, Norway
briand@simula.no
[3] Carleton University, Department of Systems and Computer Engineering
1125 Colonel By Drive, Ottawa, ON K1S5B6, Canada
labiche@sce.carleton.ca

Abstract. Model verification is the process of checking models for known problems (or anti-patterns). We propose a new approach to declaratively specify and automatically detect problems in domain-specific models using QVT (Query/View/Transformation). Problems are specified with QVT-Relations transformations from models where elements involved in problems are identified, to result models where problem occurrences are reported in a structured and concise manner. The approach uses a standard formalism, applies generically to any MOF-based modeling language and has well-defined detection semantics. We apply the approach by defining a catalog of problems for a particular but important kind of models, namely metamodels. We report on a case study where we used the catalog to verify recent revisions of the UML metamodel. We detected many problem occurrences that we analyzed and helped resolve in the (latest) UML 2.4 revision. As a result, the metamodel was found to have improved dramatically by the experts defining it.

Keywords: Smell, Anti-Pattern, Specification, Detection, UML, MOF, QVT.

1 Introduction

Model-driven engineering (MDE) is a software methodology that is based on the use of models as a primary form of expression. In such methodology, models get defined and keep evolving continuously to cope with changing system requirements. Models are defined as instances of a metamodel, a higher-level model that describes the abstract syntax of a modeling language, which can either be general-purpose like UML [1] or domain-specific (DSML) like BPMN [2]. Metamodels are themselves defined using a DSML called the Meta Object Facility (MOF) [3] that is standardized by the Object Management Group (OMG). A MOF-based metamodel consists of a set of metaclasses, their attributes and relationships, plus constraints governing their integrity. Metamodel constraints are often specified using the Object Constraint Language (OCL) [4] that is based on first-order predicate logic and set semantics.

Model verification is an integral process of MDE that is concerned with checking models to find occurrences of known problems. Problems can be of different kinds: a) syntactic problems specified by the well-formedness constraints of metamodels and their extensions (e.g., UML profiles are extensions of UML); b) semantic problems describing poor design choices that are known to have a negative impact on some aspect (e.g., implementability, maintainability, usability, performance) of models; c) convention problems, which are violations to methodological, organizational or project-specific conventions (e.g., naming conventions).

Verifying (large) models manually is a time and resource consuming activity that is also error-prone (some problems are complex, cross-cutting many model elements). A better approach is to automate model verification. Such an approach should first allow problems to be specified declaratively (leading to concise and maintainable specifications) using a generic (i.e., adaptable to any DSML), flexible (i.e., supporting arbitrary, complex problems) and standard (i.e., familiar and portable) formalism. Second, it should also allow problems to be detected automatically (using their specifications) and directly (involving no data conversion) in models. Finally, it should allow problem occurrences to be reported in a concise (i.e., easy to inspect) and structured (i.e., showing all role bindings) manner. Several approaches ([14] to [24]) have been proposed in the literature. However, none of them satisfies all of the aforementioned requirements (more details in Section 2).

In this paper, we present three contributions. First, we propose adopting the pQVT approach, which has been used for design pattern specification and detection in [5], for model verification. Similar to a design pattern, a problem is composed of interrelated and constrained model elements playing unique roles in a given context. Only this time, the context is problematic and the detection leads to finding problem (vs. pattern) occurrences. We show how pQVT can be used to specify and detect arbitrary problems of any MOF-based DSML. Problems get specified with a QVT-Relations (QVTr) [6] transformation from input models (conforming to a MOF-based metamodel), where elements involved in problems are identified, to result models (conforming to the pResults metamodel [5]), where problem occurrences are reported in a structured and concise manner. pQVT uses a standard declarative formalism and provides powerful reuse semantics, allowing for modularizing problem specifications and handling of problem variants. Thanks to QVTr's well-defined execution semantics, problems are detected by simply running the transformations, producing concise result models containing any detected problem occurrences.

Second, we investigate the power of our approach by defining a catalog of problems for a specific DSML, namely MOF. We chose to study MOF as it is used to define many popular metamodels (e.g., UML and BPMN) that tend to have a large number of issues [7]. The catalog has 113 problems in different categories: syntactic (based on MOF well-formedness rules), semantic (based on metamodeling idioms and best practices) and convention (based on conventions used for standard metamodels).

Third, we report on a case study where we specified the catalog with pQVT. The approach was found to be very adequate for expressing such a large and complex catalog in a modular and concise manner. We then used the specification to detect problems with recent revisions (2.2, 2.3 and 2.4 beta) of the standard UML metamodel. We detected and analyzed hundreds of problem occurrences, reported them to the UML 2.4 revision task force (RTF), and helped resolve 53% of them in the final

UML 2.4 revision. We also assessed the performance of the catalog and found its detection scaling very well (finishing in under a minute), given the size of the catalog and the complexity of the UML metamodel.

The rest of this paper is structured as follows: Section 2 highlights related work; the detection of problems with pQVT is described in Section 3; Section 4 presents a catalog of problems for MOF-based metamodels; a case study where the catalog was used to verify the UML metamodel is discussed in Section 5; Section 6 enumerates the limitations and future works; finally, the conclusions are given in Section 7.

2 Related Work

In the literature of model verification, a problem is often described as one of two kinds. The first is a bad smell [8], which is a symptom that possibly indicates a deeper problem. The second is an anti-pattern [9], which is a bad solution to a recurring design problem (as opposed to a good pattern like in [10]). Over the years, many smells and anti-patterns got defined. For example, Fowler [8] provided 22 code smells and Brown et al. [11] described 40 anti-patterns (e.g., Blob). Language-specific problems have also been studied. Huzar et al. [12] overviewed consistency problems for UML. Koehler and Vanhatalo [13] specified process anti-patterns for BPMN.

Several approaches to specify and detect problems have been proposed in the literature. Travassos et al. [14] introduced manual reading techniques to detect code smells. However, manual approaches do not scale for large systems. Dhambri [15] presented a semi-automatic approach that was a compromise between automatic detection, which is efficient but loses track of context, and manual inspection that is slow and subjective. Still, semi-automatic approaches cannot scale with large models.

Marinescu [16] presented an automatic metric-based approach to detect deviations from good design patterns. Metric values were compared against thresholds. One problem here is that the choice of metrics and thresholds are always controversial. Munro [17] tried to address this by empirically justifying his choices.

Some approaches used logic systems. Trcka et al. [18] used temporal logic (CTL*) to formalize data-flow anti-patterns and used solvers to detect them. Correa et al. [19] encoded smells in Prolog and detected them using an inference engine. Unlike pQVT's ability to work on models directly, these approaches need pre-processing to convert data (e.g., models) first into suitable representations. In this case, they get converted into predicates so that solvers can operate on them. This conversion is expensive and makes live integration with modeling tools harder.

Moha et al. [20] proposed a rule-based DSL to specify smells with a way to generate detection algorithms from rules. They obtained good precision and recall. The work was later extended by Khomh et al. [21] to convert specifications into Bayesian Belief Networks, which allowed specifying probabilities on different rules, improving results as they get sorted based on confidence. However, their DSL only allowed checking pre-defined constructs and focused on structural aspects of software only. In contrast, pQVT leverages OCL and thus has a higher expressive power and uses a generic detection algorithm that works by interpreting problem specifications.

Graph-based techniques have also been used. Meyer [22] converted code into Abstract Syntax Graph (ASG) representation and specified anti-patterns as template

ASG graphs to match. Feng et al. [23] represented code using an XML schema for software and defined anti-patterns as template XML documents to match. These techniques also involve converting data first into another representation before detection becomes possible. For pQVT, models are already graphs of model elements allowing QVTr transformations to process them directly without conversion.

OCL has also been used. Enckevort [24] defined rules for UML class diagrams using OCL constraints and used them to check models. One problem with OCL is the way problem occurrences are reported. Since constraints are written in the context of one metaclass, reporting is limited to elements of that metaclass violating the constraints. Other interesting elements involved in the problem cannot be reported on simultaneously. In contrast, pQVT produces result models with occurrences reporting all interesting roles. Also, as an extension to OCL, pQVT provides a more declarative syntax and complexity management features that simplifies problem specification.

In summary, approaches in previous works are not fully adequate or practical to specify arbitrary problems for MOF-based DSMLs and automate their detection. We believe our pQVT approach has a combination of capabilities that make it an adequate solution to this important problem. It is declarative, leverages a standard formalism (QVTr), applies consistently to any MOF-based DSML, has complexity management facilities, inspects models directly (no conversion needed), has well-defined detection semantics, uses an interpreted (vs. code-generated) detection algorithm, and produces strucured and concise result reports.

3 Problem Detection with pQVT

pQVT is a pattern specification and detection approach that was previously defined in [5]. In this paper we show how pQVT can be used for model verification as well. The approach is depicted in Fig. 1. Modeling problems are specified with a QVTr transformation from an input model (conforming to any MOF-based metamodel), where model elements involved in problems are identified, to a result model (conforming to pResults, Section 3.5), where problem occurrences are reported in a concise and structured manner. In the remainder of this section, we use an example modeling problem to illustrate the process of problem specification and detection with pQVT. First, we define a general template for problem specification with pQVT. Then, we use it to gradually specify the details of a modeling problem, including specifying problem roles, a problem occurrence, and problem variants if any.

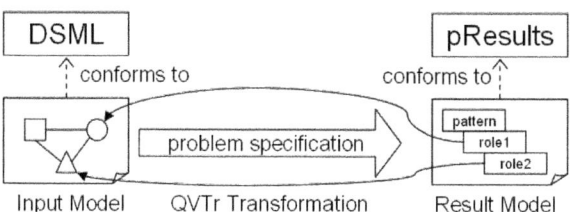

Fig. 1. Modeling problem detection with pQVT

3.1 Example Problem

The example problem is one of the UML well-formedness rules: a UML class should not define a new owner property when it already has a required one. The problem is depicted by the class diagram in Figure 2-left, where the class *Owned* is composed by two classes *Owner1* and *Owner2*, resulting in having two owner properties: *owner1* and *owner2*, respectively. According to UML semantics, an object can have a maximum of one owner reference at a time. Since *owner1* is required (has a multiplicity of 1), an *Owned* object must have reference to its owner through *owner1*, which makes *owner2* either impossible to satisfy (if it is required) or not useful (if it is optional). Figure 2-right shows a simplified subset of the UML metamodel that defines the concepts in the example problem.

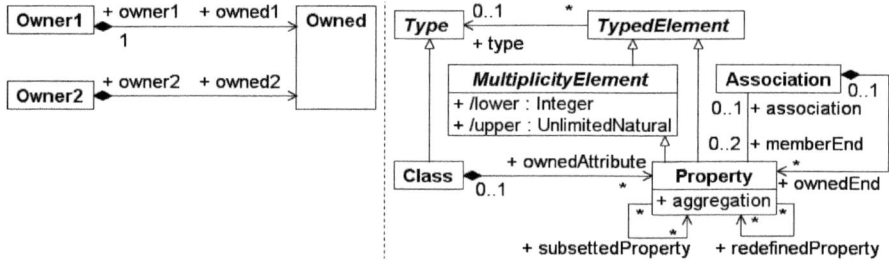

Fig. 2. The example problem (left) and a simplified subset of UML metamodel (right)

```
1 transformation Catalog (dsml:DSML, presults:pResults) {
2    top relation Problem {
3       checkonly domain dsml role:Type {/*problem role*/};
4       enforce domain presults c:Category {/*problem occurrence*/};
5       when {/*extra constraints*/}
6    }
7 }
```

Fig. 3. A template for problem specification using pQVT

3.2 Specification Template

A template for problem specification using pQVT is shown in Fig. 3. A problem catalog is specified with a QVTr *transformation* (line 1) between two models: an input *dsml* model (conforming to some MOF-based DSML), where problems are detected, and an output *presults* model (conforming to pResults, Section 3.5), where problem occurrences are reported. Each problem in the catalog is specified with a *top relation* (line 2) declaring two kinds of variables: one or more *checkonly domain* variables (line 3) specifying the problem roles (their types and constraints) to detect in the *dsml* model, and a single *enforce domain* variable (line 4) specifying a problem occurrence to report in the *presults* model. A relation can optionally have a *when* clause (line 5) specifying extra constraints for the problem.

The semantics of problem detection with pQVT is based on the execution semantics of QVTr. When a transformation is executed, each *top relation* (specifying a problem) tries to find all combinations of elements in the input *dsml* model that satisfy the constraints of the *checkonly domain* variables (the problem roles) and those in the *when* clause (extra problem constraints). For each such combination of elements, the *top relation* creates the elements specified by the *enforce domain* variable (the problem occurrence) in the *presults* model.

```
1   transformation Metamodeling (uml:UML, presults:pResults) {
2       top relation ClassWithRequiredOwnerDefinesAnotherOwner {
3           checkonly domain uml Owned:Class {
4               associationEnd = owner1:Property {},
5               associationEnd = owner2:Property {}
6           };
7           checkonly domain uml owner1:Property {
8               lower = 1
9           };
10          checkonly domain uml owner2:Property {};
11          when {
12              owner1 <> owner2;
13              owner1.otherEnd.aggregation = AggregationKind::composite;
14              owner2.otherEnd.aggregation = AggregationKind::composite;
15              owner2.subsettedProperty->excludes(owner1);
16          }
17      }
18      property Property::otherEnd : Property =
19          self.association.memberEnd->any(e | e <> self);
20      property Class::associationEnd : Set(Property) =
21          Property.allInstances()->collect(e | e.otherEnd.type = self);
22  }
```

Fig. 4. The specification of the example problem using pQVT

3.3 Problem Specification

Since the example problem is about the well-formedness of a UML model, a problem catalog is specified, in Figure 4, with a QVTr *transformation* (line 1) between an input *uml* model and an output *presults* model. The problem itself is defined with a *top relation* (line 2) within the catalog.

3.4 Role Specification

Identifying Roles. The problem description is used to identify the significant roles played by model elements in the problem. In the example problem, such roles are the *Owned* class and the *owner1* and *owner2* properties. The problem roles are therefore defined with *checkonly domain* variables (lines 3, 7 and 10) typed with corresponding metaclasses from UML (*Class* for *owner* and *Property* for *owner1* and *owner2*).

Adding Constraints. Adding more constraints to the roles enhances their precision. Simple constraints in the form of 'attribute=value' can be nested within the domain variable declarations. This is used to specify any expected values for roles' attributes (e.g., attribute *lower* of role *owner1* has a value of 1 to indicate it is required in line 8) or to specify role interrelations (e.g., properties *owner1* and *owner2* are related to class *Owned* through the attribute *associationEnd* in lines 4-5). Other constraints, more complex than simply 'attribute=value', are specified (in OCL) in the relation's *when* clause (e.g., a constraint requiring properties *owner1* and *owner2* to be distinct in line 12; two constraints requiring them to be ends of composition associations in lines 13-14; and a constraint excluding the valid case of property *owner1* being a subset of property *owner2* in line 15). Some constraints may be complex or used several times in a transformation, in which case QVTr provides reuse facilities to simplify the transformation. One such facility is a *property* (an enhancement proposed in [5]) that is initialized with an OCL expression in the context of some DSML metaclass (e.g., *Property::otherEnd* in lines 18-19 gives the other member end across an association, and *Class::associationEnd* in lines 20-21 gives the properties accessible from a class over its associations). Those facilities can then be used in constraints across the transformation (e.g., lines 4, 5, 13, 14).

Relaxing Constraints. If a constraint is over restrictive, it may not get satisfied for some valid elements. Such constraint needs to be relaxed (removed or generalized). On the other hand, an overly loose constraint may get satisfied for some invalid elements. In practice, it takes some experimentation to reach an acceptable balance. While there is no generic way for generalizing constraints, role interrelationships may be generalized by making them transitive. For example, in Figure 5, three transitive properties are defined: *allAssociationEnds* (lines 12-13) allowing *owner1* to be an owner of class *Owned* or any of its super classes (line 3); *allSubsettedProperties* (lines 14-16) allowing *owner1* to be directly or transitively subsetted by *owner2* (line 8); and *allRedefinedProperties* (lines 17-19) allowing the exclusion of the valid case of *owner2* hiding *owner1* by directly or transitively redefining it (line 9).

```
1   top relation ClassWithRequiredOwnerDefinesAnotherOwner {
2     checkonly domain uml Owned:Class {
3       allAssociationEnds = owner1:Property {},
4       associationEnd = owner2:Property {}
5     };
6     ...
7     when {...
8       owner2.allSubsettedProperties->excludes(owner1);
9       owner2.allRedefinedProperties->excludes(owner1);
10    }
11  }
12  property Class::allAssociationEnds : Set(Property) =
13    self.associationEnd->union(self.superClass.allAssociationEnds);
14  property Property::allSubsettedProperties : Set(Property) =
15    self.subsettedProperty->union(
16      self.subsettedProperty.allSubsettedProperties);
17  property Property::allRedefinedProperties : Set(Property) =
18    self.allRedefinedProperty->union(
19      self.redefinedProperty.allRedefinedProperties);
```

Fig. 5. A more general specification of the example problem using pQVT

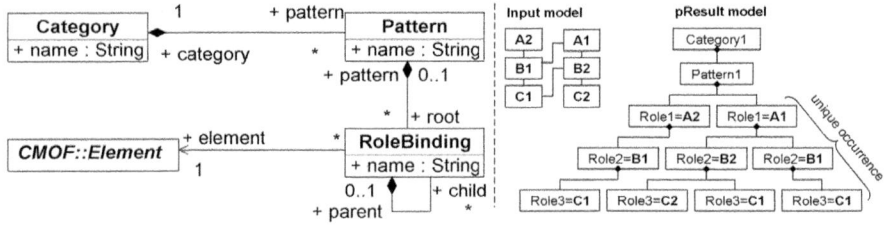

Fig. 6. pResults metamodel (left) and an example pResults model (right)

3.5 Problem Occurrence Specification

Problem detection may result in a set of problem occurrences. An occurrence is a unique mapping of roles to model elements playing those roles in a problem. The pQVT approach defines the pResults metamodel (Figure 6-left) to compactly represent occurrences of a given problem as a tree of *RoleBinding* objects under one problem (*Pattern*) object. At every level in the tree, role bindings map a unique role to a set of elements playing this role in an input model. A unique problem occurrence is a complete branch in the tree from a root to a leaf role binding. Related problem occurrences are grouped together under one *Category* object. Figure 6-right shows an example pResults model with occurrences pointing to elements in an input model.

In a pQVT problem specification, a pResuls problem occurrence is specified (Figure 7) as an *enforce domain* variable *c:Category* (line 1) that nests *p:Pattern* (line 2) that nests a *rb:RoleBinding* corresponding to each problem role (lines 3-5). The *element* attribute of each *RoleBinding* variable is assigned to the corresponding role's *checkonly domain* variable (e.g., *rb1*'s *element* in line 3 is assigned to variable *Owned* declared in line 3 of Figure 4).

```
1  enforce domain presults c:Category{ name='UML Problems',
2    pattern= p:Pattern{ name='ClassWithRequiredOwnerDefinesAnother',
3      root = rb1:RoleBinding{ name='Owned', element=Owned,
4        child = rb2:RoleBinding{ name='owner1', element=owner1,
5          child = rb3:RoleBinding{ name='owner2', element=owner2
6  }}}}};
```

Fig. 7. The specification of a problem occurrence for the example problem using pQVT

```
1  top relation ProblemWithVariants {
2    checkonly domain dsml role:Type {/*problem role*/};
3    when {/*extra conditions*/};
4    where { Variant1(role1, role2, ...);
5            Variant2(role2, role2, ...); }
6  }
7  relation Variant1 {
8    checkonly domain dsml role:Type {/*problem role*/};
9    enforce domain presults c:Category {/*problem occurrence*/};
10   when {/*extra constraints*/};
11 }
```

Fig. 8. Specification of a problem and its variants with pQVT

3.6 Variant Specification

Some problems may have variants (versions with slightly different roles and/or constraints). Specifying all variants ensures that all possible problem occurrences are detectable. However, specifying variants with separate *top relation*(s) is not efficient as it leads to duplication. Instead, a different problem specification template, shown in Figure 8, is used. In this template, the common roles (line 2) and constraints (line 3) are specified with a *top relation*, while the specific roles (line 8) and constraints (line 10) of each variant are specified with non-top *relation*(s) that get composed in the *top relation*'s *where* clause (line 4-5). A *where* clause extends a relation by composing other relations. Recall that a relation tries to find all combination of elements matching its *checkonly domain* variables. Now for each such combination, it calls the composed relations in the *where* clause. Each call binds variables from a composing relation to the *domain* variables of a composed relation. This further constrains the common roles of a problem by the extra constraints of variants. Notice also that the *enforce domain* variable is moved to the variant relation (line 9) so that problem occurrences are only reported when all constraints for a variant have been satisfied.

4 Catalog of Metamodeling Problems

In the previous section, we showed how the pQVT approach can be used to specify problems of MOF-based DSMLs, using a UML problem as an example[1]. In this section, we present a catalog of problems we defined for another DSML, namely MOF itself. We chose to study MOF because we noticed, through our involvement with OMG standards, that MOF-based metamodels tend to have a large number of problem occurrences (called issues in [7]). Obviously, some of these occurrences are symptoms of the complexity of designing a metamodel, which requires expertise. However, many other occurrences are rather due to ambiguities in MOF (and its UML foundation), the lack of documented metamodeling idioms and best practices, the lack of formally-specified conventions or simply human error.

An obvious mitigation is to use tool support to help with checking metamodels. Unfortunately, a large number of metamodels are defined using UML tools as opposed to MOF tools and only get converted to MOF as a post-processing step. The drawback is that most of these tools only implement constraints that are explicitly defined in the UML specification. They do not implement other constraints that are informally implied by the UML semantics or those that are MOF-specific. In fact, this was one of the motivations for dropping MOF's own metamodel in MOF 2.4 and using the UML metamodel directly, albeit with extra well-formedness constraints.

This led us to consider defining a catalog of MOF 2.4-based metamodeling problems. The catalog defines a total of 113 problems in four categories: UML well-formedness (33 problems), MOF well-formedness (32 problems), semantic (33 problems) and convention (15 problems). Well-formedness problems are based on constraints of the UML and MOF specifications. Semantic problems are based on metamodeling idioms and best practices. Convention problems are based on conventions used in developing standard metamodels. In the rest of this section, we elaborate on the strategy followed for defining each category. For brevity, we only show the subset of problems for which we actually detected occurrences in the case study in Section 5. A larger set of problems is provided online [26].

4.1 Well-Formedness Problems

UML Well-formedness. As mentioned above, MOF 2.4 uses the metamodel of UML 2.4, which is a general-purpose modeling language. Our first challenge was to identify the subset of the UML 2.4 metamodel that is relevant for metamodeling and collect its constraints. First, we identified a set of concrete UML metaclasses and their

---

[1] Approaches that work at the metamodel level apply equally to DSMLs and UML.

non-derived (direct and inherited) properties that have counterparts in MOF. We then compared it to the set that was actually used in defining two standard metamodels (UML 2.4 and BPMN 2.0) with UML. We noticed some differences that we had to reconcile. For example, UML used a Generalization element to specify inheritance between classes, while MOF used a direct super class reference. Finally, we validated the subset with key members of the MOF revision task force to ensure accuracy. Table 1 shows the metaclasses in this subset.

The next step was to collect the constraints that are relevant to this subset of metaclasses in UML. Some constraints were explicitly identified in the UML specification, while others had to be recovered from the described semantics. Based on those constraints, we defined 33 problems. Table 2 shows a subset of those problems. An example problem (UML2) is a classifier with an attribute hiding (as opposed to redefining) a similarly named one in a general classifier. Another example (UML8) is a property with an explicit default value even through it is derived.

Table 1. The concrete UML metaclasses used for defining metamodels

Association	Enumeration	LiteralInteger	PackageImport
Class	EnumerationLiteral	LiteralString	PackageMerge
Comment	Generalization	LiteralUnlimitedNatural	Parameter
Constraint	InstanceValue	OpaqueExpression	PrimitiveType
DataType	LiteralBoolean	Operation	Property
ElementImport	LiteralReal	Package	

Table 2. UML well-fomedness problems (excerpt)

UML1	Class With Required Owner Property Defines Another Owner
UML2	Classifier Has Attribute Not Redefining Inherited One With Same Name
UML3	Comment Has No Annotated Elements
UML4	Constraint Expression Has Parse Errors
UML5	Constraint Has No Constrained Elements
UML6	Namespace Has Indistinguishable Members
UML7	Property Has Invalid Default Value
UML8	Property Is Derived But Has Default Value

Table 3. MOF well-fomedness problems (excerpt)

MOF1	Association Does Not Have Two Member Ends
MOF2	Element Is Not Allowed In Metamodel
MOF3	Enumeration Has Operations
MOF4	Multiplicity Element Is Multi Valued But Has Default Value
MOF5	Named Element Has No Name
MOF6	Named Element Is Not Public
MOF7	Parameter Has Effect
MOF8	Typed Element Has No Type

MOF Well-formedness. Some constraints are specific to MOF and we collected them from the MOF 2.4 specification [3]. Since the UML metaclasses used for metamodeling (Table 3) have more features and richer semantics than is needed for MOF, these constraints are meant to prevent usage of those features and semantics unrelated to MOF. We then defined 32 problems corresponding to those constraints. Figure 3 shows a subset of those problems. An example (MOF1) is a class flagged as *active* since this has no meaning in a metamodel. Another example (MOF2) checks if a UML element is allowed to be in a metamodel. Notice that we only defined problems for the Complete-MOF (CMOF) variant since it is more relevant to the case study in Section 5. The Essential-MOF (EMOF) variant is more constrained and hence would need a bigger set of problems.

4.2 Semantic Problems

This category of problems defines situations that are well-formed according to the semantics of UML/MOF but could be problematic when implementing and/or using the metamodel. We collected 33 smells from experience defining metamodels over the years. Table 4 shows a subset of those smells. An example (SEM6) is a classifier having generalizations that are already implied by other generalizations, leading to redundancy. Another example (SEM14) is an operation not being flagged as a query (i.e., has no side effects). Operations are typically defined in a metamodel to facilitate querying models, especially by OCL expressions. Therefore, we need to check whether defining an operation as a non-query operation is really intended. Another example (SEM20) is a property that is required but has no default value, forcing modelers to specify a value for it every time in a model.

Table 4. Semantic problems (excerpt)

SEM1	Association Has Asymmetric Redefinition
SEM2	Association Has Asymmetric Subsetting
SEM3	Association Is Bidirectional With Asymmetric Derived Ends
SEM4	Association IsDerived Conflicts With Ends IsDerived
SEM5	Classifier Has Ambiguous Non-Owned End
SEM6	Classifier Has Redundant Generalizations
SEM7	Classifier Is Abstract With One Direct Subtype
SEM8	Constraint Has Trivial Expression
SEM9	Constraint References Non Context Element Only
SEM10	Multiplicity Element Has Redundant Lower Bound
SEM11	Multiplicity Element Has Redundant Upper Bound
SEM12	Namespace Has Identical Constraints
SEM13	Operation Could Be Converted To Derived Attribute
SEM14	Operation Is Not Query
SEM15	Property Has Different Name Than Redefined Property
SEM16	Property Has Redundant Subsetting
SEM17	Property Is Composite And Typed By Data Type
SEM18	Property IsDerived Conflicts With IsReadOnly
SEM19	Property Is Optional With Default Value
SEM20	Property Is Required With No Default Value

4.3 Convention Problems

This category defines problems that are violations to common conventions adopted when defining metamodels. One may find these conventions specified explicitly as part of metamodel specifications or one may find them implicitly applied. We have collected 15 such conventions and specified their violations as problems. Table 5 shows a subset of those problems. Some problems (CON2/3/6/7/8/9) are violations to naming conventions. Others (CON4/5) are violations to documentation conventions. Yet others (CON1/10/11/12) tighten some loose UML semantics like requiring association's member ends to be in a particular order.

Table 5. Convention problems (excerpt)

CON1	Association Member Ends Are Reversed
CON2	Association Has Non-Default Name
CON3	Classifier Name Is Part Of General Classifier Name
CON4	Named Element Has No Documentation When It Should
CON5	Named Element Has Multiple Documentations
CON6	Named Element Is Not Alphabetic
CON7	Named Element Starts With Upper Case
CON8	Operation Has Return Parameter Not Named "result"
CON9	Property Is Boolean But Does Not Start With "is"
CON10	Property Is Derived With No Derivation Constraint
CON11	Property Derivation Constraint Does Not Reference Property
CON12	Typed Element Has Default Value Literal With Type Set

5 Case Study

In this section, we report on a case study where we specified the catalog of metamodel problems presented above (Section 4) with pQVT (Section 3) and used it to verify recent revisions of the UML metamodel (defined with CMOF). The case study had three objectives. First, we wanted to assess the ability of pQVT to express a complex catalog of problems. Second, we wanted to assess the effectiveness of pQVT at detecting valid problem occurrences. The occurrences we detected in the standard UML metamodels were analyzed and results were shared with the UML Revision Task Force (RTF), which judged their validity. In fact, pQVT was used in realistic conditions to actually improve the UML 2.4 metamodel. Third, we wanted to evaluate the performance of pQVT on realistically large models to assess its scalability. The UML metamodel with about 680 classes, 623 properties and 128 operations, can be considered complex and representative of real-life metamodels.

5.1 pQVT Expressiveness

Due to the large number (113) of problems in the catalog (section 4), we cannot show all their pQVT specifications here. Instead, we collected some metrics in in Table 6 to help the reader assess the effort involved. We chose to specify each category of problems in a separate QVTr transformation to make them more manageable. Each problem was specified using a *top relation* for a total of 122 relations (four problems had variants, thus needed some extra non-top relations). Problem specifications had a total of 207 roles with a range of 1-6 roles each. UML and semantic problems involved more roles (~2) on average than MOF and convention problems (~1.5). The specifications also had a total of 324 constraints with a range of 1-11 constraints each. This means an average of 2.86 per problem and 1.56 per role, indicating that the specifications were generally concise. Constraints also varied in complexity with 64% specified using the form 'property=value' (i.e., nested in variable declarations) and 36% using other forms (i.e, in *when* clauses), indicating that the specifications were generally simple. Furthermore, 20% of constraints were simplified by using (13) queries and (16) derived properties that we defined in a reusable library and imported in the transformations. The above analysis suggests that pQVT had the expressive power and facilities needed to adequately specify such a large catalog of problems.

Table 6. Metrics of the metamodeling catalog specified with pQVT

Category (Problems)	Relations	Roles		Constraints			
		Avg.	Total	Avg.	Total	In *when*	Simplified
UML (33)	37	2.09	69	3.39	112	37	40
MOF (32)	32	1.56	50	1.59	51	22	3
Semantic (33)	36	2.03	67	3.18	105	34	20
Convention (15)	17	1.4	21	3.73	56	24	1

5.2 pQVT Effectiveness

We used the specified catalog to verify the (most recent) 2.2, 2.3 and 2.4 revisions of the standard UML metamodel. Recall that MOF 2.4 requires metamodels to be defined in UML. Therefore, we obtained those revisions from OMG as UML models. For each revision, we detected many problem occurrences: 2558 (2.2), 2120 (2.3) and 786 (2.4). A complete report is available online [26]. For 2.4, we first checked a beta revision and then based on our findings we reported problem occurrences (issues) to the UML RTF and helped resolve some of them. Finally, we checked the official 2.4 revision. Table 7 shows the number of occurrences of the identified problems. Our first observation is that the quality of the UML 2.x metamodel has been improving over revisions, which is expected given the mandate of the RTF to address issues with the metamodel. Specifically, the total number of problem occurrences has decreased by 17% from 2.2 to 2.3 and by 63% from 2.3 to 2.4. When we checked the beta revision of 2.4, we detected 1670 occurrences (omitted from Table 7 for brevity). This is a 21% reduction from 2.3 but, more importantly, a 53% reduction between the beta and official revisions of 2.4. Given that most of the metamodel changes between these two revisions (i.e., those in change ballot 11 [27]) were to address issues raised by this case study using pQVT, it shows the usefulness of automated model verification and more specifically, the effectiveness of pQVT in realistic conditions, where a standard metamodel is being revised by an official task force.

Nevertheless, different categories of the catalog varied according to the ratio of the detected occurrences getting resolved, as follows: UML (28%), MOF (100%), semantic (65%) and convention (65%). While MOF occurrences fared well given that they are not controversial, UML ones did not do as well because one of the problems

(UML4: constraints have parse errors) had a relatively large number of occurrences that required significant effort to resolve. More generally, some occurrences did not get resolved for one of the following reasons: a) the RTF ran out of time and deferred them to a future revision (e.g., UML4/8, SEM8/16/18, CON4/5); b) the cost of fixing them now (e.g., on tool migration) outweighed the value (e.g., SEM5/7/13/15, CON3/6/7/9); c) they were judged as exceptions to the rules (e.g., SEM3/19/20, CON2). An example of the latter is some associations detected in CON2 with non-default names, as the naming convention would have given them ambiguous names.

Table 7. Total number of detected problem occurrences in three revisions of UML

Prob.	2.2	2.3	2.4	Prob.	2.2	2.3	2.4	Prob.	2.2	2.3	2.4
UML1	5	58	0	SEM1	23	25	0	SEM17	6	6	0
UML2	1	1	0	SEM2	208	203	0	SEM18	21	23	11
UML3	0	7	0	SEM3	6	6	6	SEM19	4	4	2
UML4	200	190	185	SEM4	37	38	0	SEM20	0	0	1
UML5	3	3	0	SEM5	1	160	151	CON1	43	0	0
UML6	12	0	0	SEM6	1	0	0	CON2	306	10	9
UML7	3	3	0	SEM7	4	4	4	CON3	1	1	1
UML8	14	14	14	SEM8	207	208	232	CON4	7	10	6
MOF1	1	0	0	SEM9	0	1	0	CON5	58	58	62
MOF2	1	1	0	SEM10	179	186	0	CON6	5	5	5
MOF3	1	1	0	SEM11	478	483	0	CON7	5	5	6
MOF4	2	2	0	SEM12	4	4	0	CON8	122	126	0
MOF5	443	141	0	SEM13	53	55	58	CON9	7	7	7
MOF6	17	0	0	SEM14	3	0	0	CON10	19	19	0
MOF7	9	9	0	SEM15	4	8	24	CON11	9	11	0
MOF8	3	3	0	SEM16	0	0	2	CON12	22	22	0

5.3 pQVT Performance

We used the tool Medini-QVT [25] (with our performance tune-ups [5] like cashing query results) to specify and execute the QVTr transformations. We also used our pResults model viewer [5] to inspect and analyze problem occurrences. The detection was performed on a laptop with 2.4 GHz core 2 duo processor and 3G of memory running Windows XP. We recorded the average time for running each problem category on the UML metamodel (all revisions were in the same range). The times were as follows: UML (22s), MOF (8s), semantic (15s) and convention (5s). This means that it takes under a minute to run the whole catalog, which is very efficient and reasonable to repeat frequently as the analyzed model is evolving. We note that the UML category takes a bit longer due to problem UML4, which parses OCL expressions of constraints verifying their syntax.

6 Limitations and Future Work

The pQVT approach to model verification has some limitations and can still be improved further. For example, problem specifications could be made more portable, i.e.

not tied to a particular DSML. We plan to resolve this issue by investigating transformation genericity, where a generic DSML is defined for a problem domain and used to specify problems. Separate mappings can then be defined between such DSML and the real DSMLs. Another improvement could be to augment a problem specification with a way to auto-correct a problem occurrence. Another area to improve is the presentation of problem occurrences, which are currently not ordered. We plan to investigate ways to calculate importance scores for occurrences and order them accordingly, making inspection much more effective. Another possibility is to define a dedicated graphical pattern specification DSML whose models can be used to generate pQVT transformations along with all their boilerplate and idioms. Another possible work is to specify problems of other popular DSMLs, including UML profile-based ones, which could be interesting as some DSMLs are defined with UML profiles rather than MOF-based metamodels. Other case studies are also necessary to validate the flexibility and performance of the approach reported in this paper.

7 Conclusion

Model verification is an integral process of MDE concerned with checking models for known problems. Automating model verification is important as the process is resource intensive and error prone. This paper presents an approach (called pQVT) to automate the detection of problems in MOF-based models. pQVT specifies problems with a QVTr transformation from models conforming to a MOF-based DSML, where elements playing roles in problems are identified, to result models where problem occurrences are reported. The approach is declarative, leverages a standard formalism, applies to any MOF-based DSML, has well-defined detection semantics, has powerful reuse and modularization semantics and produces concise and detailed results.

In addition, the paper presents a catalog of 113 problems for MOF 2.4-based metamodels split into four categories: UML well-formedness, MOF well-formedness, semantic and convention. The catalog was formally specified using pQVT, which was found to be both adequate and concise. It was then used to detect problem occurrences in recent revisions of the standard UML metamodel. A large number of occurrences were detected and analyzed. Results show that pQVT is effective at finding real problems in realistic models as it led to a 53% reduction of the problem occurrences detected in the UML 2.4 metamodel, which were all verified and agreed upon by the UML RTF (a large majority of the identified problems resulted in changes, as we explained earlier). Finally, the case study shows that pQVT has a good performance as it could execute the entire catalog of problems on the complex UML metamodel in about one minute clearly demonstrating this is a scalable, practical technology.

Acknowledgements

The authors would like to thank the following individuals for helping review the case study: Steve Cook (Microsoft), Nicolas Rouquette (JPL) and Pete Rivett (Adaptive).

References

1. Unified Modeling Language (UML), Infrastructure v2.4. OMG ptc/2010-11-03
2. Business Process Modeling and Notation (BPMN) v2.0. OMG dtc/2010-06-05
3. Meta Object Facility (MOF) Core v2.4. OMG ptc/2010-12-08
4. Object Constraint Language (OCL) v2.2. OMG formal/2010-02-01
5. Elaasar, M., Briand, L., Labiche, L.: An Approach to Detecting Design Patterns in MOF-Based Domain-Specific Models with QVT. Technical Report SCE-10-02, Carleton University (November 2010) (submitted for publication)
6. Query/View/Transformation (QVT) v1.0. OMG formal/2008-04-03
7. OMG issues database, http://www.omg.org/issues/
8. Fowler, M.: Refactoring: Improving the Design of Existing Code, 1st edn (June 1999)
9. Koenig, A.: Patterns and Antipatterns. J. of OO Programming 8(1), 46–48 (1995)
10. Gamma, E., Helm, R., Johnson, R., Vlissides, J.: Design Patterns: Elements of Reusable Object-Oriented Software (1995)
11. Brown, W., Malveau, R., Brown, W., McCormick III, H., Mowbray, T.: Anti Patterns: Refactoring Software, Architectures, and Projects in Crisis. 1st edn (1998)
12. Huzar, Z., Kuzniarz, L., Reggio, G., Sourrouille, J.-L.: Consistency Problems in UML-Based Software Development. In: Jardim Nunes, N., Selic, B., Rodrigues da Silva, A., Toval Alvarez, A. (eds.) UML Satellite Activities 2004. LNCS, vol. 3297, pp. 1–12. Springer, Heidelberg (2005)
13. Koehler, J., Vanhatalo, J.: Process Anti-patterns: How to Avoid the Common Traps of Business Process Modeling. IBM WebSphere Developer Technical Journal (Febraury 2007)
14. Travassos, G., Shull, F., Fredericks, M., Basili, V.: Detecting Defects in Object-Oriented Designs: Using Reading Techniques to Increase Software Quality. In: Proc. of OOPSLA 1999, pp. 47–56 (1999)
15. Dhambri, K., Sahraoui, H., Poulin, P.: Visual Detection of Design Anomalies. In: Proc. of CSMR 2008, pp. 279–283 (2008)
16. Marinescu, R.: Detection Strategies: Metrics-Based Rules for Detecting Design Flaws. In: Proc. of the ICSM 2004, pp. 350–359 (2004)
17. Munro, M.: Product Metrics for Automatic Identification of "Bad Smell" Design Problems in Java Source-Code. In: Proc. of the 11th Int'l Soft. Metrics Symposium, p. 15 (2005)
18. Trcka, N., Aalst, W., Sidorova, N.: Data-Flow Anti-patterns: Discovering Data-Flow Errors in Workflows. In: van Eck, P., Gordijn, J., Wieringa, R. (eds.) CAiSE 2009. LNCS, vol. 5565, pp. 425–439. Springer, Heidelberg (2009)
19. Correa, A., Werner, C., Zaverucha, G.: Object oriented design expertise reuse: An approach based on heuristics, design patterns and anti-patterns. In: Frakes, W.B. (ed.) ICSR 2000. LNCS, vol. 1844, pp. 336–352. Springer, Heidelberg (2000)
20. Moha, N., Gueheneuc, Y.-G., Duchien, L., Le Meur, A.-F.: DECOR: A Method for the Specification and Detection of Code and Design Smells. TSE 36(1) (January/February 2010)
21. Khomh, F., Vaucher, S., Gueheneuc, Y.-G., Sahraoui, H.: A Bayesian Approach for the Detection of Code and Design Smells. In: Proc. of ICSQ 2009, pp. 305–314 (2009)
22. Meyer, M.: Pattern-based Reengineering of Software Systems. In: Proc. of WCRE 2006, pp. 305–306 (October 2006)
23. Feng, T., Zhang, J., Wang, H., Wang, X.: Software Design Improvement through Anti-patterns Identification. In: Proc. of ICSM 2004, p. 534 (2004)

24. Enckevort, T.: Refactoring UML Models: Using OpenArchitectureWare to measure UML model quality and perform pattern matching on UML models with OCL queries. In: Proc. of OOPSLA 2009, pp. 635–646 (2009)
25. Medini QVT: A Toolset for Model to Model Transformations, http://projects.ikv.de/qvt
26. Elaasar, M., Briand, L., Labiche Y.: Metamodeling Anti-Patterns (2010), https://sites.google.com/site/metamodelingantipatterns
27. UML Revision Task Force Wiki, http://www.omgwiki.org/uml2-rtf

A SysML Profile for Development and Early Validation of TLM 2.0 Models

Vaibhav Jain, Anshul Kumar, and Preeti R. Panda

Indian Institute of Technology Delhi, India
{vjain,anshul,panda}@cse.iitd.ac.in

Abstract. Use of UML for SoC design has recently generated new interest and several UML profiles for SystemC have been developed for this purpose. These profiles, however, do not focus on transaction level modeling (TLM). The TLM 2.0 standard introduces interoperability rules for the correct behavior of component models. The important challenge is to identify and debug errors in the system model occurring due to violation of these rules. In TLM model development based on SystemC or SystemC profiles these rules are usually checked during simulation stage. However, several of these rules are static in nature and can be checked before simulation. In this paper, we present a TLM profile based on SysML and show that it can facilitate in TLM model development and also helps in early validation of TLM 2.0 models by introducing checking of static TLM rules during design phase. Our approach, in effect, contributes to reducing the overall debugging efforts.

Keywords: SoC Design, TLM, UML Profile, Model Validation, MBE.

1 Introduction

UML and UML based methodologies have received significant interest from SoC community in recent times. UML, based on meta-modeling mechanism, offers customization towards a specific domain in the form of UML profiles, which provides a light-weight approach towards high-level modeling and can be seen as an effective way of modeling in the specialized domains like SoC design.

Initially, UML standards were not mature enough to be used for real-time and embedded systems domain. However, UML 2.0 standard provided a new direction towards UML based high-level modeling of embedded systems, especially for SoC design. The earlier attempts towards establishing UML as an entry level language for SoC design are reported in [5].

UML, together with OMG's model driven architecture (MDA), offers automated code generation from UML models towards a suitable target language. For SoC design, the system description language, SystemC, has emerged as the most appropriate target language for UML based modeling of SoCs. The initial contribution towards using UML with SystemC in a system design process was made by Pauwel et al. [7]. They suggested a UML based design methodology for executable SystemC models using structural diagrams only. Work of Nguyen et al. [2] contributed towards SystemC code generation from behavior diagrams like state diagrams but was limited in using SystemC stereotypes and full code generation capabilities.

Later, industry and academia suggested several UML profiles targeted towards embedded systems domain. The work by Riccobene et al. [1], proposed a UML profile for SystemC supporting structural and behavioral modeling capabilities and suggested a UML-based SoC design flow supporting HW/SW codesign. In another development, the UML profile for SoC [12] targets SoC design based on SystemC and focuses on the structural modeling. Recently, a synthesis extension to SystemC and SysML profile was proposed for SystemC models towards HW/SW co-simulation and co-synthesis [8]. OMG's recent efforts on system modeling lead to SysML profile [14] providing system modeling capabilities for domain-neutral applications. The role of SysML and its application in context of SoC design was highlighted in [6] and SystemC code generation from SysML was proposed by Prevostini et al. [4]. In another development MARTE profile [16] enhances UML capabilities for modeling RTES and can be used during UML based virtual platform development of SoCs.

Transaction level modeling (TLM) has now become an important aspect of SoC design, with TLM 2.0 as the current standard [11]. However, none of the SystemC profiles mentioned above includes TLM constructs, though examples of TLM usage have been reported [2,8]. TLM 2.0 introduces new TLM concepts and specifies a large number of rules to ensure correct operation and interoperability of TLM models. Without a proper TLM profile, the usual approach to verify TLM models against these rules is to use protocol checkers [17] at simulation time. However, several of these rules are static in nature and can be checked before simulation.

In this paper, we propose a TLM profile and show that it can facilitate checking of static TLM rules. Our strategy is based on SysML profile for TLM. We have developed this profile to support structural and behavioral modeling using the TLM 2.0 standard and to support full SystemC code generation. We aim at finding the errors in the system model as early as possible in order to reduce the overall debugging time and efforts. This is achieved by incorporating all the TLM 2.0 rules that can be statically checked as modeling constraints using the profile. These constraints are expressed using OCL (Object Constraint Language) [15].

This paper is organized as follows. Section 2 gives an overview of TLM 2.0 and the interoperability rules. Section 3 introduces our SysML profile for TLM. Section 4 presents TLM model validation aspect based on our modeling approach and Section 5 presents a modeling example demonstrating its application and results of experiments performed in this work. Section 6 closes with conclusions and future work.

2 TLM 2.0 and Rules for Interoperability

TLM captures abstract models of SoC by separating the communication and computation parts of it using well-defined interfaces. Interoperability problems can occur during TLM simulation mainly caused during interactions of non-compliant high-level components. Recently, TLM 2.0 standard [11] was introduced which especially takes care of interoperability issues. TLM 2.0 provides an interoperability layer which constitutes a generic payload[1] and a set of protocols ensuring data consistency among different communicating subsystems.

TLM 2.0 provides a strict framework to model the interactions between blocks as shown in Fig.1. A TLM 2.0 model may consists of a number of TLM modules like initiators, interconnects and targets. An initiator starts a transaction through initiator port, an interconnect which acts as a bridge/router and consists of initiator and target sockets and a target component which services memory-based read/write transaction requests through target sockets. The communication between these components takes place along the forward and backward paths. TLM 2.0 also offers different modeling styles, namely loosely-timed(LT) and approximately-timed (AT), based on the preciseness of timing information of transactions. These modeling styles can be used in conjunction with the different TLM abstraction levels.

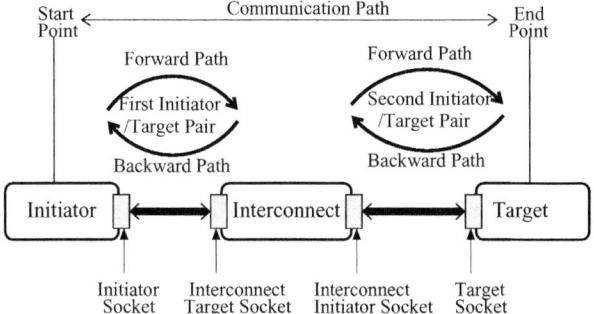

Fig. 1. TLM 2.0 Framework used for System Model

We observe that the TLM rules can be broadly categorized as suggestive rules and restrictive rules. The suggestive rules are more like guidelines to be followed during implementation of a system model for achieving the expected behavior of the transaction. For example, "*b_transport may call wait, directly or indirectly*" suggests the scope or usability of *b_transport* method. On the other hand, the restrictive rules, enforce modeling restrictions on a TLM concept, and can be further classified as static and dynamic rules. We have identified 24 such static rules in the TLM 2.0 standard.

A static rule enforces restriction on a TLM concept related to its structure and its application. For example, the rules concerning the initiator socket connection or the methods that can be realized by an initiator module can be considered as structural rules. The dynamic rules enforce restrictions on a running instance of a TLM concept and applicable during simulation time. For example, *"For base protocol, the forward and backward paths should pass through exactly the same sequence of components and sockets in opposing order"*. Clearly, the rule requires dynamic checks (simulation time) because paths are established at run time.

All these rules ensure the interoperability among high-level component models. But, identifying and debugging errors in the system model is a major

---
[1] A standard transaction object.

problem. A TLM model based on SystemC or developed using SystemC profile may fail to take into account static rules. In order to confirm this, we handcrafted an example of TLM 2.0 model having violation of each of the 24 static rules. The model was compiled and tested to find the stage at which various violations were detected. Table 1 shows results of this experiment. It was found that only 6 of the violations were detected at compile time, elaboration time and simulation time and the majority of the rules were ignored.

Table 1. TLM Rule Checking Report

Stage	Violation Count	Example
Compile Time	2	Two sockets must share the same BUSWIDTH
Elaboration Time	2	initiator socket must be connected to target socket
Simulation Time	2	b_transport should not be called from a method
Ignored	18	Initiator can not realize b_transport method

3 A SysML Profile for TLM 2.0

A UML Profile is a set of extensions to UML using the built-in extension facilities provided by UML. A UML profile is developed by extending the UML metamodel [13] and introducing domain specific concepts into it, mainly in form of stereotypes. A stereotype represents an extension to the UML metaclasses and may be parametrized with properties known as tagged values. A stereotype may also contain constraints written in OCL, specifying the structure and/or behavior restrictions of a stereotype in a well-formed model.

Our profile for TLM is based on the SysML 1.1 specification [14] and TLM 2.0 specification [11] as shown in the Fig.2. While developing the profile, we have taken the best of SysML and UML SystemC profiles [1]. The key strength of SysML lies in its physical modeling capabilities. SysML provides Block Definition Diagrams and Internal Block Definition Diagrams which are more suitable in representing TLM models in comparison to the UML diagrams. The UML SystemC profile offers structure and behavior modeling capabilities which can help in full code generation.

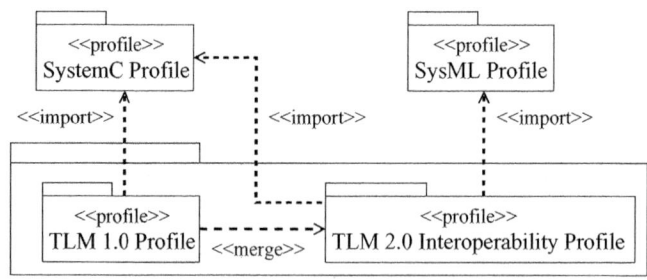

Fig. 2. TLM Profile Relationship with Other Profiles

The TLM profile imports the existing UML SystemC and SysML profiles. We have also introduced a TLM 1.0 profile and merged it with the TLM 2.0 profile. Thus, our TLM profile supports constructs and semantics of TLM 1.0 and TLM 2.0 standards. Table 2 shows examples of the stereotypes defined in the TLM profile corresponding to TLM 2.0 concepts.

Table 2. TLM Profile Stereotypes

TLM Concepts	Stereotypes	Base Stereotype(s)	Referenced Profile
Modules	≪Initiator≫	≪Block≫	SysML
	≪Interconnect≫	≪sc_module≫	SystemC
	≪Target≫		
Sockets	≪tlm_initiator_socket≫	≪FlowPort≫	SysML
	≪tlm_target_socket≫	≪sc_port≫	SystemC
	...		
Interfaces	≪tlm_blk_forward_if≫	≪sc_interface≫	SystemC
	≪tlm_non_blk_fw_if≫		
	...		
Transport Methods	≪b_transport≫	≪sc_method≫	SystemC
	≪nb_transport_fw≫		
	...		
TLM Path	≪tlm_block_fw_path≫	≪sc_connector≫	SystemC
	≪tlm_nb_fw_path≫		
	...		
Payload Object	≪tlm_generic_payload≫	≪ItemFlow≫	SysML
TLM Phase	≪tlm_phase≫	≪Enumeration≫	UML
...	...	...	...

A TLM stereotype either specialize a SysML stereotype or SystemC stereotype or both as base stereotypes. For example, Fig.3(a) shows TLM modules introduced as stereotypes in the TLM profile using an extension to the stereotypes *sc_module* and *block* defined respectively in the SystemC and SysML profiles. Fig.3(b) shows a hierarchy of TLM initiator socket stereotypes. Overall, the profile contains 38 stereotypes; each of them corresponds to a TLM concept.

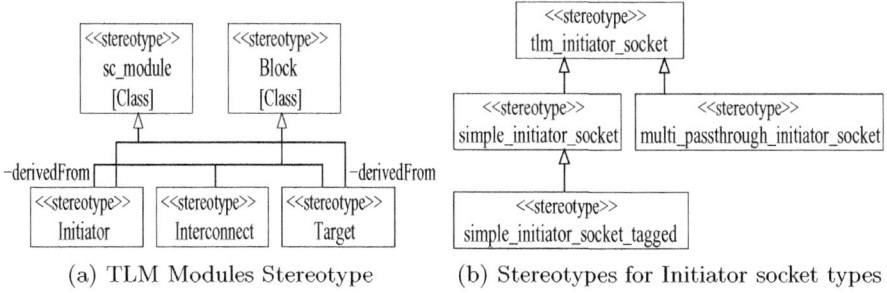

(a) TLM Modules Stereotype   (b) Stereotypes for Initiator socket types

Fig. 3. Example of TLM Stereotypes Structure

4 TLM Model Validation

The UML based model-driven development offers a unique advantage of performing model validation earlier in the design phase in comparison to other system development strategies. The model validation helps in rectifying the errors found in the model during design phase, absence of which could lead to spending more efforts and time in debugging errors in the system.

The UML based model validation ensures that during model construction, one can check that a model complies with the defined constraints and ensure that no broken cross-model reference exists. It involves checking a UML model against the UML rules as well as any constraint defined in the model expressed in the OCL. OCL can be used to express additional constraints on UML models that cannot be expressed or very difficult to express using UML diagrams alone. A constraint is basically an expression typically specifying an invariant condition that must hold for the system being modeled or a query over a object described in a model. These constraints can be added either directly to a model element or can be grouped and can be stored as global constraints.

UML modeling tools supporting OCL allow application-specific rules to be expressed as OCL constraints in a model and support validation of a UML model against such OCL constraints. In our view, an OCL expression for a TLM rule can be built in the following steps:

- Examining semantics of a TLM rule.
- Identifying the relevant part of the UML metamodel corresponds to TLM stereotype.
- Constructing an OCL expression from the UML metamodel.

4.1 Expressing TLM Rules in OCL

A TLM rule can be expressed as an OCL constraint and can be added to a stereotype representing a TLM concept in the profile. For example, let us closely examine the semantics of a TLM rule stating *"An Initiator can not realize b_transport method"*. In TLM context, an Initiator module may consists of a set of methods. According to the rule, none of these methods should be of type b_transport. Similarly, a TLM rule *"b_transport should not be called from method process"* illustrates that a b_transport method should be called either as a sc_thread or a sc_cthread context but not as a sc_method context.

Now, after examining the semantics of a TLM rule we need to express that rule into OCL. For that, we need to identify a stereotype in the profile representing a TLM concept on which that rule is applicable. Finally, we need to examine the part of the UML metamodel which consists of the stereotype definition declared in the TLM profile to get an OCL expression for that rule.

In the context of the TLM rule mentioned above, we note that in the TLM profile, an *Initiator* stereotype represents a TLM concept of an Initiator module. An *Initiator* stereotype is derived from a SysML *Block* stereotype and a SystemC profile's *sc_module* stereotype. Both the stereotypes extend a UML metaclass *Class* as shown in the Fig.4.

A SysML Profile for Development and Early Validation of TLM 2.0 Models 305

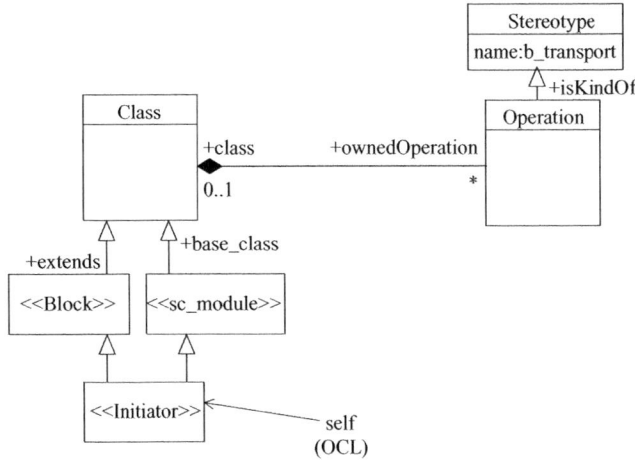

Fig. 4. Classes Diagram of Kernel package of UML metamodel

A UML metaclass *Class* owns a UML metaclass *Operation* and its attribute ownedOperation returns an ordered set of operations which are declared in a *Class* instance. An *Operation* metaclass is also derived from a metaclass *Type*. In this example, a *Type* classifier is represented by a *Stereotype* metaclass. In OCL, each classifier defined within a UML model represents a distinct OCL type. Now, in order to check whether the operation is of type *b_transport* we can use an OCL operator *OCLIsKindOf* to confirm this.

In OCL, *self* refers to the object of the classifier which is the context of the expression. In an OCL expression, the dot(.) is used to define the value of a property which could be an attribute, an association end or an operation of an object. So, finally the OCL expression can be written as

self.base_Class.ownedOperation → *forAll(e|e.oclIsKindOf(b_transport))*

Table 3. Examples of TLM Rules expressed as OCL Constraints

Constraint Element	TLM Rule	OCL Constraint
Initiator	Initiator can not realize b_transport method	self.base_Class.ownedOperation→forAll (e|not e.oclIsKindOf (b_transport))
b_transport	b_transport should not be called from method process	self.base_StateMachine.class.extension →exists(e|e.ownedEnd.type.name <>'sc_method')
nb_trans_fw	nb_transport_fw should be realized by Target	self.base_Operation.featuringClassifier →exists (e|e.oclIsKindOf(Target))
nb_bw_path	nb_transport_bw shall be called on backward path	self.realizingMessage→forAll(e| e.ownedEnd.type.name='nb_trans_bw')
tlm_dbg	tlm_dbg shall not call wait directly	self.base_StateMachine.region. subvertex→select(oclIsKindOf(State)) → forAll(s:State|s.oclIsKindOf(wait))

All OCL constraints representing TLM static rules are added into the TLM profile. Table 3 shows examples of TLM static rules expressed as OCL constraints incorporated into the proposed profile.

5 Implementation and Case Study

Fig.5 shows our UML based framework for TLM 2.0 model development, validation and code generation. We have developed a TLM profile for model validation and an XSL stylesheet for code generation. For modeling and validation purpose, we have used Magicdraw, a UML modeling tool [9]. However, our approach does not restrict to a particular modeling tool and it can be used with any UML modeling tool supporting SysML and OCL. The tool provides support for model validation and generates a validation report in case a TLM model violates any of the static rules. For code generation, we have used an Extensible Stylesheet Language Transformation (XSLT) technique [3]. The modeling tool saves a TLM 2.0 model in XML format compliant with Extensible MetaData Interchange(XMI) format. We also used an XSLT processor, *Saxon 9* [10], which processes XML documents using our XSLT stylesheets and generates executable SystemC code.

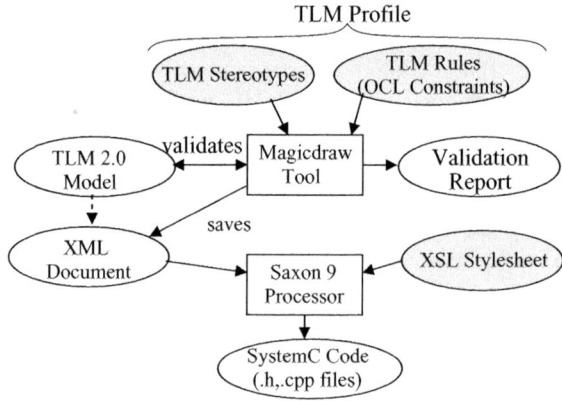

Fig. 5. A UML based Framework for TLM 2.0 Model development and validation

5.1 A Digital Photo Frame : Case Study

To illustrate the use of the TLM profile, we have developed a TLM model for a Digital photo frame (DPF) SoC. Fig.6 shows the system model of DPF. The system contains a CPU which acts as an initiator and sends requests for displaying images to the JPEG Decoder. The JPEG Decoder acts as an initiator and a target, and uses LT coding style. It forwards a request to the Memory to get the encoded JPEG image stored there. The Memory uses LT style and responds with the image data to the JPEG Decoder. The JPEG Decoder decodes the image and sends a write request to the Display controller. The Display controller follows AT 1-phase coding style. There is a system bus, which uses LT coding style and acts as interconnect between initiators and targets.

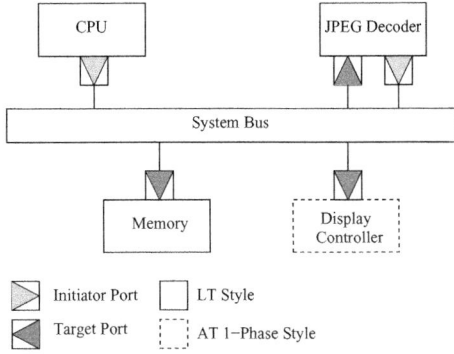

Fig. 6. TLM Model Example (A Digital Photo Frame)

Fig.7 shows system block diagram depicting the relationship among different modules represented as SysML blocks. There is a top level SystemC module *sc_top* which contains all of these modules. Fig.8 shows the connectivity between all the modules using internal block definition diagram. The Display controller uses AT-1 phase coding style and therefore uses a non-blocking interface and methods while CPU and JPEG Decoder use LT coding style and use blocking transport interfaces. The information item, *gp*, a generic payload, is used between each pair of modules.

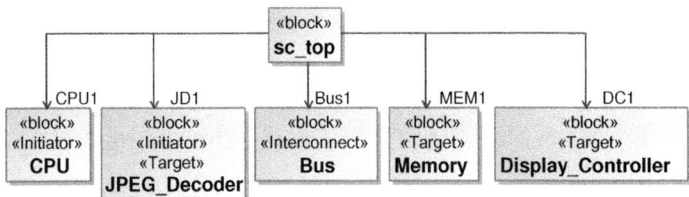

Fig. 7. Block Definition of DPF

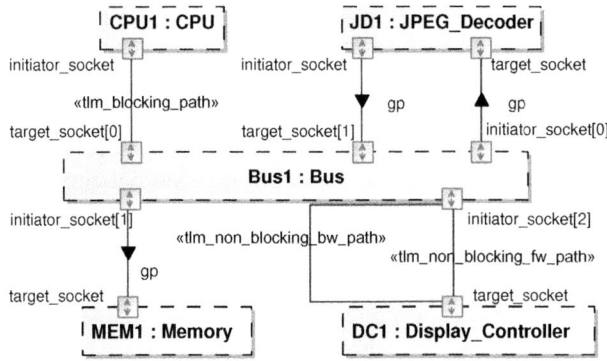

Fig. 8. Internal Block Diagram of DPF

Fig.9 depicts the behavior of CPU's Initiator *thread_process* captured in a UML statemachine. The thread reads a payload object from a request port, and sends memeory read/write request to the target by calling b_transport method. Then, it waits for the response from the target. If the transaction response is "OK", then it synchronizes itself with the target by waiting for a delay set by target and then writes the transaction object to a response port.

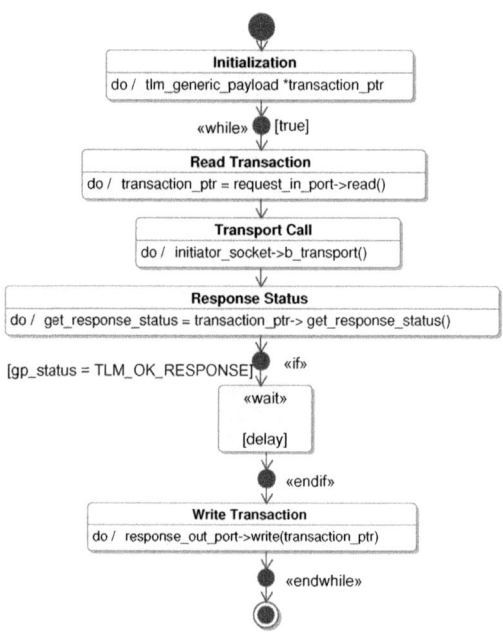

Fig. 9. Behavioral View of DPF representing CPU Initiator's Thread

5.2 TLM Static Rules Validation

Now, with the help of the UML modeling tool, Magicdraw, a TLM model designed using proposed TLM profile can be validated against all TLM static rules expressed as OCL constraints. During model validation, the tool reports the violations of the OCL constraints found in the model. In order to demonstrate this, we took the DPF model but we deliberately introduced some violations in the model. The tool highlights all the model elements of the TLM 2.0 model which violate TLM static rules as shown in the Fig.10.

Table 4 shows the outcome of the model validation performed on this model. For example, one of the error messages, states that *"Initiator must have a tlm initiator socket"*. According to TLM standard, for the correct behavior of the system, an Initiator module must have a tlm initiator socket which is missing from the CPU module.

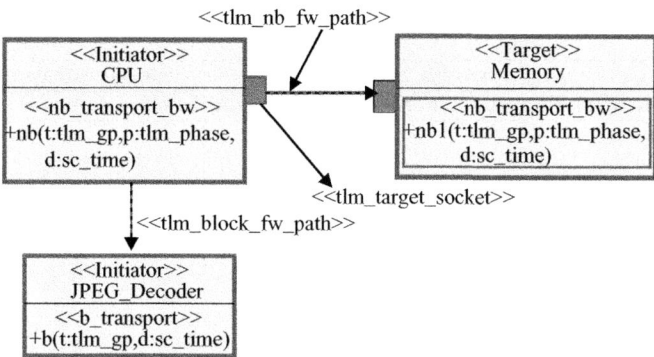

Fig. 10. Example of a Model violating TLM Rules

Table 4. Result of Model Validation performed on a model shown in Fig.10

Model Element	Error Message
CPU[Model]	Initiator must be a Block classifier
JPEG_Decoder[Model]	Initiator realizes blocking transport call
Path[CPU-Memory]	Initiator socket missing on non-blocking forward path
Memory[Model]	Target realizes non-blocking backward call
Path[CPU-JPEG_Decoder]	Initiator and Target socket missing on blocking path

5.3 Code Generation

For generation of executable SystemC code, as discussed earlier, we have used an XSLT approach where an XSLT processor parses an XMI document based on the XSLT rules specified in a XSL stylesheet. We have developed a XSL Stylesheet which contains XSLT rules organized in the form of templates.

Fig.11 shows an example of the code generated for the CPU's initiator thread process as shown in Fig.9. Table 5 shows the code generation statistics for the executable TLM model of DPF.

```
void lt_initiator::initiator_thread(void){
  tlm_generic_payload *transaction_ptr;
  while(true) {
    transaction_ptr=request_in_port->read();
    sc_time delay = SC_ZERO_TIME;
    initiator_socket->b_transport(*transaction_ptr,delay);
    gp_status = transaction_ptr->get_response_status();
    if(gp_status == TLM_OK_RESPONSE)
      wait(delay);
    response_out_port->write(transaction_ptr);
  }
}
```

Fig. 11. Code Generation Example for Fig.9

Table 5. Code Generation Statistics for DPF

Model Size		Code Generation	
Model Element Used	Diagrams Used	LOC	Time(s)
Blocks/Classes 20	BDD 1		
Operations 28	IBD 2	515	3.796
Ports 11	SM 16		
Class Instances 5			

6 Conclusions and Future Work

This paper described a UML based approach for model development and early validation of TLM 2.0 models based on a TLM profile. The TLM profile based on UML/SysML provides the foundation for the model validation and the executable SystemC based TLM models. Moreover, our approach enables modeling and code generation of TLM 2.0 models at different abstraction levels. We reported the TLM model development approach through an example of Digital Photo Frame SoC. Our work also demonstrated that with the early validation of TLM 2.0 models based on static rules we can reduce the overall debugging efforts. Although UML behavior modeling in general, requires much efforts from a designer viewpoint, but reusing the same behavior again can save overall designer's efforts. We plan to extend the UML based model validation aspect to include dynamic validation of TLM models and look at the possibility of incorporating the model refinement aspect in the current framework.

References

1. Riccobene, E., et al.: SystemC/C-based model-driven design for embedded systems. ACM Trans. Embedded Comput. Syst. 8(4) (2009)
2. Nguyen, K., Sun, Z., Thiagarajan, P., Wong, W.: Model-Driven SoC Design via Executable UML to SystemC. In: Proc. of 25th Real-Time Systems Symposium (RTSS 2004) (December 2004)
3. Prevostini, M., Zamsa, E.: SysML Profile for SoC Design and SystemC Transformation. Tech Report, ALaRI, Faculty of Informatics, University of Lugano (2007)
4. Raslan, W., Sameh, A.: Mapping SysML to SystemC. Forum on specification and Design Languages. In: FDL 2007 (2007)
5. Martin, G., Müller, W.: UML for SOC Design. Springer, New York (2005)
6. Vanderperren, Y., Dehaene, W.: SysML and Systems Engineering Applied to UML-Based SoC Design. In: 2nd UML-SoC Workshop at 42nd DAC, USA (2005)
7. Pauwels, M., et al.: A Design Methodology for the Development of a Complex SOC Using UML and Executable System Models. In: Proc. of FDL (2002)
8. Mischkalla, F., He, D., Müller, W.: Closing the gap between UML-based modeling, simulation and synthesis of combined HW/SW systems. In: Design, Automation and Test in Europe, DATE 2010 (March 2010)
9. The MagicDraw tool, http://www.nomagic.com
10. The Saxon Processor, http://www.saxonica.com

11. Open SystemC Initiative (OSCI). TLM 2.0 Language Reference Manual
12. Object Management Group (OMG). UML Profile for SoC v1.1 Specification
13. Object Management Group (OMG). UML 2.0 Superstrcuture and Infrastructure Specification
14. Object Management Group (OMG). SysML v1.2 Specification
15. Object Management Group (OMG). UML 2.2 OCL Specification
16. Object Management Group (OMG). UML Profile for MARTE specification
17. TLM 2.0 Compliance Checker, Jeda Technologies, http://www.jedatechnologies.net

Taming the Confusion of Languages

Rolf-Helge Pfeiffer and Andrzej Wąsowski

IT University of Copenhagen, Denmark
{ropf,wasowski}@itu.dk

Abstract. Large software systems are composed of diverse artifacts. The relations between these artifacts are usually not formalized, if the artifacts use different modeling or programming languages. This hinders component-oriented development, as interfaces of exchangeable components do not capture hidden artifact dependencies. We present GenDeMoG, a tool that allows for mining inter-component dependencies beyond those explicitly specified. GenDeMoG is a generic generator-generator parameterized with a high-level system model containing dependency specifications. So, unlike the language interface mechanisms, GenDeMoG is not restricted to any given kind of links. We apply GenDeMoG to a realistic case study—an open source enterprise system, OFBiz. The experiment confirms that the stereotypical opinion about unknown dependencies across artifact types is indeed correct. Just 22 specifications allowed GenDeMoG to uncover 1737 undocumented inter-component dependencies among OFBiz components.

1 Introduction

A modern enterprise system is heterogeneous—it combines development artifacts, expressed in various languages. These artifacts are *aggregated* into larger reusable entities, called components. However, when forming a system, the artifacts are not merely put together to form components, but they are interrelated via references or other dependencies. Depending on the language and the provided mechanisms, such references are either *direct* or *indirect*. Direct references are string-based references expressed by using the same datum in different locations. If at one place the datum changes, the reference is broken. *Indirect* references are established between artifacts at runtime; for example in adapter calls, such like when a Java method is calling a Prolog rule.

The larger the number of languages used at development time, the more artifacts containing references to artifacts in other languages appear. Further, since not all languages are general purpose (GPLs), many artifacts cannot use adapters to interact with code in other languages, instead they refer to other code artifacts *directly*. Usually such direct references are *implicit*, in the sense that their semantics is hidden in the execution platform (an interpreter, business logics, etc.). In contrast, *explicit* references exploit metadata of the referenced datum, for example document structure like in unified resource locators (URI). Either type of references result in dependencies between artifacts.

The proliferation of references across languages and across components causes a number of problems for software developers:

- Since inter-language dependencies are usually implicit, they require substantial domain knowledge for a developer to correctly perform simple evolution steps.

- Implicit dependencies may cross the borders of system's aggregation structure: components get coupled tighter together. When this happens, it is often not explicitly recorded in component interfaces.
- Errors caused by broken dependencies are most often only exposed at runtime; so detection of any errors requires thorough testing of the modified code—while, at least in principle, errors caused by dangling references between static artifacts, could easily be caught at compile time.

The first objective of this paper is to present GenDeMoG—a tool that allows for specifying inter-component dependency patterns for artifacts in heterogeneous systems. GenDeMoG automatically reveals the hidden dependencies using these patterns. The tool is generic. It is neither tied to certain languages nor applications. It is also non-invasive, in the sense, that it does not require that the related artifacts are modified.

Our second objective is to use GenDeMoG to analyze a larger realistic case study for the presence of unspecified dependencies, and their interaction with component structure of the system. We use *OFBiz* [10], an open-source enterprise automation software project, as the subject in this study. OFBiz is a component-based system comprising a multitude of heterogeneous languages, both general purpose languages (GPLs) like *Java*, and domain-specific languages (DSLs). We research OFBiz applications, that is programs running on the OFBiz framework. Such applications are again component-based and heterogeneous. Therefore, we identified 22 exemplary dependency patterns using 7 languages specific to OFBiz. GenDeMoG automatically revealed 1737 inter-component dependencies of the kind specified by these patterns.

The main findings of these study are that:

- There indeed exists a large number of references between OFBiz components not specified in the component description mechanism (see e.g., Fig. 1)—even though the mechanism provides for specifying such.
- These dense and circular references couple the components tightly together. This confirms the qualitative understanding (see Section 2) that evolution or refactoring of OFBiz component structure is difficult in practice.

A useful by-product of this work is an initial meta-model of Java 5 implemented in *Xtext* [14]. Since we could not find a pre-existing Xtext specification of Java, we adapted an existing ANTLR grammar, and optimized it to decrease the number of model elements created in each type, so that pattern matching, which relies on these types, is more efficient. The new Java model is available online together with GenDeMoG (http://www.itu.dk/~ropf/download/gendemog.html).

We further motivate the problem of unspecified references across languages and components using the OFBiz example in Sect. 2. In Sect. 3 GenDeMoG is introduced. Sect. 4 describes the experimental case study of applying GenDeMoG to OFBiz. We end with a discussion of future work (Sect. 5), related work (Sect. 6) and conclusion.

2 Background and Rationale

Software systems are implemented using many interrelated artifacts, expressed in multiple languages. We shall now investigate this architectural phenomenon by surveying the example of the OFBiz project. OFBiz is a component-based *framework* on top of which OFBiz *applications* are run. A standard OFBiz distribution includes 11 application core components delivering key functionalities: accounting, commonext, content, humanres, manufacturing, marketing, order, party, product, securityext, and workeffort.

Each application component contains a *component descriptor*, by convention in a file named ofbiz-component.xml, expressed in a domain specific language using an XML syntax. The descriptor defines the visibility of artifacts, their types, etc. Fig. 1 presents a fragment of the descriptor for the order component, which supports functionality around management of customer orders. The component descriptor informs the framework about the existence and location of data models and initialization data (entity-resource) or about the existence and location of business logic (service-resource). Further it declares whether a component is a web application (webapp) and allows for the specification of a set of components that it depends on (depends-on). The latter, however, is not used in the above example, nor anywhere else in core application components of OFBiz.

Implementation artifacts are expressed using DSLs and GPLs. Dependencies between heterogeneous artifacts are expressed using string-based references, since the languages themselves do not support heterogeneous interface descriptions—i.e., only few languages allow for expressing relations between language elements within the same language in a managed manner. That is, the wish to separate concerns by expressing development artifacts in different DSLs and GPLs and the lack of a uniform managed mechanism to describe relations between artifacts creates a confusion of languages.

Fig. 2 shows an example of an inter-language, inter-component, string-based dependency between a Java method call and an entity definition. A dependency (reference) goes from a class FinAccountHelper in the order component to the file entitymodel.xml in the accounting component (both red in the Figure). This reference, as many other similar, is not captured by the interface specification of Fig. 1.

Dependencies that cross component boundaries are problematic since they increase coupling and make components hard to exchange or remove, when customizing OFBiz. Still, OFBiz contains no mechanism for specification of inter-component dependencies, which could help developers by reporting violations of dependencies, or merely by documenting dependencies. The following quotes (original spelling) from the developer

```
<ofbiz-component name="order"
  xmlns:xsi="http://www.w3.org/2001/XMLSchema-instance"
  xsi:noNamespaceSchemaLocation="http://ofbiz.apache.org/dtds/ofbiz-component.xsd">
    <resource-loader name="main" type="component"/>
    <classpath type="jar" location="build/lib/*"/>
    <classpath type="dir" location="config"/>
    ...
    <entity-resource type="model" ... location="entitydef/entitymodel.xml"/>
    ...
    <entity-resource type="data" ... location="data/OrderTypeData.xml"/>
    ...
    <service-resource type="model" loader="main" location="servicedef/services.xml"/>
    ...
    <service-resource type="eca" loader="main" location="servicedef/secas.xml"/>
    ...
    <webapp name="order" title="Order" ... location="webapp/ordermgr"
        base-permission="OFBTOOLS,ORDERMGR" mount-point="/ordermgr"/>
</ofbiz-component>
```

Fig. 1. An excerpt of the Order component descriptor

```xml
<entity entity-name="FinAccount" package-name="org.ofbiz.accounting.finaccount"
  title="Financial Account Entity">
  <field name="finAccountId" type="id-ne"></field>
  <field name="finAccountTypeId" type="id"></field>
  <field name="statusId" type="id"></field>
  ...
</entity>
```
```java
public static boolean validatePin(GenericDelegator delegator,
                                  String finAccountId, String pinNumber) {
  GenericValue finAccount = null;
  try {
    finAccount = delegator.findByPrimaryKey("FinAccount",
        UtilMisc.toMap("finAccountId", finAccountId));
  } ...
```

Fig. 2. An inter-language cross-component string-based dependency: the marked string literals in the Java method validatePin refer to objects specified in the XML file on top (both red)

mailing lists show that indeed implicit coupling of components is an issue in practice (Note, these quotes are to motivate our work. We did not perform a systematic research on the OFBiz mailing lists):

> **Hansen:** *I am looking for information regarding the inter-dependency among all ofbiz components ... Is there any effective way to know this kind of information. So that I can safely remove those components I do not want without affecting the functionalities of the other components that I want to keep*
>
> **skip@theDevers:** *I recently used just the party manager in a project and deleted all the rest. Took a couple of days replacing/commenting out the dependencies...*
>
> **Hansen:** *It would be usuful to have such information (something like rpm dependency list) handy especially for those application components as they are supposed to be less dependent on other components comparing to framework components.*
> [http://ofbiz.135035.n4.nabble.com/component-dependency-td153157.html]
>
> **Mustansar Mehmood:** *My company(a service company) is considering ofbiz as their ERP/CRM/accounts Receivable system but Ofbiz seems to have a few things that my company will not be using for instance E commerce or Manufacturing/. How do we removed those applications ? and keep it running stable...*
>
> **Divesh Dutta:** *You can not remove the any of the complete application. Each module is related to another module one or other way...*
>
> **cjhorton:** *Generally, because of dependancies you don't want to 'remove' a component, but rather just 'hide' it as talked about in the links above...*
>
> [http://ofbiz.135035.n4.nabble.com/Removing-applications-from-OfBiz-td160666.html#a160669]

Our long term research agenda is to support smooth evolutions of systems with interrelated artifacts. We recognize that this cannot be solved without taking project specifics into account. Thus in this paper we present a *generic tool*, which parameterized with a *project-specific model* of a software system with its dependencies, is able to reveal unspecified relations between implementation artifacts across components. In the second part of the paper we will use this tool to further explore the nature of dependencies in an example of a mature business application, such as OFBiz.

3 GenDeMoG

This section introduces GenDeMoG a generic tool for mining an inter-component dependency graph of heterogeneous component-based software systems. GenDeMoG's architecture and other important aspects are described.

The central artifact to GenDeMoG is a *Component Descriptor Model (CDM)*. A CDM provides an external description of a component-based software system under analysis. It states which languages are used by development artifacts, what components are formed by which artifacts and, most importantly, includes the language-level patterns that describe the conditions for dependencies between development artifacts. A CDM comprises the following three sections:

Type definitions. In our work we use the terms *types* and *languages* synonymously. Types are defined by a path to a languages meta-model assigned to an alias. The alias is required to be equal to the meta-models name. GenDeMoG generally provides 2 different means of importing a language to the framework. These are first XSD meta-models and second EMF meta-models. Each language definition has to refer to its meta-meta-model.

Component List. Components are specified by a unique name. This may be a relative path to a folder containing the components artifacts or any other name. Each component declares a list of artifacts it contains. Artifacts are specified by a unique path, with respect to a single CDM. Each artifact refers further to its meta-model or the language it is instance of.

Pattern Definitions. Dependency patterns are defined by specifying a key pattern, and a reference pattern with respect to the corresponding language definitions. Patterns are specified using the EMF expression language that is used for writing model transformers and code generators in Xtend and Xpand [13,12] respectively. Key patterns always start with the keyword possibleKey and reference patterns with the keyword possibleReference and may be followed by navigations to certain model sub-elements, see the dependency pattern in Fig. 3. The second element of both pattern specifications is the respective model element type. This states the type of the possibleKey and possibleReference model element respectively. Finally, the language for key and reference patterns is specified. A separate boolean expression over key- and reference patterns defines under which condition a key and a reference pattern are in relation.

Obviously, GenDeMoG's CDM is directly tied to the meta-model hierarchy [28,16]. All used languages in a software system are defined to be instances of the same meta-meta-language (M3) (Ecore [11]). This allows for the definition of dependency patterns on meta-model level (M2) or language level. All artifacts are specified as models (on level M1) that are instances of the corresponding meta-model or languages stated in the type definitions.

```
key pattern: "possibleKey.entityName" typeOf "EntityType" in iof entitymodel
reference pattern: "possibleReference.relEntityName"
                    typeOf "RelationType" in iof entitymodel
dependency relation: "_keyPattern_ == _refPattern_"
```

Fig. 3. Example pattern

In a nutshell, a CDM lists all languages used or of interest in the software system under analysis, it lists which artifacts form components and most importantly, which language constructs induce inter-component dependencies.

Supported Languages. Since GenDeMoG allows for mining inter-component dependencies for heterogeneous languages, it is crucial to provide a mechanism for including new languages. As mentioned above all languages are based on the Ecore meta-meta-model. XSD-based language definitions can either be automatically or manually converted to Ecore-based language definitions. In the experiment (Sect. 4) we use 6 XSD-based language definitions and one Ecore-based definition. The Ecore-based Java 5 model is an initial implementation setting up on XText. Generally, there are multiple sources for predefined languages such as e.g., EMFText Syntax Zoo [3] (currently, 88 languages), the Atlant Ecore Zoo [2] (currently, 304 languages), the MoDisco Project Page [9] (currently for Java and XML documents).

Dependency Patterns. GenDeMoG mines *Key-Reference* dependencies. That is, there is a key, the definition of a certain piece of information that may be referenced. Furthermore, there are references, which are pieces of information that specify the referenced keys. In GenDeMoG such pieces of information are model elements. A key and a reference are in relation, if and only if the boolean constraint that specifies their relation evaluates to true. That is, there are no keys and references without a relation.

Dependency patterns are defined between two language elements of a certain type (type) each which in turn belongs to a certain language (in iof). Each key and reference pattern may be defined more precisely by an optional refine statement. It may be used to provide another boolean expression that needs to evaluate to true. Key patterns are referenced in the dependency patterns using the key word _keyPattern_. Reference patterns are referenced in the dependency patterns using the key word _refPattern_. A dependency pattern, with substituted _keyPattern_ and _refPattern_, is a boolean expression that evaluates to true if a dependency between a key and a reference exists. Since GenDeMoG is a generator-generator, the dependency patterns get transformed to dependency graph generator code that contains a boolean function call for the dependency relation, see Fig. 4, corresponding to the dependency relation in Fig. 3. The language for describing key and reference patterns is the *Eclipse Modeling Framework (EMF)* expression language [4].

GenDeMoG's Architecture. GenDeMoG is a generator-generator. " [It] compiles a query into a special-purpose search program, whose task is only to answer the given query. ... the input to the program generator is a general query answerer, and the output is a 'compiler' from queries into search programs." [25] The queries in our case are the dependency patterns. The 'compiler' is the *ext_gen* model transformer. It takes the dependency pattern queries from a CDM and generates *graph_gen* as special purpose search program, which in turn is a model transformer again. The following is a description of GenDeMoG's architecture using the compiler notation from [25]:

```
cached Boolean check(EntityType possibleKey, RelationType possibleReference) :
    possibleKey.entityName == possibleReference.relEntityName;
```

Fig. 4. Automatically generated code corresponding to the pattern in Fig. 3

$$graph\_gen = [\![ext\_gen]\!]_{\text{xpand}} \, [cdm, fst\_wf] \tag{1}$$

$$snd\_wf = [\![wf\_gen]\!]_{\text{xpand}} \, [cdm] \tag{2}$$

$$dep\_model = [\![graph\_gen]\!]_{\text{xtend}} \, [\{artifacts\}, snd\_wf] \tag{3}$$

Entities in $[\![\cdot]\!]$ describe semantic units, i.e., programs in a certain language (denoted as subscript) that are executed consuming the arguments in $[\cdot]$. Workflows (fst_wf, snd_wf) are programs that execute model generators and model transformers in a specified order. The first workflow calls the ext_gen code generator on the CDM. That means, that the generator-generator gets instantiated to the concrete generators for patterns. The second workflow takes the generated concrete generators and runs them on the corresponding artifacts in order to generate the dependency graph. Thus, workflows are programs that have a coordinating function and we denote them as arguments to model generators and transformers. The generated dependency model is an instance of the meta-model shown in Fig. 5. Such a dependency graph ($Tengsl$[1] model) contains a representation for each component, containing artifacts, which in turn may contain key elements and references to keys.

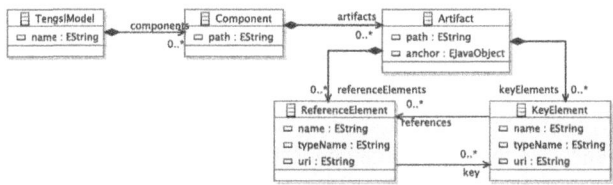

Fig. 5. Metamodel for the mined inter-component dependency graph

4 Experiment

We will now demonstrate GenDeMoG by applying it to a real-world medium-sized software system analysis scenario. This way we will extract an inter-component dependency graph for the subject system, which we will further analyze.

The Experiment Subject. OFBiz is an industrial-strength *open source enterprise automation software project licensed under the Apache License Version 2.0. By open source enterprise automation we mean: Open Source ERP, Open Source CRM, Open Source E-Business / E-Commerce, Open Source SCM, Open Source MRP, Open Source CMMS/EAM, and so on* [10]. In this experiment we have used OFBiz ver. 9.04, available at http://svn.apache.org/repos/asf/ofbiz/branches/release09.04.

OFBiz' source tree contains 6522 files, including 1122 Java source code files, 365 Groovy files, 1283 XML files, and files in various other languages. Out of 6522 files, 2289 are related to the framework only, and 1539 are owned by the 11 core application components. The tree contains more than 388000 lines in XML models, and in excess of 310 KLOC of Java code. The OFBiz project uses not less than 33 domain

---

[1] Tengsl: Icelandic for relationship.

specific languages and relies on about a dozen standards or open technologies. More than 2000 email addresses are subscribed to the OFBiz mailing list, most of these technically oriented participants ranging from core developers to technically skilled users who customize and deploy OFBiz. The project website lists (February 2011) several large customers, including internationally known brands such as telecom operators or large airlines and a multitude of smaller ones. All in all, OFBiz is a fairly representative example of an industrial quality modern enterprise system.

In this paper we focus on dependencies in OFBiz applications across the core components, i.e., inter-component dependencies. To customize an application the mentioned components can either be modified, removed, or extended and expanded by new components. We note that in case of OFBiz, the framework follows the same architectural principle as the applications built on top of it.

A typical application relies on the following 25 DSLs: componentLoader, jndiConfig, ofbizComponent, ofbizContainer, ofbizProperties, datafiles, entityConfig, entityEca, entitygroup, entitymodel, fieldtypemodel, simpleMethods, securityConfig, serviceConfig, serviceEca, serviceGroup, serviceMca, services, testSuite, regions, siteConf, widgetForm, widgetMenu, widgetScreen, and widgetTree. On top of the GPLs such like Java and Groovy [6], the FreeMarker Template Language (FTL) [5], and JavaServer Pages (JSP) [7] are used. DSLs are used to describe data models, visual application parts, and together with GPLs they are used to specify the controller level, i.e., required logics, following the model-view-controller design pattern.

The Experiment Set-up. The objective of this experiment is two-fold. First, we want to show that a large number of dependencies—precisely, direct references—exists between components and languages in a mature system like OFBiz. Second, we want to demonstrate effectiveness of GenDeMoG while revealing the dependencies. We do not aim at revealing all not specified dependencies—since this would require a substantial domain knowledge.

We are interested in dependencies within and across architectural layers. Since OFBiz follows the model-view-controller design pattern the interesting component boundaries can be divided in the following 6 categories: *model–model*, *model–view*, *view–view*, *view-controller*, *controller–controller*, and *controller—model*. We have identified patterns describing dependencies in each of these. The dependencies have been identified by studying available documentation, in particular the developer guide book [24]. We have stopped searching for more dependencies as soon as we accumulated representatives for all categories (in total 22 dependency patterns, 19 inter-language and 3 intra-language patterns). Fig. 6 shows these categories by black edges—thickness of the edge, and the numeric labels, reflect how many dependency patterns we were able to find on each of the boundaries. Note that due to the inherent incompleteness of the collection method this does not mean that proportions between dependencies in OFBiz are precisely as indicated in the figure. The diagram merely shows the characteristics of our selected sample set, and it does show *qualitatively* that there exist dependencies on each of these boundaries.

The dependency mining algorithm is applied to 642 artifacts (relevant for the patterns) belonging to the 11 core application components of OFBiz.

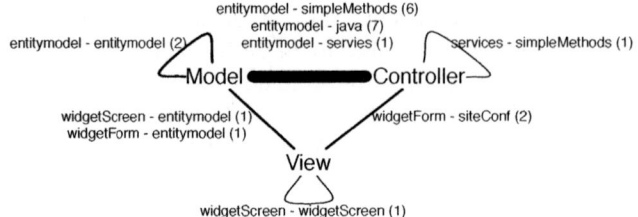

Fig. 6. Amount of dependency patterns between the parts of the MVC architecture

Fig. 7 shows an excerpt of the CDM used for this experiment. The complete model showing all included languages, components, artifacts and dependency patterns is available online at http://www.itu.dk/~ropf/download/gendemog.html.

```
1   project ofbiz at "/ofbiz_9_4"
2   ...
3   type entitymodel metamodel ".../dtd/entitymodel.xsd" typeOf XSD,
4   type simpleMethods metamodel ".../dtd/simple-methods.xsd" typeOf XSD,
5   type java3 metamodel ".../lang/xtext/Java3.ecore" typeOf Ecore
6       -P "dk.itu.sdg.lang.xtext.java3.Java3Package"
7
8   component accounting at "/ofbiz/applications/accounting" {
9     artefact "/.../accounting/.../entitymodel.xml" typeOf entitymodel,
10    ...
11    artefact "/.../accounting/.../TaxAuthorityServices.xml" typeOf simpleMethods,
12    ...
13    artefact "/.../accounting/.../UtilAccounting.jxmi" typeOf java3,
14    ...
15  }
16  ...
17  component order at "/ofbiz/applications/order" {
18    artefact "/.../order/.../entitymodel.xml" typeOf entitymodel,
19    artefact "/.../order/.../entitymodel_view.xml" typeOf entitymodel,
20    ...
21    artefact "/.../order/.../PurchaseOrderTest.jxmi" typeOf java3,
22    artefact "/.../order/.../SalesOrderTest.jxmi" typeOf java3,
23    ...
24  }
25  ...
26  /* entitymodel <-> entitymodel */
27  key pattern: "possibleKey.field.name" typeOf "EntityType" in iof entitymodel
28  reference pattern: "possibleReference.relation" typeOf "EntityType"
29      in iof entitymodel
30  dependency relation:
31      "_refPattern_.select(e|e.relEntityName == possibleKey.entityName).size > 0
32      && _keyPattern_.intersect(_refPattern_.keyMap.fieldName).size > 0"
33  ...
34  /* entitymodel <-> java */
35  ...
36  key pattern: "possibleKey.entityName" typeOf "EntityType" in iof entitymodel
37  reference pattern: "possibleReference" typeOf "PrimaryVarCall"
38      refine "_refPattern_.name.name.last() == ('getRelatedOne') &&
39      !_refPattern_.eContents.typeSelect(Arguments).isEmpty &&
40      !_refPattern_.eAllContents.typeSelect(PrimaryLiteral).isEmpty" in iof java3
41  dependency relation: "_refPattern_.eAllContents.typeSelect(PrimaryLiteral)
42      .select(e|e.literal == '\"'+_keyPattern_+'\"').size > 0" ...
```

Fig. 7. An excerpt of the CDM for the experiment

Let us survey Fig. 7 to provide further details. A CDM is defined per software system or `project` where the projects root folder is specified (`at`), see line 1. Used languages (`type`) are declared, see lines 3-6, by giving them a unique name, a path to their language specification (`metamodel`) or additionally their language package (see line 6), and stating the languages meta-meta-model (`typeOf`). Lines 8-24 show an excerpt of two component specifications (`component`) via a unique name, a path to the component's root folder (`at`), an finally the contained artifacts. Each artifact (`artefact`) is specified by a path to the artifacts location and the type of the language it is instance of (`typeOf`). Note, to minimize GenDeMoG's memory footprint, the experiment is run with preprocessed Java source code files. That is, a separate preprocessing step converted the textual Java files to an Ecore-based model representation (`jxmi`, e.g., line 13). Lines 26-42 show the declaration of two dependency patterns. We will have a closer look to the second one. Model elements that might be keys (`key pattern:`) are specified by a pattern to a model element, the model element's type (`typeOf`), and the type declaring language (`in iof`). The same holds for the specification of a reference element. In both are `possibleKey` and `possibleReference` reserved keywords. In case that a lot of model elements match the pattern definition with the corresponding type, it is possible to further refine the matching model element set (`refine`). By a boolean expression over key and reference patterns, are dependency relations defined (`dependency relation:`). In dependency relations and refine declarations are `possibleKey`, `possibleReference`, `_keyPattern_`, and `_refPattern_` reserved keywords.

Results and Analysis. A check for one pattern (out of the 22) over the 642 relevant artifacts takes about 2-3 minutes time on a 2GHz Intel Core 2 Duo Mac Book with 2GB 1067MHz DDR3 RAM.

Our 22 patterns, reveal in total 1737 inter-component dependencies (the number of elements of type ReferenceElement as per Fig. 5). These 1737 dependencies have 635 unique target elements (KeyElements). Remember, that since the list of patterns is highly incomplete, this number is a strict lower bound on the actual number of interactions between core application components in OFBiz!

It turns out that the density of dependencies varies a lot for patterns. This is visualized in Fig. 8. For example pattern number zero, leftmost in the figure, uncovers 700 dependencies, to 132 elements, while pattern number five applies rarely, uncovering only 4 dependencies to 3 key elements.

Fig. 9 shows qualitatively how dependencies are split across the components. Vertices represent components. There is an edge between two vertices if there is at least one dependency between the components in the given direction (arrow-heads point towards owners of target key elements). The only component that is independent from the remaining ones, as far the 22 dependency patterns are considered, is securityext. Note, that commonext depends on no component but is required by four others.

The graph contains a large number of cycles, and it is clear that each component depends on a handful of others. Also each has a few dependent ones. The median number of components depending on a given node is 6, while the median number of components on which a node depends is 5. This confirms quantitatively that problems indicated in the mailing list discussions (see Sect. 2) are well grounded—clearly it must be a

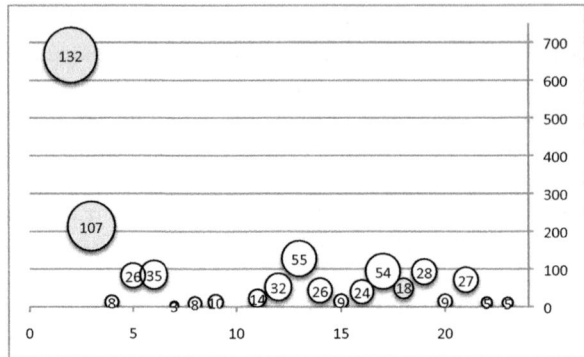

Fig. 8. Number of dependencies (vertical axis) for each pattern (horizontal axis). Number of key elements are shown in the bubbles. Grey bubbles are intra-language patterns.

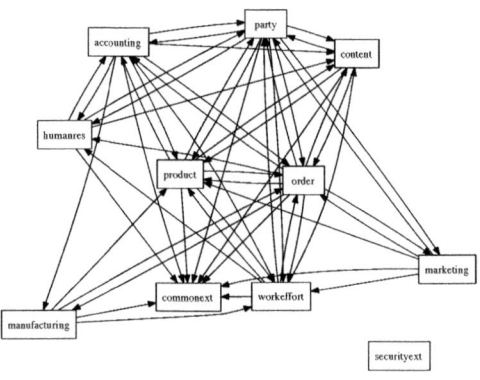

Fig. 9. Inter-component dependencies aggregated from the mined dependency graph

challenge to remove, replace or modify a component. Indeed, we have been able to confirm this coupling using merely 22 patterns!

Despite the fact that the component descriptions (ofbiz-component.xml) allow to specify component dependencies, none of the uncovered dependencies has been explicitly declared by developers. It turns out that this specification mechanism is not used in practice. This motivates further research in automatic dependency maintenance tools such as GenDeMoG.

Fig. 10 summarizes distribution of keys (referred elements) and references (referring elements) over the languages. Not surprisingly the biggest amount of keys is defined in the entitymodel DSL, which is used to define the data model. The large numbers of references outgoing from entitymodel (881) is caused by a large number of relations between the various concepts in the data model. This is natural in a data processing system. Also data modeling patterns were the easiest to identify for non-experts, so it is expected that we included some of these. As we have seen in Fig. 6—the model part

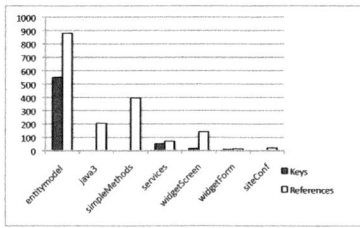

Fig. 10. Distribution of keys and references per language

of the architecture (containing the entitymodel language) has participated in the biggest share of our patterns, so it is expected that it generates most dependencies.

Finally, we have classified the dependencies that we have observed, in order to understand the circumstances in which they emerge. We observe three main categories of dependency patterns (and thus of the mined dependencies):

1. A *relation* provides a mechanism for distributed information specification within a language. For example, the relation mechanism of the entitymodel language allows specifying relations between data tables across artifact boundaries.
2. A *call* is an inter-language mechanism, where at least one language has runtime semantics and thus can call certain other code blocks or variables. For example, a Java method call that consumes a name of a data table as a parameter.
3. A *value source* is an inter-language mechanism that provides missing values to a template—for example, when displaying the value of a data field in a view.

Threats to validity. The main external threat is that OFBiz is not a representative example of an enterprise systems. We have tried to argue that it has many of typical characteristics of such systems. Moreover, we have informally confirmed that indeed it resembles commercial systems a lot, through personal communication with engineers in the ERP industry. The main reason to use OFBiz in this experiment is the unrestricted access to its source code, which would be difficult for other products (and would also make our results difficult to reproduce or compare in future).

The main internal threat lies in the selection of the 22 dependency patters. First, that they might be incorrect. Second, that they are not complete. We addressed the latter issue by deciding not to draw any conclusions about completeness. This allowed us to mitigate the former, by only focusing on the most obvious patterns, that can be extracted from the best available documentation [24].

Furthermore, GenDeMoG's algorithm can contain errors. Besides the usual testing effort aiming at establishing trust in the implementation we have manually verified that indeed the dependencies have been correctly matched by manually inspecting all of them for two selected patterns. This step has shown that 100% of dependencies have been mined correctly (no false positives). Since the mining program is automatically generated, our confidence that it operates correctly for other patterns is high.

Finally, the taxonomy of dependency kinds presented above is by design not complete, but only covers the categories that actually appeared in our 22 patterns.

5 Discussion and Future Work

Currently, GenDeMoG allows for the following:

- Non-invasive description of component-based software systems capturing used languages, components and contained artifacts.
- The definition of inter-component dependency patterns on the language level.
- Automatic generation of programs for mining inter-component dependencies.

GenDeMoG itself relies on *Eclipse Modeling Framework* (EMF) technologies, such as the model transformation language Xtend, the code generation language Xpand, and the DSL development framework Xtext.

It is specific to GenDeMoG that new languages may be included as Ecore-based models, i.e., all languages are described using the same meta-meta-language. This allows for the definition of dependency patterns on language level using one language, in this case Xtend. Importantly, this makes GenDeMoG a generic tool, i.e., applicable to a wide range of software systems. To demonstrate GenDeMoG's general applicability we have created a meta-model for Java 5 and used it in the experiment. Currently, GenDeMoG's CDM supports language dependency patterns that relate single language elements to each other. In future, we will investigate if relating single language elements is sufficiently expressive for general cases, or if language dependency patterns need to be more expressive.

One could consider relying on another meta-meta-model than Ecore, such as the *Kernel Metameta-Model* (KM3) [26]. Then, GenDeMoG's model transformations could be implemented using ATL [1], QVT [8], or the VIATRA2 [15] framework. The particular choice of modeling and model transformation technologies is not essential for the design idea behind GenDeMoG. In future, it would be interesting to investigate, whether the technologies selected were the most efficient possible for the use case. Since models become very large for large artifacts, we intend to continue improving the tool's performance. Also, further work is required to integrate GenDeMoG better into the IDE.

GenDeMoG only mines cross-component dependencies so far. It is however extremely easy to extend it so that intra-component dependencies are also searched—we have made preliminary attempts in that direction. Nevertheless, we have decided to focus on the cross-component dependencies, as they pose a much more pressing issue.

All in all, we spent two man-month for implementing GenDeMoG, setting-up the experiment, and for identifying the dependency patterns. We did not meassure more precisely how much time we spent on reading documentation and reading source code. The working time necessary to apply GenDeMoG to other software systems, i.e., to identify the corresponding dependency patterns, depends on the degree of experience a developer has with development of the system under scope.

Since GenDeMoG is generic with respect to the software systems under analysis its applicability is tied to the amount of language definitions readily available. Especially GPL definitions can be reused across projects. Hence we aim for providing definitions for languages such as Groovy, JSP, and FTL.

6 Related Work

The closest work to GenDeMoG is [20], which presents the PAMOMO tool. PAMOMO uses patterns on models for defining traces or constraints between Ecore-based models. PAMOMO only allows for pattern definition, whereas GenDeMoG supports modeling entire software projects, where the used languages, components, contained artifacts, and the dependency patterns are provided together. On top of that, we provide experimental data: we assess the tools performance applying it to a mature system, and analyzing the data that it can provide. No experimental data on a realistic case study is available in [20]. It would be interesting to investigate how PAMOMO patterns scale compared to dependency patterns in our CDM.

Macromodels [29] have been proposed to capture the meaning of relationships between models. The reference key relationship captured in the dependency graph of GenDeMoG (Fig. 5) could be defined in macromodels as well. Contrary to macromodels, we do not aim at assigning different types to dependencies. We believe, plain reference key relations are the most generic dependencies. Therefore, only those should be supported by a generic tool, such as GenDeMoG.

Similarly to macromodels, GenDeMoG allows to relate models that present different views of the system to each other. We provide evidence for this in Sect. 4. Both macromodels and megamodels [27] provide a framework, which allows for manual specification of different relations. We provide automatic mining facilities to automatically reveal dependencies.

The AM3 tool (http://eclipse.org/gmt/am3/, [27]) allows capturing and handling of traceability links between models across languages. A megamodel contains links between interrelated model elements and models. Our dependency model (Fig. 5) resembles megamodels in the sense that it is noninvasive: it captures dependency information without modifying the artifacts in question. Megamodels have been designed with DSLs in mind. GenDeMoG strives to support both DSLs and GPLs, recognizing that a truly heterogeneous system, like OFBiz, contains all kinds of artifacts. Again, we extend [27], by considering a substantial realistic case study. On the other hand it would be interesting, to see whether there are any performance gains in integration of AM3 into GenDeMoG.

Mahé [30] uses megamodels in reverse engineering for an existing software system, *TopCased*. Unlike, GenDeMoG, which is generic, his tool is geared towards specific kind of patterns and platforms. Since GenDeMoG is parameterized with models it allows for a more precise and concrete software system definition.

Favre et. al. describe a scenario of reverse engineering a software system written in C and COBOL [19]. They deploy the Obeo Reverse engineering tool that treats source code as models. They create a single model for the entire software system. This model is subsequently transformed, e.g., to a visual representation of the system. The main commonality between Favre et. al., the *Reuseware* framework [22], the *MoDisco* [17] toolkit, and GenDeMoG is that code artifacts are abstracted to Ecore-based models and further transformations are applied to these models and not directly to the source code. Reuseware and MoDisco both provide a meta-model for the Java GPL. We decided to implement and deploy our own Ecore-based Java model using XText. We did not reuse MoDisco's Java model since we are interested in a model per compilation unit and MoDisco generates one model per project from the abstract syntax tree. Our Java model is grammar based, i.e., a parser is generated out of a grammar that builds a Java model independently from the Java abstract syntax tree. We did not chose EMFText's Java model [21], since it could not be used to read the OFBiz code base.

GenDeMoG and *SmartEMF* [23] both abstract XML-based DSLs to Ecore models. They both use the same case study—the OFBiz project. However, SmartEMF requires using Prolog to express inter-model dependencies, and it does not handle reference to GPLs. Also we did not focus on customizations of OFBiz applications, but more on OFBiz applications seen as component-based systems.

Mélusine [18] is a DSL composition environment, which captures the forward-development of a software system. In contrast, GenDeMoG is concerned with existing, perhaps legacy, heterogeneous software systems, where languages are already inter-related and the hidden dependencies need to be revealed.

7 Conclusion

We have presented GenDeMoG, a generic generator-generator which allows for the non-invasive description of component-based software systems and patterns which describe language structures that result in inter-component dependencies. In particular, GenDeMoG allows for the definition of dependency patterns between artifacts in a heterogeneous system, including dependencies across boundaries between GPLs and DSLs. GenDeMoG is available online, and as a generic tool, it can be readily instantiated for other projects.

Furthermore, we have conducted an experiment, applying GenDeMoG to an industrial strength, mature case study, the OFBiz project. We are not aware of any previously published experiment that characterizes adverse impact of inter-model references on architecture in systems based on multiple modeling languages. The experiment has confirmed the informal impression, that it is difficult to manipulate OFBiz components—this is likely caused by a quite tight and circular coupling between core application components. It has also confirmed that a large number of implicit dependencies exist in the system, even though, the internal component specification mechanism of OFBiz, does support explicit specification of such. This is an indicator, that, perhaps, expectations that developers would maintain such dependencies manually are futile.

Acknowledgments. We would like to thank Peter Sestoft for the help on formalizing GenDeMoG's architecture description.

References

1. ATL - A Model Transformation Technology (January 2011),
   http://www.eclipse.org/atl/
2. AtlantEcore Zoo (January 2011),
   http://www.emn.fr/z-info/atlanmod/index.php/Ecore
3. EMFText Concrete Syntax Mapper (January 2011),
   http://www.emftext.org/index.php/EMFText

4. Expression Language Documentation (January 2011),
   http://help.eclipse.org/helios/index.jsp?topic=/org.eclipse.xpand.doc/help/r10_expressions_language.html
5. FreeMarker (January 2011), http://freemarker.org/
6. Groovy - An agile dynamic language for the Java Platform (January 2011),
   http://groovy.codehaus.org/
7. JavaServer Pages Overview (January 2011),
   http://www.oracle.com/technetwork/java/overview-138580.html
8. Model To Model (M2M) (January 2011), http://www.eclipse.org/m2m/
9. MoDisco (January 2011), http://www.eclipse.org/MoDisco/
10. OFBiz The Apache Open for Business Project (January 2011),
    http://ofbiz.apache.org/
11. Package org.eclipse.emf.ecore (January 2011),
    http://download.eclipse.org/modeling/emf/emf/javadoc/2.6.0/org/eclipse/emf/ecore/package-summary.html
12. Xpand (January 2011), http://wiki.eclipse.org/Xpand
13. Xtend documentation (January 2011),
    http://help.eclipse.org/helios/index.jsp?topic=/org.eclipse.xpand.doc/help/Xtend_language.html
14. Xtext - Language Development Framework (January 2011),
    http://www.eclipse.org/Xtext/
15. Bergmann, G., Horváth, Á., Ráth, I., Varró, D., Balogh, A., Balogh, Z., Ökrös, A.: Incremental Evaluation of Model Queries over EMF Models. In: Petriu, D.C., Rouquette, N., Haugen, Ø. (eds.) MODELS 2010, Part I. LNCS, vol. 6394, pp. 76–90. Springer, Heidelberg (2010)
16. Bézivin, J., Gerbé, O.: Towards a Precise Definition of the OMG/MDA Framework. In: Proceedings of the 16th IEEE International Conference on Automated Software Engineering, ASE 2001, p. 273. IEEE Computer Society, Washington, DC, USA (2001)
17. Bruneliere, H., Cabot, J., Jouault, F., Madiot, F.: MoDisco: a Generic and Extensible Framework for Model Driven Reverse Engineering. In: Proceedings of the IEEE/ACM International Conference on Automated Software Engineering, ASE 2010, pp. 173–174. ACM, New York (2010)
18. Estublier, J., Vega, G., Ionita, A.D.: Composing Domain-Specific Languages for Wide-Scope Software Engineering Applications. In: Briand, L.C., Williams, C. (eds.) MoDELS 2005. LNCS, vol. 3713, pp. 69–83. Springer, Heidelberg (2005)
19. Favre, J.M., Musset, J.: Rétro-ingénierie dirigée par les métamodèles : Concepts, Outils, Méthodes (June 2006)
20. Guerra, E., de Lara, J., Kolovos, D.S., Paige, R.F.: Inter-modelling: From Theory to Practice. In: Petriu, D.C., Rouquette, N., Haugen, Ø. (eds.) MODELS 2010, Part I. LNCS, vol. 6394, pp. 376–391. Springer, Heidelberg (2010)
21. Heidenreich, F., Johannes, J., Seifert, M., Wende, C.: Closing the Gap between Modelling and Java. In: van den Brand, M., Gašević, D., Gray, J. (eds.) SLE 2009. LNCS, vol. 5969, pp. 374–383. Springer, Heidelberg (2010)
22. Henriksson, J., Johannes, J., Zschaler, S., Aßmann, U.: Reuseware – Adding Modularity to your Language of Choice. In: Proc. of TOOLS EUROPE 2007: Special Issue of the Journal of Object Technology (2007)
23. Hessellund, A., Czarnecki, K., Wasowski, A.: Guided Development with Multiple Domain Specific Languages. In: Engels, G., Opdyke, B., Schmidt, D.C., Weil, F. (eds.) MODELS 2007. LNCS, vol. 4735, pp. 46–60. Springer, Heidelberg (2007)
24. Howell, R.: Apache OFBiz Development: The Beginner's Tutorial. Packt Publishing (2008)
25. Jones, N.D., Gomard, C.K., Sestoft, P.: Partial Evaluation and Automatic Program Generation (1993)

26. Jouault, F., Vanhooff, B., Bruneliere, H., Doux, G., Berbers, Y., Bezivin, J.: Inter-DSL Coordination Support by Combining Megamodeling and Model Weaving. In: Proceedings of the 2010 ACM Symposium on Applied Computing, SAC 2010, pp. 2011–2018. ACM, New York (2010)
27. Jouault, F., Bézivin, J.: KM3: A DSL for Metamodel Specification. In: Gorrieri, R., Wehrheim, H. (eds.) FMOODS 2006. LNCS, vol. 4037, pp. 171–185. Springer, Heidelberg (2006)
28. Oei, J.L.H., van Hemmen, L., Falkenberg, E., Brinkkemper, S.: The Meta Model Hierarchy: A Framework for Information Systems Concepts and Techniques (1992)
29. Salay, R., Mylopoulos, J., Easterbrook, S.: Using Macromodels to Manage Collections of Related Models. In: van Eck, P., Gordijn, J., Wieringa, R. (eds.) CAiSE 2009. LNCS, vol. 5565, pp. 141–155. Springer, Heidelberg (2009)
30. Vincent, M., Jouault, F., Bruneliere, H.: Megamodeling Software Platforms: Automated Discovery of Usable Cartography from Available Metadata

Table-Driven Detection and Resolution of Operation-Based Merge Conflicts with Mirador

Stephen C. Barrett, Patrice Chalin, and Greg Butler

Concordia University, Montreal, Quebec, Canada
{ste_barr,chalin,gregb}@cs.concordia.ca

Abstract. Decision tables are a useful technique for implementing complex decision logic, and a concise communication device. Model merging is a process that can greatly benefit from the flexibility of control, rapidity of change, and understandability of purpose that tables engender.

Heretofore, users have been cut off from the inner workings of merge tools. Among its many features, our model merging tool, Mirador, opens the process of merging to inspection and manipulation. The tool's support for user modification of the decision table rules that drive its conflict detection and resolution, as well as the possibility of adding customized table conditions and actions is the focus of this paper.

Keywords: Mirador, model merging, state-based merging, operation-based merging, decision table, conflict detection, conflict resolution.

1 Introduction

To a great extent, the success of software model-driven engineering (MDE) depends on the exploitation of automation [1], and nowhere is the necessity for automation more acute than in the case of concurrent development: modeling in parallel inevitably leads to model divergence and conflicts. Consequently, there is a great need for further research into, and development of tools that perform the synchronization and merging of models [2]. Typically merging:

1. requires a great deal of knowledgable human input [3],
2. can quickly overwhelm the user with non-relevant information [3],
3. performs only minimal detection of merge conflicts [4];
4. offers inadequate choices for conflict resolution [5];
5. cannot use semantics for conflict detection or resolution [6]; and
6. exhibits counter-intuitive behavior [3].

We believe that the unique features of our model merging tool Mirador (Sect. 3), make the following theoretical and practical contributions with regard to the above issues:

- A hybrid approach to leverage state *and* operation-based merging (Sect. 3).
- A distinction between direct and indirect merge conflicts (Sect. 4).

- Techniques for visualizing change and conflict dependencies, and breaking their cycles in order to preserve operation order and merge context for less cluttered and more intuitive merge sessions (Sect. 5).
- A decision table-driven conflict detection and automatic resolution mechanism that injects semantics into the merge process (Sect. 6).
- The addition of "both" and "rename" options for conflict resolution (Sect. 6).

2 Background

Multiple developers working in parallel inevitably alter the same artifacts, necessitating reconciliation. Under MDE the artifacts to be reconciled are models, and it is up to model merging tools to bring new versions of these diverging *replicas* (i.e., initial copies of a base model) into agreement. If the common ancestor of two versions to be merged is available, the merge can be *three-way*, which, since it addresses the so-called *add-delete problem*, is used extensively [7].

2.1 Approaches to Merging

If it relies solely on a comparison of the final states of *replica-versions*, a merge tool is *state-based*. The schematic of Fig. 1a depicts the merging of *left* and *right* versions of a common source model after extraction of their differences.

These differences comprise the changes made to the replicas. They are selected for their contributions to a more complete merge, forming an update set that is eventually applied to the source version. As many of the changes as possible are assimilated by the set, with those that induce inconsistencies or conflicts being omitted. For these, special algorithms may be invoked to remove the merge errors, but, more usually, the user is asked to do so. State-based merging is in general easier to implement, and does not require change operation recording.

Rather than having to reconstruct its updates from artifact difference as a state-based tool must do, a history, or *operation-based*, tool has access to the historical traces of change operations executed in modifying the replica-versions to be merged. The operations are of a finer grain than those produced by a straightforward "diff" of artifact states.

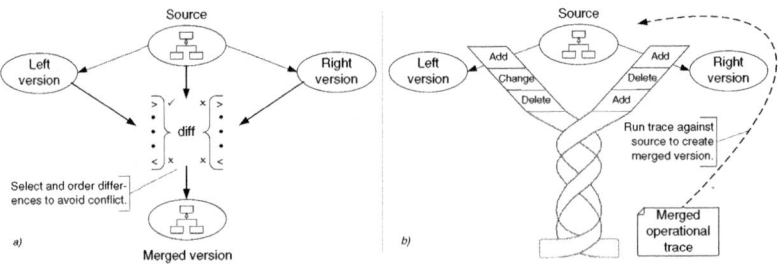

Fig. 1. State and operation-based, three-way merges

The operations from two sequences of model changes are being intertwined in Fig. 1b to create a merged *operational trace*. To avoid merge errors, operations may be included or omitted, kept in order, reordered, or interleaved. The resulting merged trace is then run against the common source to generate the merged version of the inputs. Operation-based merging makes context available to the process, but requires tight coupling with a change recording unit.

2.2 The Merge as a Transformation

Each change applied to a given model can be thought of as a function, or an operation, on that model that yields a new model. Or, alternately, as a *transformation* that takes the model and transforms it into another version of itself. A sequence of such operations then, may be functionally composed into a single transformation T. Applying T to some initial model M_I conforming to some metamodel MM_I will then produce a final model M_F conforming to some metamodel MM_F: $TM_I = (T_1 \circ \ldots \circ T_{n-1} \circ T_n)M_I = M_F$,

where T_i is one in a sequence of *subtransformations* of T.

An operation-based merge then, can be thought of as a particular path traced out on a grid of subtransformations of the left and right models [8]. The paths of this *transformation grid* that result in a consistent model are known as *weaves*. A path with an operation whose preconditions cannot be met suffers from an *inconsistency* and will fail. Weaves that terminate at the same node, but produce different outcomes are in *conflict*.

A node that hosts the same model for every one of its weaves is conflict-free and said to be *single-valued*. On the other hand, a node that hosts more than one model is in conflict and said to be *multiple-valued*. The first conflict encountered will lay out a border of multiple-valued nodes across the transformation grid called the *frontier set* [8]. It is the boundary at which operation-based merging can no longer effortlessly acquire conflict-free subtransformations.

It is often possible to re-route around inconsistencies. Conflicts however, being semantic in nature, must be resolved by: arbitrarily picking one change over the other, employing heuristics, or appealing to the user. The further the frontier set can be pushed out from the origin, the later such merge decisions can be made, and the more context there will be to make them.

Contradictory operations are at the root of conflicts, and are manifest as non-commutative operations. If subtransformations T_1 and T_2 commute globally, i.e., $T_1 \circ T_2 = T_2 \circ T_1$, or locally when operating on a removed section S, i.e., $(T_1 \circ T_2)S = (T_2 \circ T_1)S$, then the operations will not conflict. Checking operation commutativity then, is an appropriate way of detecting merge conflicts [9].

3 Merge Workflow in Mirador

Mirador is a stand-alone Java application being developed at Concordia University for the merging of software models. The tool takes a hybrid tack to the problem of merging, using state-based techniques in the front part of its workflow, and transitions to operation-based activities for the back part. It is these later phases that concern us most, but all will be described briefly.

Model Normalization and Denormalization. The first thing Mirador does is to decouple itself from the originating modeling tool or change recording unit [10]. It does this by converting all input models to a state-based, *normal-form*, which currently is Ecore. A denormalizing phase performs the reverse conversion on the merged outcome of the workflow.

Model Differencing. Next, a differencing calculation determines how each replica-version differs from its base model, identifying what elements have changed, and in what way. One difference is obtained between the base model and its left version, and another between the base and its right version. This is in preparation for transitioning back to operation-based activity, and is in contrast to the classic state-based approach, which performs a difference *between* the two replica-versions.

To make differences first class artifacts, we extend Ecore with the difference metamodel (MMD) of Cicchetti et al. [11], with two minor modifications. From each `ENamedElement` class of Ecore an `Altered` (instead of `Changed`), `Added`, and `Deleted` class are derived. Thus class `EClass` becomes the supertype for MMD classes `AlteredEClass`, `DeletedEClass` and `AddedEClass`. We also add a copy constructor to the `Altered` classes to ease building the difference model.

Model Comparison. A state-based comparison of the models to be merged is then made, the intent being to establish correspondence between their elements [12]. Identifiers can only partially determined this, as elements added separately to the versions will not possess comparable IDs. Some other model element *matching strategy* must be used. Mirador supports up to seven such strategies—including two user-defined ones—which may be selectively loaded at start-up time [13].

Operation Extraction. To bridge from state-based to operation-based work requires knowing what change operations were executed in modifying the replicas. Unfortunately, this information is obliterated by the merger's state-based front end, and must be reconstructed.

The difference metamodel makes this a fairly straightforward process. Each `Added` or `Deleted` element in a difference model results in an add or a delete operation, respectively. The `Altered` elements however, require a comparison of the updated element with its original in order to see exactly how they differ, and then the creation of an alter operation for each difference noted.

Conflict Detection. The order of element changes, and the conflicts between them are identified with the *before(a, b)* predicate where operation a must come before operation b. A conflict exists if *before(a, b)* = *before(b, a)* = *true*.

A two part decision table is used to determine the predicate outcome. First, changes to the same model (*same-side changes*) are tested only for ordering, as changes derived from model state cannot be in conflict. Then changes to opposite models (*cross-side changes*) are tested for ordering *and* conflicts. This application of *before* produces a partially ordered collection of individual and conflicting pairs of changes—a merged trace, or transformation, of change operations.

Any freedom in the ordering is exploited to move conflicts as close to the end of the transformation as permitted by the inter-dependencies. Syntactic conflicts that consist of operations that are not actually in contradiction (e.g., deletes of the same model element) are filtered out by rules of the cross-side decision table. This is a form of semantic conflict detection [9], because it considers both the meaning of an update, and the effect the update will have on the targeted item.

Conflict Resolution and Merging. This phase uses another decision table to attempt to resolve any conflicts contained in the trace of change operation received from the preceding phase. All changes and conflicts, whether resolved or not, are presented to the user in the form of a *merge plan*—a visualization of the merged model transformation, the recommendations of which the user is free to change.

The plan is an ordered list, so application of its changes to the base model is progressive, and therefore, intuitive. Also, since conflicts have been placed as far down the list as dependencies allow, any manual resolution occurs in the context of the most complete merge attainable given the conflicts. Finally, unlike other tools, which always treat conflicting changes as being mutually exclusive, Mirador can recommend—if the semantics of its updates warrant it—that *both* sides of a conflict be executed.

Model Patching. Applying a change of the merge plan effectively transforms, or patches, a copy of the base model with the change. The changes must be executed sequentially, but can be applied individually or en masse. Applying the entire plan will patch the base model up to the first unresolved conflict, skipping over any rejected changes. Application will also halt on an inconsistency error, which can occur if a change's precondition is among the rejected changes. Each application updates a view of the merged model.

4 Conflicts and the Change Plane

In Figure 2 we orient the transformation grid of [8] to resemble the classic merge diamond, with nodes representing models, and edges primitive change operations, or subtransformations. The changes along the axes comprise transformations T_L and T_R, which transform the base model M_B into left and right versions of itself. To follow a path from M_B to another node is to execute the sequence of changes that lie on the path, transforming M_B at each step. Hence, each node hosts a set of models produced by all the paths that reach it. We term this surface of subtransformations and potential models, the *change plane*. The populated plane of Fig. 2 will serve as a running example for the paper.

The essence of merging is to blend the subtransformations of the change plane into a single transformation incorporating as many changes from both sides as possible, which when applied to M_B yield a consistent model. Absent any conflicts, T_L and T_R may simply be combined in whole. Otherwise a final transformation must be cobbled together subtransformation by subtransformation, with moving forward over an edge being to *accept* the change the edge represents, and not traversing an edge being to *reject* its change.

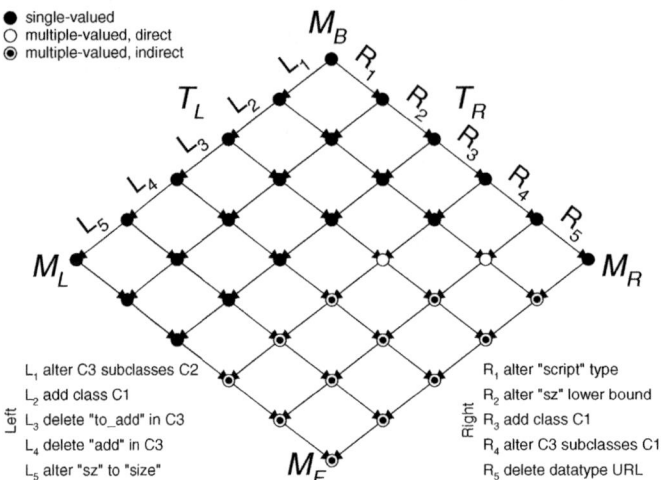

Fig. 2. Change plane overlaid with subtransformations of left and right replica-versions

Nodes marked by solid black dots are single-valued—the same model is produced by whatever path is followed to reach them (disallowing backward travel)—and are without conflict. The rest are multiple-valued, and in conflict. But not all conflicts are created equal, prompting us to make a distinction between *direct* and *indirect* multiple-valued types.

If the subtransformations that *terminate* at a node do not commute, we say that their operations are in direct conflict. Suppose model matching determines that changes L_2 and R_3 create the *same* element. If the added classes are not identical, the operations will not commute and will be in direct conflict. Then, L_3 and R_3, which *do* commute, will conflict, because the "upstream" L_2, R_3 pair cause node L_3, R_3 to host two models, making it (indirectly) multiple-valued.

In fact, every node reached by a path that passes through a direct conflict node will suffer from its conflict. This spillover is what produces the frontier set: the upper tier of multiple-valued nodes running across the plane. A direct conflict is analogous to that of the keystone in an arch: pull the keystone, and the other stones fall; resolve a direct conflict, and its indirect ones vanish. This analogy tells us that instead of 14 conflicts, we need only resolve the 2 *key conflicts*.

5 Conflict Matrix and Change Partitioning

The change plane uncovers conflicts, but not the dependencies needed to order change operations. That is the purpose of the techniques of this section. Unavoidably, references are made to decision table concepts and specifics not to be introduced until the next section. We ask the reader's indulgence.

5.1 Visualizing Relations with the Conflict Matrix

A tabular layout of the relations between change operations is helpful for determining execution order. Applying *before* to the changes of the running example in Fig. 3 yields the accompanying *conflict matrix*. Where a < or ∧ points to which of a cell's operations is to receive *positional preference*. Going against the wedge, the third row reads, "L_3 is preferred to L_4," as does going down the third column. The notation makes the symmetry along the diagonal of the matrix evident. A careful comparison will reveal that the conflicts of the matrix (marked by '×') coincide with the direct conflicts of the change plane.

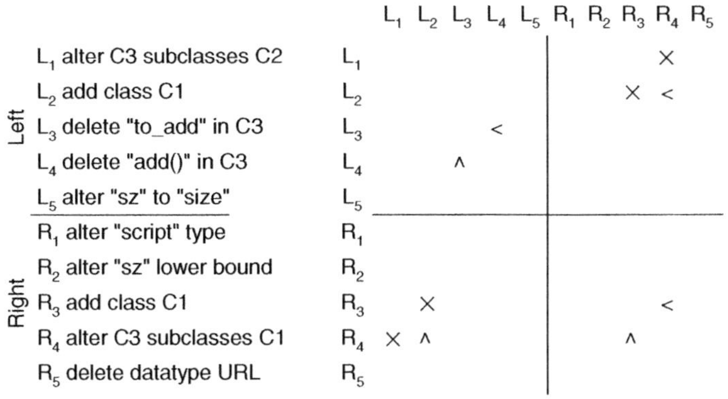

			L_1	L_2	L_3	L_4	L_5	R_1	R_2	R_3	R_4	R_5
Left	L_1 alter C3 subclasses C2	L_1									×	
	L_2 add class C1	L_2								×	<	
	L_3 delete "to_add" in C3	L_3				<						
	L_4 delete "add()" in C3	L_4		∧								
	L_5 alter "sz" to "size"	L_5										
Right	R_1 alter "script" type	R_1										
	R_2 alter "sz" lower bound	R_2										
	R_3 add class C1	R_3	×								<	
	R_4 alter C3 subclasses C1	R_4	× ∧							∧		
	R_5 delete datatype URL	R_5										

Fig. 3. Conflict matrix after application of *before* predicate to all element pairs

Quadrants II and IV depict same-side changes, and quadrants I and III, cross-side ones. Change L_3 deletes the parameter to_add from operation add(), which is in turn deleted by L_4. Because the parameter is contained by the operation, this delete-delete pair matches rule 3 of Table 1. The rule stipulates that the inner delete operation (L_3) must be done before the outer one (L_4).

Since same-side changes cannot be in conflict, there is no ambiguity over what *before* means in quadrants II and IV: an operation must come before another if it satisfies a precondition (e.g., executing L_4 first would cause L_3 to fail for lack of a target). If no decision table rules are asserted for a change pair, there are no preconditions to satisfy, and the operations may be performed in any order.

Across models the meaning is not so clear. For instance, changes L_1 and R_4 attempt to give class C3 different superclasses. Assuming single inheritance, the operations clash. But there is no a priori reason for L_1 to come before R_4, or R_4 before L_1. Still, to flag a conflict, both must assert a preference. The answer is to write the cross-side rules of *before* to take a selfish "me first" (or "last" in the case of an overwrite) attitude. In this case, rule 7 of Table 2 claims priority for L_1 in one direction, and for R_4 in the other direction, flagging a conflict.

Changes L_2 and R_3 conflict by rule 1, because the added classes are deemed to be the *same* model element (albeit with different IDs). If no conflict were raised, the model would end up with two classes of the same name. This *duplicate element problem* is a common occurrence among tools that rely solely on IDs for matching. Rule 7 also finds L_5 and R_2 to be in conflict for altering the same element, but rule 4 of Table 3 discovers that they alter different properties, and therefore causes *both* changes of the conflict to be executed.

5.2 Breaking Cycles with Conflict Partitioning

The dependencies uncovered during conflict detection (e.g., Fig. 4a) can make determining the execution order of change operations difficult, or if cycles are involved, impossible. To remedy this, *conflict partitioning* gathers conflicting changes into collectively exhaustive and mutually exclusive blocks.

This is easily accomplished by: 1) putting each pair of conflicting operations into a block with a double-headed arrow between them, 2) putting non-conflicting operations into their own block, and 3) adding single-headed arrows between blocks to reflect the ordering of the changes they contain as dictated by the conflict matrix. This procedure produces the partitioning of Fig. 4b.

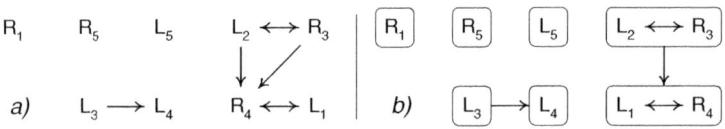

Fig. 4. *a)* Change dependencies, *b)* partitioned into mutually exclusive conflict blocks

Dependency cycles like in Fig. 5a require additional steps. Partitioning by conflict produces the blocks of Fig. 5b. The arrows signify that the upper conflict blocks are dependent on the bottom conflict—they require either L_2 or R_2 as a target for their operations. The transitive R_1–R_3–R_2 relation now makes the L_1–L_2 relation superfluous, so it may be discarded.

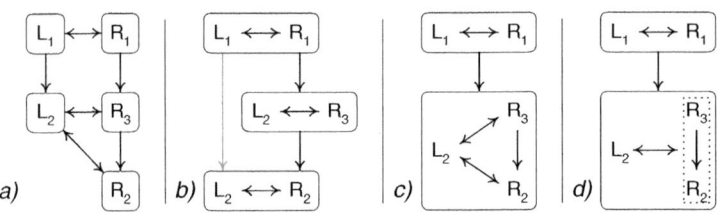

Fig. 5. *a)* Original change dependencies, *b)* non-exclusive conflicts, *c)* exclusive conflicts using a composite block, *d)* with conflicts collapsed

Though exhaustive, this partitioning is not mutually exclusive (L_2 is in two blocks). Putting the changes of the troubled blocks into a single composite block, as in Fig. 5c, fixes the non-exclusivity at the expense of reconstructing the cycle. It is broken by *collapsing* the conflicts between individual operations into a single conflict between *dependency chains*. In Fig. 5d the chain of R_3–R_2 is treated as a single operation. Collapsing conflicts lowers merge complexity at a slight loss in resolution choices—the closed nature of dependency chains precludes selecting certain combinations of operations. Usually however, the choices lost are illegal (e.g., accepting L_2 over R_3, *and* R_2 over L_2), and will not be missed.

6 Mirador Decision Tables

Decision tables provide an overview of control flow that is easy to comprehend, making for flexible and rapid program changes [14]. In Mirador, tables direct conflict detection (i.e., *before* predicate evaluation) and resolution. Three user levels are supported: the turnkey user who relies on the built-in tables; the motivated user who tweaks table rules; and the practitioner of "domain specific merging" who replaces the tables entirely with their own set.

6.1 Table Specification

Rather than use its built-in tables, Mirador can load tables from user-specified files. One such file is shown in Table 1. The main components are: conditions, actions, and rules. The names of the [Conditions] section correspond to functions to be evaluated, and those of the [Actions] section to procedures to be executed. [Table] simply provides a name and delimits tables in the same file.

Each column of desired condition outcomes forms a rule. Rules are evaluated from left to right, and condition results from top to bottom. Evaluation ends when a pattern is matched, or the rules have been exhausted. Conditions constitute the table's domain, restricting these to predicates gives a value range of *true* ('Y'), *false* ('N'), or *don't care* ('-'). This is a limited-entry type table, so the rule mask technique may be used for pattern matching [15].

A rule selects a condition for testing by placing a 'Y' or an 'N' opposite the condition's name. Conditions with a '-' are ignored. To satisfy a rule, all of its tested conditions must return the expected value. Once satisfied, a rule fires, executing the procedures of the [Actions] section directly beneath the rule, in numerical order. Actions not to be executed are marked with a '0'.

6.2 Conflict Detection and the *before* Predicate

To test change commutativity Lippe and van Oosterom define a *before* predicate [8]. Applied to two changes, the test imposes an ordering if one operation must come before the other. While adequate in preventing inconsistencies between operations on the same replica, *before* is lacking when it comes to working across replicas. This is because it is often the *second* operation of an pair that has the last word, so to speak, on the outcome. For example, if two changes rename the same (i.e., matched) attribute, the second change will prevail, making perhaps an *after* predicate more appropriate.

Rather than add a new predicate, we choose to keep the original one, but extend its semantics somewhat. Instead of implying precedence, we interpret *before* to mean that an operation has a *preferred position* with respect to another operation, or that it has a contrary purpose. This interpretation avoids same-side inconsistencies, but also raises cross-side conflicts when appropriate.

Table 1 is used by Mirador to test same-side changes for ordering. All pairings of same-side operations, except the mirror pairs, are evaluated against this table's

Table 1. Decision table for evaluating the *before* predicate of same-side model changes

```
[Table]
before_same     // Evaluates before(op1, op2) for same side change operations.
                //             +------------- Element is added to a container that itself is added.
                //             | +----------- Added class element is target of an added reference.
                //             | | +--------- Element is deleted from a container that is deleted.
                //             | | | +------- Altered class subtypes added class.
                //             | | | | +----- Catch-all rule, invokes linked decision table.
                //             | | | | |
[Conditions]    // Rule#  1   2 3 4 5
on_same_side                -   - - - N
op1_is_add                  Y   Y - Y -
op1_is_delete               -   - Y - -
op1_is_alter                -   - - - -
op1_is_class                -   Y - Y -
op2_is_add                  Y   Y - - -
op2_is_delete               -   - Y - -
op2_is_alter                -   - - Y -
op2_is_reference            -   Y - - -
op2_is_class                -   - - Y -
op1_contains_op2            Y   - - - -
op2_contains_op1            -   - Y - -
op2_is_ref_to_op1           -   Y - - -
op2_subclasses_op1          -   - - Y -
aux_match                   -   - - - Y  // Invokes auxiliary table, before cross.

[Actions]
do_true                     1   1 1 1 1  // Put op1 before op2.
```

Table 2. Decision table for evaluating the *before* predicate of cross-side model changes

```
[Table]
before_cross    // Evaluates before(op1, op2) for cross side change operations.

[Conditions]    // Rule#  1 2 3 4 5 6 7 8 9 10 11 12 13 14 15 16 17 18 19 20
elements_match            Y Y Y Y N N Y Y Y -  -  -  -  -  -  -  -  Y  N  -
op1_is_add                Y Y - - - - Y N - Y  Y  -  -  -  -  Y  -  Y  -  -
op1_is_delete             - - Y - Y - - N Y -  -  Y  Y  -  Y  -  Y  -  -  -
op1_is_alter              - - - - Y Y - N -  -  -  -  -  -  Y  -  -  -  -  -
op1_is_class              - - - - - - - - -  -  -  -  -  -  -  Y  -  -  -  -
op1_is_reference          - - - - - - - - -  -  -  -  -  -  -  -  -  Y  -  Y
op1_updates_match         - - - - Y - - - -  -  -  -  -  -  -  -  -  -  -  -
op2_is_add                Y - Y - - - N Y Y  -  Y  -  -  -  Y  -  -  Y  -  -
op2_is_delete             - Y - - - Y - N -  -  Y  -  Y  -  Y  -  Y  Y  -  -
op2_is_alter              - - - Y Y - Y N -  -  -  -  -  Y  -  -  -  -  -  -
op2_is_class              - - - - - - - - -  -  -  -  -  -  -  -  Y  -  -  -
op2_is_reference          - - - - - - - - -  -  -  -  -  -  -  Y  -  -  Y  -
op2_updates_match         - - - Y - - - - -  -  -  -  -  -  -  -  -  -  -  -
op1_contains_op2          - - - - - - - - Y  -  Y  Y  Y  -  -  -  -  -  -  -
op2_contains_op1          - - - - - - - - -  Y  -  -  -  Y  -  -  -  -  -  -
op1_is_ref_to_op2         - - - - - - - - -  -  -  -  -  -  -  Y  -  -  -  -
op2_is_ref_to_op1         - - - - - - - - -  -  -  -  -  -  -  -  Y  -  -  -
names_are_same            - - - - - - - - -  -  -  -  -  -  -  -  -  -  Y  -
containers_match          Y - - - - - - - -  -  -  -  -  -  -  -  -  -  Y  -

[Actions]
do_true                   1 1 1 1 1 1 1 1 1  1  1  1  1  1  1  1  1  1  1  0
do_false                  0 0 0 0 0 0 0 0 0  0  0  0  0  0  0  0  0  0  0  1
```

rules. If a pair of operations happen to satisfy a rule, the sole action, do_true will return a true value indicating that $op1$ claims positional preference over $op2$.

Rule 1 ensures that $op1$ will be executed before $op2$ and prevent an inconsistency, if the element added by the first change contains the element added by the second. Similarly, rule 2 fires if the class being added by $op1$ is a target of the reference added by $op2$. Rule 3 is effectively the reverse of rule 1: $op1$ is before $op2$ if both targets are being deleted and the first's target is contained by the second's. Rule 4 was added to handle the subclassing of a newly added class, as in the running example. Note that there is no need to test on_same_side for these rules, because it is implied by the nature of the tested conditions.

As the right-most rule is the last one tested, it can be used as a default, or catch-all. Thus, all cross-side operation pairs will fire rule 5, and execute condition aux_match, which is not a condition at all, but a jump to an auxiliary table containing the cross-side rules (Table 2). This *table chaining* makes it possible to modularize the tables, and can be extended to any depth.

6.3 Conflict Resolution

Once the change operations have been extracted from the difference models and arranged into a single trace, the models are essentially merged. All that remains is to resolve their key conflicts. The rules for doing this are found in Table 3.

The add C1 conflict (L_2, R_3) of Fig 3 is resolved by rule 2, which finds through the updates_are_equal condition that all properties of the added elements are equivalent, so which change to execute is arbitrary—the settable do_master action makes the choice. There is no rule to handle the alter C3 conflict (L_1, R_4), so it matches the catch-all rule 6 which returns *false*, signifying that a user decision is required. Rule 1, though not invoked by the example, is interesting: it will first rename the elements involved in a name clash of non-overlapping

Table 3. Decision table for resolving cross-side model conflicts

```
[Table]
resolve         // Executes resolve(conflict_block)

[Conditions]   // Rule#   1  2  3  4  5  6
conflict_is_simple         Y  Y  Y  Y  Y  -
conflicts_match            N  -  -  -  -  -
left_is_add                Y  Y  -  -  -  -
left_is_delete             -  -  Y  -  -  -
left_is_alter              -  -  -  Y  Y  -
right_is_add               Y  Y  -  -  -  -
right_is_delete            -  -  Y  -  -  -
right_is_alter             -  -  -  Y  Y  -
updates_are_equal          -  Y  -  -  Y  -
update_same_property       -  -  -  N  -  -
conflict_with_name         Y  -  -  -  -  -

[Actions]
do_rename                  1  0  0  0  0  0   // Rename conflicting objects
do_master                  0  1  1  0  1  0   // Execute master side change
do_left                    2  0  0  1  0  0   // Execute left side change
do_right                   3  0  0  2  0  0   // Execute right side change
do_false                   0  0  0  0  0  1   // Signify conflict is unresolved
```

changes before executing both changes. This is appropriate when two references of a class have the same role name, but target different classes.

After auto-resolution Mirador rearranges the change trace to, in effect, push out the frontier set. Then a merge plan like that of Fig. 6 is presented to the user for final approval. From here it is possible to modify automatic merge actions, execute all resolved changes, observe their effects on the merge (not shown), and resolve conflicts in the context of an almost fully merged model. Choices are made by highlighting a conflict, and pressing the "Left" or "Right" button. The user may also "Accept" or "Reject" individual changes. "Apply" will execute all changes up to and including the highlighted one. Execution stops if either an unresolved conflict or an error is encountered.

Apply Desired Changes and Resolve Conflicts				
Left Model Change Operations		Right Model Change Operations	Accept	Reject
to_add {deleted} (vKKxN_04,L)	>	script {altered} (vKKxN_E4 ,R)		
add {deleted} (vKKxN_E3,L)	<		Left	Right
	>	URL {deleted} (vKKxN_24,R)		
[[C1 {added} (_3Aq5_BC,L)]]	<	[[C1 {added} (I5_AA_BC,R)]]	Apply	Undo
[[sz {altered} (vKKxN_C4 ,L)]]	<>	[[sz {altered} (vKKxN_C4 ,R)]]		
[[C3 {altered} (vKKxN_63 ,L)]]	X	[[C3 {altered} (vKKxN_63 ,R)]]		

| Help | | | Finish | Cancel |

Fig. 6. Change operations in a merge plan after partitioning and auto-resolution

The presentation is primitive, but the merged operational trace of the running example (prior to change application) can be discerned in the figure: the deletion of to_add (L_3) occurs before deletion of its method add (L_4); the alteration of class C3 (R_4) is placed after the creation of class C1 (R_3) on which it depends, dragging its conflicting change (L_1) with it. Three conflicts can be seen at the bottom of the plan. The first (L_2, R_3), since its changes accomplish the same thing, has been arbitrarily resolved to the left. The changes of the second (L_5, R_2) alter the same element, but in a non-conflicting way, so both are selected for execution. And the third (L_1, R_4) is still conflicted over which should be the supertype of class C3—C2 or C1.

The middle column of symbols indicate the current status of the changes:

```
Single and conflicting changes
    <    (>)   - execute left (right) change
    <<  (>>)  - left (right) change executed
    !          - error executing change
Single changes only
    X          - change rejected
Conflicting changes only
    < >        - execute both changes
    << >>      - both changes executed
    X          - unresolved conflict
```

Through use of a configuration file, merges may be done without any interaction, save pressing the "Finish" button. This will match the elements, auto-resolve conflicts, order changes, and apply non-conflicting changes to the base model. The tool may also be run from the command line, sans GUI, to support what Bendix et al. refer to as *batch merging* [16].

6.4 Customizing Rules, Conditions, and Actions

Making decision table definitions accessible opens Mirador's conflict handling to modification through rule changes. It is also possible to add new table conditions or actions. The former takes adding a new `TableCondition` object in which the `testCondition()` method is overridden, while the latter involves a new `TableAction` that overrides `doAction()`. The objects must then be registered with the appropriate decision table, and provided with labels to identify them to the parser. Below are code fragments to illustrate both customizations.

```
/** Decision condition to test for changes on same side of merge. */
public TableCondition on_same_side_ =
   new TableCondition("on_same_side", new ConditionTest() {
   @Override public boolean testCondition(Object... objs) {
     return ((AtomicChangeOp) objs[0]).getMergeSide()
         == ((AtomicChangeOp) objs[1]).getMergeSide();
   }
});

/** Decision action simply sets return code of result object to true. */
public TableAction do_true_ = new TableAction("do_true") {
   @Override public boolean doAction(ActionSet steps, Object... objs) {
     steps.setMergeSide(MergeSide.BASE);
     steps.setResult(Tristate.TRUE);
     return true;
   }
};
```

7 Related Work

State-based merging relies on static models, and is exemplified by Unison [4] and Rational Rose, where operation-based tools like IceCube [17] analyze dynamic traces of replica changes. Renewed interest in operation-based merging is typified by Koegel et al. [18], and Schmidt et al. who argue for transaction based merging [19].

Lippe and van Oosterom put forth operation-based merging as a means for managing changes to object-oriented databases [8]. They described a merge as a weave of primitives in a transformation grid with two types of nodes, related operation commutation to conflict detection, and proposed three merge algorithms that hinged on the use of a *before* predicate. In Mirador we have reorient their grid, and add another dimension for matching strategies. We make a distinction between direct and indirect multiple-valued nodes, with the former identifying key conflicts. We also clarify the definition of *before* so as not to miss conflicts.

Lippe and van Oosterom did not concern themselves with model element matching, and others like Pottinger and Bernstein take it as a given [20]. But properly matching elements is vital to successful merging. Many tools like Rational Software Architect insist on unique element identifiers [3]. More flexible ideas are offered by Xing and Stroulia who heuristically measure name and structural similarity for matching [5], or Kolovos who furnishes a general comparison language [21] for which Mirador has a specialized evaluator. SiDiff, a similarity-based differencing engine described by Schmidt and Gloetzner [22], offers a framework for building comparison tools, which, like Mirador, can use multiple strategies to compare models, but only one per type.

Another framework Kompose, consists of a metamodel specific matching portion, and a generic merging potion [23]. The merge operation is state-based, and has little overlap with our work. Its conflicts must be explicitly resolved by the user, where Mirador can recognize and resolve conflicts. The matching operation, which relies on specialized signatures of element type and equality tests, has the potential to use different matching strategies, but only one per type, whereas we support up to seven. Kompose makes the common assumption that its way of matching is the *only* way, and as with most tools, cannot be overridden.

8 Conclusion and Future Work

This paper has presented an abbreviated overview of the Mirador model merging tool's workflow. Its hybrid nature, reliance on a difference metamodel, and use of multiple matching strategies were touched upon. Details of its decision table mechanism with respect to conflict detection and resolution were provided, and illustrated with a running example. Explanations of its use of several conceptual devices—change plane, conflict matrix, and conflict partition—were also given.

Our work mitigates the merging difficulties enumerated in the introduction (issue number in parenthesis). The necessity for large amounts of human input (1) stems from the tool asking the user to step in whenever difficulty is encountered, which can inundate the user with irrelevant details (2). Mirador:

- Resolves many conflicts. The ability to rapidly enhance decision tables with rules, and, if need be, new conditions and actions increases this potential.
- Reduces the number of conflicts through recognition of key conflicts, and the collapsing of conflicts in cycles.
- Orders changes to make context available and merging more intuitive.

Poor element matching can lead to surprising merge outcomes (6), and inappropriate matches result in missed or false conflicts (3). Mirador:

- Opens element matching up for user inspection and manipulation.
- Employs up to seven matching strategies, in order to make the best pairings.
- Allows customized scripts and similarity evaluators to improve matching.

Because semantics are not taken into account (5), a tool may miss more involved conflicts or raise false ones. The same deficiency also precludes their automatic resolution, which in the case of a false conflict, may mean executing both changes, a choice most tools do not provide (4). Mirador:

- Detects and resolves conflicts through decision tables, which can take semantics into account, and are amenable to modification.
- Uses semantics to filter out syntactic pseudo conflicts.
- Automatically resolves five classes of conflicts.

- Adds "both" and "rename" to the normal conflict resolution options of "left," "right," "accept" and "reject."

Work remains to be done on Mirador: normalization only supports Ecore and Fujaba models; the change application panel is crude, and batch mode reports rudimentary; the decision tables are still being refined with new rules, conditions, and actions as situations are discovered; and the sometimes subtle interaction of rules points to a need for tool support, or the use of a rule engine like the Epsilon Merging Language [24]. Replacement of the Ecore based normal-form by UML2 [25] will allow Mirador to merge model types other than class diagrams.

References

1. Selic, B.: The pragmatics of model-driven development. IEEE Softw. 20(5), 19–25 (2003)
2. Schmidt, D.C.: Guest editor's introduction: Model-driven engineering. IEEE Comput. 39(2), 25–31 (2006)
3. Barrett, S., Chalin, P., Butler, G.: Model merging falls short of software engineering needs. In: MoDSE 2008: Internat. Workshop on Model-Driven Software Evolution (April 2008)
4. Pierce, B.C., Vouillon, J.: What's in Unison? A formal specification and reference implementation of a file synchronizer. Technical Report MS-CIS-03-36, University of Pennsylvania, Philadelphia, PA, USA (February 2004), http://www.cis.upenn.edu/~bcpierce/papers/unisonspec.pdf
5. Xing, Z., Stroulia, E.: UMLDiff: an algorithm for object-oriented design differencing. In: ASE 2005: 20th IEEE/ACM Internat. Conf. on Automated Software Engineering, pp. 54–65. ACM, New York (November 2005)
6. Cicchetti, A., Ruscio, D.D., Pierantonio, A.: Managing model conflicts in distributed development. In: Busch, C., Ober, I., Bruel, J.-M., Uhl, A., Völter, M. (eds.) MODELS 2008. LNCS, vol. 5301, pp. 311–325. Springer, Heidelberg (2008)
7. Mens, T.: A state-of-the-art survey on software merging. IEEE Trans. on Softw. Eng. 28(5), 449–462 (2002)
8. Lippe, E., van Oosterom, N.: Operation-based merging. ACM SIGSOFT Softw. Eng. Notes 17(5), 78–87 (1992)
9. Saito, Y., Shapiro, M.: Replication: Optimistic approaches. Technical Report HPL-2002-33, Hewlett-Packard Laboratories (March 2002), http://www.hpl.hp.com/techreports/2002/HPL-2002-33.pdf
10. Barrett, S., Chalin, P., Butler, G.: Decoupling operation-based merging from model change recording. In: ME 2010: Internat. Workshop on Models and Evolution (October 2010)
11. Cicchetti, A., Ruscio, D.D., Pierantonio, A.: A metamodel independent approach to difference representation. Journal of Object Technology 6(9), 165–185 (2007), http://www.jot.fm/contents/issue_2007_10/paper9.html
12. Treude, C., Berlik, S., Wenzel, S., Kelter, U.: Difference computation of large models. In: ESEC-FSE 2007: 6th Joint Meeting of the European Software Engineering Conference and the ACM SIGSOFT Symposium on the Foundations of Software Engineering, pp. 295–304. ACM, New York (September 2007)

13. Barrett, S., Butler, G., Chalin, P.: Mirador: a synthesis of model matching strategies. In: IWMCP 2010: Internat. Workshop on Model Comparison in Practice (July 2010)
14. Pooch, U.W.: Translation of decision tables. ACM Comput. Surv. 6(2), 125–151 (1974)
15. King, P.J.H.: Conversion of decision tables to computer programs by rule mask techniques. Commun. ACM 9(11), 796–801 (1966)
16. Bendix, L., Koegel, M., Martin, A.: The case for batch merge of models issues and challenges. In: ME 2010: Internat. Workshop on Models and Evolution (October 2010)
17. Kermarrec, A.M., Rowstron, A., Shapiro, M., Druschel, P.: The IceCube approach to the reconciliation of divergent replicas. In: PODC 2001: 20th Annual ACM Sympos. on Principles of Distributed Computing, pp. 210–218. ACM, New York (August 2001)
18. Koegel, M., Helming, J., Seyboth, S.: Operation-based conflict detection and resolution. In: CVSM 2009: Workshop on Comparison and Versioning of Software Models, pp. 43–48. IEEE Computer Society, Los Alamitos (2009)
19. Schmidt, M., Wenzel, S., Kehrer, T., Kelter, U.: History-based merging of models. In: CVSM 2009: Internat. Workshop on Comparison and Versioning of Software Models, pp. 13–18. IEEE Computer Society, Los Alamitos (May 2009)
20. Pottinger, R.A., Bernstein, P.A.: Merging models based on given correspondences. In: VLDB 2003: 29th Internat. Conf. on Very Large Data Bases, VLDB Endowment, pp. 862–873 (September 2003)
21. Kolovos, D.S.: Establishing correspondences between models with the epsilon comparison language. In: Paige, R.F., Hartman, A., Rensink, A. (eds.) ECMDA-FA 2009. LNCS, vol. 5562, pp. 146–157. Springer, Heidelberg (2009)
22. Schmidt, M., Gloetzner, T.: Constructing difference tools for models using the SiDiff framework. In: ICSE 2008: Companion of the 30th Internat. Conf. on Software Engineering, pp. 947–948. ACM, New York (May 2008)
23. Fleurey, F., Baudry, B., France, R., Ghosh, S.: A generic approach for automatic model composition. In: MoDELS 2007: 11th Internat. Workshop on Aspect-Oriented Modeling, Berlin, Germany, pp. 7–15. Springer, Heidelberg (September 2007)
24. Kolovos, D.S., Rose, L., Paige, R.F., Polack, F.A.: The Epsilon Book. Website of the Epsilon subproject of the Eclipse GMT project (2010),
http://www.eclipse.org/gmt/epsilon/doc/book
25. UML2. Website of the UML2 subproject of the Eclipse MDT project (May 2010),
http://www.fujaba.de/home.html

Improving Naming and Grouping in UML

Antonio Vallecillo

GISUM/Atenea Research Group, Universidad de Málaga, Spain
av@lcc.uma.es

Abstract. The package is one of the basic UML concepts. It is used both to group model elements and to provide a namescope for its members. However, combining these two tasks into a single UML concept can become not only too restrictive but also a source of subtle problems. This paper presents some improvements to the current UML naming and grouping schemata, using the ideas proposed in the reference model of Open Distributed Processing (ODP). The extensions try to maintain backwards compatibility with the existing UML concepts, while allowing more flexible grouping and naming mechanisms.

1 Introduction

The UML [1] is probably the most widely used modeling notation nowadays. It is currently applied for the specification of many different kinds of systems and is supported by a wide range of tools. However, UML is far from being a perfect notation. It has grown too much to accommodate too many concepts and languages. The need for backwards compatibility with previous versions, and the OMG's design-by-committee approach to standardization have not helped much either. This has resulted in a large, complex and brittle metamodel for UML, which represents a challenge for all its stakeholders—in particular for its users and for the UML tool builders. More importantly, some of its basic concepts were probably developed with some restricted usages in mind. The problem is that they are now challenged by the new MDE requirements, which are stretching these concepts beyond their original intent.

In this paper we are concerned with the limitations of one of the basic UML concepts, the Package, which is used in UML to group model elements and to provide a namescope for its members. Although combining these two goals into a single UML concept can be appropriate in some cases, in general its proves to be too restrictive for organizing model elements in a flexible way because it ties elements with names, and names with packages. Thus, the UML grouping mechanism only allows non-overlapping classifications of model elements, and there is no easy way to implement federated modeling [2]. Furthermore, the two operations associated to these objectives (PackageMerge and PackageImport) become jeopardized by the limitations of UML packaging. For instance, name resolution does not work well under the presence of PackageImport, something critical in the case of OCL expressions and constraints [3]. Several semantic problems have also been reported for PackageMerge in [4,5].

This paper proposes some improvements of the current UML naming and grouping mechanisms, trying to respect backwards compatibility with the existing concepts. Import and merge operations will also be re-defined using the new concepts presented in this paper. Our proposal is based on existing international standards of Open Distributed Processing (ODP) [6,7]. ODP offers a set of mature and well-defined concepts and solutions for coping with the inherent complexity of the specification of large distributed applications. In particular, we base our proposal on the ODP Naming standard [8], and on the organizational concepts defined in the ODP foundations [6, Part 2].

The structure of this paper is as follows. After this introduction, section 2 provides a summary of the Package element and the import and merge relationships defined in UML 2. Section 3 presents the problems that we have detected with them. Section 4 introduces our proposal and the concepts and mechanisms that we have defined to address these problems. Then, section 5 discusses how our proposal can extend the current UML notation. Finally, section 6 compares our work with other related proposals, and section 7 draws some conclusions.

2 The UML Package and Its Related Operations

The package is the mechanism available in UML for grouping modeling elements (including other packages) and it also provides a namespace for its members. A namespace is an element in a UML model that contains a set of elements that can be identified by name [1, clause 7.3.34]. The namespace is a named element itself. A package owns its members, with the implication that if a package is removed from a model, so are the elements owned by the package.

There are two package operations related to grouping and naming: PackageImport and PackageMerge. A package import is a relationship that identifies a package whose members are to be imported by a namespace. It allows the use of unqualified names to refer to package members from other namespaces [1, clause 7.3.39]. Owned and imported elements have a visibility that determines whether they are available outside the package.

Conceptually, a package import is equivalent to individually importing each member of the imported namespace using the ElementImport operation, which identifies an element in another package. This allows the element to be referenced using its name without any qualifier, as if they were owned elements. Elements defined in an enclosing namespace are also available using their unqualified names in the enclosed namespaces.

When importing an element it is possible to use an alias for it (to, e.g., avoid name clashes), and to decide whether the imported element can be further imported or not by other packages (the visibility of the imported element has to be either the same or more restricted than that of the referenced element).

Element importation works by reference, i.e., it is not possible to add features to the element import itself, although it is possible to modify the referenced element in the namespace from which it was imported [1, clause 7.3.15]. In case of name clashes with internal elements, the imported elements are not added to the importing namespace, and the name of those elements must be qualified in order to be used. In case of a name clash with an outer name in the importing namespace, the outer name is hidden, and the unqualified name refers to the imported element (the outer name can be accessed from this moment on using its qualified name). If more than one element with the same name is imported to a namespace as a consequence of multiple element or package imports, the elements are not added to the importing namespace.

A package merge defines how the contents of one package (the source) are extended by the contents of another package (the target) [1, clause 7.3.40], combining them together. Thus, the contents of the receiving package are (implicitly) modified and become the result of the combination of the two packages. In other words, the receiving package and its contents represent both the operand and the results of the package merge, depending on the context in which they are considered.

PackageMerge is normally used to integrate the features of model elements defined in different packages that have the same name and are intended to represent the same concept. It is extensively used in the definition of the UML metamodel, allowing an incremental definition of the metaclasses by which each concept is extended in increments, with each increment defined in a separate merged package. By selecting which increments to merge, it is possible to obtain a custom definition of a concept for a specific end [1]. In terms of semantics, there is no difference between a model with explicit package merges, and a model in which all the merges have been performed.

The resulting model contains the duplicate-free union of the two merged packages, matching elements by names and types, and joining together all their features (properties, references, operations, constraints, etc.). In case of any kind of conflicts, the merge is considered ill-formed and the resulting model that contains it is invalid.

The result of combining the merge and import operations is also defined in UML. Importing a receiving package of a merge will import the combined contents of the merge (because the receiving package contains the result of the merge operation), while importing a merge package (i.e., the target of the merge) will only import its contents. In case of an element import owned by the receiving package of a merge, it will be transformed into a corresponding element import in the resulting package. Imported elements are not merged (unless there is also a package merge to the package owning the imported element or its alias).

3 Current Limitations of the UML Package

As we mentioned above, the fact that the same concept (the Package) provides at the same time the grouping and naming mechanisms for the UML language, together with the complex semantics of import and merge operations, may lead to some problems and restrictions. These are described in this section.

3.1 Ownership of Packaged Elements

In UML, a package owns its grouped elements [1]. This imposes a hierarchical decomposition of the model elements into a tree structure (not a graph), in which a model element can belong to at most one package.

Although the use of tree structures greatly simplifies the handling and grouping of model elements, it becomes a strong limitation if a modeler wants to group model elements according to different classifications, each one using a different criteria. For example, we could organize our model elements depending on whether they represent structural or behavioural features of the system being modeled (e.g., the software architecture in one package, the specification of the interactions in another). Another organization can divide the model elements depending on whether they represent internal elements of the system, or part of the interfaces with other systems. We could also classify the model elements depending on their level of criticality, or the project phase they belong to. Forcing one organizational structure is not acceptable: normally there is no single classification that fits all conceptual dimensions in which modeling elements can be organized.

A proper grouping schema for organizing models should be able to allow modeling elements to belong, in principle, to more than one group.

3.2 Naming Schema

A UML package also provides a namespace for its members. In UML, a namespace is an element that owns a set of elements that can be identified by name.

The fact that UML elements may have at most one name can be a strong limitation in some contexts, for example in heterogeneous federated environments. In such cases there is no single global naming schema in which only one selected naming convention applies to all entities, and there is no single authority that administers all names. We cannot ignore the existing independently developed naming schemes already in use, or the ones currently being proposed.

Moreover, there are many situations in which the name of an element depends on the context in which it is used, so names cannot be fixed and absolute.

A proper naming schema should be able to accommodate these different naming schemata and allow their interconnection, while at the same time maintaining name unambiguity in each context of use.

3.3 Name Resolution

Another problem of the current UML naming schema has to do with name resolution, due to the semantics of ElementImport operation. The situation gets even worse under the presence of PackageImport and PackageMerge operations, as mentioned in [3].

This is a critical issue for those languages, such as OCL [9], that provide navigation facilities to refer to specific model elements. The environment of an OCL expression defines what model elements are visible and can be referred to from the expression. Such references are done by name, using either single names or package-qualified names. In principle the UML and OCL naming schemata are aligned, although it is not completely clear whether they are fully compatible or not, specially when import or merge operations are in place with their complex rules and with aliasing. MOF languages also have complex visibility rules, again aggravated by the importing relationships that can exist on a model. For example, the same package can have two distinct interpretations depending on its role as a source or as a target of a package merge or import relationship. The context-sensitive interpretation of a package has subtle implications for the name resolution of OCL constraints in the context of a package with two distinct interpretations about its extent [3].

There are other problematic situations that can lead to undesirable consequences, due to the potential side-effects of the import operation. For example, suppose a package P containing a constraint C that refers to a class A in an outer package. If P now imports another package Q that contains a class named A, the name resolution rules will hide the old class A and resolve name A to the newly imported class. This could easily break the constraint or, even worse, inadvertently change its behaviour. Another undesirable situation can happen if package P contains another constraint C' that refers to a class B, which does not exist in P but is imported from package R. If the newly imported package Q also contained a class named B, the semantics of the import operation would make the name B unresolvable (because multiple imports of the same name are not allowed), and hence constraint C' would not work any more. An additional problem with these side-effects is that most tools do not give any warning to the user about them.

3.4 PackageMerge Problems

The PackageMerge operation presents several problems mainly due to its complex semantics, as initially pointed out in [4]. The work in [5] provides a thorough analysis of this operation and its problems, proposing a set of solutions for those that can be resolved, and identifying those that cannot. PackageMerge is not a simple operation, and in fact, the UML documentation discourages its use by casual system modelers. It is said to be intended for expert metamodelers to help them define their metamodels using a modular approach, which allows adding features to existing classes by merging them with others that define the extensions.

Furthermore, to our knowledge there is no general tool support for it. At least we do not know of any UML modeling tool that allows you drawing a «merge» dependency between two packages and then changes the receiving one according to the result of the operation (as it happens with UML Generalization, despite the fact that the UML manual mentions that these two operations should behave similarly in that way).

4 The Proposal

4.1 A More Flexible Grouping Schema

In order to allow a more flexible grouping schema for modeling elements, we will adopt one of the concepts defined in ODP, the **group**. A group is "a set of objects with a particular relationship that characterizes either the structural relationship among objects, or an expected common behaviour" [6, Part 2, clause 10.1].

Figure 1 shows our proposal of a new grouping schema for UML model elements. The central element is the Group, which is related[1] to a set of GroupableElements that represent the model elements that can be grouped together. The characterizing relation that defines the criteria that the members should fulfil to belong to the group is expressed by an optional UML constraint. All groupable elements (including groups) are named elements (see section 4.2). There is also another constraint (not shown here) that forbids cycles in the membership relation, that is, we do not allow groups to contain themselves or to contain other groups that contain them.

Figure 1 also shows how the Package becomes just an specialization of a Group, in which the members belong to exactly one package (itself). Our proposal allows model

---

[1] The Membership relationship is represented here by an association, although other UML modellers would have used an aggregation. Given the loose semantics of the UML aggregation, we have preferred to use an association.

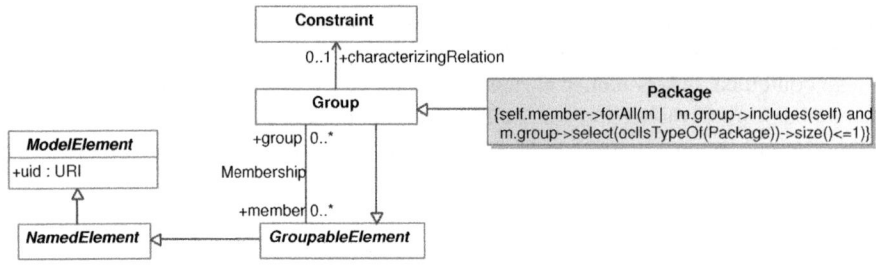

Fig. 1. A new grouping schema for UML model elements

elements to belong to several groups, hence supporting overlapping organizations of model elements. This grouping schema is similar to the classification schema used by Google Gmail, which associates *labels* to mail messages. Such labels act as groups that identify the relations that characterize their member elements. Any Gmail message may have several associated labels, one for each of the groups it belongs to. Selecting a particular label lists all the member messages associated to that label. Similarly, our model elements can be associated to more than one group, avoiding the tyranny of the dominant classification currently required by UML.

4.2 A More Powerful Naming Schema

Our proposed naming schema is based on the ODP Naming standard [8], which provides a *context-relative* naming schema for large, open, federated and heterogeneous systems and environments. In a context-relative naming schema, multiple naming contexts can apply to entities in different domains. These naming contexts can be related to one another, hence allowing us to refer from one naming context to an entity in another.

To achieve this we need to introduce an intermediate level of indirection between an entity and its name, which is given by a *Naming Action*.

Figure 2 shows the main elements of the proposed naming schema, representing in a class diagram the core part of the ODP naming schema tailored to our specific environment. The elements in that diagram correspond to the concepts defined in [8]:

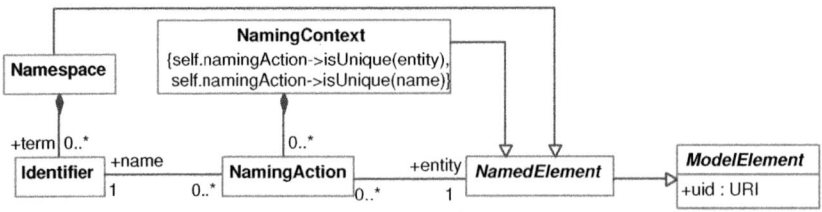

Fig. 2. A new naming schema for UML model elements

- A **name** is is a term which, in a given naming context, refers to an entity. In this paper we will assume that names are represented by Strings, although it would be possible to use other representations such as symbols, images, icons, etc.
- An **identifier** is an unambiguous name, in a given naming context.
- A **namespace** is a set of terms, usable as names, generated by a naming convention.
- A **naming context** establishes a relation between names and entities (in our case, model elements that are subject to naming). Such a relation is composed by a set of pairs "(name,entity)" that defines how the entities are named in this particular context. Such pairs are represented by naming actions. The fact that naming contexts are also named entities enables the relationship between naming contexts.
- A **naming action** is an action that associates a term from a name space with a given entity. All naming actions are relative to a naming context.

Note that for simplicity in this paper we do not allow direct synonyms (entities with several names) nor homonyms (names associated to several entities) within the same naming context, as expressed by the two constraints in the NamingContext class. These constraints could be relaxed to take into account not only the names but also the element types when comparing elements, although in this paper we will use just names.

A very simple and common example of the use of multiple naming contexts can be found in mobile phones. Every person assigns a name to each number in his/her mobile phone's contact list, hence defining a unique naming context. For example, the name I have assigned in my cellular phone to my wife's phone number ("wife") is different from the name that each of my children have assigned to it ("mum" and "mammy", respectively). But we all refer to the same number. Analogously, the same name "ICE" is normally used in all phones to refer to the number to call in case of an emergency, although this number is different for almost everyone. In our terminology, each phone defines a naming context, and each entry in a phone's contact list is nothing but a naming action in that context.

Another example of naming contexts can be found in natural languages. Figures 3 and 4 show two examples of this, using our representation in UML. The first one shows how two model elements are named in the English context. The second figure shows one element being named in six different contexts (only the naming actions are shown, with the references to the related elements shown in their slots).

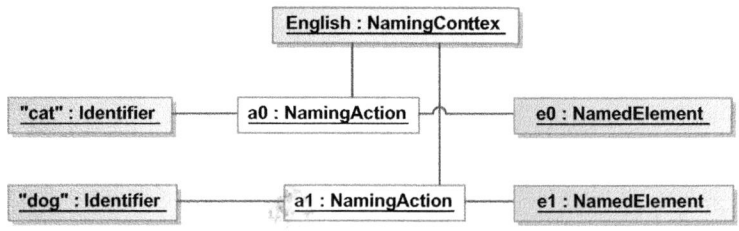

Fig. 3. An example of a naming context with two entities and their associated names

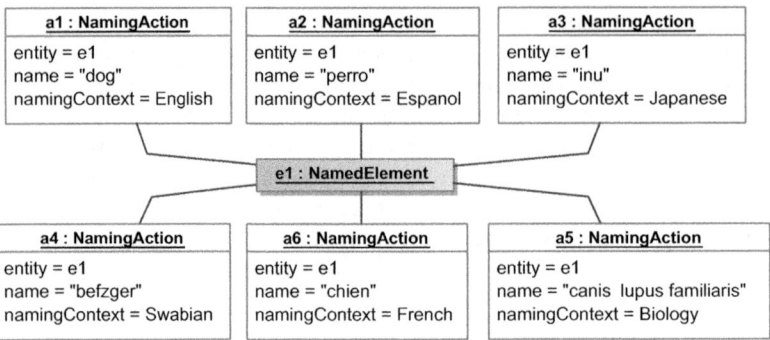

Fig. 4. An example of multiple names for an entity in several naming contexts

The fact that a naming context can be itself named in another context implies an interesting level of indirection by nesting naming contexts. In this way entities that belong to more that one nested domain may be referred to using different names. For example, figure 5 shows how the entity called "dog" in English and "perro" in Spanish, can also be called "Inglés::dog" in the Spanish naming context, because the English context is called "Inglés" in Spanish. Similarly, from the English context a dog can be called both a "dog" and a "Spanish::perro". (We are using "::" as separator for composing names.)

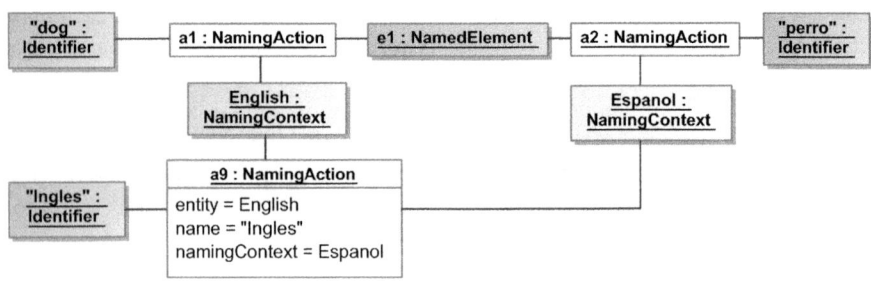

Fig. 5. An example of multiple names for an entity in several naming contexts

4.3 Name Resolution

As defined in ODP, name resolution is the process by which, given a name and an initial naming context, an association between a name and the entity designated by the name can be found. In general this is a difficult process, because it can potentially match multiple elements. In our current proposal naming contexts do not allow synonyms, so the name of every model element is unique in that context. Then we assume that its name will be the only one defined by the appropriate naming action. The following operation **resolve()** implements name resolution:

```
context Identifier::resolve(C : NamingContext) : NamedElement
   body:  self.namingAction->any(namingContext = C).entity
```

Of course, this operation can evaluate to UndefinedValue if the name does not correspond to any model element in the context (for instance, "bfgtrr".resolve(English). This can be checked by operation canResolve():

```
context Identifier::canResolve(C : NamingContext) : Boolean
   body:  self.namingAction->exists(namingContext = C)
```

The opposite operation name(), that given a model element and a context returns a name, is not so simple. We could naively think of the following operation:

```
context NamedElement::name(C : NamingContext) : Identifier
   body:  self.namingAction->any(namingContext = C).name
```

However, it can also be the case of a model element that is not named in a given context C, but there is another context D in which the element is named (as, say, "x"), and the context D is named "d" in C. Then, the element can be indirectly named in context C as "d::x". Thus, finding the name of an element which is not directly named in a naming context may result in 0, 1 or more names for the element (depending on how many other contexts define a name for it). This is also a complex process because it may involve cycles (if context D names context E and context E names D) which need to be detected to avoid infinite names. Besides, names in general federated schemata can have different incompatible naming conventions. Here we propose a simple approach when looking for names, returning the first one we find if the name can be resolved in the naming context, either directly or indirectly in other referenced naming contexts. For a discussion of the general process for name resolution, the interested reader is referred to the ODP Naming standard [8].

4.4 Putting It All Together

Figure 6 shows the complete picture of our proposal. Once we have individually defined the grouping and naming mechanisms, the question is how to combine them.

We mentioned in section 4.1 that a Group is a NamedElement (see also figure 1), and therefore it can be addressed by its name, being part of the naming schema. Moreover, it is natural to expect that a group provides a naming context for their member elements (although not in an exclusive way, as the UML Package does). Thus we have defined a relationship between Group and NamingContext that establishes how the group assigns names to its members. A Group is related to one NamingContext, the one that provides unambiguous names to its members. The cardinality at the other end of the association means that a NamingContext can provide names for more than one group. That is, several groups can of course share the same naming context for assigning names to their members.

The following constraint forces all members of a group to be named in the naming context associated to the group. If we want a group with elements from different naming contexts, it is just a matter of creating a naming context that imports them (see 5.1).

```
context Group inv AllMembersNamed:
self.namingContext.namingAction.entity->includesAll(self.member)
```

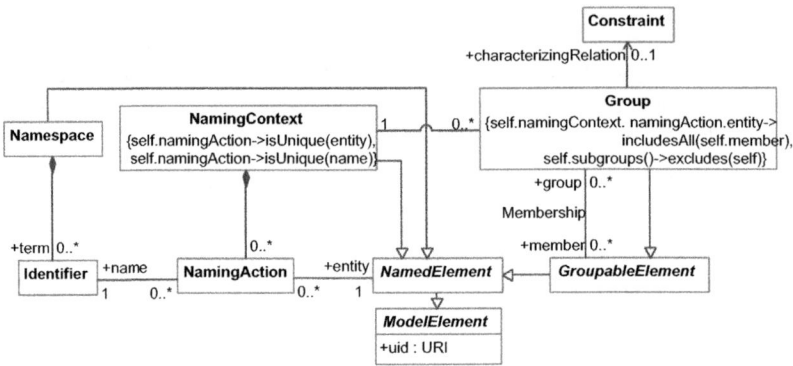

Fig. 6. A summary of the proposed combined naming and grouping schemata

5 Back to the Future

Let us discuss in this section how our proposal can fit with the current UML language and its Package element. In section 4.1 we already mentioned that a package can be considered a special kind of group, whose members belong to exactly one group (itself). We showed this in figure 1, where Package inherits from Group.

Figure 7 provides more details, showing how our proposal can extend the current UML PackageableElement metaclass and its relation with Package. We can see how PackageableElement inherits from GroupableElement, as Package inherits from Group. Similarly, the composition relation between a package and its members is just a subset of the Membership association.

Regarding the provision of a namescope to its members, in the current version of UML, metaclass NamedElement contains an attribute called name (of type String) with the name of that element. In our proposal this attribute has been moved to a property called name of the naming action that assigns a name to an element in a given context, which plays the same role. Still it is obvious to derive the value of the name attribute for a PackageableElement using the relationship between its owner package (which is a Group) and the associated NamingContext.

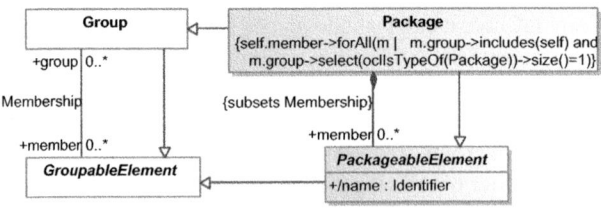

Fig. 7. Extensions to current UML metaclasses

```
context PackageableElement::name : Identifier
  derive: self.name(self.group.namingContext))
```

Furthermore, the following invariant should hold for packages and their members:

```
context Package inv:
  self.member->forAll(m | m.name = m.name(self.namingContext))
```

Note that, in that invariant, the operation name() is always defined for the context associated to the Package, because the AllMembersNamed constraint holds.

Finally, the selection of a concrete syntax for the new Group element is outside the scope of this paper, although any variation of the concrete syntax of the UML Package that showed that overlapping is possible could work well. For simplicity we will use the UML symbol for Package, stereotyped as «group» to represent groups.

Packages and groups can be used together in a specification. In fact, we think that they provide their best advantages when combined together because each one has its own specific goal. Thus, a very few packages can be responsible for owning the modeling elements, managing their lifecycles and also providing the basic naming contexts for them. Groups become very useful for organizing the model elements according to different categories and/or views in a flexible and structured way.

5.1 Redefining Package Import

The two importing operations in UML are defined by ElementImport and PackageImport relationships. Their goal is to be able to use unqualified names to refer to external members that belong to other packages [1, clause 7.3.39].

The need for such importing operations in UML is due to the strong coupling in UML between names and elements, and between elements and packages. In our proposal we have loosened these relationships, decoupling names from elements, and elements from their groups. Therefore, to use an unqualified name to refer to an entity from a group, in our proposal it is enough to add its name to the naming context associated to the group.[2] The following operation specifies this action. It returns a boolean value indicating whether the operation has succeeded or not.

```
context NamingContext::
         import(n : Identifier, e : NamedElement) : Boolean
  post: if (self.namingAction.name->excludes(n)
           and self.namingAction.entity->excludes(e))
        then result = true and self.namingAction->
              includes (na | na.name = n and na.entity = e)
        else result = ( n.resolve(self) = e )
        endif
```

This operation checks whether the name or the entity already exist in the naming context, but are not related to each other, and if not, a naming action that relates them is added. Otherwise the operation returns false, meaning that the operation has failed.

---
[2] This operation reflects what normally happens in natural languages when they adopt a term from other languages if they do not have a precise name for a given entity. In English, examples of these names include expresso, siesta, baguette or bonsai, to name a few.

This operation also provides the possibility of importing a complete NamingContext, because a naming context is itself a NamedElement.

Despite it now being an operation on naming contexts, we could also define the corresponding operation import() on groups:

```
context Group::import(n : Identifier, e : NamedElement): Boolean
  body: self.namingContext.import(n,e)
```

Then, if we had a group A that imports the names of the member elements of a group B (via an «import» relation), the semantics of this operation is now given by the OCL expression A.import(B). Note that this operation has a possible side-effect if several groups share the same naming context: if one group imports an element, it becomes imported to all the groups. However, this is not a problem because of the difference between *importing* one element and *including* it as a member of a group. Importing an element allows referring to it by its name, i.e., it is an operation on naming contexts and not on groups. Including an element (using operations include() or union(), for instance) means adding it to the set of members of the group. Elements can be added by identifier, name or both. We show here the include() operation using identifiers. The other operations are similar. Remember that constraint AllMembersNamed requires included elements to be named in the corresponding naming context.

```
context Group::include ( n : Identifier )
  pre: n.canResolve(self.namingContext)
  post: self.member->includes(n.resolve(self.namingContext))
```

One of the benefits of having a well-defined semantics of all these operations specified in OCL, is that they can now be easily implemented and checked by UML modeling tools. Moreover, the fact that these operations return a boolean value indicating whether a conflict has been found or not during the import operation allow modeling tools to warn users about conflicts—in contrast to current UML PackageImport and ElementImport operations, which do not warn the users about their side-effects in case of conflicts. This is of special importance in large models with many elements, possibly developed by different people in different locations, in which name conflicts can easily pass unnoticed.

The way in which the conflicts are resolved falls outside the scope of this paper, and depends on what we want the import() operation to do in case of name clashes. To illustrate this issue, let us suppose two groups One and Two, each of them with a different naming context, and with four elements that globally refer to six entities $\{e_1, ..., e_6\}$. This is informally shown in figure 8, where dependencies represent graphically the naming contexts of these two groups before the import operation:

One.namingContext = $\{(A, e_1), (B, e_2), (C, e_3), (D, e_4), ...\}$
Two.namingContext = $\{(A, e_1), (B, e_3), (C, e_5), (E, e_6), ...\}$

If we want group One to import the names of Two (for calculating the union of both, for example), two conflicts appear for names B and C, each of them with a particular kind of problem. It is clear that after the import operation the resulting naming context of One will contain naming actions $\{(A, e_1), (D, e_4), (E, e_6)\}$. However, the way to resolve the other two names and how to create a new name for the sixth entity depends solely on the user, who should decide what to do with the clashes.

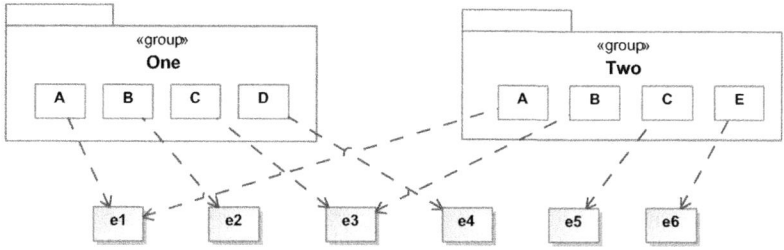

Fig. 8. An example of two overlapping groups

Is it worth noting that in our proposal one could, as an alternative, just name the contexts in each other, and thus avoid the import operation altogether.

5.2 Merging Groups

Decoupling the names from the entities they refer to allows to uncover a semantic distinction between the import and merge operations. While the former deals with the names of the model elements, the latter deals with the elements themselves (as it happened with include and union operations). In fact, several elements of the UML packages to be merged are expected to share names, because they are supposed to represent the same entities but from different perspectives. In theory a package merge is just aimed at the *extension* of the receiving package with the duplicate-free union of the two packages. This should work in a similar way as the Generalization. However, when it comes to the details the situation gets really complex. The handling of the constraints on the model elements and the potential inconsistences between conflicting requirements on the elements to merge complicates the semantics of this operation (see the good discussion presented in [5]). In addition, Generalization works on classes, while PackageMerge works on packages, i.e., sets of model elements. This is a subtle but crucial difference that introduces further problems. Finally, the side-effects of this operation on the receiving package (whose elements are implicitly, but not explicitly modified) complicates the naming operations and the navigation of elements, as mentioned above.

We propose a different approach to group (and thus package) merging, based on the creation of a new group whose members are the result of the merge. These elements can be either previous elements (if they are not modified by the merge—for instance those that belong to just one of the groups) or newly created elements, resulting from the individual merges. On the one hand this approach allows the use of a more powerful merge operation between individual elements, such as the ones proposed for merging DB schema, generic model merging or ontology merging defined by Pottinger and Bernstein in [10], the class merging operation as defined in MetaGME [11], or the epsilon merge operation [12]. On the other hand, this approach allows groups and elements to maintain their properties and avoids undesirable side-effects. The fact that each group can have its own naming context solves the problem of finding names to the new entities created after the merge: they maintain in the new context the names they had before.

Figure 9 shows how the new operation works on the two groups described in figure 8. We can see that the resulting group has 5 elements (and not six as it would happen if instead of merging we had used the union operation), named {A..E}. The elements these names refer to is specified by the resulting naming context:

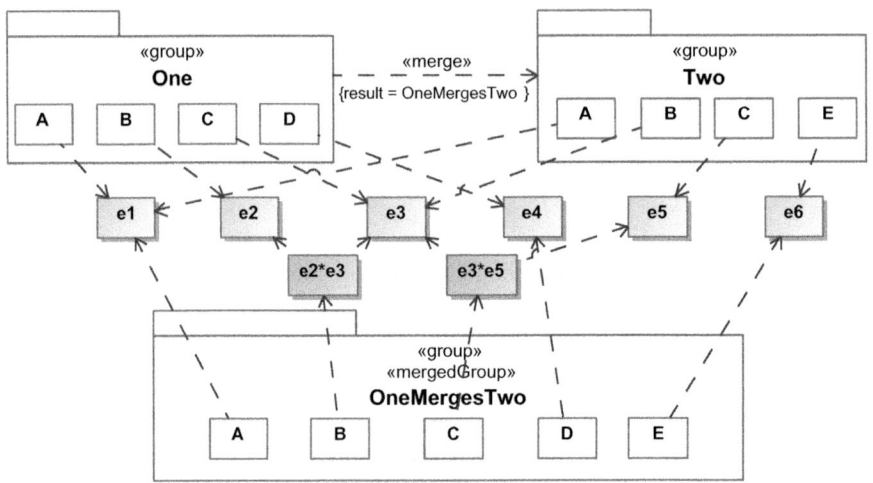

Fig. 9. Merging the two models

OneMergesTwo.namingContext = $\{(A, e_1), (B, e_2 * e_3), (C, e_3 * e_5), (D, e_4), (E, e_6)\}$

Name A refers to the same element e_1 in groups One and Two and therefore it remains the same in the resulting group. Names D and E become part of the result without changes because they belong only to one of the two groups to merge. Names B and C are part of the resulting group, but they now refer to the elements obtained by merging e_2 with e_3 and e_3 with e_5, respectively (whose ids we have called e2*e3 and e3*e5). As mentioned before, the way in which these elements are calculated from the original ones is outside the scope of the paper. In general, any merging algorithm can do the job, although the simplest way would be to use one based on multiple inheritance such as the one described in [11].

A new tag definition (result) of stereotype «merge» on the dependency identifies the group that receives the result of the merge. Such a group should not exist beforehand, and is created to accommodate the merge. The new group is stereotyped «mergedGroup» precisely to indicate that it is the result of a merge. This stereotype has two tag definitions (named receivingGroup and mergeGroup, not shown in the diagram), that refer to the two groups involved in the merge operation.

This merge operation does not provide full backwards compatibility with the original PackageMerge operation, in order to avoid some of its problems. The new operation does not have any side-effects, and also is flexible w.r.t. the way in which the elements are merged. Furthermore, it is worth noting that modifying the members of a group as a result of a merge operation does not make sense in this new context, because a group does not own its members—it only provides references to them. One could still define another semantics for this operation that behaved as the previous one in the case of packages (which own their members).

6 Related Work

This proposal is influenced by the naming concepts developed by ISO/IEC for the RM-ODP framework [8], which in turn come from the ANSA project in the nineties [13]. These concepts were defined to cope with the heterogeneity of naming schemata existing in any open distributed system, with possible federated applications, and prove to be very useful for providing a more flexible naming schema to UML—required to enable, for example, federated modeling with UML.

There have always been several currents in the modeling community to improve UML. Probably the most active proposals now come from the OMG's UML revision task force that works on the definition of UML 3; from the group working on fUML [14] for a proper and well-founded subset of the UML 2 metamodel—which provides a shared foundation for higher-level UML modeling concepts; and from the OMG's Architecture Ecosystem SIG [2], whose goal is to manage the alignments between different OMG recommendations (such as UML and SysML, or UML and BPMN), and also aims at achieving federated modeling [15]. The proposal presented here aims at contributing to the work of these groups.

The merging of groups and packages is influenced by our previous work on combining Domain Specific Visual Languages [16]. Model merging can provide a solution to language combination in some cases, and package merge is one of the possible ways to achieve model merge. Regarding the way the individual elements are merged, we allow the use of any of the existing algorithms, such as the ones described in [10,11,12].

7 Conclusions

In this work we have presented a proposal for new UML naming and grouping mechanisms, which are currently provided in UML by the single concept **Package**. Our proposal addresses some of the limitations that the UML mechanisms have, because UML tightly couples elements with names, and names with packages. Our proposal allows elements to belong to more than one group, and to have more than one name in different contexts; it can accommodate different naming schemata and permit their interconnection while maintaining name unambiguity in each context; and enables the proper definition of grouping and naming operations such as import. One of the major advantages of our proposal is that it tries to respect as much as possible the current version of UML, extending it for backwards compatibility. A second major strength is that it is faithfully based on international standards (by ISO/IEC and ITU-T), making use of mature ideas which are developed with the consensus of major international parties and organizations. Plans for future work include dealing with synonyms and with UML inheritance as part of naming context.

Acknowledgements. The author would like to thank Peter Linington, Martin Gogolla and Pete Rivett for their very useful comments and criticisms on earlier versions of this paper, and to the anonymous reviewers for their helpful suggestions. This work is supported by Spanish Research Projects TIN2008-03107 and P07-TIC-03184.

References

1. Object Management Group. Unified Modeling Language 2.3 Superstructure Specification (May 2010), OMG doc. formal/2010-05-05
2. Object Management Group. Architecture Ecosystem Special Interest Group (December 2009), http://www.omgwiki.org/architecture-ecosystem/
3. Chimiak-Opoka, J.D., Demuth, B., Silingas, D., Rouquette, N.F.: Requirements analysis for an integrated OCL development environment. In: Proc. of the OCL Workshop at MODELS 2009. ECEASST, vol. 24 (2009)
4. Zito, A., Diskin, Z., Dingel, J.: Package merge in UML 2: Practice vs. Theory? In: Wang, J., Whittle, J., Harel, D., Reggio, G. (eds.) MoDELS 2006. LNCS, vol. 4199, pp. 185–199. Springer, Heidelberg (2006)
5. Dingel, J., Diskin, Z., Zito, A.: Understanding and improving UML package merge. Software and System Modeling 7, 443–467 (2008)
6. ISO/IEC. RM-ODP. Reference Model for Open Distributed Processing, ISO/IEC 10746, ITU-T Rec. X.901-X.904 (1997)
7. ISO/IEC. Information technology – Open distributed processing – Use of UML for ODP system specifications, ISO/IEC IS 19793, ITU-T X.906 (2008)
8. ISO/IEC. Information Technology — Open Distributed Processing — Naming Framework, ISO/IEC IS 14771, ITU-T Rec. X.910 (1999)
9. Object Management Group. Object Constraint Language (OCL) Specification. Version 2.2 (February 2010), OMG doc. formal/2010-02-01
10. Bernstein, P.A., Pottinger, R.A.: Merging models based on given correspondences. In: Proc. of VLDB 2003, Berlin, Germany, pp. 862–873 (2003)
11. Emerson, M., Sztipanovits, J.: Techniques for metamodel composition. In: Proc. of the Workshop on Domain Specific Modeling at OOPSLA 2006, pp. 123–139 (2006)
12. Kolovos, D., Rose, L., Paige, R.: The Epsilon book, U. York (2010), http://www.eclipse.org/gmt/epsilon/doc/book/
13. van der Linden, R.: The ANSA naming model. Architecture report APM.1003.01, ANSA (July 1993), http://www.ansa.co.uk/ANSATech/93/Primary/100301.pdf
14. Object Management Group. Semantics of A Foundational Subset For Executable UML Models (fUML). Version 1.0 – Beta 3 (June 2010), OMG doc. ptc/2010-03-14
15. Casanave, C.: Requirements for Federated Modeling. White paper. Model Driven Solutions (January 2011), http://bit.ly/dUGiVf
16. Vallecillo, A.: On the combination of domain specific modeling languages. In: Kühne, T., Selic, B., Gervais, M.-P., Terrier, F. (eds.) ECMFA 2010. LNCS, vol. 6138, pp. 305–320. Springer, Heidelberg (2010)

Aspect-Oriented Model Development at Different Levels of Abstraction

Mauricio Alférez[1], Nuno Amálio[2], Selim Ciraci[3], Franck Fleurey[4], Jörg Kienzle[5], Jacques Klein[2], Max Kramer[6], Sebastien Mosser[7], Gunter Mussbacher[8], Ella Roubtsova[9], and Gefei Zhang[10]

[1] Universidade Nova de Lisboa, Portugal
mauricio.alferez@di.fct.unl.pt
[2] University of Luxembourg
{nuno.amalio,jacques.klein}@uni.lu
[3] University of Twente, The Netherlands
ciracis@ewi.utwente.nl
[4] SINTEF IKT, Norway
Franck.Fleurey@sintef.no
[5] McGill University, Canada
Joerg.Kienzle@mcgill.ca
[6] Karlsruhe Institute of Technology, Germany
max.kramer@student.kit.edu
[7] INRIA Lille - Nord Europe
sebastien.mosser@inria.fr
[8] SCE, Carleton University, Canada
gunter@sce.carleton.ca
[9] Open University of the Netherlands and
Munich University of Applied Sciences, Germany
ella.roubtsova@ou.nl,ella.roubtsova@hm.edu
[10] Ludwig-Maximilians-Universität München and
arvato systems, Germany
gefei.zhang@pst.ifi.lmu.de

Abstract. The last decade has seen the development of diverse aspect-oriented modeling (AOM) approaches. This paper presents eight different AOM approaches that produce models at different level of abstraction. The approaches are different with respect to the phases of the development lifecycle they target, and the support they provide for model composition and verification. The approaches are illustrated by models of the same concern from a case study to enable comparing of their expressive means. Understanding common elements and differences of approaches clarifies the role of aspect-orientation in the software development process.

Keywords: Aspect-oriented modeling, localization of concerns, composition, verification, localization of reasoning.

1 Introduction

Separation of concerns is a key software engineering principle that helps to reduce complexity, improve reusability, and simplify evolution. Aspect-oriented software development (AOSD) takes traditional support for separating concerns a step further by allowing developers to modularize their descriptions along more than one dimension [14].

Drawing inspiration from aspect-oriented programming research, AOM brings the aspect-orientation to design, analysis and requirements phases of software development. Aspect-oriented modeling (AOM) approaches, in particular, aim to provide means for

- *localizing of crosscutting concerns* at the level of models to guarantee traceability of concerns across the software development lifecycle and reuse of different realizations of a concern within and across software models;
- *verification* of models with crosscutting concerns;
- *localizing of reasoning* on models of concerns about the behaviour of the whole model.

This paper surveys a set of AOM approaches working at different levels of abstraction. The aim is to compare the techniques of localization of aspects and the techniques of reasoning on aspect models and identify research challenges in AOM. Section 2 identifies the abstraction level of each of eight different AOM approaches and illustrates each of the approaches with a model of the same concern. All chosen approaches have demonstrated their scalability by taking the challenge of modelling the case study of a crisis management system (CMS) [8]. Section 3 discusses the approaches and identifies future directions for AOM research.

2 AOM at Different Levels of Abstraction

2.1 Authentication Concern

The description of the authentication concern is taken from the requirements for a Crisis Management System [8]. This concern is modelled and used for correctness analyses in all compared AOM approaches.

```
The system authenticates users on the basis of the access policies when they first access
any components or information. If a user remains idle for 30 minutes or longer, the system
shall require them to re-authenticate.

Use Case: AuthenticateUser
    Scope: Car Crash Crisis Management System
    Primary Actor: None
    Secondary Actor: CMSEmployee
    Intention: The intention of the System is to authenticate the CMSEmployee to allow access.

    Main Success Scenario:
        1. System prompts CMSEmployee for login id and password.
        2. CMSEmployee enters login id and password into System.
        3. System validates the login information. Use case ends in success.
    Extensions:
        2a. CMSEmployee cancels the authentication process. Use case ends in failure.
        3a. System fails to authenticate the CMSEmployee.
        3a.1 Use case continues at step 1.
        3a.1a CMSEmployee performed three consecutive failed attempts.
            Use case ends in failure.
```

2.2 Feature Abstractions

In Variability Modelling Language for Requirements (VML4RE) [1] the *Authentication* concern is *localized* as one reusable feature identified by its name "Authentication"(Figure 1). Feature model visualizes the dependencies between the *Authentication* feature and the *Session Handling* and *Administration* features. *Authentication* requires the *UserAdministration* feature because the system authenticates users on the basis of access policies associated to them. Feature model also identifies *Authentication* as an optional feature.

The VML4RE specification is a good starting point for concern modelling. Different requirements models can be created to describe the features, using notations of UML2.0 or approaches presented in this overview. For example, if the *Authentication* feature is selected for a specific product according to the VML4RE specification in Figure 1, the requirements specification will include the specification concern called "Authentication" in the chosen specification notation (e.g. a use case specification or a sequence diagram). Also, according to combinations of more than one feature it is possible to apply concerns that modify or add new parts in the requirements specifications. Features do not specify system internals, they only capture requirements for a system, so the *verification* of the system's behaviour and *any reasoning* about it *are not applicable* at the level of feature modelling.

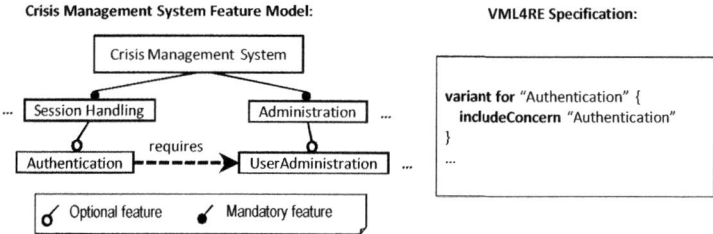

Fig. 1. VML4RE model

2.3 Use Cases

At the level of use case modelling the *Authentication* use case is described step by step. As it is recognized as a reusable unit, it should contain pointcut designators (instructing where, when, and how to invoke the advice) and join points (defining places in the model where an advice should be inserted) [13]. Such concepts do not exist in conventional use case notations.

Aspect-oriented User Requirements Notation (AoURN) [12] supports conventional concepts of use case and workflow modelling techniques but also enables localizing of aspects. The primary goal of AoURN is to model any functional or non-functional concern of the system under development that can be expressed with scenarios.

Fig. 2 depicts the AoURN scenario model for the *Authentication* concern. The authentication scenario starts at the *authenticate* start point and ends either at

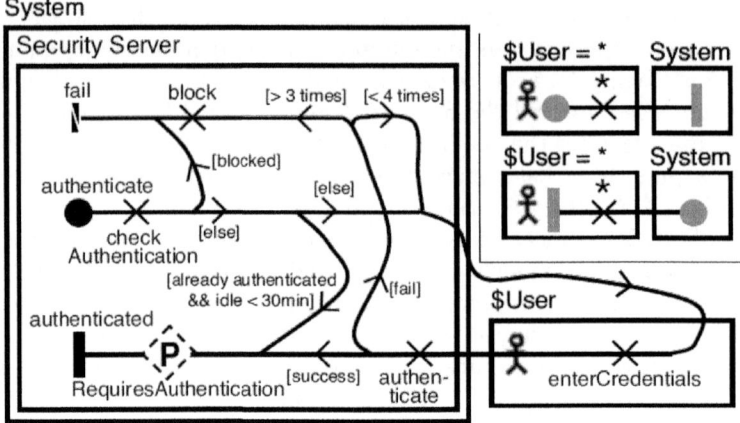

Fig. 2. AoURN model

the *authenticated* or *fail* end point. Various conditions are checked: the *User* may have to *enter credentials*, and the *System* may *authenticate* or *block* the *User*. The pointcut stub *RequiresAuthentication* represents all locations where the Authentication concern is to be applied. At one glance, it is apparent that the concern is to be applied before these locations since the concern-specific behaviour occurs before the pointcut stub. In this case, a simple sequential composition is desired, but AoURN scenario models can be composed in many different ways (e.g., as alternatives, optionally, in parallel, in loops, or in an interleaved way). The composition rules are exhaustive in that their expressiveness is only restricted by the AoURN scenario language itself.

Patterns define the actual locations where the concern is to be applied: in this case, each time there is an interaction between an actor and the *System* as shown in the two sub-models above the *User* component. The variable *$User* defined in the patterns allows the concern to reuse the matched component.

AoURN models involve neither detailed data nor message exchanges. This makes them well suited for the early stages of the software development process. AoURN scenario definitions can be analyzed, enabling regression-testing of the scenario model. AoURN combines aspect-oriented modeling with goal-oriented modelling allowing to model the reasons for choosing a concern using goal models.

Use cases identify abstract actions coming from the environment and abstract responses of the system, driving the system from one state to another, but do not capture system local storage and the internal behavior. While it is possible to validate use case models, system *verification* and *local reasoning* on aspects about the whole system behaviour are *not applicable* at the level of use cases. Further system specification involves choices. Actions may become operations, messages, or events recognized by objects and aspects. Depending on these choices, different modelling techniques may be used.

2.4 Classes and Sequence Diagrams

Reusable Aspect Models (RAM) [7] describes the structure and behaviour of a concern using class, state and sequence diagrams. Fig. 3 shows how the structural view of the *Authentication* concern associates *Session* objects with |*Authenticatable* objects.

The *Authentication* behavior is described in *state views* and *message views*. State views detail the method invocation protocol of objects using state diagrams. Message views specify the message passing between objects using sequence diagrams. For example, the *login* message view in Fig. 3 shows how a *session* object is instantiated upon a successful login attempt. The *requireLogin* message view demonstrates how method invocations of |*methodRequiringLogin* of an |*Authenticatable* object are disallowed if no session is currently established. To apply the authentication aspect, the mandatory instantiation parameters must be mapped to model elements of the base model. For instance, to enable user authentication, the mapping |*Authenticatable* → *User*, |*methodRequiringLogin* → * *(..) would ensure that no public method of a *User* object can be invoked before the user authentication.

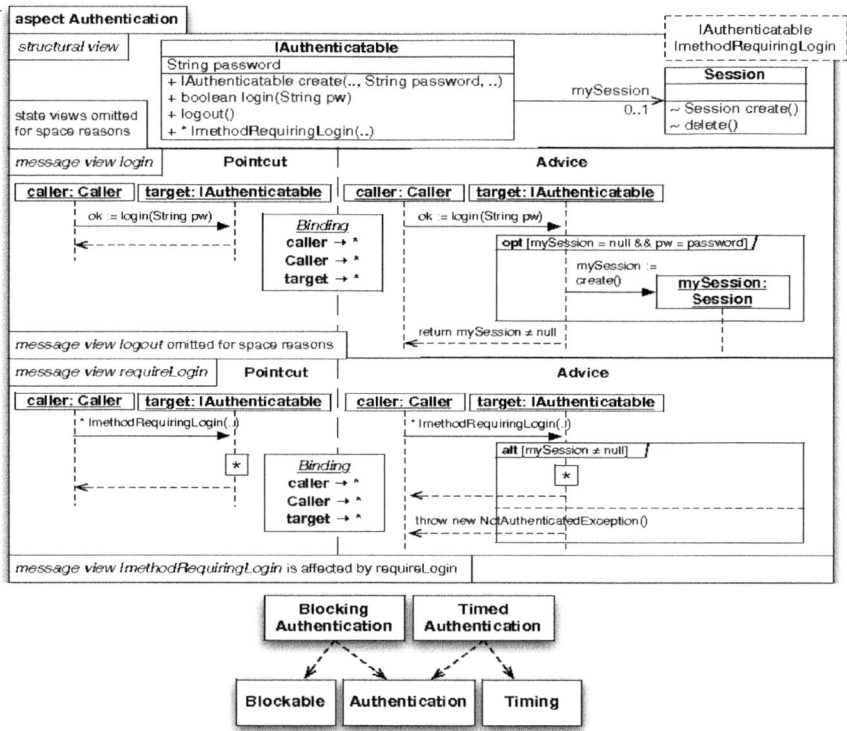

Fig. 3. RAM model

To reuse structure and behavior of low-level aspect models in models that provide more complex functionality, the RAM approach supports the creation of complex aspect dependency chains. Blocking authentication and timed authentication are modeled by reusing the aspects *Authentication*, *Blockable* and *Timing* (see bottom of Fig. 3).

GrACE (Graph-based Adaptation, Configuration and Evolution) approach expresses the base and concerns models as class and sequence diagrams. The specification also contains an activator action and the execution constraint, a sequence of method invocations, expressed with Computational Tree Logic (CTL). With this input, GrACE simulates the execution and the composition of the input diagrams starting from the activator action. The end result of this is the execution tree where each branch is a possible composition showing all the methods invoked in it [5]. Then, a verification algorithm verifies whether the input execution constraints is violated or not. In case it is violated, a feedback is provided to the user. In this way, the user can verify the behavior of the concerns in the composed model. For simulation, GrACE specializes graph-based model checking by defining a model called Design Configuration Model (DCM) for representing UML based AOMs with graphs, and modeling OO- and AspectJ-like execution semantics with graph-transformation rules over this model.

GrACE uses the mapping from Theme/UML [6] to a Domain Specific Language. Hence, the concerns are modeled as "themes" in Theme/UML. Fig. 4 presents an excerpt from the sequence diagram of the theme *Authenticate*, which defines a pointcut to the template method *fireStart*. The advice for this pointcut is defined in the method *beforeInvoke()*, which checks if the user is already authenticated.

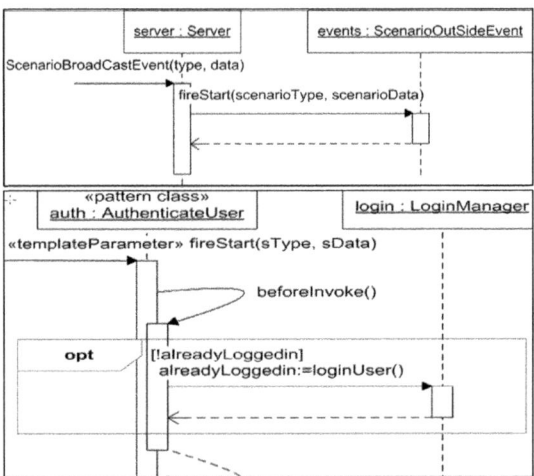

Fig. 4. GrACE:Sequence diagrams

The themes are converted to DCMs for *verification*. GrACE toolset includes a prototype tool which automates the conversion from Theme/UML to DCM. Fig. 5 shows the graph-based DCM of the theme *Authenticate*. The node labeled *AspectType* with the attribute name *AuthenticateUser* represents the template class *AuthenticateUser*. The node with the attribute *toMethod* set to *fireStart* that is connected to the aspect type node represents the template parameter of the theme *Authenticate*.

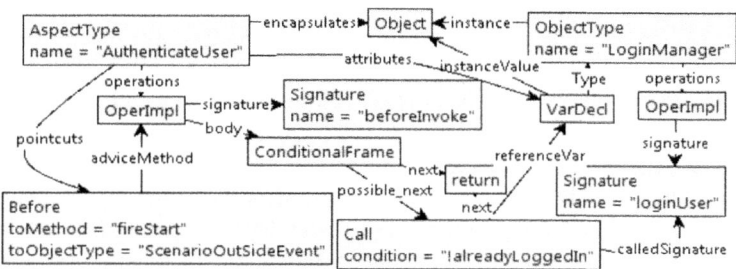

Fig. 5. GrACE:DSM Authenticate

To illustrate composition of aspects, Fig. 6 presents an excerpt of the execution tree generated from the simulation of the base model and the theme *Authenticate* shown in Fig 4. At state $S5$, this excerpt starts with the dispatch of the method

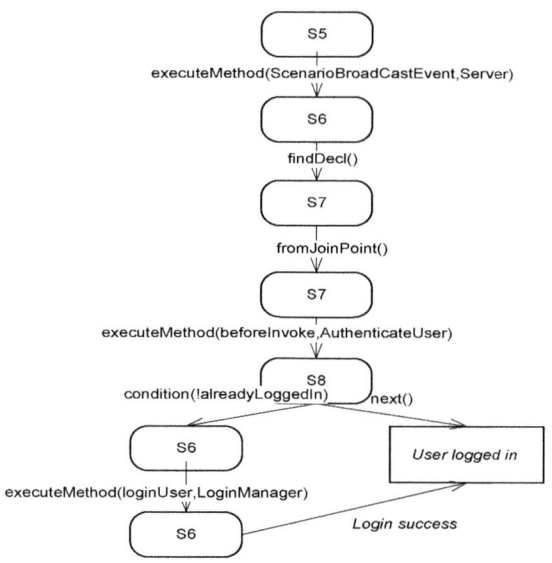

Fig. 6. GrACE:Execution tree

Server.ScenarioBroadCastEvent(). In the activation bar of this method, the first action is a call action. Hence, the transformation rule *findDecl* matches at state *S6* and identifies *ScenarioOutSideEvent.fireStart()* as the receiver of the call. Because the aspect *AuthenticateUser* defines a pointcut to this method, the transformation rule *formBeforeJoinPoint* matches and gives the execution to the advice.

2.5 Classes and State Machines

A UML Behaviour State Machine (BSM) usually presents behaviour of one classifier. Aspects extend the behaviour specified for classifiers. HiLA modifies the semantics of BSM allowing classifiers to apply additional or alternative behaviour. The High-Level Aspects (HiLA) approach [15] introduces AspectJ-like constructs into UML state machines. The basic static structure usually contains one or more classes. Each base state machine is attached to one of these classes and specifies its behavior. HiLA offers two kinds of aspects to modify such a model. Static aspects directly specify a model transformation of the basic static structure of the base state machines. Dynamic (high-level) aspects only apply to state machines and specify additional or alternative behaviour to be executed at certain "appropriate" points of time in the base machines execution.

Fig. 7 presents the scenario of the *Authentication* concern. Modeling with HiLA is a top-down process. The main success scenario of a (behavioral) concern is modeled in the base machine: first the user enters his credentials (*EnterCredentials*), which are then validated (in *stateAuthenticate*). The extension for authentication failures is modeled with the pattern *whilst* (stereotype *whilst*). State *Authenticate* is active. If the current event is wrong (tagged value *"trigger = wrong"*, then the advice is executed, which forces the base machine to go to state *EnterCredentials*, where the user can try again.

The history-based extension, which allows the system to accept at most three trials to log in is modeled in *Three Trials*. The history property $f3$ counts how often its pattern, which specifies continuous sequences containing three and no) final state occurrences, are contained in the execution history so far. The pointcut selects the points of time just *before* state EnterCredentials gets active. If $f3 = 1$, is satisfied, which means that the user has already tried to log in three times unsuccessfully and now tries to authenticate again, the advice takes the base

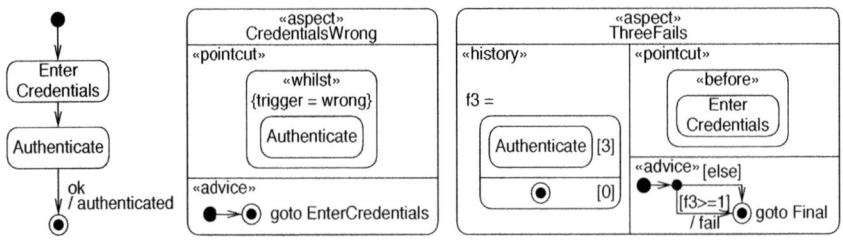

Fig. 7. HiLA model

machine to the final state (label *goto Final*), and ends in failure (signal *fail*). Otherwise the advice does not do anything.

Aspects are composed together by the weaving process. Additional behaviors defined by *whilst* aspects are woven as additional transitions. History-awareness is achieved by entry actions to keep track of states activation; *before* (and *after*) aspects are woven into transitions selected by the pointcut.

HiLA uses formal methods of model validation. The application of aspects to BSM results in another UML state machine which is analyzed using the model checking component of Hugo/RTmodel checking tools. Hugo/RT translates the state machine and the assertions into the input language of a back-end model checker SPIN. SPIN then *verifies* the given properties presented in Linear Temporal Logic.

2.6 Services

The ADORE framework[1] is an approach to support aspect-oriented business processes modeling, using the orchestration of services paradigm.

Models describing business–driven processes (abbreviated as *orchestrations*, defined as a set of partially ordered activities) are composed with process fragments (defined using the same formalism) to produce a larger process. *Fragments* realize models with little behavior and describe different aspects of a complex business process. ADORE allows a business expert to model these concerns separately, and use automated algorithms to compose them.

Using ADORE, designers can define *composition units* (abbreviated as *composition*) to describe the way fragments should be composed with orchestrations. The merge algorithm used to support the composition mechanism[11] computes the set of actions to be performed on the orchestration to automatically produce the composed process. When the engine detects shared join points, an automatic *merge* algorithm is triggered to build a *composed* concern. ADORE also provides a set of *logical rules to detect conflicts* inside orchestrations and fragments (*e.g.*, non-deterministic access to a variable, interface mismatch, lack of response under a given condition set).

We represent in Fig.8 the initial orchestration dealing with the *authentication* concern. It represents the base success scenario, as described in the requirements. To model blocking the user after 3 failed attempts, we use the fragment depicted in Fig.9. The composition algorithm produces the final behavior by integrating the fragment into the legacy orchestration.

2.7 Mixins

A Protocol Model [10] of a system is a set of protocol machines (PMs) that are composed to model the behavior of the system. Fig. 10 shows a protocol model of the security concern composed from PMs *Employee Main, Clock, Singleton, Password Handler* and *Want Time Out*.

---
[1] *http://www.adore-design.org*

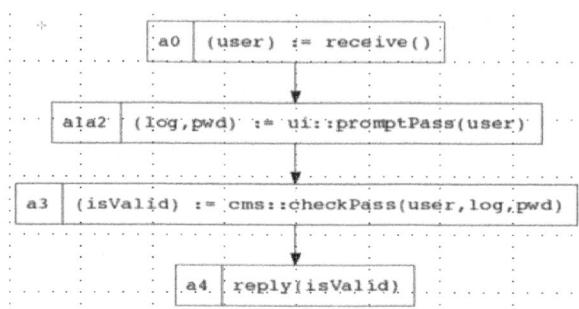

Fig. 8. Orchestration:cms:authUser

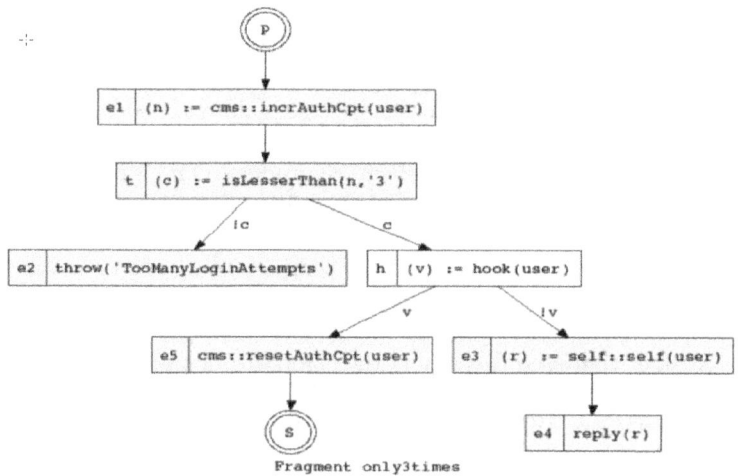

Fig. 9. Authentication concern in an ADORE model

The specification of a PM is described in a textual file as it is shown below for machine *Employee Main*.

```
BEHAVIOUR Employee Main
     ATTRIBUTES Employee Name: String, !Employee Status: String,
            (Security Password: String), Max Tries: Integer
     STATES created, deleted
     TRANSITIONS @new*!Create Employee=created,
               created*Session Event=created,
               created*!Set Password=created,
               created*Log In=created, created*Log Out=created,
               created*Time Out=created, created*Reset=created,
               created*Delete Employee=deleted
     EVENT Create Employee
          ATTRIBUTES Employee: Employee Main,
               Employee Name: String,Security Password: String,
               Max Tries: Integer
     EVENT Delete Employee
          ATTRIBUTES Employee: Employee Main
```

```
EVENT Set Password
      ATTRIBUTES Employee: Employee Main,
      Security Password: String, Max Tries: Integer
EVENT Log In
      ATTRIBUTES Employee:: Employee Main, Password:String
EVENT Log Out
      ATTRIBUTES Employee: Employee Main
EVENT Time Out
      ATTRIBUTES Employee: Employee Main
GENERIC OUT
    MATCHES Time Out, Log Out
```

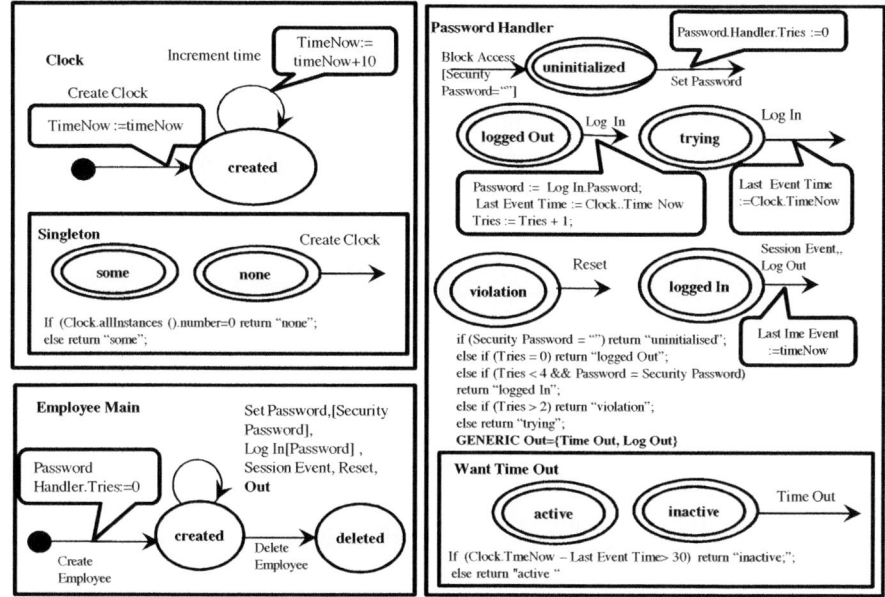

Fig. 10. Protocol Model of the Authentication Concern

The graphical presentation is a secondary artefact; it does not contain all the elements of the specification. The specification of a PM includes its *local storage* and the *alphabet* of *event types*. The local storage is represented as a set of its attributes. For example, attribute *Password Handler.Tries* for the PM *Employee Main*. Each event type is specified by metadata. For example, event *Set Password* contains attribute *Security Password: String*.

An event instance comes from the environment and it is atomic. Instances of PMs are created with happening of events. PM instances can be included into other PMs. A PM instance behaves so that it either accepts or refuses an event from its alphabet, depending on its state and the state of other included machines. Events that are not in its alphabet are ignored. To evaluate the state a machine may read, *but not alter*, the local storage of the included machines.

The complete system is composed using CSP parallel composition [4] extended by McNeile [10] for machines with data. This composition techniques serves as a natural weaving algorithm for aspects. The alphabet of the composed machine is the union of the alphabets of the constituent machines; and the local storage of the composed machine is the union of the local storages of the constituent machines. When presented with an event the composed machine will accept it if and only if all its constituent machines, that have this event in their alphabet, accept it. If at least one of such machines refuses the event it is refused by the composed machine. The concept of event refusal is critical to implement CSP composition for composition of protocol machines. This allows for modelling of the situation when events occur and the system cannot accept them.

Join points are often events. *Password Handler* specifies join points for the *Authentication* concern. A *Session Event* is accepted if the *Password Handler* is in state *logged in*, when both machines *Employee Main* and *Password Handler* may accept it.

Quantification on events is defined by *generalized events*, e.g. event $Out = \{LogOut, TimeOut\}$. Quantification on states is defined as derived states. State abstractions specified with derived states are allowed to be used in join point specifications. For example, the state *logged In* is derived as *"If (Tries $<=$ 4 && Password = Security Password)"*, and as a result the generic event Out representing events *Time Out* and *Log Out* becomes possible.

The CSP composition based algorithm is used for aspect weaving and *simulation*. It produces system traces from parts of traces of aspects with te Modelscope tool. This algorithm guarantees that the order of accepted events in traces of aspects is not changed in the result of their composition (see the proof in [9]). The aspect interference of composed aspects may block some traces of aspects, but it will not change the order of events in them. This property of *local reasoning* [9] provided by the PM approach prevents appearance of invasive aspects and eases the reuse and evolution of protocol models.

2.8 Contracts

The Visual Contract Language (VCL) [2,3] takes an approach to behaviour modelling that is based on *design by contract*. A VCL model is organized around packages, which are reusable units encapsulating structure and behaviour. Packages represent either a traditional module or an aspect. VCL's package composition mechanisms allow larger package to be built from smaller ones.

Figure 11 presents the VCL package *Authentication*, which localizes part of the *authentication* concern. *Authentication* extends package *Users*. State structures of a package are defined in the package's *structural diagram* (SD); together they define the package's state space. The SD of package *Authentication* (Fig. 11(b)) says that a *User* of package *Users*[2] is associated with a *Session* through the relational-edge *HasSession*. In addition, the diagram includes an invariant *HasSessionIfLoggedIn*, stating that each session must be associated with a user that is *logged-in* [3]. Figure 11(c) gives the global behaviour diagram of package *Authentication* with the global observe operation *UserIsLoggedIn*, which says whether a user is logged-in or not; this is described using a VCL assertion diagram (Fig. 11(d)).

---

[2] A blob defines a set of objects.

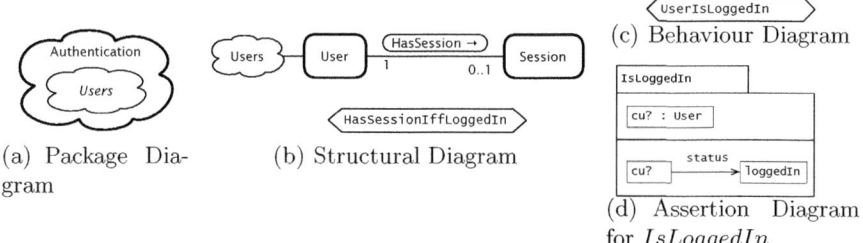

(a) Package Diagram

(b) Structural Diagram

(c) Behaviour Diagram

(d) Assertion Diagram for *IsLoggedIn*

Fig. 11. VCL package *Authentication*, addressing the authentication concern

Authentication operations (*Login* and *Logout*) are defined in VCL package *AuthenticationOps*, which extends package *Authentication* (Fig. 12). Operations that perform state changes are defined in contract diagrams, composed of a pre- and a post-condition. Figure 12(c) shows two contract diagrams for blob *User*. Operation *LoginOk* says in the pre-condition that a login is successful if the password given as input (*pw?*) matches the password of the user being authenticated (*u?.pw*); post-condition says that the status of the user is *loggedIn*, the number of passwords misses is 0, and the operation reports success (value *loginOk*) to its environment (output *r!*). Operation *Logout* says that provided the user status is logged in (pre-condition), then the user status is changed to logged-out (post-condition).

Figure 13 presents package *Authorisation*, which puts two aspects together: *Authentication* and *AccessControl* (see [3]). This package defines the observe operation *UserLoggedInAndHasPerm*, which checks whether a user is logged in and has the right permissions to execute some task; this puts together the observe operations *UserHasPerm* of *AccessControl* and *UserIsLoggedIn* of *Authentication*. VCL's contracts and assertions are modules that can be combined using logical operators.

Aspects are composed using *join extension*, which is illustrated in Fig. 14. In join extension, there is a contract that describes the joining behaviour of an aspect (a *join contract*) that is composed with a group of operations placed

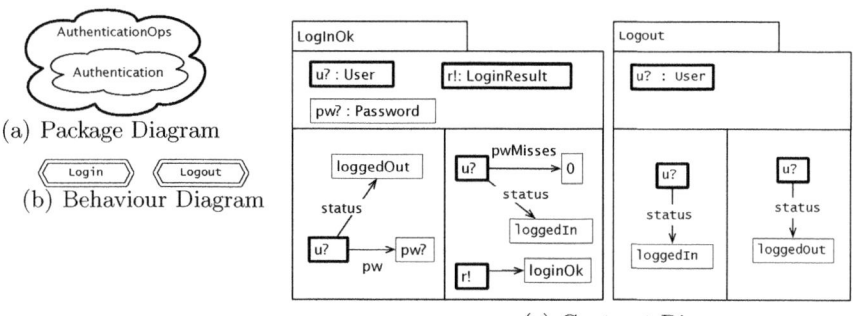

(a) Package Diagram

(b) Behaviour Diagram

(c) Contract Diagrams

Fig. 12. VCL package *AuthenticationOps*, addressing the authentication concern

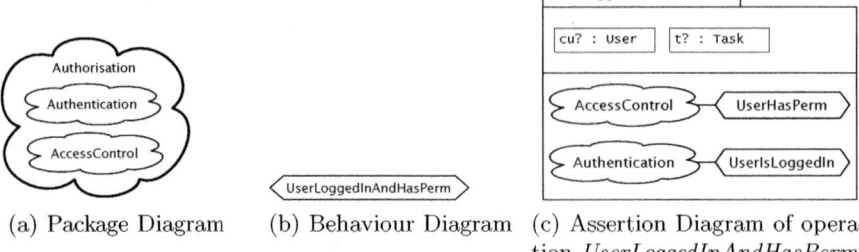

Fig. 13. VCL package *Authorisation*

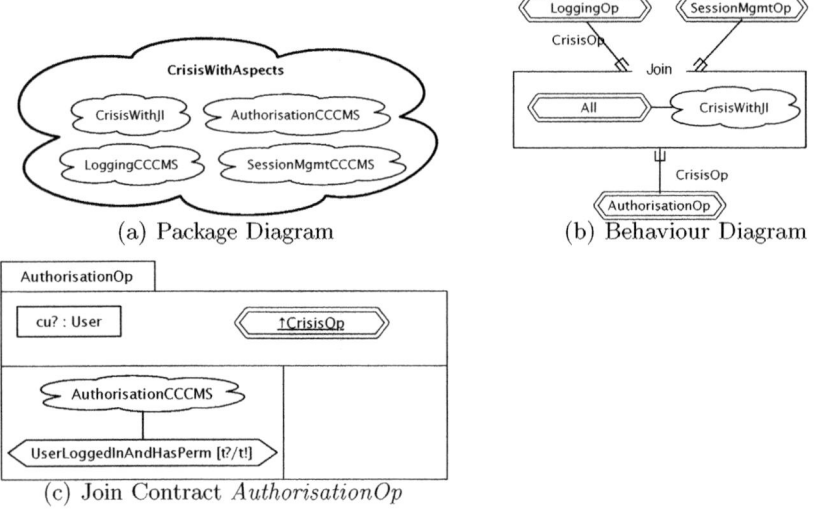

Fig. 14. VCL package *CrisisWithAspects*

in a *join-box*. All operations of package *CrisisWithJI* are conjoined with join contracts *LoggingOp*, *SessionMgmtOp* and *AuthorisationOp*. Join contract *AuthorisationOp* specifies the extra behaviour of the *Authorisation* concern by adding an extra pre-condition to all operations of package *CrisisWithJI*; this specifies that the users executing operations of package *CrisisWithJI* must be logged-in and have the required permissions to execute that task.

VCL is designed with a formal Z semantics and so it has the potential for *verification* and global *reasoning* using theorem proving.

3 Discussion and Conclusion

Our overview shows how aspect-orientation is used at different levels of abstraction. All approaches achieved localization of concerns and better traceability of requirements in models.

Table 1. AOM approaches at different levels of abstraction

Abstraction	Localization of concerns	Verification	Localization of reasoning
Features	VML4RE	n.a.	n.a.
Use cases	AoURN	n.a.	n.a.
Classes, sequence diagrams	RAM. GrACE	+	-
Classes, state machines	HiLA	+	-
Services, orchestration	Adore	rule based	-
Mixins	Protocol Modelling	+	+
Contracts	VCL	+	-

Each abstraction level supports its own composition technique and this technique defines the possibilities of reasoning on models. The modelling techniques that use the same composition techniques as programs, i.e. sequential compositional composition, alternative, cycle and inheritance have an execution tree as a result of model composition and need to use verification techniques for model analysis. The modelling techniques that use the ideas of design by contract need to rely on theorem proving for system analysis. In general, the localization of reasoning on aspects cannot be achieved with these composition forms as it cannot be achieved in programs [13]. The result of composition has to be analyzed to ensure correctness of behaviour. The modelling techniques with the mixins semantics and the CSP composition (used also in some programming languages [13]) localize reasoning on aspects and objects, and the behaviour of aspects survives in the result of composition. So, the choice of composition semantics is the major challenge of the AOM research.

The models in the presented approaches show that using aspects in models always increases fragmentation of models. This simplifies model construction, but does not simplify model understanding. However, fragmentation of complex models of real size applications is unavoidable. The experience of the presented approaches shows that any investment into tool support, allowing for search in sets of model fragments and model simulation, improves model understanding and transforms the fragmentation into an advantage.

References

1. Alférez, M., Santos, J., Moreira, A., Garcia, A., Kulesza, U., Araújo, J., Amaral, V.: Multi-View Composition Language for Software Product Line Requirements. In: van den Brand, M., Gašević, D., Gray, J. (eds.) SLE 2009. LNCS, vol. 5969, pp. 103–122. Springer, Heidelberg (2010)
2. Amálio, N., Kelsen, P.: Modular Design by Contract Visually and Formally using VCL. In: VL/HCC 2010 (2010)
3. Amálio, N., Kelsen, P., Ma, Q., Glodt, C.: Using VCL as an Aspect-Oriented Approach to Requirements Modelling. TAOSD VII, 151–199 (2010)
4. Hoare, C.A.R.: Communicating Sequential Processes. Prentice-Hall, Englewood Cliffs (1985)

5. Ciraci, S., Havinga, W.K., Aksit, M., Bockisch, C.M., van den Broek, P.M.: A Graph-Based Aspect Interference Detection Approach for UML-Based Aspect-Oriented Models. Technical Report TR-CTIT-09-39, Enschede (September 2009)
6. Clarke, S., Walker, R.J.: Generic Aspect-Oriented Design with Theme/UML. In: Aspect-Oriented Software Development, pp. 425–458. Addison-Wesley, Reading (2005)
7. Kienzle, J., Abed, W.A., Klein, J.: Aspect-Oriented Multi-View Modeling. In: AOSD 2009, pp. 87–98. ACM Press, New York (March 2009)
8. Kienzle, J., Guelfi, N., Mustafiz, S.: Crisis Management Systems: a Case Study for Aspect-Oriented Modeling. TAOSD 7, 1–22 (2010)
9. McNeile, A., Roubtsova, E.: CSP Parallel Composition of Aspect Models. In: AOM 2008, pp. 13–18 (2008)
10. McNeile, A., Simons, N.: Protocol Modelling. A Modelling Approach that Supports Reusable Behavioural Abstractions. SoSyM 5(1), 91–107 (2006)
11. Mosser, S., Blay-Fornarino, M., Riveill, M.: Web Services Orchestration Evolution: A Merge Process For Behavioral Evolution. In: Morrison, R., Balasubramaniam, D., Falkner, K. (eds.) ECSA 2008. LNCS, vol. 5292, pp. 35–49. Springer, Heidelberg (2008)
12. Mussbacher, G., Amyot, D.: Extending the User Requirements Notation with Aspect-oriented Concepts. In: Reed, R., Bilgic, A., Gotzhein, R. (eds.) SDL 2009. LNCS, vol. 5719, pp. 115–132. Springer, Heidelberg (2009)
13. Filman, R., Elrad, T., Clarke, S., Akşit, M.: Aspect-Oriented Software Development. Addison-Wesley, Reading (2004)
14. Tarr, P., Ossher, H., Harrison, W., Stanley, J., Sutton, M.: N Degrees of Separation: Multi-Dimensional Separation of Concerns. In: ICSE 1999 (1999)
15. Zhang, G., Hölzl, M.: HiLA: High-Level Aspects for UML State Machines. In: Ghosh, S. (ed.) MODELS 2009. LNCS, vol. 6002, pp. 104–118. Springer, Heidelberg (2010)

MBSDI 2011
3rd International Workshop on
Model-Based Software and Data Integration

Ralf-Detlef Kutsche[1] and Nikola Milanovic[2]

[1] TU Berlin and Fraunhofer FIRST, Germany
rkutsche@cs.tu-berlin.de
[2] Model Labs GmbH, Germany
nikola.milanovic@modellabs.de

1 Goals

... to continuously develop the community of partners from academia and industry in the area of model-based software and data integration...

Our workshop, after the success of MBSDI 2008 (Berlin) and 2009 (Sydney), will be the third of its kind, directly addressing collaborative development of methodologies and tools for Model-Based Software and Data Integration (MBSDI). Our additional focus in the 2011 issue of MBSDI will be the emerging field of domain modeling and domain ontologies, as an important aid in (semi-) automated understanding software and data components and their potentials for integration. DSLs and, particularly, Domain Specific Modeling Languages (DSMLs) will be a special focus area in MBSDI 2011.

2 Description of the Workshop

Integration of data from heterogeneous and distributed sources, and, at the same time, integration of software components, subsystems and systems, in order to achieve full interoperability, is one of the major challenges and research areas in software industry since decades, as well as the most significant IT cost driving factor. Thus, an increasing need and market pressure to reduce time-to-market and cost of integration solutions is present everywhere.

The reason for the ever growing relevance of software integration is the dynamic nature of today's business operations, where fast enterprise decision making is essential. However, the relevant data and functions, based on which decisions should be made, are distributed over many heterogeneous and autonomous systems. Retrieving this data and processing it, in order to generate the added value services, requires an expensive and tedious software development process. In the previous years, it could be demonstrated that model-based software engineering (MBSWE) offers not only the methodology but also standardized (meta)tools and platforms for enterprise-wide and cross-enterprise integration of software solutions with the ultimate goal of (semi)automatic generation of added-value such as business intelligence components and others.

Contributions with a strong theoretical and technical background, as well as contributions focusing on domain knowledge and practical/industrial experience, both are in the center of our interest. Particularly, software and data integration solutions in the context of health care, education, production/logistics, finance and publishing are welcome, as they coincide with the focus domains of our research initiative. However, to extend this spectrum, other application domains, like e.g. automotive or avionics, are most welcome, too.

3 Topics

The MBSDI 2011 topics include the areas listed below:

- Models and Metamodels in Software and Data Integration
- Domain Specific Modeling Languages
- Domain (Ontology) Engineering
- Model Management: Consistency, Merging and Evolution/Synchronization
- Model & Artifact Repositories
- Model Transformation: Languages, Frameworks
- Integration (Meta-)Tools, and Tool Integration
- ECLIPSE-based Modeling Frameworks
- Software Interoperability: Middleware Platforms & Standards
- Integration/Composition of Software Components, Systems & Services
- Data & Information Integration (Matching, Merging, Federation)
- Semantic Integration using Ontologies
- Service Oriented Architecture: Concepts for Systems Integration
- SLA, Negotiation, Orchestration
- Performance and Dependability Aspects of Data and Software Integration
- Component and Service Interaction Patterns
- Runtime Environments and Software Monitoring
- Standards for Software & Information Modeling
- Model-Based Software Evolution & Migration
- Domain Ontologies in Integration Scenarios
- Business Processes and Software Integration in Concrete Applications
- Cross-Enterprise Business Integration/ Collaboration
- Integrated Domain Applications, as e.g. in the Domains of Health Care, Education, Publishing, Finance, Production/Logistics, Automotive, Avionics etc.

MELO 2011 - 1st Workshop on Model-Driven Engineering, Logic and Optimization

Jordi Cabot[1], Patrick Albert[2], Grégoire Dupé[3],
Marcos Didonet del Fabro[4], and Scott Lee[5]

[1] AtlanMod research team
INRIA - École des Mines de Nantes
[2] Ilog Research Project
IBM France
[3] Mia-Software
[4] Univ. Federal do Paraná
[5] CEA-List
Jordi.Cabot@inria.fr, Albertpa@fr.ibm.com,
gdupe@mia-software.com, marcos.ddf@inf.ufpr.br,
Scott.Lee@cea.fr

Abstract. The main goal of this workshop is to bring together two different communities: the Model-Driven Engineering (MDE) community and the logic programming community, to explore how each community can benefit from the techniques of the other. Are both communities friends or foes?

1 Model-Driven Engineering, Logic and Optimization: Friends or Foes?

The widesepread application of MDE in all kinds of domains (e.g. critical sytems, software product lines, embedded systems,...) has triggered the need of new techniques to solve optimization, visualization, verification, configuration,... problems at the model level. Instead of reinventing the wheel, most of these problems could be solved by reexpressing the modeling problem as a logic programming problem. As an example, verification (satisfiability) of large static models can be addressed by reexpressing the model as a constraint satisfaction problem to be solved by state-of-the-art constraint solvers.

Similarly, logic programming can benefit from the integration of MDE principles. As in any other domain, introduction of MDE would help to raise the abstraction level at which the problem is described (e.g. by providing domain-specific languages that allow non-technical users to specify the problem using a vocabulary closer to the domain), improve the separation of concerns by using different model-based views of the problem at different levels of detail, achieve tool independence (e.g. by following a typical PIM-PSM separation where, for instance, at the PIM level we could define tool-independent logic programming metamodels), increase reusability, ...

The main goal of this workshop is to bring together these two different communities: the Model-Driven Engineering (MDE) community and the logic programming community in a first joint workshop to explore how each community can benefit from the techniques of the other. We refer to the logic programming community in a broad sense (i.e. including Constraint Logic Programming, Answer-Set Programming but also ontology and semantic web aspects). The growing interest in the bidirectional relationship between MDE and logic-based techniques makes us believe that both communities could benefit a lot from having a workshop where to exchange experiences and research lines on these topics.

2 Relevant Topics

Topics of interest for the workshop include:

- Modeling and generation of constraint problems,
- Interoperability between constraint technical spaces,
- Constraint metamodels,
- Constraint Independent Model-Platform Independent Model-Platform Specific Model for Constraint Logic Programming,
- Domain Specific Languages for Constraint Logic Programming,
- Semantics of Business Vocabularies and Business Rules (SBVR),
- Business Process Modeling Notation(BPMN),
- MDE in satisfaction and planning problems,
- Model Checking,
- Model Optimization,
- Using Constraint Programming or Operational Research to compute Software Product Line solutions,
- Using MDE to represent Software Product Line problems and solutions,
- Comparing combination of MDE and Constraint Programming/Operational Research for Software Product Line.

3 Organization

The workshop will attract researchers with an MDE and/or logic programming background and interested in the use of new techniques (either MDE or logic-based) to improve current research problems in their domain. Technical papers (full papers, short papers and position papers) describing original solutions, empirical evaluation papers and experience/industrial papers presenting problems or challenges encountered in practice are welcome.

All papers will be reviewed by an international programme committee: Raphael Chenouard (Ecole Centrale de Nantes, France), Robert Clarisó (Open University of Catalonia, Spain), Sophie Demassey (Ecole des Mines de Nantes, France), François Fage (INRIA, France), Sebastien Gerard (CEA-List, France), Alfonso Pierantonio (University of L'Aquila, Italy), Antonio Ruiz-Cortés (University of Seville, Spain), Daniel Varró (Budapest University of Technology and Economics, Hungary), Jules White (Virginia Tech, USA)

Accepted papers are published online in the workshop web page. It is planned that the final versions of accepted papers will be published as online proceedings on the CEUR Workshop Proceedings publication service

The Third Workshop on Behaviour Modelling - Foundations and Applications

Ella Roubtsova[1], Ashley McNeile[2], Ekkart Kindler[3], and Mehmet Aksit[4]

[1] Open University of the Netherlands and
Munich University of Applied Sciences, Germany
ella.roubtsova@ou.nl,ella.roubtsova@hm.edu
[2] Metamaxim Ltd,UK
ashley.mcneile@metamaxim.com
[3] Technical University of Denmark
eki@imm.dtu.dk
[4] TU Twente, The Netherlands
aksit@ewi.utwente.nl

Recent trends in software system development point to the growing importance of behaviour modelling.

These trends are:

- The growing role of business process management and workflow;
- The growing importance of Service-Orientation as an architectural principle, with consequent emphasis on well defined interaction between software components;
- The importance of interfaces, contracts and service level agreements in defining and managing of behaviour integration both within and across organizational boundaries;
- The growing variety of business intelligence applications and their increasing complex behavioural requirements.

To meet the challenges presented by these trends we must be able to determine which behaviour modelling techniques are applicable to a given situation, and be able to use multiple techniques in combination. This requires suitable and simple compositional semantics so that the various models used to describe the behaviour of a complex system can be put together. Behaviour modelling attracts more attention as the research community understands that behaviour modelling concepts are different from programming concepts and can be used to create programming languages of the next generation.

The Third Workshop on Behaviour Modelling - Foundations and Applications brings together experts from academia and industry who are interested in

- Evaluation of goals and application area of different modelling techniques;
- Direct execution of behavioural models;
- Code generation from behavioural models;

- Usability results of different modelling techniques;
- Lessons learned from case studies with emphasis on what such cases show about how modelling can be improved;
- Composition and decomposition of behavioural models;
- Combination of different behaviour modelling approaches;
- Application of formal reasoning to behavioural models.

This workshop is already the third one in this serie. The first workshop took place in 2009 in the University of Twente, Enschede, the Netherlands [1]. The second workshop was organized in University of Pierre & Marie Curie, Paris, France, in 2010 [2]. The goal of the workshop serie is to make contributions in the area of software and systems behaviour modelling to address the demands of todays systems and applications requirements.

The first two workshops examined:

- the use Abstract State Machines for service modelling;
- some limitations of UML based behavioural approaches for needs of real-time modelling, interactive business process modelling, service-orientation and aspect-orientation;
- transformation of the UML models into formal modelling approaches (Coloured Petri Nets, pi-calculus);
- compositional behaviour modelling in business processes;
- the application of Design-by-Contract approach to modelling of collaborated distributed services;
- the use of Protocol Contracts for modelling of choreography of collaborated distributed services
- the application of Business Rules Modelling approaches for behaviour modelling of services.

The conclusion that may be drawn from the set of the papers presented at two workshops [1,2] is that the modelling of interaction and integration of system models is the most problematic aspect of behaviour modelling approaches. The challenge now is to increase understanding of these issues in the modelling community as a whole, so that we can work together towards better solutions. The Third Workshop on Behaviour Modelling - Foundations and Applications continues to examine how to analyze and classify system behaviour modelling semantics and how to use and combine behaviour modelling approaches effectively.

References

1. BM-MDA 2009: Proceedings of the First International Workshop on Behaviour Modelling in Model-Driven Architecture. ACM, New York (2009) ISBN 978-1-60558-503-1
2. BM-FA 2010: Proceedings of the Second International Workshop on Behaviour Modelling: Foundation and Applications. ACM, New York (2010) ISBN 978-1-60558-961-9

Process-Centred Approaches for Model-Driven Engineering (PMDE) – First Edition

Reda Bendraou[1], Redouane Lbath[2],
Bernard Coulette[2], and Marie-Pierre Gervais[3]

[1] LIP6, Université Pierre & Marie Curie, France
`reda.bendraou@lip6.fr`
[2] Université Pierre de Toulouse le Mirail, France
`Lbath@univ-tlse2.fr, Bernard.Coulette@univ-tlse2.fr`
[3] LIP6, Université Paris Ouest, France
`marie-pierre.gervais@lip6.fr`

Abstract. On one hand, the process engineering community has developed a large background on how to specify, to execute and to improve processes. On the other hand, the model-driven engineering community brings new techniques for easing the construction of languages and applications, editors and compilers. The goal of the PMDE workshop is to bring together experts from both communities to discuss the complementarity of these domains and how they can be combined together for a better software productivity and reliability. The workshop will invite contributions from both academia and the industry and will present the emerging research topics with their main challenges.

1 Introduction

Despite the benefits brought by the Model-Driven Engineering approach, the complexity of today's applications is still hard to master. Building complex and trustworthy software systems in the shortest time-to- market remains the challenging objective that competitive companies are facing constantly. A more challenging objective for these companies is to be able to formalize their development processes in order to analyze them, to simulate and execute them, and to reason about their possible improvement.

The PMDE Workshop aims to gather researchers and industrial practitioners working in the field of Model- Based Engineering, and more particularly on the use of processes to improve software reliability and productivity.

The PMDE workshop will invite papers presenting research results or work-in-progress in all areas of process- based approaches for model-driven engineering, including:

- Modelling software and systems processes for model-driven engineering
- Domain-Specific Languages (DSL) for modelling software and systems processes
- Transformation-based process modelling: structural and behavioural aspects

- MDE Process patterns: modelling and application
- MDE Process patterns for reuse: definition, search methods, application of patterns
- Process models refactoring and composition
- Process lines and MDE
- Verification of process models
- MDE process enactment and simulation
- MDE Process resource management
- Process metrics for model-driven engineering
- Management of distributed MDE processes
- MDE process evolution: static evolution, process models refactoring, dynamic process evolution, process deviations management
- Process-centred MDE tools
- Description of case studies based on MDE processes, experimentations on real projects, empirical studies

2 Submissions and Selection Process

We ask for papers in PDF format and not exceeding 10 pages in the LNCS style. The paper should present original research work related to the above-cited topics and should not be published or submitted simultaneously to other workshops, conferences or journals. Industrial papers are welcome. Each paper will be blindly reviewed by three members of the program committee.

3 Program committee

- Colin Atkinson (University of Mannheim, Mannheim, Germany)
- Behzad Bordbar (University of Birmingham, UK)
- Jacky Estublier (University of Grenoble, France)
- Christian Haerdt (EADS, Germany)
- Jason Xabier Mansell (TECNALIA - ICT/European Software Institute, Spain)
- Larrucea Uriarte Xabier (TECNALIA - ICT/European Software Institute, Spain)
- Leon J. Osterweil (University of Massachusetts, USA)
- Richard Paige (University of York, UK)
- Kakade Rupesh (General Motors Technical Centre, India)
- Garousi Vahid (University of Calgary Alberta, Canada)

4 Workshop Organizers

- Bendraou Reda (LIP6, France)
- Lbath Redouane (IRIT, France)
- Coulette Bernard (IRIT, France)
- Gervais Marie-Pierre (LIP6, France)

Third International Workshop on Model-Driven Product Line Engineering (MDPLE 2011)

Goetz Botterweck[1], Andreas Pleuss[1],
Julia Rubin[2], and Christa Schwanninger[3]

[1] Lero, University of Limerick, Ireland
{goetz.botterweck,andreas.pleuss}@lero.ie
[2] IBM Research, Haifa, Israel
mjulia@il.ibm.com
[3] Siemens CT, Germany
christa@kircher-schwanninger.de

Abstract. MDPLE workshop series focuses on exploring the present and the future of Model-Driven Software Product Line Engineering techniques. The main goal of MDPLE is to bring together researchers and industrial participants in order to discuss current research in Model-Driven Product Line Engineering and to identify emerging research topics. The workshop aims to foster the discussion between experts with background in model-driven engineering and experts from software product line domain.

The third edition of MDPLE is held in conjunction with the Seventh European Conference on Modeling Foundations and Applications (6-9th of June, 2011, Birmingham, UK).

Keywords: Product line engineering, software product lines, variability management, model-driven development.

1 Introduction

The fundamental premise of product line engineering (PLE) is that the investment in a family of products pays off later by allowing systematic, efficient derivation of products. This should be auto-mated as much as possible, which can be achieved via model-driven engineering (MDE) techniques.

Research in PLE and MDE has many intersections. PLE leverages MDE to specify variability, domain concepts, configurations and more. (Semi-) automated product derivation requires mappings between the models on different abstraction layers and model transformations to derive an implementation from a configuration.

In addition, latest research shows the increasing need for concepts to deal with very large and evolving systems. Product lines can no longer rely on an immutable scope but need to be considered as evolving systems which can span over organizational boundaries. Thus, there is a need to apply and investigate latest concepts from MDE like model-driven evolution and co-evolution, consistency management, multi-paradigm modeling, etc.

In this workshop we aim to bring together researchers and practitioners to foster the exchange of concepts and ideas between them to address these challenges. We are interested in the application of concepts from MDE to Product Line Engineering, including: modelling of software product lines; variability modelling; evolution of product lines; complexity handling and scalability; automated and interactive tool-support; aspect-oriented approaches; multiple binding time and run-time variability; advanced approaches and process models (e.g., multiple product lines and organisations); integrated handling of multiple models; and variability-aware validation approaches.

2 Submissions and Selection Process

We accepted two types of submissions: (1) regular papers (max. 12 pages) presenting original research and/or experience reports and (2) short papers (max. 6 pages) describing ongoing research, new results, and future trends. We explicitly encouraged submission of case studies and experience reports from industry where such techniques have been applied in industrial practice and on a larger scale.

All papers submitted to the workshop must be unpublished original work and must not have been submitted anywhere else for publication. Submissions were selected based on the relevance to the workshop topics and the suitability to trigger discussions.

3 Program Committee

David Benavides, University of Seville, ES; Manfred Broy, TU Munich, DE; Deepak Dhungana, Siemens CT, AT; Laurence Duchien, Lille University, FR; Ulrich W. Eisenecker, University of Leipzig, DE; Paul Grünbacher, JKU Linz, AT; Herman Hartmann, Univ. of Groningen, NL; Patrick Heymans, Univ. of Namur - FUNDP, BE; Jaejoon Lee, University of Lancaster, UK; Richard Paige, University of York, UK; Klaus Pohl, University Duisburg-Essen, DE; Andreas Rummler, SAP Research, DE; Klaus Schmid, University of Hildesheim, DE; Tim Trew, independent, UK; Frank van der Linden, Philips, NL; Andrzej Wasoswki, IT University Copenhagen, DK; and the workshop organizers.

4 Workshop Organizers

Goetz Botterweck, Lero, Univ. of Limerick, IE
Andreas Pleuss, Lero, Univ. of Limerick, IE
Julia Rubin, IBM Haifa Research Lab, IL
Christa Schwanninger, Siemens CT, DE

Agile Development with Domain Specific Languages

Bernhard Rumpe, Martin Schindler,
Steven Völkel, and Ingo Weisemöller

Software Engineering
RWTH Aachen University, Germany
http://www.se-rwth.de/

1 Introduction

An increasing number of software development projects uses domain specific languages (DSLs) at least at one stage. Such languages allow domain experts to take part in the product development, and they can often contribute to improved efficiency. As a drawback, the development of a DSL is a complex and error-prone software development process itself, which causes additional efforts and costs. Moreover, the actual software product and the DSL are often developed concurrently, and the requirements for the DSL may change according to the needs of developers of the actual product. Therefore, we have to address two interdependent development processes: the product development process, in which we may need to react on requirement changes by the customer quickly, and the language development process, in which we want to define an adaptable and extensible DSL.

In this tutorial, we sketch preliminary considerations about the use of DSLs, important methods and techniques that are crucial for defining the language, and basic technologies for code generation. In our tutorial, we also introduce concepts for the modular definition of DSLs, quality assurance, and the integration of a DSL into software development processes. Both our tutorial and this summary build on our tutorial *Generative Software Development* presented at the ICSE 2010, respectively on the corresponding summary [4].

2 Usage of DSLs in Software Development Processes

There is already a considerable number of successfully applied domain specific languages. In the requirements and analysis phase, requirements specification languages that are close to natural languages have been introduced. Architectural description languages and the UML play an important role in system design. Matlab/Simulink is a wide spread language for the implementation of electronic control units in the automotive industry.

The development of a domain specific language and the corresponding tools is a software development process itself, which may be expensive and error-prone. Therefore, the introduction of a DSL is particularly useful in the development of large and complex products [1]. In smaller development processes, the improvements in terms of efficiency and software quality may not be sufficient to compensate the initial costs that are caused by the DSL development. If in contrast the complexity, size and lifetime of the software product are sufficiently large, the development of high-quality languages and language instances can substantially contribute to a more efficient and valuable software system.

3 Development of Domain Specific Languages

The development of precise DSLs and accompanying tools like MontiCore [3] contain concepts of metamodels or grammars (syntax), context conditions (static analysis and quality assurance) as well as possibilities to define the semantics of a language. Instances of most DSLs can be mapped to models in different languages or executable programs by model transformations and code generators. The growing number and complexity of DSLs is addressed by concepts for the modular and compositional development of languages and their tools.

As a first step the language has to be defined precisely. This includes a description of the valid words of the language, which is determined by its syntax and by context conditions. These are often described by means of context free grammars, attribute grammars, symbol tables and constraints.

The language definition also includes a description of the semantics of the language [2]. This is often implemented by means of transformations, with code generators as an outstandingly important special case. In the case of executable models, the target language is often a general purpose language such as Java or C++, and the runtime semantics of the source model are the runtime semantics of the generated code. Most model-to-text-transformations are implemented by means of template languages such as Freemarker. Transformations can be executed locally on the developer's machine, or remote as a transformation service, where the latter reduces the technical efforts required for using a DSL.

In addition to the language definitions, developers need tools to describe and transform models in the DSL, and the process must be adopted to the usage of the new language. Moreover, measures for quality assurance of documents in the language are required. Once these steps in language and tool development have been completed, the DSL is ready to be used in other software development processes.

References

1. Deursen, A., Klint, P.: Little Languages: Little Maintenance? Journal of Software Maintenance: Research and Practice 10, 75–92 (1998)
2. Harel, D., Rumpe, B.: Meaningful Modeling: What's the Semantics of "Semantics"? Computer 37(10), 64–72 (2004)
3. MontiCore Website, http://www.monticore.de/
4. Rumpe, B., Schindler, M., Völkel, S., Weisemöller, I.: Generative software development. In: Proceedings of the 32nd International Conference on Software Engineering (ICSE 2010), vol. 2, pp. 473–474. ACM, New York (March 2010), tutorial summary

Incremental Evaluation of Model Queries over EMF Models: A Tutorial on EMF-IncQuery*

Gábor Bergmann, Ákos Horváth,
István Ráth, and Dániel Varró

Budapest University of Technology and Economics,
Department of Measurement and Information Systems,
H-1117 Magyar tudósok krt. 2, Budapest, Hungary
{bergmann,ahorvath,rath,varro}@mit.bme.hu

Keywords: incremental pattern matching, EMF, model query.

1 Introduction

Model driven development platforms such as the industry leader Eclipse Modeling Framework (EMF) greatly benefit from pattern matching, as it supports various usecases including model validation, model transformation, code generation and domain specific behaviour simulation. Pattern matching is a search for model elements conforming to a given pattern that describes their arrangement and properties, e.g. finding a violation of a complex well-formedness constraint of a domain specific modeling language.

Two major issues arise in pattern matching: (i) it can have significant impact on runtime performance and scalability; and (ii) it is often tedious and time consuming to (efficiently) implement manually on a case-by-case basis. The latter is typically addressed by a declarative query language (e.g., EMF Query, OCL) processed by a general-purpose pattern matching engine.

2 EMF-IncQuery

The current tutorial introduces a declarative model query framework over EMF called EMF-INCQUERY [1], using the graph pattern formalism (from the theory of graph transformations) as its query language and relying on incremental pattern matching for improved performance. Graph patterns represent conditions (or constraints) that have to be fulfilled by a part of the instance model. A basic graph pattern consists of *structural constraints* prescribing the existence of nodes (EObjects) and edges (EReference and EAttribute instances) of a given type. Additional features include pattern composition, negation, and attribute constraints.

The advantage of declarative query specification is that it achieves (effective) pattern matching with much less time-consuming, manual coding effort than

---
* This work was partially supported by the SecureChange (ICT-FET-231101) European Research Project.

ad-hoc model traversal. While EMF-INCQUERY is not the only technology providing declarative queries over EMF (think of EMF Query or MDT-OCL), it has a distinguishing feature, namely *incremental pattern matching*.

In case of incremental pattern matching, matches of a pattern are explicitly stored and remain available for immediate retrieval throughout the lifetime of the EMF ResourceSet. Even when the EMF model is modified, these caches are continuously and automatically kept up-to-date using the EMF Notification API. This maintenance happens without additional coding, and works regardless how the model was modified (graphical editor, programmatic manipulation, loading a new EMF resource, etc.). In many scenarios this technique provides significant speed-up at the cost of increased memory consumption.

Additionally, some shortcomings of EMF are mitigated by capabilities of EMF-INCQUERY, such as cheap enumeration of all instances of a type regardless where they are located in the resource tree. Another such use is navigation of EReferences in the opposite direction, without having to augment the metamodel with an EOpposite, which is problematic if the metamodel is beyond our control.

While EMF-INCQUERY might not be the tool best suited for every single model query problem, it offers some great and unique features in a range of use cases, some of which will be demonstrated in the tutorial.

3 Tutorial

In this tutorial, we give an overview of the EMF-INCQUERY system, demonstrating how the technology can be applied, and discuss gains and trade-offs. We will show how cheap pattern matching can have significant performance advantages in a number of scenarios, such as model validation (model editors can continuously evaluate complex well-formedness constraints and give efficient, immediate feedback), model transformation (determining the applicability of declarative transformation rules), and simulation of dynamic domain-specific models (identifying the possible model evolutions). These will be illustrated using a case study of on-the-fly well-formedness constraint evaluation in UML models.

Our target audience includes experts already working with EMF based query or model transformation technologies like EMF Query or ATL and programmers/educators who wish to learn about a new EMF based query technology. The tutorial will build on a basic understanding of EMF and graph patterns to explain these technicalities and will focus on a software engineer's viewpoint on using our framework.

Reference

1. Bergmann, G., Horváth, A., Ráth, I., Varró, D.: Incremental evaluation of model queries over EMF models. In: Petriu, D., Rouquette, N., Haugen, O. (eds.) MODELS 2010. LNCS, vol. 6394, pp. 76–90. Springer, Heidelberg (2010), http://viatra.inf.mit.bme.hu/incquery

Integrated Model Management with Epsilon

Dimitrios S. Kolovos, Richard F. Paige,
Louis M. Rose, and James Williams

Department of Computer Science, University of York,
Deramore Lane, York, YO10 5GH, United Kingdom
{dkolovos,paige,louis,jw}@cs.york.ac.uk

Abstract. This paper provides a summary of the contents of the ECMFA 2011 tutorial titled "Integrated Model Management with Epsilon". The aim of the tutorial is to provide an overview of the principles, practices and standards related to MDE and present the Epsilon model management platform, which provides an extensible architecture and set of consistent and interoperable task-specific model management languages and tools for automating a wide range of MDE operations.

1 Goals and Structure

Model-Driven Engineering (MDE) raises models to first-class development artefacts, used throughout the systems engineering lifecycle. MDE inherently relies on automated model management; an MDE process can involve different kinds of model management operations such as model-to-model and model-to-text transformation, model validation, comparison, merging, refactoring and evolution. The aim of the tutorial is to provide an overview of the principles, practices and standards related to MDE and present the Epsilon model management platform[1], a mature and well-established component of the Eclipse GMT project, which provides an extensible architecture and set of consistent and interoperable task-specific model management languages and tools for automating a wide range of MDE operations.

The tutorial will be structured as follows; the order in which content is listed is the approximate order of planned presentation. We envision the tutorial to be split in two parts; items 1-5 below will be covered in the morning session, while items 6-8 will be covered in the afternoon session.

1. Introduction to Model-Driven Engineering: a brief overview of the principles, practices, standards, and tools relevant to MDE. These include standards such as the OMGs MDA and UML, and tools such as Eclipse EMF and GMF.
2. Model Management and its Relationship to MDE: the basic principles of model management, including the need for repositories and MDE tool chains, which support a variety of MDE scenarios.

---
[1] http://www.eclipse.org/gmt/epsilon/

3. Requirements for Model Management: where we give an overview of typical scenarios for model management from both a customers perspective, and from a technology perspective. Example scenarios include updating, querying, transforming, and analysing models.
4. The Epsilon Platform: an introduction to the principles, motivation, architecture, and development tools of the Epsilon platform. A demonstration of the basic functionality of the platform within Eclipse will be given. The focus will be on describing the infrastructure through which different drivers (supporting different modelling technologies) and language reuse is achieved.
5. Epsilon Languages and Tools: detailed presentation of the fundamental languages and development tools of Epsilon, including:
    - the base navigation and modification language, the Epsilon Object Language;
    - the Epsilon Transformation Language, for model-to-model transformation;
    - the Epsilon Comparison Language, for model comparison;
    - the Epsilon Merging Language, for model merging;
    - the Epsilon Validation Language, for model validation;
    - the Epsilon Wizard Language, for model refactoring, refinement, and update;
    - the Epsilon Generation Language, for model-to-text transformation;
    - the Epsilon Flock language, for model evolution;
    - EuGENia, for constructing GMF-based graphical editors for Domain Specific Languages;
    - model management workflows in Epsilon, via integration with Ant.

    Short demonstrations of the languages, with examples, will be provided. As well, a discussion on the process and techniques used to develop additional languages will be presented.
6. Case Studies: a selection of case studies and applications of Epsilon.
7. Future Evolution and Development: an outlook to future developments, plans, and applications of Epsilon, including an overview of other interesting applications within the MDE community.

2 Objectives

At the end of the tutorial, participants will:

- understand the challenges of large-scale MDE, and the need for scaleable model management technology;
- appreciate the benefits and side-effects of using a platform of integrated languages (Epsilon) for model management.
- understand the basic tasks of model management, and how Epsilon contributes solutions;
- obtain some basic familiarity with the languages of the Epsilon platform, and how they can be used to solve realistic problems.

Creating Domain-Specific Modelling Languages That Work: Hands-On

Juha-Pekka Tolvanen

MetaCase
Ylistönmäentie 31, FI-40500 Jyväskylä, Finland
jpt@metacase.com

Abstract. A horrible lie exists in our industry today: it says that defining a graphical DSL is difficult and time intensive. In this tutorial, we will lay bare this fallacy and demonstrate how simple and quick it is to create domain-specific modelling languages and their generators. Through a hands-on approach, we define a modelling language and related generators in a few hours. More than just a technical exercise, we will show how this reflects industry experiences in various domains and companies.

Keywords: Domain-specific modelling, domain-specific language, metamodeling, code generation, language workbench.

1 Tutorial Description

Domain-Specific Languages and Model-Driven Development have moved from scattered successes, through industry hype, to increasingly widespread practical use. Well-attested benefits include raising the level of abstraction, improving productivity, and improving quality [1, 2]. The main questions are no longer what or why, but where and how.

This tutorial will teach participants about Domain-Specific Modelling (DSM) and code generation, where they can best be used (and where not), and how to apply them effectively to improve software development. The main part of the tutorial applies a hands-on approach in which participants define a domain-specific modelling language and related generators. We will focus on creating modelling languages that enable true model-driven engineering in which working code is generated from models:

- The language is based on the concepts of the problem domain, not the solution domain
- The scope of the language is narrowed down to a particular domain
- The language minimizes the effort needed to create, update and check the models
- The language supports communication with users and customers

At the end of the tutorial participants will have implemented several versions of the language - each time raising the level of abstraction. More than just a technical exercise, we will show how this reflects industry experiences in various domains, including telecom, consumer electronics and home automation.

2 Tutorial Requirements

2.1 Required Equipment

For the hands-on part it is recommended that everyone has a personal laptop, but it is also possible to work in pairs. Language creation can be done in any technology or tool that is available for the participants. For the rest organizers will provide tools [3] for language creation (supporting the following operating systems: Windows XP/Vista/7, Mac OS X Snow Leopard (or Panther/Tiger with X11 support installed), Linux (any contemporary basic distribution should work, but Ubuntu and SuSE are the recommended ones).

2.2 Pre-requisites

Participants should have experience on using at least one modelling and/or code generation tool. Experience on using some metamodeling tools is not needed.

3 Tutorial Goals

Participants will learn how to define modelling languages that enable full code generation from models. In addition to demonstrating industrial cases, during collaborative group work session participants will apply the principles of language and generator creation in practice: We seek in good design abstractions, capture them to a metamodel and define the language including constrains and concrete syntax. At the end of the session participants will try the language they created to model some applications.

References

1. Sprinkle, J., Mernik, M., Tolvanen, J.-P., Spinellis, D.: What Kinds of Nails Need a Domain-Specific Hammer? IEEE Software, 15-18 (July/August 2009)
2. Kelly, S., Tolvanen, J.-P.: Domain-Specific Modeling: Enabling full code generation. Wiley, Chichester (2008)
3. MetaCase, MetaEdit+ Workbench 4.5 SR1 User's Guide (2009), http://www.metacase.com/support/45/manuals/

Author Index

Aksit, Mehmet   381
Albert, Patrick   160, 379
Alférez, Mauricio   361
Al-Hilank, Samir   19
Ali, Shaukat   115
Amálio, Nuno   361

Babau, Jean-Philippe   270
Bajwa, Imran S.   132
Ballagny, Cyril   3
Barbier, Franck   3
Barbier, Gabriel   160
Barrett, Stephen C.   329
Behjati, Razieh   236
Bendraou, Reda   383
Bergmann, Gábor   389
Blanc, Xavier   85
Botterweck, Goetz   385
Briand, Lionel   115, 236, 282
Butler, Greg   329

Cabot, Jordi   160, 379
Cariou, Eric   3
Chalin, Patrice   329
Champeau, Joël   270
Ciraci, Selim   361
Colombo, Pietro   97
Combemale, Benoît   35
Coulette, Bernard   383

da Silva, Marcos Aurélio Almeida   85
Delande, Olivier   85
Del Fabro, Marcos Didonet   160, 379
Dogui, Aymen   189
Dolques, Xavier   189
Doux, Guillaume   160
Drexler, Johannes   19
Dupé, Grégoire   379

Elaasar, Maged   282
Ellner, Ralf   19
Exertier, Daniel   85

Falleri, Jean-Rémy   189
Farcet, Nicolas   270

Feugas, Alexandre   3
Fleurey, Franck   361

Gervais, Marie-Pierre   383
Gessenharter, Dominik   205
Gogolla, Martin   221
Goldschmidt, Thomas   172
Gonnord, Laure   35
Greenyer, Joel   144

Haugen, Øystein   253
Horváth, Ákos   389
Huchard, Marianne   189

Jain, Vaibhav   299
Jung, Martin   19
Jürjens, Jan   52

Khendek, Ferhat   97
Kienzle, Jörg   361
Kindler, Ekkart   381
Kips, Detlef   19
Klein, Jacques   361
Kolovos, Dimitrios S.   391
Kramer, Max   361
Kumar, Anshul   299
Kutsche, Ralf-Detlef   377

Labiche, Yvan   282
Lavazza, Luigi   97
Lbath, Redouane   383
Lee, Mark G.   132
Lee, Scott Uk-Jin   160, 379
Le Noir, Jerome   85
Ludwig, Marie   270

Marchal, Loïc   52
McNeile, Ashley   381
Mens, Tom   69
Milanovic, Nikola   377
Møller-Pedersen, Birger   253
Mosser, Sebastien   361
Mussbacher, Gunter   361

Nebut, Clémentine   189
Nejati, Shiva   236

Ochoa, Martín 52

Paige, Richard F. 391
Panda, Preeti R. 299
Pfeiffer, Rolf-Helge 312
Pfister, François 189
Philippsen, Michael 19
Pinna Puissant, Jorge 69
Pleuss, Andreas 385
Pook, Sebastian 144

Ráth, István 389
Rauscher, Martin 205
Rieke, Jan 144
Rose, Louis M. 391
Roubtsova, Ella 361, 381
Rubin, Julia 385
Rumpe, Bernhard 387
Rusu, Vlad 35

Schäfer, Wilhelm 1
Schindler, Martin 387

Schmidt, Holger 52
Schwanninger, Christa 385
Selic, Bran 236
Svendsen, Andreas 253

Tolvanen, Juha-Pekka 393

Uhl, Axel 172

Vallecillo, Antonio 221, 345
Van Der Straeten, Ragnhild 69
Varró, Dániel 389
Völkel, Steven 387

Wąsowski, Andrzej 312
Weisemöller, Ingo 387
Williams, James 391

Yue, Tao 115, 236

Zhang, Gefei 361

GPSR Compliance

The European Union's (EU) General Product Safety Regulation (GPSR) is a set of rules that requires consumer products to be safe and our obligations to ensure this.

If you have any concerns about our products, you can contact us on ProductSafety@springernature.com

In case Publisher is established outside the EU, the EU authorized representative is:

Springer Nature Customer Service Center GmbH
Europaplatz 3
69115 Heidelberg, Germany

Batch number: 09478804

Printed by Printforce, the Netherlands